FREE SPEECH IN THE UNITED STATES

FREE SPEECH IN THE UNITED STATES

BY

ZECHARIAH CHAFEE JR.

Langdell Professor of Law
in Harvard University

ORIGINALLY PUBLISHED BY HARVARD UNIVERSITY PRESS

ATHENEUM 1969 NEW YORK

THIS BOOK IS GRATEFULLY DEDICATED

TO

ABBOTT LAWRENCE LOWELL

WHOSE WISDOM AND COURAGE
IN THE FACE OF UNEASY FEARS AND STORMY CRITICISM
MADE IT UNMISTAKABLY PLAIN
THAT SO LONG AS HE WAS PRESIDENT
NO ONE COULD BREATHE THE AIR OF HARVARD
AND NOT BE FREE

PREFACE TO SECOND PRINTING

THE WRITING OF THIS BOOK was completed before Russia and the United States entered the war. These two events have affected the bearing of a few scattered passages, and created new conditions for the application of the principles determining the limits of free speech, but the principles remain the same. What I wrote during the national defense emergency about the great value of open discussion holds equally good during actual hostilities. This seems to me particularly true of the final chapters.

This war is not going to be like the last. The methods of fighting are very different, and the kind of talk which may be sought out for suppression will, I think, be just as different. There is not likely to be the same questioning of the causes of the war as in 1917. The events of December 7th leave very little room for argument on that score. Although employment relations may cause some disputes, radical labor will not be so outspoken as before, for the expenditures and policies of the New Deal have gone a long way to satisfy the old platforms of the I.W.W. and the socialist farmers. In 1942 the trouble seems likely to arise more from criticism of our associates, England and Russia, or from criticism of the disposition of the armed forces and the supply of munitions. Also the time may come, as in the Civil War, when some citizens will favor ending hostilities at once by a negotiated peace, while the administration and the majority are determined to struggle on for a decisive victory. Opposition to the government on such matters is sure to arouse resentment and fears and vigorous demands for prosecutions and other forms of suppression. Then it will be necessary for thoughtful Americans to remember the national tradition of free speech. Great is the value of united opinion in war, but it cannot be effectively obtained by persecution. It is equally important that the war should be waged with as few mistakes as possible, and that it should be ended at the right time. The ultimate decision of all such questions is more likely to be wise if it be shaped by an informative and informed public opinion. And that means that both sides must have a fair chance to speak out.

Most of all, we need an immense amount of thinking and talking about the kind of world we want after the war. Victory is not enough unless it brings a just and enduring peace. American civilization cannot stand an endless outpouring of billions for defense during a patched-up peace. The problem is enormously difficult. In 1919 we tried to put together the pieces and failed. Now there are very few pieces to put together. There will have to be a big, fresh start, and its success will depend on the continued support of the American people for a good many years after the fighting is over. Any plan framed by a few leaders, however wisely, will fail unless it responds to widespread thoughts and desires of us ordinary men and women. Whatever plan be proposed, it will involve drawbacks, and citizens must first have become ready to accept those drawbacks as preferable to the horrors of a third World War. That means they must be made thoroughly aware through long discussion in speech and print of the nature of the plan. The seed Wilson sowed was perhaps better than we knew in the short time it was before us. At all events, it fell on thin soil and was blown away. If the new seed of 1943 or 1944 or 1945 is to take firm root, the soil must first be ploughed long and deeply back and forth by the impact of ideas, until it is prepared for fertile growth.

So far I have stressed the responsibilities of the authorities and ordinary citizens to preserve this liberty. Now I want to speak of responsibilities of the men who wish to talk. They are under a strong moral duty not to abuse the liberty they possess. All I have written goes to show that the law should lay a few restraints upon them, but that makes it all the more important for them to restrain themselves. They are enjoying a great privilege, and the best return which they can make is to use that privilege wisely and sincerely for what they genuinely believe to be the best interests of their country. It is not going to be an easy task during the next few years to maintain freedom of speech unimpaired. There will be hard times ahead, perhaps even periods of disaster, during which many devoted citizens will readily believe that the safety of the nation demands the suppression of all criticism against those in authority. This tendency toward suppression will be immensely strengthened if speakers and writers use their privilege of free discussion carelessly or maliciously, so as to further their own ambitions or the immediate selfish interests of their particular minority. By abusing liberty of speech, they may easily further its abolition. I should be very slow to lock such men up or confiscate their pamphlets, but I do say that they owe it to the framers of the First Amendment who gave them this privilege, they owe it to all their fellow citizens and particularly to the few who share their own views, to think long and hard before they express themselves, so as to be sure that they speak fruitfully. It is hopeless for the law to draw the line between liberty and license. Judges and juries cannot look into the heart of a speaker or writer and tell whether his motives are patriotic or mean. But the man can look into his own heart and make that decision before he speaks out. Whatever efforts of this sort unpopular persons make will do much to maintain the vitality of the First Amendment.

There is another danger to the American tradition of open discussion, against which unpopular speakers and writers should be constantly on their guard. If our enemies win this war, the First Amendment will be the first to disappear. These speakers and writers will have no opportunity to criticize their future rulers. There will be no newspapers in which to publish their views, no platforms on which to speak, no Supreme Court to protect them by a test of clear and present danger. Yetta Stromberg and Angelo Herndon and Harry Bridges will no longer have nice distinctions drawn in their favor by judges in gowns; they will merely be dumped into concentration camps or sent to the scaffold. More temperate opponents will be dragged down along with them. The only political party will be the party in power. Therefore, those who propose to criticize governmental policies during war should be ever aware of the fact that criticism carries risks. Attacks may weaken the power of the leaders to obtain the support of the rank and file. Even at this price, the risks of criticism must be run for the sake of its benefits, for the sake of being sure that the war is waged in the best possible way. Still it is the responsibility of the critics to be sure that the risks are as small as possible and the benefits are as great as possible. Hence they should take plenty of time and effort before they speak to be sure that their criticisms are based upon ascertained or highly probable facts, and that the judgments based thereon are formed calmly and without malice. They should be sure to frame their remarks so as to persuade their hearers to correct the mistakes which are pointed out and not merely arouse them to a useless or dangerous resentment.

The Bill of Rights belongs to us all. Majorities and minorities alike, we must henceforward give the best that is in us to preserve these ten amendments together with the rest of the Constitution and everything else that we hold dear.

Z. C. Jr.

Cambridge, Massachusetts

April 6, 1942

PREFACE

LATE LAST AUTUMN my fellow Syndics of the Harvard University Press asked me to replace my book on *Freedom of Speech*, which was published in 1920 and has long been very difficult to obtain. The growing danger of a recurrence of the conditions discussed in that book led me to interrupt a long piece of work and respond to their request, although the pressure of other tasks has not allowed me to do as much as I wished. What I have done is to fuse together in this book all my ideas past and present on freedom of speech.

This book is designed to be less technical than my earlier writing. One of the main purposes of the 1920 book was to supply material to lawyers engaged in cases involving free speech; until it was published, they had few sources of information on this branch of the law. Today, this need of the practitioner is met by numerous court decisions and articles in legal periodicals, encyclopaedias, etc. Hence I am now directing myself to all thoughtful citizens, whether lawyers or laymen. In both revision and fresh writing, I have endeavored to phrase every paragraph so that it will be intelligible to a man or woman without legal training.

Part I, A Survey of Freedom of Speech in 1920, covers the same ground as my book of that year. Although the material has been revised throughout and although I still hold all the views there stated, it seems best to let these chapters continue to speak as of 1920 in the face of conditions of that time which may easily be repeated in the near future. Hence events since 1920 are rarely mentioned in the text; later occurrences that seem relevant are referred to in the footnotes. Part II, The First Decade of Peace, deals with several important decisions between 1920 and 1930. These chapters originally appeared in my book *The Inquiring Mind* (1928), but have been much revised. Part III, The Second Decade of Peace, contains hitherto unpublished discussion of decisions and legislation between 1930 and 1940. In Part IV, Wider Horizons, legal restrictions on freedom of speech are surveyed as a whole, first vertically and then horizontally. The chapter on The History

of the Law of Sedition is largely taken from my article on
"Sedition" in the *Encyclopaedia of the Social Sciences*, by the
kind permission of the publishers, Macmillan & Co. of New
York. The chapter on Methods of Controlling Discussion in
Peace Time is mostly based on my contribution to *Freedom in
the Modern World*, edited by Horace Kallen and published by
Coward-McCann Co. of New York, who have allowed me to
reprint the material here. The passage on Plays and Books is
taken by permission from the *Bill of Rights Review*. The discussions of motion-picture censorship and some other topics
are now printed for the first time. Part V, Free Speech Today,
sets forth some general reflections which have been accumu-
lating in my mind during the twenty years since I first wrote
on the subject. The book does not attempt to collect material
after March 31, 1941.

The chronological arrangement of the various parts involves
some disadvantages. For example, the deportation of radical
aliens in 1920 is presented in Part I, while recent deportation
legislation comes in Part III, many pages later. However, I
have tried to connect separated passages by abundant cross-
references.

During the preparation of the present book I have read over
the reviews of my 1920 book, with particular attention to unfavorable criticisms. Four types of such criticisms have received much thought on my part.

In the first place, several discriminating reviews by other
law teachers took issue on technical points with my discussion
of Supreme Court decisions under the Espionage Act. Although
reflection has not altered my main conclusions, these reviews
have led me to reshape the presentation of some passages, particularly in the chapter on the Abrams case. For the most part
it did not seem desirable to restate in detail the views of legal
writers opposed to my position, but I have taken pains to cite
the work of such men in footnotes and indicate their attitude
so that their work may be easily accessible to the reader, who
can then make up his own mind.

Next, I was charged with excessive solicitude for the persons
who were prosecuted and deported. This charge was most
fairly expressed by my friend Arthur D. Hill: "The half-baked

young men and women who suffered imprisonment for foolish talk were as inevitably victims of the war as the French children who were killed by German bombs, and their wrongs will seem to most of us to rank low in the scale of war-time suffering." There is some truth in this comment, but it seems to me unsound to regard the persons who are actually suppressed as the sole victims of suppression. In several pages in the present book I have pointed out that the imprisonment of "half-baked" agitators for "foolish talk" may often discourage wise men from publishing valuable criticism of governmental policies. Consequently, what might be well said is not said at all. Unfettered discussion of war aims in 1918 might have produced a better treaty, rallied liberals around President Wilson to carry the United States into the League of Nations, and saved English children from German bombs in 1941. Thus unremitting regard for the First Amendment benefits the nation even more than it protects the individuals who are prosecuted. The real value of freedom of speech is not to the minority that wants to talk, but to the majority that does not want to listen.

Thirdly, I was accused of being too harsh toward the promoters of suppression — legislators, judges, officials, and groups of private persons. This was best phrased by Professor H. L. McBain: "There is nothing more intolerable — or for that matter more usual — than intolerance of intolerance." I am incapable of deciding how much this charge is justified. One cannot get outside himself to do his thinking, or his feeling either. At all events, such criticisms have led me to reconsider carefully the facts of each case and my judgment thereon. I have tried to place myself in the position of the men who incited, conducted, and upheld the prosecutions and deportations. Whenever possible I have put their own words before the reader. I have endeavored to avoid the error of passing judgment on exciting events as if they were taking place in the peaceful room where I was writing about them. Beyond this I cannot go. I am incapable of speaking calmly about what I believe to be injustice. And of all human sins, cruelty is to me one of the very worst.

Finally, my close analysis of the various tests laid down by the District Courts and the Supreme Court and my endeavor to frame a precise definition of the limits of constitutional free

speech were criticized as being somewhat scholastic and unsuited to the turmoil of war. Thus Professor McBain acutely
observed: "Legal precepts cannot change human nature. And
the stuff of courts is human stuff." And my associate, Professor T. R. Powell, in the wisest of all the reviews I received,
said: "Nine men in Washington cannot hold a nation to ideals
which it is determined to betray. Whether justice is done to
the particular defendant is important, but in the long run less
important than whether a nation does justice to itself." These
criticisms have affected the present book in two ways. I have
devoted much attention to the procedure by which constitutional rights are safeguarded; and I have often stressed the
fact that the ultimate security for free and fruitful discussion
lies in the tolerance of private citizens. Indeed, my main purpose in writing this new book is to make such men and women
realize the great value of their own tolerance to the welfare of
the nation.

It has been a pleasurable experience to rewrite and try to
make better what I did twenty years ago. All of us after some
conversation have thought of replies which we would make if we
could only go back and start the whole thing over again. The
preparation of this book has been like gratifying such a wish.

On the other hand, as I have once more immersed myself at
the age of fifty-five in the exciting events in which I participated at thirty-five, I have constantly missed many friends
then close. I think most of Walter Pollak whose unfailing joy
in life prevented his zeal for human rights from ever degenerat-
ing into cynicism or bitterness. I recall Albert DeSilver, whose
wealth and time were always at the service of those in trouble.
I remember the long day in Judge Anderson's office when lunch
had to be sent in while he read to the little group of lawyers of
all sides the draft of his opinion depicting deportation raids.
Memories of two leisurely talks on the North Shore with Justice Holmes come to mind, though naturally they left free
speech undiscussed. The frequent letters from Judge Amidon
have been reread and quoted in these pages. I should like to
hear again the words of vigorous encouragement from Albert
J. Beveridge. John Graham Brooks, whose age never kept him
from living with younger men in the present, taught me out of

his long experience that there is no single or easy remedy for
any human maladjustment. Thomas Nelson Perkins showed
me that denunciation of undesirable legislation at a hearing is
sometimes not the best way to defeat the bill. And while most
of us sat around talking about the wrongs of various victims of
suppression, Jessie Wilson Sayre crossed the waters of Boston
Harbor in January to visit the deportees crowded on Deer
Island, and Mrs. Glendower Evans spent many days with
prisoners in their cells. To all these men and women I now
acknowledge my indebtedness.

And I cannot fail to mention one other man, now dead, whom
I never knew personally, but who was much in my thoughts
during the months when I first wrote on freedom of speech.
The name of Woodrow Wilson occurs many times in this book,
not often with praise. Indeed, the material published since his
death which I have used here only serves to place his participation in war-time suppression in a more unfavorable light than
before. There are few sadder books than Ray Stannard Baker's
two biographical volumes on *The War Years*. Woodrow Wilson,
the man and the prophet, has turned into a series of fifteen-
minute appointments. When war begins, all thinking stops.
However, my subject touches only a small part of Wilson's
work, and what I have said of him in the text necessarily fails
to disclose my whole opinion of the man. So I take this opportunity to say some things which would be inappropriate in the
body of the book.

Around 1918 a group of Republicans gathered in the Union
League Club in New York were denouncing Wilson for this and
that. When the discussion reached a peak of vituperation, one
of the number who had hitherto kept silent — I like to think
that it was Elihu Root — suddenly remarked, "And there is
one thing above all, gentlemen, for which we can never forgive
him, and that is his consummate ability."

It was more than ability, it was vision. He saw clearly what
ought to be done, though he sometimes lacked the shrewdness
or wisdom to know how to do it. For instance, some of his most
fatal blunders are described in this book. But the blunders
must never be allowed to blind us to the vision. The Peace
without Victory speech before we entered the World War,
which I have quoted at the head of Chapter II, describes the

tragedy of the years between two wars. And in the equally great speech at St. Louis on September 5, 1919, he said in urging our membership in the League:

All the nations that Germany meant to crush and reduce to the status of tools in her own hands have been redeemed by this war and given the guarantee of the strongest nations of the world that nobody shall invade their liberty again. If you do not want to give them that guarantee, then you make it certain that without your guarantee the attempt will be made again, and if another war starts like this one, are you going to keep out of it? If you keep out of this arrangement, that sort of war will come soon.

Twenty years later, almost to the day, this prophecy was fulfilled.

My book has been written with the hope that this time we may avoid his mistakes and make real his vision.

Z. C. Jr.

CAMBRIDGE, MASSACHUSETTS
June 30, 1941

CONTENTS

PART I

A SURVEY OF FREEDOM OF SPEECH IN 1920

PART II

THE FIRST DECADE OF PEACE: 1920–1930

PART III

THE SECOND DECADE OF PEACE: 1930–1940

PART IV

WIDER HORIZONS

PART V

1941

PART I

A SURVEY OF FREEDOM OF SPEECH IN 1920

Yet, Freedom! yet thy banner, torn, but flying,
Streams like the thunder-storm against the wind.

CHAPTER 1

FREEDOM OF SPEECH IN THE CONSTITUTION

> *And though all the winds of doctrine were let loose to*
> *play upon the earth, so Truth be in the field, we do in-*
> *juriously by licensing and prohibiting to misdoubt her*
> *strength. Let her and Falsehood grapple; who ever knew*
> *Truth put to the worse, in a free and open encounter?*
>
> MILTON, Areopagitica.

NEVER in the history of our country, since the Alien and Sedition Laws of 1798, has the meaning of free speech been the subject of such sharp controversy as during the years since 1917. Over nineteen hundred prosecutions and other judicial proceedings during the war, involving speeches, newspaper articles, pamphlets, and books, were followed after the armistice by a widespread legislative consideration of bills punishing the advocacy of extreme radicalism. It is becoming increasingly important to determine the true limits of freedom of expression, so that speakers and writers may know how much they can properly say, and governments may be sure how much they can lawfully and wisely suppress.

This book is an inquiry into the proper limitations upon freedom of speech, and is in no way an argument that any one should be allowed to say whatever he wants anywhere and at any time. We can all agree from the very start that there must be some point where the government may step in, and my main purpose is to make clear from many different angles just where I believe that point to lie. We ought also to agree that a man may believe that certain persons have a right to speak or other constitutional rights without at all identifying himself with the position and views of such persons. In a country where John Adams defended the British soldiers involved in the Boston Massacre and Alexander Hamilton represented British Loyalists and General Grant insisted upon amnesty for Robert E. Lee, it is surprising how between 1917 and 1920 it was impossible for any one to uphold the rights of a minority without subjecting himself to the accusation that he shared their opinions. If he urged milder treatment of conscientious objectors, he was a pacifist. If he held that the treaty with Germany should not violate the terms of the armistice, he was a pro-German. This popular argument reached its climax when an opponent of the disqualified Socialist assemblymen informed the world that he had always suspected Charles Evans Hughes of being disloyal.

I am not an atheist, but I would not roast one at the stake as in the sixteenth century, or even exclude him from the witness stand as in the nineteenth. Neither am I a pacifist or an anarchist or a Socialist or a Bolshevik. I have no sympathy myself with the views of most of the men who have been imprisoned since the war began for speaking out. My only interest is to find whether or not the treatment which they have received accords with freedom of speech. That principle may be invoked just as eagerly in future years by conservatives. Whatever political or economic opinion falls within the scope of the First Amendment ought to be safeguarded from governmental interference by every man who has sworn to uphold the Constitution of the United States, no matter how much he disagrees with those who are entitled to its protection or how lofty the patriotism of those who would whittle away the Bill of Rights into insignificance.

A friend of Lovejoy, the Abolitionist printer killed in the Alton riots, said at the time:

We are more especially called upon to maintain the principles of free discussion in case of unpopular sentiments or persons, as in no other case will any effort to maintain them be needed.[1]

The free speech clauses of the American constitutions are not merely expressions of political faith without binding legal force. Their history shows that they limit legislative action as much as any other part of the Bills of Rights. The United States Constitution as originally drafted contained no guaranty of religious or intellectual liberty, except that it forbade any religious test oath and gave immunity to members of Congress

[1] Edward Beecher, *Alton Riots* (Alton, Ill., 1838).

for anything said in debates. Pinckney, of South Carolina, had sought to insert a free speech clause, grouping liberty of the press with trial by jury and habeas corpus as "essentials in free governments." His suggestion was rejected by a slight majority as unnecessary, in that the power of Congress did not extend to the press, a natural belief before Hamilton and Marshall had developed the doctrine of incidental and implied powers. Hamilton himself defended the omission on the ground that liberty of the press was indefinable and depended only on public opinion and the general spirit of the people and government for its security, little thinking that he himself would frame a definition now embodied in the constitutions of half the states.[2] The citizens of the states were not satisfied, and the absence of the guaranty of freedom of speech was repeatedly condemned in the state conventions and in outside discussion. Virginia, New York, and Rhode Island embodied a declaration of this right in their ratifications of the federal Constitution. Virginia expressly demanded an amendment and Maryland drafted one in its convention, basing it on a very significant reason, to be mentioned shortly. At the first session of Congress a Bill of Rights, including the present First Amendment, was proposed for adoption by the states, and became part of the Constitution December 15, 1791. Massachusetts, Virginia, and Pennsylvania already had similar provisions, and such a clause was eventually inserted in the constitutions of all other states. Thus the guaranty of freedom

[2] The various types of free speech clauses are given in *Index Digest of State Constitutions* (*N. Y. State Cons. Conv. Comm.*, 1915), pp. 700–702, 956–958. Twenty-three state constitutions follow Hamilton (note 60, *infra*) in making truth a defense to criminal libel if published with good motives. The first was the New York Constitution of 1821, Art. 7, § 8. See *Reports of New York Constitutional Convention of 1821*, pp. 167, 487. All but five states have a clause resembling another sentence of the New York section: "Every citizen may freely speak, write, and publish his sentiments, on all subjects, being responsible for the abuse of that right; and no law shall be passed, to restrain, or abridge the liberty of speech, or of the press." Massachusetts, Mississippi, New Hampshire, Vermont, and South Carolina retain a short clause much like the federal Constitution. The express exception of "abuse" was first made by Pennsylvania in 1790 (note 32, *infra*); but since I regard such an exception as implied in the United States form, I have assumed in this book that there is no difference in legal effect. The effect of the Hamiltonian clause is discussed by Henry Schofield, "Freedom of the Press in the United States," *Essays on Constitutional Law & Equity*, II, 510, 536, first published in 1914 and cited hereafter as Schofield.

of speech was almost a condition of the entry of four original states into the Union, and is now declared by every state to be as much a part of its fundamental law as trial by jury or compensation for property taken by eminent domain. Such a widely recognized right must mean something, and have behind it the obligation of the courts to refuse to enforce any legislation which violates freedom of speech.

We shall not, however, confine ourselves to the question whether a given form of federal or state action against pacifist and similar utterances is void under the constitutions. It is often assumed that, so long as a statute is held valid under the Bill of Rights, that document ceases to be of any importance in the matter, and may be henceforth disregarded. On the contrary, a provision like the First Amendment to the federal Constitution,

Congress shall make no law respecting an establishment of religion, or prohibiting the free exercise thereof; or abridging the freedom of speech, or of the press; or the right of the people peaceably to assemble, and to petition the Government for a redress of grievances

is much more than an order to Congress not to cross the boundary which marks the extreme limits of lawful suppression. It is also an exhortation and a guide for the action of Congress inside that boundary. It is a declaration of national policy in favor of the public discussion of all public questions. Such a declaration should make Congress reluctant and careful in the enactment of all restrictions upon utterance, even though the courts will not refuse to enforce them as unconstitutional. It should influence the judges in their construction of valid speech statutes, and the prosecuting attorneys who control their enforcement. The Bill of Rights in a European constitution is a declaration of policies and nothing more, for the courts cannot disregard the legislative will though it violates the Constitution.[3] Our Bills of Rights perform a double func-

[3] A. V. Dicey, *Law of the Constitution* (8th ed.), p. 130: "This curious result therefore ensues. The restrictions placed on the action of the legislature under the French constitution are not in reality laws, since they are not rules which in the last resort will be enforced by the Courts. Their true character is that of maxims of political morality, which derive whatever strength they possess from being formally inscribed in the constitution and from the resulting support

tion. They fix a certain point to halt the government abruptly with a "Thus far and no farther"; but long before that point is reached they urge upon every official of the three branches of the state a constant regard for certain declared fundamental policies of American life.[4]

Our main task, therefore, is to ascertain the nature and scope of the policy which finds expression in the First Amendment to the United States Constitution and the similar clauses of all the state constitutions. We can then determine the place of that policy in the conduct of war, and particularly the war with Germany. The free speech controversy during the war chiefly gathered about the federal Espionage Act, discussed at length in the next chapter. This statute, which imposes a maximum of twenty years' imprisonment and a $10,000 fine on several kinds of spoken or written opposition to the war, was enacted and vigorously enforced under a Constitution which provides: "Congress shall make no law . . . abridging the freedom of speech, or of the press."

Clearly, the problem of the limits of freedom of speech in war time is no academic question. On the one side, thoughtful men and journals were asking how scores of citizens could be imprisoned under this Constitution only for their open disapproval of the war as irreligious, unwise, or unjust. On the other, federal and state officials pointed to the great activities of German agents in our midst and to the unprecedented extension of the business of war over the whole nation, so that, in the familiar remark of Ludendorff, wars are no longer won by armies in the field, but by the *morale* of the whole people. The widespread Liberty Bond campaigns, and the shipyards, munition factories, government offices, training camps, in all

of public opinion. What is true of the constitution of France applies with more or less force to other polities which have been formed under the influence of French ideas."

Probably some Americans anticipated only the same effect from our bills of rights, not realizing that an unconstitutional statute would be held unenforceable. Spencer said in the North Carolina Convention: "If a boundary were set up, when the boundary is passed, the people would take notice of it immediately." — *Elliot's Debates* (2d ed.), IV, 175.

[4] "No doubt our doctrine of constitutional law has had a tendency to drive out questions of justice and right, and to fill the mind of legislators with thoughts of mere legality, of what the constitution allows." — J. B. Thayer, *Legal Essays*, p. 38.

parts of the country, were felt to make the entire United States a theater of war, in which attacks upon our cause were as dangerous and unjustified as if made among the soldiers in the rear trenches. The government regarded it as inconceivable that the Constitution should cripple its efforts to maintain public safety. Abstaining from countercharges of disloyalty and tyranny, let us recognize the issue as a conflict between two vital principles, and endeavor to find the basis of reconciliation between order and freedom.

At the outset, we can reject two extreme views in the controversy. First, there is the view that the Bill of Rights is a peace-time document and consequently freedom of speech may be ignored in war. This view has been officially repudiated.[5] At the opposite pole is the belief of many agitators that the First Amendment renders unconstitutional any Act of Congress without exception "abridging the freedom of speech, or of the press," that all speech is free, and only action can be restrained and punished. This view is equally untenable. The provisions of the Bill of Rights cannot be applied with absolute literalness, but are subject to exceptions.[6] For instance, the prohibition of involuntary servitude in the Thirteenth Amendment does not prevent military conscription, or the enforcement of a "work or fight" statute. The difficulty, of course, is to define the principle on which the implied exceptions are based, and an effort to that end will be made subsequently.

Since it is plain that the true solution lies between these two extreme views, and that even in war time freedom of speech exists subject to a problematical limit, it is necessary to determine where the line runs between utterances which are protected by the Constitution from governmental control and those which are not. Many attempts at a legal definition of that line have been made, but two mutually inconsistent

---

[5] Report of the Attorney General of the United States (1918), p. 20: "This department throughout the war has proceeded upon the general principle that the constitutional right of free speech, free assembly, and petition exist in war time as in peace time, and that the right of discussion of governmental policy and the right of political agitation are most fundamental rights in a democracy."

[6] Robertson v. Baldwin, 165 U. S. 275, 281 (1897); Selective Draft Law Cases, 245 U. S. 366, 390 (1918); Claudius v. Davie, 175 Cal. 208 (1917); State v. McClure, 30 Del. 265 (1919).

theories have been especially successful in winning judicial acceptance, and frequently appear in the Espionage Act cases.

One theory construes the First Amendment as enacting Blackstone's statement that "the liberty of the press . . . consists in laying no *previous* restraints upon publications and not in freedom from censure for criminal matter when published." [7] The line where legitimate suppression begins is fixed chronologically at the time of publication. The government cannot interfere by a censorship or injunction *before* the words are spoken or printed, but can punish them as much as it pleases *after* publication, no matter how harmless or essential to the public welfare the discussion may be.[8] This Blackstonian definition is sometimes urged as a reason why civil libels should not be enjoined,[9] so that on this theory liberty of the press means opportunity for blackmailers and no protection for political criticism. Of course, if the First Amendment does not prevent prosecution and punishment of utterances, no serious question could arise about the constitutionality of the Espionage Act.

This Blackstonian theory dies hard, but it ought to be knocked on the head once for all. In the first place, Blackstone was not interpreting a constitution, but trying to state the English law of his time, which had no censorship and did have extensive libel prosecutions. Whether or not he stated that law correctly, an entirely different view of the liberty of the press was soon afterwards enacted in Fox's Libel Act, discussed below, so that Blackstone's view does not even correspond to the English law of the last hundred and twenty-five years. Furthermore, Blackstone is notoriously unfitted to be an authority on the liberties of American colonists, since he upheld the right of Parliament to tax them, and was pronounced by one of his own colleagues to have been "we all know, an anti-republican lawyer." [10]

Not only is the Blackstonian interpretation of our free

---

[7] Blackstone, *Commentaries*, IV, 151.

[8] My article in 32 *Harvard Law Review* at 938 contains additional material on the Blackstonian definition.

[9] See Roscoe Pound, "Equitable Relief Against Defamation and Injuries to Personality," 29 *Harvard Law Review* 651.

[10] Blackstone, *Commentaries*, I, 109; Willes, J., in Dean of St. Asaph's Case, 4 Doug. 73, 172 (1784).

speech clauses inconsistent with eighteenth-century history, soon to be considered, but it is contrary to modern decisions, thoroughly artificial, and wholly out of accord with a common-sense view of the relations of state and citizen. In some respects this theory goes altogether too far in restricting state action. The total prohibition of previous restraint would not allow the government to prevent a newspaper from publishing the sailing dates of transports or the number of troops in a sector. It would forbid the removal of an indecent poster from a billboard. Censorship of moving pictures before exhibition has been held valid under a free speech clause.[11] And whatever else may be thought of the decision under the Espionage Act with the unfortunate title *United States* v. *The Spirit of '76*,[12] it was clearly previous restraint for a federal court to direct the seizure of a film which depicted the Wyoming Massacre and Paul Revere's Ride, because it was "calculated reasonably so to excite or inflame the passions of our people or some of them as that they will be deterred from giving that full measure of co-operation, sympathy, assistance, and sacrifice which is due to Great Britain, as an ally of ours," and "to make us a little bit slack in our loyalty to Great Britain in this great catastrophe."

On the other hand, it is hardly necessary to argue that the Blackstonian definition gives very inadequate protection to the freedom of expression. A death penalty for writing about socialism would be as effective suppression as a censorship. The government which holds twenty years in prison before a speaker and calls him free to talk resembles the peasant described by Galsworthy:

The other day in Russia an Englishman came on a street-meeting shortly after the first revolution had begun. An extremist was addressing the gathering and telling them that they were fools to go on fighting, that they ought to refuse and go home, and so forth. The crowd grew angry, and some soldiers were for making a rush at him; but the chairman, a big burly peasant, stopped them with

[11] Mutual Film Corporation *v.* Industrial Commission of Ohio, 236 U. S. 230, 241 (1915). See *infra*, Chapter XIV, section v, for a discussion of the possible unconstitutionality of film censorship in view of a Supreme Court decision in 1931.

[12] 252 Fed. 946 (D. C. S. D. Cal., 1917), Bledsoe, J. See also Goldstein *v.* U. S., 258 Fed. 908 (C. C. A. 9th, 1919); *infra*, page 55.

these words: "Brothers, you know that our country is now a country of free speech. We must listen to this man, we must let him say anything he will. But, brothers, when he's finished, we'll bash his head in!"[13]

Cooley's comment on Blackstone is unanswerable:

. . . The mere exemption from previous restraints cannot be all that is secured by the constitutional provisions, inasmuch as of words to be uttered orally there can be no previous censorship, and the liberty of the press might be rendered a mockery and a delusion, and the phrase itself a byword, if, while every man was at liberty to publish what he pleased, the public authorities might nevertheless punish him for harmless publications, . . . Their purpose [of the free-speech clauses] has evidently been to protect parties in the free publication of matters of public concern, to secure their right to a free discussion of public events and public measures, and to enable every citizen at any time to bring the government and any person in authority to the bar of public opinion by any just criticism upon their conduct in the exercise of the authority which the people have conferred upon them. . . . The evils to be prevented were not the censorship of the press merely, but any action of the government by means of which it might prevent such free and general discussion of public matters as seems absolutely essential to prepare the people for an intelligent exercise of their rights as citizens.[14]

If we turn from principles to precedents, we find several decisions which declare the constitutional guaranty of free speech to be violated by statutes and other governmental action which imposed no previous restraint, but penalized publications after they were made.[15] And most of the decisions in

[13] John Galsworthy, "American and Briton," 8 *Yale Review* 27 (October, 1918). *Cf.* Boswell's *Johnson*, ed. G. B. Hill, IV, 12.

[14] Cooley, *Constitutional Limitations* (7th ed.), pp. 603, 604.

[15] These pre-war state cases invalidated statutes punishing school superintendents for political speeches; making an employer liable for damages if he failed to furnish a discharged employee with a written statement of the true reason for discharge; punishing voters' leagues for commenting on a candidate for office without disclosing the names of all their informants; invalidating the nomination of candidates by conventions or any other method except primaries; punishing disbursements outside a candidate's own county except through a campaign committee. Other cases quashed contempt proceedings for criticism of judge for past decision. Some of these decisions are open to dispute on the desirability of the statutes, and some are opposed by other cases for that reason, but in their repudiation of the Blackstonian test they furnish unquestioned authority. The Blackstonian test is also inconsistent with many

which a particular statute punishing for talking or writing is sustained do not rest upon the Blackstonian interpretation of liberty of speech,[16] but upon another theory, now to be considered. Therefore, the severe punishments imposed by the Espionage Act might conceivably violate the First Amendment, although they do not interfere with utterances before publication.[17]

A second interpretation of the freedom of speech clauses limits them to the protection of the use of utterance and not of its "abuse." It draws the line between "liberty" and "license." Chief Justice White rejected:

the contention that the freedom of the press is the freedom to do wrong with impunity and implies the right to frustrate and defeat the discharge of those governmental duties upon the performance of which the freedom of all, including that of the press, depends. . . . However complete is the right of the press to state public things and discuss them, that right, as every other right, enjoyed in human society, is subject to the restraints which separate right from wrong-doing.[18]

A statement of the same view in another peace case was made by Judge Hamersley of Connecticut:

Every citizen has an equal right to use his mental endowments, as well as his property, in any harmless occupation or manner; but he has no right to use them so as to injure his fellow-citizens or to endanger the vital interests of society. Immunity in the mischievous use is as inconsistent with civil liberty as prohibition of the harmless use. . . . The liberty protected is not the right to perpetrate acts of licentiousness, or any act inconsistent with the peace or safety of the State. Freedom of speech and press does not include the abuse of the power of tongue or pen, any more than freedom of other

decisions of the United States Supreme Court after 1924, which invalidated statutes on free speech grounds; these decisions are discussed in Chapters IX, X, and XI.

[16] Examples in such cases of express repudiation of the Blackstonian doctrine are found in Schenck v. United States, 249 U. S. 47 (1919); State v. McKee, 73 Conn. 18 (1900); State v. Pioneer Press Co., 100 Minn. 173 (1907); Cowan v. Fairbrother, 118 N. C. 406, 418 (1896).

[17] Title XII of the Espionage Act does impose previous restraint on publications which violate the Act by authorizing the Postmaster General to exclude them from the mails. See *infra*, Chapter II, section VI; Chapter VII, section II.

[18] Toledo Newspaper Co. v. United States, 247 U. S. 402, 419 (1918).

action includes an injurious use of one's occupation, business, or property.[19]

The decisions in the war were full of similar language,[20] of which a few specimens will suffice:

In this country it is one of our foundation stones of liberty that we may freely discuss anything we please, provided that that discussion is in conformity with law, or at least not in violation of it.

No American worthy of the name believes in anything else than free speech; but free speech means, not license, not counseling disobedience of the law. Free speech means that frank, free, full, and orderly expression which every man or woman in the land, citizen or alien, may engage in, in lawful and orderly fashion.

No one is permitted under the constitutional guaranties to commit a wrong or violate the law.

Just the same sort of distinction was made by Lord Kenyon during the French revolution:

The liberty of the press is dear to England. The licentiousness of the press is odious to England. The liberty of it can never be so well protected as by beating down the licentiousness.

This exasperated Sir James Fitzjames Stephen into the comment, "Hobbes is nearly the only writer who seems to me capable of using the word 'liberty' without talking nonsense." [21]

A slightly more satisfactory view was adopted by Cooley, that the clauses guard against repressive measures by the several departments of government, but not against utterances which are a public offense, or which injure the reputation of individuals.

We understand liberty of speech and of the press to imply not only liberty to publish, but complete immunity from legal censure and punishment for the publication, so long as it is not harmful in its character, when tested by such standards as the law affords.[22]

[19] State v. McKee, 73 Conn. 18, 28 (1900).

[20] Mayer, J., in United States v. Phillips, Bull. Dept. Just. No. 14, 5 (S. D. N. Y., 1917); and United States v. Goldman, Bull. Dept. Just. No. 41, 2 (S. D. N. Y., 1917); Van Valkenburgh, J., in United States v. Stokes, Bull. Dept. Just. No. 106, 12 (W. D. Mo., 1918). See also United States v. Pierce, Bull. Dept. Just. No. 52, 22 (S. D. N. Y., 1917), Ray, J.; United States v. Nearing, Bull. Dept. Just. No. 192, 4 (S. D. N. Y., 1917), Mayer, J.; United States v. Wallace, Bull. Dept. Just. No. 4, 4 (Iowa, 1917), Wade, J.

[21] History of the Criminal Law, II, 348 n.

[22] Cooley, Constitutional Limitations, 7th ed., p. 605; quoted by Hough, J., in Fraina v. United States, 255 Fed. 28, 35 (C. C. A. 2d, 1918).

To a judge obliged to decide whether honest and able opposition to the continuation of a war is punishable, these
generalizations furnish as much help as a woman forced, like
Isabella in *Measure for Measure*, to choose between her
brother's death and loss of honor, might obtain from the
pious maxim, "Do right." What is abuse? What is license?
What standards does the law afford? To argue that the federal
Constitution does not prevent punishment for criminal utterances begs the whole question, for utterances within its protection are not crimes. If it only safeguarded lawful speech,
Congress could escape its operation at any time by making
any class of speech unlawful. Suppose, for example, that
Congress declared any criticism of the particular administration in office to be a felony, punishable by ten years' imprisonment. Clearly, the Constitution must limit the power of
Congress to create crimes. But how far does that limitation
go?

Shall we say that the constitutional guaranties must be
interpreted in the light of the contemporary common law;
and that Congress and the state legislatures may punish as
they please any speech that was criminal or tortious before
1791? [23] We can all agree that the free speech clauses do not
wipe out the common law as to obscenity, profanity, and
defamation of individuals. But how about the common law
of sedition and libels against the government? Was this left
in full force by the First Amendment, although it was the
biggest of all the legal limitations on discussion of public
matters before the Revolution? No doubt conditions in 1791
must be considered, but they do not arbitrarily fix the division
between lawful and unlawful speech for all time.

Clearly, we must look further and find a rational test of
what is use and what is abuse. Saying that the line lies between them gets us nowhere. And "license" is too often
"liberty" to the speaker, and what happens to be anathema
to the judge.

One of the strongest reasons for the waywardness of trial
judges during the war was their inability to get guidance from
precedents. There were practically no satisfactory judicial

[23] See Cooley, *op. cit. supra*, pp. 604, 612 ff.; Schofield, p. 511; Sutherland, J.,
in the Grosjean case, quoted *infra*, Chapter XI, section IV.

discussions before 1917 about the meaning of the free speech clauses. The pre-war courts in construing such clauses did little more than place obvious cases on this or that side of the line. They told us, for instance, that libel and slander were actionable, or even punishable, that indecent books were criminal, that it was contempt to interfere ·with pending judicial proceedings, and that a permit could be required for street meetings; [24] and on the other hand, that some criticism of the government must be allowed, that a temperate examination of a judge's opinion was not contempt, and that honest discussion of the merits of a painting caused no liability for damages. But when we asked where the line actually ran and how they knew on which side of it a given utterance belonged, we found little answer in their opinions.

Even frequently quoted statements by Justice Holmes in his first Espionage Act decisions are open to the same adverse criticism — they tell us that plainly unlawful utterances are, to be sure, unlawful:

The First Amendment . . . obviously was not intended to give immunity for every possible use of language. . . . We venture to believe that neither Hamilton nor Madison, nor any other competent person then or later, ever supposed that to make criminal the counselling of a murder . . . would be an unconstitutional interference with free speech.[25]

The most stringent protection of free speech would not protect a man in falsely shouting fire in a theater and causing a panic.[26]

How about the man who gets up in a theater between the acts and informs the audience honestly, but perhaps mistakenly, that the fire exits are too few or locked? He is a much closer parallel to Frohwerk or Debs. How about James Russell Lowell when he counseled, not murder, but the cessation of murder, his name for war? The question whether such perplexing cases are within the First Amendment or not cannot be solved by the multiplication of obvious examples, but only by the development of a rational principle to mark the limits of constitutional protection.

[24] But as to such permits, see Hague v. C.I.O., 307 U. S. 496 (1939), discussed in Chapter XI, section VIII.

[25] Frohwerk v. United States, 249 U. S. 204 (1919).

[26] Schenck v. United States, 249 U. S. 47 (1919).

"The gradual process of judicial inclusion and exclusion," [27] which has served so well to define other clauses in the federal Constitution by blocking out concrete situations on each side of the line until the line itself becomes increasingly plain, was of very little use for the First Amendment before 1917. The pre-war cases were too few, too varied in their character, and often too easily solved to develop any definite boundary between lawful and unlawful speech.

Fortunately, we did get during the war years three very able judicial statements which take us far toward the ultimate solution of the problem of the limits of free speech, one by Judge Learned Hand in 1917 and two by Justice Holmes in 1919.[28] I shall return to these in the next two chapters.

For the moment, however, it may be worth while to forsake the purely judicial discussion of free speech, and obtain light upon its meaning from the history of the constitutional clauses and from the purpose free speech serves in social and political life.

The framers of the First Amendment make it plain that they regarded freedom of speech as very important; "absolutely necessary" is Luther Martin's phrase. But they say very little about its exact meaning. That should not surprise us if we recall our own vagueness about freedom of the seas. Men rarely define their inspirations until they are forced into doing so by sharp antagonism. Therefore, it is not until the Sedition Law of 1798 made the limits of liberty of the press a concrete and burning issue that we get much helpful expression of opinion on our problem.[29] Before that time, however, we have a few important pieces of evidence to show that the words were used in the Constitution in a wide and liberal sense.

On October 26, 1774, the Continental Congress issued an address to the inhabitants of Quebec, declaring that the English

[27] Miller, J., in Davidson v. New Orleans, 96 U. S. 97, 104 (1877).
[28] Masses Pub. Co. v. Patten, 244 Fed. 535 (S. D. N. Y., 1917); Schenck v. United States, 249 U. S. 47 (1919); Abrams v. United States, 250 U. S. 616, 624 (1919), Holmes dissenting.
[29] Anderson, "The Enforcement of the Alien and Sedition Laws," *Annual Report of the American Historical Association*, 1912, p. 115; Beveridge, *Life of John Marshall*, vols. II, III, *passim*; Carroll, "Freedom of Speech and of the Press in the Federalist Period; The Sedition Act," 18 *Michigan Law Review* 615 (1920).

colonists had five invaluable rights, representative government, trial by jury, liberty of the person, easy tenure of land, and freedom of the press:

The last right we shall mention regards the freedom of the press. The importance of this consists, besides the advancement of truth, science, morality and arts in general, in its diffusion of liberal sentiment on the administration of government, its ready communication of thoughts between subjects, and its consequential promotion of union among them, whereby oppressive officials are shamed or intimidated into more honorable and just modes of conducting affairs.[30]

In 1785 Virginia, which was the first state to insert a clause protecting the liberty of the press in its constitution (1776), enacted a statute drawn by Jefferson for Establishing Religious Freedom.[31] This opened with a very broad principle of toleration: "Whereas, Almighty God hath created the mind free; that all attempts to influence it by temporal punishments or burthens, or by civil incapacitations, tend only to beget habits of hypocrisy and meanness." Though this relates specifically to religion, it shows the trend of men's thoughts, and the meaning which "liberty" had to Jefferson long before the bitter controversy of 1798.

Benjamin Franklin,[32] in discussing the brief "freedom of speech" clause in the Pennsylvania Constitution of 1776, said in 1789 that if by the liberty of the press were to be understood merely the liberty of discussing the propriety of public measures and political opinions, let us have as much of it as you please. On the other hand, if it means liberty to calumniate another, there ought to be some limit.

The reason given by the Maryland convention of 1788 to the people for including a free speech clause in the proposed federal Bill of Rights was: "In prosecutions in the federal courts, for libels, the constitutional preservation of this great and fundamental right may prove invaluable." [33]

[30] Journal of the Continental Congress (ed. 1800), I, 57; quoted by Chief Justice Hughes in Near v. Minnesota, 283 U. S. at 717 (1931).

[31] See note 61, infra.

[32] Works, ed. A. H. Smyth, X, 36 ff. See Pa. Cons. (1776), c. I, sect. 12; Pa. Cons. (1790), Art. IX, sect. 7. Another article on free speech is reprinted in Sparks's edition of Franklin's Works, II, 285, with some doubts as to its genuineness. See infra, Chapter XIV.

[33] Elliot's Debates (2d ed.), II, 511; see the same argument in newspaper

The contemporaneous evidence in the passages just quoted shows that in the years before the First Amendment freedom of speech was conceived as giving a wide and genuine protection for all sorts of discussion of public matters. These various statements are, of course, absolutely inconsistent with any Blackstonian theory that liberty of the press forbids nothing except censorship. The men of 1791 went as far as Blackstone, and much farther.

If we apply Coke's test of statutory construction, and consider what mischief in the existing law the framers of the First Amendment wished to remedy by a new safeguard, we can be sure that it was not the censorship. This had expired in England in 1695, and in the colonies by 1725.[34] They knew from books that it destroyed liberty of the press; and if they ever thought of its revival as within the range of practical possibilities, they must have regarded it as clearly prohibited by the First Amendment.[35] But there was no need to go to all the trouble of pushing through a constitutional amendment just to settle an issue that had been dead for decades. What the framers did have plenty of reason to fear was an entirely different danger to political writers and speakers.

For years the government here and in England had substituted for the censorship rigorous and repeated prosecutions for seditious libel, which were directed against political discussion, and for years these prosecutions were opposed by liberal opinion and popular agitation. Primarily the controversy raged around two legal contentions of the great advocates for the defense, such as Erskine and Andrew Hamilton. They argued, first, that the jury and not the judge ought to decide whether the writing was seditious, and secondly, that the truth of the charge ought to prevent conviction. The real issue, however, lay much deeper. Two different views of the relation of rulers and people were in conflict. According to one view, the rulers were the superiors of the people, and there-

---

letters given in *Pennsylvania and the Federal Constitution*, ed. J. B. McMaster and F. D. Stone, pp. 151, 181. The second letter suggests the possibility of a prohibitive stamp tax as in Massachusetts to crush the press.

[34] Macaulay, *History of England*, chap. xxi; C. A. Duniway, *Freedom of Speech in Massachusetts*, p. 89 n. See *infra*, Chapter XIII, at note 3.

[35] See Near *v.* Minnesota, 283 U. S. 697 (1931), discussed in Chapter XI, section III.

fore must not be subjected to any censure that would tend to diminish their authority. The people could not make adverse criticism in newspapers or pamphlets, but only through their lawful representatives in the legislature, who might be petitioned in an orderly manner. According to the other view, the rulers were agents and servants of the people, who might therefore find fault with their servants and discuss questions of their punishment or dismissal, and of governmental policy.

Under the first view, which was officially accepted until the close of the eighteenth century, developed the law of seditious libel. This was defined as "the intentional publication, without lawful excuse or justification, of written blame of any public man, or of the law, or of any institution established by law." There was no need to prove any intention on the part of the defendant to produce disaffection or excite an insurrection. It was enough if he intended to publish the blame, because it was unlawful in him merely to find fault with his masters and betters. Such, in the opinion of the best authorities, was the common law of sedition.[36]

It is obvious that under this law liberty of the press was nothing more than absence of the censorship, as Blackstone said. All through the eighteenth century, however, there existed beside this definite legal meaning of liberty of the press, a definite popular meaning: the right of unrestricted discussion of public affairs. There can be no doubt that this was in a general way what freedom of speech meant to the framers of the Constitution. Thus Madison, who drafted the First Amendment, bases his explanation of it in 1799 on "the essential difference between the British Government and the American constitutions." In the United States the people and not the government possess the absolute sovereignty, and the legislature as well as the executive is under limitations of power. Hence, Congress is not free to punish anything which was criminal at English common law. A government which is "elective, limited and responsible" in all its branches may

[36] Madison, Report on the Virginia Resolutions, 1799, *Elliot's Debates* (2d ed.), IV, 596 ff.; Stephen, *History of the Criminal Law*, II, 299, 353, and chap. xxiv, *passim*; Schofield, II, 511 ff., gives an excellent summary with especial reference to American conditions.

The eighteenth-century controversy concerning seditious libel prosecutions will be more fully discussed in Chapter XIII.

well be supposed to require "a greater freedom of animadver-sion" [37] than might be tolerated by one that is composed of an irresponsible hereditary king and upper house, and an omnipotent legislature.

This contemporary testimony corroborates the conclusions of Professor Schofield:

One of the objects of the Revolution was to get rid of the English common law on liberty of speech and of the press. . . . Liberty of the press as declared in the First Amendment, and the English common-law crime of sedition, cannot co-exist.[38]

There are a few early judicial decisions to the contrary, but they ought not to weigh against the statements of Madison and the general temper of the time. These judges were surely wrong in holding as they did that sedition was a common-law crime in the federal courts, and in other respects they drew their inspiration from British precedents and the British bench instead of being in close contact with the new ideas of this country. "Indeed," as Senator Beveridge says, "some of them were more British than they were American." "Let a stranger go into our courts," wrote one observer, "and he would almost believe himself in the Court of the King's Bench." [39] Great as was the service of these judges in establishing the common law as to private rights, their testimony as to its place in public affairs is of much less value than the other contemporary evi-dence of the men who sat in the conventions and argued over the adoption of the Constitution. The judges forgot the truth emphasized by Maitland: "The law of a nation can only be studied in relation to the whole national life." I must there-fore strongly dissent, with Justice Holmes,[40] from the posi-tion sometimes taken in arguments on the Espionage Act, that the founders of our government left the common law as to seditious libel in force and merely intended by the First Amend-

[37] Madison's Report on the Virginia Resolutions, *Elliot's Debates* (2d ed.), IV, 596–598. As draftsman of the Amendment, Madison's views about its in-terpretation carry great weight, although they were written down eight years after its adoption and may have been somewhat modified during the interval by his opposition to the Sedition Act of 1798. The same distinction was made by Erastus Root, *Report of the New York Constitutional Convention of 1821*, p. 489. See also *Speeches of Charles Pinckney* (1800), pp. 116 ff.

[38] Schofield, II, 521–522, 535.   [39] Beveridge's *Marshall*, III, 23–29.

[40] Abrams *v.* U. S., 250 U. S. 616 (1919).

ment "to limit the new government's statutory powers to penalize utterances as seditious, to those which were seditious under
the then accepted common-law rule." [41] The founders had
seen seventy English prosecutions for libel since 1760, and
fifty convictions under that common-law rule, which made
conviction easy.[42] That rule had been detested in this country
ever since it was repudiated by jury and populace in the famous
trial of Peter Zenger, the New York printer, the account of
which went through fourteen editions before 1791.[43] The close
relation between the Zenger trial and the prosecutions under
George III in England and America is shown by the quotations
on reprints of the trial and the dedication of the 1784 London
edition to Erskine, as well as by reference to Zenger in the
discussions preceding the First Amendment. Nor was this the
only colonial sedition prosecution under the common law, and
many more were threatened. All the American cases before
1791 prove that our common law of sedition was exactly like
that of England, and it would be extraordinary if the First
Amendment enacted the English sedition law of that time,
which was repudiated by every American and every liberal
Englishman,[44] and altered through Fox's Libel Act by Parliament itself in the very next year, 1792. We might well
fling at the advocates of this common law view the challenge
of Randolph of Roanoke, "whether the common law of libels
which attaches to this Constitution be the doctrine laid down
by Lord Mansfield, or that which has immortalized Mr. Fox?" [45]
The First Amendment was written by men to whom Wilkes
and Junius were household words, who intended to wipe out
the common law of sedition, and make further prosecutions
for criticism of the government, without any incitement to
law-breaking, forever impossible in the United States of
America.

[41] W. R. Vance, in "Freedom of Speech and the Press," 2 *Minnesota Law
Review*, 239, 259.

[42] May, *Constitutional History of England* (2d ed.), II, 9 n.

[43] 17 How. St. Tr. 675 (1735); Rutherford, *John Peter Zenger* (New York,
1904). See also the life of Zenger's counsel, Andrew Hamilton, by William
Henry Loyd, in *Great American Lawyers*, I, 1.

[44] May, *Constitutional History of England*, vol. II, chap. ix; Stephen, *History of the Criminal Law*, vol. II, chap. xxiv.

[45] Beveridge's *Marshall*, III, 85.

It must not be forgotten that the controversy over liberty of the press was a conflict between two views of government, that the law of sedition was a product of the view that the government was master, and that the American Revolution transformed into a working reality the second view that the government was servant, and therefore subjected to blame from its master, the people. Consequently, the words of Sir James Fitzjames Stephen about this second view have a vital application to American law.

To those who hold this view fully and carry it out to all its consequences there can be no such offense as sedition. There may indeed be breaches of the peace which may destroy or endanger life, limb, or property, and there may be incitements to such offenses, but no imaginable censure of the government, *short of a censure which has an immediate tendency to produce such a breach of the peace*, ought to be regarded as criminal.[46]

In short, the framers of the First Amendment sought to preserve the fruits of the old victory abolishing the censorship, and to achieve a new victory abolishing sedition prosecutions.

The repudiation by the constitutions of the English common law of sedition, which was also the common law of the American colonies, has been obscured by some judicial retention of the two technical incidents of the old law after the adoption of the free speech clauses. Many judges, rightly or wrongly, continued to pass on the criminality of the writing and to reject its truth as a defense,[47] until statutes or new constitutional provisions embodying the popular view on these two points were enacted.[48] Doubtless, a jury will protect a popular attack on the government better than a judge, and the admission of truth as a defense lessens the evils of suppression. These procedural changes help to substitute the modern view of rulers for the old view, but they are not enough by themselves to establish freedom of speech. Juries can

[46] Stephen, *History of the Criminal Law*, II, 300. The italics are mine. See also Schofield, II, 520 ff.

[47] Duniway, *supra*, chap. ix; Commonwealth *v.* Clap, 4 Mass. 163 (1808); Commonwealth *v.* Blanding, 3 Pick. (Mass.) 304 (1825).

[48] Examples are: Pa. Cons. 1790, Art. 9, § 7; N. Y. Session Laws, 1805, c. 90; N. Y. Cons., 1821, Art. VII, § 8; Mass. Laws, 1827, c. 107. See Schofield, II, 540 ff.

suppress much-needed political discussion in times of intolerance, so long as the substantive common law or a statute defines criminal utterances in sweeping and loose terms. Sedition prosecutions went on with shameful severity in England [49] after Fox's Libel Act [50] had given the jury power to determine criminality. The American Sedition Act of 1798, which President Wilson declares to have "cut perilously near the root of freedom of speech and of the press," [51] entrusted criminality to the jury and admitted truth as a defense. On the other hand, freedom of speech might exist without these two technical safeguards.

The essential question is not, who is judge of the criminality of an utterance, but what is the test of its criminality. The common law and the Sedition Act of 1798 made the test blame of the government and its officials, because to bring them into disrepute tended to overthrow the state. The real issue in every free speech controversy is this: whether the state can punish all words which have some tendency, however remote, to bring about acts in violation of law, or only words which directly incite to acts in violation of law.

If words do not become criminal until they have "an immediate tendency to produce a breach of the peace," there is no need for a law of sedition, since the ordinary standards of criminal solicitation and attempt apply. Under those standards the words must bring the speaker's unlawful intention reasonably near to success. Such a limited power to punish utterances rarely satisfies the zealous in times of excitement like a war. They realize that all condemnation of the war or of conscription may conceivably lead to active resistance or insubordination. Is it not better to kill the serpent in the egg? All writings that have even a remote tendency to hinder the war must be suppressed.

Such has always been the argument of the opponents of

[49] Brown, *The French Revolution in English History*, pp. 118–162.
[50] 32 Geo. 3, c. 60 (1792): "On every such [criminal libel] trial the jury sworn to try the issue may give a general verdict of guilty or not guilty upon the whole matter put in issue . . . and shall not be required or directed by the Court or judge . . . to find the defendant . . . guilty merely on the proof of publication by such defendant . . . of the paper charged to be a libel, and of the sense ascribed to the same in such indictment or information."
[51] Woodrow Wilson, *History of the American People*, III, 153.

free speech. And the most powerful weapon in their hands, since the abolition of the censorship, is this doctrine of indirect causation, under which words can be punished for a supposed bad tendency long before there is any probability that they will break out into unlawful acts. Closely related to it is the doctrine of constructive intent, which regards the intent of the defendant to cause violence as immaterial so long as he intended to write the words, or else presumes the violent intent from the bad tendency of the words on the ground that a man is presumed to intend the consequences of his acts. When rulers are allowed to possess these weapons, they can by the imposition of severe sentences create an *ex post facto* censorship of the press. The transference of that censorship from the judge to the jury is indeed important when the attack on the government which is prosecuted expresses a widespread popular sentiment, but the right to jury trial is of much less value in times of war or threatened disorder when the herd instinct runs strong, if the opinion of the defendant is highly objectionable to the majority of the population, or even to the particular class of men from whom or by whom the jury are drawn.

Under Charles II trial by jury was a blind and cruel system. During the last part of the reign of George III it was, to say the least, quite as severe as the severest judge without a jury could have been. The revolutionary tribunal during the Reign of Terror tried by a jury.[52] It is worth our frank consideration, whether in a country where the doctrine of indirect causation is recognized by the courts twelve small property-holders, who have been through an uninterrupted series of patriotic campaigns and are sufficiently middle-aged to be in no personal danger of compulsory military service, are fitted to decide whether there is a tendency to obstruct the draft in the writings of a pacifist, who also happens to be a Socialist and in sympathy with the Russian Revolution. This, however, is perhaps a problem for the psychologist rather than the lawyer.

Another significant fact in sedition prosecutions is the

[52] Stephen, *History of the Criminal Law*, I, 569.

well-known probability that juries will acquit, after the excitement is over, for words used during the excitement, which are as bad in their tendency as other writings prosecuted and severely punished during the critical period. This was very noticeable during the reign of George III. It is also interesting to find two juries in different parts of the country differing as to the criminal character of similar publications or even the same publication. Thus Leigh Hunt was acquitted for writing an article, for the printing of which John Drakard was convicted. The acquittal of Scott Nearing and the conviction by the same jury of the American Socialist Society for publishing his book form an interesting parallel.[53]

The manner in which juries in time of excitement may be used to suppress writings in opposition to the government, if bad tendency is recognized as a test of criminality, is illustrated by the numerous British sedition trials during the wars with Revolutionary France and Napoleon, after the passage of Fox's Libel Act. For instance, in the case just mentioned, Drakard was convicted for printing an article on the shameful amount of flogging in the army, under a charge in which Baron Wood emphasized the formidable foe with whom England was fighting, and the general belief that Napoleon was using the British press to carry out his purpose of securing her downfall.

It is to be feared, there are in this country many who are endeavoring to aid and assist him in his projects, by crying down the establishment of the country, and breeding hatred against the government. Whether that is the source from whence the paper in question springs, I cannot say, but I advise you to consider whether it has not that tendency. You will consider whether it contains a fair discussion — whether it has not a manifest tendency to create disaffection in the country and prevent men enlisting into the army — whether it does not tend to induce the soldier to desert from the service of his country. And what considerations can be more awful than these? . . .

The House of Parliament is the proper place for the discussion of subjects of this nature . . . It is said that we have a right to discuss the acts of our legislature. That would be a large permission

[53] Judge Mayer decided that there was not such inconsistency in the two verdicts as to warrant a new trial. American Socialist Society v. United States, 260 Fed. 885 (1919).

indeed. Is there, gentlemen, to be a power in the people to counteract the acts of the parliament, and is the libeller to come and make the people dissatisfied with the government under which he lives? This is not to be permitted to any man — it is unconstitutional and seditious.[54]

The same emphasis on bad tendency appears in Lord Ellenborough's charge at Leigh Hunt's trial, although it failed to secure his conviction.

Can you conceive that the exhibition of the words "One Thousand Lashes," with strokes underneath to attract attention, could be for any other purpose than to excite disaffection? Could it have any other tendency than that of preventing men from entering into the army? [55]

The same desire to nip revolution in the bud was shown by the Scotch judges who secured the conviction of Muir and Palmer for advocating reform of the rotten boroughs which chose the House of Commons and the extension of the franchise, sentences of transportation for seven and fourteen years being imposed.

The right of universal suffrage, the subjects of this country never enjoyed; and were they to enjoy it, they would not long enjoy either liberty or a free constitution. You will, therefore, consider whether telling the people that they have a just right to what would unquestionably be tantamount to a total subversion of this constitution, is such a writing as any person is entitled to compose, to print, and to publish.[56]

American sentiment about sedition trials was decisively shown by an expedition to New South Wales to rescue Muir, a sort of reverse deportation.

In the light of such prosecutions it is plain that the most vital indication that the popular definition of liberty of the

---

[54] 31 How. St. Tr. 495, 535 (1811).

[55] 31 How. St. Tr. 367, 408, 413 (1811).

[56] May, *Constitutional History*, II, 38–41, on the trials of Muir and Palmer; Brown, *The French Revolution in English History*, p. 97. Fourteen years appears to have been the longest sentence for sedition imposed in Scotland during the French wars. Four years was the longest in England. See note 80 in Chapter II, *infra*, for sentences under the Espionage Act. Compare with these charges that of Van Valkenburgh, J., in United States *v.* Rose Pastor Stokes, *infra*, and the remarks of Judge Clayton in the Abrams trial in Chapter III.

press, unpunishable criticism of officials and laws, has become a reality, is the disappearance of these doctrines of bad tendency and presumptive intent. In Great Britain they lingered until liberalism triumphed in 1832,[57] but in this country they disappeared with the adoption of the free speech clauses.

The revival of those doctrines is a sure symptom of an attack upon the liberty of the press.

Only once in our history prior to 1917 has an attempt been made to apply those doctrines. In 1798 the impending war with France, the spread of revolutionary doctrines by foreigners in our midst, and the spectacle of the disastrous operation of those doctrines abroad — facts that have a familiar sound today — led to the enactment of the Alien and Sedition Laws.[58] The Alien Law allowed the President to compel the departure of aliens whom he judged dangerous to the peace and safety of the United States, or suspected, on reasonable grounds, of treasonable or secret machinations against our government. The Sedition Law punished false, scandalous, and malicious writings against the government, either House of Congress, or the President, if published with intent to defame any of them, or to excite against them the hatred of the people, or to stir up sedition or to excite resistance of law, or to aid any hostile designs of any foreign nation against the United States. The maximum penalty was a fine of two thousand dollars and two years' imprisonment. Truth was a defense, and the jury had power to determine criminality as under Fox's Libel Act. Despite the inclusion of the two legal rules for which reformers had contended, and the requirement of an actual intention to cause overt injury, the Sedition Act was bitterly resented as invading the liberty of the press. Its constitutionality was assailed on that ground by Jefferson, who pardoned all prisoners when he became President; Congress eventually repaid all the fines; and popular indignation at the Act and the prosecutions wrecked the Federalist party. In those prosecutions words were once more made punishable for their judicially supposed bad tendency, and the judges re-

[57] That they may not have wholly disappeared even yet is indicated by the definition of sedition in Stephen's *Digest of Criminal Law*, which should have no application to American law. See also House Judiciary Hearings on S. 3317 etc., 66th Cong., 2d Sess., p. 277.

[58] Act of June 25, 1798, 1 Stat. 570; Act of July 14, 1798, 1 Stat. 596.

duced the test of intent to a fiction by inferring the bad intent
from this bad tendency.

Whether or not the Sedition Act was unconstitutional, and
on that question Jefferson seems right, it surely defeated the
fundamental policy of the First Amendment, the open discussion of public affairs. Like the British trials, the American
sedition cases showed, as Professor Schofield demonstrates,[59]
"the great danger . . . that men will be fined and imprisoned,
under the guise of being punished for their bad motives, or
bad intent and ends, simply because the powers that be do
not agree with their opinions, and spokesmen of minorities
may be terrorized and silenced when they are most needed
by the community and most useful to it, and when they stand
most in need of the protection of the law against a hostile,
arrogant majority." When the Democrats got into power, a
common-law prosecution for seditious libel was brought in
New York against a Federalist who had attacked Jefferson.
Hamilton conducted the defense in the name of the liberty
of the press.[60] This testimony from Jefferson and Hamilton,
the leaders of both parties, leaves the Blackstonian interpretation of free speech in America without a leg to stand on. And
the brief attempt of Congress and the Federalist judges to
revive the crime of sedition had proved so disastrous that it
was not repeated during the next century.

The lesson of the prosecutions for sedition in Great Britain
and the United States during this revolutionary period, that
the most essential element of free speech is the rejection of
bad tendency as the test of a criminal utterance, was never
more clearly recognized than in Jefferson's preamble to the
Virginia Act for establishing Religious Freedom. His words
about religious liberty hold good of political and speculative
freedom, and the portrayal of human life in every form of art.

---

[59] Schofield, *op. cit.*, II, 540, and 541, note 43.
[60] People *v.* Croswell, 3 Johns. Cas. 337 (1804). New York had then no
constitutional guarantee of liberty of the press, but Hamilton urged that under
that right at common law truth was a defense and the jury could decide on
criminality. He defined liberty of the press as "The right to publish, with impunity, truth, with good motives, for justifiable ends though reflecting on government, magistracy, or individuals." See Schofield, *op. cit.*, II, 537 ff., for
criticism of this definition as not in the common law and as too narrow a definition of the conception of free speech. However, it is embodied in many state
constitutions and statutes. Two out of four judges agreed with Hamilton.

To suffer the civil Magistrate to intrude his powers into the field of opinion, and to restrain the profession or propagation of principles on supposition of their ill tendency, is a dangerous fallacy, which at once destroys all religious liberty, because he being of course judge of that tendency, will make his opinions the rule of judgment, and approve or condemn the sentiments of others only as they shall square with or differ from his own.[61]

Although the free speech clauses were directed primarily against the sedition prosecutions of the immediate past, it must not be thought that they would permit unlimited previous restraint. They must also be interpreted in the light of more remote history. The framers of those clauses did not invent the conception of freedom of speech as a result of their own experience of the last few years. The idea had been gradually molded in men's minds by centuries of conflict. It was the product of a people of whom the framers were merely the mouthpiece. Its significance was not fixed by their personality, but was the endless expression of a civilization.[62] It was formed out of past resentment against the royal control of the press under the Tudors, against the Star Chamber and the pillory, against the Parliamentary censorship which Milton condemned in his *Areopagitica*, by recollections of heavy newspaper taxation, by hatred of the suppression of thought which went on vigorously on the Continent during the eighteenth century. Blackstone's views also had undoubted influence to bar out previous restraint. The censor is the most dangerous of all the enemies of liberty of the press, and ought not to exist in this country unless made necessary by extraordinary perils.

Moreover, the meaning of the First Amendment did not crystallize in 1791. The framers would probably have been horrified at the thought of protecting books by Darwin or Bernard Shaw, but "liberty of speech" is no more confined to the speech they thought permissible than "commerce" in another clause is limited to the sailing vessels and horse-

[61] Act of December 26, 1785, 12 Hening's *Statutes at Large of Virginia* (1823), c. 34, page 84. Another excellent argument against the punishment of tendencies is found in Philip Furneaux, *Letters to Blackstone* (2d ed.), pp. 60–63 (London, 1771) ; quoted in State *v.* Chandler, 2 Harr. (Del.) 553, 576 (1837), and in part by Schofield, II, 523.

[62] 1 Kohler, *Lehrbuch des Bürgerlichen Rechts*, I, § 38.

drawn vehicles of 1787. Into the making of the constitutional conception of free speech have gone, not only men's bitter experience of the censorship and sedition prosecutions before 1791, but also the subsequent development of the law of fair comment in civil defamation, and the philosophical speculations of John Stuart Mill. Justice Holmes phrases the thought with even more than his habitual felicity.[63] "The provisions of the Constitution are not mathematical formulas having their essence in their form; they are organic living institutions transplanted from English soil."

It is now clear that the First Amendment fixes limits upon the power of Congress to restrict speech either by a censorship or by a criminal statute, and if the Espionage Act exceeds those limits it is unconstitutional. It is sometimes argued that the Constitution gives Congress the power to declare war, raise armies, and support a navy, that one provision of the Constitution cannot be used to break down another provision, and consequently freedom of speech cannot be invoked to break down the war power.[64] I would reply that the First Amendment is just as much a part of the Constitution as the war clauses, and that it is equally accurate to say that the war clauses cannot be invoked to break down freedom of speech. The truth is that all provisions of the Constitution must be construed together so as to limit each other. In a war as in peace, this process of mutual adjustment must include the Bill of Rights. There are those who believe that the Bill of Rights can be set aside in war time at the uncontrolled will of the government.[65] The first ten amendments were drafted by men who had just been through a war. The Third and Fifth Amendments expressly apply in war. A majority of the Supreme Court declared the war power of Congress to be restricted by the Bill of Rights in Ex parte *Milligan*.[66] If the

[63] Gompers v. United States, 233 U. S. 604, 610 (1914).

[64] United States v. Marie Equi, Bull. Dept. Just., No. 172, 21 (Ore., 1918), Bean, J.

[65] Henry J. Fletcher, "The Civilian and the War Power," 2 *Minnesota Law Review* 110, expresses this view. See also Ambrose Tighe, "The Legal Theory of the Minnesota 'Safety Commission' Act," 3 *Minnesota Law Review* 1.

[66] 4 Wallace (U. S.) 2 (1866). It may be that military tribunals are necessary where the machinery of the civil courts cannot adequately meet the situation (3 *Minnesota Law Review* 9), but the civil courts must eventually decide whether their machinery was adequate or not. Otherwise, in any war, no matter

First Amendment is to mean anything, it must restrict powers which are expressly granted by the Constitution to Congress, since Congress has no other powers.[67] It must apply to those activities of government which are most liable to interfere with free discussion, namely, the postal service and the conduct of war.

The true meaning of freedom of speech seems to be this. One of the most important purposes of society and government is the discovery and spread of truth on subjects of general concern. This is possible only through absolutely unlimited discussion, for, as Bagehot points out, once force is thrown into the argument, it becomes a matter of chance whether it is thrown on the false side or the true, and truth loses all its natural advantage in the contest. Nevertheless, there are other purposes of government, such as order, the training of the young, protection against external aggression. Unlimited discussion sometimes interferes with these purposes, which must then be balanced against freedom of speech, but freedom of speech ought to weigh very heavily in the scale. The First Amendment gives binding force to this principle of political wisdom.

Or to put the matter another way, it is useless to define free speech by talk about rights. The agitator asserts his constitutional right to speak, the government asserts its constitutional right to wage war. The result is a deadlock. Each side takes the position of the man who was arrested for swinging his arms and hitting another in the nose, and asked the judge if he did not have a right to swing his arms in a free country. "Your right to swing your arms ends just where the other man's nose begins." To find the boundary line of any right, we must get behind rules of law to human facts. In our

how small or how distant, Congress could put the whole country under military dictatorship.

[67] United States Constitution, Art. I, § 1: "All legislative powers herein granted shall be vested in a Congress." Amendment X: "The powers not delegated to the United States by the Constitution, nor prohibited by it to the States, are reserved to the States respectively or to the people."

"This government is acknowledged by all to be one of enumerated powers. The principle that it can exercise only the powers granted to it, would seem too apparent." — Marshall, C.J., in McCulloch v. Maryland, 4 Wheaton (U. S.) 316, 405 (1819). See also Taney, C.J., in Ex parte Merryman, Taney, 236, 260 (1861), and Brewer, J., in Kansas v. Colorado, 206 U. S. 46, 81 (1907).

problem, we must regard the desires and needs of the individual human being who wants to speak and those of the great group of human beings among whom he speaks. That is, in technical language, there are individual interests and social interests, which must be balanced against each other, if they conflict, in order to determine which interest shall be sacrificed under the circumstances and which shall be protected and become the foundation of a legal right.[68] It must never be forgotten that the balancing cannot be properly done unless all the interests involved are adequately ascertained, and the great evil of all this talk about rights is that each side is so busy denying the other's claim to rights that it entirely overlooks the human desires and needs behind that claim.

The rights and powers of the Constitution, aside from the portions which create the machinery of the federal system, are largely means of protecting important individual and social interests, and because of this necessity of balancing such interests the clauses cannot be construed with absolute literalness. The Fourteenth Amendment and the obligation of contracts clause, maintaining important individual interests, are modified by the police power of the states, which protects health and other social interests. The Thirteenth Amendment is subject to many implied exceptions, so that temporary involuntary servitude is permitted to secure social interests in the construction of roads, the prevention of vagrancy, the training of the militia or national army. It is common to rest these implied exceptions to the Bill of Rights upon the ground that they existed in 1791 and long before, but a less arbitrary explanation is desirable. Not everything old is good. Thus the antiquity of peonage does not constitute it an exception to the Thirteenth Amendment; it is not now demanded by any strong social interest. It is significant that the social interest in shipping which formerly required the compulsory labor of articled sailors is no longer recognized in the United States as sufficiently important to outweigh the individual interest in free locomotion and choice of occupation. Even treaties

[68] This distinction between rights and interests clarifies almost any constitutional controversy. The distinction originated with von Ihering. See John Chipman Gray, *Nature and Sources of the Law* (2d ed.), pp. 17 ff.; Roscoe Pound, "Interests of Personality," 28 *Harvard Law Review* 453.

providing for the apprehension in our ports of deserting foreign seamen have been abrogated by the La Follette Seamen's Act. The Bill of Rights does not crystallize antiquity. It seems better to say that long usage does not create an exception to the absolute language of the Constitution, but demonstrates the importance of the social interest behind the exception.[69]

The First Amendment protects two kinds of interests in free speech. There is an individual interest, the need of many men to express their opinions on matters vital to them if life is to be worth living, and a social interest in the attainment of truth, so that the country may not only adopt the wisest course of action but carry it out in the wisest way. This social interest is especially important in war time. Even after war has been declared there is bound to be a confused mixture of good and bad arguments in its support, and a wide difference of opinion as to its objects. Truth can be sifted out from falsehood only if the government is vigorously and constantly cross-examined, so that the fundamental issues of the struggle may be clearly defined, and the war may not be diverted to improper ends, or conducted with an undue sacrifice of life and liberty, or prolonged after its just purposes are accomplished. Legal proceedings prove that an opponent makes the best cross-examiner. Consequently it is a disastrous mistake to limit criticism to those who favor the war. Men bitterly hostile to it may point out evils in its management like the secret treaties, which its supporters have been too busy to unearth. If a free canvassing of the aims of the war by its opponents is crushed by the menace of long imprisonment, such evils, even though made public in one or two newspapers, may not come to the attention of those who had power to counteract them until too late.[70]

[69] This paragraph rests on Butler v. Perry, 240 U. S. 328 (1916); Robertson v. Baldwin, 165 U. S. 275, 281 (1897); Bailey v. Alabama, 219 U. S. 219 (1911); Act of March 4, 1915, c. 153, § 16 [22 U. S. C. A. (1926), § 258]; Hurtado v. California, 110 U. S. 516 (1884).

[70] "Senator Borah — 'Then we had no knowledge of these secret treaties so far as our Government was concerned until you reached Paris?'

"The President — 'Not unless there was information at the State Department of which I knew nothing.'" — *New York Times*, Aug. 20, 1919.

In 1940 we learned that on May 18, 1917, Arthur J. Balfour delivered to Secretary of State Lansing a long document telling much about the secret treaties with Italy and Russia. — *Foreign Relations of the United States: The*

The history of the years between 1914 and 1919 shows how the objects of a war may change completely during its progress, and it is well that those objects should be steadily reformulated under the influence of open discussion not only by those who demand a military victory, but by pacifists who take a different view of the national welfare. Further argument for the existence of this social interest becomes unnecessary if we recall the national value of the opposition in former wars.

The great trouble with most judicial construction of the Espionage Act is that this social interest has been ignored and free speech has been regarded as merely an individual interest, which must readily give way like other personal desires the moment it interferes with the social interest in national safety. The judge who has done most to bring social interests into legal thinking said years ago, "I think that the judges themselves have failed adequately to recognize their duty of weighing considerations of social advantage. The duty is inevitable, and the result of the often proclaimed judicial aversion to deal with such considerations is simply to leave the very ground and foundation of judgments inarticulate and often unconscious." [71] The failure of the courts in the past to formulate any principle for drawing a boundary line around the right of free speech not only threw the judges into the difficult questions of the Espionage Act without any well-considered standard of criminality, but also allowed some of them to impose standards of their own and fix the line at a point which makes all opposition to this or any future war impossible. For example:

No man should be permitted, by deliberate act, or even unthinkingly, to do that which will in any way detract from the efforts

---

Lansing Papers, II, 19–32 (1940). In January, 1918, Balfour wrote President Wilson a letter specifically discussing the secret treaty with Italy. On April 28, 1918, Colonel House recorded in his diary a conversation with Balfour about the nature and scope of the secret treaties. President Seymour of Yale comments: "The mystery of Wilson's statement to the Senate Foreign Relations Committee . . . remains unsolved." — *Foreign Affairs*, XIX, 416 (1941). The statements by R. S. Baker, *Woodrow Wilson and the War Settlement*, I, 34, must now be considered superseded.

[71] Oliver Wendell Holmes, "The Path of the Law," 10 *Harvard Law Review* 457, 467. (Holmes, *Collected Legal Papers*, p. 184.)

which the United States is putting forth or serve to postpone for a single moment the early coming of the day when the success of our arms shall be a fact.[72]

The true boundary line of the First Amendment can be fixed only when Congress and the courts realize that the principle on which speech is classified as lawful or unlawful involves the balancing against each other of two very important social interests, in public safety and in the search for truth. Every reasonable attempt should be made to maintain both interests unimpaired, and the great interest in free speech should be sacrificed only when the interest in public safety is really imperiled, and not, as most men believe, when it is barely conceivable that it may be slightly affected. In war time, therefore, speech should be unrestricted by the censorship or by punishment, unless it is clearly liable to cause direct and dangerous interference with the conduct of the war.

Thus our problem of locating the boundary line of free speech is solved. It is fixed close to the point where words will give rise to unlawful acts. We cannot define the right of free speech with the precision of the Rule against Perpetuities or the Rule in Shelley's Case, because it involves national policies which are much more flexible than private property, but we can establish a workable principle of classification in this method of balancing and this broad test of certain danger. There is a similar balancing in the determination of what is "due process of law." We can insist upon various procedural safeguards which make it more probable that a tribunal will give the value of open discussion its proper weight in the balance. Fox's Libel Act is such a safeguard, and others will be considered in the next chapter. And we can with certitude declare that the First Amendment forbids the punishment of words merely for their injurious tendencies. The history of the Amendment and the political function of free speech corroborate each other and make this conclusion plain.

[72] United States v. "The Spirit of '76," 252 Fed. 946. Another good example is United States v. Schoberg, Bull. Dept. Just., No. 149.

CHAPTER 2

WAR-TIME PROSECUTIONS

*First of all, . . . it must be a peace without victory.
. . . Victory would mean peace forced upon the loser, a
victor's terms imposed upon the vanquished. It would
be accepted in humiliation, under duress, at an intolerable
sacrifice, and would leave a sting, a resentment, a bitter
memory upon which terms of peace would rest, not permanently, but only as upon quicksand. Only a peace
between equals can last. Only a peace the very principle
of which is equality and a common participation in a
common benefit. The right state of mind, the right feeling between nations, is as necessary for a lasting peace
as is the just settlement of vexed questions of territory
or of racial and national allegiance.* WOODROW WILSON,
Address to the Senate, January 22, 1917.

ON April 6, 1917, Congress declared war against Germany. On May 18 it enacted the Selective Service Act
for raising a National Army. The people, by an overwhelming
majority, believed conscription to be a necessary and just
method of waging an unavoidable war, and the machinery for
enforcing the draft by civilian aid was admirably planned.
"The result," says Attorney General Gregory,[1] "was that the
ultimate opposition to the draft by those liable was surprisingly
small, considering the persistent propaganda carried on against
the policy of the law and against its constitutionality." And
his Assistant, Mr. John Lord O'Brian, adds, "No anti-draft
propaganda had the slightest chance of success." The decision of the Supreme Court sustaining the validity of the statute [2]
merely fulfilled the general expectation.

Besides the military and civilian organization for reaching
the men who were liable to registration and subsequently called

[1] Report of the Attorney General, 1917, p. 74; "Civil Liberty in War Time,"
John Lord O'Brian, 42 Rep. N. Y. Bar Assn. 275, 291 (1919), cited hereafter
as O'Brian.
[2] Selective Draft Law Cases, 245 U. S. 366 (1918).

into service, the government had at its disposal several criminal statutes enacted during the Civil War. These it could and did use to punish conspiracies by Emma Goldman and others aiming to resist recruiting and conscription by riots and other forcible means, or seeking by speeches and publications to induce men to evade the draft.[3] In some respects, however, these statutes were felt by the Department of Justice to be incomplete. (1) It was not a crime to persuade a man not to enlist voluntarily. (2) Inasmuch as one man cannot make a conspiracy all by himself, a deliberate attempt by an isolated individual to obstruct the draft, if unsuccessful, was beyond the reach of the law. except when his conduct was sufficiently serious to amount to treason. The treason statute, the only law on the books affecting the conduct of the individual, was of little service,[4] since there was considerable doubt whether it applied to utterances. Therefore, although it is probable that under the circumstances the existing conspiracy statutes would have taken care of any serious danger to the prosecution of the war, new legislation was demanded.

If the government had been content to limit itself to meeting the tangible needs just mentioned, the effect on discussion of the war would probably have been very slight, for treason, conspiracies, and actual attempts constitute a direct and dangerous interference with the war, outside the protection of freedom of speech as defined in the preceding chapter. Two additional factors, however, influenced the terms of the new statutes, and even more the spirit in which they were enforced. First came the recollection of the opposition during the Civil War, which was handled under martial law in so far as it was suppressed at all. Some persons, full of old tales of Copper-

---

[3] These statutes are now 18 U. S. C. A. (1926), §§ 4, 6, 88, 550; see *infra* Chapter IV, section 1. World War conspiracy cases thereunder include Emma Goldman *v.* United States, 245 U. S. 474 (1918); Wells *v.* U. S., 257 Fed. 605 (C. C. A., 1919); U. S. *v.* Phillips, Bull. Dept. Just., No. 14 (1917); Bryant *v.* U. S., 257 Fed. 378 (C. C. A., 1919); Orear *v.* U. S., 261 Fed. 267 (C. C. A., 1919); U. S. *v.* Reeder, Bull. Dept. Just., No. 161 (1918).

[4] O'Brian, 277. The treason statute is now 18 U. S. C. A. (1926), §§ 1, 2; see Warren, "What is Giving Aid and Comfort to the Enemy?" 27 *Yale Law Journal* 331 (1918). The legal scope of treason is discussed in Chapter VI, section 11. World War treason cases include U. S. *v.* Werner, 247 Fed. 708 (1918); U. S. *v.* Robinson, 259 Fed. 685 (1919); U. S. *v.* Fricke, 259 Fed. 673 (1919).

heads, were eager to treat all opponents of this war as spies and traitors. A bill was actually introduced into the Senate which made the whole United States "a part of the zone of operations conducted by the enemy," and declared that any person who published anything endangering the successful operation of our forces could be tried as a spy by a military tribunal and put to death. President Wilson wished to head off such legislation as unwise and unconstitutional.[5] A turmoil would arise if army officers could thus dispose of the liberties and lives of civilians. Any control of the government over civilians outside actual war areas ought to be exercised through judges and juries. And yet the legal advisers of the administration felt that the conspiracy statutes were not enough to enable the ordinary courts to handle on a large scale dangerous activities short of treason. So it would be easier to resist pressure to take matters away from judges and juries, if a new criminal statute gave judges and juries wider and stiffer powers. The second factor was the fear of German propaganda, and the knowledge of legislation and administrative regulations guarding against it in Great Britain and Canada.[6] Although we did not adopt the British administrative control, which combined flexibility with possibilities of despotism, it was easy to forget our own policy of non-interference with minorities and put the United States also in a position to deal severely with written and spoken opposition to the war.

I. THE ESPIONAGE ACTS OF 1917 AND 1918

> *I approve of this legislation but . . . I shall not expect or permit any part of this law to apply to me or any of my official acts, or in any way to be used as a shield against criticism.* WOODROW WILSON, letter of April 25, 1917.

The result of these various influences was the third section of Title I of the Espionage Act. As originally enacted on

[5] On this Chamberlain bill and similar proposals, see Thomas F. Carroll, "Freedom of Speech and of the Press in War Time: The Espionage Act," 17 *Michigan Law Review* 621, 663 note (1919); cited hereafter as Carroll. The bill seems clearly unconstitutional under *Ex parte* Milligan, 4 Wallace 2 (1866); see note 66 in Chapter I.

[6] As to England, see 31 *Harvard Law Review* 296 (by Laski); Laski, *Authority in the Modern State*, p. 101. As to Canada, see Carroll, at 621 note.

June 15, 1917 (and still in force in 1940), this section established three new offenses:

(1) Whoever, when the United States is at war, shall willfully
make or convey false reports or false statements with intent to
interfere with the operation or success of the military or naval
forces of the United States or to promote the success of its enemies
(2) and whoever, when the United States is at war, shall willfully
cause or attempt to cause insubordination, disloyalty, mutiny, or
refusal of duty, in the military or naval forces of the United States,
(3) or shall willfully obstruct the recruiting or enlistment service
of the United States, to the injury of the service or of the United
States, shall be punished by a fine of not more than $10,000 or
imprisonment for not more than twenty years, or both.[7]

Although most of the Espionage Act deals with entirely
different subjects, like actual espionage, the protection of
military secrets, and the enforcement of neutrality in future
conflicts between other nations, the section just quoted is
buttressed by several provisions. Section 4 of the same Title
(50 U. S. C. A. § 34) punishes persons conspiring to violate
section 3, if any one of them does any act to effect the object
of the conspiracy. Title XI (18 U. S. C. A. §§ 611–633)
authorizes the issue of search warrants for the seizure of
property used as the means of committing a felony, which
would include violations of the section just quoted. It was
under this provision that the moving-picture film was confiscated in the *Spirit of '76* case,[8] and raids were made on the
offices of anti-war organizations. Finally, Title XII (18 U. S.
C. A. §§ 343, 344) makes non-mailable any matter violating
the Act, or advocating treason, insurrection, or forcible resistance to any law of the United States, directs that it shall
not be conveyed or delivered, and imposes heavy penalties
for attempting to use the mails for its transmission.

Eleven months later the Espionage Act was greatly expanded
by a second statute. Attorney General Gregory thought the
original 1917 Act did not go far enough in some respects. He
stated that although it had proved an effective instrumentality

---

[7] Act of June 15, 1917, c. 30, Title I, § 3, now 50 U. S. C. A. (1926), § 33.
The numerals are inserted by me. As to the provisions of this statute against
real spying, see Gorin *v.* United States, 61 Sup. Ct. 429 (1941).

[8] See *supra*, Chapter I, at nn. 12, 72; *infra*, Chapter II, at n. 37.

against deliberate or organized disloyal propaganda, it did not reach the individual casual or impulsive disloyal utterances. Also some District Courts gave what he considered a narrow construction of the word "obstruct" in clause 3, so that, as he described it, "most of the teeth which we tried to put in were taken out." [9]

These individual disloyal utterances, however, occurring with considerable frequency throughout the country, naturally irritated and angered the communities in which they occurred, resulting sometimes in unfortunate violence and lawlessness and everywhere in dissatisfaction with the inadequacy of the Federal law to reach such cases. Consequently there was a popular demand for such an amendment as would cover these cases.[10]

The history of subsequent events shows what is likely to happen in times of panic, when sedate lawyers ask for "just a wee drappie mair of suppression, and where's the harm in that." The Attorney General requested only a brief amendment of the Espionage Act by the addition of attempts to obstruct the recruiting service, and the punishment of efforts intentionally made to discredit and interfere with the flotation of war loans. The Senate Committee on the Judiciary, being thus stirred up, took the bit in its teeth, and decided to stamp on all utterances of a disloyal character. It went for a model of legislation affecting freedom of discussion to a recent sweeping sedition statute of the state of Montana, and inserted most of its clauses into the new federal law.

This amendment of May 16, 1918 (repealed in 1921),[11] which is sometimes called the Sedition Act, inserted "attempts to obstruct" in the third of the original offenses, and added nine more offenses, as follows: (4) saying or doing anything with intent to obstruct the sale of United States bonds, except by way of bona fide and not disloyal advice; (5) uttering, printing, writing, or publishing any disloyal, profane, scurrilous, or abusive language, or language intended to cause

[9] 4 *American Bar Association Journal*, 306.

[10] The history of the amendment is taken from Report of the Attorney General of the United States (1918), 18; O'Brian, 302. See Montana Laws, 1918, sp., c. 11, now Mont. Rev. Stat. (1935), § 10737.

[11] 40 Stat. 553 (1918). As to the repeal in 1921, see 41 Stat. 1359–1360; 60 *Congressional Record*, 293–4, 4207–8.

contempt, scorn, contumely or disrepute as regards the form of government of the United States; (6) or the Constitution; (7) or the flag; (8) or the uniform of the Army or Navy; (9) or any language intended to incite resistance to the United States or promote the cause of its enemies; (10) urging any curtailment of production of any things necessary to the prosecution of the war with intent to hinder its prosecution; (11) advocating, teaching, defending, or suggesting the doing of any of these acts; and (12) words or acts supporting or favoring the cause of any country at war with us, or opposing the cause of the United States therein. Whoever committed any one of these offenses during the war was liable to the maximum penalty of the original Act, $10,000 fine or twenty years' imprisonment, or both.

The 1918 amendment was fortunately repealed on March 3, 1921. The original Espionage Act of 1917 was expressly left in force; and it will be operative if the United States enter the second World War.

The Espionage Act of 1918 has been defended on the ground that previously when the public found that many obnoxious utterances were regarded by United States district attorneys as outside the simple Act of 1917, loyal people would take matters into their own hands. Two lynchings and many horse-whippings and tar-and-featherings had occurred, and over two hundred miners, mostly members of the I. W. W., were forcibly deported from their homes in Bisbee, Arizona, into the desert.[12] Congress responded to this outcry, it is said, by the passage of the 1918 amendment. Doubtless some governmental action was required to protect pacifists and extreme radicals from mob violence, but incarceration for a period of twenty years seems a very queer kind of protection.

This amendment came so late in this war that all the big cases, except the Abrams prosecution, turned on the meaning

[12] See note 10. Many cases of mob violence are listed on pp. 5–13 of *Wartime Prosecutions and Mob Violence* (New York, 1919). The Bisbee deportations were held not to be a federal crime in United States v. Wheeler, 254 Fed. 611 (1918), affd. in 254 U. S. 281 (1920); see 34 *Harvard Law Review* 554, 53 *id.* at 1038–1041, 19 *Michigan Law Review* 558. The defendants were then acquitted by an Arizona jury. The judge's charge is reprinted in 6 *Journal of the American Bar Association* 99 (October, 1920); see 21 *Columbia Law Review* 71. Compare 1 *Bill of Rights Review* 145 (1941).

of the three original offenses of the 1917 Act or on "attempts
to obstruct." As the Abrams case is reserved for a chapter by
itself, I shall hereafter in this chapter confine myself to those
three offenses except when I expressly refer to the statute of
1918.

2. MASSES PUBLISHING CO. *v.* PATTEN

> *The framers of the First Amendment knew that the
> right to criticise might weaken the support of the Govern-
> ment in a time of war. They appreciated the value of a
> united public opinion at such a time. They were men
> who had experienced all those things in the war of the
> Revolution, and yet they knew too that the republic
> which they were founding could not live unless the right
> of free speech, of freedom of the press was maintained
> at such a time. They balanced these considerations and
> then wrote the First Amendment.*
>
> JUDGE CHARLES F. AMIDON.

The Espionage Act of 1917 seems on its face constitutional
under the interpretation of the First Amendment reached in
this book; but it may have been construed so extremely as to
violate the Amendment. Furthermore, freedom of speech is
not only a limit on Congressional power, but a policy to be
observed by the courts in applying constitutional statutes to
utterances. The scope of that policy is determined by the same
method of balancing social interests. The boundary line of
punishable speech under this Act was consequently fixed at
the point where words come close to injurious conduct by that
judge who during the war gave the fullest attention to the
meaning of free speech, Judge Learned Hand, of the Southern
District of New York.

In *Masses Publishing Co.* v. *Patten* [13] Judge Hand was
asked to enjoin the postmaster of New York from excluding
from the mails the August issue of *The Masses*, a monthly
revolutionary journal, which contained several articles, poems,
and cartoons attacking the war. When notified of the exclusion,
the publisher had offered to delete any passages pointed out

---

[13] 244 Fed. 535 (S. D. N. Y., 1917). On Wilson's opinion of the exclusion
of the *Masses* from the mails, see R. S. Baker, *Woodrow Wilson*, VII, 165 n.

by the postmaster, but was refused such information. After suit was started, the postmaster, while objecting generally that the whole purport of the number was unlawful, since it tended to encourage the enemies of the United States and hamper the government in the conduct of the war, specified four cartoons, entitled "Liberty Bell," "Conscription," "Making the World Safe for Capitalism," and "Congress and Big Business"; also a poem, which declared Emma Goldman and Alexander Berkman, who were in prison for conspiracy to resist the draft, to be "elemental forces" —

> Like the water that climbs down the rocks;
> Like the wind in the leaves;
> Like the gentle night that holds us.

He also objected to three articles admiring the "sacrifice" of conscientious objectors, and praising Goldman and Berkman as "friends of American freedom."

The Espionage Act, it will be remembered, made nonmailable any publication which violated the criminal provisions of the section already quoted. One important issue was, therefore, whether the postmaster was right in finding such a violation. The case did not raise the constitutional question whether Congress could make criminal any matter which tended to discourage the successful prosecution of the war, but involved only the construction of the statute, whether Congress had as yet gone so far. Judge Hand held that it had not and granted the injunction. He refused to turn the original Act, which obviously dealt only with interference with the conduct of military affairs, into a prohibition of all kinds of propaganda and a means for suppressing all hostile criticism and all opinion except that which encouraged and supported the existing policies of the war, or fell within the range of temperate argument. As Cooley pointed out long ago, you cannot limit free speech to polite criticism, because the greater a grievance the more likely men are to get excited about it, and the more urgent the need of hearing what they have to say.[14] The normal test for the suppression of speech

[14] Cooley, *Constitutional Limitations* (7th ed.), p. 613. Bagehot said in 1844: "If it were said . . . that the interference of the state was . . . to restrict . . . only the improper method of propagating opinions, my answer is,

in a democratic government, Judge Hand insists, is neither the justice of its substance nor the decency and propriety of its temper, but the strong danger that it will cause injurious acts. The Espionage Act should not be construed to reverse this national policy of liberty of the press and silence hostile criticism, unless Congress had given the clearest expression of such an intention in the statute.

Congress had shown no such intention in the Act of 1917, according to Judge Hand. Moreover, whether or not it could create a personal censorship of the press under the war power, it had not yet done so. Since the portions of *The Masses* selected by the postmaster did not actually advocate violence, he had no right to suppress the magazine "on the doctrine that the general tenor and animus of the paper were subversive to authority and seditious in effect."

The tradition of English-speaking freedom has depended in no small part upon the merely procedural requirement that the state point with exactness to just that conduct which violates the law. It is difficult and often impossible to meet the charge that one's general ethos is treasonable.

Judge Hand places outside the limits of free speech one who counsels or advises others to violate existing laws. Language is not always exempt from punishment. "Words are not only the keys of persuasion, but the triggers of action, and those which have no purport but to counsel the violation of law cannot by any latitude of interpretation be a part of that public opinion which is the final source of government in a democratic state." It is also true, he says, that any discussion designed to show that existing laws are mistaken in means or unjust in policy may result in their violation. Nevertheless, if one stops short of urging upon others that it is their duty or their interest to resist the law, he should not be held to have attempted to cause illegal conduct. If this is not the test, the 1917 Act punishes every political agitation which can

that if this were so, Government ought to interfere with the improper ways of maintaining *all* opinions. At least nothing can be more one-sided than that Government should interfere with one side of a controversy to preserve proper decorum, and let the other be as abusive and slanderous as it pleases." — *Works*, X, 128.

be shown to be apt to create a seditious temper. The language of the statute proves that Congress had no such revolutionary purpose in view.

According to this view, criminality under the Espionage Act of 1917 would be determined by an objective test, the nature of the words used. The jury could pass on this much better than on questions of political and economic tendency. Moreover, the Act would have a meaning easily understood by the opponents of the war. They could safely engage in discussion of its merits and the justice of war policies, so long as they refrained from urging violation of laws. The Act, thus interpreted, does not go to the limits of Congressional power as I have construed them. Under some circumstances an expression of opinion which does not counsel any unlawful act may be highly dangerous. Even Mill would punish a statement that grain-dealers are starvers of the poor, or that private property is robbery, when delivered orally to an excited mob assembled before the house of a grain-dealer.[15] A scathing analysis of the incompetence of the commanding general circulated among the troops on the eve of battle would be a direct and dangerous interference with the war. But military law would deal with this offense within the lines, and the law of illegal assembly will come into play elsewhere, as in Mill's case. There is no need to make the expression of opinion in itself criminal. It has not been so normally in this country, especially not under federal law, and the Espionage Act of 1917 (unlike that of 1918) contains nothing to indicate such an interference with the attainment and dissemination of truth. That statute by its terms fills in the gap between the treason and the conspiracy laws by reaching the individual who actually attempts or incites interference with the war, whether by acts like assaulting a recruiting officer or by words whose tenor shows that they have very little to do with the social interest in truth, since they do not discuss the merits of the war, but counsel immediate and injurious acts. In other words, Congress was punishing dangerous acts and such words as had all the effect of acts, because they could have no other purpose but a direct and dangerous interference with the war.

[15] Mill, *Liberty*, opening ot chap. iii.

There was during the war no finer judicial statement of the right of free speech than these words of Judge Hand:

Political agitation, by the passions it arouses or the convictions it engenders, may in fact stimulate men to the violation of law. Detestation of existing policies is easily transformed into forcible resistance of the authority which puts them in execution, and it would be folly to disregard the causal relation between the two. Yet to assimilate agitation, legitimate as such, with direct incitement to violent resistance, is to disregard the tolerance of all methods of political agitation which in normal times is a safeguard of free government. The distinction is not a scholastic subterfuge, but a hard-bought acquisition in the fight for freedom.

Look at the Espionage Act of 1917 [16] with a post-armistice mind, and it is clear that Judge Hand was right. There is not a word in it to make criminal the expression of pacifist or pro-German opinions. It punishes false statements and reports — necessarily limited to statements of fact — but beyond that does not contain even a provision against the use of language. It differs entirely from the Act of 1918, and from state laws making utterances criminal for their own sake as nuisances or breaches of the peace. Utterances (except false statements) are punishable, if at all, because of their relation to specified acts. Clauses 2 and 3 punish successful interference with military affairs and attempts to interfere, which would probably include incitement. The tests of criminal attempt and incitement are well settled.[17] The first requirement is the intention to bring about the overt criminal act. But the law does not punish bad intention alone, or even everything done with a bad intention. A statute against murder will not be construed to apply to discharging a gun with the intention to kill a man forty miles away. Writing a letter to a firm in San Francisco requesting a shipment of liquor into Alaska is not an attempt to import liquor into Alaska until it is brought near the borders, headlands, or waters of that territory. Attempts and incitement to be punishable must come dangerously near success, and bad intention is merely one modifying factor in determining whether

[16] See section 1, *supra*, for text of the Act.
[17] Joseph H. Beale, "Criminal Attempts," 16 *Harvard Law Review* 491; U. S. *v.* Stephens, 12 Fed. 52. See also 32 *Harvard Law Review* 417.

the actual conduct is thus dangerous. A speaker is guilty of solicitation or incitement to a crime only if he would have been indictable for the crime itself, had it been committed, either as accessory or principal.[18] Of course his liability when nothing really happens will not be greater than if his conduct leads to actual crime. Now even in that event, at common law the utterer of written or spoken words is not criminally liable merely because he knows they will reach those who may find in them the excuse for criminal acts. The assassin of President McKinley may have been influenced by the denunciatory cartoons of "Willy and his Papa" in the Hearst newspapers, but the artist was not an accessory to the murder.

Wharton, a leading writer on criminal law, shows how wise the common law was in refusing to establish any rule of indirect causation with respect to utterances:

> For we would be forced to admit, if we hold that solicitations to criminality are generally indictable, that the propagandists, even in conversation, of agrarian or communistic theories are liable to criminal prosecutions; and hence the necessary freedom of speech and of the press would be greatly infringed. It would be hard, also, we must agree, if we maintain such general responsibility, to defend, in prosecutions for soliciting crime, the publishers of Byron's *Don Juan*, of Rousseau's *Emile*, or of Goethe's *Elective Affinities*. Lord Chesterfield, in his letters to his son, directly advises the latter to form illicit connections with married women; Lord Chesterfield, on the reasoning here contested, would be indictable for solicitation to adultery. Undoubtedly, when such solicitations are so publicly and indecently made as to produce public scandal, they are indictable as nuisances or as libels. But to make bare solicitations or allurements indictable as *attempts*, not only unduly and perilously extends the scope of penal adjudication, but forces on the courts psychological questions which they are incompetent to decide, and a branch of business which would make them despots of every intellect in the land.[19]

On the contrary, the rule has always been that, to establish criminal responsibility, the words uttered must constitute dangerous progress toward the consummation of the independent offense attempted and amount to procurement,

---

[18] See Beale, *supra*, 16 *Harvard Law Review* 491, 505. Under the federal statutes he would be a principal. 18 U. S. C. A. § 550.

[19] Wharton, *Criminal Law* (2d ed.), vol. I, § 179.

counsel, or command to commit the forbidden acts.[20] This standard can be applied, not only to attempts to cause insubordination and obstruction of the draft, where the ultimate result would be a crime, but also to the persuasion of men not to volunteer. Their failure to enlist is not a crime, but it is a serious injury to the government. The speaker is interfering with the right of the army to a free labor market, in a manner analogous to picketing and boycotting in private business, which often constitute civil wrongs, compensated by damages.[21] Such interference may justly be made criminal, but only if it is direct and dangerous, for the measure of liability ought not to be larger than for solicitation to a criminal result like evasion of the draft.[22]

Consequently, no one should have been held under clauses 2 and 3 of the Espionage Act of 1917 who did not satisfy these tests of criminal attempt and incitement. As Justice Holmes said in *Commonwealth* v. *Peaslee*,[23] "It is a question of degree." We can suppose a series of opinions, ranging from "This is an unwise war" up to "You ought to refuse to go, no matter what they do to you," or an audience varying from an old women's home to a group of drafted men just starting for a training camp. Somewhere in such a range of circumstances is the point where direct causation begins and speech becomes punishable as incitement under the ordinary standards of statutory construction and the ordinary policy of free speech, which Judge Hand applied. Congress could push the test of criminality back beyond this point, although eventually it would reach the extreme limit fixed by the First Amendment, beyond which words cannot be restricted for their remote tendency to hinder the war.[24] In other words, the ordinary tests punish agitation just before it begins to boil over; Congress could change those tests and punish it when it gets really hot, but it is unconstitutional to interfere when it is merely

[20] Blackstone's *Commentaries*, IV, 36.

[21] Gompers *v.* Bucks Stove and Range Co., 221 U. S. 418 (1911); Vegelahn *v.* Guntner, 167 Mass. 92 (1896).

[22] See Hand in U. S. *v.* Nearing, 252 Fed. 223, 227 (1918). The same principle applies to interference with Liberty Bond sales under the 1918 Act.

[23] 177 Mass. 267, 272 (1901). See also his opinion in Swift *v.* United States, 196 U. S. 375, 396 (1905).

[24] See the quotation from Justice Brandeis, pp. 90–91, *infra*.

warm. And there is not a word in the 1917 Espionage Act
to show that Congress did change the ordinary tests or make
any speech criminal except false statements and incitement
to overt acts. Every word used, "cause," "attempt," "obstruct,"
clearly involves proximate causation, a close and direct relation to actual interference with the operations of the army and
navy, with enlistment and the draft. Finally, this is a penal
statute and ought to be construed strictly. Attorney General
Gregory's charge that judges like Learned Hand "took the
teeth" out of the 1917 Act [25] is absurd, for the teeth the government wanted were never there until other judges in an
excess of patriotism put in false ones.

Nevertheless, Judge Hand was reversed [26] on a point of
administrative law, that the postmaster's decision must stand
unless clearly wrong; [27] and, in addition, the Circuit Court of
Appeals thought it desirable to reject his construction of the
Espionage Act and substitute the view that speech is punishable under the Act "if the natural and reasonable effect of
what is said is to encourage resistance to law, and the words
are used in an endeavor to persuade to resistance." Judge
Hand's objective test of the nature of the words was considered
unsound. Advice in direct language was repudiated as a requisite of guilt. Judge Hough used the Sermon on the Mount as
a precedent for the government's war policy: "It is at least
arguable whether there can be any more direct incitement
to action than to hold up to admiration those who do act. . . .
The Beatitudes have for some centuries been considered highly
hortatory, though they do not contain the injunction: 'Go
thou and do likewise.' " It is possible that the upper court
did not intend to lay down a very different principle from
Judge Hand, but chiefly wished to insist that in determining
whether there is incitement one must look not only at the
words themselves but also at the surrounding circumstances
which may have given the words a special meaning to their
hearers. Judge Hand agreed with this, and regarded Mark

[25] See note 9 *supra*.

[26] Masses Pub. Co. *v.* Patten, 245 Fed. 102 (C. C. A. 2d, 1917), Hough, J.,
stayed the injunction; *ibid*. 246 Fed. 24 (C. C. A. 2d, 1917), Ward, Rogers,
and Mayer, JJ., reversed the order granting the injunction.

[27] See 32 *Harvard Law Review* 417, 420; *infra*, section VI, Censorship.

Antony's funeral oration, for instance, as having counseled violence while it expressly discountenanced it. However, the undoubted effect of the final decision in *Masses* v. *Patten* was to establish the old-time doctrine of remote bad tendency in the minds of district judges throughout the country. By its rejection of the common-law test of incitement, it deprived us of the only standard of criminal speech there was, since there had never been any well-considered discussion of the meaning of "freedom of speech" in the First Amendment.

As a result of this and similar decisions, the district judges ignored entirely the first element of criminal attempt and solicitation, that the effort, though unsuccessful, must approach dangerously near success. They repudiated the test of guilt under the Act laid down by Judge Hand, that the words must in themselves urge upon their readers or hearers a duty or an interest to resist the law or the appeal for volunteers, and substituted the test that the words need only have a tendency to cause unrest among soldiers or to make recruiting more difficult. The remaining element, intention to cause the bad overt action, they retained. This new standard of guilt allowed conviction for any words which had an indirect effect to discourage recruiting and the war spirit, like the poem about Emma Goldman and the wind, if only the intention to discourage existed. Intention thus became the crucial test of guilt in any prosecution of opposition to the government's war policies, and this requirement of intention became a mere form since it could be inferred from the existence of the indirect injurious effect.[28] A few judges, notably Amidon of North Dakota, swam against the tide, but of most Espionage Act decisions what Jefferson and Stephen and Schofield said about the prosecutions under George III and the Sedition Act of 1798 can be said once more, that men were punished without overt acts, with only a presumed intention to cause overt acts, merely for the utterance of words which judge and jury thought to have a tendency to injure the state. Judge Rogers was right in saying [29] that the words of the

[28] Masses Pub. Co. *v.* Patten, 246 Fed. 24, 39 (1917), Ward, J.; and Rogers, J.: "The court does not hesitate to say that, considering the natural and reasonable effect of the publication, it was intended willfully to obstruct recruiting."

[29] *Id.* 29.

Espionage Act of 1917 bear slight resemblance to the Sedition
Law of 1798, but the judicial construction is much the same,
except that under the Sedition Law truth was a defense.

3. THE DISTRICT COURT CASES

*The effect of the prosecutions under this Act has, no
doubt, been beneficial in maintaining law and order*
Report of the Attorney General, 1919.

The revival of the doctrines of bad tendency and constructive intent always puts an end to genuine discussion of public
matters. It is unnecessary to review the two thousand Espionage Act prosecutions in detail, but a few general results
may be presented here. The courts treated opinions as
statements of fact and then condemned them as false because
they differed from the President's speech or the resolution of
Congress declaring war. Their construction of this first clause
of the Act will be considered in connection with the Supreme
Court decisions. Under the second and third clauses against
causing insubordination or obstructing recruiting, only a few
persons were convicted for actually urging men to evade the
draft or not to enlist. Almost all the convictions were for
expressions of opinion about the merits and conduct of the
war.

It became criminal to advocate heavier taxation instead of
bond issues, to state that conscription was unconstitutional
though the Supreme Court had not yet held it valid, to say
that the sinking of merchant vessels was legal, to urge that
a referendum should have preceded our declaration of war, to
say that war was contrary to the teachings of Christ. Men
have been punished for criticising the Red Cross and the
Y. M. C. A., while under the Minnesota Espionage Act it has
been held a crime to discourage women from knitting by the
remark, "No soldier ever sees these socks." [30] It was in no

[30] State *v.* Freerks, 140 Minn. 349 (1918). Among the many cases illus-
trating the statements of this paragraph, I cite the following convictions:
Sandberg (revd. in 257 Fed. 643); Miller (Bull. 104); Nagler (Bull. 127, 252
Fed. 217); Goldsmith (Bull. 133); Kaufman (Bull. 134); Weist (Bull. 169);
Kirchner (Bulls. 69, 174, 255 Fed. 301); Shaffer (Bull. 125, 190, 255 Fed. 886);
Albers (Bull. 191, 263 Fed. 27); Krafft (Bull. 6, 84, 249 Fed. 919, 247 U. S. 520);
Boutin (251 Fed. 313); Granzow (revd. in 261 Fed. 172); Hitchcock (Bull.

way necessary that these expressions of opinion should be addressed to soldiers or men on the point of enlisting or being drafted. Most judges held it enough if the words might conceivably reach such men. They have made it impossible for an opponent of the war to write an article or even a letter in a newspaper of general circulation because it will be read in some training camp where it might cause insubordination or interfere with military success. He cannot address a large audience because it is liable to include a few men in uniform; and some judges have held him punishable if it contains men between eighteen and forty-five, since they may be called into the army eventually; some have emphasized the possible presence of shipbuilders and munition-makers. All genuine discussion among civilians of the justice and wisdom of continuing a war thus becomes perilous.

Judge Van Valkenburgh, in *United States* v. *Rose Pastor Stokes*,[31] even made it crimii.al to argue to women against a war, by the words, "I am for the people and the government is for the profiteers," because what is said to mothers, sisters, and sweethearts may lessen their enthusiasm for the war, and "our armies in the field and our navies upon the seas can operate and succeed only so far as they are supported and maintained by the folks at home." The doctrine of indirect causation never had better illustration than in his charge. It shows how a very able judge of large experience can be swept from his moorings by war passion. Furthermore, although Mrs. Stokes was indicted only for writing a letter, the judge admitted her speeches to show her intent, and then denounced to the jury in the strongest language the opinions expressed

122); Weinsberg (Bull. 123); Denson (Bull. 142); Von Bank (Bull. 164, revd. in 258 Fed. 641); White (265 Fed. 17). A few of these convictions have been reversed as noted above and most of the other sentences were considerably reduced by the President after the armistice, but that does not excuse the conduct of the trial courts. See also the Supreme Court cases discussed *infra*.

A great many of the Espionage Act cases have never been reported in detail in print. The total number of persons convicted was stated by the Attorney General in his annual Reports as 877, out of 1,956 cases commenced. His Reports also show pardons and commutations of sentences.

A main source for these prosecutions is Bulletins of the Department of Justice on the Interpretation of War Statutes, cited herein as Bull. For other sources, see 32 *Harvard Law Review* 417.

[31] United States *v.* Stokes, Bull. 106 (Mo. 1918), revd. in 264 Fed. 18 (C. C. A. 8th, 1920)

in those speeches as destructive of the nation's welfare, so that she may very well have been convicted for the speeches and not for the letter.

Just as Lord Kenyon, while trying a man who happened to sympathize with the French Revolution, went out of his way to emphasize its massacres as a consequence of theories like the defendant's,[32] so Judge Van Valkenburgh denounced the Russian Revolution as "the greatest betrayal of the cause of democracy the world has ever seen," and made use of Mrs. Stokes' declared sympathy with that Revolution, an offense not punishable even under the Espionage Act, to show how dangerous it was for her to talk about profiteers.

Of course, the jury convicted Mrs. Stokes after such a charge. They found that the words, "I am for the people, and the government is for the profiteers," were a false statement, known to be false and intended and calculated to interfere with the success of our military and naval forces, that they were an attempt to cause insubordination in those forces, and that they obstructed recruiting. The judge sentenced her in April, 1918, to ten years in prison. The Circuit Court of Appeals set aside this conviction in March, 1920, but it stood all through the last part of the war as a stern example that it was a heinous crime to discuss profiteering, because of "the possible, if not probable effect on our troops."

A case in the Second Circuit makes it equally perilous to urge a wider exemption for conscientious objectors because this tends to encourage more such objectors, a close parallel to the English imprisonment of Bertrand Russell.[32a]

Many men were imprisoned for arguments or profanity used in the heat of private altercation, on a railroad train, in a hotel lobby, or at that battle-ground of disputation, a boarding-house table.[33] In one case,[34] two strangers came to a

[32] Rex v. Cuthell, 27 How. St. Tr. 642, 674 (1799).

[32a] Fraina v. United States, 255 Fed. 28 (C. C. A. 2d, 1918), for conspiracy and not under the Espionage Act; Rex v. Bertrand Russell, Littell's *Living Age*, Feb. 15, 1919, p. 385.

[33] For instance, Sandberg, Albers, Goldsmith, Denson, all cited *supra*, note 30. But Judge Bourquin refused to let the jury pass on such evidence in the case of V. Hall, involving "kitchen gossip and saloon debate." — 248 Fed. 150.

[34] U. S. v. Harshfield, 260 Fed. 659 (C. C. A. 8th, 1919), reversing the conviction. In Schoberg v. U. S., 264 Fed. 1, under 1918 Act, three elderly

farmhouse and asked the owner if he could let them have some gasoline, saying that they had been stranded out in the country. He not only gave them the gasoline, but invited them to dinner. An argument arose during the meal, and the farmer used scurrilous and presumably unpatriotic language in the presence of his guests, two hired men, two nieces, and some children. The guests reported his language, and he was convicted of a willful attempt to cause disloyalty, insubordination, mutiny, and refusal of duty in the military and naval forces of the United States. Even unexpressed thoughts were prosecuted through an ingenious method of inquisition. A German-American who had not subscribed to Liberty bonds was visited in his house by a committee who asked his reasons and received a courteous reply that he did not wish either side to win the war and could not conscientiously give it his aid. He was thereupon arrested and held in confinement until released by a district court.[35]

A few concrete cases of convictions that have been upheld on appeal will show how the Espionage Act operates to punish expressions of opinion.

J. P. Doe, son of the great Chief Justice of New Hampshire, while living in Colorado because of bad health, mailed an "endless chain" letter, to be sent "to friends of immediate peace," which stated that although the President and Secretary of State had said Germany had broken her promise to end submarine warfare, Germany had made no such promise, but had reserved in the *Sussex* note complete liberty of decision as to the future. Doe's statement was a legitimate inference from the note, whatever its bearing on the merits of our position — and this he did not discuss. Yet he was convicted for it, the alleged intent to obstruct recruiting being evidenced by passages from a long personal letter to his sister. The Court of Appeals said it was a fair construction of the circular that Doe intended to convey the idea that the United States was wrong in relying on the alleged promise as a cause of war; "such an argument would have a direct tendency to

German Americans, hobnobbing together in the cobbler's shop of one of them and growling about the war, were convicted by means of a dictagraph.

[35] United States *v.* Pape, 253 Fed. 270 (1918). To the same effect is State *v.* Ludemann, 143 Minn. 126 (1919).

obstruct the recruiting and enlistment service." Doe was sentenced to eighteen months in prison.[36]

Robert Goldstein, who had been connected with D. W. Griffith in producing "The Birth of a Nation," a well-known moving-picture film of the Civil War, planned a similar presentation of the Revolution in a film called "The Spirit of '76," which contained such scenes as Patrick Henry's Speech, the Signing of the Declaration of Independence, and Valley Forge. After a year and a half of work the picture was finished, just before the outbreak of our war with Germany. The film was displayed in Los Angeles to the usual audience, which was not shown to contain either soldiers or sailors. The government thereupon indicted Goldstein for presenting a play designed and intended to arouse antagonism, hatred, and enmity between the American people (particularly the armed forces) and the people of Great Britain (particularly their armed forces) when Great Britain was "an ally" of the United States, because one scene, the Wyoming Massacre, portrayed British soldiers bayoneting women and children and carrying away girls. The film was seized, the business was thrown from prosperity into bankruptcy with a loss of over $100,000, and Goldstein was convicted of attempting to cause insubordination, etc., in the armed forces and sentenced to ten years in the federal penitentiary at Steilacoom, Washington. His punishment for depicting the origin of this nation was commuted to three years.[37]

Rev. Clarence H. Waldron, of Windsor, Vermont, was charged with handing to five persons, among whom were a woman, two men apparently above military age, and another clergyman, a pamphlet to show where he himself stood on the war. The judge in his charge quoted such statements as the following from the pamphlet:

Surely, if Christians were forbidden to fight to preserve the Person of their Lord and Master, they may not fight to preserve themselves, or any city they should happen to dwell in. Christ has no kingdom here. His servants must not fight.

I do not say that it is wrong for a nation to go to war to preserve

[36] Bull. No. 55 (Colo.), affd. in 253 Fed. 903 (C. C. A. 8th, 1918).

[37] 258 Fed. 908 (C. C. A. 9th, 1919); see Bull. 33. As to the film seizure, see *supra*, Chapter I at nn. 12, 72; Chapter II at n. 8.

its interests, but it is wrong to the Christian, absolutely, unutterably wrong.

Under no circumstances can I undertake any service that has for its purpose the prosecution of war.

Mr. Waldron was convicted for causing insubordination and obstructing recruiting, and sentenced to fifteen years in prison.[38]

D. H. Wallace, an ex-British soldier, was sentenced to twenty years for saying:

That when a soldier went away he was a hero and that when he came back flirting with a hand organ he was a bum, and that the asylums will be filled with them; that the soldiers were giving their lives for the capitalists, that 40 per cent of the ammunition of the allies or their guns was defective because of graft.[39]

Wallace went insane and died in jail.

D. T. Blodgett was given the same sentence by the same judge, Wade, for circulating a pamphlet urging the voters of Iowa not to reëlect the Congressmen who voted for conscription, and reprinting an argument of Thomas E. Watson, of Georgia, against the constitutionality of the Draft Act. This was before its validity had been upheld by the Supreme Court. Judge Wade charged that the government had passed the Espionage Act, "realizing that it must protect the feeling and spirit of the American people against the work of those who defy authority; it was not intended for ninety-five per cent of the American people, but necessary for the few who will not heed the judgment of the ninety-five per cent; who assume to know more than all the others put together. It is not a harsh Act." He recalled the draft riots of the Civil War, and suggested that Blodgett had felt that a little mutiny might aid his political cause. "Just look at this that he wants drafted men to buy":

In Washington City it is a carnival, a wild extravagance; an orgy of prodigal waste; a Bacchanalian revel of men who act as though they were drunk on power and had lost every sense of shame, duty and responsibility. The huge appropriations made will accrue to the benefit of the classes. Great is the gathering of the vultures at

[38] Bull. 79. Waldron was pardoned after a year in prison.
[39] Bull. 4 (Iowa).

the National Capital, for never before has there been such a carcase inviting them to the feast. Three thousand millions of dollars in one appropriation, and the vultures fiercely shrieking for more.

"There is no better way," said the judge, "of unsettling the confidence of the people and stirring their souls against the war than to paint it as a war of capitalism, organized by capitalists and for capitalists, and painting the officers of the government as representing willing tools of Wall Street. There is no better way." [40]

Undoubtedly in all these cases intention to cause insubordination or obstruct recruiting was made a test of guilt. It may seem to many persons that so long as a speaker talks with such a purpose it makes no difference whether he satisfies Judge Hand's objective standard by saying, "Don't enlist, don't register, shoot over the enemies' heads," or whether he confines himself to statements about the horrors of a modern battlefield and opinions about the legality of the German entry into Belgium. Very likely the moral quality of the two methods is the same; the tendency to prevent enlistment may be the same. But the reason that makes it, if not unconstitutional, at least very unwise to punish the second type of utterance, the expression of fact or opinion, is that it is only by absence of penalties for such utterances that a self-governing people can learn and disseminate the truth on public affairs. The first type of utterance, on the other hand, has practically no value for such a purpose. When the public is interested, bad motives ought not to deprive it of the benefit of what is said. Opposition to governmental action through discussion, like opposition to private action through law-suits, is the alternative to the use of force. If the law should require litigants to have good motives, it might as well shut up the courts. In the same way, truth is truth, and just as valuable to the public, whether it comes from the most enthusiastic supporter of the war or from a pro-German, and in order to get the truth, conflicting views must be allowed. What a pacifist says about the extravagance of Congress or bad camp conditions during the influenza epidemic or the desire of France for the left bank of the Rhine, may be worth

[40] Nelles, *Espionage Act Cases*, p. 48.

hearing and acting on, and it will be just as important, although he does it with the hope of hindering the war. If disclosures like those made by Admiral Sims about the conditions of the navy are true, they would have been very valuable if made by some private citizen during the war, and no less so if printed in Berger's *Milwaukee Leader*.[41] So long as the speaker creates no great danger of losing the war, so long as the discouraging effects of his utterances can be checked by the draft organization, government orators like the four-minute men, and the general loyalty, it is wiser to let him talk for the sake of possible good.

The last case reviewed, Judge Wade's trial of Blodgett, brings out my point clearly. Every one will admit that Congress may properly consider ending a war. If so, the men to favor this must be elected, as many of them were in 1864; and the election will be a poor expression of the popular will unless it is preceded by discussion of the merits of beginning and continuing the war. Moreover, that discussion will have little value for the formation of opinion if the presence of a man within draft age brings it within the scope of the Espionage Act, and if those who oppose the war vigorously are cowed into silence by twenty-year sentences. It must never be forgotten that the Espionage Act of 1917 will be in force in all future wars, and the next one may be as questionable as those of 1812 and 1846.

The same considerations apply to the right of petitioning Congress and high officials, which is expressly secured by the First Amendment. Twenty-seven South Dakota farmers were opposed to the draft and believed that an unduly high quota was exacted from their county. They petitioned various state officers, asking a new arrangement, a referendum on the war, payment of war expenses from taxation, and repudiation of war debts. As an alternative they threatened defeat to the officers, their party, and the nation. Foolish as this petition was, it stated a grievance which deserved inquiry. Instead, the twenty-seven were sentenced to more than a year in prison. This conviction Attorney General Gregory declares to have been "one of the greatest deterrents against the spread of hostile propaganda, and particularly that class of propaganda

[41] As to this anti-war newspaper, see Chapter VII, section II.

which advanced and played upon the theme that this was a capitalists' war." Yet after it had served this suppressive purpose, and reached the Supreme Court, he confessed that the conviction was erroneous.[42]

In the same way, punishment of alleged evil tendency coupled with unlawful intention limits the general influence of the press on legislation and administrative policies, which is a recognized part of American democracy. Undoubtedly, the statement which appeared in many conservative newspapers, that $640,000,000 had been spent on aeroplanes without a single machine in France, had as great a tendency to weaken the national morale as any event of the war. The District Court test made it criminal for an editor to mention that fact if a jury subsequently found that his purpose was to turn public opinion against the war. It is true that no prosecutions were brought on that account, but were we any worse off without them? Was it not an advantage to have the fact as widely known as possible so as to produce a complete alteration of government methods? And so with respect to the territorial and commercial aims of our associates in the war, which caused us so much concern after the armistice. In short, the truth may be told with a bad purpose, but it is none the less truth; and the most dangerous falsehoods (like the report of the premature armistice, which probably cost a very great loss of production of munitions) may be committed from motives of the highest patriotism. Even on the assumption, which I shall soon show to be questionable, that all the persons convicted under the Espionage Act intended to hinder the war, intention is a very poor test of the truth and value of reports and opinions, and in effect results in the punishment of men, not for any actual or probable injury, but for their state of mind.

The needlessness of these hundreds of prosecutions in the District Courts is shown by the experience of Massachusetts. This state contained a large training camp and naval bases.

[42] United States v. Baltzer, Bull. 3 (S. D.), revd. in 248 U. S. 593; Report of Attorney General, 1918, 48. Jared Peck was indicted under the Sedition Act of 1798 for circulating a petition to Congress for the repeal of the Act. — Beveridge's *Marshall*, III, 42 n. Contrast the protection of the right of petition in Spayd v. Ringing Rock Lodge, 270 Pa. 67 (1921); noted in 35 *Harvard Law Review* 332, 6 *Minnesota Law Review* 241, 14 A. L. R. 1446.

Thousands of soldiers embarked from Boston for France. We had innumerable factories for the manufacture of munitions and other war supplies. We had in our midst a large foreign-born population, much of it unfriendly, by race at least, to the Allied cause, much of it possessing radical views. The United States District Attorney in Massachusetts, George W. Anderson, refused to institute a single prosecution although much was said and written which would have been punished elsewhere. No record exists of a single bomb explosion, act of sabotage, or evasion of the draft, or desertion, which may be traced to such an unpunished utterance. There is not one bit of evidence that the cause of the war suffered in Massachusetts because this District Attorney disregarded clamor and adhered to liberal principles.[43]

4. THE HUMAN MACHINERY OF THE ESPIONAGE ACTS

If there be a scintilla of real evidence *that seditious rags are infecting the Native Army, nobody would refuse suppression. Only you won't forget that in moments of excitement, such as this may become, people are uncommonly liable to confuse suspicions and possibilities with certainty and reality.*

MORLEY, Letter to the Viceroy of India.

A less obvious but not less vital objection to the District Court test is its unfitness for practical administration. Even if we decide that the man who makes discouraging utterances in war time with a bad intention deserves punishment, we ought not to lay down a rule of law to punish him unless we can be sure that in its actual operation it will catch him and let the man with good intention go. A rule is not desirable simply because it reads well. It must also work well. The law is not self-operating and it cannot pick out the bad man automatically. It must discover him through human machinery, and the defects of this machinery are the very greatest reason for preserving an immunity of speech from prosecution far wider than the District Court test.

"We have to consider," said Macaulay of a theory of crim-

---

[43] Anderson was appointed United States Circuit Judge in November, 1918. See Chapter V, section III, for his later contribution to freedom of speech.

inal law very similar to this test,[44] "not merely the goodness of the end, but also the fitness of the means. . . . There is surely no contradiction in saying that a certain section of the community may be quite competent to protect the persons and property of the rest, yet quite unfit to direct our opinions."

Jefferson pointed out in the Virginia Toleration Statute, quoted in the first chapter,[45] the unfitness of this machinery for discriminating between utterances of good tendency and utterances of bad tendency. Its unsuitability to separate good from bad intention is just as great.[46] The trouble with the District Court test is that in making intention the crucial fact in criminality it exposes all who discuss heated questions to an inquiry before a jury as to their purposes. That inquiry necessarily is of the widest scope and if the general attitude of the person is singular and intransigeant, there is an insufficient protection. You cannot tell a man's intention by looking at his forehead, you must look through it to the inside of his head; and no judge and jury are capable of looking through the skull of a man who has done nothing but talk to see what goes on inside. As a canny English judge remarked during the Wars of the Roses: "The thought of man is not triable; for the Devil himself knoweth not the mind of man."

It is true that intention is material in other crimes, such as murder; but in dealing with an overt criminal act like killing the intention is evidenced by many other acts, which are a kind of fact with which the jurymen are familiar and capable of dealing. On the other hand, the intention in making utterances is evidenced (1) by inferences drawn from the supposed bad tendency of the words themselves, and (2) by other utterances, which will also be viewed under the obnoxious test of bad tendency. For instance, in the Stokes and Doe cases [47]

[44] Essay on Southey's *Colloquies*. The whole is worth rereading today, especially the warning against a Paul Pry government, declaring what we shall think and what we shall drink.   [45] See *supra*, Chapter I, at n. 61.

[46] "It seems to me perfectly clearly established, that no official yet born on this earth is wise enough or generous enough to separate good ideas from bad ideas, good beliefs from bad beliefs, and that the utmost that anybody can ask of a government, is that if it is efficient it should detect and run down criminal acts; that beyond reaching words which are the direct and immediate incitement to criminal acts, no government dare go." — Walter Lippmann, *Bulletin of the League of Free Nations Association*, March, 1920.

[47] *Supra*, Chapter II, at nn. 31, 36.

the judge admitted speeches or letters not included in the indictment. In many cases opinions expressed before the United States entered the war were also admitted — opinions which the defendants then shared with many persons who afterwards supported the war. No matter how carefully the judge instructs the jury to disregard such prior language except as evidence of intention, it is undoubtedly human nature for a jury to lump together all the utterances, inside and outside the indictment, and then decide whether or not the defendant deserves punishment for everything he said. The Abrams case in the next chapter will bring this out very clearly.

The parallelism with the French revolutionary trials is often curiously close. Just as Lord Ellenborough could see no motive for Leigh Hunt's attack on flogging in the army except to cause a mutiny,[48] so the District Court judges have often been ready to infer a similar criminal intent from talk of profiteering or Wall Street. It is easy for the supporters of a war to class all its opponents as traitors, forgetting that some of them argue against it merely because they cannot bear to see what seems to them a needless conflict cripple or destroy the lives of thousands of their fellow-countrymen. A lawyer who defended many Espionage Act cases tells me that there was much speculation among his clients as to whether they actually possessed the requisite criminal intent. A few of them admitted to him that they had it, and there is not much question that some of the utterances which were prosecuted were made with the purpose of obstructing recruiting or the draft, although the danger of their doing so was usually non-existent. But it is impossible to read over the various cases without coming to the conclusion that most of the defendants had no real intention to cause trouble, and were only engaged in heated altercations or expounding economic doctrines.

A saw is a very good thing, but not to shave with, and a judge and jury are an excellent instrument to pass on overt acts. They are also well fitted to decide the effect of words upon the reputation of an individual, when the harmfulness of the language can be easily tested by common-sense standards, and its counterbalancing benefit to the public, if any, is indicated by well-established principles of law as to privilege and

[48] *Supra*, Chapter I, at n. 55.

fair comment. But they are not trained and they are not able to apply such vague and misleading tests of the criminality of utterances as bad tendency and presumptive intent.

It is on this account that I have spent so much time in emphasizing the difference between Judge Hand's test and the District Court test, in what may seem to many of my readers a mere interest in technicalities, far removed from the broad principles of freedom of speech. They forget that the technical rules of the common law are often the greatest safeguards of freedom. As Sir Henry Maine said, "Substantive law has at first the look of being gradually secreted in the interstices of procedure." [49] It is only necessary to recall the tremendous importance to human liberty of such procedural regulations as the Habeas Corpus Act, Fox's Libel Act,[50] and the rule that no man shall be compelled to give evidence against himself. This is the great value of Judge Hand's test, which was the only sort of rule about war-time utterances which should have been permitted. If it was not the correct interpretation of the language of the Espionage Act, then a statute with different language ought to have been passed. Even if not the only constitutional construction, it was the only workable construction. His rule gave the jury something definite to consider — the actual nature of the words and the danger of interference with the armed forces. The District Court test left them nothing but speculation upon the remote political and economic effect of words and the probable condition of mind of a person whose ideas were entirely different from their own.

In peaceable and quiet times, our legal rights are in little danger of being overborne; but when the wave of power lashes itself into violence and rage, and goes surging up against the barriers which were made to confine it, then we need the whole strength of an unbroken Constitution to save us from destruction.[51]

Judge Hand's test would have been a sea-wall against these surging waves, but the District Court test was nothing but a mud-bank which was rapidly swept away.

No one reading the simple language of the Espionage Act

---

[49] *Early Law and Custom*, p. 389.
[50] Quoted *supra*, Chapter I, n. 50.
[51] Jeremiah Black, arguing in *Ex parte* Milligan, 4 Wallace 2, 75 (1866).

of 1917 could have anticipated that it would be rapidly turned into a law under which opinions hostile to the war had practically no protection. Such a result was made possible only by the District Court test and by the tremendous wave of popular feeling against pacifists and pro-Germans during the war. This feeling was largely due to the hysterical fear of spies and other German propaganda. All of us on looking back to 1917 and 1918 are now sure that the emotions of ourselves and every one else were far from normal. During a war all thinking stops. I remember hearing one woman in a railroad train say to another, "Yes, my brother was going to France with the Y. M. C. A., but the sailing of his boat has been put off and put off. I don't like to say that it's German propaganda, but it certainly looks like it."

Mr. John Lord O'Brian, Assistant to the Attorney General in the prosecution of the most important Espionage Act cases, gives a vivid account of the false stories of enemy activities within the United States, put forth through the medium of press dispatches, pamphlets of patriotic societies, and occasionally speeches on the floor of Congress:

A phantom ship sailed into our harbors with gold from the Bolsheviki with which to corrupt the country; another phantom ship was found carrying ammunition from one of our harbors to Germany; submarine captains landed on our coasts, went to the theater and spread influenza germs; a new species of pigeon, thought to be German, was shot in Michigan; mysterious aeroplanes floated over Kansas at night, etc. Then there were the alleged spies themselves — Spoermann, alleged intimate of Bernstorff, landed on our coasts by the U-53, administrator of large funds, caught spying in our camps, who turned out to be a plumber from Baltimore. Several other alleged spies caught on the beaches signaling to submarines were subsequently released because they were, in the several cases, honest men, one of whom has been changing an incandescent light bulb in his hotel room, another of whom was trying to attract the attention of a passerby on the beach, etc. There was no community in the country so small that it did not produce a complaint because of failure to intern or execute at least one alleged German spy. These instances are cited, not to make light of the danger of hostile activities, nor to imply that incessant vigilance was not necessary in watching the German activities, but to show how impossible it was to check that kind of war hysteria and war excitement which found expression in impatience with the civil courts and the oft-recurring and false statement that this government showed undue leniency toward enemies within our gates.[52]

Yet not one case under this part of the statute shows the slightest evidence that the speeches or pamphlets subjected to prosecution were actuated by German money or German plans. Mr. O'Brian says it is doubtful if even the I.W.W. had any degree of German support.

Besides this fear of spies another influence which made fair trials under the Espionage Act very difficult was the passion for becoming spies. Not only did the American Protective League act as auxiliary to the Department of Justice, but as the same authority says:

Throughout the country a number of large organizations and societies were created for the purpose of suppressing sedition. All of these were the outgrowth of good motives and manned by a high type of citizens. The membership of these associations ran into the hundreds of thousands. One of them carried full page advertisements in leading papers from the Atlantic to the Pacific, offering in substance to make every man a spy chaser on the payment of a dollar membership fee. These associations did much good in awakening the public to the danger of insidious propaganda, but no other one cause contributed so much to the oppression of innocent men as the systematic and indiscriminate agitation against what was claimed to be an all-pervasive system of German espionage.[53]

It is obvious that the presence of members of these societies on juries made a just determination of such vague facts as the bad tendency of utterances and the intention of the defendant impossible. Once more we have a curious parallelism with the experiences of England during the French Revolution:

Another agency was evoked by the spirit of the times, dangerous to the liberty of the press, and to the security of domestic life. Voluntary societies were established in London and throughout

[52] 52 N. Y. Bar Assn. Rep. 281 (1919). Judge G. W. Anderson, who was U. S. District Attorney in Massachusetts in 1917, says, "More than ninety-nine per cent of the advertised and reported pro-German plots never existed." — 21 *New Republic* 251.

[53] O'Brian, pp. 279, 292, 297. On the I.W.W., p. 299.

the country, for the purpose of aiding the executive Government in the discovery and punishment of seditious writings or language. . . . These societies, supported by large subscriptions, were busy in collecting evidence of seditious designs, often consisting of anonymous letters, often of the report of informers, liberally rewarded for their activity. They became, as it were, public prosecutors, supplying the Government with proof of supposed offenses, and quickening its zeal in the prosecution of offenders. Every unguarded word at the club, the market-place or the tavern, was reported to these credulous alarmists and noted as evidence of disaffection.

Such associations were repugnant to the policy of our laws, by which the Crown is charged with the office of bringing offenders to justice, while the people, represented by juries, are to judge, without favor or prejudice, of their guilt or innocence. But here the people were invited to make common cause with the Crown against offenders, to collect the evidence, and prejudge the guilt. How then could members of these societies assist in the pure administration of justice, as jurymen and justices of the peace? In the [rural regions] especially was justice liable to be warped.[54]

Attorney General Gregory corroborates Mr. O'Brian's statement:

The department has also been hampered by the circulation of unfounded reports, running into the hundreds, of supposed unpunished alien enemy activities in the way of fires alleged to have been caused by enemy agents, alleged uses of poison by enemy agents, alleged uses of ground glass, alleged damage to Red Cross supplies, etc. In view of the necessity for constant vigilance on the part of the public, it has not always seemed advisable to this department to enter into controversies as to the truth of these irresponsible reports.[55]

It was with the nation in the atmosphere above described that the laws affecting free speech received the severest test thus far placed upon them in our history. It is obvious that a country full of would-be spies chasing imaginary spies and finding only pro-Germans and pacifists is a very unfit place for the decision of those psychological questions which, as Wharton pointed out,[56] inevitably arise from the prosecution of utterances. It may be helpful to examine briefly the effect

---

[54] May, *Constitutional History*, II, 36.
[55] Report, 1918, p. 23.   [56] See note 19, *supra*.

of this atmosphere upon the three main parts of the human machinery through which the Espionage Act necessarily operated, namely, the prosecuting officials, the juries, and the trial judges.

a. The Prosecuting Officials

The Assistants to the Attorney General in charge of the administration of the Espionage Act were John Lord O'Brian of Buffalo, so frequently quoted in these pages, and Alfred Bettman of Cincinnati. Although these men enforced the statute in accordance with the District Court test, which in my opinion made the maintenance of a real freedom of speech impracticable, nevertheless they were firm believers in that principle and singularly free from the effects of war emotion. In particular, great praise must be given to their thorough investigation of hundreds of convictions, as a result of which the sentences imposed by the judges were in many instances commuted by the President to a small fraction of their original length.[57] Unfortunately, it was very hard for these officials in Washington to impress their ideas of fairness and open discussion upon some of their subordinates and upon the public, and consequently to keep control of prosecutions throughout the country. Mr. O'Brian sums up this local situation:

It has been quite unnecessary to urge upon the United States Attorneys the importance of prosecuting vigorously, and there has been little difficulty in securing convictions from juries. On the contrary, it has been necessary at all times to exercise caution in order to secure to defendants accused of disloyalty the safeguard of fair and impartial trials. In addition to the causes already recited there were the patriotic agitations continually being carried on by the Liberty Loan speakers, four-minute men and others, all of which worked the whole country up to a pitch of intense patriotism, resulting in instinctive aversion toward anyone even under suspicion for disloyalty.

The situation became much worse after the May, 1918, amendment. Despite the very wide scope given by judges to the original Espionage Act, this did after all require the forbidden speeches and pamphlets to have *some* connection with

[57] Report of the Attorney General, 1919, Exhibit 21.

the raising of armed forces. So a sensible or busy United States district attorney always had a good excuse ready for getting rid of overzealous patrioteers: "This fellow you want prosecuted didn't say anything about the army or navy. I don't see any federal offense here. It's just a matter for the police or the county attorney." Consequently, before the amendment isolated disloyal utterances had been handled in many parts of the country under a rather loose interpretation of state laws or city ordinances providing light punishments for disorderly conduct. The 1918 Act killed this excuse, and threw a great burden upon the comparatively small law machinery of the federal government. It was almost impossible for the United States district attorneys to keep abreast of the complaints.

The general publicity given the statute through the newspapers and, in many cases, through employers, who circularized their employees with copies of the act (calling attention to the dangers of strike activities), fanned animosities into flame, vastly increasing the amount of suspicion and complaints throughout the country. This, in turn, resulted in a large increase in the amount of prosecutions, backed up by strong local patriotic sentiment. Up to the time that this statute went into practical operation the United States Attorneys throughout the country, except in genuine cases of treason, had each acted as the supreme law official of his district, exercising on his own account full discretion in all matters as to prosecution.[58]

Under these circumstances, on May 23, 1918, the Attorney General issued to all United States attorneys a circular about the amended Act. It stated that the prompt and aggressive enforcement of the Act was of the highest importance, but it was also of great importance that it should be administered with discretion and should not be permitted to become the medium whereby efforts were made to suppress honest, legitimate criticism of the administration or discussion of government policies, or for personal feuds or persecution.[59]

It is obvious that this circular simply transferred the strain from the judge and jury to another portion of the human machinery, the district attorney, who is a government official

[58] O'Brian, 304, 305, 309. See the facts of some of the local cases in *War-time Prosecutions*, 27 ff., listing 126 convictions under local laws (a few under state sedition statutes).

[59] Report of the Attorney General, 1918, p. 674.

and not expected to be impartial. Opinions will differ as to the wisdom of enacting a very broad and severe criminal statute and then letting individual prosecutors enforce it or not as they think best. The plausible argument for such a system is that it enables the government to imprison the really dangerous men easily, and ignore the numerous other persons who happen to be covered by the statute. But can we be sure that all the unimportant violators will be left alone? It was well said by Judge Amidon that this circular "converts every United States attorney into an angel of life and death clothed with the power to walk up and down his district, saying, 'This one will I spare, and that one will I smite.' If the law leaves it to the district attorney to determine when an act shall be prosecuted as a crime and when it shall not be, how is a citizen to know when he is exercising his constitutional right, and when he is committing a crime? Of course such conduct in administering criminal law, punishable by imprisonment for twenty years, simply converts government into a government of men and not of law."

The Department of Justice eventually realized this, wide divergencies appearing in the theories entertained by the various prosecuting attorneys, so that the Attorney General about a month before the end of the war issued a circular directing district attorneys to send no more cases to grand juries under the Espionage Act of 1918 without first submitting a statement of facts to the Attorney General and receiving by wire his opinion as to whether or not the facts constituted an offense under the Act.[60] "This circular," says Mr. O'Brian, "is suggestive of the immense pressure brought to bear throughout the war upon the Department of Justice in all parts of the country for indiscriminate prosecution demanded in behalf of a policy of wholesale repression and restraint of public opinion." Doubtless this second circular made it possible for the Attorney General to weed out mere "clamor" cases, but it came too late in the war to have any practical effect. Until that time all persons who were opposed to the war were practically at the mercy of the local district attorneys, and under the District Court test of the 1917 Act or the express language of the 1918 Act prosecution almost invariably resulted in conviction.

[60] *Id.;* O'Brian, p. 306.

b. The Juries

For the human machinery broke down at a second point — the jury. It is sometimes suggested that a jury trial gives a sufficient protection for freedom of speech, and that public sentiment will inevitably reflect itself in verdicts of acquittal if the prosecution seems unjust.[61] It is undoubtedly true that in England freedom of discussion is, as Dicey says, "little else than the right to write or say anything which a jury, consisting of twelve shopkeepers, think it expedient should be said or written." In my first chapter, however, I have endeavored to show that this protection is entirely inadequate and that the constitutional provision must mean much more. It is only in times of popular panic and indignation that freedom of speech becomes important as an institution, and it is precisely in those times that the protection of the jury proves illusory. As the Assistant to the Attorney General admits, "There has been little difficulty in securing convictions from juries."

Judge Amidon said after much experience in Espionage Act cases:

Only those who have administered the Espionage Act can understand the danger of such legislation. When crimes are defined by such generic terms, instead of by specific acts, the jury becomes the sole judge, whether men shall or shall not be punished. Most of the jurymen have sons in the war. They are all under the power of the passions which war engenders. For the first six months after June 15, 1917, I tried war cases before jurymen who were candid, sober, intelligent business men, whom I had known for thirty years, and who under ordinary circumstances would have had the highest respect for my declarations of law, but during that period they looked back into my eyes with the savagery of wild animals, saying by their manner, "Away with this twiddling, let us get at him." Men believed during that period that the only verdict in a war case, which could show loyalty, was a verdict of guilty.

[61] E.g., W. R. Vance in 2 *Minnesota Law Review* 260; 33 *Harvard Law Review* 448. In England freedom of speech is necessarily protected only by jury trial plus the common law rules of criminal attempt and solicitation, unlawful meetings, etc. See Dicey, *Law of the Constitution*, chapters vi and vii. Without the guidance of these rules the jury would be far less valuable. Hence the merit of Judge Hand's test.

There are strong indications of other influences which accentuated the effect of the general war emotion, of circumstances which resemble the situation in England during the French Revolution, when the juries were chosen largely from men much opposed to the prisoners.[62] Mr. O'Brian tells [63] how the administration of the Act was affected by economic conflicts growing out of the activities of the Non-Partisan League and the I.W.W. Although the Attorney General insisted upon the doctrine that guilt was personal and refused to proscribe any group as such, the effect on juries in federal and state prosecutions was probably serious. For instance, in the trial of the president of the Non-Partisan League, under the Minnesota Espionage Act, the jury was chosen out of a total panel picked from among the voters by the County Commissioner. Although the farmers of Jackson County were sharply divided into members of the Non-Partisan League and bitter opponents with practically no neutrals, and the League candidate had barely lost the last election, the panel of one hundred and forty-four contained not a single member of the League, but consisted of men from sections of the county which League organizers and speakers were barred from visiting. The defense had only four peremptory challenges. The jury was not segregated, but was subjected to the heat of popular discussion during the trial.[64]

This was not a federal case, but similar problems are raised by the method of selecting juries in the United States courts. As long ago as the Sedition trials of 1798 the method of securing indictments and convictions met with public condemnation because of the men from whom and by whom the jury were chosen. Beveridge says,

In many states the United States Marshals selected what persons they pleased as members of the grand juries and trial juries. These officers of the National courts were, without exception, Federalists;

---

[62] May, II, 36, 87.

[63] O'Brian, p. 295.

[64] See on the Townley trial: C. R. Johnson, *New Republic*, XX, 18 (Aug. 6, 1919); Judson King, *Nation*, CIX, 143 (Aug. 2, 1919); *Weekly Review*, I, 230 (July 26, 1919). An impartial account of the Non-Partisan League is Arthur Ruhl, "The North Dakota Idea," *Atlantic Monthly*, CXXIII, 686 (May, 1919). See also section VII of this chapter; Chapter VII, section I.

in many cases, Federalist politicians. When making up juries they selected only persons of the same manner of thinking as that of the marshals and judges themselves. So it was that the juries were nothing more than machines that registered the will, opinion, or even inclination of the National judges and the United States District Attorneys. In short, in these prosecutions, trial by jury in any real sense was not to be had.[65]

It would certainly be improper without a very elaborate investigation to assert that such conditions existed in federal juries during the war. The method of selection varied so much that generalization is impossible. There can be no doubt, however, that in some districts a wide power of selection, otherwise than by lot, was exercised by the officials. Federal juries in civil cases were often stated by members of the bar to be superior in quality to state juries, and this was accounted for by the practice of the officials to go through the lists carefully and exclude persons considered undesirable. Although this method may not have been exercised with any desire to prejudice the jury in Espionage Act cases, the jury might naturally be limited to men of means who were not likely to understand at all the position of a person opposed to the war for economic reasons. On the other hand, federal jurors in New York City were said by a member of the Department of Justice to be inferior to those in the state courts. The government had more difficulty there in securing convictions in war cases than almost anywhere else, and this was attributed by some of the government counsel to the presence on the jury list of many persons with radical tendencies of thought. Without framing any conclusions myself on this extremely delicate matter, I shall present statements made on behalf of two prominent defendants.

Max Eastman in his account of the Debs case spoke from the

[65] Beveridge's *Marshall*, III, 42. F. M. Anderson, "The Enforcement of the Alien and Sedition Laws," *Report of the American Historical Association* (1912), p. 125, says that the grand juries were composed preponderantly, if not exclusively, of Federalists; that the Callender trial jury was drawn in a manner that went far toward justifying the charge of packing; and that other juries could scarcely be called impartial. See also 32 *West Virginia Law Quarterly* 72 (1925); United States *v.* Wood, 299 U. S. 123 (1936); People *v.* Wismer, 58 Cal. App. 679 (1922).

point of view, obviously partisan but worth attention, of one who had himself been on trial under the Espionage Act:

As to the jury . . . they were about seventy-two years old, worth fifty to sixty thousand dollars, retired from business, from pleasure, and from responsibility for all troubles arising outside of their own family. An investigator for the defense computed the average age of the entire venire of 100 men; it was seventy years. Their average wealth was over $50,000. In the jury finally chosen every man was a retired farmer or a retired merchant, but one, who was a contractor still active. They were none of them native to leisure, however, but men whose faces were bitterly worn and wearied out of all sympathy with a struggle they had individually surmounted.[66]

Berger's counsel made the following statement to the Committee of the House of Representatives:

On the selection and composition of the jury, I want to say that out of a panel that was examined of fully 50 there was only one laboring man who appeared, out of a 90 per cent. population of that judicial district, on the panel, and he was promptly treated as though he were a spy in camp. The jury was made up of a number of insurance brokers of the city of Chicago, of a number of very wealthy farmers, retired farmers, I think five, all men of much acreage and wealth in Illinois, and two bankers. Racially, it was utterly unrepresentative. I mean the whole panel was utterly unrepresentative of the racial, national, or industrial composition of the masses of the people in that district. . . . It is the marshal's personal selection. It is the most extraordinary thing and the judicial system of our country ought to be corrected, because he is the appointee of the civil administration.[67]

Whether or not these accusations were accurate, they certainly present a problem in the trial of persons of radical inclinations, which must be solved in the future with considerable thought. The solution should not only give justice, but be so plain as to satisfy all classes, in so far as that is possible, that they are getting justice.

[66] "The Trial of Eugene Debs," 1 *Liberator*, No. 9 (November, 1918), 9.

The charge of Mayer, J., in United States *v.* Phillips, Bull. 14, was so favorable to the defendant that, I am informed by an eyewitness, an acquittal was generally expected in the court-room, but the defendants were convicted.

[67] Victor L. Berger: Hearings before the Special Committee, I, 636. See Wurts, "The jury System under Changing Social Conditions," 47 *American Law Review* 67 (1913); Mamaux *v.* United States, 264 Fed. 816 (C. C. A. 6th, 1920).

c. *The Trial Judges*

The third point at which the human machinery breaks down in the enforcement of a sedition law is the trial judges. Some of the English charges against agitators have already been mentioned. It is well known that one of the worst features of the Sedition Act of 1798 was its administration by the Federalist judges, which afterwards caused a determined assault upon the National Judiciary. In their charges to grand juries, they lectured and preached on religion, on morality, on partisan politics. At the trials, freedom of speech was ignored, no distinction was made between fact and opinion, and prosecutions for "wholly justifiable political criticisms — some of them trivial and even amusing" were allowed to go to the jury. Although the deportment of the judges, with the exception of Chase, was substantially correct and the charges were usually right in what they said, convictions followed because of what was omitted or because the jury should have been prevented by a direction of acquittal from passing on the cases at all.[68]

Some Espionage Act charges which merit a similar criticism have already been mentioned, and make it plain that, in contrast to the Civil War judges who stood rock-ribbed for legality,[69] a few men on the United States bench during the World War felt it to be their duty to deliver stump speeches to the jury as if they were soliciting subscriptions to a Liberty Loan. One more instance may be given.

Judge Aldrich in a New Hampshire case charged:

These are not times for fooling. The times are serious. Nobody knows what is going to happen to our institutions within the next year, or the next month. Out West they are hanging men for saying such things as this man is accused of saying. They are feeling outraged by such expressions to such extent that they are taking the law into their own hands. Now, that is a very bad thing to do. We do not want that in New Hampshire, but we do want a courageous enforcement of the law.[70]

[68] Beveridge's *Marshall*, III, 30 n.; II, 421; and III, 29–49 *passim*; F. M. Anderson, *op. cit.*, p. 126.

[69] *E.g.*, Taney's decision in *Ex parte* Merryman, Taney, 246 (1861); and the release of the Copperhead Milligan, 4 Wallace 2 (1866).

[70] United States *v.* Taubert, Bull. 108. He was sentenced to three years for obstructing bond sales by saying, "This was a Morgan war and not a war of the people." There is nothing about bonds in the 1917 Act, but Judge

Besides this attitude toward opposition to the war in general, some judges expressed an attitude on economic questions which seriously affected not only the enforcement of the Espionage Act but of the Deportation law as well. A considerable portion of hostility to the declaration of war and conscription was due to the belief of radicals that it represented a sacrifice of working-class lives for the benefit of the wealthy. This belief was voiced by many members of the Non-Partisan League, the Socialist Party, and the Industrial Workers of the World. Sympathy with the Russian Revolution was also a complicating factor. It was clearly the duty of the judges to keep their minds free from economic prejudices, and to warn the jury that just because a defendant held unpopular radical views this in no way affected his guilt for interference with the war. Of course judges, like other men, are entitled to definite opinions on vital controversies of the day, and most of them will naturally favor only gradual changes in the present order, but the increasingly frequent part which radicalism is playing in legal proceedings of various kinds, and particularly in sedition prosecutions during and since the war, makes it essential that the judge hearing such cases shall have a scholarly and dispassionate attitude and an ability to discriminate between different schools of revolutionary thought. The warning of Justice Holmes in 1913 deserves reprinting:

When twenty years ago a vague terror went over the earth and the word socialism began to be heard, I thought and still think that fear was translated into doctrines that had no proper place in the Constitution or the common law. Judges are apt to be naif, simple-minded men, and they need something of Mephistopheles. We too need education in the obvious — to learn to transcend our own convictions and to leave room for much that we hold dear to be done away with short of revolution by the orderly change of law.[71]

Consequently, it is a cause for grave concern when we find Judge Albert B. Anderson, who later enjoined the coal strike, using this language from the bench, even though in the particular case he made a very good decision:

Aldrich held it covered them because an army could not be raised without them and "the Government must not be embarrassed in those respects by unreasonable opposition."

[71] Holmes, *Collected Legal Papers*, p. 295.

I think that about the least commendable sort of folks I know are these Russians, who have fled to this country, and are not anything like satisfied with what they have here. Why? Because we do not give them everything they want. Mary Antin was here not long ago and delivered an address, but she didn't simply want the Jews to have their rights. The trouble with Mary Antin is that she wanted the Jews to have everything that we have got; and that is the way with this gentleman. . . . I do not like the word "Socialist" or these Socialists. The Socialist always flatters himself when he calls himself a Socialist. He means to leave the impression that he is more generous and more unselfish than the average run of men; but he doesn't want to be called an anarchist. . . . If I had time I would like to have somebody explain what it means except for the "have-nots" to take it away from the "haves." That is all there is to it; so I have not much patience with that sort of thing or soap-box orators. Why don't they go hire a hall? [72]

One fears that he will not always add as he wisely did:

Free speech means the right to say foolish things as well as the right to say sensible things.

Judge Wade said in sentencing Mrs. O'Hare:

Well, I tell you, if that is the sort of stuff the socialist party stands for, if its gospel is the gospel of hate, and contempt of religion and charity, it has not any place on the American soil either in times of war or times of peace.[73]

The feeling against the I.W.W. was very bitter in the West, and convictions were numerous. One of these was reversed because Judge Wolverton in Oregon charged:

The I.W.W. is a disloyal and unpatriotic organization. Adherents thereof owe no allegiance to any organized government, and so far as the government is concerned the organization itself is thoroughly bad.[74]

[72] United States v. Zimmerman, Nelles, *Espionage Act Cases*, pp. 10–12. The judge ordered the jury to acquit. On this judge's coal strike injunction of 1919, see Chafee, *The Inquiring Mind*, pp. 198–207.

[73] Nelles, p. 47.

[74] Kumpula v. United States, 261 Fed. 49. Another case of reversal for the prejudicial attitude of the court is Rutherford v. United States, 258 Fed. 855. See "Lawless Enforcement of Law," 33 *Harvard Law Review* 956; "Unfairness in Prosecutions," 4 *Reports of the National Commission on Law Observance and Enforcement* (Wickersham Commission) 263 ff. (1931).

The remarks of Judge K. M. Landis about German Americans, made before

Contrast with this language the words of Judge Amidon in trying a member of the Non-Partisan League:

The head and front of it is that the speech tended to array class against class. I have been on this earth quite a spell myself. I never have known of any great reform being carried through where the people whose established condition would be disturbed by the carrying out of the reform did not say that the people who were trying to bring about the reform were stirring up class against class. That is an argument that I know to be at least 3,500 years old from my knowledge of history, and it is repeated in every effort to change an existing condition.[75]

The number of Espionage Act judges who were guilty of actually prejudicial conduct at the trials was comparatively few, and in many respects the judges deserved the praise which Mr. O'Brian awarded them for giving great latitude to the defendant's proof [76] and urging upon the jury the necessity for the dispassionate consideration of evidence. The defect was, for the most part, not so much in what they said as in what they did not say. In the first place, despite the vagueness of the District Court test, common sense ought to have led them to withdraw many more cases of remote language from the jury, as Justice Brandeis forcibly insisted in his *Tageblatt* opinion.[77] And whenever there was enough apparent relation to the raising of armies to justify the submission of the evi-

he presided at the Berger trial, led the Supreme Court to reverse the conviction, because they showed an "objectionable inclination or disposition of the judge" which disqualified him from sitting. — Berger *v.* United States, 255 U. S. at 28 (1921).

[75] United States *v.* Brinton, Bull. 132. On possible dangers from the participation of the Department of Justice in the selection and promotion of United States judges, see Works, *Juridical Reform* (New York, 1919), pp. 123 ff.; Chafee, *The Inquiring Mind*, p. 210, n. 20.

[76] O'Brian, p. 310. On the importance of such a policy in political criminal trials, see the next chapter; Robert Ferrari in 3 *Minnesota Law Review* 365; and 66 *Dial* 647 (June 28, 1919). Compare the opportunity given Debs, Nearing, Eastman, and even the I.W.W.'s at Chicago to speak in their own defense with the refusal of the Minnesota state court to hear Townley, when at the close of his case he arose in the hot night with coat off to address the jury. — 109 *Nation* 144.

[77] See page 91, *infra. Cf.* O'Brian, p. 309: "The chief difficulty on any trial has naturally been the question of what *quantum of evidence* would, as a matter of law, justify submitting to the jury the question of unlawful intent and the question of the reasonable and natural result of the utterance complained of."

dence to the jury, the trial judge should have cautioned them against convicting because the words might possibly and in-directly cause discontent in the forces or a refusal to enlist. The juries needed much more careful guidance on the issue of intent and far more discretion should have been exercised in the admission of prior utterances, because of the danger that the jury would convict the defendant as an undesirable citizen, who, taken all in all, ought to be shut up.[78] Further-more, whenever a charge did mention freedom of speech, it was almost sure to say or imply that this right had nothing to do with opposition to war and put such opposition in the same class with extreme utterances like advocacy of a natural right to kill men or outrage women. Almost no emphasis was laid on the desirability of wide discussion so long as there was no real interference with the raising of armies, even discussion by those opposed to the war. The charge of Judge Augustus Hand in the trial of Max Eastman was a notable exception:

Every citizen has a right, without intent to obstruct the recruiting or enlistment service, to think, feel, and express disapproval or abhor-rence of any law or policy or proposed law or policy, including the Declaration of War, the Conscription Act, and the so-called sedition clauses of the Espionage Act; belief that the war is not or was not a war for democracy; belief that our participation in it was forced or induced by powers with selfish interests to be served thereby; belief that our participation was against the will of the majority of the citizens or voters of the country; belief that the self-sacrifice of persons who elect to suffer for freedom of conscience is admirable; belief that war is horrible; belief that the Allies' war aims were or are selfish and undemocratic; belief that the Hon. Elihu Root is hostile to socialism, and that his selection to represent America in a socialistic republic was ill-advised.

It is the constitutional right of every citizen to express his opinion about the war or the participation of the United States in it; about the desirability of peace; about the merits or demerits of the system of conscription, and about the moral rights or claims of conscientious objectors to be exempt from conscription. It is the constitutional right of the citizen to express such opinions, even though they are opposed to the opinions or policies of the administration; and even

---

[78] Admissibility of such utterances has been contested, but see the Abrams decision. *Cf.* People *v.* Molyneux, 168 N. Y. 264, a famous case of the other view. See Wigmore on Evidence (3d ed., 1940), vol. II, §§ 302, 369.

though the expression of such opinion may unintentionally or indirectly discourage recruiting and enlistment.[79]

In one matter over which they had complete control, the District Court judges must bear a lasting blame. The only proceedings in our law comparable to the Espionage Act sentences are the sedition prosecutions under George III, with which so many parallels have been found. Indeed, at this point the parallelism breaks down. The longest sentences for sedition in England were four years, and even Scotch judges like Braxfield did not exceed fourteen years, of transportation and not imprisonment. Our judges condemned at least eleven persons to prison for ten years, six for fifteen years, and twenty-four for twenty years.[80] Judge Van Valkenburgh summed up the facts with appalling correctness in view of the virtual life terms imposed under the Espionage Act, when he said that freedom of speech means the protection of "criticism which is made friendly to the government, friendly to the war, friendly to the policies of the government." [81]

[79] Nelles, pp. 29, 30. As this charge was not reprinted in the Bulletins of the Department of Justice, it had no effect upon other district judges, except possibly in United States v. Debs, which permitted "reasonable and tempered discussions." — Bull. 166, p. 12. Judge Clayton refused to repeat Judge Hand's words in his Abrams charge.

Another good statement was made by Judge Julius M. Mayer, in an alien enemy internment case after the armistice: "Vital as is the necessity in time of war not to hamper acts of the executive in the defense of the nation and in the prosecution of the war, of equal and perhaps greater importance, is the preservation of constitutional rights." — Ex parte Gilroy, 257 Fed. 110, 114 (1919).

[80] These figures include only sentences in the reported cases. They do not include the I.W.W.s sentenced in Chicago, sixteen of them to twenty years, and thirty-three to ten years; or many unreported cases with long sentences, e.g., twenty-six at Sacramento for ten years. No allowance is made for reversals and commutations in appraising the work of the trial judges; indeed, there could be no more biting comment on their conduct than the enormous reductions in scores of sentences recommended by the Department of Justice. See Reports of U. S. Atty. Gen. for details.

[81] United States v. Rose Pastor Stokes, Bull. 106, p. 14.

5. THE SUPREME COURT DECISIONS

> *To me it seems simply a case of flagrant mistrial, likely to result in disgrace and great injustice, probably in life imprisonment for two old men, because this court hesitates to exercise the power, which it undoubtedly possesses, to correct, in this calmer time, errors of law which would not have been committed but for the stress and strain of feeling prevailing in the early months of the late deplorable war.*
>
> JUSTICE CLARKE, dissenting in the *Tageblatt* case.

.The Espionage Act did not come before the Supreme Court until 1919, after the fighting was ended and almost all the District Court cases had been tried. It was too late for anything our highest Court said to lessen the restrictive effect of the Act upon the discussion of public affairs during the war. Thus we cannot rely on the Supreme Court as a safeguard against the excesses of war legislation. A statute enacted early in a war is likely to receive its first authoritative interpretation many months later when the war is over. During the period when the statute is actually operating, it will possess meaning given to it by prosecuting officials and lower court judges. The nine Justices in the Supreme Court can only lock the doors after the Liberty Bell is stolen.

However, the necessarily belated views of the Supreme Court have much importance for the future, especially when the statute, like the Espionage Act of 1917, applies to succeeding wars. So we shall examine six decisions upholding convictions under the Act,[82] three unanimously in the spring of 1919 and three by a divided Court in the winter of 1919–1920.[83]

The first decision in the earlier group and the most influential upon the later development of constitutional law was

---

[82] Three less important criminal cases under the Act were Sugarman *v.* United States, 249 U. S. 130 (1919); Stilson *v.* United States, 250 U. S. 583 (1919); O'Connell *v.* United States, 253 U. S. 142 (1920). On the abortive Baltzer case, see *supra*, at note 42. The Milwaukee Leader case under the mail section of the Act is treated in Chapter VII, section II.

[83] For an able review of all these cases, which is more favorable to the government's position than I am, see J. P. Hall, "Free Speech in War Time," 21 *Columbia Law Review* 526 (1921).

Schenck v. *United States.*[84] This was one of the few reported prosecutions under the Act where there clearly was incitement to resist the draft. The defendants had mailed circulars to men who had passed exemption boards, which not only declared conscription to be unconstitutional despotism, but urged the recipients in impassioned language to assert their rights. Such utterances could fairly be considered a direct and dangerous interference with the power of Congress to raise armies, and were also counseling unlawful action within Judge Hand's interpretation of the statute. Consequently, no real question of free speech arose. Nevertheless, the defense of constitutionality was raised, and denied. Judge Holmes, speaking for the unanimous Court, lays down a test of great value for determining the true scope of the First Amendment:

> We admit that in many places and in ordinary times the defendants in saying all that was said in the circular would have been within their constitutional rights. But the character of every act depends upon the circumstances in which it is done. . . . *The question in every case is whether the words used are used in such circumstances and are of such a nature as to create a clear and present danger that they will bring about the substantive evils that Congress has a right to prevent.* It is a question of proximity and degree. When a nation is at war many things that might be said in time of peace are such a hindrance to its effort that their utterance will not be endured so long as men fight and that no Court could regard them as protected by any constitutional right.

Although "the substantive evils" are not specifically defined, they mean successful interference with the particular power of Congress that is in question — in this instance, the war power. Since Congress is authorized to declare war and raise armies, it can expedite its task by punishing those who actually keep men out of the service, whether by starting a draft riot or by effectually persuading men not to register or not to enlist. And Congress can go one step farther. Besides punishing overt acts of interference with the war, it can prevent such acts from occurring by penalizing unsuccessful efforts to interfere, whether they are acts or words. But this desire to head off actual injury to the government is, we have seen, the

[84] Schenck *v.* United States, 249 U. S. 47 (1919). The italics are mine. No data have been found on sentence or commutation.

basis of all suppression of discussion, unless it is limited very narrowly. In order to give force to the First Amendment, Justice Holmes draws the boundary line very close to the test of incitement at common law and clearly makes the punishment of words for their remote bad tendency impossible. He shows the close relation between freedom of speech and criminal attempts by borrowing a phrase from his own opinion in a leading Massachusetts attempt case, "It is a question of degree." [85]

The Supreme Court's opinion in the Schenck case lends much support to the views of Judge Learned Hand in the *Masses* case. Justice Holmes does interpret the Espionage Act somewhat more widely than Judge Hand, in making the nature of the words only one element of danger, and in not requiring that the utterances shall in themselves satisfy an objective standard. Thus he loses the great administrative advantages of Judge Hand's test. But though the decision, like many District Court cases, allows conviction for expressions of opinion uttered with a bad intention, it imposes additional requirements, which most trial courts had neglected. Words are criminal under the second and third clauses of the Act only because of their relation to the armed forces, and that relation must be so close that the words constitute "a clear and present danger" of injury to the raising of those forces or of mutiny and similar breaches of discipline.

Words and intentions (the Supreme Court here held) are not punishable for their own sake, or merely for their tendency to discourage citizens at war. Thus the opinion, especially the italicized sentence, substantially coincides with the conclusion reached by our investigation of the history and political setting of the First Amendment.[86] The concept of freedom of speech received for the first time an authoritative judicial interpretation in accord with the purpose of the framers of the Constitution.

The next decision, in the Frohwerk case,[87] illustrates one of the commonest reasons why appeals from sedition convictions

[85] Commonwealth *v.* Peaslee, 177 Mass. 267, 272 (1901). See *supra*, at n. 23.
[86] *Supra*, last two paragraphs of Chapter I. To the same effect was Schofield in 1914; see *supra*, Chapter I, at n. 38.
[87] Frohwerk *v.* United States, 249 U. S. 204 (1919). The sentence of ten years was afterwards commuted by the President to a year.

prove unsuccessful — the lack of good old-fashioned lawyer-like work by the defense counsel. An unpopular pacifist or radical often finds it hard to get a competent lawyer. Eloquent praise of the blessings of free speech amounts to little, unless counsel also possesses a firm grasp of the technical issues involved and tries the case so as to bring out those issues clearly and get them on the printed record which goes to the appellate court. The main issue in such a prosecution is usually not the unconstitutionality of the statute as a whole, but whether what the defendant said or did, when connected with the surrounding circumstances, falls within the terms of the statute as properly construed in the light of the free speech clause. Therefore, it is essential for counsel for the accused to establish at the trial with accuracy and completeness just what the accused said or did, among what persons and when and where and how.[88] The prisoner's lawyer keeps his eyes on the jury, but he must always keep his mind on the appellate court.

The Frohwerk case brings out the disastrous consequences of an unsatisfactory record. Frohwerk had inserted several articles in the *Missouri Staats-Zeitung* on the constitutionality and merits of the draft and on the purposes of the war. Even in the Department of Justice there was considerable question whether these did not merely advocate a change in governmental policy as distinguished from an obstruction of such policy, and no special effort appeared to reach men who were subject to the draft. Justice Holmes said that there might have been cause for reversal, if more evidence had been presented on the record. However, on the inadequately prepared record as it stood, the evidence might conceivably have been sufficient to sustain a conviction, since the circumstances and the intention, though not the words *per se*, might satisfy the danger test.

It may be that all this might be said or written even in time of war in circumstances that would not make it a crime. We do not lose our right to condemn either measures or men because the country is at war. . . . But we must take the case on the record as it is, and of that record it is impossible to say that it might not have been

---

[88] An illuminating example of the value of such an adequate record to the accused is furnished by the opinion of Hughes, C.J., in De Jonge v. Oregon, 299 U. S. 353 (1937), discussed in Chapter XI, section v.

found that the circulation of the paper was in quarters where a little breath would be enough to kindle a flame and that the fact was known and relied on by those who sent that paper out.

Great historical interest attaches to the last of the earlier decisions, which sustained the conviction of Eugene V. Debs, the most famous person imprisoned under the Espionage Act.[89] Debs's utterances are hard to reconcile with the Supreme Court test of "clear and present danger," but Justice Holmes was willing to accept the jury's verdict as proof that actual interference with the war was intended and was the proximate effect of the words used. It is regrettable that he felt unable to go behind the verdict. Judge Westenhaver's charge gave the jury such a wide scope that Debs was probably convicted for an exposition of socialism, merely because the jury thought his speech had some tendency to bring about resistance to the draft.

The proper construction of the Espionage Act of 1917 is far more important than its constitutionality. There can be little doubt that it is constitutional under any test if construed naturally, but it had been interpreted by many lower courts in such a way as to violate the free speech clause and the plain words of the statute, to say nothing of the principle that criminal statutes should be construed strictly. If the Supreme Court test had been laid down in the summer of 1917 and followed in charges by the District Courts, the most casual perusal of the utterances prosecuted makes it sure that there would have been many more acquittals. Instead, bad tendency

[89] Debs *v.* United States, 249 U. S. 211 (1919). Debs began serving his sentence of ten years on April 13, 1919, at the age of sixty-three. At the 1920 election while in prison he received 919,799 votes as the Socialist candidate for President for the fifth time, more than when he had last run in 1912. On Christmas Day, 1921, he was released by President Harding, without restoration of citizenship. See Report of the Attorney General, 1922, 416; *Dictionary of American Biography*, V, 183 ff.

The statements on p. 86 about the reasons why Justice Holmes wrote the opinions of the Court in the Debs and other early Espionage Act cases have been confirmed by his letter of April 5th, 1919, to Sir Frederick Pollock about the Debs case: "There was a lot of jaw about free speech, which I dealt with somewhat summarily in an earlier case — Schenck *v.* United States. . . . As it happens I should go farther probably than the majority in favor of it, and I daresay it was partly on that account that the Chief Justice assigned the case to me." — *Holmes–Pollock Letters*, II, 7.

and presumed intent were the tests of criminality, tests which this book has endeavored to prove wholly inconsistent with freedom of speech and any genuine discussion of public affairs.

The Debs decision showed clearly the evils of the broad construction of the Espionage Act, which rejected Judge Learned Hand's objective standard of the meaning of the words used. Debs was convicted of an attempt to cause insubordination in the army and obstruct recruiting, yet no provocation to any such definite and particular acts was proved. He spoke to a convention of Socialists in support of their economic views, instancing the war as the supreme curse of capitalism. In a few sentences he approved the conduct of persons convicted of like offenses, saying, for example, that if Mrs. Stokes was guilty so was he. Her conviction has since been reversed. Not one word was designed for soldiers, not one word urged his hearers to resist the draft, objectionable as he considered it. Undoubtedly he admitted at his trial that he had obstructed the war: "I abhor war. I would oppose the war if I stood alone. When I think of a cold, glittering steel bayonet being plunged in the white, quivering flesh of a human being, I recoil with horror." But the only question before the jury was whether he had tried to obstruct it in the ways made unlawful in the statute. If all verbal or written opposition to the war furnishes a basis for conviction, because it is dangerous under the circumstances and indicates a criminal mind, then none but the most courageous will dare speak out against a future war.

"It is useless," wrote Ernst Freund,[90] "to over-emphasize the substantive limitations of the Constitution; the real securities of rights will always have to be found in the painstaking care given to the working out of legal principles. So long as we apply the notoriously loose common law doctrines of conspiracy and incitement to offenses of a political character, we are adrift on a sea of doubt and conjecture. To know what you may do and what you may not do, and how far you may go in criticism, is the first condition of political liberty; to be permitted to agitate at your own peril, subject to a jury's guessing at motive,

[90] Ernst Freund, "The Debs Case and Freedom of Speech," 19 *New Republic* 13 (May 3, 1919); and the correspondence, *id.* 151 (May 31, 1919).

tendency and possible effect, makes the right of free speech a precarious gift."

These three decisions in March, 1919, came as a great shock to forward-looking men and women, who had consoled themselves through the war-time trials with the hope that the Espionage Act would be invalidated when it reached the Supreme Court. They were especially grieved that the opinions which dashed this hope were written by the Justice who for their eyes had long taken on heroic dimensions. Looking backward, however, we see that Justice Holmes was biding his time until the Court should have before it a conviction so clearly wrong as to let him speak out his deepest thoughts about the First Amendment.

Meanwhile the cause of freedom of speech surely profited from his serving as spokesman for all the Justices in the Schenck case, far more than if he had voted for reversal. For subsequent decisions prove that he would then have been in a small minority and would not have been able (as he actually was) to announce with the backing of a unanimous Supreme Court the rule of clear and present danger. That rule now serves as a guiding principle for the future, and ought to make impossible hereafter a repetition of the worst decisions of the trial courts under the Espionage Act of 1917.

This book will constantly return to the Schenck test for help in determining what kinds of speech or writing ought to be immune from the operation of peace-time sedition laws.

The opportunity for which Justice Holmes had been waiting came eight months after Debs went to prison, in *Abrams* v. *United States*. The story of that case will be told in the next chapter. Then and thenceforth Justice Holmes and Justice Brandeis parted company with the majority of the Court.

In the opening months of 1920 came two more decisions, which proved that freedom of speech had not yet been made secure in the Supreme Court by the "clear and present danger" test. These two cases were chiefly concerned with the first clause of the Espionage Act of 1917, punishing willfully published "false reports and statements with intent to interfere with the operation or success of the military or naval forces of the United States or to promote the success of its enemies."

The first of these cases (the fifth important Espionage Act

decision) was *Schaefer* v. *United States*.[91] This involved the conviction of five officers of the corporation issuing the *Philadelphia Tageblatt*, a German-language newspaper. After an acquittal on the charge of treason for publishing fifteen articles, which were surely unpatriotic in tone, glorifying German strength and success, abusing our allies, and attacking the sincerity of the United States, they were indicted under the Espionage Act for the same utterances and all found guilty. Two defendants were discharged by the Supreme Court for want of responsibility for the articles.[92] Three convictions (two for five years, one for two years) were affirmed by a majority of six speaking through Justice McKenna; Justice Brandeis filed a dissenting opinion on behalf of himself and Justice Holmes; and Justice Clarke, who had spoken for the majority in the Abrams case, now also dissented, not because he found any violation of the First Amendment, but upon the ground that the Act had been misinterpreted by the trial court, whose charge "was so utterly unadapted to the case . . . as to be valueless or worse as a direction to the jury."

This newspaper was so poor financially that it was not able to have any telegraphic service, and consequently filled its columns with clippings from other newspapers. As it did not print so many columns as they, it was necessarily obliged to cut and condense both the headlines and the body of the articles. It did not indicate the source of its articles or imply that they were complete copies. The falsity alleged by the government was not that the articles which were published were false in fact, but merely that they differed from the originals, and had been altered or mistranslated so as to bear a changed meaning which was depressing or detrimental to patriotic ardor. For instance, in the translation of a speech of Senator La Follette, predicting bread-lines as a consequence of the failure to tax profiteers, the word *Brot-riots* was used instead of *Brodreihen*.[93] The wide divergence of opinion in the Court is indicated by Justice McKenna's statement, "There could be no

[91] 251 U. S. 468 (1920). Sentences five and two years; no pardon or commutation noted.

[92] This part of the Schaefer case has an important bearing on the problem of guilt by association, discussed in Chapter XII, section 1 of this book.

[93] For more details see the Supreme Court opinions, and United States *v.* Werner, 247 Fed. 768.

more powerful or effective instruments of evil than two German newspapers organized and conducted as these papers were organized and conducted," as against that of Justice Brandeis, "To hold that such harmless additions to or omissions from news items, and such impotent expressions of editorial opinion, as were shown here, can afford the basis even of a prosecution, will doubtless discourage criticism of the policies of the Government."

A comparison of the opinions of Justice McKenna and Justice Brandeis offers a valuable study in judicial methods and the two ways of solving any problem of freedom of speech. Of course we shall not find in a member of the Supreme Court that total ignoring of the social interest in discussion, which blots many District Court cases. The difference between the two Justices is a difference in the degree of emphasis placed upon that interest and in their approach to the case. Since the limits of the right of freedom of speech in war time necessarily involve a conflict between the danger of defeat and the desirability of public knowledge of the truth about the war, it makes all the difference in the world whether the judge who sets out to determine those limits starts from the unqualified language of the First Amendment (which, unlike the Habeas Corpus clause, makes no exception of invasion),[94] and seeks to give to public opinion as much scope as is possible in view of the danger and the precise words of the statute; or whether he is primarily concerned to avert all influences which might conceivably delay or forfeit victory and is anxious not to go any farther to permit words of that tendency than seems absolutely necessary if we are to have any discussion about the war at all. Again, it makes all the difference in the world whether this judge is satisfied to say, "Free speech is not an absolute right, and when it or any right becomes wrong by excess is somewhat elusive of definition," without seeking to define it; or whether he insists that the preservation of this right must inevitably depend on restricting the latitude allowed to the human machinery administering the law.

Justice McKenna approaches the problem from the side

---

[94] "Not one of these safeguards [in the Bill of Rights] can the President, or Congress, or the Judiciary disturb, except the one concerning the writ of *habeas corpus.*" — Field, J., in *Ex parte* Milligan, 2 Wallace 125.

of the war power. The restraints of the Espionage Act are for him neither excessive nor ambiguous; they are directed against conduct which might cause our armies "to operate to defeat and the immeasurable horror and calamity of it." He is surprised that the Constitution should have been invoked to protect "the activities of anarchy or of the enemies of the United States." This is an argument always used to undermine freedom of speech, for if that right does not protect criticism hostile to the government it has little value. During the periods when such criticism is most needed, it is invariably denounced by the supporters of the government as revolution or treason. Only wide discussion and time can tell whether the activities of the opponents of our wars, James Russell Lowell, the Hartford Convention, William Graham Sumner, Vallandigham, were the activities of the enemies of the United States or of its friends.

On the other hand, Justice McKenna entrusts freedom of speech to the jury's sense of fairness rather than to any guiding principles. He considers that the trial judge gives sufficient protection to this constitutional right if he admonishes the jury to decide impartially after close attention to the evidence. To all the passages in the defendants' newspaper, Justice McKenna applies the eighteenth-century tests of bad tendency and presumptive intent to see whether the evidence can justify the convictions. The only remoteness which he recognizes seems to depend on the will of the jury. For example, the reprint from a Berlin newspaper entitled "Yankee Bluff," which ridiculed the possibility of our aiding the Entente, so slow were our war preparations, might "chill . . . the ardency of patriotism and make it . . . in hopelessness relax energy both in preparation and in action." What was its purpose if not that? Success is unnecessary. The tendency of the articles and their efficacy were enough to constitute the offense; this is all that "intent" and "attempt" mean. To require more would, he thinks, make the law useless, for it was passed in precaution, and the consequences of its violation might appear only in disaster. In other words, any newspaper editor who reprints German bragging is liable to imprisonment unless he can furnish a clean bill of health as to his loyal intentions.

Justice McKenna also regards it as criminal to say that the war was commenced without the people's consent. Of an article attacking "the pro-British policy of the Government" he says, in language that leaves no room for questioning as to the righteousness of any war:

Its statements were deliberate and willfully false, the purpose being to represent that the war was not demanded by the people but was the result of the machinations of executive power, and thus to arouse resentment to it and what it would demand of ardor and effort. In final comment we may say that the article in effect justified the German aggressions.

Justice Brandeis, on the other hand, starts from the danger-test of freedom of speech in the Schenck case and from the actual words of the Espionage Act. He even goes back to an important circumstance preceding the statute, the recommendation of the War College for legislation to prevent injurious disclosures on military matters, which helps explain the meaning of the "false statements clause."

Willfully untrue statements which might mislead the people as to the financial condition of the Government and thereby embarrass it; as to the adequacy of the preparations for war or the support of the forces; as to the sufficiency of the food supply; or willfully untrue statements or reports of military operations which might mislead public opinion as to the competency of the army or navy or its leaders (see "The Relation Between the Army and the Press in War Time," War College Publication, 1916); or willfully untrue statements or reports which might mislead officials in the execution of the law, or military authorities in the disposition of the forces. Such is the kind of false statement and the only kind which, under any rational construction, is made criminal by the act.

And in connection with the "Yankee Bluff" article, Justice Brandeis applies the same tests of danger and statutory wording to the recruiting clause of the 1917 Act, confirming the interpretation of that clause advanced earlier in this chapter.[95]

It is not apparent on a reading of this article . . . how it could rationally be held to tend even remotely or indirectly to obstruct recruiting. But as this court has declared . . . the test to be applied — as in the case of criminal attempts and incitements — is not the

[95] Pages 48–49, *supra*.

remote or possible effect. There must be the clear and present danger. Certainly men judging in calmness and with this test presented to them could not reasonably have said that this coarse and heavy humor immediately threatened the success of recruiting.

The most important part of the Brandeis opinion is the repeated criticism of the administration of the statute in the trial below. The jury, however much instructed to be calm and unbiased, were authorized to convict for any words which would lessen "our will to win, or, as it is generally expressed, our will to conquer." Jurymen need something more than "a sense of duty and a sense of justice." They need hard and fast tests of criminality, which will bring home to them the standard of "clear and present danger." And in this case that test should have prevented the evidence, so remote is it, from going to the jury at all. After quoting the words of the unanimous Court in the Schenck case, Justice Brandeis says:

This is a rule of reason. Correctly applied, it will preserve the right of free speech both from suppression by tyrannous, well-meaning majorities and from abuse by irresponsible, fanatical minorities. Like many other rules for human conduct, it can be applied correctly only by the exercise of good judgment; and to the exercise of good judgment, calmness is, in times of deep feeling and on subjects which excite passion, as essential as fearlessness and honesty. The question whether in a particular instance the words spoken or written fall within the permissible curtailment of free speech is, under the rule enunciated by this Court, one of degree. And because it is a question of degree the field in which the jury may exercise its judgment is, necessarily, a wide one. But its field is not unlimited. The trial provided for is one by judge *and* jury; and the judge may not abdicate his function. If the words were of such a nature and were used under such circumstances that men, judging in calmness, could not reasonably say that they created a clear and present danger that they would bring about the evil which Congress sought and had a right to prevent, then it is the duty of the trial judge to withdraw the case from the consideration of the jury; and if he fails to do so, it is the duty of the appellate court to correct the error.

Then he emphasizes a principle which has often been ignored in sedition trials, and which might have affected the Debs decision, as well as the Abrams case, that the appellate court ought not to determine the nature and possible effect of a speech or writing simply by culling here and there a sentence and presenting it separated from the context. The speech or writing ought to be read as a whole, and often considered with other evidence which may control its meaning.

Finally, Justice Brandeis warns the Court, in a passage which I shall quote later with reference to peace-time sedition laws, that the sweeping application of a criminal statute to utterances with scant regard for the First Amendment will have disastrous consequences for freedom of speech in future periods of excitement.

The last Supreme Court decision under the criminal sections of the Espionage Act, and the least defensible, was *Pierce* v. *United States.*[96] This was a prosecution of three Socialists, for being local distributors in Albany of "The Price We Pay," a highly colored pamphlet by St. John Tucker, a prominent Episcopal clergyman. It was published by the national office of the Socialist Party at Chicago, and contained much in the way of denunciation of war in general, the pending war in particular, something in the way of assertion that under Socialism things would be better, little or nothing in the way of fact or argument to support the assertion.[97] Seven judges through Justice Pitney sustained the conviction, while Justice Brandeis dissented with the concurrence of Justice Holmes.

The principal ground of conviction was the false statements clause of the Espionage Act of 1917. Justice Brandeis pointed out that the danger-test applies to this clause as much as to the other two, and that three additional elements of crime must be established: (1) The statement or report must be of something capable of being proved false in fact. The expression of an opinion, for instance, whether sound or unsound, may conceivably afford a sufficient basis for the charge of attempting to cause insubordination, disloyalty or refusal of duty, or for the charge of obstructing recruiting; but, because an opinion is not capable of being proved false in fact, a statement of opinion cannot be made the basis of a prosecution under this clause. (2) The statement or report must be proved to be

---

[96] 252 U. S. 239 (1920). No data found as to sentences or pardons. *Cf.* United States *v.* Baker, 247 Fed. 124 (1917) (directed acquittal of other persons for publishing same pamphlet).

[97] The whole pamphlet is reprinted in the dissenting opinion of Brandeis, J

false. (3) The statement or report must be known by the defendant to be false when made or conveyed.

Justice Pitney did not reject these requirements. However, he culled out of the long pamphlet three passages (five sentences in all) as constituting the false statements or reports.

1. Into your homes the recruiting officers are coming. They will take your sons of military age and impress them into the army. . . .
And still the recruiting officers will come; seizing age after age, mounting up to the elder ones and taking the younger ones as they grow to soldier size.

2. The Attorney General of the United States is so busy sending to prison men who do not stand up when the Star Spangled Banner is played, that he has no time to protect the food supply from gamblers.

3. Our entry into it was determined by the certainty that if the allies do not win, J. P. Morgan's loans to the allies will be repudiated, and those American investors who bit on his promises would be hooked.

Only the last passage need detain us. The first was clearly true, since the Schenck case had held "recruiting" to include the draft, though a regular army major gravely testified at the trial that it had only to do with the volunteer service. The prediction that older and younger persons would be drafted was, of course, fulfilled. Yet the point was left to the jury. The second passage was not literally true, because civilians were not and could not be subjected to federal prosecutions for sitting during the National Anthem; but such an obviously figurative way of saying that the Attorney General was devoting important time to trivial sedition cases could not properly be regarded as a statement of fact within a twenty-year criminal penalty.[98]

Justice Pitney held that these passages satisfied the requirements laid down by Justice Brandeis.

On the points of intention and proximate cause (clear and present danger of unlawful acts), Justice Pitney said:

If its probable effect was at all disputable, at least the jury fairly might believe that, under the circumstances existing, it would have

---

[98] Under a local law, J. W. Beckstrom of Chicago was, after the Pierce trial, fined $50 for refusing to stand when the "Star-Spangled Banner" was played in a theater. — *War-time Prosecutions*, p. 30.

a tendency to cause insubordination, disloyalty, and refusal of duty in the military and naval forces . . . . Evidently it was intended, as the jury found, to interfere with the conscription and recruitment services; to cause men eligible for the service to evade the draft; to bring home to them, and especially to their parents, sisters, wives, and sweethearts, a sense of impending personal loss, calculated to discourage the young men from entering the service; to arouse suspicion as to whether the chief law officer of the Government was not more concerned in enforcing the strictness of military discipline than in protecting the people against improper speculation in their food supply; and to produce a belief that our participation in the war was the product of sordid and sinister motives, rather than a design to protect the interests and maintain the honor of the United States.

One rubs his eyes and wonders whether he has dreamed himself back into the eighteenth century.

The most dangerous aspect of this case, however, is the decision that the opinion about the economic cause of the war is a false statement and known to be false by men who had nothing to do with writing it and merely served as errand-boys to pass it out. Justice Pitney said:

Common knowledge (not to mention the President's Address to Congress of April 2, 1917, and the Joint Resolution of April 6 declaring war, which were introduced in evidence) would have sufficed to show at least that the statements as to the causes that led to the entry of the United States into the war against Germany were grossly false; and such common knowledge went to prove also that defendants knew they were untrue. That they were false if taken in a literal sense hardly is disputed.

Justice Pitney is a great equity judge, and often a man is held subject to the equitable rights of others because he ought reasonably to know of them though in fact he does not, but such constructive notice has never before been made the basis of criminal responsibility. For example, a man purchasing land cannot get rid of a heavy recorded mortgage just because he was ignorant of it; but if he resells the land without mentioning this still unknown mortgage he is innocent of obtaining money under false pretenses. Yet the Supreme Court is willing to say that men who wrangled with their neighbors for years about the capitalistic causes of the war and clung to their views with pig-headed devotion knew they were wrong just because they were in a small minority.

Consider where this leads. If opinions about the origin and justice of a war are to be regarded as false statements whenever the jury find them erroneous, the proof of truth or falsity involves logically all available evidence about the causes of the war, a staggering task. The proof of historical causes surely ought 'not to be limited to such official hearsay evidence as the President's Message or the Resolution of Congress, for then conviction would be a foregone conclusion. Furthermore, neither by sight nor by hearing can the jury investigate this "question of fact." It is a matter of inference from the complex and obscure political, economic, and social conditions of the nation or even of the world. The data for such a judgment, even if a jury had the very slightest capacity for making it, are not available during a war or for years afterwards.[99] Imagine John Bright or James Russell Lowell trying to convince a jury that the Crimean or the Mexican War was due to sinister motives, a question on which men are still disputing.

What minority opinion can be safe in war time under Justice Pitney's test? Surely, language which is immune from civil defamation suits as comment on a public matter ought to be equally immune from the sterner rigors of the federal penitentiary. If everything an opponent of a war says is to be adjudged false because the jury and the Supreme Court disagree with it, and then he is declared to know it is false because most people think it so, the whole value of the First Amendment as a means of learning the truth about future wars is lost.

Into this technical reasoning, which virtually ignores the standard of clear and present danger and revives the District Court test of remotely injurious tendency, cuts the common sense of Justice Brandeis. The so-called statement of fact about the Morgan loans is, he says, merely a conclusion or deduction from facts. True, it is not a conclusion of law, but it is not an evidentiary fact. In its essence it is the expression of

[99] According to the Pierce case in 1920, it was a criminal falsehood to say that we entered the war to save the Morgan loans. During the hearings of the Nye committee of the Senate in 1934, it was almost a crime to say that we did *not* enter the war to save the Morgan loans. Compare with Pitney's opinion the summary of these hearings in Beard, *America in Midpassage* (1939), pp. 402 ff.

a judgment, like the statements of many so-called historical facts. There is no exact standard of absolute truth by which to prove the assertion false. Himself a strong supporter of the war, he recognizes nevertheless the possibility of divergent views:

The cause of a war — as of most human action — is not single. War is ordinarily the result of many co-operating causes, many different conditions, acts and motives. Historians rarely agree in their judgment as to what was the determining factor in a particular war, even when they write under circumstances where detachment and the availability of evidence from all sources minimizes both prejudice and other sources of error. For individuals, and classes of individuals, attach significance to those things which are significant to them. And, as the contributing causes cannot be subjected, like a chemical combination in a test tube, to qualitative and quantitative analysis so as to weigh and value the various elements, the historians differ necessarily in their judgments. One finds the determining cause of war in a great man, another in an idea, a belief, an economic necessity, a trade advantage, a sinister machination, or an accident. It is for this reason largely that men seek to interpret anew in each age, and often with each new generation, the important events in the world's history.

Not all who voted in Congress for the declaration of war did so for the President's reasons, and the previous debate, Justice Brandeis reminds us, included many statements that the vast loans were instrumental in causing a sentiment through the nation in favor of war.

However strongly we may believe that these loans were not the slightest makeweight, much less a determining factor, in the country's decision, the fact that some of our representatives in the Senate and the House declared otherwise on one of the most solemn occasions in the history of the Nation, should help us to understand that statements like that here charged to be false are in essence matters of opinion and judgment, not matters of fact to be determined by a jury upon or without evidence; and that even the President's address, which set forth high moral grounds justifying our entry into the war, may not be accepted as establishing beyond a reasonable doubt that a statement ascribing a base motive was criminally false. All the alleged false statements were an interpretation and discussion of public facts of public interest. . . . To hold that a jury may make punishable statements of conclusions or of opinion, like those· here involved, by declaring them to be statements of facts and to be false would practically deny members of small political parties freedom of criticism and of discussion in times when feelings run high and the questions involved are deemed fundamental.

It is extremely ominous for future wars that the Supreme Court at the close of the World War was so careless in its safeguarding of the fundamental human need of freedom of speech, so insistent in this sphere that the interests of the government should be secured at all costs. Progress is possible only through a genuine application of the great principle behind the First Amendment which the majority Justices in the Abrams, Schaefer, and Pierce decisions reduced almost to a pious hope.

The fundamental right of free men to strive for better conditions through new legislation and new institutions will not be preserved, if efforts to secure it by argument to fellow citizens may be construed as criminal incitement to disobey the existing law — merely, because the argument presented seems to those exercising judicial power to be unfair in its portrayal of existing evils, mistaken in its assumptions, unsound in reasoning or intemperate in language.[100]

6. CENSORSHIP AND EXILE

> *The Postmaster General . . . is as anxious as I am to see that freedom of criticism is permitted up to the limit of putting insuperable obstacles in the way of the Government in the prosecution of the war. . . . He is inclined to be most conservative in the exercise of these great and dangerous powers.*
>
> WOODROW WILSON, Letters of October, 1917.[101]

The federal government can restrict speech during war in other ways besides punishment. It possesses a virtual censorship over all criticism of its policies, and exercises this power at the arbitrary will of an administrative official, who is of course directly interested to preserve those policies from attack, especially when they touch his own department. That this official is not called a censor is immaterial. Under the Espionage Act the Postmaster General can exclude from the

---

[100] Brandeis, J., in Pierce *v.* United States, *supra.*
[101] R. S. Baker, *Woodrow Wilson*, VII, 313, 318.

mails, the only profitable and often the only possible means of effective publication, anything which he considers to be in violation of the statute.[102] In no case during the war did any court set aside his decision by injunction or mandamus after Judge Hand was reversed as to the *Masses*. Some judges said that they would not review the Postmaster General's ruling unless it was clearly wrong, which meant never. Others declared that an opponent of the war did not come into court with clean hands and therefore could not get judicial relief even though the ruling was illegal. And the power of the Postmaster General is not limited to the particular issue of the periodical which he declares non-mailable. For instance, after Mr. Burleson had suppressed the August number of the *Masses*, he refused to admit the September or any future issues to the second-class mailing privilege, even if absolutely free from any objectionable passages, on the ground that since the magazine had skipped a number, *viz.*, the August number, it was no longer a periodical, since it was not regularly issued! He took the same position as to Berger's *Milwaukee Leader*, and in both instances the courts sustained him, thus confirming his right to drive a newspaper or magazine out of existence for one violation as determined by him.[103]

Let us now see what Mr. Burleson considered to violate the Espionage Act. By no means did he limit himself to pro-German and pacifist articles and books, like Latzko's *Men in War*. He suppressed an issue of the *Public* for urging that more money be raised by taxes and less by loans. He suppressed

---

[102] The 1917 Espionage Act, still in force, allowed any letter, newspaper, book, etc., which violated the three substantive provisions of this statute, to be excluded from the mails. 18 U. S. C. A. § 343. The 1918 amendment extended the Postmaster General's powers still further. First, it added as non-mailable matter anything within the nine new offenses then created (see *supra* section 1). Second, if "upon evidence satisfactory to *him*" the Postmaster General thought anybody had mailed anything violating the Act, he could prevent that person or concern from *receiving* any mail at all, however innocent. Without any jury trial or hearing before a judge, the citizen in question became for the post-office an outlaw. 40 Stat. 554 (1918), repealed by 41 Stat. 1360 (1921).

See *supra* section II for the *Masses* case. See also the Trading with the Enemy Act, § 19, for war-time regulation of the foreign language press (50 U. S. C. A. 300).

[103] For the subsequent history of the *Milwaukee Leader* case in the Supreme Court, see Chapter VII, section II, which discusses the desirability of vesting absolute control of the mails in a single official.

Lenin's *Soviets at Work*, a purely economic pamphlet, although we were not at war with Russia. He suppressed the *Nation* of September 14, 1918, either for criticizing the great slacker round-up in New York City, which Mr. O'Brian states to have been in contravention of specific instructions from the Attorney General and a mistake which could not be condoned,[104] or more probably for attacking Mr. Gompers. He censored any adverse comment on the affairs of the British Empire. He censored a pamphlet by Lajpat Rai on India. He censored the *Freeman's Journal and Catholic Register* for reprinting Jefferson's opinion that Ireland should be a republic; the *Gaelic American* for denouncing the felicitous remarks of F. E. Smith during his flying trip to this country, and saying, "The clear-headed, keen-witted Yankees who read his bitter attack on the Irish will not wonder at the Irish for refusing to fight for a government of which Smith is a member"; and the *Irish World* for expressing the expectation that Palestine would not be a Jewish kingdom but on the same footing as Egypt, and for stating that the trend of French life and ideals for a century had been toward materialism. And finally, Thorstein Veblen's *Imperial Germany and the Industrial Revolution*, which was published in 1915, was recommended by Mr. Creel's Committee on Public Information as containing damaging data about Germany, and then excluded by Mr. Burleson from the mails.

It is clear that exclusion from the mails practically destroys the circulation of a book or periodical, and makes free speech to that extent impossible. To say, as many courts do, that the agitator is still at liberty to use the express or the telegraph,[105] recalls the remark of the Bourbon princess when the Paris mob shouted for bread, "Why don't they eat cake?"

Still another method of suppression of opinion was used. Not only did we substantially revive the Sedition Act of 1798, but the Alien Act as well. Aliens were freely deported under statutes passed during the war, to be discussed in a later chapter. In a future war any alien convicted of violating the Espio-

---

[104] O'Brian, p. 292.

[105] This alternative is even less valuable when the government controls the express and the telegraph. The *New York World* was denied the opportunity to use the telegraph to distribute a criticism of Mr. Burleson. *Collier's Weekly*, May 17, 1919, p. 16.

nage Act can be deported at once. Even naturalized citizens
were often brought within the reach of this power. For example, a former German subject who was naturalized in 1882
refused in 1917 to contribute to the Red Cross and the Young
Men's Christian Association because he would do nothing to
injure the country where he was brought up and educated.
His naturalization certificate was revoked after thirty-five
years on the presumption that his recent conduct showed that
he took the oath of renunciation in 1882 with a mental reservation as to the country of his birth. Thereupon he became liable
to deportation as an enemy alien.[106]

7. STATE ESPIONAGE ACTS

> *Him that escapeth the sword of Hazael shall Jehu slay.*
> The First Book of Kings.

One would have supposed that the federal Espionage Act
was a sufficient safeguard against opposition to the war, but
many states were not satisfied with either its terms or its enforcement, and enacted similar but more drastic laws of their
own.[107] These were particularly common is western states,
where feeling ran high against the Non-Partisan League or
the I.W.W. The most important of these statutes, that of
Minnesota, made it unlawful to say "that men should not enlist
in the military or naval forces of the United States or the
State of Minnesota," or that residents of that state should not
aid the United States in carrying on war with the public enemies.[108] There were a very large number of prosecutions and

[106] United States v. Wursterbarth, 249 Fed. 908 (N. J., 1918). See also
35 *Harvard Law Review* at 444; 6 A. L. R. 407; 18 *id.* 1185; United States v.
Herberger, 272 Fed._278 (Wash., 1921).

[107] These statutes are listed in Appendix III. On the constitutionality of
the Minnesota war statute and similar laws, see Chapter VII, section 1. On the
Non-Partisan League and Townley, see *supra* at note 64; *American Labor Year
Book*, 1919–20, pp. 280–289.

Other state cases arising out of war utterances involved breaches of the
peace; municipal ordinances regulating newspapers (see Pound, *Cases on
Equitable Relief against Defamation*, 2d ed., p. 44 n.); conspiracy to compel
newsdealer to handle distasteful newspaper; libel in war controversy; expulsion of college student for pacifism (*id.* 108); ordinance prohibiting German
opera (*infra*, Chapter IV, note 29); ordinance making opponent of war a
vagrant (*Ex parte* Taft v. Shaw, 284 Mo. 531; 27 *Illinois Law Review* 67).

[108] Minn. Laws, 1917, c. 463. This was superseded in 1919 by a still more

many convictions under this statute, chiefly of members of the Non-Partisan League, culminating in the condemnation of its president, A. C. Townley.

Even if state acts like that in Minnesota are constitutional,[109] they are still extremely undesirable because they conflict very seriously with national war policies. If a man deserves to be prosecuted for his anti-war activities it is fair to presume that the Department of Justice will have him indicted under the ample provisions of the Espionage Act, and it is important that the control of proceedings should be in the hands of the Department, without parallel prosecutions by independent state officials. On the other hand, if Congress and the federal officials think it wise to allow much discussion of war aims and economic aspects, it is very unfortunate that their policy should be hampered by bitter prosecutions based on an entirely different policy and growing out of local hysteria or directed against opinions which are objectionable to influential political or economic groups in the state. Mr. O'Brian contrasts the federal policy of restraint against members of the Non-Partisan League and adherence to the fundamental principle that guilt is personal and that no class of individuals will be proscribed as a class, with the sweeping and severe action of Minnesota:

The result of its adoption increased discontent and the most serious cases of alleged interference with civil liberty were reported to the federal government from that state. Our view was that, while cases of individual guilt must be prosecuted with severity, class movements cannot be controlled or molded by indictments. Arbitrary repression or interference often adds to their dynamic force. But unfortunately the constructive teachings and arguments of persuasion necessary to deal with movements of this character were not at any time in evidence in these disturbed districts of the country.

If hostilities had continued for another year, these local statutes might have produced an alarming effect upon the output of the grain-producing states by breeding a suppressed but no less active hatred of the war in the Non-Partisan League,

---

drastic act, to take care of future wars. — Laws, 1919, c. 93; Mason's Minn. Stat. (1927), § 9972.

[109] So held in Gilbert v. Minnesota, 254 U. S. 325 (1920), discussed in Chapter VII, section 1.

and might also in jailing members of the I.W.W., whom the Department of Justice was leaving alone, have blocked the conciliatory work of Colonel Disque in the spruce forests and of other federal agents in the copper regions.[110]

8. REFLECTIONS DURING A TECHNICAL STATE OF WAR [111]

We have seen the war powers, which are essential to the preservation of the nation in time of war, exercised broadly after the military exigency had passed and in conditions for which they were never intended, and we may well wonder in view of the precedents now established whether constitutional government as heretofore maintained in this republic could survive another great war even victoriously waged.   CHARLES EVANS HUGHES,
Address at Harvard Law School, June 21, 1920.

The Espionage Act of 1917, as interpreted by the Supreme Court, suppresses free speech for all opponents of a war, but allows militant newspapers and politicians to block, by unbounded abuse, the efforts of the President to end a war by a just settlement. Congress reached the same result by the 1918 amendment, since repealed, making it criminal to "oppose the cause of the United States" in any war.

The original Espionage Act [112] is not limited to this war. The pacifists and Socialists were perhaps wrong about that, but they may be right next time. They might have been right in 1919, had we been drawn into war with Mexico as carelessly as England was drawn into the war with Spain over Jenkins' ear. Balance military necessity in such a case against the harm of suppressing truth by a ten-year sentence. The government can argue better than its opponents, if it has any case at all, and at its back are public opinion, the press, the police, the army, to prevent their words from causing unlawful acts. And though national welfare doubtless demands that a just

[110] O'Brian, pp. 296, 299; Report to the President of the President's Mediation Commission.

[111] The war between the United States and Germany was terminated by Congress on July 2, 1921. — 42 Stat. 105. Thus nearly two-thirds of the war was after the armistice; and the Espionage Act of 1917 was in force throughout, including the postal censorship.

[112] Still in force as 50 U. S. C. A. § 33.

war be pushed to victory, it also demands that an unjust war be stopped. The only way to find out whether a war is unjust is to let people say so.

We can no longer cherish the delusion that the First Amendment protects open discussion of the merits and methods of a war. We can predict with certainty what will happen in the next war from what happened in the last war, because exactly the same statute is in force. Although on its face it does not seem to make discussion criminal, yet the sweeping judicial interpretations of it which the government lawyers obtained from the Supreme Court, and wider still from the District Courts, will be constantly cited as precedents for punishing expressions of opinion about the merits and conduct of the next war, or about the justice and wisdom of continuing it beyond any given stage.[113]

The 1918 clauses punishing attacks on the Constitution and our form of government raise still stronger objections, if they be ever revived in a future war. They have nothing to do with war. They may be used during some petty struggle to arrest and imprison for twenty years an excitable advocate of the repeal of a Prohibition Amendment or the abolition of the Senate. If there was one thing which the First Amendment was meant by our ancestors to protect, it was criticism of the existing form of government and advocacy of change, the kind of criticism which George III's judges punished. Even if the Act permits temperate discussion, which is doubtful, in view of the words about causing "contempt . . . or disrepute," it still abridges free speech, for the greater the need of change, the greater the likelihood that agitators will lose their temper over the present situation. It is impossible to speak respectfully of that portion of our Constitution and form of government which is represented by the electoral college, and much hatred was justly directed to the clause for the return of fugitive slaves. Other parts may prove equally objectionable in the course of years. Particularly dangerous are the 1918 clauses about defamation of the army and navy. They would surely be invoked by advocates of compulsory military service

---

[113] "I do not speak of what is past and gone; but in case of a future war what results will follow from your decision indorsing the Attorney General's views?" — Jeremiah Black, arguing in *Ex parte* Milligan (1866).

against their opponents, if they wished to take advantage of any hostilities to fasten conscription upon the nation as a continuous policy. They make any scathing criticism of military methods a very perilous matter in future wars even for the most loyal and eminent civilians (no intent to favor the enemy being required by the statute), and raise the army and navy into a privileged position beyond the range of ordinary outspoken discussion, such as is enjoyed by no civilians. This is what the French army wanted during the Dreyfus affair. Furthermore, if the language used does bring the army or navy into contempt, it is absolutely immaterial that the charge made is true.

That these predictions of what will happen in a petty war are by no means exaggerated is proved by what was done under the Espionage Act in 1919 and 1920 when there was no war at all — except by a legal fiction.[114] First, the Attorney General, a year after the armistice, raided and closed the office of the *Seattle Union-Record*, because it urged the workers to kick the governing class into the discard at the next election, and said that the Centralia shootings [115] were the culmination of a long series of illegal acts by ex-service men, pleading for law and order on the part of rich and poor alike. Secondly, thirteen months after the armistice, Mr. Burleson still kept the *New York Call* and the *Milwaukee Leader* from the mails. Thirdly, fourteen months after all fighting had stopped three men were tried in Syracuse for distributing circulars in the autumn of 1919, describing ill-treatment of political prisoners, calling an amnesty meeting, and requesting that letters be written to the President and members of Congress. The leaflets quoted the First Amendment, *Ex parte* Milligan, and a speech by President Wilson. The defendants were convicted and sentenced to eighteen months in prison for disloyal language about our form of government and the military forces, language designed to bring them and the Constitution into contempt, inciting resistance to the United States, and obstruction of recruiting.[116]

The Espionage Act prosecutions break with a great tradi-

[114] See 274 Fed. 749 (Call) ; Chapter VII, section II (Leader). The succeeding Republican Postmaster General, Will H. Hays, readmitted both the *Call* and the *Leader* to the mails.
[115] As to Centralia, see Chapter IV, note 2.
[116] United States *v.* Steene, 263 Fed. 130.

tion in English and American law. Only once before has the United States tried to punish political crimes, and the Sedition Act of 1798 with its maximum of two years' imprisonment wrecked the Federalist party. The Mexican War produced the Biglow Papers, and every stanza in the opening poem would have violated a separate clause of the Espionage Act of 1918, if the slaveholders had drafted such a statute. We fought the Civil War with the enemy at our gates and powerful secret societies in our midst without an Espionage Act.

When the disloyal press was curbed by Burnside and his subordinates, they received sharp telegrams of revocation from Lincoln. The irritation produced by such acts was in his opinion "likely to do more harm than the publication would do." Undoubtedly he permitted a very large number of arbitrary arrests by Seward and Stanton, or under martial law in the border states. "Must I shoot a simple soldier boy who deserts, while I must not touch a hair of a wily agitator who induces him to desert?" But Lincoln's policy, apart from all questions of its legality, was very different in nature from most of the Espionage Act prosecutions and sentences. He was proceeding against men who were so far within the test of direct and dangerous interference with the war that they were actually causing desertions, and even then he acted to prevent and not to punish. Vallandigham was sent through into the Confederate lines, and left unmolested on his return. Lincoln would not have allowed an old man, a Presidential opponent and the choice of nine hundred thousand American citizens, to lie in prison for sincere and harmless even though misguided words, over a year after the last gun was fired.

If the North was a dictatorship, says Rhodes, the South was a socialized state, which was much closer to the situation of all the countries engaged in the World War. There the newspapers were probably under closer control, but there were no prosecutions.

And so in England. Bright and Cobden in the Crimean War, Morley and Lloyd George in the Boer War, were untouched. Even in the World War, though the terms of the Defense of the Realm Act were more sweeping than our statute, the administration was less severe. Those who enforced it allowed a wide range of discussion and imposed brief sentences, though they sat within sound of the German guns. And of all the nations at war, we alone, three thousand miles from the conflict, still refused in 1920 a general amnesty to political prisoners.[117]

Undoubtedly some utterances had to be suppressed. We were passing through a period of danger, and reasonably supposed the danger to be greater than it actually was, but the prosecutions in Great Britain during a similar period of peril in the French Revolution have not since been regarded with pride. Action in proportion to the emergency was justified, but we censored and punished speech which was very far from direct and dangerous interference with the conduct of the war. The chief responsibility for this must rest, not upon Congress which was content for a long period with the moderate language of the Espionage Act of 1917, but upon the officials of the Department of Justice and the Post-office, who turned that statute into a drag-net for pacifists, and upon the judges who upheld and approved this distortion of law. It may be questioned, too, how much has actually been gained. Men have been imprisoned, but their words have not ceased to spread.[118] The poetry in the *Masses* was excluded from the mails only to be given a far wider circulation in two issues of the *Federal Reporter*. The mere publication of Mrs. Stokes' statement in the *Kansas City Star*, "I am for the people and the Government is for the profiteers," was considered so dangerous to the morale of the training camps that she was sentenced to ten years in prison, and yet it was repeated by every important newspaper in the country during the trial. There is an unconscious irony in all suppression. It lurks behind Judge Hough's comparison of the *Masses* to the Beatitudes,[119] and in the

---

[117] This was granted in Italy on November 19, 1918, before the signing of peace and in Germany before the armistice. The French amnesty was October 24, 1919. Sentences under the British Defense of the Realm Act had all expired before 1920, being very short; the longest, three years, was commuted to one year. This note comprises only seditious utterances in the war, not treasonable acts like the Bonnet Rouge affair or Irish convictions since the armistice. Many Espionage Act prisoners, including Debs, were not released until Christmas, 1921.

[118] *Cf.* a similar experience of the Emperor Tiberius, in Tacitus, *Annals*, IV, c. 35: "Punitis ingeniis, gliscit auctoritas." "A man who preaches in the stocks will always have hearers enough." — Dr. Johnson.

[119] See p. 49, *supra*.

words of Lord Justice Scrutton during this struggle against autocracy: "It had been said that a war could not be conducted on the principles of the Sermon on the Mount. It might also be said that a war could not be carried on according to the principles of Magna Charta." [120]

Those who gave their lives for freedom would be the last to thank us for throwing aside so lightly the great traditions of our race. Not satisfied to have justice and almost all the people with our cause, we insisted on an artificial unanimity of opinion behind the war. Keen intellectual grasp of the President's aims by the nation at large was very difficult when the opponents of his idealism ranged unchecked while the men who urged greater idealism went to prison. In our efforts to silence those who advocated peace without victory we prevented at the very start that vigorous threshing out of fundamentals which might today have saved us from a victory without peace.

[120] Ronnfeldt *v.* Phillips, 35 T. L. R. 46 (1918, C. A.). The last paragraph of this chapter stands exactly as it was written in June, 1919. See 32 *Harvard Law Review* at 973.

CHAPTER 3

THE ABRAMS CASE

The expedition [to North Russia] was nonsense from the beginning. SECRETARY OF WAR NEWTON D. BAKER.[1]

I was in command of the United States troops sent to Siberia and, I must admit, I do not know what the United States was trying to accomplish by military intervention. GENERAL WILLIAM S. GRAVES.[2]

UNLIKE the other Supreme Court decisions, which arose under the original Espionage Act of 1917, the Abrams case involved the more sweeping provisions of the 1918 amendment.[3] The defendants were not prosecuted for pacifist or

[1] From a letter of 1929, quoted in R. S. Baker, *Woodrow Wilson*, VIII (1939), 284, n. 1. See also Secretary Baker's Foreword to Graves, cited in the next footnote.

[2] Graves, *America's Siberian Adventure* (1931), p. 354.

[3] Abrams v. United States, 250 U. S. 616 (1919). The sources of the trial are given in my article in 33 *Harvard Law Review* 747 (1920), which contains a fuller statement of the facts; see corrections and additions in 35 *id.* 9 (1921). For the repercussions of this chapter (as first published) upon free speech at Harvard, see S. E. Morison, *Three Centuries of Harvard* (1936), pp. 464 ff.; Henry Copley Green, "A Fight for Freedom, 1921," 8 *History Reference Bulletin*, No. 23, sec. 2 (November 1934); 35 *Harvard Law Review* 9 (1921).

A valuable analysis of the Supreme Court decision is made by T. R. Powell, "Constitutional Law in 1919–1920," 19 *Michigan Law Review* 283, 288 ff. (1921).

Able comments in support of the majority opinion will be found in Day Kimball, "The Espionage Act and the Limits of Legal Toleration," 33 *Harvard Law Review* 442 (1920); J. P. Hall, "Free Speech in War Time," 21 *Columbia Law Review* 526 (1921); E. S. Corwin, "Freedom of Speech and Press under the First Amendment," 30 *Yale Law Journal* 48 (1920); same, "Constitutional Law in 1919–1920," 14 *American Political Science Review* 635, 655 ff. (1920); H. F. Goodrich, "Does the Constitution Protect Free Speech?" 19 *Michigan Law Review* 487 (1921). A vigorous attack on Justice Holmes's dissenting opinion, which is significant to show how war can upset a first-class thinker, is J. H. Wigmore's "Freedom of Speech and Freedom of Thuggery, in War-Time and Peace-Time," 14 *Illinois Law Review* 539 (1920), which was written after a distinguished military career in Washington as colonel on the staff of the Judge Advocate General. Justice Holmes, who was wounded at Ball's Bluff, Antietam, and Fredericksburg, is said to have remarked after reading

pro-German utterances, as in the general run of Espionage Act cases, but for agitation against the government's policy in despatching American troops to Vladivostok and Murmansk in the summer of 1918. The case deserves extensive presentation because it brings out the serious difficulties of trying political offenses satisfactorily in our courts.

In the early morning of August 23, 1918, loiterers at the corner of Houston and Crosby streets in New York City were surprised to see the air full of leaflets thrown from a window of a manufacturing building close by. One set of leaflets was in English, as follows: [4]

THE
HYPOCRISY
OF THE
UNITED STATES
AND HER ALLIES

"Our" President Wilson, with his beautiful phraseology, has hypnotized the people of America to such an extent that they do not see his hypocrisy.

Know, you people of America, that a frank enemy is always preferable to a concealed friend. When we say the people of America, we do not mean the few Kaisers of America, we mean the "People of America." You people of America were deceived by the wonderful speeches of the masked President Wilson. His shameful, cowardly silence about the intervention in Russia reveals the hypocrisy of the plutocratic gang in Washington and vicinity.

The President was afraid to announce to the American people the intervention in Russia. He is too much of a coward to come out openly and say: "We capitalistic nations cannot afford to have a proletarian republic in Russia." Instead, he uttered beautiful phrases about Russia, which, as you see, he did not mean, and secretly, cowardly, sent troops to crush the Russian Revolution.

---

this article: "Colonel Wigmore may be a better lawyer than I am, but I think I know a little more about war than he does."

The minority opinion is supported in a note by Sir Frederick Pollock, 36 *Law Quarterly Review* 334 (1920). See *Holmes-Pollock Letters*, II, 29, 31, 32, 42, 44, 45, 48, 65 (1941). American views to the same effect are by K. N. Llewellyn, 29 *Yale Law Journal* 337 (1920); C. E. Clark (now U. S. Circuit Judge), 30 *id.* 68; L. G. Caldwell, 14 *Illinois Law Review* 601 (1920); Gerard C. Henderson, *New Republic*, XXI, 50 (Dec. 10, 1919).

[4] Errors of punctuation, etc., are preserved. Both leaflets measure 12 × 4½ inches, one page, printed on one side.

Do you see how German militarism combined with allied capitalism to crush the Russian Revolution?

This is not new. The tyrants of the world fight each other until they see a common enemy — WORKING CLASS — ENLIGHTMENT as soon as they find a common enemy, they combiné to crush it.

In 1815 monarchic nations combined under the name of the "Holy Alliance" to crush the French Revolution. Now militarism and capitalism combined, though not openly, to crush the russian revolution.

What have you to say about it?

Will you allow the Russian Revolution to be crushed? You: Yes, we mean YOU the people of America!

THE RUSSIAN REVOLUTION CALLS TO THE WORKERS OF THE WORLD FOR HELP.

The Russian Revolution cries: "WORKERS OF THE WORLD! AWAKE! RISE! PUT DOWN YOUR ENEMY AND MINE!"

Yes friends, there is only one enemy of the workers of the world and that is CAPITALISM.

It is a crime, that workers of America, workers of Germany, workers of Japan, etc., to fight the WORKERS' REPUBLIC OF RUSSIA.

AWAKE! AWAKE, YOU
WORKERS OF THE WORLD!
REVOLUTIONISTS

P. S. It is absurd to call us pro-German. We hate and despise German militarism more than do your hypocritical tyrants. We have more reasons for denouncing German militarism than has the coward of the White House.

The other leaflet was in Yiddish, and was thus translated:

WORKERS — WAKE UP.

The preparatory work for Russia's emancipation is brought to an end by his Majesty, Mr. Wilson, and the rest of the gang; dogs of all colors!

America, together with the Allies, will march to Russia, not, "God Forbid," to interfere with the Russian affairs, but to help the Czecho-Slovaks in their struggle against the Bolsheviki.

Oh, ugly hypocrites; this time they shall not succeed in fooling the Russian emigrants and the friends of Russia in America. Too visible is their audacious move.

Workers, Russian emigrants, you who had the least belief in the honesty of our government must now throw away all confidence, must spit in the face the false, hypocritic, military propaganda which has fooled you so relentlessly, calling forth your sympathy, your help, to the prosecution of the war. With the money which you have loaned or are going to loan them, they will make bullets not only for the Germans but also for the Workers Soviets of Russia. Workers in the ammunition factories, you are producing bullets, bayonets, cannon, to murder not only the Germans, but also your dearest, best, who are in Russia and are fighting for freedom.

You who emigrated from Russia, you who are friends of Russia, will you carry on your conscience in cold blood the shame spot as a helper to choke the Workers Soviets. Will you give your consent to the inquisitionary expedition to Russia? Will you be calm spectators to the fleecing blood from the hearts of the best sons of Russia?

America and her Allies have betrayed (the workers). Their robberish aims are clear to all men. The destruction of the Russian Revolution, that is the politics of the march to Russia.

Workers, our reply to the barbaric intervention has to be a general strike! An open challenge only will let the government know that not only the Russian Worker fights for freedom, but also here in America lives the spirit of revolution.

Do not let the government scare you with their wild punishment in prisons, hanging and shooting. We must not and will not betray the splendid fighters of Russia. Workers, up to fight.

Three hundred years had the Romanoff dynasty taught us how to fight. Let all rulers remember this, from the smallest to the biggest despot, that the hand of the revolution will not shiver in a fight.

Woe unto those who will be in the way of progress. Let solidarity live!   THE REBELS.

The Military Intelligence Police sent two army sergeants, who climbed from floor to floor of the building asking questions until at a hat factory on the fourth story they arrested Rosansky, a young Russian, who eventually confessed that he had thrown out the leaflets. The Military Police with his aid captured six other Russians, five men and a girl. The oldest man, Abrams, was twenty-nine; the youngest, Lipman, twenty-one, the same age as the girl, Molly Steimer. The group lived in a bare apartment three flights up a rear staircase on East 104th Street. A police instructor examined the prisoners in the presence of several army sergeants. They refused to tell where the pamphlets were printed, but the Military Police discovered that they had a motor-driven press and a small hand press in the basement of 1582 Madison Avenue, where mis-printed pamphlets and corrected proof lay crumpled upon the floor.

The prisoners, one of whom died before trial, were indicted for conspiracy to violate four clauses of the Espionage Act of 1918.[5] The Department of Justice had prevented several other prosecutions of so-called Bolshevists for opposition to the government's Russian policy, inasmuch as no war had been declared against Russia. However, the appeal of the Abrams group to munitions workers for a general strike was regarded as more serious.

I. THE DISTRICT COURT

> SCOTCH POLITICAL PRISONER: *All great men have been reformers, even our Savior himself.*
> LORD BRAXFIELD: *Muckle he made o' that, he was hanget.*

The trial of Abrams and his associates, except Schwartz, began on October 10, 1918, in the United States Court House in New York City, before Judge Clayton of the Northern and Middle Districts of Alabama. Henry De Lamar Clayton was then sixty-one years of age. Belonging to a distinguished Ala-bama family, he had graduated from the State University and practised law in Montgomery. For eighteen years he repre-sented Alabama in Congress, serving eventually as Chairman of the Judiciary Committee of the House and giving his name to the well-known Clayton Act. In 1914 he was appointed to the United States bench. This was his first prominent Espionage Act case.

There were in the Southern District of New York three judges with extensive experience in the difficulties of war legislation — Mayer, and Learned and Augustus Hand.[6] In the Abrams trial, six persons risked the best part of their lives upon the decision of the perplexing problems of freedom of speech. The position of the defendants could hardly be under-

---

[5] The conspiracy section of the Espionage Act is Act of June 15, 1917, c. 30, Title I, § 4 [50 U. S. C. A. (1926), § 34]. The 1918 amendment to § 3 is sum-marized *supra*, Chapter II, section 1.

[6] See *supra*, pp. 25 n., 49 n.; 42–49; 78–79.

stood without some acquaintance with the immigrant population of a great city, some knowledge of the ardent thirst of the
East Side Jew for the discussion of international affairs. Yet
because the New York dockets were crowded the Abrams case
was assigned to a judge who had tried no important Espionage
Act case, who was called in from a remote district where people
were of one mind about the war, where the working class is
more conspicuous for a submissive respect for law and order
than for the criticism of high officials, where Russians are
scarce and Bolshevists unknown.

The government was represented by Francis G. Caffey,
United States Attorney, with John M. Ryan and S. L. Miller,
Assistant United States Attorneys, of counsel. Harry Weinberger of New York appeared for the defendants. The jury
was duly empaneled and sworn on Monday, October 14, and
the trial ended on Wednesday, October 23.

The overt acts were proved without contradiction. Soon
after United States troops were ordered to Vladivostok in the
first week of August, 1918, the group had begun meeting in
their bare "third-floor back," and decided to protest against
the attack on the Russian Revolution, with which as anarchists
or socialists they strongly sympathized. After printing five
thousand copies of each leaflet they stopped for lack of funds.
They had distributed about nine thousand leaflets, throwing
them in the streets where there were the most working people
or passing them around at radical meetings. There was no
evidence that one person was led to stop any kind of war
work or even that the leaflets reached a single munitions
worker.

The defense, besides contending that the Espionage Act was
unconstitutional, maintained that it was not violated, and in
particular that the criminal intent required by express terms
of the statute of 1918 did not exist. Each count of the indictment covered a conspiracy to violate one clause of the Act
as italicized below, as follows, according to the language of
the statute. Certain phrases in the indictment which are not
in the Act are enclosed in brackets.

Whoever, when the United States is at war, . . . shall willfully
utter, print, write, or publish

(Count 1) any disloyal, . . . scurrilous, or abusive language about the form of government of the United States, . . .

(Count 2) or any language intended to bring the form of government of the United States . . . into contempt, scorn, contumely, or disrepute, . . .

(Count 3) or . . . any language *intended to incite, provoke, or encourage resistance to the United States* [*in said war with the German Imperial Government*], . . .

(Count 4) or shall willfully by utterance, writing, printing, publication, . . . urge, incite, or advocate any curtailment of production in this country of any thing or things, product or products [to wit, ordnance and ammunition necessary or essential to the prosecution of the war in which the United States may be engaged [to wit, *said war with the Imperial German Government*], *with intent* by such curtailment *to cripple or hinder the United States in the prosecution of the war*, . . .

shall be punished by a fine of not more than $10,000 or imprisonment for not more than twenty years or both.

The first [7] and second counts may be dismissed from further discussion. The Supreme Court refused to pass on their constitutionality; but this did not benefit the prisoners, because twenty-year sentences could be sustained if they were properly convicted under either the third or fourth count.[8] Justice Clarke contented himself with suggesting that the distinction between abusing our form of government and abusing the President and Congress, the agencies through which it must

[7] The corresponding clause of the statute resembles the Sedition Act of 1798, but is far more severe in its penalty and its elimination of such defenses as truth and good motives.

[8] 250 U. S. at 619. Compare Stromberg *v.* California, 283 U. S. at 367 (1931), discussed in Chapter XI. The multiplication of overlapping counts in a sedition indictment creates serious risks of unfairness. In tangible crimes like assault with a dangerous weapon, recklessly negligent injury, etc., the jury is familiar with the fences between the different counts and can be trusted to find its way around with discrimination. But a series of charges against a single speech or leaflet phrased in the vague language of the successive clauses of a sedition statute amounts to piling up as many bad names as possible to fling at the accused. The jurymen are only too likely to roll the counts together, and then decide whether the prisoner is an undesirable citizen (or worse yet, an undesirable alien). If so, they may bring in a verdict of guilty all down the line for good measure. So if a fair-minded prosecutor wants to promote freedom of speech but believes that the utterance creates a real danger of disastrous acts, *e.g.*, munition strikes, he should base the indictment on the statutory clause which best describes that danger, and be reluctant to throw in a string of trivial offenses in addition. The first two counts in the Abrams indictment should have been dropped before the trial, not in the Supreme Court.

function in time of war, might be only "technical." If so, these sections of the Espionage Act must have been more frequently violated in Wall Street than in Harlem.

Since most of the controversy about this case revolves around the fourth count of the indictment, we can confine ourselves to that. Aside from questions of constitutionality, the government had to establish the specific criminal intent required by the indictment and the Espionage Act. (1) It had to prove intention to publish the pamphlets. This the government undoubtedly did. (2) Under the fourth count it had to prove intention to produce curtailment of munitions, because the words "urge, incite, advocate" create an offense analogous to criminal solicitation, which involves a specific intent to bring about the overt act. There are a few sentences in the Yiddish leaflet which show such an intention, although it is open to question whether an incidental portion of a general protest which is not shown to have come dangerously near success really constitutes criminal solicitation or amounts to advocating. (3) Anyhow, the main task of the government was to establish an additional *intention to interfere with the war with Germany*. The question whether it proved anything more than an intention to obstruct operations in Russia is the vital issue of fact in the case.

Since we had not declared war upon Russia, protests against our action there could not be criminal unless they were also in opposition to the war with Germany. There are two conceivable theories of guilt, which might connect the leaflets with the war. The first theory is that the despatch of troops to Siberia was "a strategic operation against the Germans on the eastern battle front," so that any interference with that expedition hindered the whole war. The second theory is that the circulars intended to cause armed revolts and strikes and thus diminish the supply of troops and munitions available against Germany on the regular battle front.

Clearly the second theory is the only legitimate basis for conviction. The alternative argument, that opposition to the armed occupation of neutral territory and assertions of its illegality are *per se* criminal, is clearly a travesty on the defense of Belgium and a violation of the right of freedom of speech. Hence this first theory has been rejected by the majority Supreme Court opinion in the Abrams case, by the government's brief, and by writers [9] who support the decision. They have adopted the second theory of guilt and have taken it for granted that the jury followed the same course. If so, the convictions represent a finding of fact by the jury that the defendants intended to interfere with operations against Germany itself. Nevertheless, the record of the trial makes it highly probable that these defendants were convicted on just the other theory — for trying to hinder the Russian expedition.

As a state trial, this case cannot be understood without reference to the atmosphere in which the defendants wrote the circulars and the jury reached their verdict. I have no desire to venture into the Serbonian bog of the Russian Revolution, but a few undisputed facts must be recalled.[10] On January 8, 1918, two months after the establishment of the Soviet Government, President Wilson declared as the sixth of his Fourteen Points that Russia must have "an unhampered and unembarrassed opportunity for the independent determination of her own political development," and that the treatment accorded her by her sister nations during the months to come would be "the acid test of their good-will." On March 11 he telegraphed the Pan-Soviet Congress, promising that Russia should be secured "complete sovereignty and independence in her own affairs." Four months later a small body of American marines joined in the occupation of Murmansk, and shortly afterwards American troops were sent to Vladivostok. On August 3, an official statement from Washington announced that military intervention in Russia would only add to the confusion there and dissipate our forces on the western front. Consequently, we would not interfere with the political sovereignty of Russia or intervene in her local affairs, but would merely send a few thousand men to Vladivostok in coöperation with Japan and other Allies, who would be asked to give a similar assurance.

A few days later Abrams and his friends wrote and printed

[9] Mr. Wigmore is a possible exception and may regard all Bolshevism as within the Espionage Act. — 14 *Illinois Law Review* 439 ff.

[10] The documents are in R. S. Baker, *Woodrow Wilson*, vol. VIII, chapter iii (1939); Graves, *America's Siberian Adventure* (1931); *Russian-American Relations*, ed. Cumming and Pettit (New York, 1920). See Charles Cheney Hyde, "The Recognition of the Czechoslovaks as Belligerents," 13 *Amerian Journal of International Law* 93 (1919).

the leaflet headed, "The Hypocrisy of the United States and her Allies."

The Soviet government failed to distinguish between military intervention and the arrival of foreign troops on Russian soil. The diplomatic breach was complete. Soon afterwards the newspapers were filled with accounts of Bolshevist atrocities. In September the United States recognized the Czechoslovaks as a belligerent government warring against Germany and Austria, with their capital in Washington and their chief army in Siberia, so that the seacoast of Bohemia was evidently the Pacific Ocean. On September 15 the United States Committee on Public Information published nation-wide in the press the documents [11] collected by its representative, Mr. Edgar Sisson, which were stated to show that the present heads of the Bolshevist government were merely hired German agents. No one who recalls the widespread popular identification of the Soviet government with Germany in the summer and early autumn of 1918 can doubt that an October jury would inevitably regard pro-Bolshevist activities as pro-German, and consequently apply the first or Russian theory of guilt, besides having a prejudice against the defendants as sympathizers with the Russian Revolution. This prejudice could only be overcome by an exposition of the Russian situation from sources which had as yet found no expression in the newspapers.

Early on Friday, October 18, the fifth day of the actual trial, the government rested. Mr. Weinberger opened the case to the jury on behalf of the defendants, and called to the witness stand Colonel Raymond Robins, who had recently spent six months in Russia with the Red Cross and knew the Bolshevist leaders intimately. After a dozen introductory questions, the United States attorney objected to further examination, and the witness thereafter was obliged to remain silent while the defendants' counsel ran through a series of thirty unanswered

[11] *War Information Series, No. 20* (October, 1918); the documents, without the historical report, are in *Bolshevik Propaganda*, etc., p. 1125. The documents appeared in the public press by installments, beginning September 15, 1918. See the *New York Times* of that date. But see R. S. Baker, *Woodrow Wilson*, VIII, 402, n. 2: "The original documents later disappeared. Early in October Balfour sent the President a confidential message that English experts and authorities had gone over the Sisson papers carefully and had come to the conclusion that they were forgeries."

questions in order to get them on the record. This was repeated
with Albert Rhys Williams, who had also been in Russia in
1917–1918 and acted for the Soviets in foreign affairs. It was
not considered worth while to call Edgar Sisson at all. The
admissibility of the evidence of these three witnesses raises
problems that go to the heart of the case.

The first theory of guilt raised the complex question whether
the Russian expedition was a part of the war. If this was a
political question which must be answered in the affirmative
on the mere *ipse dixit* of the government, the existence of a
war enables the government to withdraw the most remote and
questionable policies from the scope of ordinary discussion
simply by labeling them a war matter. The annexation of
Mexico to prevent its becoming a base for German operations,
the use of American troops to put down strikes in England
or Sinn Fein in Ireland, were no more remotely connected with
the war with Germany than the Russian affair. On the other
hand, if the relation of such an expedition to the war was put
in issue to be decided by the jury, the defense ought to have
been allowed to call witnesses to disprove it. On this account,
in the Abrams case, Raymond Robins and other eyewitnesses
of Russian affairs were summoned to prove that the Bolshevist
and Czechoslovak situation was such that our intervention
was not anti-German; but this testimony and all questions
of the constitutionality of intervention were excluded by Judge
Clayton with the remark, "The flowers that bloom in the spring,
tra la, have nothing to do with the case."

This phase of the trial is very important for its demonstration of the enormous difficulties of proof into which we have
brought ourselves in the United States by creating political
crimes. Before the Espionage Act our criminal law punished
men almost entirely for acts which take place in the tangible
world and are proved by the evidence of our five senses. This
Act punishes men for words which cause no injury, but have a
supposedly bad tendency to harm the state, and also for intentions which are regarded as evil. Now, bad tendency and
bad intention cannot be seen or heard or touched or tasted or
smelled. They are, as we have seen, a matter of inference from
the complex and obscure background of general conditions.
Consequently, that background becomes, whether we admit

witnesses or not, an issue in the case. The rules of evidence for the trial of overt criminal acts prove almost useless. Common sense makes it plain that a knowledge of Russian affairs was essential to a jury with the attitude of that moment, obliged to interpret the repeated references to Russia in the circulars, and as we shall see, told often by the judge that the defendants were guilty if their pamphlets were issued for the purpose of preventing the government from carrying on its operations in Russia.

All prosecutions for words will involve us in the same awkward dilemma that was suggested in connection with the "false statements" clause in the Pierce case.[12] If we follow the logical course just indicated and allow the alleged promoter of sedition to bring in a mass of evidence from Russia or other dark and distant regions to show that neither he nor his utterances are liable to cause even remote injury to the national welfare, the prosecution is justly entitled to call other witnesses to establish the evil character of the agitation. Every sedition trial will be a rag-bag proceeding like the 1919 hearings about Bolshevism before the Overman Committee of the Senate.[13] As Judge Clayton pointed out in the Abrams trial, the admission of Raymond Robin's testimony would open up a Pandora's box. The district attorney would offer on his side to prove that Trotsky had been bought by the German Government.

To use a vulgar expression, it would be "swiping" them on the other hand, and we would forget all about the issues in this case, and we would find ourselves trying Lenine and Trotsky, which is something I do not intend to do. I have enough trouble trying these people here in the United States, and God knows I am not going into Russia to try to try anybody there.

On the other hand, if for the sake of speed and convenience we adopt the policy of Judge Clayton and exclude general testimony as to bad tendency, pinning the evidence down to the facts of publication and the precise intention of the defendants, we shall often do a grave injustice to the prisoners. The jury

[12] Page 95, *supra*.

[13] Bolshevik Propaganda, Hearings before a sub-committee of the Judiciary Committee of the U. S. Senate, 65th Cong. 3d sess. and thereafter, pursuant to Sen. Res. 439 and 469 (1919). This is cited in this book as Bolshevik Propaganda. It contains the testimony of Raymond Robins and others on Russian internal affairs.

and even the judge may bring to the trial preconceived views of the bad tendency and evil purpose of utterances opposed to the existing economic and social order or to war policies supported by the great mass of the population. If no counter-evidence to show that the opinions of the defendants may be reasonable or honest is admitted from third persons like Raymond Robins, these presuppositions must inevitably remain. Even if a defendant is allowed a wide scope in testifying in his own behalf, he is often the sort of man whose arguments carry little weight. In other words, in spite of the judge's desire to exclude outside evidence on either side as to bad tendency and bad intention from the case, such evidence in favor of a bad tendency and a bad intention is often automatically admitted the moment that the jury enter the box, and no system of challenges can avoid it. During a war they have for months been supplied with evidence by the government and the loyal press, diametrically opposed to the utterances for which the prosecution is brought. Unless something is done to tear the tribunal out of the fabric of public sentiment, a conviction is almost certain to result in prosecutions for political crimes, where the ordinary tests of the five senses play no part and men are forced to judge of the opinions and character of the prisoners by their own opinions and character as formed in the furnace of war. What Mr. Robins has since said and written makes it clear that his evidence would have been highly valuable to the defense.

Despite the practical inconveniences of such testimony as his in political prosecutions, it is the method pursued in countries where political crimes have existed when unknown in the United States. France, for instance, allows a "free defense," as in the *Affaire Dreyfus*. The defendant is not only allowed to say anything in his own favor, but may bring forward any witnesses he pleases, who express themselves fully and unhindered. Strange as it seems to us, the results are said to be very satisfactory.[14] Consequently, if we are going to continue

[14] Robert Ferrari, "The Trial of Political Prisoners Here and Abroad," 66 *Dial* 647 (June 28, 1919). The same method is pursued in French murder cases where "the honor of the family" is a defense, and perhaps instances like the Thaw trial show it is not wholly unknown in this country. See Walter F. Angell, "A Providence Lawyer at the Caillaux Trial," *Providence Daily Journal*, Aug. 21, 1914.

to prosecute men for the bad political tendency of their disloyal or anarchistic utterances, we may have to adopt a similar
wide-open policy in justice to the defendants.

Better far to reject both horns of the dilemma and refuse
altogether to make tendency a test of criminality. If we are
not willing to allow the free defense, we ought to abolish
political crimes by the repeal of the Espionage Act and all
other sedition statutes.

In the absence of any established technique for political
crimes in this country, the exclusion of the Robins testimony is
understandable, especially as it did not bear directly on the only
legitimate theory of guilt; but this only made it all the more
imperative that Judge Clayton should repeatedly during the
trial and in his charge insist to the jury that opposition to our
Russian policy was not in itself a crime. He ought to have
cleared Russia and Bolshevism out of the case for good and
all, and pounded home the proposition that the only issue
under the third and fourth counts (which alone should have
gone to the jury, if anything went at all) was whether the
defendants intended by inducing strikes in munition factories
and other forms of protest to interfere with the supply of munitions *for use against Germany*. No one who will put himself
back into the atmosphere of October, 1918, can doubt that
the jury would naturally regard pro-Bolshevist activities as
pro-German, and that it was the duty of Judge Clayton to
warn them explicitly against the Russian theory of guilt, and
confine their attention to the pro-German theory. There is no
adequate warning on this in the record.[16] Instead, Judge Clayton himself repeatedly proclaimed the unsound theory of guilt,
that if the defendants intended to oppose the government's
Russian policy, they had *ipso facto* violated the law.

Before the defendants had put in any material testimony,
he said:

Now the charge in this case is, in its very nature, that these defendants, by what they have done, conspired to go and incite a
revolt; in fact, one of the very papers is signed "Revolutionists,"
and it was for the purpose of avoiding — a purpose expressed in the

---

[16] In 35 *Harvard Law Review* at 13–15 I have set out in full passages in
the stenographic minutes of the trial which may have had a slight effect on
the jury with respect to the issue of specific intent.

paper itself — the purposes of the Government and raising a state of public opinion in this country of hostility to the Government of the United States, so as to prevent the Government from carrying on its operations and prevent the Government from recognizing that faction of the Government of Russia, which the Government has recognized, and to force the Government of the United States to recognize that faction of the Government in Russia to which these people were friendly.

Now, they cannot do that. No man can do that, and that is the theory that I have of this case, and we might as well have it out in the beginning.

The court did tell the jury that this statement was not part of the evidence and should be disregarded in passing on the issues of fact, but the harm was done and he took no steps to present any concrete alternative view. The second and legitimate theory of guilt was never stated by him, and it is doubtful if he himself ever realized the distinction or what really was in issue. Instead, he continued to apply the Russian theory in his cross-examination of Lipman, for it is one of the remarkable features of this case that most of the cross-examination of the prisoners was not by the district attorney, but by the court, who sometimes broke in upon the direct examination before half a dozen questions had been asked.[16] Lipman was testifying in response to his counsel that he had written the English pamphlet because the President after sending the telegram of sympathy to the Soviets had a few weeks later despatched a military expedition to Russia. Judge Clayton took over the witness:

"The President, you thought, and all that he was doing ought to be stopped and broken up?" "I thought when I know he is elected by the people they should protest against intervention. . . . I did not want to break up. I called for a protest, which as I understand it, from my knowledge of the Constitution, the people of America had a right to protest." . . .

"Did you not intend to incite or provoke or encourage resistance to the Government of the United States?" "Not to the Government — never did."

"Who was acting for the Government if the President was not?"

[16] On questioning of witnesses by the trial judge, see 30 *Yale Law Journal* 196 (1920); 4 Reports National Commission on Law Observance & Enforcement (Wickersham Commission) 320 ff. (1931).

"I thought it was the Congress and Senate that was supposed to represent the people of America."

"The President is the executive head . . . You intended to incite opposition to what the President did?" "I did not. I intended to enlighten the people about the subject, for, as I stated, the papers were afraid to state it, and I thought it was the right time."

". . . The Government acts through the President, and you intended to incite opposition to what he was doing?" "I intended to incite opposition to every wrong act I understood to be wrong."

"You had the specific intention to make public opinion and arouse public opinion against intervention in Russia?" "Yes."

When the judge also kept saying that the defendants' opinion of the legality of the President's action could not justify them in breaking the law, he made their anti-interventionist propaganda seem a crime in itself, and there was no need for the jury to consider whether they had any intention to prevent the shipment of munitions to the western front. There is nothing in the charge about such an intention, nothing to exclude Russian operations from the scope of the war. Therefore, it is very probable that the defendants were convicted on an erroneous theory of guilt, simply because they protested against the despatch of armed forces to Russia.

However, it is maintained that the defendants did intend to hinder the fighting against Germany and so were properly convicted on the second theory of guilt. There are three classes of evidence in the case bearing on their intention.

First, the two pamphlets speak for themselves. Both plainly protest against our Russian policy and not against the war. The English circular emphatically repudiates the charge of pro-Germanism. It is nearly all expository, but throws in a few general exhortations which have been tossed about in every socialistic hall and street-meeting since the Communist Manifesto in 1848. Military imagery ought not to be taken literally in radical propaganda, any more than in church hymns. The Yiddish leaflet is more specific and has a few sentences calling for a general strike, which can no more be kept out of a radical pamphlet than King Charles's head could be barred from Mr. Dick's Memorial. We ought to hesitate a long while before we decide that Congress made such shopworn exuberance criminal. Very likely, as Justice Clarke says,

"This is not an attempt to bring about a change of administration by candid discussion," [17] — but how much political discussion is candid? If nothing but candid discussion is protected by the First Amendment, its value for safeguarding popular review of official acts is *nil*. And even if words like "fight" and "revolution" indicate violence, though often used in a grandiose vein, the advocacy of strikes and violence is not a crime under this indictment unless intended to resist and hinder the war with Germany.

Second, as subsidiary evidence of evil intention Justice Clarke relied on a yellow paper with handwriting taken from Lipman when arrested, and some typewritten sheets found in a closet in Abrams' rooms. In these long discussions wholly concerned with the wrongs suffered by Russia at the hands of Germany and ourselves, he pounced on a few sentences about keeping the allied armies busy at home so that there would be no armies to spare for Russia, or saying that if arms are used against the Russian people, "so will we use arms, and they shall never see the ruin of the Russian revolution." [18] Justice Clarke then commented:

These excerpts sufficiently show, that while the immediate occasion for this particular outbreak of lawlessness, on the part of the defendant alien anarchists, may have been resentment caused by our government sending troops into Russia as a strategic operation against the Germans on the eastern battle front, yet the plain purpose of their propaganda was to excite, at the supreme crisis of the war, disaffection, sedition, riots, and, as they hoped, revolution, in this country for the purpose of embarrassing and if possible defeating the military plans of the Government in Europe.

Thus the defendants entered prison with the prospect of staying fifteen or twenty years largely because of scattered passages in manuscripts for which they were not indicted, and which they had neither printed or distributed. There is not the slightest testimony that Lipman ever showed them to anybody after dashing them off. Moreover, the typewritten sheets

[17] 250 U. S. at 622. Bagehot points out the danger of such a test: "The effect of all legislative interference in controversies has ever been to make an approximation to candor compulsory on one side but to encourage on the other side violence, calumny, and bigotry." — *Works*, Longmans' ed., X, 127.

[18] The significant passages from both manuscripts are in 250 U. S. at 622.

were plainly a first draft for the English leaflet, and in revision all Justice Clarke's objectionable passages vanished. It is going pretty far to condemn an author for what he leaves out.

Thirdly, we have the testimony of the defendants on the vital issue, whether they intended to defend the Russian Revolution by the methods of impulsive youth or intended to hinder us in our war against German militarism. All were born in Russia and had remained citizens of that country during their few years in the United States. All were anarchists except Lipman, and he was a socialist. Nothing in the case rebuts the natural inference that such persons were devoted to Russian radicalism and bitterly hostile to Imperial Germany.

Abrams said that he had offered his services to the President to go to Russia and fight Germany, but permission had been refused; that he would help send propaganda from Russia to Germany to start a revolution there, as he had done on the border of Austria and was sent to Siberia for it. As to the appeal for strikes, he called upon the workers here not to produce bayonets to be used against the workers in Russia.

"I say it is absurd I should be called a pro-German, because in my heart I feel it is about time the black spot of Europe should be wiped out."

"You are opposed to German militarism in every form?" "Absolutely."

"You would overthrow it and help overthrow it if you could?" "First chance."

The other defendants testified to the same effect, even Molly Steimer, the most inflexible, whose creed was that any human being should be free to live anywhere on earth that he or she desired. There is not a word in the whole *Record* to show that any prisoner was opposed to the war with Germany or desired Germany to win it or had any intention except an absorbing desire to protest against intervention in Russia.

It is hard to see how the jury could have convicted on this evidence if they had been instructed that a specific intent to hinder the war with Germany was necessary, but the judge did virtually nothing except repeat the words of the statute. He gave no explanation of the importance of this specific intent. He did not distinguish it from a general intention to publish the leaflets. Instead, the judge charged, "People who have circulars to distribute, and they intend no wrong, go up and down the streets circulating them." During the trial, although the defendants' counsel reminded him that Russian meetings in New York had been broken up, Judge Clayton said he would leave it to the jury whether throwing pamphlets out of windows squared with good, honest intention, and whether being anarchists and wanting to break up all government squared with honesty and sincerity of purpose. Soon afterward he stated:

> If it were a case where the defendant was indicted for homicide, and he was charged with having taken a pistol and put it to the head of another man and fired the pistol and killed the man, you might say that he did not intend to do that.
> But I would have very little respect for a jury that would come in with a verdict that he didn't have any intent.

Plainly these rulings of Judge Clayton ignored the specific intent to oppose or hinder the war with Germany, as demanded by the statute; he authorized the jury to convict the defendants for intention to publish the pamphlets and a generally bad mind.

The verdict against Abrams, three other men, and Molly Steimer was guilty on all four counts. The sixth prisoner was acquitted, for insufficient evidence of connection with the leaflets. The district attorney's office, which thought he had distributed leaflets at radical meetings, cites his acquittal as evidence of the fairness of the jury.

One more feature of the trial demands attention. Legal historians have always taken interest in the criminal judge who jests with the lives of men.[19]

> "You keep talking about producers," said Judge Clayton to Abrams. "Now may I ask why you don't go out and do some producing? There is plenty of untilled land needing attention in this country."

[19] Judge Clayton's words are taken *verbatim* from the *New York Times*, which on October 18 said editorially, "Judge Henry D. Clayton deserves the thanks of the city and of the country for the way in which he conducted the trial," and praised his "half-humorous" methods.

. . . The witness said that he was an anarchist and added that Christ was an anarchist.

"Our Lord is not on trial here. You are. . . ." [20]

"When our forefathers of the American Revolution —— " the witness began, but that was as far as he got.

"Your what?" asked Judge Clayton.

"My forefathers," replied the defendant.

"Do you mean to refer to the fathers of this nation as your forefathers? Well, I guess we can leave that out, too, for Washington and the others are not on trial here."

Abrams explained he called them that because, "I have respect for them. We all are a big human family, and I say 'our forefathers.' . . . Those that stand for the people, I call them father."

The day after conviction the prisoners were called before Judge Clayton for sentence. The court said:

"I am not going to permit anybody to start anything to-day. The only matter before this court is the sentencing of these persons. There will be no propaganda started in this court, the purpose of which is to give aid and comfort to soap-box orators and to such as these miserable defendants who stand convicted before the bar of justice."

When Lipman, the socialist, stepped forward to address the court and started to harangue about democracy, "You don't know anything about democracy," said Judge Clayton, "and the only thing you understand is the hellishness of anarchy." . . .

"These defendants took the stand. They talked about capitalists and producers, and I tried to figure out what a capitalist and what a producer is as contemplated by them. After listening carefully to all they had to say, I came to the conclusion that a capitalist is a man with a decent suit of clothes, a minimum of $1.25 in his pocket, and a good character.

"And when I tried to find out what the prisoners had produced, I was unable to find out anything at all. So far as I can learn, not one of them ever produced so much as a single potato.[21] The only thing they know how to raise is hell, and to direct it against the government of the United States. . . .

[20] See the quotation at the head of this section, page 112. On Braxfield's trials of Muir and others for sedition, see Henry Cockburn, *Memorials of His Time*; Brown, *French Revolution in English History*; Robert Louis Stevenson, *Some Portraits by Raeburn* and *Weir of Hermiston*; *supra* Chapter I, at n. 56.

[21] Abrams and Lachowsky bound books, Lipman produced furs, Rosansky produced hats, Molly Steimer produced shirtwaists.

"But we are not going to help carry out the plans mapped out by the Imperial German Government, and which are being carried out by Lenine and Trotsky. I have heard of the reported fate of the poor little daughters of the Czar, but I won't talk about that now. I might get mad. I will now sentence the prisoners."

Rosansky was given three years in prison, Molly Steimer fifteen years and $500 fine, Lipman, Lachowsky, and Abrams twenty years (the maximum), and $1,000 on each count. If they had actually conspired to tie up every munition plant in the country, and succeeded, the punishment could not have been more.[22]

"I did not expect anything better," said Lipman.

"And may I add," replied the judge, "that you do not deserve anything better."

2. THE SUPREME COURT

> *In this case sentences of twenty years imprisonment have been imposed for the publishing of two leaflets that I believe the defendants had as much right to publish as the Government has to publish the Constitution of the United States now vainly invoked by them.*
>
> JUSTICE HOLMES.

Seven judges of the Supreme Court were for affirmance of these convictions, Justice Clarke delivering the majority opinion. Justice Holmes read a dissenting opinion, in which Justice Brandeis concurred. The Supreme Court had only a limited power to correct any errors that may have occurred at the trial.[23] It could not revise the sentences. It could not set aside the verdict merely because its judges would have found differently on the facts themselves. Only two questions were clearly before the court: (1) the existence of the requisite

---

[22] It would not be treason, for lack of overt acts. (See Chapter VI, section II.) An actual conspiracy could be punished under the Espionage Act only by the twenty-year sentence here imposed on three of the male defendants. The general statute on conspiracy to destroy by force the government of the United States imposes only six years. — 18 U. S. C. A. § 6. Conspiracies to limit the production of necessaries were punished under the Lever Act by two years. — 40 Stat. 279.

[23] I have here modified somewhat the views formerly expressed as to the technical legal problems, and am indebted to my colleague Livingston Hall for several very helpful suggestions.

evidence of specific intent under the third and fourth counts
(the others being disregarded); (2) whether the two corresponding clauses of the Espionage Act could constitutionally
be interpreted to apply to the publication of these leaflets.

Enough will be said if I limit myself mainly to the fourth
count,[24] for urging by printing and publication curtailment of
production of ordinance and ammunition necessary or essential
to the prosecution of the war against Germany, *"with intent by
such curtailment to cripple or hinder the United States in the
prosecution of the war."*

The required specific intent to hinder the war with Germany
is worked out by Justice Clarke in this way:

> It will not do to say . . . that the only intent of these defendants
> was to prevent injury to the Russian cause. Men must be held to
> have intended, and to be accountable for, the effects which their acts
> were likely to produce. Even if their primary purpose and intent
> was to aid the cause of the Russian Revolution, the plan of action
> which they adopted *necessarily* involved, before it could be realized,
> defeat of the war program of the United States, for the obvious effect
> of this appeal, if it should become effective, as they hoped it might,
> would be to persuade persons . . . not to aid government loans and
> not to work in ammunition factories . . .[25]

In order to analyze this reasoning about intent, let us block
out three different types of situations. First, A for a joke
yelled "Fire!" in a crowded theater. Many of the audience
rushed for the doors in panic and a girl was trampled to death.
Undoubtedly A is liable for manslaughter. When A protests
that he intended no harm to anybody and least of all a fatality,

[24] As to the third count Justice Clarke said that "the language of these
circulars was obviously intended to provoke and encourage resistance to the
United States in the war." — 250 U. S. at 624. As proof of this intent, he
relied chiefly on the manuscripts which I have already considered to be insig-
nificant. I have not troubled to deal further with this count because my whole
chapter indicates that the leaflets did not intend to provoke any resistance to
the United States as the third count required. Whatever action was really urged
in the leaflets boiled down to munitions strikes to help Russia, and they are
covered by the fourth count discussed in the text. Justice Holmes said: "Resistance to the United States means some forcible act of opposition to some
proceeding of the United States in pursuance of the war. . . . There is no hint
at resistance to the United States as I construe the phrase." — 250 U. S. at 629
(1919).
[25] 250 U. S. at 621. Italics mine.

the judge might reply in a hackneyed legal phrase, "The prisoner must be taken to have intended the natural and probable consequences of his acts." [26] Now, this statement is obviously a roundabout and fictitious way of stating the correct proposition that a man is often held responsible for the natural and probable consequences of his act, whether or not he intended those consequences. His intention, as to what happened after his act, is immaterial. The defendant would be properly convicted, but the judge's reasoning would be wrong.

The Abrams case cannot be classified in this first situation, although Justice Clarke's second sentence hints in that direction. Why not? Because although in manslaughter and several other crimes any real intention of the defendant to do the resulting harm may be ignored where there is recklessness, this is not true when the offense charged is created by a statute which expressly requires an intent to cause a specific kind of injury. In such crimes, a man is not punished for the probable consequences of his act unless the tribunal finds that he really did have those consequences in mind.[27] Or, to put the matter another way, it is not enough for the defendant to do an act which is considered objectionable unless he actually has the mental state described in the statute.

My second situation illustrates the principles just stated. B is indicted under a federal statute providing that "If any person intending to devise any scheme to defraud, to be effected by correspondence with any person, shall, in and for executing such scheme," use the mails he shall be punishable on conviction. B, who is not a physician, has operated under the name of Boston Medical Institute, an establishment carrying on an extensive correspondence about the treatment of alleged diseases. The testimony of medical experts shows that his course of treatment is not helpful, and may cause serious nervous conditions, so that it is clear that his patrons have paid their money without any adequate return. The trial judge

---

[26] Rex v. Harvey, 2 B. & C. 257 at 264 (1823). Cf. Regina v. Martin, 14 Cox C. C. 633 (1881). See Jeremiah Smith, "Surviving Fictions," 27 *Yale Law Journal* 147, 156 (1917); H. F. Goodrich, "Does the Constitution Protect Free Speech?" 19 *Michigan Law Review* 487, 497 (1921).

[27] In People v. Landman, 103 Cal. 577, 580 (1894), Garoutte, J., said: "When a specific intent is an element of the offense, no presumption of law can ever arise that will decide this question of intent."

charges: "The law presumes that every man intends the natural and legitimate and necessary consequences of his acts. Wrongful acts, knowingly or intentionally committed, can neither be justified nor excused on the ground of innocent intent. The intent to injure or defraud may be presumed upon an unlawful act which results in loss or injury, if proved to have been knowingly committed." B's conviction must be reversed on appeal, because no such rule as the trial judge stated is applicable to this type of case. B cannot be properly convicted unless he really intends to defraud his patrons. If he is just a muddle-headed person who ignorantly and obstinately believes in the value of his treatment then he is not guilty of the statutory crime, however harmful his conduct appears to the court and the public.[28]

As between the first and second situations, it is clear that the Abrams case is much more like the second. But before we decide to place it in the second situation, which will necessarily make the prisoners innocent, we must give our attention to a third situation. C throws a brick at a man behind a plate-glass window, which is of course broken. He is indicted for intentional destruction of property. He defends himself by saying that he merely intended to hit the man, and did not want to break the window. This defense is clearly bad. C's principal desire may have been to hit the man, but that necessarily involved smashing the window; and if he knows this fact he has a secondary intention to break the glass even though he would much rather not have done so.[29] Similarly, when a man was indicted for assault on another with intent to disfigure him by biting off his ear, it was useless for him to argue that he intended only to injure but not to disfigure. The disfigurement was a necessary and obviously a known consequence of the intended act.[30] These cases differ from those in the second group, because there the harmful results were only probable

[28] Hibbard v. United States, 172 Fed. 66 (C. C. A. 7th, 1909), noted in 18 Ann. Cas. 1044. To the same effect are Dobbs's Case, 2 East P. C. 513 (1770); Rex v. Knight, 2 East P. C. 510 (1782); Baender v. Barnett, 255 U. S. 224 (1921); United States v. Moore, 2 Lowell (U. S.) 232 (Mass. 1873); Hairston v. State, 54 Miss. 689 (1877); and many other decisions.

[29] Cf. Rex v. Pembliton, 12 Cox C. C. 607 (1874). A shooting analogy is given in 33 Harvard Law Review 444 n.

[30] State v. Clark, 69 Iowa 196 (1886).

and perhaps unknown to the accused, while here the harmful results are inevitable, as the accused realizes.

The majority opinion in the Abrams case substantially takes the position that the defendants were like C and the ear-biter. Thus the first sentence quoted from Justice Clarke urges that aiding Russia was not the only intent of these defendants. It is argued that they had two intents: (1) to curtail production of munitions in order to help Russia, (2) to bring about interference with the war against Germany, which they knew would inevitably result from such curtailment during the process of accomplishing the first object; that it is immaterial which intent was principal and which was subordinate so long as both intentions were in their minds when they distributed the leaflets.

There are several answers to this argument that one who intends a curtailment of munitions for any purpose must know that fewer munitions will hinder the war and therefore must *ipso facto* intend to hinder the war. First, the analogy of the stone-throwing and biting cases just stated is too simple to have a proper application to free speech situations like the Abrams case. There is no such obvious and mechanical chain of cause and effect in complex social conditions, and the obscure factors involved are entirely beyond the capacity of a jury to decide. The argument supposes (1) that the hindrance of the war was inevitable, (2) that this inevitable consequence must have been in the defendants' minds. Both steps are very questionable, and the opinion of a jury on either step should have no weight with an appellate court. As to the first step, Justice Clarke's assumption that the defendants' plan "*necessarily* involved the defeat of the war program" merely states his own opinion on an issue which cannot be proved by legal evidence and as to which reasonable men might well think differently. Justice Holmes says, "An intent to prevent interference with the Revolution in Russia might have been satisfied without any hindrance to carrying on the war in which we were engaged." Thus a very short strike that stopped intervention would have caused a very small loss in munitions for shipment to France, which would have been enormously offset by the release of troops and equipment previously diverted to Russia; and a different Russian policy might have created greater liberal enthusiasm in this country and elsewhere for the President's war aims.[31] The second step ignores the defendants' belief that a friendly Soviet government would render valuable aid in attacking Imperial Germany by war, or at least by propaganda, which was proved effective by the German collapse within a fortnight after the conviction of Abrams and his friends.

Secondly, if every curtailment of munitions, whatever its purpose, is necessarily criminal under this Act, because of its alleged obvious and inevitable effect on the war, why does the Espionage Act take pains to limit the crime to "curtailment . . . *with intent . . . to cripple or hinder the United States in the prosecution of the war*"? [32] This clause is superfluous and meaningless, if every advocacy of curtailment involves such an intent. This clause about intent in a very severe criminal statute, and especially a statute limiting popular discussion, must mean what any layman who wished to urge a strike in war time lawfully would assume it to mean, that interference with the war must not be the object of his exhortation, the purpose at which he aims. Such a man would be entrapped if "intent" means an incidental, undesired, and at the most a vaguely considered consequence of his utterances.[33] Strikes are not ordinarily illegal, and it would be startling if Congress in 1918 intended to prohibit all incitement to them during the war. Naturally the statute confined itself to strikes and similar measures that were specifically planned to interfere with the war.

[31] Justice Brandeis considered that Wilson's public statement about intervention in Siberia was "unnatural" to him and that it "marked the beginning of his mistakes, all of which came in the latter part of his administration, and were due to physical and mental overstrain." — R. S. Baker, *Woodrow Wilson*, VIII, 316 n.

[32] It is significant that Justice Clarke omits this clause in quoting the indictment, and possibly he overlooked it altogether and assumed that intent to advocate curtailment of war essentials was the only intent specified in the Act.

[33] Holmes, J., 250 U. S. at 627: "When words are used exactly, a deed is not done with intent to produce a consequence unless that consequence is the aim of the deed — unless the aim to produce it is the proximate motive of the specific act. . . ." The Sabotage Act of 1918 punishes defective manufacture of war essentials only if there is intent to interfere with the war or reason to believe that the act will interfere with it. — 40 Stat. 534; 50 U. S. C. A. § 102. The amendment of Nov. 30, 1940, which includes peace-time sabotage, requires intent to interfere, etc., with national defense. See S. B. Warner, "The Model Sabotage Prevention Act," 54 *Harvard Law Review* 602, 624 ff. (1941).

This is not, as has been charged, a confusion of intent and motive.[34] The distinction which I have drawn is between intent in its broadest sense (including both results desired and results known to be the necessary concomitants of the desired results), on the one hand; and, on the other hand, intent in the more narrow sense, limited to results actually desired. Even if we concede the dubious contention of the majority that the aims of the Abrams group "*necessarily* involved defeat of the war program of the United States," still the strong reasons set out by Holmes should limit "intent" in a statute affecting freedom of speech so as to mean only desired results. In other words, if we let our decision as to guilt depend on speculations as to what unwanted consequences are necessarily caused by the accomplishment of a purpose legitimate in itself, we are far from provable facts and our conclusions about punishable utterances are sure to be much swayed by our own fears and beliefs. Hence it is much wiser to group these free speech cases requiring a specific intent with the second situation described above (the Medical Institute case), although they are not exactly the same.

To return to the facts of the Abrams case. The primary intent of the defendants, as Justice Clarke expressly recognizes, was to help Russia. The defendants desired to produce certain tangible results, notably protest meetings, which in turn were desired to produce another tangible result, the end of intervention. Their motive was love for Russia. They also desired as a part of their machinery of protest to produce a general strike. They may properly be said to have intended all these results. But interference with the war was at the most an incidental consequence of the strikes, entirely subordinate to the longed-for consequence of all this agitation, withdrawal from Russia. And such incidental consequences should not be the main basis for punishments restricting open discussion.

In other words, this argument of inevitable hindrance proves too much. If these defendants were guilty under the fourth count, so was every other person who advocated curtailment

---

[34] "Justice Holmes' Dissent," 1 *Review* 636 (Dec. 6, 1919). The interrelation between intent and motive is discussed and illustrated by W. W. Cook, "Act, Intention and Motive," 26 *Yale Law Journal* 645 at 654 ff. (1917).

in the production of war essentials, no matter what his purpose. The machinists in Bridgeport who struck in defiance of the arbitration of the National War Labor Board violated the Espionage Act, although they intended to obtain higher wages. The Smith and Wesson Company violated it in refusing to continue to manufacture pistols under another arbitration, although they intended to retain an open shop.[35] The coal miners in the autumn of 1919 violated that Act in calling a strike. The government should have threatened all these people with the twenty-year penalty of the Espionage Act instead of acting under its general war statutes or imposing the milder rigors of the Lever Act and an injunction.[36]

To sum up, the Supreme Court was construing not only a criminal statute which must be applied in a fashion which the laymen who are menaced. by it will readily understand, but also a statute limiting discussion and hence to be carefully interpreted in the light of the First Amendment. It ought not to be assumed that Congress meant to make all discussion of any governmental measure criminal in war time simply because of an incidental interference with the war. As Justice Holmes says, "Congress certainly cannot forbid all effort to change the mind of the country." The danger of the majority view is that it allows the government, once there is a war, to embark on the most dubious enterprises, and gag all but very discreet protests against such enterprises. To give extreme concrete examples: Irish munition workers could not have been urged to strike had our government been sending arms to Dublin Castle, because this would have lessened munitions for France, since a machinist could not be sure that any particular shell or gun was going to Ireland. Incitement to armed resistance to an executive edict nationalizing women would be opposition that might paralyze the war, and therefore easily suppressed under this Act.

The majority opinion dismisses this matter of constitutionality in two sentences, citing decisions on the Espionage Act of 1917 to establish the validity of the far more objectionable provisions of the Act of 1918.[37] Furthermore, the Court did

---

[35] See these two cases in Report of the Activities of the War Department in the Field of Industrial Relations During the War (Washington, 1919), 32–35.
[36] 40 Stat. 279.   [37] 250 U. S. at 619.

not have to declare the clauses involved in the third and fourth counts void. Indeed, they are probably constitutional when construed in accordance with the First Amendment. It is the same situation that Judge Hand pointed out in *Masses* v. *Patten*: [38] it is a question of giving valid legislation a construction which will permit discussion outside the precise terms of the Act. These leaflets were political agitation on matters not directly related to the war with Germany,[39] and about the invasion of a country against which Congress had not declared war. The specific intent clause of the statute punishes agitation against the war. Therefore, the Act should not have been stretched to cover the leaflets. The First Amendment requires doubts to be resolved in favor of innocence, especially in the absence of "clear and present danger." Discussion of public matters should be left as wide as possible, when not expressly forbidden by Congress. Hence it was erroneous for the Court to construe the Act so as to make the remote bad tendency and possible incidental consequences of these pamphlets a valid basis for conviction.

The decision of the majority worked injustice to the defendants, but its effect on the national ideal of freedom of speech should be temporary in view of its meager discussion and the enduring qualities of the reasoning of Justice Holmes. Although a dissenting opinion, it must carry great weight as an interpretation of the First Amendment, because it is only an elaboration of the principle of "clear and present danger" laid down by him with the backing of a unanimous court in *Schenck* v. *United States*. This principle is greatly strengthened since the Abrams case by Justice Holmes's magnificent exposition of the philosophic basis of this article of our Constitution:

Persecution for the expression of opinions seems to me perfectly logical. If you have no doubt of your premises or your power and want a certain result with all your heart you naturally express your wishes in law and sweep away all opposition. To allow opposition by speech seems to indicate that you think the speech impotent, as

---

[38] 244 Fed. 535, 538 (1917). See pp. 43–44, *supra*.

[39] Secretary of War Newton D. Baker wrote in 1929: "The expedition [to North Russia] was nonsense from the beginning and always seemed to me to be one of those side shows born of desperation and organized for the purpose of keeping up home morale rather than because of any clear view of the military situation. . . ." — R. S. Baker, *Woodrow Wilson*, VIII, 284 n.

when a man says that he has squared the circle, or that you do not care whole-heartedly for the result, or that you doubt either your power or your premises. But when men have realized that time has upset many fighting faiths, they may come to believe even more than they believe the very foundations of their own conduct that the ultimate good desired is better reached by free trade in ideas — that the best test of truth is the power of the thought to get itself accepted in the competition of the market, and that truth is the only ground upon which their wishes safely can be carried out. That at any rate is the theory of our Constitution. It is an experiment, as all life is an experiment. Every year if not every day we have to wager our salvation upon some prophecy based upon imperfect knowledge. While that experiment is part of our system I think that we should be eternally vigilant against attempts to check the expression of opinions that we loathe and believe to be fraught with death, unless they so imminently threaten immediate interference with the lawful and pressing purposes of the law that an immediate check is required to save the country. . . . Only the emergency that makes it immediately dangerous to leave the correction of evil counsels to time warrants making any exception to the sweeping command, "Congress shall make no law abridging the freedom of speech." Of course I am speaking only of expressions of opinion and exhortations, which were all that were uttered here, but I regret that I cannot put into more impressive words my belief that in their conviction upon this indictment the defendants were deprived of their rights under the Constitution of the United States.

The preceding chapters have been written in support of this danger-test as marking the true limit of governmental interference with speech and writing under our constitutions, but an able and thoughtful criticism of Justice Holmes's dissent [40] makes it imperative to say something more on the subject. In the first place, the First Amendment is very much more than "an expression of political faith." It was demanded by several states as a condition of their ratification of the Federal Constitution, and is as definitely a prohibition upon Congress as any other article in the Bill of Rights. The policy behind it is the attainment and spread of truth, not merely as an abstraction, but as the basis of political and social progress. "Freedom of speech and of

[40] "The Espionage Act and the Limits of Legal Toleration," 33 *Harvard Law Review* 442 (January, 1920), by Day Kimball.

the press" is to be unabridged because it is the only means of testing out the truth. The Constitution does not pare down this freedom to political affairs only, or to the opinions which are held by a majority of the people in opposition to the government. A freedom which does not extend to a minority, however small, and₁ which affords them no protection when the majority are on the side of the government, would be a very partial affair, enabling the majority to dig themselves in for an indefinite future. The narrow view that the amendment does not protect a few of the people against the force of public opinion throws us back to the English trials during the French Revolution, ánd the Sedition Law of 1798, for which the United States through many years showed its repentance by pardoning all prisoners and repaying to them the fines imposed. These were none the less injurious to the cause of truth because they had the sanction of the majority.

Undoubtedly, although we are not infallible, we must assume certain opinions to be true for purposes of action; but this does not make it right or desirable to assume that they are true for the purpose of crushing those who hold a contrary doctrine.

There is the greatest difference between presuming an opinion to be true, because, with every opportunity for contesting it, it has not been refuted, and assuming its truth for the purpose of not permitting its refutation.[41]

The vote of the majority of the electorate or the legislature is the best way to decide what beliefs shall be translated into immediate action, and the government must resist if its opponents begin to carry on the conflict of opinions by breaking heads instead of counting them. But it is equally inadvisable for the government to seek to end a contest of ideas by imprisoning or exiling its intellectual adversaries. Force seems like force to its victim, whether or not it has the sanction of law. No one will question that the government must resist a revolt, however Utopian in purposes, but the inference that logically it must also condemn all utterances "aimed at such subversion or tending solely thither" ignores the difference

[41] Mill, *Liberty*, chap. II.

of degree emphasized by the First Amendment. It is the unfailing argument of persecutors. The opinions to which they object are always conceived to aim at revolution, violence, and nothing else, although such utterances are usually in large part the exposition of political and economic views. The advocates of parliamentary reform in England were condemned on just such reasoning. To throw overboard the danger-test, and permit "the suppression, whenever reasonably necessary, of utterances whose aims render them a menace to the existence of the state," inevitably substitutes jail for argument, since the determination of the vague test of "menace" depends on the tribunal's abhorrence of the defendant's views. It is no answer that this tribunal (outside of the crushing powers of the postoffice and of the immigration officials in deportation cases) is a jury. A fitness to apply a common-sense standard to alleged criminal acts bears no resemblance to a capacity to appraise the bad political and social tendency of unfamiliar economic doctrines during panic. The Abrams case shows the capacity of a judge to decide such a question. The only tribunal which can pass properly on the menace of ideas is time.

We must fight for some of our beliefs, but there are many ways of fighting. The state must meet violence with violence, since there is no other method, but against opinions, agitation, bombastic threats, it has another weapon — language. Words as such should be fought with their own kind, and force called in against them only to head off violence when that is sure to follow the utterances before there is a chance for counter-argument. To justify the suppression of the Abrams agitation because the government could not trust truth to win out against "the monstrous and debauching power of the organized lie" overlooks the possibility that in the absence of free discussion organized lies may have bred unchecked among those who upheld the course of the government in Russia.

The lesson of *United States* v. *Abrams* is that Congress alone can effectively safeguard minority opinion in times of excitement. Once a sedition statute is on the books, bad tendency becomes the test of criminality. Trial judges will be found to adopt a free construction of the act so as to reach objectionable doctrines, and the Supreme Court will probably be unable to afford relief.

Most of the discussion of the Abrams case has turned on the question whether the decision of the United States Supreme Court affirming these convictions was right or wrong. It seems to me much more important to consider the case as a whole, and ask how the trial and its outcome accord with a just administration of the criminal law.

The systematic arrest of civilians by soldiers on the streets of New York City was unprecedented, and the seizure of papers without a warrant was illegal. The trial judge ignored the fundamental issues of fact, took charge of the cross-examination of the prisoners, and allowed the jury to convict them for their Russian sympathies and their anarchistic views. The maximum sentence available against a formidable pro-German plot was meted out by him to the silly, futile circulars of five obscure and isolated young aliens, misguided by their loyalty to their endangered country and ideals, who hatched their wild scheme in a garret, and carried it out in a cellar. "The most nominal punishment" was all that could possibly be inflicted, in Justice Holmes's opinion, unless Judge Clayton was putting them in prison not for their conduct but for their creed. Yet they were sentenced for their harmless folly to spend the best years of their lives in American jails.[42] The injustice was none the less because our highest court felt powerless to wipe it out. The responsibility was simply shifted to the pardoning authorities[43] and to Congress, which can refuse to revive the Espionage Act of 1918, so that in future wars such a trial and such sentences for the intemperate criticism of questionable official action[44] shall never again occur in these United States.

[42] See Morley's indignation at the "thundering sentences" for sedition in India. *Recollections*, II, 269.

[43] In November, 1921, the prisoners were released on the condition of their return to Russia at their own expense. — Report of the Attorney General, 1922, p. 398. See *id.* 1921, p. 717.

[44] On armed intervention without Congressional authority, see the state papers of Seward and Fish in J. B. Moore, *Digest of International Law*, VI, 23 ff., and Moorfield Storey, "A Plea for Honesty," 7 *Yale Review* 260 (1918): "If any nation were to do any of these things to the United States, we should not doubt that it was making war on us."

CHAPTER 4

POST-WAR SEDITION LAWS

> *If there be any among us who wish to dissolve this union, or to change its republican form, let them stand undisturbed, as monuments of the safety with which error of opinion may be tolerated where reason is left free to combat it. I know indeed that some honest men have feared that a republican government cannot be strong; that this government is not strong enough. But would the honest patriot, in the full tide of successful experiment, abandon a government which has so far kept us free and firm on the theoretic and visionary fear that this government, the world's best hope, may, by possibility, want energy to preserve itself? I trust not. I believe this, on the contrary, the strongest government on earth.*
>
> JEFFERSON, First Inaugural Address.

LONG before the armistice it became clear that the problem of freedom of speech would not end with the war, but would be raised for us in a different aspect and with added difficulties by the unaccustomed prevalence and outspoken expression of radical ideas. This phenomenon was bound to result from the war. The routine of the day's work ordinarily holds in check the eternal antagonism of the "have-nots" to the "haves," but habits of mechanical obedience and adjustment to the prevailing scheme of life were suddenly destroyed for many by the rapid shift to new scenes and occupations and a novel conviction of the power of unskilled labor. The immense amount of thought and discussion caused by the war during the three years preceding our entry has been often remarked. Such an overhauling directed popular attention to the part played by economic factors in the origin and conduct of the war. Many extreme radicals claimed therefrom fresh proof of the economic interpretation of history and the class struggle. The official emphasis on democracy against autocracy inevitably stimulated discussion of those two concepts and their application to industrial and other non-political fields. Labor programs in England and France crossed the ocean. Then came one of the earthquakes of history, the Russian Revolution, from whose remote influence it was as impossible for us to escape as from the French Revolution which produced the Alien and Sedition Laws of 1798. Jefferson's *First Inaugural* states the controversy of today:

During the throes and convulsions of the'antient world, dur^r the agonis^d spasms of infuriat^d man, seeking through blood & slaughter his long lost liberty, it was not wonderful that the agitation of the billows should reach even this distant & peaceful shore: that ye sh^d be more felt & fear^d by some, & less by others, & sh^d divide opinions as to measures of safety.

Much of this radicalism had identified itself with the opposition to the war, and thereby been involved in prosecutions under the Espionage Act and the state laws. A few members of the Non-Partisan League were tried in the federal courts, and its leaders and several of the rank and file were convicted in Minnesota. Much use was made against Debs, Berger, and Mrs. O'Hare of the St. Louis Socialist platform, with its declaration for "continuous, active, and public opposition to the war, through demonstrations, mass petitions, and all other means within our power." The Industrial Workers of the World, whose creed was syndicalism, had taken advantage of the nation's hour of need to withhold assistance which they felt under no obligation to give. Their position was stated to Carleton Parker in plain language by one of their chiefs.

You ask me why the I.W.W. is not patriotic to the United States. If you were a bum without a blanket; if you had left your wife and kids when you went West for a job, and had never located them since; if your job never kept you long enough in a place to qualify you to vote; if you slept in a lousy, sour bunk-house, and ate food just as rotten as they could give you and get by with it; if deputy sheriffs shot your cooking cans full of holes and spilled your grub on the ground; if your wages were lowered on you when the bosses thought they had you down; if there was one law for Ford, Suhr, and Mooney [three radical leaders then in prison], and another for Harry Thaw; if every person who represented law and order and the nation beat you up, railroaded you to jail, and the good Christian people cheered and told them to go to it, how in hell do you expect a man to be patriotic? This war is a business man's war and we don't see why we should go out and get shot in order to save the lovely state of affairs that we now enjoy.

Parker, Colonel Disque in the spruce forests, and the President's Mediation Commission had striven with much success to bring these irreconcilables into the great stream of national effort. Others thought coercion a better method to end the dangerous menace of sabotage and the recurrent strike. W. D. Haywood and one hundred more members of the I.W.W. were convicted and imprisoned under long sentences for threats and designs of tangible obstruction to war work.

This union of hostility to the war with strange economic and political doctrines set its mark on the later war legislation. The amended Espionage Act of 1918 included the clauses about defamation of our form of government and curtailment of production which played such a prominent part in the Abrams case. A federal Sabotage Act was enacted.[1] States punished the advocacy of syndicalism and sabotage in their war statutes or more often by separate acts. Much of this legislation extended automatically to peace-time utterances, and when it did not, it was easy and natural to adapt it for that purpose by the omission of a few military phrases. In the legislative sessions which followed the armistice, emergency laws against new crimes labeled as anarchy and criminal syndicalism were adopted by state after state with a striking coincidence of phraseology.

This coercive legislation was held by its supporters to have unanswerable justification in the succeeding outrages of 1919. A large number of bombs addressed to federal officials and judges were seized in the mails, and the houses of Attorney General Palmer and several other individuals prominent in sedition prosecutions and legislation were wrecked by explosions, one of which caused loss of life. There was much street fighting at May Day parades in Boston and Cleveland, and a clash of very obscure origin between the I.W.W. and

---

[1] 50 U. S. C. A. §§ 101–3, applicable only in war. This was amended on Nov. 30, 1940, by the addition of provisions operative during peace. See S. B. Warner, "The Model Sabotage Prevention Act," 54 *Harvard Law Review* at 624–628 (1941).

the American Legion in Centralia, Washington, resulted in the death of five ex-service men, four shot and one lynched.[2]

During most of 1919 and the early months of 1920, the Department of Justice and Congressional committees to investigate Bolshevism, the New York Lusk committee to investigate seditious activities, and various patriotic societies were gathering and pouring into the news a mass of evidence about the large number of dangerous radicals and revolutionary periodicals and pamphlets in the United States. The press was full of arrests of Reds, and raids on Red headquarters, and deportations of Reds, and hidden stores of arms and ammunition which always eluded discovery. Attorney General Palmer led the repeated demands for wider and severer statutes to meet "the Red menace," and above all a federal Sedition Act enforceable in time of peace.

The presence in our midst of new forces that make for disorder and violence renders it desirable to review the resources of our law for dealing with insurrection, bombs, and assassination, and to examine calmly recent and pending legislation to prevent the promotion of anarchy. The disruption of our social and economic fabric by revolution, or even the continual recurrence of local outrages, would be so disastrous that they ought to be prevented in the' wisest and most effective manner. Many persons take it for granted that any statute which is directed against those evils must be beneficial. That does not necessarily follow. If an emergency really exists, it behooves us all to keep cool, and consider with great care any new laws or proposals for legislation, to see whether they are actually needed to combat the danger, whether they will really meet it, and whether in the haste and excitement of the moment our legislators may not be going much too far.

[2] On the May Day parade in Boston (Roxbury) see Comm. *v.* Frishman, 235 Mass. 449 (1920). The decision on the Centralia affair is State *v.* Smith, 115 Wash. 405 (1921). One side of the story appears in Lampman, *Centralia Tragedy and Trial* (1920, distributed by the American Legion). But for quite different accounts from these, see Chaplin, *The Centralia Conspiracy* (3d ed., 1924, distributed by the Defense Committee); *The Centralia Case: A Joint Report on the Armistice Day Tragedy* (1930, prepared by committees of the Federal Council of Churches, National Catholic Welfare Conference, and American Rabbis); Brissenden, "Industrial Workers of the World," 8 *Encyclopaedia of the Social Sciences* at 15–16 (1932).

This country has been able without any anarchy acts to cope with several insurrections like Shay's Rebellion and the Dorr War, a considerable amount of anarchy, and a great many turbulent strikes. May it not be that a wise and vigorous enforcement of the ordinary criminal law will meet most, if not all, of the present danger?

I. THE NORMAL LAW AGAINST VIOLENCE AND REVOLUTION

As far as state prosecutions are concerned, there has been very little need of specific legislation against anarchy and criminal syndicalism. Actual violence against government, life, and property is punishable everywhere. Those who plan or counsel such violence are liable even if they do not actively participate. When several policemen were killed by a bomb at the Haymarket in Chicago in 1886, Spies and other anarchists were convicted and executed though it was clear that some one else threw the bomb. Nor is it necessary that any criminal act shall take place. An unsuccessful attempt at a serious crime or a definite solicitation of another to commit it is punishable under the general criminal law. Chief Justice Morton of Massachusetts said in 1883, while upholding the sentence of one Flagg for urging another without success to burn down a barn: "It is an indictable offense at common law to counsel and solicit another to commit a felony or other aggravated offense, although the solicitation is of no effect, and the crime counseled is not in fact committed." [3] Consequently the normal law of the states and the District of Columbia, apart from any legislation against anarchy, enables the police and the courts to deal vigorously with actual or threatened insurrection, explosions, or assassination. The president and other federal officials are protected against bodily violence by these local laws, in or out of Washington. Thus the assassin of President McKinley was convicted in the New York courts. · If national safety requires such crimes to be punishable in federal as well as state courts, Congress

[3] Comm. v. Flagg, 135 Mass. 545 (1883). If the normal law of any state is incomplete, a definite provision as to criminal attempt or solicitation will meet the need far more wisely than the enactment of a vague and sweeping act against anarchy. State decisions are collected in 35 A. L. R. 961 (1925); *American Jurisprudence* (1938), XIV, 846.

(as I shall argue later) probably has the power so to provide.[4] Finally, almost every state has a statute or rule of the common law punishing a person who conspires with one or more associates to commit any crime, and often no overt act need have been committed. Such a conspiracy law seems sufficiently sweeping to reach a group which plans the destruction of property or life or any sort of violent revolution.

No new Congressional legislation is needed to make criminal any scheme to overthrow the United States Government by bombs or any other means. A glance at the first eight sections of the federal Criminal Code suffices to prove this.[5] Levying war against the United States is treason punishable with death, and recruiting or enlisting for armed hostility against the United States is a serious crime. Conduct short of insurrection is penalized in section 6. "If two or more persons . . . conspire to overthrow, put down, or to destroy by force the Government of the United States, or to levy war against them, or to oppose by force the authority thereof, or by force to prevent, hinder, or delay the execution of any law of the United States," they are each liable to six years in prison or $5,000 fine or both. It is of course well settled that conspiracy does not have to succeed to be punishable. All that is required is a common design to use force against the government; no overt act is then necessary to constitute guilt. If any further protection against threatened revolution is needed, it is furnished by section 37 of the Criminal Code, which punishes with two years in prison or $10,000 fine, or both, conspiracy "to commit any offense against the United States," if any party "do any act to effect the object of the conspiracy." The act may be entirely innocent in itself, and may consist in speech or publication.[6]

Section 6 of the Criminal Code was enacted during the Civil War and was thought adequate to meet the real dangers of the Reconstruction Period in the South. Indeed, William M. Evarts said of this statute in 1868: "It is a law wholly improper in time of peace, for, in the extravagance of its

---

[4] See section VII of this chapter. The state conspiracy statutes are listed in Appendix III.

[5] 18 U. S. C. A. (1926) §§ 1–8.

[6] *Id.*, § 88. On section 6, see *Arguments and Speeches of W. M. Evarts* (1919), I, 470.

comprehension, it may include much more than should be made criminal, except in times of public danger." However, Attorney General Palmer, in asking Congress for a new sedition law, alleged two defects in this section, which in his opinion destroy its usefulness in dealing with a serious radical situation.[7] First, the section is limited to conspiracies of two or more persons, and does not reach the isolated individual who threatens to overthrow the government. It may be a breach of the peace under state law but it is not in 1920 a federal crime if one man, all by himself, goes and hires a hall and tells his audience to start a revolution.[8] This solitary talker was frequently held up at post-war Congressional hearings as an example of existing danger to the country, until Mr. Alfred Bettman answered out of his long experience with sedition prosecutions during war service in the Department of Justice:

This man does it all by himself. Nobody encourages him. No organization supports or inspires him. He thinks up a rebellion all by himself. He hires a hall all by himself. Nobody helps him pay for it. He makes his speech all by himself. Nobody introduces him. He makes his speech. And nothing happens. That is your case. *Nothing happens.* Well, nothing happens.[9]

The second peril to which section 6 is said to leave us exposed is that even several persons can get out a revolutionary pamphlet without necessarily being guilty of conspiracy. For example, the El Ariete Society of Buffalo anarchists circulated a Spanish manifesto which abused our officials and form of government and advocated the organization of soviets, anarchy, and the destruction of the institutions of society. However, a prosecution for conspiracy under section 6 was quashed, because the court found nothing urging the use of violence to usher in this bright New Day. For all the manifesto said, it might be sent out to bring about "a change of government by propaganda — by written documents."[10] So Attorney General

[7] Investigation Activities of the Department of Justice, 6.

[8] In 1941 it might be a federal crime under Title I of the Alien Registration Act of 1940, discussed in Chapter XII, section 1.

[9] 21 *New Republic* 314 (February 11, 1920).

[10] U. S. *v.* Aso, Investigation Activities of the Department of Justice, pp. 15–22.

Palmer wanted new federal legislation to reach such publications.

A circular which is part of any plot to overthrow the government by unlawful acts would be punishable under section 6. This is plainly shown by a conviction under this section for conspiracy to circulate pamphlets advocating resistance to military conscription.[11] On the other hand, a statute applying to the Ariete manifesto would necessarily make it criminal to express economic views and aims different from those which now prevail. Whether such legislation is desirable will soon be discussed, but clearly it is not needed to meet any present danger of revolution. If there is any real revolutionary plot afoot by Bolshevists, anarchists, or any one else, they can be tried, convicted, and sentenced to six years in prison under section 6 of the Criminal Code; and if six years is not time enough a simple amendment of this section can make it longer.

One other feature of the existing federal law deserves attention. The chief danger from anarchists arises through the use of explosives, and if these are kept under federal control the country will be reasonably safe from bombs and dynamite. On October 6, 1917, Congress passed an elaborate statute making it unlawful, when the United States is at war, to manufacture, distribute, store, use, or possess explosives, fuses, detonators, etc., except under specified regulations which include a requirement for a government license given only after full information. This law was used during the war to impose sentences of eighteen months on bomb plotters who were shipping explosives without a license.[12] The statute is automatically suspended during peace, but Congress would do well to continue it, and could, it seems, accomplish this constitutionally under its powers to regulate interstate and foreign commerce and to conserve material needed for army and navy use. Under this statute it would be practically impossible for unauthorized persons to secure enough explosives to cause extensive damage.

---

[11] Wells v. U. S., 257 Fed. 605 (C. C. A., 1919). See Chapter II, note 3.

[12] Now 50 U. S. C. A. §§ 121–143; see Inspector Thomas J. Tunney, in *Bolshevik Propaganda*, p. 28. The Neutrality Act of 1939 set up a National Munitions Control Board with wide peace-time powers over the manufacture of explosives. — 22 U. S. C. A. § 245j — 11.

With these suggested amendments to the federal statutes to protect the lives and persons of United States officials and regulate the use of explosives in peace, the normal law will be entirely adequate to guard us against dangerous anarchy. Violence, direct and dangerous provocation to violence, and conspiracies to bring about violence will be severely punished, and the instruments of outrage will be removed.

2. THE NORMAL CRIMINAL LAW OF WORDS

I have dwelt at such length upon the ordinary law in order to make it clear that sedition and anarchy acts, insofar as they are not unnecessary duplication of that law, go far beyond it and impose an entirely different test of criminality. To restate the matter in accordance with the reasoning in the first chapter, the normal criminal law is interested in preventing crimes and certain non-criminal interferences with governmental functions like refusals to enlist or to subscribe to bonds. It is directed primarily against actual injuries. Such injuries are usually committed by acts, but the law also punishes a few classes of words like obscenity, profanity, and gross libels upon individuals, because the very utterance of such words is considered to inflict a present injury upon listeners, readers, or those defamed, or else to render highly probable an immediate breach of the peace. This is a very different matter from punishing words because they express ideas which are thought to cause a future danger to the State.

Undoubtedly, the existence of these verbal peace-time crimes subjects the argument of my first chapter to an acid test. They are too well-recognized to question their constitutionality, but I believe that if they are properly limited they fall outside the protection of the free speech clauses as I have defined them. My reason is not that they existed at common law before the constitutions, for a similar argument would apply to the crime of sedition, which was abolished by the First Amendment. The existence of a verbal crime at common law shows the presence of a social interest which must be weighed in the balance, but the free speech guaranties, as I have argued at length, enact a countervailing social interest in the attainment and dissemination of truth, which was insufficiently recognized by the common law. Nor do I base my conclusion on the historical fact that the framers of the constitutions wanted to safeguard political discussion, because their own statements of freedom of speech in the address to the people of Quebec, the Virginia Toleration Statute, and the opening clause of the First Amendment itself, prove that they also wanted to safeguard scientific and religious freedom, both of which would be greatly restricted by a sweeping application of the common law of obscenity and blasphemy. The true explanation is that profanity and indecent talk and pictures, which do not form an essential part of any exposition of ideas, have a very slight social value as a step toward truth, which is clearly outweighed by the social interests in order, morality, the training of the young, and the peace of mind of those who hear and see. Words of this type offer little opportunity for the usual process of counter-argument. The harm is done as soon as they are communicated, or is liable to follow almost immediately in the form of retaliatory violence. The only sound explanation of the punishment of obscenity and profanity is that the words are criminal, not because of the ideas they communicate, but like acts because of their immediate consequences to the five senses. The man who swears in a street car is as much of a nuisance as the man who smokes there. Insults are punished like a threatening gesture, since they are liable to provoke a fight. Adulterated candy is no more poisonous to children than some books. Grossly unpatriotic language may be punished for the same reasons. The man who talks scurrilously about the flag commits a crime, not because the implications of his ideas tend to weaken the Federal Government, but because the effect resembles that of an injurious act such as trampling on the flag, which would be a public nuisance and a breach of the peace. This is a state but not a federal crime, for the United States has no criminal jurisdiction over offenses against order and good manners, although Congress may possibly have power to regulate the use of the national emblem. It is altogether different from sedition.

The absurd and unjust holdings in some of these prosecutions for the use of indecent or otherwise objectionable language furnish a sharp warning against any creation of ·new verbal crimes. Thus, the test of obscenity is very vague, and many decisions have utterly failed to distinguish nasty talk or the sale of unsuitable books to the young from the serious discussion of topics of great social significance. The white slave traffic was first exposed by W. T. Stead in a magazine article, "The Maiden Tribute." The English law did absolutely nothing to the profiteers in vice, but put Stead in prison for a year for writing about an indecent subject. When the law supplies no definite standard of criminality, a judge in deciding what is indecent or profane may consciously disregard the sound test of present injury, and proceeding upon an entirely different theory may condemn the defendant because his words express ideas which are thought liable to cause bad future consequences. Thus musical comedies enjoy almost unbridled license, while a problem play is often forbidden because opposed to our views of marriage. In the same way, the law of blasphemy has been used against Shelley's *Queen Mab* and the decorous promulgation of pantheistic ideas, on the ground that to attack religion is to loosen the bonds of society and endanger the state.[13] This is simply a roundabout modern method to make heterodoxy in sex matters and even in religion a crime. A Washington decision punishing a man for a newspaper article tending to defame George Washington is a serious restriction on historical writing.[14] Those of us who feel strongly that faith in the teachings of Christ means a better world must still recognize that others deplore the evils of superstition, and concede that the value of Christianity is one of the very questions which ought to be freely debated. Hence the authorities should be very reluctant to punish the contrary-minded, even though the prosecution be rested on some non-religious ground like the offensiveness of the defendant's irreligious language or the tendency of blasphemy to produce a breach of the peace.

This breach of the peace theory is peculiarly liable to abuse when applied against unpopular expressions and practices. It makes a man a criminal simply because his neighbors have no self-control and cannot refrain from violence. The *reductio*

[13] Austin W. Scott, "The Legality of Atheism," 31 *Harvard Law Review* 289 (1917). On blasphemy and criminal libel, see *infra*, Chapter XIV, note 7.

[14] People *v.* Haffer, 94 Wash. 136 (1916), under statute. Even such a conservative as Dr. Johnson opposed liability for defamation of the dead.

ad absurdum of this theory was the imprisonment of Joseph Palmer, one of Bronson Alcott's fellow-settlers at "Fruitlands," not because he was a communist, but because he persisted in wearing such a long beard that people kept mobbing him, until law and order were maintained by shutting him up.[15] A man does not become a criminal because some one else assaults him, unless his own conduct is in itself illegal or may be reasonably considered a direct provocation to violence.[16]

Thus all these crimes of injurious words must be kept within very narrow limits if they are not to give excessive opportunities for outlawing heterodox ideas.

Besides these special classes of words which cause present injury, the normal law punishes speech as an attempt or solicitation, although it falls short of actual injury; but the first chapter has shown that this is only when the words come somewhere near success and render the commission of actual crime or other tangible obstruction of state activities probable unless the state steps in at once and penalizes the conduct before it ripens into injury. The law of attempts and solicitation is directed not against the words but against acts, and the words are punished only because that is the necessary way to avoid harmful acts. When A urges B to kill C and tells him how he can do it, this has nothing to do with the attainment and dissemination of truth, and besides there is genuine danger that the murder will take place long before discussion will prove it to be a mistaken scheme.

The two conspiracy cases mentioned in connection with the federal Criminal Code bring out neatly the boundary of the normal criminal law. The anti-draft pamphlets fell within its range because of the danger created by their language and the surrounding circumstances, and although unlike solicitations to murder they served a social interest in criticizing the policies of the war, this was outweighed by the pressing peril to the social interest in the enforcement of war legislation. On the other hand, the Ariete manifesto was simply intemperate discussion of fundamental economic and political questions; and even if it had a remote tendency to injure the country by causing a revolution some day, there was obviously plenty of time to present the other side before the revolution arrived.

---

[15] Clara E. Sears, *Bronson Alcott's Fruitlands*, chap. iv.
[16] See the discussion of the right of assembly in Chapter XI, section VIII.

3. THE DIFFERENCE BETWEEN THE NORMAL LAW AND THE NEW LEGISLATION

> *We have seen and heard of revolutions in other States. Were they owing to the freedom of popular opinions? Were they owing to the facility of popular meetings? No, sir, they were owing to the reverse of these; and therefore, I say, if we wish to avoid the danger of such revolutions,.we should put ourselves in a state as different from them as possible.* CHARLES JAMES FOX, 1795.

The normal law protects us from dangerous anarchy, but sedition and anarchy acts reach out to the futile soap-box orator who advocates violence and in most cases to the Ariete manifesto which does not. These statutes are not directed against those who commit or actually plan violence, but against those who express or even hold opinions which are distasteful to the substantial majority of citizens. Some of them are so sweeping as to suppress agitation which is neither dangerous nor anarchistic. The people may be led to accept such statutes because they fear anarchy, but they will soon find that all sorts of radical and even liberal views have thereby become crimes. These acts have been drafted by men who are so anxious to avoid any disturbance of law and order that they have punished by long prison terms and heavy fines not only provocation to the use of force, but also the promulgation of any ideas which might possibly if accepted cause some one to use force.

In the past the American law has shown little sensitiveness to revolutionary utterances in time of peace, and has wisely treated most fulminations against the social fabric like a pot-shot at a man ten miles away. However, as Judge Hand pointed out,[17] all vigorous criticism of the form of government or the economic system or particular laws may by arousing passion or engendering conviction of the iniquity of existing conditions lead indirectly to violence. Even an ardent oration urging the repeal of a statute may lead hearers to disobey it. We are always tempted to apprehend such results from opinions to which we are opposed. It is easy to believe that doctrines very different from our own are so objectionable that they could

[17] See p. 46, *supra*.

only come into operation through force, so that their advocates must necessarily favor criminal acts. The difference between the expression of radical views and direct provocation to revolution is only a difference of degree, but it is a difference which the normal criminal law regards as all-important.

There are always men who want the law to go much farther and nip opinions in the bud before they become dangerous because they may eventually be dangerous. Thus, when Colley Cibber produced his adaptation of "Richard III," the Master of the Revels expunged the whole first act, fearing that the distresses of Henry VI would put weak people too much in mind of James II, also exiled in France.[18] Such an attitude is particularly common in a period of unrest like 1919, especially during a foreign revolution or after assassinations, when coercion and violence follow each other in a vicious circle. We have seen how George III's judges transported men who wanted to abolish rotten boroughs and the limited franchise, because if the people of Great Britain possessed the same privileges as the French they might destroy the Constitution and imitate the Reign of Terror. Restoration France, after the assassination of the Duc de Berri, passed a law to suppress any journal "if the spirit resulting from a succession of articles would be of a nature to cause injury to the public peace and the stability of constitutional institutions." It was only with the disappearance of these *proces de tendance* that the press once more became free, and under the Republic one could urge a change in the form of government to monarchy or empire with impunity.[19]

Abolition of slavery could never be mentioned in the antebellum South because it might cause a negro uprising. A similar sensitiveness to possible bad results led to the prohibition of "Mrs. Warren's Profession" and "September Morn." Since almost any controversial opinion has some dangerous tendencies, it is obvious that its suppression on that account

---

[18] Johnson's *Lives of the Poets* (ed. G. B. Hill), III, 292 n.

[19] A. Esmein, *Éléments de droit constitutionnel* (6 ed.), 1145, 1149. Ernst Freund in 19 *New Republic* 14 (May 3, 1919). In the same way the New York post-office objected to the general tenor and animus of *The Masses* as seditious without specifying any particular portion as objectionable, although the periodical offered to excerpt any matter so pointed out. — Masses Pub. Co. v. Patten, 244 Fed. 535, 536, 543 (1917).

puts an end to thorough discussion. Writings which do not actually urge illegal acts should never be made criminal except perhaps in great emergencies like war or revolt when the mere statement of the author's view creates a clear and present danger of injurious acts. In time of peace the limitation of the punishment of speech to direct provocation to crime is the essential element of the freedom of the press.

The normal criminal law is willing to run risks for the sake of open discussion, believing that truth will prevail over falsehood if both are given a fair field, and that argument and counter-argument are the best method which man has devised for ascertaining the right course of action for individuals or a nation. It holds that error is its own cure in the end, and the worse the error, the sooner it will be rejected. Attorney General Gregory defended the Espionage Act on the ground that propaganda is especially dangerous in a country governed by public opinion.[20] I believe this to be wholly wrong. Free discussion will expose the lies and fallacies of propaganda, while in a country where opinion is suppressed propaganda finds subterranean channels where it cannot be attacked by its opponents.

Russia under the Czar took no risks. It was afraid to wait for a clear and present danger of violence. It put the ax to the root of the tree. Five powerful methods were developed to reach anarchy and revolution in their earliest stages. The government censored and suppressed books and periodicals; it raided houses and seized men and their papers without process; it prosecuted them for their expression of opinions and for their membership in radical societies; it deported them to Siberia or abroad; it devised ingenious methods of weeding them out of the Duma.

These are not American methods. During the whole of the nineteenth century, not one of them was used against radicals in the United States. It is the American habit to take a chance on queer and objectionable opinions. Roger Williams did it when he discarded religious qualifications for office and citizenship, which even England was afraid to abandon wholly for another two hundred and fifty years. It is easy for us to forget now what a tremendous risk the founder of Rhode Island was

[20] Report of the Attorney General, 1918, p. 21.

thought to run and did run in those days of wild beliefs. The "livelie experiment" of religious freedom described in the Charter, which it was much on his heart to hold forth, was a very lively experiment indeed in its early years. And in the past the same courage has marked our policy toward radicalism. Anarchy and communism are nothing new in this country — we have had them in all varieties, foreign and domestic, since the days of Brook Farm until we lived safely through thirty-four years of Emma Goldman. The normal law, which refrains from punishing words for their bad political tendency, has carried us through far worse crises than the period following the armistice. In the midst of the great railroad strikes of 1877, when unemployment was very large, a big communist meeting was permitted in New York. The Seventh Regiment was kept in a conspicuous readiness to put down any actual disorder, but there was no interference with anything that was said. The speakers indulged in the wildest kind of talk, but it fell flat on the meeting just because there was no chance for a row.[21] Arthur Woods used the same wise policy when he became police commissioner of New York City during the hard times of the summer of 1914. Under his predecessor the police had been breaking up anarchistic meetings in Union Square every Saturday afternoon and the feeling was excited, defiant, and bitter. Threats were not disguised that since the police had "acted like agents of the capitalists," the crowds would come next time prepared to answer clubs and revolvers with bombs. Mr. Woods took office, and told the police to interfere in any actual disturbance, but not otherwise. Next Saturday, a large force of police was held within available distance, and a hundred plain-clothes men were scattered singly through the meeting, on the watch for signs of violence so that they could nip any attempt in the bud, but beyond that they were only to try to maintain an atmosphere of quiet and calm and radiate good nature. Mr. Woods says:

The change of method was almost unbelievably successful. There was no disorder; the crowd was very large but very well behaved, and at the end of the meeting when everything was over and many had gone home, three cheers were proposed and given for the police.

[21] J. F. Rhodes, *History of the United States*, VIII, 41.

A significant though less exciting incident occurred in Bowling Green Park. An earnest young woman was urging revolution to a noonday crowd calmly puffing their cigars in the spring sunshine, when one listener began to object to her continuing. The crowd at once closed in, and trouble seemed imminent. The policeman on duty walked up to the listener, who said, "Do you hear what she's saying, officer? Why don't you stop her? If you don't, I will." "Now see here," the policeman replied, "she isn't violating any law, and as long as she doesn't, I'm going to protect her in her meeting. If you want to hold a meeting, go over to the other side of the street, and I'll protect you too." [22]

This courage, this tolerance, this friendly coöperation between government and people, with its visible creation of loyalty, this is the true Americanism. And the issue before us today is whether in a period of prosperity and tremendous demand for labor we shall throw overboard the American laws and the American methods which carried us safely through the turbulent early years of our history, through Reconstruction, through panics and Populism with its widespread agitation among the native-born population, and shall now shaking and shivering in every wind of doctrine that blows from Bolshevist Russia imitate even in part any of the five methods with which Czarist Russia fought radicalism up to the day of her stupendous ruin.

To this issue in its various aspects I shall devote almost all of the remainder of this book.

The interpretation of freedom of speech which I have endeavored to establish in the opening chapter applies in peace as in war. The various interests, individual and social, must once more be balanced against one another with full regard to the social interests in progress and the attainment and dissemination of truth. The resultant boundary-line of permissible speech is drawn back of the point where overt acts of injury to the state occur but not far from that point. The test laid down by the United States Supreme Court in the Schenck case still holds good:

The question in every case is whether the words used are used in such circumstances and are of such a nature as to create a clear and

[22] Arthur Woods, *Policeman and Public*, pp. 73–78.

present danger that they will bring about the substantive evils that Congress (or the state legislature) has a right to prevent.

The power of the government to restrict discussion is undoubtedly less in time of peace than in time of war because war opens dangers that do not exist at other times. The strength of the state in war time is chiefly occupied in fighting the enemy. In a great war the chances of success are uncertain, and a slight set-back due to hostile opinion at home may cause defeat. It is hard enough for the government to resist the human desire not to enlist and not to fight, without outside incitement from adverse views of the war. Thus, there are very plausible reasons for limiting the social interest for which I earnestly contend, the need of continuous contact with the facts and with sound conclusions. In peace, however, the social interest mainly affected by discussion is not the sorely-beset endeavor to save the country from a powerful enemy, but the interest in order. With this interest the mass of the population earnestly sympathizes. It is protected by an enormous body of otherwise unoccupied police and soldiers, who are now available to check any actual violence. This interest in order is not opposed by troops and guns from abroad but only by words, which it can afford to tolerate, confident in the support of public opinion. In war an evil and wholly unfounded opposition at home may upset the state. In peace, those who love disorder for its own sake are so few that a revolution is improbable unless there are very strong reasons for discontent. If the agitation is without merit the state can afford to ignore it. If it has merit the state cannot afford to suppress it without a hearing. Consequently, in peace governmental interference should be delayed as in the New York meeting of 1877 until the last possible moment before violence occurs.

Sometimes in peace other social interests besides order come into play and strengthen the case for restriction. Thus, the interest in morals is concerned with moving-picture plays and books for the young. Street meetings may interfere with the public traffic besides causing a greater probability of violence than do books. Once more, it is a question of balancing the interests, and it may be worth while to arrange for meetings in less-used side streets in the noon-hour or in specified public parks, even at some sacrifice of traffic. After all, a democracy may wisely refuse to regard the streets only as a place where people exercise and go out to make money. Parades and soap-box orators and big meetings make them an open-air school, which prepares directly for citizenship.

The state anarchy acts are the first break with the American tradition in time of peace. Most of them are not willing to run any risk as to opinions generally considered objectionable, but make opinions in themselves and for their own sake a crime, although there is no direct and dangerous interference with order and only a remote possibility that violence will ensue. The first chapter has shown the evils of bad political tendency as a test of criminality. These statutes in large part revive that test, and are not directed against bad acts, but are designed to protect the minds of grown men and women from bad talk and bad thoughts.

4. THE RED FLAG

There are several types of state sedition statutes.[23] The simplest is the red flag law, adopted by thirty-two states by 1920 (and one more in 1921). The New York statute [24] makes it a misdemeanor to display the banner "in any public assembly or parade as a symbol or emblem of any organization or association, or in furtherance of any political, social, or economic principle, doctrine or propaganda." Other states go much further and forbid the display of the red flag anywhere. Some shrewdly guard against the wearing of red neckties or buttons or the evasive adoption of a green flag [25] by punishing the use of any emblem of any hue if it is "distinctive of bolshevism, anarchism, or radical socialism"; [26] or indicates "sympathy or support of ideals, institutions, or forms of government, hostile, inimical, or antagonistic to the form or spirit of the constitution, laws, ideals, and institutions of this state or of

[23] All the state legislation mentioned in this chapter is listed in Appendix III.

[24] N. Y. Laws, 1919, c. 409; now N. Y. Penal Law, § 2095-a. This was held unconstitutional by a lower court in 1934. People v. Altman, 241 App. Div. 858.

[25] Testimony of Inspector Tunney and Raymond Robins, in *Bolshevik Propaganda*, II, 838.

[26] Kans. Laws, 1919, c. 184; now Kans. Gen. Stat., 1935, §§ 21 — 1305-6.

the United States." [27] It is plain to any lawyer that when a vague and very wide range of commonplace and harmless conduct is made criminal merely on the basis of a bad intention, a man is condemned for his thoughts and nothing else. He may never have expressed those thoughts until they were brought out under cross-examination in a sedition trial. He is convicted simply by the jury's guess at the inside of his head. Men should be punished for what they do and not for what they think.

The way in which the red flag causes disorder is explained by Inspector Thomas J. Tunney, who played a prominent part in the Abrams case and certainly cannot be considered unduly favorable to radicals:

SENATOR OVERMAN. What effect does that red flag have on a crowd?

MR. TUNNEY. It has the effect of creating a feeling on the part of Americans that they would like to assassinate everybody carrying the red flag; or at least, a large number of them feel that way.

SENATOR OVERMAN. What effect does it have on the people who are in sympathy with carrying the red flag?

MR. TUNNEY. It simply enthuses them, and they indulge in cheering and waving it in the air.[28]

Since any gathering of radicals is likely to be attacked, the easiest way to preserve the peace is to forbid and break up such gatherings. Therefore, it may be contended that a meeting which is not otherwise illegal may become so solely because it will excite violent and unlawful opposition.[29] This is the doctrine of the long-beard case over again. Let us see how it works out with respect to meetings. The Salvation Army holds a service in a public place, knowing that a mock-organization called the Skeleton Army intends to molest it. The Skeleton Army appears, and begins to throw stones. The members of the Salvation Army are arrested by the police for holding an

[27] W. Va. Laws, 1919, c. 24; now W. Va. Code, 1937, §§ 5913–14. See also Wash. Laws, 1919, c. 181; now Rem. Rev. Stat. Wash., 1932, §§ 2563 — 7–8.
[28] *Bolshevik Propaganda*, pp. 10, 11.
[29] See Dicey, *Law of the Constitution*, chap. vii, "The Right of Public Meeting." The Salvation Army case is Beatty *v.* Gillbanks, 9 Q. B. D. 308 (1882). German opera riots, Star Opera *v.* Hylan, 109 N. Y. Misc. 132 (1919), discussed in 18 *Michigan Law Review* 245 and 34 *Harvard Law Review* at 397. Opposed to my view of red flag riots, P. *v.* Burman, 154 Mich. 150 (1908).

unlawful assembly. Obviously they must be released. Their guilt cannot be determined by the intolerance of wrong-doers. Apart from the question of permits, and special regulation by ordinances and statutes, the police cannot treat a meeting as unlawful simply because it may probably or naturally lead others to attack it. And if a permit is refused on that ground alone, a small number of intolerant men by passing the word around that they intend to start a riot can prevent any kind of meeting, not only of radicals who want a revolution, but of socialists, of moderates like the Committee of '48, of negroes, of novel religious sects, of Freemasons in an anti-masonic community. Indeed, on any such theory a gathering which expressed the sentiment of a majority of law-abiding citizens would become illegal because a small gang of hoodlums threatened to invade the hall. The proper remedy for these emergencies is police protection, to which men are entitled in public places, whether they are there singly or in groups.

There is, however, a well-recognized exception to this principle. If the meeting is going to cause trouble, not just because of the unpopularity of its views but because it expresses them in offensive ways, it may be unlawful *per se*. This is an analogy to the verbal crimes already discussed. For example, the "Pillars of Fire" were not allowed by the Mayor of Plainfield, New Jersey, to hold street meetings for abusing Roman Catholics. They must hire a hall where no one would be forced to listen to them. It is sometimes supposed that a parade displaying the red flag is illegal at common law for the same reason that it would be if it carried an abusive caricature of the Pope, but the situations are not truly parallel. The red flag is not offensive in itself. Nobody minds it at an auction sale or a railroad crossing. The onslaught is not on an object but on the unpopular ideas of those who carry it, because most of us consider that such ideas have a tendency to produce injury in the future. This only brings us back to the point that a meeting is not illegal just for unpopularity. Bad tendency must not be a test of criminality.

The policy behind even the mildest form of the red flag legislation resembles the rule of the British Government that the Uganda tribes must not wear war-paint except on the chief's birthday. If Americans cannot be trusted any more than African natives to avoid the psychological effects of color, well and good. So far, the exact meaning of the red flag seems rather obscure. Some explain it thus:

The red flag means revolution, nothing else. It means bloodshed; it cannot be interpreted otherwise.[30]

Others say it stands for the brotherhood of workingmen throughout the world.[31] It might be desirable to find out which is right before we forbid it. There is no doubt that its display is sometimes accompanied by much lawlessness — chiefly on the part of the supporters of law and order. Until the opponents of force can restrain themselves from mobbing any parade which carries a red flag, it may be wise to prohibit its use. We ought to remember, however, that if it is made a forbidden symbol its emotional appeal when displayed in secret is immeasurably heightened.

Massachusetts once had a law prohibiting a red or black flag. This was repealed because it made the Harvard crimson illegal. It is to be hoped that other portions of this land of the brave will also be willing to face valiantly a piece of cloth. There is much merit in the North Dakotan remark that the only animal that is afraid of a red flag has a fence around him.

The man who insists on waving the red flag on all occasions has just as little common sense. Those who want to remake society on a basis of fellowship and mutual agreement may fairly be asked to begin by yielding something to the wishes of their neighbors. It is an undoubted fact that most people do dislike seeing the red flag in a parade or over a building, but if the Stars and Stripes are beside it nearly all their objection vanishes. A decent respect for the opinions of mankind ought to lead the radical to do this much for the happiness of others. Even if he is so thoroughly a man without a country that he has no attachment for the government which guards

[30] Hayden, J., in Roxbury Riot trials of May, 1919, as reported in *Boston Herald*; see Rugg, C.J., in Comm. *v*. Karvonen, 219 Mass. 30 (1914).

[31] This is the explanation of all radicals whom I have questioned. It is confirmed by the expert and conservative opinion of Professor Samuel N. Harper, *Bolshevik Propaganda*, p. 101: "I think it is little more than a tradition . . . representing this mental protest . . . against what they consider the injustices of the present organization of society."

his home and educates his children, at least like a foreign vessel in our ports he might out of courtesy raise our banner beside his own. I do not believe that a man should be arrested for carrying a solitary red flag in the street any more than for wearing a sweater at a dance, but ordinary politeness ought to keep him from doing either. Surely, it is worth while for the radical to take the conciliatory step I suggest, and thus produce a friendlier atmosphere in the mass of the population, which may gain converts for his views and will certainly induce many thoughtful men to coöperate with him in the more moderate of his schemes for a better world.[32]

5. CRIMINAL ANARCHY AND CRIMINAL SYNDICALISM

A much more important group of statutes takes its origin from the New York Anarchy Act of 1902, which was enacted soon after the assassination of President McKinley.[33] Criminal anarchy is there defined as "the doctrine that organized government should be overthrown by force or violence, or by assassination . . . , or by any unlawful means." It is a felony to advocate this doctrine by speech or writing, and to join any society or any meeting for teaching or advocating it. The act can be rigorously enforced, because the owner or person in charge of any room or building who knowingly permits a meeting therein is severely punished, and the editor or proprietor of a periodical or publisher of a book which contains anarchistic matter is liable unless it was printed without his knowledge and authority and disavowed immediately. This statute lay idle for nearly twenty years,[34] but there have been several prosecutions in the winter of 1919–20. Especially significant is the sentence of Benjamin Gitlow, a former Socialist member of the New York Assembly, to an imprisonment of five to ten years for advocacy of a general strike.[35] The Washington statute

[32] Red-flag laws were held partially invalid in Stromberg v. California, 283 U. S. 359 (1931), discussed in Chapter XI, section 1; In re Hartman, 182 Cal. 447 (1920) (Los Angeles ordinance); People v. Altman, supra, note 24. Compare Comm. v. Karvonen, supra, note 30.

[33] N. Y. Penal Law, §§ 160–166.

[34] The only case was a slander suit, in which "anarchist" was held a charge of crime. Von Gerichten v. Seitz, 94 App. Div. 130 (1904). For similar defamation suits in other states, based on charges of radicalism, see 51 A. L. R. 1071 (1927).

[35] The later phases of this important case, which went to the United States Supreme Court, are discussed in Chapter IX.

of 1909 is very similar, but also makes it criminal to circulate
any document having a tendency to encourage the commission of any breach of the peace or disrespect for law or any
court. The ridiculous possibilities of such legislation are proved
by the conviction of one Fox for encouraging disrespect for
law by an article, "The Nude and the Prudes," declaring
bathing suits superfluous. Justice Holmes found nothing unconstitutional in the prosecution, but caustically remarked, "Of
course, we have nothing to do with the wisdom of the defendant,
the prosecution, or the act." [36] The first danger to be avoided
in legislation against sedition is the imposition of heavy penál-
ties for slight offenses. Such penalties create that very hatred
of our system of laws which it is our object to avoid.

Another pre-war statute, in New Jersey, punishing the advocacy of unlawful destruction of property or injury to persons,
is much more restricted in its scope, and has been construed
to enact the common law of criminal solicitation with an increased penalty. It was used to punish labor leaders in Paterson who urged clubbing strike-breakers out of the silk mills
and using chemicals and other devices to make the product
unmerchantable.[37] The Massachusetts anti-anarchy act of
1919 is very similar; it specifically penalizes the advocacy of
killing, destruction of property, or violent revolution.[38] This
Massachusetts act was reduced to its present form by repeated
protests from liberals. Instead of legislating against anarchy
and other radical doctrines as opinions, the Massachusetts and
New Jersey statutes prohibit incitement to definite serious
criminal acts. Such codifications of the common law serve
some desirable purpose in letting speakers and writers know
what they must not do. If these statutes are construed strictly
like other penal statutes and applied with common sense and

[36] Wash. Laws, 1909, c. 249, §§ 311–316; now Rem. Rev. Stat. Wash., 1932,
§§ 2562–63, 2564–68; State v. Fox, 71 Wash. 185 (1912); Fox v. Washington,
236 U. S. 273 (1915).

[37] N. J. Laws, 1908, c. 278; now 2 N. J. Stat. Ann. §§ 173 — 10–11. Some
of the New Jersey cases show that even such a narrow statute may be mis-
applied by the trial courts.

[38] Mass. Laws, 1919, c. 191; now Mass. G. L. (1932), c. 264, § 11. This
statute has lain practically idle for twenty-two years since its passage. The
only prosecution known to me was against Bimba in 1926; and this was dropped
during his appeal from a fine of $100. See Chafee, *The Inquiring Mind*, pp.
108 ff.

a realization, as Charles Evans Hughes put it, that "Hyde Park meetings and soap-box oratory constitute the most efficient safety-valve against resort by the discontented to physical force," [39] then they will enable New Jersey and Massachusetts to deal vigorously with any real danger of lawlessness without at the same time turning revolutionary opinions into crimes.

Most of the legislation between 1917 and 1920 has, however, been far more extensive. About one third of the states have applied the New York statutory scheme to the new crime of criminal syndicalism, which (to quote the much enforced California statute) is the "doctrine . . . advocating, teaching or aiding and abetting the commission of crime, sabotage [herein defined], or unlawful acts of force and violence or unlawful methods of terrorism as a means of accomplishing a change in industrial ownership or control, or effecting any political change." (A few states add "or for profit.") The advocacy of this doctrine by spoken or written words or personal conduct, the issue or circulation of any book or document teaching the doctrine, and membership in any organization which advocates it are among the offenses punishable by imprisonment for ten years or longer. These acts are almost uniform in phraseology, Idaho having apparently supplied the original model. Some states depart from this type into much vaguer language. Thus, Arizona in an act which Governor Hunt allowed to become law without being willing to put his name to it makes it criminal to advocate the violation of "the constitutional or statutory rights of another as a means of accomplishing industrial or political ends." [40] Montana punishes in peace all the non-military crimes mentioned in the federal Espionage Act of 1918 as well as "any language calculated to incite or inflame resistance to any duly constituted state authority." [41] West Virginia makes criminal any teachings in sympathy with or favor of "ideals hostile to those now or henceforth existing under the constitution and laws of this state." [42]

[39] Brief for N. Y. Socialist Assemblymen, p. 41 (see Chapter VI).

[40] Ariz. Laws, 1918, sp., c. 13; repealed in 1928.

[41] Mont. Laws, 1919, c. 77; now Rev. Codes Mont., 1935, §§ 10737–39. On the 1918 Espionage Act, see *supra*, Chapter II, section 1.

[42] W. Va. Code, 1937, § 5912; see note 27.

These are but brief extracts from the legislation which was enacted or invoked in almost every state between 1917 and 1920. These statutes are, for the most part, different from the normal criminal law in three ways: (1) they label opinions as objectionable and punish them for their own sake because of supposedly bad tendencies without any consideration of the probability of criminal acts; (2) they impose severe penalties for the advocacy of small offenses as much as for serious crimes; (3) they establish a practical censorship of the press *ex post facto*. These statutes are no dead letter. In several states prosecutions have been numerous, and maximum sentences often imposed.[43]

In addition, city ordinances have occasionally been proposed or enacted against radicals. Mayor Hylan of New York wanted an ordinance to punish owners of buildings permitting an assemblage advocating "policies tending to incite the minds of people to a proposition likely to breed a disregard for law," and a Boston ordinance to forbid the display of anything that was sacrilegious or tended to promote immorality was also unsuccessful, but the Mayor of Toledo is said to have prohibited any meeting anywhere in the city "where it is suspected a man of radical tendencies will speak." An ordinance in Eureka, California, made it unlawful to distribute membership cards, pamphlets, handbills, or songs of the organization "known as the Industrial Workers of the World, or the I.W.W.," under a penalty of $500 fine or six months imprisonment or both.[44]

The problem of the constitutionality of the state anarchy and syndicalism acts varies with different types of provisions: (1) Some clauses seem directed against a "clear and present danger" of unlawful conduct within the Supreme Court's test in the Schenck case, although the punishments may be unnecessarily severe. The open and direct advocacy of assassination, sabotage, and destruction of property surely satisfies this

---

[43] Illinois and New York were active up to 1920. Since 1920 prosecutions have been especially numerous in California and Oregon. See *infra* Chapter X, section I, on the California statute. The Oregon statute was repealed in 1937. For United States Supreme Court decisions on these state statutes see Chapters IX, X, section II, and XI, sections V and VI.

[44] This ordinance was held invalid in an interesting opinion by Hart, J. *In re* Campbell, 64 Cal. App. 300 (1923).

test; and some other doctrines of revolutionary syndicalism, although more vague and much less likely to be realized in action, probably lie within the range of legislative discretion. At any rate, state courts seem very unlikely to declare such kinds of speech protected by their constitutions. The worse the nature of the threats, the more their emptiness is disregarded by judges. (2) On the other hand, the clauses of syndicalism statutes which make it criminal *ipso facto* to belong to an organization like the Industrial Workers of the World, although the accused has never expressed any agreement with the violent portions of its economic theory, raise serious difficulties. This is not punishing a man for what he does, or even for what he says, but for what some one else says, which he may possibly not approve. There are so many reasons why a workman is led to join the labor union to which his fellows belong, that the law should hesitate to attribute to him an active support of every plank in its platform. (3) When the anarchy acts go still farther and punish discussions of a remote general strike, or condemn words and symbols which are inoffensive in themselves, for their bad social, economic, or political tendencies, they clearly infringe the danger-test and ought to be declared void.[45]

But I do not think we ought to let the discussion of sedition laws turn on the controversy whether they are unconstitutional. The free speech clauses, as I said at the outset of this book, are a declaration of American policy as well as an extreme limit upon legislative power. Even if the statute be constitutional, the most important questions still remain: (1) whether it is wise and expedient and in accord with American traditions; (2) how it shall be construed. What I have already said about the state anarchy and syndicalism statutes has

---

[45] For numerous state cases upholding validity, see Notes, 1 A. L. R. 336, 20 *id.* 1535; 73 *id.* 1494 (and supplementary annotations). An alien was held to have no constitutional right of free speech in State *v.* Sinchuk, 96 Conn. 605 (1921), disapproved in 31 *Yale Law Journal* 422 and in 20 *Michigan Law Review* 538.

Sedition statutes were considered invalid by state judges in State *v.* Diamond, 27 N. M. 477 (1921); dissenting opinions in State *v.* Tachin, 93 N. J. L. 485 (1919); State *v.* Gabriel, 95 N. J. L. 337 (1921); *Ex parte* Meckel, 87 Tex. Cr. 120 (1920) (war statute). See 20 *Columbia Law Review* 232 (1920).

As to United States Supreme Court decisions, see Chapters IX, X, and XI. On guilt by association, see Chapter XII, section 1.

bearing on these two points; but the problem of sound policy is even more important for every thoughtful American in considering a federal peace-time Sedition Law.

6. THE FEDERAL SEDITION BILLS OF 1919–1920

Nothing less than a very great national danger should lead us to abandon the American policy of courage and tolerance and reënact the first Sedition Act in time of peace since the disaster of 1798. The burden of proof rests fairly on those who advocate such a doubtful step. It has already been shown that it is not called for by any immediate danger of revolution, since the Criminal Code will deal with that, and indeed what has been said of the enormously exaggerated accounts of pro-German plots during the war ought to show that any "Red menace" is probably a similar panic.

If the Attorney General had limited himself to proposing a statute punishing successful and unsuccessful attacks upon federal officials and property, he would have performed a real service in filling gaps in the federal law against violence. Legislation against his hypothetical man who approaches the Chief Justice with a bomb in his hand would not affect freedom of speech. But Mr. Palmer asked much more than this when he sought to legislate out of existence various kinds of theories and doctrines, on the ground that they might conceivably lead to future assaults and revolutions. In a circular letter sent to the editors of leading magazines, the Attorney General said:

The Department, as far as existing laws allow, intends to keep up an unflinching war against this movement no matter how cloaked or dissembled. We are determined that this movement will not be permitted to go far enough in this country to disturb our peace or create any widespread distrust of the people's government.

There is a menace in this country. It may not be the menace of revolution. . . . My one desire is to acquaint people like you with the real menace of evil-thinking which is the foundation of the Red movement.[46]

Besides the draft Sedition Act recommended by the Attorney General, which went so far as to punish writings which "tend

[46] Reprinted in 110 *Nation* 190 (February 14, 1920).

to indicate sedition," Congress had about seventy similar bills under consideration during the winter of 1919–20. The House Judiciary Committee recommended for immediate enactment a measure with a death penalty and a sweeping postal censorship. Other bills imposed a maximum of twenty years in prison for unlawful discussion; in addition aliens were to be deported, and naturalized citizens were to be denaturalized and turned loose on the world as men without a country. Indeed, Senator McKellar of Tennessee wanted to go one step farther and deport native-born Americans to a penal colony in Guam, so that we also might have our Devil's Island or Siberia.

Energetic opposition to all these bills by the American Federation of Labor and many kinds of other organizations and by the most conservative newspapers and periodicals prevented any of them from becoming law. Congress adjourned in June, 1920, without any enactment.

In order to raise the problems of a federal peacetime Sedition Act fairly, I am going to assume for purposes of discussion that Congress may eventually have before it a very simple measure, from which all the obviously objectionable features of the bills just described will be eliminated. This hypothetical bill is limited by its terms to the advocacy of (1) assassination of federal officials; and (2) the use of "force or violence" for the overthrow of our government or all governments, or the attainment of changes in our Constitution and laws. It punishes the individual who urges such "force or violence" orally or in writing, and also any one who imports from abroad or transports from state to state any book or other printed matter which advocates such "force or violence." It is improbable that power will be given to the Postmaster General to exclude such material from the mails, for the strongest hostility to the bills of 1919–20 was directed to such a power. Even if it be said that the Blackstonian test does not forbid the government to control the use of its own machinery, the post-office, it is clear to every newspaper that its exclusion from the mails is equivalent to an absolute censorship. The same considerations apply to a censorship of the foreign-language press, although this presents special problems and dangers. Consequently, the bill before us for discussion imposes no previous restraint, but

makes the advocacy of "force or violence" a crime, punishable
by a long term in prison and a heavy fine.[47]

Two questions are raised. (1) How far is such a measure
constitutional? (2) How far is it wise and expedient?

7. THE CONSTITUTIONALITY OF A FEDERAL SEDITION LAW

The constitutional problem involves three points, affirmative power to punish, the treason clause, and the free speech
clause.[48]

1. What clause in the Constitution gives the United States
power to punish seditious utterances? The states face no
such difficulty, for they possess all power that is not expressly
denied to them by their constitutions, and can reach objectionable writings under their general police power and criminal
jurisdiction. The United States government, on the other hand,
has only the powers which are expressly granted to it by its
organic document. Most of the discussion in 1787–88 over
the need of a free speech clause in the federal Constitution
and most of the controversy over the constitutionality of the
Sedition Act of 1798 turned on this point. Much has happened
since, however, to indicate that the United States has this power
to punish verbal opposition unless prohibited by some negative
clause in the Constitution. The epoch-making decisions of
Marshall show that the government does not have to rely on
any one specific grant of power. The Constitution as a whole
creates a nation with officers and functions and in Article I,
section 8, gives to Congress the right "to make all laws which
shall be necessary and proper for carrying into execution the
foregoing powers, and all other powers vested by this Con-

[47] The sedition clauses of the Alien Registration Act of 1940, reprinted *infra*
Chapter XII, section 1, closely resemble most features of the hypothetical bill
(though the 1940 Act has a membership clause, and does not punish importation
or interstate transportation). Consequently, most of the arguments about constitutionality and wisdom in the rest of this chapter apply to the federal
statute in force in 1941.

[48] For a full discussion with citation of cases, see H. W. Biklé, "The Jurisdiction of the United States over Seditious Libel," 41 *American Law Register*
(N. S.) 1 (1902). His conclusions as to the First Amendment differ very
much from mine. See also Wallace, "Constitutionality of Sedition Laws," 6
Virginia Law Review 385 (1920); Hart, "Power of Government over Speech
and Press," 29 *Yale Law Journal* 410 (1920).

stitution in the government of the United States, or in any department or officer thereof." Consequently, no express provision is required to enable the government to operate one or more national banks, or exclude aliens from its shores. Its courts can punish contempts committed against them. The United States Supreme Court has already decided in the Neagle case that the federal government has power to protect the lives of its judges engaged in the discharge of judicial duties, and in other decisions that it can safeguard even prisoners in its custody. The same principle applies to the President or any other official, and it seems immaterial whether they are at the moment occupied with business. Their work may be hindered by threats and other utterances as well as by acts. Similarly, words which interfere with express functions of the government like the war power fall within its criminal jurisdiction. The conviction of Emma Goldman for issuing pamphlets urging disobedience to the draft, and all the Espionage Act cases prove this beyond question. It is of course true that revolutionary speeches do not affect any specific function of the government, but they do affect its existence, the most important result of the Constitution. Therefore, on this point I conclude that the United States has affirmative power to protect its own life and the lives of its officers, not only from revolution and assassination, but also from attempts and solicitation directed toward these ends, and even from discussion which might have a remote tendency to produce such evils, unless that power is restricted by either the treason clause or the First Amendment.

2. Section 3 of Article III, which relates to the judicial power of the United States, provides:

Treason against the United States, shall consist only in levying War against them, or in adhering to their Enemies, giving them Aid and Comfort. No Person shall be convicted of Treason unless on the Testimony of two Witnesses to the same overt Act, or on Confession in open Court. The Congress shall have Power to declare the Punishment of Treason, but no Attainder of Treason shall work Corruption of Blood, or Forfeiture except during the Life of the Person attainted.

We can here disregard the question what is treason in war when there are "enemies." In peace, treason is narrowly limited in this country to "levying war," and Chief Justice Marshall decided in the case of Aaron Burr that that crime requires an actual assemblage of forces. Consequently, the conduct we have in mind is not punishable as treason under our Constitution. Does this prevent it from being punishable otherwise? Under the English treason statute of Edward III, very many kinds of action which interfered with the state were defined as treason. The courts construed these clauses very widely to reach as "constructive treasons" conduct very remote from the defined crimes.[49] This practice became so notorious that the framers of the Constitution wisely prevented it by rejecting most of the English categories and narrowly restricting the evidence on which conviction can be secured. Can Congress accomplish these undesired results by calling the same conduct, not treason, but sedition or something else?

For example, under the English statute it was treason to "compass or imagine the death of our lord the king." This was interpreted to include threats against him. By analogy, it would be treason to threaten the life of the President, if our Constitution had not definitely provided otherwise. Congress in 1917 created the crime of threats against the President.[50] Is such a statute an unconstitutional evasion of the treason clause?

Again, if the *Biglow Papers* were not "aid and comfort to the enemy" — a problem to which I shall return in the sixth chapter — could Congress treat them as severely as if they were treasonable by creating the crime of seditious libel with a punishment of death? A similar question was put to the counsel for the United States in the Abrams case by Justice Brandeis, who got the reply, "Of course, we wouldn't go that far." But if Congress and the Department of Justice have power to go that far, the value of the treason clause is considerably weakened. All the acts which were constructive treasons under the English law could be made criminal without even the security of two witnesses or the provisions against corruption of the blood and forfeiture.

On the other hand, it is argued that the treason clause is

---

[49] Stephen, *History of the Criminal Law*, vol. II, chap. xxiii, on High Treason. As to treason in war, see *infra*, Chapter VI, section II.

[50] Discussed *infra*, at note 64.

not placed among the restrictions on Congress. It simply prevents the courts from construing the word "treason" in a statute to extend beyond the constitutional definition, even if the statute gives it a wider definition. Congress is not prohibited from punishing on other grounds and under other names crimes which were treason in England, if these are within the federal criminal jurisdiction. The same act might be both treason and something else. Thus killing the king was treason and murder. Congress can punish the murder of the President but not the treason. Or rather, it can punish it not as murder, but as an interference with an express function of the government. It is settled that the United States can prevent assaults on federal judges, though that is analogous to treason in England. Counterfeiting money was treason there, and is punishable under here as a different crime by the express provision in Article I, section 8, of the Constitution. The Espionage Act, which rests on the war power, was held applicable in the Frohwerk case to conduct which was treason in England.[51]

This argument seems to me more satisfactory when applied to active interferences with specific functions of the government lying within express powers of Congress than when extended to utterances which have a tendency to weaken the sovereignty of the state as a whole. Are they treason in England plus something else? Was it not this tendency to weaken the government which made them constructive treason, and when they cannot be criminal on that account, does not all ground of jurisdiction fail?

This is a problem somewhat foreign to my province, so that I prefer not to state a definite conclusion, which can only be reached after more judicial interpretation of the treason clause.

3. The First Amendment seems clearly to be violated by many clauses in federal sedition bills of 1919–20, which punish words merely for their assumed tendency to produce bad consequences in the remote future, for instance, a heavy penalty on "printed matter . . . whereby the use of force . . . is . . . defended . . . as a means towards the accomplishment

---

[51] Frohwerk v. United States, 249 U. S. at 210 (1919).

of industrial, economic, social, or political change, or whereby
an appeal is made to racial prejudice the intended or probable
result of which appeal is to cause rioting or the resort to force
and violence within the United States . . . ." The first clause
would affect every history of the American Revolution, Macaulay's *History of England*, and W. R. Thayer's *Life of Cavour*.
The second would suppress all but the most carefully guarded
presentations of the wrongs of the negro.[52] This attempt to
enlist popular support for attacks on radicalism by uniting fear
of the blacks to fear of the reds has become a favorite device
of late. Attorney General Palmer hinted that negroes must
not be allowed to join radical organizations. The Lusk Committee seized an unanswered letter *to* the Rand School suggesting the spread of socialism among the negroes (without
a word about violence) and presented it as a menacing scheme
adopted *by* the School "for the spreading of Bolshevist propaganda among negroes in the South," so that the *New York
Times* ran front-page head-lines: "Moves to Close the Rand
School — District Attorney Takes Steps Toward Revoking
Radical Institution's Charter — Planned Negro Uprising." [53]

The Sedition Act of 1798 was also a violation of the First
Amendment, especially as it included criticism of the Presi-
dent and Congress, which was very remotely injurious to the
United States.[54]

If, however, we consider a simpler federal bill such as I have
suggested, which, like the Massachusetts and New Jersey Acts
stated above, eliminates all clauses obviously punishing bad
tendency and penalizes only the advocacy of force and violence,
much more difficult questions of constitutionality arise. It
may be helpful to examine various kinds of utterances suc-
cessively. If one directly incites another to murder an official,
and the murder takes place, the speaker is, of course, punish-

[52] For restrictions of race-irritation in moving-picture films, see W. Va. Laws,
1919, c. 117; Epoch Producing Corp. *v*. Davis, 19 Ohio N. P. (N. S.) 465
(1917) (forbidding *The Birth of a Nation* in Cleveland). But see Dearborn
Pub. Co. *v*. Fitzgerald, 271 Fed. 479 (N. D. Ohio, 1921) (invalidating Cleveland
ordinance prohibiting sale of anti-Jewish newspaper).

[53] *New York Times*, June 28, 1919; see also July 9. Compare Herndon *v*.
Lowry, 301 U. S. 242 (1937), discussed in Chapter XI, section vi.

[54] See *supra*, Chapter I, at n. 58. Biklé admits it was probably invalid for
the reason stated above.

able. The same holds good even if the incitement proves un-successful. If the speaker does not solicit any particular person, but eloquently appeals to a large audience for some new Charlotte Corday, or if, naming no specific victim, he urges the assassination of an indefinite number of men from some hated group, the case is not altered. Even if he alleges the loftiest motives, the social interest in truth and progress is far outweighed by the interest in order, and there is a direct interference with the safety of life. When he does not ask for any future killing, but merely glorifies such an event in the past, the danger lessens and the power to punish becomes more uncertain.[55] The time elapsed is perhaps an element. A distinction might be drawn between praise of the assassin of McKinley and "Cæsar had his Brutus, Charles the First his Cromwell." Yet even Patrick Henry's speech might be held advocacy of force and within the hypothetical Sedition Law. A further step is the discussion of tyrannicide as an abstract proposition of morality. Mill was willing to allow the fullest liberty even for this,[56] but it is probable that assassination is so easily carried out that there is always a sufficiently clear and present danger of its occurrence to bring such discussions within the range of legislative discretion.

Advocacy of revolution is much less dangerous except in extraordinary times of great tension. The chances of success are so infinitesimal that the probability of any serious attempt following the utterances seems too slight to make them punish-able by the federal government. This is especially true if the speaker urges revolution at some future day, so that no im-mediate check is required to save the country. Even if several men talk like this with very bad intentions, they should not be held guilty of conspiracy under section 6 of the United States Criminal Code unless the danger-test is satisfied. There is no "clear and present danger" in a revolution announced for 1976.

The federal government has nothing to do with the ques-tion whether such discussion is a public nuisance or a breach of the peace under state law. Johann Most was convicted

---

[55] For opposing views on the question whether praise of a criminal can be considered incitement to crime, see Masses Pub. Co. v. Patten, 244 Fed. 535; 245 Fed. 102.

[56] Mill, *Liberty*, note at opening of chap. ii.

on both sides of the Atlantic for advocacy of assassination,[57] but those decisions are based on present injury to the peace and not on danger to the rulers. When, however, the audience joins in the speaker's inflammatory utterances the assembly becomes unlawful, and may possibly constitute a conspiracy under the federal Criminal Code. Thus Most, at a New York meeting on the morrow of the Spies executions, doomed to an early death the prosecuting attorney, the trial judge, the Supreme Court of Illinois, "the highest murderers in the land — the Supreme Court of the United States," and the Governor of Illinois. His hearers exhibited warm approval, and when he said, "The day of revolution is not far distant," one of the audience rose and said excitedly: "Why not to-night, for we are ready and prepared?" The address by itself appears to have been deemed insufficient to support a criminal prosecution, but he was convicted of participating in an unlawful assembly.[58] Possibly there was also a conspiracy within the United States Criminal Code, but the absence of any real danger to the federal government makes this improbable.

This case shows how much the danger of utterances is affected by surrounding circumstances as well as by the words used. A soap-box orator on a street-corner shouting to casual passers-by is far less perilous than if he delivers the same address in a hall overcrowded with sympathetic listeners. A pamphlet is less dangerous than any speech, a book than a pamphlet. A threat of revolution over the family tea-table is innocuous. Every one will admit that these considerations affect the wise drafting and enforcement of sedition legislation, and some at least hold that they may decrease the danger from objectionable utterances until they sink below the minimum limit of Congressional power. Thus, Freund says:

The doctrine that crime may under given conditions become justifiable or that it may have a tendency to arouse the public conscience should not in itself be held to constitute a crime. It is clear that an exposition of social wrong or injustice must be allowed, nor can the necessary liberty of agitation be said to be overstepped by appeals to sentiment rather than to reason; and if it is said that appeal to

[57] Reg. v. Most, 7 Q. B. D. 244 (1881); P. v. Most, 171 N. Y. 423 (1902).
[58] P. v. Most, 128 N. Y. 108 (1891); see Freund on the Police Power, §§ 476–478. On Spies and the Haymarket explosion, see Chapter XIII, note 12.

sentiment is appeal to passion and must lead to disorder and violence, it must be answered that this was always the plea upon which
political agitation was formerly suppressed. Not even the fact that
an adherent of the doctrine commits a crime is conclusive that the
teaching of the doctrine amounts to incitement; for the crime may
as well have been induced by a morbid brooding over conditions
which are the cause of social discontent. . . . The constitutional
guaranty of freedom of speech and press and assembly demands the
right to oppose all government and to argue that the overthrow of
government cannot be accomplished otherwise than by force. . . .
It is probably true to say . . . that it is impossible to strike at
anarchism as a doctrine without jeopardizing valuable constitutional
rights.

Nevertheless, the Abrams and Schaefer decisions in the
Supreme Court should deter any one from predicting unconstitutionality under the First Amendment for the hypothetical
statute I have been considering, which is carefully limited to
advocacy of "force and violence." The "nature of the words
used" may be held to create sufficient danger to support the
restriction on freedom of speech. Moreover, the real issues
of constitutional law, as in *Masses* v. *Patten* and the Abrams
trial, are likely to arise from a loose construction of the statute,
even if its wording is valid. Therefore, I consider it a much
more fertile subject of discussion to turn to the wisdom and
policy of a federal sedition law against the advocacy of "force
and violence."

8. THE WISDOM AND EXPEDIENCY OF A FEDERAL SEDITION LAW

> *No one knows what blasphemy is or what sedition is,*
> *but all know that they are vague words which can be*
> *fitted to any meaning that shall please the ruling powers.*
> WALTER BAGEHOT.

"No man," said Attorney General Palmer, "can go further
than I will go in his earnestness to protect the people in the
guaranty of free speech." Nevertheless, he insisted that there
must be a deadline, and this he found it easy to draw at the
place where there is a threat or promise or necessary implica-
tion of the use of physical force or violence. So long as Congress does no more than punish this sort of language, how can

any one reasonably object? The public seems at first sight to get no benefit from such talk, and clearly the speaker has no claim to encouragement. Men may well inquire how the interest of society in the attainment of truth and progress is served by threats to kill officials, blow up buildings, and bring in the dictatorship of the proletariat with a holocaust of vengeance. Consequently, the question whether a law against the advocacy of force and violence is wise may be thought to admit only of an affirmative answer.

I believe, however, that the problem is far less simple than it seems. Although the opponent of the proposed legislation apparently occupies a very bad position, that of standing up for force and violence, yet it may be possible to show that such legislation is dangerous, far more dangerous than the agitation it expects to suppress. If a federal law against violent talk and writings which create no immediate danger of injurious action is not only constitutional but highly desirable and necessary, why is it that we have had only one such law in the past, and that one a stupendous failure? Even the state laws against inflammatory utterances as breaches of the peace have been used very sparingly against soap-box orators and revolutionary literature. We have refused to make arrests unless there was a real danger that the lawlessness which was advocated would immediately take place. Surely, there · is nothing to be ashamed of in urging a continuance of this traditional American policy.

Most of us believe that our Constitution makes it possible to change all bad laws through political action. We ought to disagree vehemently with those who urge violent methods, and whenever necessary take energetic steps to prevent them from putting such methods into execution. This is a very different matter from holding that all discussion of the desirability of resorting to violence for political purposes should be ruthlessly stamped out. There is not one among us who would not join a revolution if the reason for it be made strong enough. Californians would take up arms against a constitutional amendment or treaty for the cession of California to an Oriental power. And talk about violence is far more common. Tobacco would not be prohibited like alcohol without some murmurs of a fight from the most peaceable citizens.

The United States is the last place on earth where mere talk about resistance and revolution ought to be treated as inherently vicious and intolerable. The founders of the colonies broke the religious laws of England before they came here and some of them engaged in a large-sized rebellion. The founders of the United States urged the destruction of property by the destruction of tea and the burning of stamped paper. They went further. They advocated the overthrow of this or any other government by force and violence when they adopted a well-known document which reads, "That whenever any form of government becomes destructive of these ends, it is the right of the people to alter and abolish it."

If a federal statute against the advocacy of force and violence had been enacted in the Abolition period, several distinguished citizens of Massachusetts would have been criminals. Wendell Phillips advocated opposition to the Fugitive Slave Law, and his statue is in the Public Gardens of Boston. William Lloyd Garrison did so, and his statue is on Commonwealth Avenue. The Overseers of Harvard College dismissed a law teacher, Edward G. Loring, because he carried out his oath of office as United States Commissioner by enforcing that law, and for the same reason both houses of the Massachusetts legislature requested the Governor to remove him from a probate judgeship, and he was removed. Theodore Parker, George L. Stearns, Thomas Wentworth Higginson, and Frank B. Sanborn contributed funds to send John Brown to Harper's Ferry to use force and violence.

These men believed that some bad laws are so powerfully supported that the only way to obtain their repeal is to violate them. They believed that no decent man could sit silent and inactive while the Fugitive Slave Law was enforced. Perhaps they were all of them wrong. Some of them were clearly liable as accessories to criminal acts. I insist that such acts must be punished, however noble the motive. But we cannot honor and praise these men for their courageous onslaughts on established evils, and at the same time pronounce it a heinous crime for any one today to urge the removal of wrongs by force. Above all, we cannot draw a distinction between those days and ours on the ground that the government was bad then and is now good. I believe that to be true, but time alone will prove which is right, the left-wing Socialist or I. We must not forget how Braxfield justified his ferocious sentences by saying that the British Constitution of 1794 was the best in the world. The law and order men of 1774 and 1854 did not consider their governments and laws bad. They would have been glad to incarcerate Otis and Adams, Garrison and Sumner, if they had had a sedition act in force. Yet the advocates of repression in those days were not a race of tyrants. They were respectable citizens just like ourselves. They were merely mistaken. Can we be any more sure of our infallibility than of theirs? And how do we know that we are infallible until we hear the men on the other side, however excitable and given to threats?

This is not indifferentism. We must take our stand for private property if we believe in it, put our backs to the wall, and fight for it with all our strength. Nevertheless, there are many ways of fighting. The American policy is to meet force by force, and talk by talk.

Furthermore, as soon as the danger-test is abandoned, bad tendency inevitably becomes the standard of criminality. Any attempt to distinguish between liberty and license will break down in administration for sheer vagueness, and sooner or later officials will swing toward the view of Lord Holt in 1704:

If men should not be called to account for possessing the people with an ill opinion of the government, no government can subsist; for it is very necessary for every government, that the people should have a good opinion of it. And nothing can be worse to any government, than to endeavor to produce animosities as to the management of it. This has always been looked upon as a crime, and no government can be safe unless it be punished.[59]

England in the eighteenth century and Russia in the nineteenth [60] applied this test of bad tendency. The United States has hitherto preferred to follow the principle of Madison:

Some degree of abuse is inseparable from the proper use of everything; and in no instance is this more true, than in that of the press.[61]

[59] Tuchin's Case, Holt 424 (1704).
[60] See the summary of Russian law in Freund, *op. cit.*, § 471 note.
[61] Report on the Virginia Resolutions, *Elliot's Debates* (2 ed.), IV, 598. Marshall told Talleyrand the same truth, Beveridge, II, 329.

Consequently, President Wilson's Message of December, 1919, was attempting the impossible when it supported a federal sedition bill on this ground: "With the free expression of opinion and with the advocacy of political change, however fundamental, there must be no interference, but toward passion and malevolence tending to incite crime and insurrection under guise of political evolution there should be no leniency." No one has yet invented a gun which will kill a wolf in sheep's clothing and will not hit a sheep. We should all be glad to have a law, "Bad men shall be imprisoned," if it would work, but we know that it would not. A law against "passion and malevolence" is just as bad.

Acts of violence committed by or attributed to radicals are sometimes urged as a reason for enacting sedition legislation. For example, in 1919–20 the Centralia shootings and the bomb explosions near Attorney General Palmer's house and J. P. Morgan's office were often cited as arguments for drastic suppression of radical speeches, pamphlets, and parades. This line of reasoning needs to be carefully qualified by remembrance of the fact that harsh suppression may cause a bitter resentment which will in turn produce more violence. The remedy may merely speed the disease. Some of the violent outbreaks in 1919–20 may have been partly in retaliation for preceding severe restraints on open discussion, such as the long imprisonment of Debs, heavy sentences for red-flag paraders, wholesale raids on I.W.W. and Socialist headquarters by American Legionnaires, and the vigorous enforcement of statutes against syndicalism. By all means, the men responsible for violent outbreaks must be discovered and tried and soundly punished. It is an altogether different matter to make these affairs the basis of further suppression. The advocates of such a policy are doing their best to get this country into the vicious circle of outrages — coercion, coercion — outrages, outrages — coercion, from which John Morley spent his whole official career vainly trying to extricate Ireland and India.[62]

Contrast the American policy of punishing acts and letting talk run to waste. Until 1917 we stuck by the schoolboy maxim, "Sticks and stones will break my bones, but words

[62] See especially the thoughtful letter on the Phoenix Park murders, in his *Recollections*, I, 178.

will never hurt me." Recent riots which have nothing to do with radicalism show that our criminal machinery is very unsuccessfully dealing with acts of violence. That is its absorbing task. It has less time than ever to bother with the men who merely talk. If there is any immediate danger of revolution, the government should be employing the Criminal Code instead of fooling around with a sedition law. If there is no such danger (as thoughtful officials will usually admit), then, much as every one of us dislikes the advocate of force and violence, we shall be wise if we seek remedial and not punitive methods to make his talk of no effect. In particular, let me mention three concrete reasons why a sedition law will fail to accomplish its purpose of getting the really bad man and leaving valuable discussion untouched.

a. A Sedition Law is applied in ways which were wholly unexpected when it was enacted

In the first place, simple as a law against incitement to force and violence appears on its face, it will be a very difficult statute to construe unless the courts adhere closely to the ordinary rules of criminal attempt. Of course, the man who shouts, "We want to kill the President and blow up the Capitol," presents no difficulties, and he is the man whom most people who discuss the proposed statute suppose it is meant to reach. The vital point which I want to drive in hard is that these few plain cases, which anybody would call advocacy of "force and violence," will form only a very small part of the prosecutions actually brought under the sedition statute. For instance, Attorney General Palmer wanted to use such a law to imprison the editors of radical newspapers who had, he said, "a subtle way" of placing their propaganda for the overthrow of the government before their readers, but the reader understands what is meant. The question is whether he or any one else can draft a statute which makes it possible for fallible human beings to distinguish good attacks on the government from bad attacks which sound as if they were good. Jeffreys, Braxfield, and Kenyon thought they were punishing "passion and malevolence," but posterity has condemned them for interfering with the "advocacy of orderly political change."

Whatever law is passed will be used to prosecute speeches

and books full of general language. The question whether such language is advocacy of force and violence must of course be determined by a judge and jury. Judges and jurymen are trained to decide about overt acts, but problems of "subtle" propaganda are an entirely different matter. The normal law of criminal attempt offers to this tribunal a considerable amount of tangible fact. There is, of course, a mental element, the intention of the defendant to bring about the criminal act, but in addition the jury must find a clear and present danger to society in view of the nature of the words *and the surrounding circumstances*. Now, unless the proposed sedition law practically codifies the ordinary rules of attempt, the most tangible factor of the crime disappears; the jury can disregard the absence of danger in the external situation, and merely frame their own views about the intention of the prisoner and the tendency of his words. This must be so, for the federal act is expressly intended to prevent the remote possibility of revolution and punish violent language for its own sake. Consequently, the jury are cut loose entirely from overt acts and the world of the five senses. They are adrift on a sea of speculation.

At the very outset the same controversy will arise as in *Masses* v. *Patten*. It is the old question of Mark Antony's funeral oration. It is natural to assume that advocacy of force and violence means that the defendant must utter words which are violent on their face like "bombs" and "blood"; that the words taken by themselves must be directly provocative of assassination and revolution. This assumption is sure to break down in practice. *Masses* v. *Patten* and other Espionage Act cases indicate that if an unpopular speaker or pamphleteer uses the ordinary language of political agitation, the jury will still be allowed to convict him so long as they find that he intended to cause violence and that this was "the natural and reasonable effect" of his delusively innocent words.[63]

Let me illustrate this danger of loose interpretation from the experience of the courts with an existing federal statute, which looks absolutely clear-cut. This law (already mentioned) punishes with imprisonment up to five years a willful "threat to take the life of the President or inflict bodily harm

---

[63] *Masses* v. Patten, 246 Fed. at 38, revg. 244 Fed. at 540; Schaefer *v.* United States, 251 U. S. 466. See *supra*, Chapter II, sections II and V.

upon him." [64] What could be plainer? At once we think of the need of shutting up the man who writes the President that he will be shot unless a certain bill is vetoed. But that is not the way this statute has worked out. The President does not need to know about the threat. If it is in a letter, nobody needs to see the threat except the officials who open the letter. Thus the element of dangerous circumstances is eliminated, and everything turns on the mere use of words no matter how remote from acts. What words constitute a threat? Let us see what kind of persons have been convicted under this statute. A Syracuse woman of German descent, exasperated by her fellow-employees who continually picked on her and called her the Kaiser, finally burst out that she would poison the President if she had him there. She pleaded guilty before Judge Ray, and was fined $300, "not because the court regarded her as a dangerous person, but to show all quick-tempered or alien-minded persons that they must not threaten to do the President bodily harm or utter unpatriotic sentiments in such times as these." [65] In another case, the words were, "I wish Wilson was in hell, and if I had the power I would put him there." The judges held this revolting language to be a threat to kill the President, because how could he be in hell unless he were dead? [66]

The kind of language which will be held to advocate force and violence under a peace-time Sedition Law may be clearly foreshadowed by the construction which the Supreme Court in the Abrams decision put upon the exhortation:

Workers of the World! Awake! Rise! Put down your enemy and mine! Yes, friends, there is only one enemy of the workers of the world and that is Capitalism.

[64] Act of Feb. 14, 1917, c. 64 [18 U. S. C. A. § 89, collecting numerous decisions thereunder]; see 32 *Harvard Law Review* 724. Every reported case under this statute was in 1917 or 1918, except one in 1921. Another simple statute which has been unexpectedly construed is the last sentence of 18 U. S. C. A. § 334, declaring "matter . . . tending to incite arson, murder, or assassination" to be indecent and hence non-mailable. This was used by Postmaster General Burleson to deny second-class mailing privileges to a well-known Socialist newspaper, the *New York Call.* See Burleson *v.* United States, 274 Fed. 949 (1921) ; *infra,* Chapter VII, section II.

[65] A Memorandum concerning Political Prisoners within the Jurisdiction of the Department of Justice in 1919, p. 22 (in Harvard Law School Library).

[66] U. S. *v.* Clark, Bull. 101; affd., 250 Fed. 449 (C. C. A., 1918).

Here was not a word to indicate violence or negative the use of political and economic pressure, but Justice Clarke declared:

This is clearly an appeal to the workers of this country to arise and put down by force the Government of the United States.

If he was right, the traditional language of socialism becomes advocacy of "force or violence," as has already been held of the general strike under the similar terms of the New York Anarchy Act. If Justice Clarke was wrong, lesser judges may err. In either case, the federal Sedition Law will become a drag-net for every form of radicalism. We have traveled very far from the realm of overt acts.

It is unnecessary to repeat the argument of the first chapter and the experience of the eighteenth century in England, that the risk of the suppression of opinion is very great when the bad political tendency of words and the bad intention of the defendant become the only tests of criminality. Furthermore, we must not forget that we can never be sure that the tendency is bad or the intention evil. These are not visible facts. We have to depend on the opinions of the judge and jury as to the merits of the tendency and the morality of what they can guess about the inside of a man's head. Of course, one evidence and often the main evidence of bad intention will be the supposed bad tendency of the language he employs. In short, any peace-time Sedition Law is open to exactly the objections which Jefferson stated in the Virginia Toleration Act,[67] that when the expression of opinion is made criminal, the tribunal will acquit or convict accordingly as the sentiments of the prisoner square with or differ from its own.

To recapitulate, we began to discuss the Sedition Law with the assumption that it would punish only the man who talks out-and-out revolution and whom we know to intend out-and-out revolution. Such a man seems entitled to no protection. Now we see that we are not dealing with such a man at all. We must encounter much vaguer language and we can never be sure that a man's mind is bad. In its actual application the law must necessarily convict any man whom the judge and jury consider to be using language of bad political tendency with a bad intention, whether or not the judge and jury are

[67] Chapter I, at note 61, *supra*.

right. The desirability of the statute ought to depend very largely on the question whether human beings are likely to be right in forming such a judgment. The answer is that history shows they are very liable to be wrong.

Without the slightest imputation of corruption or malice, we can all agree that a juryman's judgment of the remote political and economic effects of a book or speech is inevitably warped by his own views to a much greater degree than if he is determining the path of a bullet or the value of a house or even the effect of a line on a woman's reputation. And the moral quality of another's mind is even more difficult to determine fairly when there is no criminal act, as in ordinary crimes, to check it up by. A bad intention is easily inferred from what we consider bad opinions. The consequence of such vague standards is that objectionable men and doctrines are easily decided to be advocating violence. Thus, a Winnipeg strike leader was prosecuted in 1919 for sedition, solely on the ground in one count of the indictment that he "seditiously" published two verses of Isaiah, beginning, "Woe unto them that decree unrighteous decrees." [68] Intention, that is, presumed intention, becomes the essence of the crime, and the thing actually done immaterial. Once more, the prisoner is convicted, not for what he does but for what he thinks.

Whether we believe that the Espionage Act decisions were necessary in time of war or not, we ought to hesitate to enact in peace a statute which is sure to be construed as widely as the simple words of the 1917 Act, and to subject all adverse criticism of the government to the risk of suppression so forcibly presented by Justice Brandeis in an Espionage Act case: [69]

The jury which found men guilty for publishing news items or editorials like those here in question must have supposed it to be within their province to condemn men not merely for disloyal acts but for a disloyal heart; provided only that the disloyal heart was evidenced by some utterance. To prosecute men for such publications reminds of the days when men were hanged for constructive treason. To hold that such harmless additions to or omissions from

---

[68] "Quoting Isaiah in Winnipeg," A. V. Thomas, 109 *Nation* 850 (January 3, 1920). The case was afterwards dropped. 110 *ibid.* 292.

[69] Schaefer *v.* U. S., 251 U. S. 466, 493 (1920), dissenting opinion.

news items, and such impotent expressions of editorial opinion, as
were shown here, can afford the basis even of a prosecution will
doubtless discourage criticism of the policies of the Government. To
hold that such publications can be suppressed as false reports, subjects to new perils the constitutional liberty of the press, already
seriously curtailed in practice under powers assumed to have been
conferred upon the postal authorities. Nor will this grave danger end
with the passing of the war. The constitutional right of free speech
has been declared to be the same in peace and in war. In peace, too,
men may differ widely as to what loyalty to our country demands;
and an intolerant majority, swayed by passion or by fear, may be
prone in the future, as it has often been in the past, to stamp as disloyal opinions with which it disagrees. Convictions such as these,
besides abridging freedom of speech, threaten freedom of thought
and of belief.

b. A Sedition Law prevents the discovery of grievances which need removal

Secondly, men who use revolutionary language should not
be suppressed in the absence of very serious and pressing
danger, because they almost always have a grievance. Very
few people want to smash things for the fun of it like small
boys breaking windows. Whether the grievance is well founded
or not, the defenders of the existing order ought to know about
it so that they may correct it or show by counter-argument that
it does not exist. The agitator would be much wiser and more
effective if he expressed his case calmly without threats, but
we ought not to punish him for this mistake. He is not an
educated man, he is not a lawyer, he is not accustomed to
weighing his words carefully, and he is only too apt in a heated
argument to let himself go. And on the whole, society gains if
he is free to do so. The worse the grievance, the more likely
the victim is to get angry and urge violent measures. Yet
that is the grievance which most needs removal.[70] Reformers
who get excited are pretty sure to take the position that force

[70] See the thoughtful statement by Judge Cooley in his *Constitutional Limitations* (7 ed.), p. 613, of the great danger of a rule against intemperate discussion, ending: "If they exceed all the proper bounds of moderation, the consolation
must be, that the evil likely to spring from the violent discussion will probably
be less, and its correction by public sentiment more speedy, than if the terrors
of the law were brought to bear to prevent the discussion." Mill adds very
strong arguments against the same rule at the close of chapter ii of his *Liberty*.

is justifiable if peaceful methods fail to gain what they consider right. Even the supporters of existing institutions have
been known to lose their tempers and suggest lamp-posts and
ropes. In the past we have felt it wiser to let, the opponents
of the government talk than to cause much greater bitterness
in them and in their friends by throwing them into prison. Nor
will this treatment silence those who are really dangerous. A
friend of mine wants all "Bolshevists" shut up till the jails
are so crowded that their feet hang out of the windows, but the
daily letters from political prisoners in the radical newspapers
show that their tongues hang out too. Putting radicals to death
is the only way to get rid of them, and for that we have lost
our nerve. Anything less only increases their power for harm.
If they can say, "This government of capitalists denies us a
decent life and now it won't even let us tell our wrongs," the
natural conclusion is, "If it will not let us talk, our only resort
is to fight." A passage in President Wilson's Message to Congress in December, 1919, hammers this truth home:

The only way to keep men from agitating against grievances is to
remove the grievances. An unwillingness even to discuss these matters
produces only dissatisfaction and gives comfort to the extreme elements in our country which endeavor to stir up disturbances in order
to provoke Governments to embark upon a course of retaliation and
repression. The seed of revolution is repression.

c. *A Sedition Law often suppresses much good with a little bad*

Thirdly, a Sedition Act will suppress much discussion which
is not within its terms at all. Men assume that such a law
affects only a speech or a book which devotes itself entirely to
the advocacy of violence. This is not so. For instance, any
small conservative group in the community which wants to
prevent radical agitators from bringing disagreeable facts to
public attention will be enabled by such a statute to go through
their speeches and pamphlets with a fine-tooth comb and probably find a sentence here or there which can be interpreted
(in the light of the Abrams decision) as advocating revolution.
Thus, it will be possible to imprison almost any radical agitator
in the absence of any real danger of revolution. Of course,
trivial offenses will not be punished in ordinary times; but
during the excitement of a great strike or some other wide-

spread unrest the partisans of law and order will hardly be able to resist the temptation to make use of this law to bottle up labor leaders and other agitators whom they fear and dislike. Witness the sentences of ten, fifteen, twenty years imposed upon leading Socialists under the Espionage Act, so that further activity on their part is conveniently prevented during the time they are likely to live. And in a government of laws and not of men, no one human being ought to be entrusted with the power to give or withhold the heavy sentences of a Sedition Law for the light offenses included within its provisions.

The effect of a Sedition Law upon books is even more injurious. An *ex post facto* censorship of the press is created by the provision that a book which advocates force and violence must not be sold or imported from abroad or transported from state to state. It may be asked, why should any one honestly want to possess a book which urges revolution or even the violation of law? Why should we allow such books to come into the country or be put on sale? But it ought to be remembered that a book falls under the penalties of the law if only a part of it is revolutionary. There are many books and pamphlets which for the most part contain elaborate discussions of social and economic questions, which it is very desirable to read. Here and there the writer is so impressed with the hopelessness of legal change in the present system that he advocates resort to force if nothing else serves. That alone will render circulation of the whole book a heinous crime under this Act. Many of the classics of modern economics will be put on this new Index Expurgatorius. The law will prevent a loyal citizen from obtaining from abroad or another state the works of Marx, Proudhon, Bakunin, or Stirner, and will make it criminal for a loyal bookseller to buy these books for him.

One particular instance will show the evil of such a statute. Harvard University has been collecting in its library all books, pamphlets, posters, and other material relating to the Russian Revolution. After the French Revolution nothing of the sort was attempted for many years, and in consequence all collections of documents of that period are very imperfect. It is the intention of the Harvard Library to avoid such a loss in the case of the Russian Revolution, which everybody, no matter what his opinion of it may be, recognizes as one of the great events in the history of the world. Most of the sedition bills of 1919–20 would make it a crime to import a large part of this material from Russia or even transport it from New York to Cambridge.[71]

Furthermore, if any one who obtains this revolutionary material runs the risk of long imprisonment, sober men who would read and refute it will leave it alone, and it will still fall into the hands of agitators who are willing to take chances. The bulk of the people will be virtually ignorant of what the left-wing radicals are really planning. One of the most effective weapons against anarchy was an exhaustive article in the *New York Times* of June 8, 1919, translating anarchistic passages from the foreign language press. It warned the American people of the thought which we ought to seek to counteract by education, Americanization, constructive propaganda, and the cure of grievances. Such an article would be criminal under most of the proposed legislation. The Attorney General's Report to the Senate could not be distributed because of its extracts from the revolutionary press. Prosecutions of radical newspaper editors cannot be fully reported in the daily press, so that the public cannot know what men are convicted for, and it will be possible for the government under cover of such a practice to withhold from the people knowledge of punishment for legitimate political discussion. Even officials cannot lawfully import revolutionary literature under these bills, and an exception in their favor would be an insult to the citizens of the United States. This law is a kindergarten measure which assumes that the American people are so stupid and so untrustworthy that it is unsafe to let them read anything about anarchy and criminal syndicalism because they would immediately become converted.[72] Above all, we shall not be

---

[71] Under Title I, § 4, of the Alien Registration Act of 1940 many of such books and pamphlets can now be seized from the Harvard Library under a search warrant, and destroyed. See Chapter XII, section 1.

[72] Similar considerations applied to a proposed provision of the Hawley tariff bill of 1929, allowing customs inspectors to confiscate any important book, pamphlet, picture, etc. "advocating or urging treason, insurrection or forcible resistance to any law of the United States." Customs officials who had already excluded Voltaire's *Candide* and Rousseau's *Confessions* as obscene might easily rule out *Das Kapital* if given such new powers. See *New York Times*, May 31, 1929; editorial in St. Louis *Post-Dispatch*, June 1, 1929. On revision, the quoted words stayed in the Act, but customs inspectors were de-

able to meet this great danger of lawlessness if we refuse to look the enemy in the face. The habits of the ostrich are instinctive in many human beings, but they have not been conspicuous for success.

Even if we could wisely dispense with these left-wing books, much less radical publications will become criminal if advocacy of revolution by force and violence is punished. For example, one of the sanest discussions of contemporary thought, which has had a large sale in this country, is Bertrand Russell's *Proposed Roads to Freedom*. Further distribution will become a crime because of its extracts from the Communist Manifesto of 1848: "The Communists disdain to conceal their views and aims. They openly declare that their ends can be attained only by the forcible overthrow of all existing social conditions. Let the ruling classes tremble at a Communistic revolution."

Or take his quotation from an anarchist song:

> Si tu veux être heureux,
> Nom de Dieu!
> Pends ton propriétaire.[73]

Of course, any anti-socialistic book which gives an adequate historical account of its opponents will fall under the same condemnation.

And we shall have some surprises nearer home. It is advocacy of revolution by force and violence to write: "I hold a little rebellion now and then is a good thing, and as necessary in the political world as storms in the physical." [74] Out go the works of Thomas Jefferson. It is advocacy of change of government by assassination to say, "The right of a nation to kill a tyrant in cases of necessity can no more be doubted than to hang a robber, or kill a flea." [75] Jefferson is followed

---

prived of any power of deciding about books; court proceedings are now required in order to confiscate or destroy the book for obscenity or for the grounds stated above. Either party can demand a jury trial. — 19 U. S. C. A. § 1305. Interesting judicial decisions under this section are United States *v. Married Love*, 48 F. (2d) 821 (Woolsey, J., 1931); United States *v.* One Book Called *Ulysses*, 5 F. Supp. 182 (Woolsey, J., 1933), affd. in 72 F. (2d) 705 (Augustus N. Hand, J., 1934, Manton, J., dissenting and saying, "The people need and deserve a moral standard; it should be a point of honor with men of letters to maintain it"). [73] Russell, *op. cit.*, pp. 17, 53.

[74] *Writings of Jefferson* (ed. P. L. Ford), IV, 362; see also pp. 370 and 467.

[75] *Works of John Adams* (ed. C. F. Adams), VI, 130.

by his old antagonist, John Adams, the author of the Sedition Law of 1798. The Declaration of Independence will be barred in this country as it was once upon a time in the Philippines, since it is a most eloquent advocate of change in the form of government by force without stint or limit. And the censorship can hardly overlook Lincoln's First Inaugural:

> This country with its institutions belongs to the people who in-habit it. Whenever they shall grow weary of the existing government, they can exercise their constitutional right of amending it, or their revolutionary right to dismember or overthrow it.

It may be objected that of course no one will be prosecuted for selling such books. Perhaps not, but do we as a fair-minded people want a statute under which the very ideas which will be immune when cloth-bound in a respectable bookstore will constitute a penitentiary offense in a Yiddish handbill?

If this legislation is to be enforced with any impartiality, it must necessarily cut us off from our own revolutionary heritage and from the economic and political thought of Europe in our own time. Since August 1914 this nation has entered into the affairs of the world for the realization of noble aims. It cannot do this and at the same time propose to pass its existence for the next score of years like some Lady of Shalott, shut off from the turbulent life of European mankind.

Much more could be said, but I hope it is now clear that the really bad man is only an incidental victim of any federal Sedition Law in time of peace. Indeed, it is only too probable that he will be ingenious enough to hide his tracks and escape. Meanwhile, the law will suppress the discussion of public questions at point after point.

During the war the advocates of strong measures assured those who thought our traditional freedom of speech in peril that suppression would disappear when the fighting stopped. They remarked with Lincoln that a man could not contract so strong an appetite for emetics during temporary illness as to persist in feeding upon them during the remainder of his healthful life.[76] The war is over in 1920, actually if not tech-

---

[76] Letter to Erastus Corning and others (June 12, 1863), *Works of Lincoln* (ed. Nicolay and Hay), VIII, 309.

nically, the Espionage Act has suspended any widespread operation till the next conflict, but nearly every state in the Union has proceeded to make the expression of certain opinions criminal, and Congress came near passing a much more rigorous Espionage Act for times of peace. The truth is that persecution of unpopular doctrines is not an emetic at all, but a drug. A nation cannot indulge in an orgy of intolerance and console itself like Rip Van Winkle with the thought that "This time doesn't count!" Nobody enjoyed gasless Sundays or sugarless coffee so much that we are likely to continue them in peace, but the pleasure of being able to silence the pro-Germans and pacifists and Socialists who had irritated us in 1915 and 1916 was so agreeable in 1917 and 1918 that it will be abandoned with extreme reluctance, and we long for more suppression to satisfy the appetite which has been created contrary to our former national tradition of open political discussion.

Consequently we ought to cross-question acutely our present conviction that the repression of ideas is essential to the public safety, and ask ourselves how far that conviction results from the mood of the moment. Indeed, it may be conjectured that just as some soldiers were given ether to make them go "over the top" better, so a nation cannot enter whole-heartedly into the horrors of a war without some benumbing of its reasoning powers, from which it may not yet have recovered. Is it not psychologically probable that our minds have been so shaken by excitement, fear, and hatred, so stretched to one absorbing purpose, that they are slow to return to normal, and that we still crave something to fear and hate, some exceptional cause for which we can continue to evoke enthusiasm?

A very serious situation confronts us. For three years the government has pursued the policy advocated by Judge Van Valkenburgh when he tried Rose Pastor Stokes for her denunciation of profiteering: [77] "The President could not stop in the face of the enemy and effect domestic reforms. We do not ordinarily clean house and hang out the bedding when there is a thunderstorm on. We wait until it is over, go dirty a little longer." A good deal of soiled linen has accumulated, and the consequences are far from agreeable. The discussion of the radicals is bound to be doubly violent because it was

[77] Bull. 106, p. 18.

postponed, and now it can be postponed no longer unless we mean to suppress it altogether. By doing that we shall not end it, but only drive it underground.

A Sedition Law is not the proper way to deal with anarchy. Outside of a few intellectuals, anarchy is the creation of discontent, and this law will increase discontent. Nothing adds more to men's hatred for government than its refusal to let them talk, especially if they are the type of person anarchists are, to whom talking a little wildly is the greatest joy of life. Besides, suppression of their mere words shows a fear of them, which only encourages them to greater activity in secret. A widespread belief is aroused that the government would not be so anxious to silence its critics unless what they have been saying is true. A wise and salutary neglect of talk, coupled with vigorous measures against plans for actual violence and a general endeavor to end discontent, is the best legal policy toward anarchy and criminal syndicalism.

To quote from an extra-judicial decision of Justice Holmes: [78]

With effervescing opinions, as with the not yet forgotten champagnes, the quickest way to let them get flat is to let them get exposed to the air.

Undoubtedly, there are elements in our population, small in number, but reckless and aggressive, who are ready to act on incitement to revolution; but the real danger lies in the existence of large masses of unthinking radicals. This danger cannot be met directly by clubbing such men into loyalty. We must first understand the causes of their discontent, studying with open minds all the existing information, and then take constructive steps to end that discontent and substitute positive ideals for those we want to drive out. To modernize an old illustration from Herbert Spencer, any one who has watched a tinsmith mend a crumpled mud-guard on an automobile will observe that he never pounds the protuberant spot. To do so would either be ineffective or would simply raise a hump at some other place. Instead, he begins at a distance and hammers all around the critical point, gradually drawing the metal away from it until all is symmetrical as before.

[78] Letter to the Harvard Liberal Club, reprinted in 21 *New Republic* 250, and *Boston Herald*, January 13, 1920.

There should be no legislation against sedition and anarchy. We must legislate and enforce the laws against the use of force, but protect ourselves against bad thinking and speaking by the strength of argument and a confidence in American common sense and American institutions, including that most characteristic of all, which stands at the head of the Bill of Rights, freedom of thought.

If we have taken reasonable precautions against violence, we should not be disappointed at not securing absolute unanimity among our population on political and economic matters. If Americanism means anything concrete, it certainly means tolerance for opinions widely different from our own, however objectionable they seem to us. Such is the tradition handed down to us by Roger Williams and Thomas Jefferson. In the past we have been proud to believe that the arguments for law and order, the common sense of the American people, including those who have come from Europe to help build our industries, and the noble qualities of our institutions, would win out over any revolutionary talk or writing. The proposed Sedition Bills show a serious distrust in these three great stabilizing forces of American life. Not for the sake of the radicals, but for our own sake, should we oppose this unprecedented legislation, whose enforcement will let loose a horde of spies and informers, official and unofficial, swarming into our private life, stirring up suspicion without end, making all attacks on government either impotent or unsafe. The supporters of this gag-law assume that our patriotism and our institutions are so weak as to crumble away at any talk of revolution. Surely that time has not come, will never come. Let us put an end once for all to this cowardice, and take to heart the words of a great English Liberal: [79]

We talk much — and think a great deal too much — of the wisdom of our ancestors. I wish we could imitate the courage of our ancestors. They were not ready to lay their liberties at the feet of the Government upon every vain or imaginary alarm.

[79] Lord John Russell, quoted in G. W. E. Russell, *Prime Ministers*, N. Y., 1919, 21.

CHAPTER 5

THE DEPORTATIONS

> *It was we laid the steel on this land from ocean to ocean:*
> *It was we (if you know) put the U.P. through the passes*
>
> *Bringing her down into Laramie full load*
> *Eighteen mile on the granite anticlinal*
> *Forty-three foot to the mile and the grade holding:*
>
> *It was we did it: hunkies of our kind:*
> *It was we dug the caved-in holes for the cold water:*
> *It was we built the gully spurs and the freight sidings:*
>
> *Who would do it but we and the Irishmen bossing us?*
> *It was all foreign-born men there were in this country:*
> *'It was Scotsmen Englishmen Chinese Squareheads Aus-*
> *trians . . .*
> ARCHIBALD MacLEISH, Burying Ground by the Ties.

SO LONG as Congress refused to follow the disastrous precedent of 1798 and enact a peace-time Sedition Law, the federal government could not do much to suppress "evil-thinking" on the part of citizens. However, it could curb radical foreigners in our midst by seizing upon a new Alien Law and using it with relentless vigor. The hostility to immigrant workers, which had long been smouldering in this country, was now suddenly combined with hostility to heterodox thinkers and burst into a conflagration of hysterical hatred. Gone was the age-long welcome to the distressed and discontented laborers of Europe. Instead, a nationwide outcry arose for wholesale deportations.

The first conspicuous event was the sailing of the transport *Buford* on December 21, 1919, with two hundred and forty-nine Russians. This was followed in January by a carefully prepared roundup in all parts of the country in which over four thousand persons were arrested under deportation charges.

The right of the federal government to punish peace-time sedition is open to doubt, but there can be no question of its affirmative power to exclude aliens from this country or to deport them after they are admitted. Although no clause in the Constitution expressly gives this power, it has been held by the United States Supreme Court in the Chinese Exclusion Cases to be an incident of the sovereignty and right of self-preservation necessarily conferred by the Constitution upon the government it created.[1]

I. THE STATUTE AS TO DEPORTABLE RADICALS

Various classes of aliens besides the Chinese have long been subject to exclusion and expulsion for such obvious objections as conviction of crime, insanity, pauperism, etc., but it was not until 1903 that the possession or expression of opinions was first made a disqualification. In consequence of the death of President McKinley, Congress refused entry to the United States to anarchists, persons advocating the forcible overthrow of our government or all government, or the assassination of public officials, as well as persons disbelieving in or opposed to all organized government or belonging to organizations teaching such disbelief or opposition.[2] Other types of extreme radicals were added by subsequent legislation.[3] The statute in force in 1919–20, enacted toward the close of the war, specified the following proscribed classes:

(1) Aliens who are anarchists; (2) aliens who believe in or advocate the overthrow by force or violence of the Government of the United States or of all forms of law; (3) aliens who disbelieve in or are opposed to all organized government; (4) aliens who advocate or teach the assassination of public officials; (5) aliens who advocate or teach the unlawful destruction of property; (6) aliens who are members of or affiliated with any organization that entertains a belief in, teaches, or advocates the overthrow by force or violence of the Government of the United States or of all forms of law, or that entertains or teaches disbelief in or opposition to all organized government, or that advocates the duty, necessity, or propriety of the unlawful assaulting or killing of any officer or officers, either of specific individuals or of officers generally, of the Government of the

[1] Nishimura Ekiu *v.* U. S., 142 U. S. 651, 659 (1892); see other cases in 1 Willoughby on the Constitution (2d ed.), §§ 183–187 (1929).

[2] Act, March 3, 1903, c. 1012, §§ 2, 38.

[3] Act, February 20, 1907, c. 1134, §§ 2, 38; Act, February 5, 1917, c. 29.

United States or of any other organized government, because of his or their official character, or that advocates or teaches the unlawful destruction of property.[4]

Not only are such aliens refused admission and put out if they succeed in getting in; but also aliens who acquire these views or join these associations after their entry into this country can be deported. There is no time limit, no matter how long before 1918 they came to the United States.[5]

Like the federal "force and violence" bills discussed in the preceding chapter, this statute at first sight seems to apply to really bad men, and to effect nothing but desirable results. Once again, however, we ought to defer judgment until we have examined the actual operation of the statute. A law is much more than its words; it is what human beings do with those words.

2. THE ADMINISTRATIVE MACHINERY FOR DEPORTING RADICALS

> *"I'll be judge. I'll be jury,"*
> *Said cunning old Fury;*
> *"I'll try the whole cause,*
> *And condemn you to death."* — Alice in Wonderland.

The most important question with any legislation which affects human happiness is, what kind of men administer its provisions? Are they a judge, a jury, a government official, a secret council, a star chamber? By thus spotting the type of men involved, we can estimate how their training and circumstances are likely to affect the wisdom, discrimination, and impartiality of the decisions which transform bare words into hard facts.

[4] Act of October 16, 1918, c. 186 (numerals inserted by me). This was amended on May 10 and June 5, 1920, after the events narrated in this chapter, to include aliens convicted under the Espionage Act and other war statutes, or for advocating sabotage or injury to property or assaults on officials. Giving or lending money is proof of advocacy or membership. — 8 U. S. C. A. §§ 137, 157. On this 1920 statute, see John Lord O'Brian, "The Menace of Administrative Law," *Reports of the Maryland Bar Association,* 1920, 153, 159 ff. The deportation statutes were made still wider and more drastic by the Alien Registration Act of 1940 (8 U. S. C. A. §§ 137, 155, as amended), discussed *infra,* Chapter XII, section 1.

[5] Cases on the absence of a time-limit are collected in 8 A. L. R. 1286 (1920), with supplementary citations.

The answer to this question in our problem lies in the following sentence:

In every case where any person is ordered deported from the United States under the provisions of this Act, or by any law or treaty, the decision of the Secretary of Labor shall be *final*.[6]

No judge or jury passes on the important question whether an alien who has lived here for many years actually holds or has expressed any of the objectionable views specified as grounds for deportation. No judge or jury decides whether he belongs to an objectionable organization or whether it really is objectionable. All these vital issues of fact are determined by the Secretary of Labor, or more often by his subordinates, the immigration officials. And there is for all practical purposes no appeal from those officials to any court, not even to the Supreme Court of the United States. The law takes the position that deportation is not a criminal proceeding and involves no punishment. It is simply an exercise of the right of every sovereign state to determine who shall reside within its borders. Therefore, the foreigner who is expelled without a hearing in court, no matter how long he has lived in the United States, no matter if he must leave a house and other cherished possessions behind him, no matter if his wife and children are American citizens, is not deprived of life, liberty, or property without due process of law.

Exclusion of a newly arrived alien by administrative fiat is not a serious hardship, for he simply returns to his old life and takes up the threads where he recently dropped them, but expulsion after long residence is another affair. Liberty itself, long-established associations, the home, are then at stake. This power to tear a man up by the roots is now extended from such definite facts as the race and birthplace of a Chinese to such vague facts as the opinions and political affiliations of a European. Whatever the constitutional powers of the government, it ought not to deprive a man of liberty and happiness without being sure after a thorough and impartial investigation that the alien actually falls within a proscribed class.

[6] 8 U. S. C. A. § 155, italics mine. The Bureau of Immigration was transferred to the Department of Justice on June 14, 1940, and the final decision is now vested by law in the Attorney General.

It is popular to brush aside complaints against our deportation procedure on the ground that he is only an alien; if he wants to acquire a home here, why does he not become naturalized? He cannot be naturalized for five years, and even after that time his omission ought not to make him an outlaw. He should not be dragooned into citizenship, and incidentally citizens acquired through pressure are not always desirable. A foreigner often has honest and even praiseworthy motives for retaining his old loyalties. He may desire to return to his birthplace in his old age after he has saved a competence by building roads and railways for us, or he may be waiting here with the hope that a tyranny at home will be overthrown. Surely, we do not reproach Americans who spend their lives in England or France without renouncing their allegiance. Why should we regard similar conduct by foreigners in this country as worse than crime, for even criminals would not receive such harsh and summary treatment? We have no business to act and talk as if we owed absolutely nothing to our unnaturalized immigrants. Many of them were brought in at the earnest desire of the very persons and corporations who have been loudly calling for more deportations. For years these foreigners have done our dirty work, and we might at least give them an impartial trial before we throw them out neck and heels. An alien must expect to be expelled, if he furnishes legal cause, just as he must expect to be punished for an offense, but in each case we should be proud as citizens of a free land to furnish him the best legal machinery we can devise to ascertain whether or not the ground for governmental action really exists.

Let us now look more closely at the method which we actually employ to determine the political and economic views of an alien. Is it likely to be as fair as a jury trial? Even that, I have tried to show in the previous chapters, is a hazardous means for the investigation of another man's words and opinions, and often liable to err. What are the dangers of error and unfairness in deportation tribunals?

The commonest complaint against deportation hearings is the absence of a jury, but I doubt if an alien charged with embracing forbidden doctrines really suffers on that account, at least in times of excitement. The popular clamor against radicals in January, 1920, and the results of contemporaneous sedition trials against native Americans make it highly probable that juries would have rejoiced in the opportunity of shipping out of the country any alien whose political and economic views veered from strict orthodoxy.

The dangers of unfairness in deportation procedure lie deeper, and may be grouped under three headings. The practices in operation in January, 1920, will serve as illustrations of the risks that need consideration.[7] In future crises, it will be important to determine whether the same risks still persist under the procedure existing at such times.

1. Much depends on the rank and qualities of the official charged with deciding whether the alien falls within the statutory classes of deportable evil-thinkers. Perhaps the best person whom the law could select for such a purpose would be an official, if he were judicially-minded, versed in the history of European thought since the French Revolution, and sure of keeping his livelihood whatever his verdict. Such an official would surely be superior to a jury, and he would be better than most judges. But the official who passed on the alien's ideas in 1920 was one of a number of officers called inspectors of immigration, connected with the office of the Commissioner.

2. To what extent is the official who determines the alien's guilt protected from bias? In criminal trials the judge and jurymen enter the case for the first time when they take their places in the courtroom. They start as neutrals. The attack on the prisoner is entrusted to other agents of the law — the police who arrest and collect evidence, the grand jury which indicts, the district attorney who prepares and presents the side of the government. The importance of this segregation of functions was realized centuries ago in the days of

---

[7] See Immigration Rules of May 1, 1917, Rule 22; the full description by Holt, J., in Bosny v. Williams, 185 Fed. 598 (1911); and material cited *infra*, note 14.

Three valuable monographs have been published since 1930, which use numerous records of individual deportation cases and personal observation of the work of the Bureau of Immigration as their basis for discussing existing or needed safeguards against unfairness in deportation hearings: Van Vleck, *The Administrative Control of Aliens: A Study in Administrative Law and Procedure* (Commonwealth Fund, 1932); Oppenheimer, *The Administration of the Deportation Laws of the United States* in 2 Rep. Nat. Commn. Law Observance & Enforcement (Wickersham Commn.) (1931); Jane P. Clark, *Deportation of Aliens from the United States to Europe* (Columbia University Press, 1931).

"hanging judges" like Jeffreys. Yet the outstanding feature of deportation procedure in January, 1920, was the union of these inconsistent mental attitudes of prosecuting and judging in a single man — the immigration inspector. United States Judge Holt thus describes the practice:

Complaint that an alien is in this country in violation of law is usually made by one of these inspectors. The information upon which he bases the charge may have been obtained by himself upon investigation, or may have been furnished to him by others. Frequently such information is furnished by the city police, or by enemies of the person charged, acting through malice or revenge. Affidavits are obtained and are sent by the inspector to the Secretary at Washington, who, if he thinks a proper case is made out, issues a warrant for the arrest of the persons charged. This warrant is usually intrusted for execution to the inspector who has made the charge, and he subsequently usually takes entire charge of the case. . . . The whole proceeding is usually substantially in the control of one of the inspectors, who acts in it as informer, arresting officer, inquisitor, and judge.[8]

3. How far does the prisoner possess other safeguards customary in criminal trials? Some of these are listed in the Sixth Amendment to the Constitution:

the right to a . . . public trial . . . ; to be confronted with the witnesses against him; to have compulsory process for obtaining witnesses in his favor, and to have the Assistance of Counsel for his defence.

Although the Amendment does not apply to deportation cases, the specified privileges are just as helpful to fairness there as in criminal trials, where three additional safeguards are customary: (a) The prisoner charged with crime has plenty of time to prepare his defense, including his own testimony, before the case against him is presented to the tribunal which is to pass on his guilt. (b) An independent court stenographer makes the record of all the evidence, free from control by the prosecutor or anybody else, so that the judgment of the trial tribunal is reviewed by higher authorities on the basis of an accurate and impartial picture of the whole case. (c) The presence of newspaper reporters followed by

[8] Bosny v. Williams, *supra*, note 7. Compare monographs there cited.

publication of the proceedings in the press serves as an informal but strong check on browbeating, unfair twisting of the witnesses, and other practices common in the days of secret state trials.

In the deportation procedure of January, 1920, some of these safeguards were imperfectly preserved and others were wholly lacking. The proceedings were in secret. The public was excluded, so was the press, so were the alien's wife and children. So was any defense lawyer until the inspector saw fit to let him in. After the alien was taken into custody, he was held in seclusion and not permitted to consult counsel until he had first been examined by the inspector, under oath, and his answers put on the record.[9] Thus the alien could be rigorously cross-examined without any legal advice, not only about what he had done and said but also about what he thought. His inability to speak English and the inspector's frequent inability to speak anything else made the record often unsatisfactory, when so much turned on the alien's expression of his own views on intricate questions of ethics, economics, and political theory; but the Secretary of Labor saw nothing else. Furthermore, this record was sometimes made by the inspector himself, and he might stop it whenever he wished, after a good case was made out. Like a policeman, like a district attorney, it was his business to get results.

"After this preliminary investigation has proceeded as far as the inspector wishes," says Judge Holt, "the aliens are then informed that they are entitled to have counsel, and to give any evidence they wish in respect to the charge." Thereafter a further hearing was held, where the inspector might give more evidence and the alien could appear by counsel and offer defense evidence, which he at last had a chance to collect. This second hearing looked more like an ordinary trial, but this could not wipe out the possibilities of injustice in the earlier defenseless hearing. Although that was officially

[9] Low Wah Suey v. Backus, 225 U. S. 460 (1912), held this rule valid. See books cited *supra*, note 7. The new regulations of Dec. 31, 1940, are much fairer. 6 Fed. Reg. 70, § 19.6(d)(i). The alien's answers during the inspector's preliminary examination no longer go into the record, except under special conditions. Thus the decision of deportability is now based only on the testimony at the formal hearing, where the alien has a definite right to have his lawyer present.

termed a "preliminary investigation" or "preliminary statement," it formed a vital part of the record and probably often served to make up the inspector's mind, so that the alien's lawyer arrived too late to be of much use. The proceedings were rarely reported in the newspapers, since they were not open, so that public opinion could not easily be focused on an unjust case. Once the alien was deported, all mistakes and wrongs were covered by the intervening ocean.

3. THE RAIDS OF JANUARY, 1920

> *A Dukhobor tried to go naked in the streets of London. A policeman set out gravely to capture him, but found himself distanced because of his heavy clothing. Therefore he divested himself, as he ran, of garment after garment, until he was naked; and so lightened, he caught his prey. But then it was impossible to tell which was the Dukhobor and which was the policeman.*
>
> CHARLES P. HOWLAND.

Such is the machinery which Attorney General Palmer set in motion to bring thousands of radicals within the provisions of the Alien Act of 1918. Powerful as this machinery is, it is subjected by the law to three limitations in the interests of liberty. (1) The Act provides that arrest must be on a warrant signed by the Secretary of Labor; and the issue of the warrant is carefully regulated by the Immigration Rules, which require it to be based on "some substantial supporting evidence." [10] (2) The Fourth Amendment to the Constitution reads thus:

The right of the people to be secure in their persons, houses, papers, and effects, against unreasonable searches and seizures, shall not be violated, and no Warrants shall issue, but upon probable cause, supported by Oath or affirmation, and particularly describing the place to be searched, and the persons or things to be seized.

Consequently, a house or meeting-hall cannot be searched, and radical books and pamphlets cannot be seized for use in deportation proceedings, unless the officials have a search warrant issued in accordance with some statute and particularly describing the material to be seized. An arrest warrant against

[10] Immigration Rules, 1917, 22 (3).

an alien for deportation does not satisfy the Constitution; and
a fortiori a citizen's property is immune from seizure even if
he be arrested, since the arrest is obviously unlawful. The
Supreme Court has made repeated use of this Amendment to
prevent the use of evidence which has been improperly seized.[11]
(3) The alien must be given a fair administrative trial, in
accordance with the Rules.[12]

The raids of January, 1920, are described in the opinion of
Judge George W Anderson in the Colyer case,[13] which should

[11] An example is Silverthorne Lumber Co. *v.* United States, 251 U. S. 385
(1920). On unreasonable searches and seizures generally, see Chapter XIV,
note 5. On search warrants, see Chapter XII, at note 93.

The Fourth Amendment is not limited to criminal proceedings and so
must apply in deportation proceedings. Bilokumsky *v.* Tod, 263 U. S. 149, 155
(1923). Searches and seizures without a valid search-warrant violate the Constitution, except in certain carefully limited situations like searching the person,
immediate premises, or automobile of a person lawfully arrested for a *crime*.
See Carroll *v.* United States, 267 U. S. 132 (1925); Elias *v.* Pasmore, [1934]
2 K. B. 164. Deportability is not a crime.

Moreover, it is doubtful if a valid search-warrant could have been obtained
to authorize the seizures of books and pamphlets in the 1920 raids. There was
apparently no search-warrant statute on the books in 1920 (or in 1941 for that
matter) specifically applicable to deportation proceedings. The Secretary of
Labor (or Attorney General since 1940) has no power under any Act of Congress to issue search-warrants in immigration cases. A judicial search-warrant
under the general provisions of 28 U. S. C. A. § 377 necessitates judicial proceedings, whereas deportation is administrative. The elaborate statutory provisions about search-warrants (18 U. S. C. A. §§ 611–633) relate to proceedings
on a criminal charge or proceedings against the property or documents themselves as unlawful, *e.g.*, illegal liquor or material violating the Espionage Act as
in the *Spirit of '76* case, *supra* p. 10. No such charge was laid in the 1920
raids. Some search-warrants for guns were issued; these could not cover the
seizure of printed matter. Observe that since 1940 subversive pamphlets, etc.,
can be seized from aliens or citizens under the criminal provisions of the Alien
Registration Act, Title I, § 4 (18 U. S. C. A. § 12); see Chapter XII, section 1,
infra.

Illegal searches and seizures were a ground for the release of alien deportees
in *Ex parte* Jackson (1920), quoted *infra* at n. 40, I.W.W.; and in the Colyer
case, 265 Fed. at 44–45 (1920), Communists. As to other occurrences see Clark,
op. cit. supra note 7, pp. 326–327; Oppenheimer at 77–78.

[12] Bilokumsky *v.* Tod, 263 U. S. 149, 155 and note (1923).

[13] Colyer *v.* Skeffington, 265 Fed. 17 (D. Mass. 1920), cited hereafter as
Colyer opinion. The government did not appeal from Judge Anderson's findings
of fact as to the unfairness of the proceedings by the Department of Justice and
the immigration officials. In another portion of the opinion, it was held that
Colyer and a few other Communists who were fairly treated should be discharged, because the Communist Party did not advocate force and violence.
As to these aliens, Judge Anderson was reversed by the Circuit Court of Appeals,
which held that this was a question for the Secretary of Labor to decide. 277
Fed. 129 (C. C. A. 1st, 1922).

be read in full to get an adequate picture of what happened. The following extracts must here suffice:

Kelleher [head of the local Bureau of Investigation in Boston] says that he had operating, practically under his control, for this raid, from 300 to 500 men. This may fairly be assumed to be a moderate estimate. Most of these were agents of the Department of Justice and policemen of the various cities and towns. The plan was to make up a list of the persons intended to be arrested in a particular community; for the police and Department of Justice agents thereupon, generally without warrants, to go about to the halls or homes where these people were, arrest them, and bring them to the concentration point — commonly a police station. When halls were raided, the occupants were, as required by the instructions, lined up against the wall and searched. Many citizens were gathered into the net in this fashion, and brought to the various police stations. At the concentration points the sifting process went on during the night. Blanks for questionnaires had been prepared, answers to which were sought and generally obtained from the arrested persons. . . .

Assistant Superintendent West of the Boston Bureau of Investigation estimates that the total number of persons actually arrested on this raid was approximately 600. This also must be taken to be a moderate estimate. The circumstances under which the raid was carried on make it impossible for him or any other person to know with any approximate accuracy the number of persons arrested. Weighing his evidence in connection with the other testimony adduced before me, I am convinced that a much larger number of people was arrested — probably from 800 to 1,200. . . .

Necessarily a raid of this kind, carried out with such disregard of law and of properly verified facts, had many unexpected and some unintended results. For instance, in a hall in Lynn 39 people were holding a meeting to discuss the formation of a co-operative bakery. About half of them were citizens. But the Lynn police, acting under the instructions of the Department of Justice, raided this hall and arrested the entire 39, held them over night in cells at the police station, and then had them docketed as "suspects" and 38 of them discharged.

There were also incidents of the arrests of women under conditions involving great hardship. For instance, the witness Mrs. Stanislas Vasiliewska, the mother of three children, aged 13, 10, and 8, was arrested in a hall in Chelsea, taken in the police patrol wagon with her eldest girl to the police station, and both put with another woman into one cell. About midnight they took her child and sent her home alone to a remote part of the city. Mrs. Vasiliewska was taken the next day to the wharf, where, with Mrs. Colyer, she was confined for about 6 hours in a dirty toilet room. She was then taken to Deer Island, where she was kept 33 days. . . .

The witness Minnie Federman was arrested at her home at 6 o'clock in the morning. Several men, showing her no warrant, entered her room where she was in bed. She was told to get out of bed and dress, which she did in a closet. Then she was taken in a police wagon to the police station after they had searched her premises, apparently for I.W.W. literature. When they found that she was a naturalized citizen, she was allowed to go.

In Nashua a hall was raided and about 13 women taken, 6 or 7 of whom were released at the police station; 5 of them kept from Friday night to Saturday afternoon in one cell, without a mattress.

It was under such terrorizing conditions as these that these aliens were subjected to questionnaires, subsequently used as, and generally constituting an important part of, the evidence adduced against them before the immigration inspectors. Pains were taken to give spectacular publicity to the raid, and to make it appear that there was great and imminent public danger, against which these activities of the Department of Justice were directed. The arrested aliens, in most instances perfectly quiet and harmless working people, many of them not long ago Russian peasants, were handcuffed in pairs, and then, for the purposes of transfer on trains and through the streets of Boston, chained together. The Northern New Hampshire contingent were first concentrated in jail at Concord and then brought to Boston in a special car, thus handcuffed and chained together. On detraining at the North Station, the handcuffed and chained aliens were exposed to newspaper photographers and again thus exposed at the wharf where they took the boat for Deer Island. The Department of Justice agents in charge of the arrested aliens appear to have taken pains to have them thus exposed to public photographing.

Private rooms were searched in omnibus fashion; trunks, bureaus, suit cases, and boxes broken open; books and papers seized. I doubt whether a single search warrant was obtained or applied for. . . .

At Deer Island the conditions were unfit and chaotic. No adequate preparations had been made to receive and care for so large a number of people. Some of the steam pipes were burst or disconnected. The place was cold; the weather severe. The cells were not properly equipped with sanitary appliances. There was no adequate number of guards or officials to take a census of and properly care for so many. For several days the arrested aliens were held practically *incommunicado*. There was dire confusion of authority as between the immigration forces and the Department of Justice forces, and the

city officials who had charge of the prison. Most of this confusion
and the resultant hardship to the arrested aliens was probably unin-
tentional; it is now material only as it bears upon the question of
due process of law, shortly to be discussed. Undoubtedly it did have
some additional terrorizing effect upon the aliens. Inevitably the
atmosphere of lawless disregard of the rights and feelings of these
aliens as human beings affected, consciously or unconsciously, the
inspectors who shortly began at Deer Island the hearings, the basis
of the records involving the determination of their right to remain
in this country.

In the early days at Deer Island one alien committed suicide by
throwing himself from the fifth floor and dashing his brains out in
the corridor below in the presence of other horrified aliens. One was
committed as insane; others were driven nearly, if not quite, to the
verge of insanity. . . .

The picture of a non-English-speaking Russian peasant arrested
under circumstances such as described above, held for days in jail,
then for weeks in the city prison at Deer Island, and then summoned
for a so-called "trial" before an inspector, assisted by the Department
of Justice agent under stringent instructions emanating from the
Department of Justice in Washington to make every possible effort
to obtain evidence of the alien's membership in one of the proscribed
parties, is not a picture of a sober, dispassionate, "due process of
law" attempt to ascertain and report the true facts.

Beyond this, I shall speak only of the extent to which the
three principles of personal liberty previously set forth were
observed in these raids and the hearings that followed. My
discussion is not based upon the evidence of aliens or journalists, however credible, but upon the statements of sworn officials of the United States, and so far as possible upon the
testimony of Attorney General A. Mitchell Palmer.[14]

[14] The only sentence based on an unofficial source is that on Detroit conditions; see *infra*, note 19. The other sources used are as follows: (1) *Attorney
General A. Mitchell Palmer on Charges Made against Department of Justice*,
etc., Hearings before House Committee on Rules, 66th Cong., 2d Sess., Parts 1
and 2 (1920), cited hereafter as Palmer Deportations Testimony. (2) *Investigation of Administration of Louis F. Post, in the Matter of Deportation of
Aliens*, Hearings before House Committee on Rules, 66th Cong., 2d Sess., on
H. Res. 522, Parts 1 and 2 (1920), cited hereafter as Post Deportations Testimony. (3) Instructions and testimony of government officials in Colyer opinion.
(4) Similar official material in *Report upon the Illegal Activities of the United
States Department of Justice*, by twelve lawyers (National Popular Government
League, Washington, May, 1920).

The signers of the Report last cited included Professor (now Mr. Justice)

The Attorney General was the prime mover in the raids. The Secretary of Labor, who was ill, and Assistant Secretary Louis F. Post are not stated by Mr. Palmer to have been informed of his plans "for the apprehension of members of the Communist Party and the Communist Labor Party." The Attorney General was aided by a member of his own Department, J. W. Abercrombie, who had been detailed to serve as solicitor to the Department of Labor. Since Mr. Abercrombie had the powers of Acting Secretary of Labor when his superiors were absent or otherwise occupied, he signed 3,000 warrants for the arrest of persons alleged by affidavits of Department of Justice agents to be members of the two Communist parties. The Commissioner General of Immigration instructed the immigration officials that the aliens covered by the warrants would be arrested simultaneously by the Department of Justice and "held on local charges" until the officials had served the warrants that night or the following day. The agents would assist in serving warrants, perfecting detention arrangements, and providing evidence, but they could not legally conduct the deportation hearings, since this duty was delegated by statute to the immigration inspectors.

The character of the raids is best shown by the Instructions issued by Mr. Palmer's Bureau of Investigation to his Secret Service men throughout the country.[15] (Observe that arrest warrants and search warrants are totally ignored.)

INSTRUCTIONS

Our activities will be directed against the radical organizations, known as the Communist Party of America and the Communist Labor Party of America, also known as Communists.

Frankfurter and the writer, who had both appeared as friends of the court (*amici curiae*) in the Colyer case. Charles E. Hughes said of this Report: "Very recently information has been laid by responsible citizens at the bar of public opinion of violations of personal rights which savor of the worst practices of tyranny." — Address at Harvard Law School, June 21, 1920. For the subsequent Senate hearings, see *Charges of Illegal Practices of the Department of Justice*, Hearings before Subcommittee of Senate Judiciary Committee, 66th Cong., 3d Sess. (1921); the writer's testimony is at pp. 165–207 therein. For reports of the subcommittee by Senator T. J. Walsh of Montana and Senator Sterling of South Dakota, see 64 Cong. Rec. 3005–3027 (Feb. 5, 1923).

[15] Reprinted in Colyer opinion, and *New York Times*, Jan. 3, 1920 (front page)

The strike will be made promptly and simultaneously at 8:30 P.M. in all districts. The meeting places of the Communists in your territory, and the names and addresses of the officers and heads that you are to arrest, are on the attached lists.

You will also arrest all active members where found.

Particular efforts should be made to apprehend all the officers, irrespective of where they may be, and with respect to such officers, their residence should be searched and in every instance all literature, membership cards, records and correspondence are to be taken.

When a citizen is arrested as a communist, he must be present with the officers searching his home at the time of the search.

Meeting rooms should be thoroughly searched.

Locate and obtain the charter. All records, if not found in the meeting rooms, will probably be found in the home of the recording secretary or financial secretary, but in every instance, if possible, records should be found and taken.

All literature, books, paper, pictures on the walls of the meeting places, should be gathered together and tagged with tags which will be supplied you, with the name and address of the person by whom obtained and where obtained.

In searching meeting places, a thorough search should be made and the walls sounded.

It is an order of the Government that violence to those apprehended should be scrupulously avoided.

Immediately upon the apprehension of the alien, or citizen, search him thoroughly. If found in groups in a meeting room, they should be lined up against the wall and searched. Particular efforts should be made to obtain membership cards on the persons who are taken.

Make an absolute search of the individual. No valuables, such as jewelry and monies, to be taken away from those arrested.

After a search has been made of the person arrested you will take all the evidence you have obtained from his person and place it in an envelope, which will be furnished you, placing the name, address, contents of the envelope, by whom taken and where on the outside of the envelope and deliver to me with the alien.

Everybody will remain on duty until relieved, without exception.

Flashlights, string, tags and envelopes should be carried, as per instructions.

In searching rooms of an alien pay particular attention to everything in the room and make a thorough search thereof.

You are also warned to take notice "that no violence is to be used."

You will communicate with me by telephone from your several districts, the number of the telephone herewith given.

Attached you will find a list of those to be apprehended in your district and you will also apprehend all those found arrested with these names at the time of the arrest, whom you find to be active members of the Communist party.

You are also instructed to use reasonable care and good judgment.

The Attorney General's agents carried out their instructions faithfully. The resulting violations of the three principles of personal liberty already mentioned are authenticated by official testimony, as follows:

First, aliens and citizens found in a Communist hall on the night of raids, whether they were members of the organization or not, were seized without any warrant whatever.[16] In New England alone a hundred such persons were imprisoned for several days while the officials telegraphed for warrants to cover them, and hundreds more were not released for many hours. The Attorney General testified on the nation-wide situation:

Where the aliens were assembled at their meeting places and an actual meeting of the Communist Party was in progress the agents of the Department of Justice did take into custody all aliens attending that meeting. It is quite likely that warrants had not been obtained for all such persons, but it is sufficient, it seems to me, that when an alien is apprehended in the commission of the unlawful act that the action of the government officer taking him into custody is warranted. Certainly it could be claimed that if the government officers had visited a meeting place and had permitted aliens found there for whom warrants had not been previously obtained to depart, that they had been derelict in' their duty.

The Attorney General also stated that when persons applied at the Hartford jail to see their friends who had been arrested at a Communist meeting, the visitors were properly arrested and locked up in the jail; for their coming to inquire was *prima facie* evidence of affiliation with the Communist Party.[17]

Mr. Palmer's contention was that his agents faced the same situation as a policeman who witnesses a robbery. If he goes

---

[16] Even where warrants of arrest were used, their legality seems dubious. When 3,000 warrants were issued in bulk, it is hard to see how there could have been compliance with the rule requiring "some substantial supporting evidence" for every warrant. Probably the main evidence consisted of lists of suspected Communists. As to the arrest of citizens, see note 21.

[17] Palmer Deportations Testimony, 69, 76, 115.

to the station house for a warrant the offender will vanish. The
agents "did the safe thing" in arresting every alien apparently
a Communist. This analogy is clearly unsound. For many
crimes a warrant is necessary to arrest, and a deportable alien
is not a criminal at all. Neither he nor a citizen can be deprived of his liberty upon considerations of expediency which
are not the law of the land. Congress made that law, and it
explicitly required that the alien be taken into custody "upon
the warrant of the Secretary of Labor."

Secondly, the property of aliens and citizens was overhauled
and seized without search warrants. Attorney General Palmer
denied that any person or place was searched over the objection of an individual. Naturally an ignorant alien confronted
by a posse of detectives at night would hesitate to object to
anything. Moreover Mr. Palmer's statement was contradicted
by the peremptory language of the Instructions and the sworn
testimony of his own agents.[18] The silence of the press with
respect to the repeated violations of the Fourth Amendment
in raids on radical headquarters contrasts significantly with
the numerous editorial protests during Prohibition against
illegal seizures of liquor and stills.

Thirdly, the hearings before the immigration inspectors were
often unfair. This was in large measure due, not to the fault
of the inspectors, but to the unprecedented pressure of work
and the absence of adequate protection for the rights of the
alien. For nearly a year before the raids aliens had been entitled to counsel throughout the deportation hearings. The old
procedure (described in the preceding section of this chapter),
which deprived them of counsel during the important preliminary hearings, had been considered so harsh by Secretary Wilson that he abolished it early in 1919. On December 29, 1919,
just four days before the raids and during the Secretary's
illness, the old harsh rule was revived. This sudden change in
the law was made through the efforts of the Department of
Justice; and the Attorney General later defended it on the
ground that the examination of an alien, when under the advice
of counsel, "got us nowhere." As soon as the Secretary of
Labor realized what was happening, he restored the right to
counsel; but this was not until January 27, after most of the

---

[18] See also a citizen's account of the raids in 265 Fed. at 40–42.

examinations were completed. Meanwhile, the inspectors heard the evidence without the help of counsel for the defense; and on the other hand, for the first time in the experience of immigration officials (at least in New England), an agent of the Department of Justice was present through every hearing. The alien stood alone before an administrative official, confronted by a member of the force of detectives who had sworn out the warrant against him and accomplished his arrest. Thus the government after issuing warrants for the arrest of 3,000 persons suddenly repealed a rule so as to affect those specific persons and deprive them of rights which were guaranteed to them, not indeed by the Constitution, but by the existing law of the land.

The value of the evidence obtained in this way was also materially affected by the treatment which the aliens underwent before and during their trials. The police dragged many men out of their homes in the dead of night. The aliens, none of them under any criminal charge and many of them held without warrants, were taken on trains and through the streets in handcuffs and chains.[19] The prisoners were herded in vastly overcrowded quarters without sufficient clothing and food. For instance, the Mayor of Detroit described as "intolerable in a civilized city" conditions in the police "bull pen," a room 24 by 30 feet, where over a hundred men were kept for a week. Bail was often fixed at very high amounts; for instance, $10,000, although $500 is the normal sum specified in the Immigration Rules. The men arrested were separated for days from their wives and children, who were left without support by the government. Instead, they were, Mr. Palmer assured us,[20] "looked after by the most prominent charitable organization of their own creed in their locality. It is no part of the Attorney General's duty to look after the families of the violators of our laws." This apology recalls the British General Dyer, who found shooting into a crowd at Amritsar a still more satisfactory way to get rid of sedition, and remarked that picking up the wounded was no affair of his — that was the business of the hospitals.

[19] Palmer Deportations Testimony, 115. On Detroit, Barkley, "Jailing Radicals in Detroit," 110 *Nation* 136 (Jan. 31, 1920). On Boston, Colyer opinion.
[20] See his circular letter in 110 *Nation* 190 (February 14, 1920).

The public approval of these raids rests on a belief that all the thousands of men arrested were dangerous foreigners who advocated violence. Yet the daily press shows the eventual release for want of evidence of over a third of those seized. And a cursory glance at Mr. Palmer's Instructions shows that the character of an individual had absolutely nothing whatever to do with his arrest. The most harmless person was to be seized if suspected of membership in the specified political parties. And although there was no law authorizing the arrest of citizens, these instructions directed that all Communists should be seized, expressly including citizens.[21] Elsewhere it was ordered that if citizens were arrested "through error," they should be referred to the local authorities. Thus United States officials would arrest American citizens for prosecution under the harsh state anti-anarchy acts.

That President Wilson authorized these measures seems impossible. The Attorney General carried through the greatest executive restriction of personal liberty in the history of this country during the President's illness. Even so the British Cabinet took advantage of the illness of their head, Lord Chatham, to make one of the worst onslaughts on freedom in modern England, the expulsion of Wilkes from the House of Commons in 1768. Macaulay's second essay on Chatham gives the facts:

His colleagues for a time continued to entertain the expectation that his health would soon be restored, and that he would emerge from his retirement. But month followed month, and still he remained in mysterious seclusion. . . . They at length ceased to hope or to fear anything from him; and, though he was still nominally Prime Minister, took without scruple steps which they knew to be diametrically opposed to all his opinions and feelings.

The sequel to the raids made it plain that few of the aliens arrested by the Department of Justice would be deported. In the absence of the President, a sharp conflict between Mr. Palmer and the Department of Labor soon developed. Secretary Wilson released all the aliens imprisoned as members of

[21] Many citizens were actually arrested; for example, Peter Frank, born in Ohio, whose only organization was the Shoe Workers' Union, was dragged out of his house in Lynn at 1 A.M. and held *incommunicado* for several days. See Colyer opinion; Barkley, *supra* note 19.

the Communist Labor Party, holding that organization not to be within the deportation statute. Many of those arrested as members of the Communist Party were released by Assistant Secretary Post because their membership was not proved.[22] Judge Anderson in the Colyer case decided after an exhaustive survey of the New England raids that most of the aliens there ordered deported must be discharged for want of a fair trial.

Two comments may be made upon these raids. First, they show the mess we get into when we set out to repress objectionable ideas. Secondly, although it is undoubtedly true (as the Attorney General contended) that the laws requiring warrants for arrest, forbidding searches, and allowing counsel make deportations more difficult, even in the case of dangerous revolutionists, every rule on behalf of personal liberty necessarily diminishes the efficiency of government. Mr. Palmer adopted the attitude of the men he denounced. Because the law hindered the result he wished to accomplish and thought desirable, he disregarded the law.

4. GOVERNMENT SPIES

> *The man who is not a radical at twenty will be a spy at forty.*   Italian proverb.

The existence of spies is one of the worst evils of sedition legislation, whether directed toward prosecution or deportation. Espionage goes with an Espionage Act. Informers have been the inseparable accompaniment of government action against the expression of cpinion since the delators of Tiberius.[23] The state cannot reach such crimes without them. It needs no great force of eavesdroppers to report murders and robberies. The overt act marks the offense, and if a detective is required at all it is either to chase the criminal, to ward off bomb-plots and assassinations, or to discover who is committing especially ingenious thefts. But if political utterances are made criminal, secret police are indispensable to discover that the crime has been committed at all.

[22] For Post's account of the raids, see his *Deportations Delirium of Nineteen-Twenty* (Chicago: C. H. Kerr & Co., 1923), reviewed by Charles P. Howland in 38 *Harvard Law Review* 135 (1924) and by Senator T. J. Walsh of Montana in *New Republic* (Feb. 20, 1924).

[23] Merivale, *The Romans under the Empire*, c. 44.

We do not need to go out of Anglo-Saxon countries to Russia for examples of this system in actual operation. The accounts of the historic English sedition trials are full of the employment of spies at the meetings of political societies. And the spy often passes over an almost imperceptible boundary into the *agent provocateur*, who instigates the utterances he reports, and then into the fabricator, who invents them. There was plenty of this in England, and the same kind of liar, Captain Zaneth of the North West Mounted Police, was exposed in Canada in 1920 after convicting one of the Winnipeg strike leaders on a charge of seditious conspiracy.[24] This dirty business is the price a government must pay for the suppression of political crime. Are we willing to pay that price?

"The freedom of a country," writes Sir Erskine May, "may be measured by its immunity from this baleful agency." [25] We have never had it before in the United States, but there is disquieting evidence that this inevitable machinery of sedition-hunters is already at work. At the end of the instructions which W. J. Flynn, Director of the Bureau of Investigation in the Department of Justice, issued on August 12, 1919, "to all special agents and employees," ordering an investigation of the promotion of sedition and revolution; which should be particularly directed to aliens with a view of obtaining deportation cases, we find this enigmatic passage:

Special agents will constantly keep in mind the necessity of preserving the cover of our confidential informants, and in no case shall they rely upon the testimony of such cover informants during deportation proceedings.[26]

Who these "cover informants" were is disclosed by the *New York Times* [27] in its account of the raids on the Communists four months later:

[24] J. A. Stevenson, "A Set-back for Reaction in Canada," 110 *Nation* 292 (March 6, 1920).
[25] May, *Constitutional History of England*, II, 150. For facts about English spies at political meetings, see Brown, *French Revolution in English History*, index *sub* Spies; Hammond, *The Skilled Labourer, 1760–1832*, pp. 341–376 (1919).
[26] *Investigation Activities of the Department of Justice*, 66th Cong., 1st Sess., Senate Document No. 153 (1919), p. 34.
[27] January 3, 1920. For additional evidence as to the activities of these informants, see the testimony of Captain Swinburne Hale in *Rule Making in*

For months Department of Justice men, dropping all other work, had concentrated on the Reds. Agents quietly infiltrated into the radical ranks, slipped casually into centers of agitation, and went to work, sometimes as cooks in remote mining colonies, sometimes as miners, again as steel workers, and, where the opportunity presented itself, as "agitators" of the wildest type. Although careful not to inspire, suggest, or aid the advancement of overt acts or propaganda, several of the agents, "under cover" men, managed to rise in the radical movement, and become, in at least one instance, the recognized leader of a district.

The letter of instructions about the raids from Chief Burke of the Bureau of Investigation to his Boston agent, December 27, 1919, whatever its precise meaning, shows that United States employees were active and influential members of both Communist parties:

If possible, you should arrange with your under-cover informants to have meetings of the Communist Party and the Communist Labor Party held on the night set. . . . This, of course, would facilitate the making of the arrests.

It is to be hoped that these men have been as "careful" as the *Times* reporter says, but we would do well to recall one more warning from May:

The relations between the Government and its informers are of extreme delicacy. Not to profit by timely information were a crime; but to retain in Government pay, and to reward spies and informers, who consort with conspirators as their sworn accomplices, and encourage while they betray them in their crimes, is a practice for which no plea can be offered. No Government, indeed, can be supposed to have expressly instructed its spies to instigate the perpetration of crime; but to be unsuspected, every spy must be zealous in the cause which he pretends to have espoused; and his zeal in a criminal enterprise is a direct encouragement of crime. So odious is the character of a spy, that his ignominy is shared by his employers, against whom public feeling has never failed to pronounce itself, in proportion to the infamy of the agent, and the complicity of those whom he served.[28]

Order the Consideration of S. 3317, Hearings before House Committee on Rules, 66th Cong., 2d Sess., on H. Res. 438 (1920); Colyer opinion; Palmer Deportations Testimony, 48, 87 ff., 199; Report upon Illegal Practices.

[28] May, *id.*, II, 151–152. See Graham Wallas, *Francis Place* (New York, 1919), p. 121.

A very sinister opportunity is afforded to the enemies of any radical organization to send spies into its councils for the purpose of inducing the insertion of violent clauses in its program or other publications. Once this is accomplished, all alien members of the organization are presented with the alternatives of immediate resignation or deportation; to say nothing of the fact that citizen members may face prosecution under a state syndicalism statute or perhaps under a future federal Sedition Act. The clauses in deportation and syndicalism statutes making mere membership a basis for severe penalties render it so easy to destroy any organization in the way I have suggested that the temptation may not be resisted in times of excitement. Indeed, Judge Anderson believed that some of the extreme planks in the Communist Party Platform, which Secretary Wilson thought to bring this party within the terms of the Deportation Act, might possibly have been inserted by spies in this very manner. Even though the government which employs the spy may strongly discountenance such practices, the spy may nevertheless be impelled to use them through his affiliations with an unscrupulous employers' association or detective agency or conservative union, which has everything to gain by wrecking the radical group in such an easy and thoroughgoing way.

5. A REVIEW OF DIFFERENT TYPES OF RADICALS HELD FOR DEPORTATION

> *Give me your tired, your poor,*
> *Your huddled masses, yearning to breathe free,*
> *The wretched refuse of your teeming shore:*
> *Send these, the homeless, tempest-tossed, to me:*
> *I lift my lamp beside the golden door.*
> EMMA LAZARUS, inscription on the
> base of the Statue of Liberty.

The public is in error in assuming that all the aliens arrested for deportation were dangerous characters. Some of those expelled to Europe were undoubtedly turbulent persons like Emma Goldman, but not all the persons who were held to come within the Deportation Act were of the same sort. In order to make it plain just what kind of men the government tried to deport, I shall review the actual decisions relating to three types of radical aliens — Communists, Industrial Workers of the World, and anarchists.

a. Communists

The Communist Labor Party and the Communist Party, which were the chief objective of the raids of January, 1920, seceded from the Socialist Party in September, 1919, taking with them several state Socialist organizations, and a very large number of left-wing Socialists. Mr. Gordon Watkins, of the University of Illinois, reports the following estimates of the size of the three parties: Socialist Party after the secession, 39,000; Communist Labor Party, 10,000 to 30,000; Communist Party, 30,000 to 60,000, of whom 25,000 belonged to foreign-language federations which were predominantly Russian in their constituency.[29] The Secretary of Labor ruled that all the aliens in the Communist Party were *ipso facto* liable to deportation under the Act of 1918, as members of or affiliated with an "organization that entertains a belief in, teaches or advocates the overthrow by force or violence of the government of the United States."[30] The Attorney General's Instructions in the raids of January, 1920, evidently put the Communist Labor Party in the same class. Consequently, a card from either party found on an alien furnished the immigration officials with what they called "a perfect case." Yet, Secretary Wilson took a different view of the Communist Labor Party and held it outside the Act.

These various decisions raise two questions: (*a*) When does an organization advocate force and violence? (*b*) if it does so,

[29] Watkins, "The Present Status of Socialism in the United States," 124 *Atlantic Monthly* 821 (December, 1919).

[30] *In re* Englebrert Preis, January 24, 1920, reprinted in *Sedition*, Hearing before House Judiciary Committee, 66th Cong., 2d Sess. (1920), p. 17; cited hereafter as House Judiciary Hearings. All the important administrative decisions are reprinted in three pamphlets of Hearings before a Subcommittee of the House Committee on Immigration and Naturalization at the same session, entitled *Communist and Anarchist Deportation Cases, I.W.W. Deportation Cases, Communist Labor Party Cases.* See Skeffington v. Katzeff, 277 Fed. 129 (C. C. A. 1st, 1922). For a recent review of Communist deportations, see Note, 48 *Yale Law Journal* 111 (1938). As to the problem of administrative finality on this issue of criminality of the Communist Party, see *infra* Chapter XIII, note 5.

can all its members be justly subjected to painful consequences?

(*a*) The difficulties of the first question have already been pointed out in the preceding chapter, and the Program of the Communist Party affords a practical illustration thereof. Although this Program [31] plainly intends that the proletariat shall "conquer and destroy the bourgeois parliamentary state" and substitute a very different political and economic system, there is not a word either in it or in the Party Manifesto which expressly says that the conquest is to be by force and violence. The Secretary of Labor, admitting that such a violent purpose is essential to bring the organization within the scope of the Act, found it inferentially in various passages, for example:

Participation in parliamentary campaigns, which in the general struggle of the proletariat is of secondary importance, is for the purpose of revolutionary propaganda only.

The conquest of the power of the state is accomplished by the mass power of the proletariat. Political mass strikes are a vital factor in developing this mass power, preparing the working class for the conquest of capitalism.

Mass action, in the form of general political strikes and demonstrations, unites the energy and forces of the proletariat, brings proletarian mass pressure upon the bourgeois state. Out of this struggle develops revolutionary mass action, the means for the proletarian conquest of power.

And then, to make the violent purpose still more clear in his eyes, a passage was cited from the Manifesto of the Communist International, which the Communist Party was said to accept as part of its policy:

The revolutionary era compels the proletariat to make use of the means of battle which will concentrate its entire energies, namely,

[31] *American Labor Year Book*, 1919–20, edited by Alexander Trachtenberg, published by Rand School of Social Science, New York, pp. 416–419. Also in House Judiciary Hearings, pp. 78–80, which contains many other important documents relating to the two Communist parties. Thus the platforms and manifestos, which were supposed to endanger our government when printed by Communists, were widely distributed in government documents. And no harm resulted; quite the contrary. Similarly, the State of New York in 1919–20 condemned several men to prison for being concerned with these long-winded exhortations, and in 1939 reprinted many more radical manifestos in an 800-page volume at public expense! *Report of the Joint Legislative Committee to*

mass action, with its logical resultant, direct conflict with the governmental machinery in open combat. All other methods, such as revolutionary use of bourgeois parliamentarism, will be of only secondary significance.

From such quotations the Secretary of Labor drew this summary:

It is apparent, that the Communist Party is not merely a political party seeking the control of affairs of state, but a revolutionary party seeking to conquer and destroy the state in open combat. And the only conclusion is that the Communist Party of America is an organization that believes in, teaches, and advocates the overthrow by force or violence of the government of the United States.

This is certainly a delicate task of interpretation, more befitting a theologian or a Shakespearean scholar than a practical office-holder. We are a long way from the man against whom the Deportation Act was supposed to protect us — the alien who urges his hearers to blow up the Capitol this afternoon, kidnap the President tonight, and elect Commissars on the Mall tomorrow. An alternative exegesis of the sacred texts, which has at least as much probability as the Secretary's commentary, is that the combat is to be through proletarian control over industry, which will be used not merely to obtain bigger wages and shorter hours but also to put the government into such an uncomfortable position that it will surrender all its powers to the working class and shut up shop. A third and cynical view is that this bombastic militant phraseology, which has been going the rounds since 1848, has boiled down to mean little more nowadays than a dream of indefinite large-scale political and economic effort on the part of those· who feel down-trodden — "We'll get even with those prosperous skunks someday, somehow!"

Who would be bold enough to say on oath that these documents do contemplate violence or do exclude violence? The dream is too vague to analyze.

No doubt phrases like "revolutionary class struggle" do at least express the hope of big strikes sometime or other for political ends, with a general strike looming in the remoter distance. Such strikes like any other strike may lead to vio-

---

Investigate the Administration and Enforcement of the Law, Legislative document (1939) No. 98.

lence, but few Secretaries of Labor will admit that advocacy of a strike is *per se* "advocacy of force and violence." The general strike may be more effective against a government than an armed rebellion, and Congress can, if it wants, deal severely with those who urge a general strike; but then Congress ought to say so in plain English. It did not.

Objectionable as the purposes and methods of the Communist Party seem to all who have faith in our system of representative government and in the possibility of progress through public opinion and the ballot, those purposes and methods do not fall with any certainty under the "force and violence" clauses of sedition and deportation statutes. The contrary argument of Secretary Wilson and several judges runs like this: "Communists do not advocate political methods. Therefore, they advocate violent methods. Q. E. D." One might as well argue that since Communists are not Democrats, they must be Republicans. Non-political methods of overturning a government are not necessarily criminal and violent methods. Francis Place, the tailor, overturned the government of England in 1832 and precipitated a revolution which the voters had failed to accomplish simply by posting placards urging the people to start a run on the banks. There is a middle method of political change between the ballot and the bomb, namely economic pressure, and that, however unwise or injurious in nature, may very well be the method of the Communist Party. It advocates the overthrow of our government, but not by force and violence.

The Communist Labor Party Program has the same talk about "the conquest of political power by the workers," "the class struggle," "action of the masses." It favors "the establishment of the Dictatorship of the Proletariat" by making "the great industrial battle its major campaigns, to show the value of the strike as a political weapon." [32] It is a revolutionary working-class party, but there is nothing in its Platform or Program which expressly advocates force or violence. And so we are back again among delicate problems of textual interpretation.

[32] *American Labor Year Book*, cited note 31, pp. 414–416. See Secretary Wilson's opinion in favor of Communist Labor Party, Post Deportations Testimony, 152. Contrast convictions of members under anti-anarchy acts of states.

Undoubtedly there are men in both Communist parties who would use force to get rid of their opponents. Every party has such men. Billy Sunday, a well-known evangelist, preached, "If I had my way with these ornery wild-eyed Socialists and I.W.W.'s, I would stand them up before a firing squad and save space on our ships." Guy Empey, a popular author, told his hearers to get rid of Bolsheviks; "the necessary implements can be obtained at any hardware store." A Republican official in Massachusetts wanted to shoot Bolsheviks and traitors every morning, at least in war time, and the next morning he would have a trial to see if they were guilty. But such men do not turn their party into a party of force and violence.

There is no sure test of what a party does advocate. The utterances of a leader may represent only his personal view and be rejected by his associates. Even platforms have never been taken very seriously in any party. The law has got itself into a bad mess by starting investigations into the opinions of associations, the vaguest kind of inquiry imaginable. The expulsion of hundreds of workingmen from their homes in the United States (or their punishment under severe sedition laws) ought not to turn on this sort of guesswork.

(b) Even if Secretary Wilson is right in his ruling that some of the tenets of the Communist Party advocate force and violence, it does not necessarily follow that all its members are supporters of violence. It is true that persons joining the Communist Party signed a statement of allegiance to its platform, but this ought not to be taken as conclusive that they favor violence, especially as there is no express mention of violence in that document and the party had not then been declared illegal. The facts show that many persons are affiliated with this party for various innocent reasons. Some believe in peaceful industrial action as the only cure for social ills, some join because their friends do, others without being members of the party frequent its headquarters (and so may be held to be affiliated) to take lessons in physical geography or because the Communist restaurant has better meals at cheap prices than any other place. In Massachusetts, many persons were members of the Communist Party because they belonged to the local state Socialist organization when it seceded and turned Communist in September, 1919, and their year's Socialist member-

ship had not yet expired.[33] Many such men fall within
Secretary Wilson's ruling just as much as the real revolutionists, very few of whom seem to have been caught. When
hundreds were lined up together after the raids, the *New York
Times* reported, "They were a tame, unterroristic looking
crowd, and their appearance bore out the statements of opera-
tives that not a man had tried to put up a fight."

The novel idea for our law, that guilt is not necessarily personal but can result from mere association, will be discussed
at length in the twelfth chapter of this book.

When we count how few persons out of the many thousands
arrested were actually deported as Communists and estimate
which of the few deported were really bad, then we can ask
ourselves whether it was worth while (instead of picking out
the conspicuously dangerous aliens for expulsion in the ordinary course) to go through all the enormous expense, all the
spying, arresting, and herding, to save the country from men
who in ordinary peace-time conditions were advocating a revolution at some distant and indefinite day through legislative
and other propaganda and occasional future unspecified and
improbable general strikes.

b. Industrial Workers of the World

The Industrial Workers of the World, more generally known
as the I.W.W. and nicknamed the Wobblies, began in Chicago
in June, 1905, at a convention called to form one great industrial union embracing all industries.[34] The meeting arose from

[33] Judge Anderson said, 265 Fed. at 50: "The rank and file of the less educated membership knew little or nothing about the controversy, or the nature
and extent of the change, if any, in the Program and principles of the party.
Some of them regarded it simply as a change of name; others knew there was
some sort of little understood change in Program and purpose. But the great
mass of the former Socialists who had thus become alleged Communists had no
real comprehension of any important or material change either in their associations or in the political or economic purposes sought to be achieved by their
negligibly weak organizations. Social, educational purposes, and race sympathy,
rather than political agitation, constituted the controlling motives with a large
share of them. They joined the local Russian or Polish or Lithuanian Socialist
or Communist Club, just as citizens join neighborhood clubs, social or religious,
or civic, or fraternal."
[34] This description is based on Brissenden, *The I.W.W.* (2d ed. 1917). See
also his article in 8 *Encyclopaedia of the Social Sciences* 13 (1932). Some re-
semblances will be noted on the economic side between the I.W.W. and the C.I.O.

a conviction that the autocracy and craft form of unionism then embodied in the American Federation of Labor made solidarity impossible and hindered contests with the increasingly integrated organizations of employers.

On its strictly economic side the I.W.W. involved a single card for all members, a common defense fund, and centralized control of policy. It planned energetic campaigns to draw in the 90 per cent of workers hitherto unorganized, notably farm laborers. In 1919 it comprised seventeen subsidiary industrial unions (oil workers, fishery workers, etc.) and a General Recruiting Union. If a subsidiary union or local was involved in a strike, the central board could call out any other subsidiary. Any strike settlement between such a subsidiary and employers was not to be considered binding until approved by the central board, so that collective bargains could be easily disregarded.

The I.W.W. also had a revolutionary side, which Brissenden describes as follows: "They ask that industry be democratized by giving the workers — all grades of workers — exclusive control in its management. They ask to have the management of industrial units transferred from the hands of those who think chiefly in terms of income to those who think in terms of the production process, . . . 'Let the workers run the industries.' " (Observe the contrast with the Communist demand for control of industry by the state, albeit a proletarian state.) This purpose was expressed in the preamble to the constitution in fiery terms, beginning:

The working class and the employing class have nothing in common. There can be no peace so long as hunger and want are found among millions of working people and the few, who make up the employing class, have all the good things of life.

Between these two classes a struggle must go on until the workers of the world organize as a class, take possession of the earth and the machinery of production and abolish the wage system.

The I.W.W. has been conspicuous and turbulent rather than successful. From a peak of 100,000 members in 1912, it fell to about 35,000 in 1919 — mostly non-dues-paying. Its strength has lain among New England textile-workers, and miners and migratory agricultural laborers on the Pacific Coast. Local unpopularity on account of its missionary activities among the masses of low-paid and hitherto unorganized workers was in-

creased by its militant strike tactics, by its frequent conflicts
with police about free speech on street-corners, and by elusive
and very damaging practices like sabotage and burning crops
of unsympathetic farmers. Because of its poaching among
A. F. of L. members, it is hated by organized labor. Its hand
is against every man, and every man's hand against the I.W.W.

Detested practices like sabotage are not in the constitution
of the organization, but are described in inflammatory leaflets.
Hence the question has been constantly raised whether they
are advocated by the organization as such, or only by particular organizers and members. The state sedition prosecutions
usually attributed them to the organization, and also treated
the preamble as advocating violence and destruction of property.[35] Both the Department of Justice and the Secretary of
Labor reached the opposite conclusion.[36] "Its constitution and
by-laws have been adroitly drawn so as to avoid the possibility
of construing it as teaching either anarchy or sabotage." Consequently, mere membership is not a ground for deportation.
However, many alien leaders, organizers, and distributors of
literature have been deported;[37] and if they urged sabotage
they were undoubtedly within the Act. One judge canceled the
naturalization of an I.W.W. organizer, who at the time he became a citizen approved of sabotage and indorsed the preamble
and constitution of the organization.[38] The judge said that
since the I.W.W. is "opposed to all forms of government, advocates lawlessness, and constructs its own morals, which are not
in accord with those of well-ordered society," but are "adapted
by design to the demoralization and degradation thereof," its
adherents must *ipso facto* be guilty of fraud in declaring that
they are attached to the principles of the United States Constitution. Therefore, they cannot become citizens, and if they do,
the right can be taken away and deportation follows.

[35] For example State *v.* Moilen, 140 Minn. 122 (1918); State *v.* Lowery, 104
Wash. 520 (1918), which refused to admit in evidence the Report of the President's Mediation Commission.

[36] Investigation Activities, etc., 33; letter of W. B. Wilson to John E. Milholland, 110 *Nation* 327 (March 13, 1920). Sabotage may be punishable by
federal statute. See Chapter IV, note 1.

[37] *Ex parte* Bernat and Dixon, 255 Fed. 429 (1918); Guiney *v.* Bonham, 261
Fed. 582 (C. C. A., 1919). *Cf.* U. S. *ex rel.* Grau *v.* Uhl, 262 Fed. 532 (1919).

[38] U. S. *v.* Swelgin, 254 Fed. 884 (1918). On denaturalization generally, see
Chapter II, note 106.

When we consider the wisdom of coercion against the propagandist activities of the I.W.W., as distinct from the commission of sabotage and other violence, which of course must be vigorously punished, the basic question is whether the organization is fundamentally revolutionary or really a queer sort of labor union. The use of deportation to break up unions seems to me wholly wrong. It is said, for instance, that when the Chinese workers in New York chop suey restaurants organized a union and struck on New Year's Eve, 1918, the leaders were arrested for deportation.[39] The facts of another case are given in the decision of a United States Judge, Bourquin, who discharged the alien held for deportation:

From August, 1918, to February, 1919, the Butte Union of the Industrial Workers of the World was dissatisfied with working places, conditions, and wages in the mining industry, and to remedy them was discussing ways and means, including strike if necessary. In consequence, its hall and orderly meetings were several times raided and mobbed by employers' agents, and federal agents and soldiers duly officered, acting by federal authority and without warrant or process. The union members, men and women, many of them citizens, limited themselves to oral protests, though in the circumstances the inalienable right and law of self-defense justified resistance to the last dread extremity. There was no disorder save that of the raiders. These, mainly uniformed and armed, overawed, intimidated,· and forcibly entered, broke, and destroyed property, searched persons, effects, and papers, arrested persons, seized papers and documents, cursed, insulted, beat, dispersed, and bayoneted union members by order of the commanding officer. They likewise entered petitioner's adjacent living apartment, insulted his wife, searched his person and effects, and seized his papers and documents, and in general, in a populous and orderly city, perpetrated a reign of terror, violence, and crime against citizen and alien alike, and whose only offense seems to have been peaceable insistence upon and exercise of a clear legal right.[40]

This policy opens up dangerous possibilities of influence not only by employers but also by rival conservative unions to secure the annihilation of radical labor organizations through wholesale arrests and expulsions. The eventual disappearance

[39] *American Labor Year Book*, 1919–20, p. 113.
[40] *Ex parte* Jackson, 263 Fed. 110 (1920). The whole opinion should be read.

of the I.W.W. is highly desirable, but is the deportation of all intelligent alien members the best method to obtain that result?

The government ought not to be satisfied to base drastic action merely on an examination of the literature of the organization by men who are unfamiliar with its economic background. An alternative plan for dealing with the very difficult problem of this organization would be a vigorous suppression and punishment of sabotage, while the federal government before deporting any more members should ascertain the possibility of curing the causes of the revolutionary character of the I.W.W. A good deal of the viciousness in tactics arises from the continued existence of a large body of migratory labor, homeless, wifeless, jobless. The government has at hand for purposes of consultation men like Brissenden who have studied the I.W.W. carefully. Such a conference might evolve a new and more satisfactory policy.

For example, deportation does not seem quite the right way to handle the case of John Meehan,[41] who was arrested in Everett, Washington, in May, 1917, for violation of a local anti-billboard law, and then ordered deported as an I.W.W. to England, from which country he had come twenty-four years before. After eighteen months of incarceration he was landed, hatless, penniless, and with insufficient clothing, in England, where he had neither kith nor kin.

c. Anarchists

Anarchists have long been subject to exclusion and expulsion. If the term be taken in the popular sense of supporters of bomb-throwing and assassination generally, the statute is undoubtedly constitutional, and was so held by the Supreme Court in sustaining the exclusion of an Englishman named Turner.[42] The case possesses some literary interest, for one of his counsel was Edgar Lee Masters, whose acid-bitten portraits of life at Spoon River indicated possibilities of improvement in American life.

It is well known, however, that anarchism has no necessary connection with violence. It really means the belief which

[41] Charles Recht (counsel for Meehan), *American Deportation and Exclusion Laws*, p. 9.
[42] Turner *v.* Williams, 194 U. S. 279 (1904).

opposes every kind of forcible government and favors the abolition of all coercion over the individual by the community [43] Philosophical anarchists argue that most governmental action is required because of inequalities in property, and point to many activities of life where these inequalities do not operate and coercion has been found unnecessary. For example, if a number of friends are cruising on a sloop, they require no policeman to keep order or compel each person to do his allotted task. Mutual agreement and the desire to achieve praise and avoid blame from one's companions furnish sufficient incentive to right action. The anarchist looks forward to the time when life will be such a perpetual holiday, and hopes to convert all men to the same faith in human nature. While waiting and working for the millennium, he will, with rare exceptions, think it consistent with his theories to render obedience to existing laws, until they shall disappear forever. Kropotkin and Tolstoy in Russia, Herbert Spencer and Bertrand Russell in England, have at least been strongly influenced by this view that all government is evil. It is obvious that such men and many others have no desire to employ force to end force, but seek to attain their ideal system gradually and peacefully through discussion and education.

These philosophical anarchists caused much perplexity in the early days in this country, even to such a strong champion of soul-liberty as Roger Williams, who argued for their suppression in his celebrated letter of 1655 to the people of Providence:

There goes many a ship to sea, with many hundred souls in one ship, whose weal and woe is common, and is a true picture of a commonwealth or a human combination or society. It hath fallen out sometimes that both Papists and Protestants, Jews and Turks, may be embarked in one ship; upon which supposal I affirm, that all the liberty of conscience that ever I pleaded for, turns upon these two hinges — that none of the Papists, Protestants, Jews, or Turks, be forced to come to the ship's prayers or worship, nor compelled from their own particular prayers or worship, if they practise any. I further add, that I never denied that, notwithstanding this liberty, the commander of this ship ought to command the ship's course, yea, and also command that justice, peace, and sobriety, be kept and

---

[43] Bertrand Russell, *Proposed Roads to Freedom*, p. 32.

practised, both among the seamen and all the passengers. If any of the seamen refuse to perform their services or passengers to pay their freight; if any refuse to help, in person or purse, toward the common charges or defense; if any refuse to obey the common laws and orders of the ship, concerning their common peace or preservation; if any shall mutiny and rise up against their commanders and officers; if any should preach or write that there ought to be no commanders or officers, because all are equal in Christ, therefore no masters nor officers, no laws nor orders, nor corrections, nor punishments; — I say, I never denied, but in such cases, whatever is pretended, the commander or commanders may judge, resist, compel, and punish such transgressors, according to their deserts and merits. This, if seriously and honestly minded, may, if it so please the Father of Lights, let in some light to such as willingly shut not their eyes.[44]

However, when government became stronger in this country and stood ready to punish any of these men who actually disobeyed the law, it was realized that they presented no danger merely because of their thought and teachings. Many Quakers in the Colonies refused to participate in government because of the New Testament teachings of non-resistance. A similar philosophy was held by many great Americans in the 1840's when as Emerson said, with a twinkle in his eye, every reading man went round with a draft of a new community in his waistcoat pocket. The famous settlements at Brook Farm and Fruitlands were peopled by just such persons. Thoreau was this kind of anarchist.

The Deportation Act undoubtedly applies to these peaceful disbelievers in organized government as well as to the bombers, but the power of Congress to expel them has never been squarely upheld by the Supreme Court. In the Turner decision, which involved only the exclusion of a violent anarchist, Chief Justice Fuller said nothing at all about expulsion, but suggested in passing that Congress could refuse to admit even innocent anarchists if it was of the opinion "that the *tendency* of the general exploitation of such views is so dangerous to the public weal that aliens who hold and advocate them would be undesirable additions to our population." On the other hand, Justice Brewer, in concurring, expressly refused to determine the right of an alien if only a philosophical anarchist, "one

<hr/>

[44] Moses Coit Tyler, *History of American Literature*, I, 261.

who simply entertains and expresses the opinion that all government is a mistake, and that society would be better off
without any." [45]

The public does not realize that it is men of this type as
well as violent anarchists whom the government is now sending
out of the country after long residence, during which they have
necessarily remained aliens since the law forbids their naturalization. Take, for instance, the case of Frank R. Lopez, a
Spaniard of the Ferrer school. This man had been in the
United States seventeen years, belonged to the A. F. of L., was
married, had a son born in this country, owned his own home,
and had always been a law-abiding member of society. Yet he
was ordered deported to Spain because he held and expounded,
in speech and writing, views which the court expressly stated
to be only philosophical anarchism and in no sense advocacy
of a resort to force and revolution.[46] Judge Rogers emphasized
the point that Lopez had never become naturalized, overlook-
ing the fact that if he had become a citizen our courts would
take his naturalization papers away from him on the ground
that they were obtained by fraud.[47] Lopez told the court:

I have done nothing wrong; I call it an injustice; if a man is
going to be punished for his thoughts and ideas, it is an injustice.

Thus the Deportation Act expressly authorizes men to be
thrown out of this country after long residence for ideas which
they have never expressed to a single person until they were
subjected to an inquisition by the immigration inspector. Such
a law suppresses not only freedom of speech but freedom of
thought. The following entry added by the Inspector to the
testimony of Louis Gyori, who was ordered deported because
he expected a revolution which will compel every one to work
but will only come at some uncertain time when the majority
want it, is very significant:

Very careful and steady questioning was necessary to bring out
the alien's beliefs, political and industrial.

[45] 194 U. S. at 294, 296; italics mine.
[46] Lopez v. Howe, 259 Fed. 401 (C. C. A. 2d, 1919), giving much of the
alien's testimony; appeal dismissed in 254 U. S. 613 (1920). See also *Ex parte*
Pettine, 259 Fed. 733 (1919); 21 *New Republic* 98, 356; 12 A. L. R. 197 (1920)
(cases on various kinds of deported radicals in supplementary annotations).
[47] U. S. v. Stuppiello, 260 Fed. 483 (1919).

6. THE DEPORTATIONS AND THE BILL OF RIGHTS

> *America is West and the wind blowing.*
> *America is a great word and the snow,*
> *A way, a white bird, the rain falling,*
> *A shining thing in the mind and the gulls' call.*
> *America is neither a land nor a people,*
> *A word's shape it is, a wind's sweep —*
> *America is alone: many together,*
> *Many of one mouth, of one breath,*
> *Dressed as one — and none brothers among them:*
> *Only the taught speech and the aped tongue.*
> *America is alone and the gulls calling.*
>
> ARCHIBALD MACLEISH, American Letter.

Having thus shown that the deportation statute has been put into force against men who are in no way advocates of violence, I now return to the general question of the wisdom of expelling men from this country because of mere membership in a society considered objectionable or because they express or have in their minds peaceful ideas which are regarded as having a bad political tendency.

Drastic deportations are commonly defended on the ground that the power of Congress to decide what aliens shall remain in this country is unrestricted by the Constitution. Chief Justice Fuller suggests that if Congress can shut out all aliens, it can therefore shut out any group of aliens it pleases. This kind of reasoning leads into queer places.[48] Because a Republican Congress can refuse to naturalize all aliens, can it therefore refuse to naturalize those who express the intention of casting a Democratic vote at the next election?

Our interest, however, is in wisdom rather than constitutionality, not in what the government *cannot* do but in what it *ought not* to do. Much that is constitutional may be unwise. The Bill of Rights, as urged at the outset of this book, is not only a boundary which Congress and officials must not cross, but an exhortation and a guide for their action inside that boundary. So let us leave aside all questions of the possible unconstitutionality of some deportation measures. Our pur-

---

[48] A similar argument about a city's right to exclude radical speakers from parks was rejected in Hague *v.* C. I. O., 307 U. S. 496 (1939). See Chapter XI, section VIII.

pose shall be, instead, to consider the expulsion of men with unpopular ideas in the light of the fundamental national policies declared in the First and Fifth Amendments.

Aliens are "persons" within the Fifth Amendment, which establishes the principle that their liberty and property must not be taken away except "by due process of law," that is, by methods free from arbitrariness and appropriate to the emergency. Thus the government could not turn the aliens whom it wished to deport loose in an open boat on the Atlantic, or carry them across the border into Mexico and leave them wandering in the desert. No one would consider this a reasonable way of returning them to their own country. Moreover, the method of classifying aliens for deportation is as important as the manner of expulsion. If Congress has unlimited power to remove alien members of any group it chooses, all aliens of Jewish race, if they happen to be unpopular at the moment, can be ousted no matter how long they have been in the United States. The Supreme Court has repeatedly decided that the mere existence of a legislative power, such as taxation, does not sanction a discriminatory exercise of that power against a group such as all red-headed men, who are selected arbitrarily without reasonable relation to the facts and the needs of society. In particular, it would be undesirable to classify the objects of any recognized Congressional power solely for the purpose of accomplishing a result which the First Amendment was framed to prevent. For example, Congress can tax all incomes, but an income tax of 50 per cent on Socialist college professors alone would be a convenient but obviously unsound device to block open discussion and the search for truth. Furthermore, the power of Congress over the expulsion of aliens should be used much more cautiously than the power to refuse them admission, because the deprivation of liberty and property is so much greater after an alien has once been admitted and become settled in this country.

At this point I must prepare to meet the argument that the deportation or exclusion of radicals has nothing to do with freedom of speech. Thus Chief Justice Fuller said in the anarchist case:

It is, of course, true that if an alien is not permitted to enter this country, or, having entered contrary to law, is expelled, he is in fact cut off from worshiping or speaking or publishing or petitioning in the country, but that is merely because of his exclusion therefrom. He does not become one of the people to whom these things are secured by our Constitution by an attempt to enter forbidden by law.[49]

This argument is bad because it regards freedom of speech as purely the individual interest of the alien. We have seen in the first chapter that it is also a social interest of the community as a whole. When an active-minded alien is barred out or put out, persons already here are seriously affected because they are denied the privilege of listening to and associating with a foreign thinker. Furthermore, the progress of the country as a whole may be gravely retarded. Truth is truth, whether it comes from a citizen or an alien, and the refusal to admit a wise foreigner, especially if there is a postal censorship on books, may simply result in our remaining ignorant. Massachusetts in the middle of the eighteenth century would have been unwilling to allow Bishop Berkeley to settle in her midst, but if Rhode Island had also refused to admit him, it would have impoverished American thought. Refusal to admit Bertrand Russell would operate in the same way. Roman Catholic citizens of the United States would surely be aggrieved by a law barring all future immigrants of that faith. Therefore, freedom of speech is necessarily affected by the exclusion of aliens for their opinions, and such exclusion is unconstitutional unless the social interest in the attainment of truth is outweighed in the balance by the other interests involved. The First Amendment does not read, "No citizen shall be deprived of freedom of speech." It prohibits all laws "abridging the freedom of speech or of the press."

What has been said applies still more forcibly to the expulsion of long-established aliens for their views and utterances. This has always been a favorite method of dealing with the heterodox. Almost all the wholesale deportations of history, just like Mr. Palmer's January raid, have been an effort to overcome "evil thinking." Spain expelled the Moors; England in the reign of Edward I banished fifteen thousand Jews;

[49] *Supra*, note 42. See State *v.* Sinchuk, 96 Conn. 605 (1921) (freedom of speech not applicable to alien prosecuted for sedition); adversely criticized in 31 *Yale Law Journal* 422 and 20 *Michigan Law Review* 538.

and Louis XIV in 1685 drove out the Huguenots from France. In 1891 President Harrison called the attention of Congress to the action of Russia, a friendly nation, in banishing thousands of Jews.[50] Although there are many precedents in history for the wholesale expulsion of Communists, they are not precedents which we should be proud to follow.

Therefore, the deportations may infringe the national policy expressed by the First Amendment, even if they do not transcend the extreme limits of constitutional power. Indeed, the problem of unpopular aliens in our midst is only one aspect of the much broader problem: what is the wisest attitude that a nation can take toward heterodox thinkers of all sorts? Of course, the Bill of Rights does not deny to the government the power of self-preservation. Some opinions may be so dangerous to the nation that men holding them may be kept out if they seek entrance, and if they are already here they may be imprisoned or (when aliens) expelled. On the other hand, we must never forget that foreigners as well as citizens share in what John Stuart Mill calls [51] "the importance, to man and society, of a large variety in types of character, and of giving full freedom to human nature to expand itself in innumerable and conflicting directions."

So we must determine the limits of freedom of speech in relation to deportations according to the principles laid down in the first chapter. Let us outline the conflicting factors which affect the expulsion of radical aliens, with the hope of aiding the discovery of a wise solution.

In favor of deportation are, first, the desire of society for order, which was considered in the last chapter, and besides this, the interest of the nation in keeping its population free from elements which are considered undesirable additions to our present and future stock. The same social need found expression in the Chinese Exclusion Acts. It is this second factor which makes the power of Congress over aliens so wide. The war power should, I have endeavored to show, be used against utterances only to ward off dangerous acts, but this power over immigration is primarily directed to dangerous persons. It is

[50] Moore's *Digest of International Law*, VI, 358; this has reference to Russian subjects. On American Jews expelled from Russia, see *id.*, IV, 111 ff.
[51] Mill, *Autobiography* (World's Classics, ed. Laski), p. 215.

concerned less with what men do than with what they are —
whether they are diseased, crippled, of psychopathic inferi-
ority, liable to become a public charge. The danger-test of the
Schenck case still holds good, but in a new form. Congress
may wisely act now, although there is "no clear and present
danger" of violence, for "the substantive evil which Congress
has the right to prevent" is in this problem the presence of
persons who are so undesirable that they ought to be denied
or deprived of an American domicile.

Undoubtedly, men may be undesirable and dangerous persons because of their ideas as well as physical and mental
derangements. On the other hand, the need of society for
truth and progress must come into play, and in determining
who are undesirable we must be ever on our guard against
applying the test of conjectural and remote tendencies. It is
not at all the same provable question of fact as heart trouble
or insanity.[52] For instance, much of the reasoning in the philosophical anarchist cases, which stigmatize the doctrine as
"inimical to civilization," is purely speculative, and smacks of
the eighteenth-century sedition trials. And the organization
clauses, in expelling men who are not undesirable themselves
just because they have undesirable associates, carries the logic
of national integrity one step beyond the standard of individual suitability for residence in America.

The record of philosophical anarchists shows that they are
no more prone to disorder than any religious sect, and whatever we may think of their ultimate faith, they may be of great
benefit to society, both for their constructive schemes of voluntary organization and for their pointed criticisms of the evils
of existing governments. Let me offset the reasoning of Roger
Williams with another ship-parable (ships being rather appropriate in this chapter):

A sailor related to me [writes Benjamin Constant] that he was
once on board a vessel with a passenger who had frequently made
the same voyage. This passenger pointed out to the captain a rock
hidden beneath the waves, but the captain would not listen to him.
On his insisting upon it, the captain had him thrown into the sea.

[52] See American School of Magnetic Healing *v*. McAnnulty, 187 U. S. 94
(1902), and the quotations from Justice Brandeis in the Pierce case, pp. 96–97,
supra.

This energetic measure put an end to all remonstrances, and nothing could be more touching than the unanimity that reigned on board, until, suddenly, the vessel touched the reef, and was wrecked. They had drowned the giver of the warning, but the reef remained.[53]

Another reason against wholesale deportation for ideas is that we have a national reputation to live up to, which we should hesitate to sacrifice. We have drawn millions of workers to our soil, not merely by the material magnet of high wages, but by the great hope of freedom from all the tyranny of European empires. After priding ourselves for over a century on being an asylum for the oppressed of all nations, we ought not suddenly to jump to the position that we are only an asylum for men who are no more radical than ourselves. Suppose monarchical England had taken such a position toward the Republican Mazzini or the anarchist Kropotkin.

Think of the example which these deportation raids set to less orderly nations, this resorting to methods which we have repeatedly declared to be a violation of international law when used against Americans abroad.[54] We can no longer take that position. If Mexico should conclude that certain Americans there had advocated a revolution in that country by force and violence, or a "clean-up" by the United States (by force), then it could seize our fellow-citizens from their beds at midnight, throw them into Black Holes like the Detroit bull-pen, separate them from their families, let their business go to pieces, turn their wives and children over to the local charities, and ship them in an army transport to New Orleans, knowing that every act would be supported by precedents of what was done in this country in January, 1920.

Finally, in deciding whether radical deportations should be carried out further, we ought to consider two classes of people in this country — first, ourselves; secondly, all the aliens.

That deportations are very popular with American citizens is undeniable, far more so than the proposed federal sedition

[53] Louis Blanc, *Letters on England* (London, 1866), I, 438.

[54] *Cf.* with the raids of January, 1920, the case of Scandella, an American citizen thrown out of Venezuela (Moore's *Digest of International Law*, IV, 108). Other examples of arbitrary expulsion are the Hollander case in Guatemala (*id.*, p. 102); and the Bluefields cases in Nicaragua (*id.*, p. 99). Several arbitrations on expulsion are contained in Moore's *Digest of International Arbitrations*, IV. chap. lx.

bills. How can we account for this astonishing desire to reverse our national policy? Besides the nervous effect of the war, the shock of the Russian Revolution, the unpreparedness for wide intellectual divergencies, of which I shall speak more fully in the next chapter, there is, I suspect, another element. Genuinely grateful as we all are in our thinking moments to our immigrant population, most of us have a hidden emotion which comes to the surface in a time of excitement, the wish that we did not have in our midst these foreigners who are so different from ourselves. The basis of dislike is normally unlikeness.[55] It is just the same feeling that led Dr. Johnson to say that the experience of a lifetime had convinced him that most foreigners were fools. We are going through the old Know-Nothing affair over again.

This instinct is normally controlled by a recognition of what immigration has done for the United States. It is not true that the aliens owe us everything and we owe them nothing. They have no vote, but they have hands and muscles. They have come here at our request, often at our earnest solicitation, to dig our sewers, cart our garbage, weave our cloth, build our roads and railways. And they have minds like ourselves. Absence of citizenship means the loss of the vote, but does it give us the moral right after a man is admitted to prescribe what he shall think, under penalty of banishment from his new home, and perhaps forcible return to the secret police from whom he fled? Or worse yet, to send him back years after his arrival here to the country he left as a small boy?

Doubtless, a policy of hands-off will result in the presence of a few dangerous agitators springing up in the great army of workers, but we should be willing to take the foam with the beer. This is not the first time that restless spirits, many of whom had been actually engaged in the labor wars of Europe, have carried the instinct of industrial strife and violence with them to their new country.[56] We lived through it until 1919 in confident serenity. We believed that the unrest brought

---

[55] "The Nervousness of the Jew," Dr. A. Myerson, 4 *Mental Hygiene* 65 (January, 1920); Bagehot elaborates the point in his essay on "The Metaphysical Basis of Toleration."

[56] See account of the Molly Maguires in Rhodes, *History of the United States*, vol. VIII.

from the other side of the ocean would eventually be dissipated by contact with American life. The radical shows the same change under a fostering environment as the Jew, who is rapidly becoming assimilated to his neighbors. "What persecution could not do through the centuries, toleration does in a generation." [57] A savings bank account, a steady job, and plenty of good-humored toleration and friendly help and encouragement, will bring into harmony with our ideals all but a few heated theorists, who are not likely to be such a menace to our national safety that we cannot counteract them by sound reasoning. Secretary Wilson favored this very method:

I look upon any alien who comes to this country and advocates the use of force for the overthrow of our Government as being in exactly the same position as an invading enemy, and that it is no undue hardship to send him back to the country whence he came. Nevertheless, I would not deal with the subject matter in that way. In dealing with it during the period of the war the policy of the Department of Labor was to send high-class, intelligent working men, who had lived the lives and spoke the language of the workers themselves, into the places where working men congregate, carrying a counter-propaganda puncturing the fallacy of the philosophy of force as applied to democratic institutions.[58]

Some such approach appears more fruitful than deportation for treating the problem of radical aliens. That it is a problem, I do not deny. But it is only a small phase of what really worries us — the possibility of extensive unrest in our midst. Extremists among citizens are more numerous and more serious than alien extremists. Hence deportation ought to be considered in relation to the broad problem of unrest. If we stand off and view deportation as one of the methods of social readjustment, it is not very satisfactory. In the first place, it is a wooden device. It imposes exactly the same drastic penalty on dangerous persons and trivial offenders. The constant outcry for better and bigger deportations recalls the single cure urged by the Queen of Hearts in *Alice in Wonderland* for every difficulty — "Off with his head!" Secondly, if we look at the world as a whole, we can hardly expect to clean it up by the simple

[57] Myerson, note 55.
[58] Letter to John E. Milholland, reprinted in 110 *Nation* 326 (March 13, 1920).

process of having every nation dump its rubbish over the fence into some other nation's back yard. And finally, it is probable that deporting a few radicals just scratches the surface of unrest and spreads the infection.

The last years have taught us that the melting-pot will not entirely take care of itself. Just as the merits of free trade in goods are lessened if the normal processes of competition are checked by monopolies and dumping, so free trade in ideas requires that the barriers to the interchange of argument presented by illiteracy and foreign languages shall somehow be broken down. Aliens cannot be forced to love this country. They will love it rather because it does not employ force except against obviously wrongful overt acts. They will love it as the home of wise tolerance, of confidence in its own strength and freedom. Undoubtedly there has been much discontent in certain groups of aliens in recent years. It has been accentuated by the excitement of the Russian Revolution, which must eventually subside. We are not likely to decrease this discontent by dragging men away from their families and either shipping them abroad or releasing them after many bitter days in prison. The relatives and friends of those deported will not have any increased love for our government. And the inevitable lack of humaneness in such a governmental policy causes a deep resentment among radical citizens. The raids become a text for more agitators, who speak to men and women who now have a real reason for wanting to get rid of the existing form of government. It is not the soapbox orators, but a horde of official spies and midnight housebreakers, who bring our government into hatred and contempt.

CHAPTER 6

PURIFYING THE LEGISLATURE

> *If Charles wished to prosecute the five members, a bill against them should have been sent to a grand jury.*
> MACAULAY, Essay on Hallam.

I
T IS ONE of the unfortunate results of governmental action against freedom of speech that the persons who retain sufficient courage to come into conflict with the law are often of a heedless and aggressive character, which makes them unattractive and devoid of personal appeal. Too often we assume that such persistent trouble-makers are the only persons injured by a censorship or a sedition law, and conclude from the indiscreet and unreasonable qualities of their speech and writing that after all the loss to the world of thought has been very slight. Too often we forget the multitude of cautious and sensitive men, men with wives and children dependent upon them, men who abhor publicity, who prefer to keep silent in the hope of better days. We cannot know what is lost through the effect upon them of repression, for it is simply left unsaid. Tolstoy once wrote:

You would not believe how, from the very commencement of my activity, that horrible Censor question has tormented me! I wanted to write what I felt; but at the same time it occurred to me that what I wrote would not be permitted, and involuntarily I had to abandon the work. I abandoned, and went on abandoning, and meanwhile the years passed away.

The agitator's effort is made on behalf of those thoughtful men as well as for his own sake; and if he wins, the gain to truth comes, not perhaps from his ideas, but from theirs. The men and women mentioned in this book, whom reflection has made me consider victims of unwise and often illegal suppression, are not indeed political prisoners whose ideals I can share, as I might those of Silvio Pellico or Grotius, and it may be that even

after due allowance has been made for the natural blindness
of a contemporary to the merit of their thinking, that only
one or two among them, like Bertrand Russell, are men whose
work has enduring worth. Yet the views and even the personal
qualities of the victims of persecution have little relation to the
justice of their cause. Few objects of intolerance have touched
such a low level of thought and action, few have rendered more
numerous and more valuable services to liberty than John
Wilkes.

1. JOHN WILKES

> *In his person though he were the worst of men, I*
> *contend for the safety and security of the best.*
>   LORD CHATHAM.

"That name," says Trevelyan, "which was seldom out of
the mouths of our great-grandfathers for three weeks together,
had been stained and blotted from the first." A rake and a
prodigal, unfaithful to the wife whose fortune he looted for
use in election briberies, lacking in genuine devotion to any
political ideal, he nevertheless by sheer pluck and impudence
led the fight to establish in the law of all English-speaking countries five great principles of freedom: the immunity of political
criticism from prosecution; the publicity of legislative debates;
the abolition of outlawry, which condemned a man in his absence; the protection of house and property from unreasonable
searches and seizures; and the right of a duly elected representative of a constituency to sit in the legislature unless disqualified by law, no matter what personal objections his
colleagues may have to his opinions and writings or to his
previous convictions for sedition. So great were his achieve-
ments that he became a household word on this side of the
Atlantic. One of the largest cities in Pennsylvania is named
for him. Colonial patriots repeatedly toasted "Wilkes and
Number 45" at tavern dinners. Men called their children after
him. My great-grandfather named his three sons Wilkes, Pitt,
and Liberty. In the eyes of our forefathers he was the most
conspicuous combatant against the doctrine, so obnoxious to
them, that men might be maltreated, imprisoned, exiled, disfranchised, for the supposedly evil tendencies of their political

opinions. The preceding chapters have shown the gradual revival of that doctrine in our midst, first in war and then in peace, first against pacifists and pro-Germans, then against radical aliens, until finally the war with "evil-thinking" brought us to the point of governmental action against radical citizens with a constantly diminishing standard of radicalism, and even the last of the great principles for which Wilkes fought amid the applause of our ancestors was in grave peril — the right of the people to choose their representatives.

On the 23rd of April, 1763, appeared No. 45 of the *North Briton*, commenting upon the king's speech and upon the unpopular peace recently concluded with France. The *North Briton* was conducted by Wilkes, who had played a large part through this newspaper in driving Lord Bute from office and now castigated his successor, George Grenville, of Stamp Act fame. Other journalists abused public men under such disguises as the use of initials, but the *North Briton* called them by name. The Ministry resolved to prosecute for libel, but it was unknown who was the libeler, since those responsible for the newspaper had kept their identity concealed. Lord Halifax, one of the Secretaries of State, issued what was then called a general warrant, directing four messengers to take a constable, search for the authors, printers, and publishers, and seize them when found, together with their papers.

In three days they arrested forty-nine persons on suspicion, many of them as innocent as Lord Halifax himself. Among them was the printer of No. 45. From the seized papers Wilkes was discovered to be the real offender, and he was carried off to the Secretaries of State. As soon as he was out of his house, the messengers took entire possession of it, broke into his desk with the aid of a blacksmith, dumped his papers including his will and pocket-book into a sack, and went off with them without even taking an inventory. Wilkes brought an action, not against the messengers, but against the man higher up, the Under Secretary of State, who had personally superintended the execution of the warrant.[1] Wilkes recovered £1,000. Then he went still higher, and sued the Cabinet Minister who had issued the warrant, for false imprisonment, obtaining £4,000 damages. His associates brought similar actions. It is

[1] Wilkes *v.* Wood, 19 How. St. Tr. 1167 (1763).

said that altogether these suits cost the Grenville Government
£100,000. The law of these cases that search must be by warrant describing the property to be seized is embodied in the
Fourth Amendment to the Constitution of the United States.[2]

Then the Grenville Government, which had found Wilkes
such an expensive opponent, lodged an information against him
for seditious libel on account of what would now be considered
an ordinary political editorial. He was a member of the House
of Commons. The House ordered the newspaper to be burned
by the common hangman and summoned Wilkes to attend for
further proceedings. Meanwhile the government encouraged
bullies to make way with him. Forced into a duel, he fled to
France. Evidence was taken of his being the author and publisher of the *North Briton*, No. 45, and he was expelled for the
seditious libel published during his term as member of Parliament. This expulsion, although perhaps legal, was precipi-
tate and vindictive, for Wilkes was about to be tried for his
offense, and the House might at least have waited for his conviction, instead of prejudging his cause and anticipating his
legal punishment.[3] Later he was convicted in his absence, and
outlawed for contumacy.

Four years went by, the general election of 1768 was approaching, and Wilkes returned from exile to stand for Parliament. After a defeat in the City of London, he presented
himself as a candidate for Middlesex. The working people
allowed no man to travel to the polls without a paper in his
hat inscribed, "Number 45. Wilkes and Liberty!" Convict
and outlaw as Wilkes was, his vote was overwhelming.

After his election, Wilkes surrendered himself into custody,
and went to jail. Lord Mansfield reversed the outlawry, and
Wilkes was sentenced, on the original charge of seditious libel,
to nearly two years in prison. Obviously, the King should have
pardoned him. His sentence was unwarranted, and its re-
mission would have relegated him, as Trevelyan puts it, "to
an obscurity whence, but for the infatuation of his enemies,
he would never have emerged." A feeble speaker, he would

---

[2] Quoted *supra*, p. 204. For references on illegal searches and seizures, see
Chapter XIV, note 5. The leading English case is Entick *v.* Carrington, 19
How. St. Tr. 1029 (1765). For illegal seizures in deportation raids, see Chap-
ter V, sections II, III.

[3] May, *Constitutional History*, I, 312.

have been negligible; in the words of Junius, "a silent senator, and hardly supporting the eloquence of a weekly newspaper." But the King and the Cabinet were his implacable enemies, and he was left in prison. And, then going back forty years to the precedent of a member who had been expelled for forgery, the House of Commons declared Wilkes's seat to be vacant by a vote of two hundred and nineteen to one hundred and thirty-seven.

A new election was held, and though still in prison, he was reëlected. The House next day voted that, having been expelled, he was incapable of serving in Parliament. A third election followed with the same result. Burke told his fellow-members that Wilkes had grown great by their folly, and Townshend reminded his hearers "that a heavy account would some day be exacted from them if they continued to postpone all useful legislation for the sake of a frivolous and interminable squabble." But the election was declared null and void without a division. An opponent was produced for the fourth election in one Luttrell, who drew one vote to Wilkes's four, but was declared by the House of Commons to be member for Middlesex, after a debate in which even George Grenville rallied to the support of his old enemy, Wilkes, with such vehemence that when he sat down he spat blood, shortening his life to diminish the majority against the lawfully elected candidate. Blackstone tried to show that Wilkes was disqualified by common law, but was confuted by a passage in the early editions of his *Commentaries* (he carefully altered it in the next edition in 1773), which said that every British subject not in certain specified classes was "eligible of common right." The majority was forced to rely on precedents from the Great Civil War, when the majority expelled the minority and was itself expelled in turn, until the House of Commons was reduced to forty-six members. Luttrell's election was confirmed, against the petition of the Middlesex electors, and the King prorogued Parliament.

Burke expounded the principle involved in Wilkes's exclusion in his *Thoughts on the Present Discontents*. The only check on arbitrary power is the presence here and there on the benches of members endowed with a "spirit of independence carried to some degree of enthusiasm, an inquisitive

character to discover, and a bold one to display, every corruption and every error of government." Such qualities are
distasteful to those in power, and Wilkes was the example
chosen to discourage others, just as the arrest of five members by Charles I, if successfully conducted, would have
stifled liberty as effectually as the execution of fifty. The
question was whether the people or the government should
select the legislature. The leading Whigs stood behind Burke,
and denounced the position that a resolution of any branch
of the legislature could "make, alter, suspend, abrogate, or
annihilate the law of the land."

Of all the statements of the cause of Wilkes, that of Burke
in debate has the greatest value for our own time:

Accumulative crimes are things unknown to the courts below. In
those courts two bad things will not make one capital offense. This
is a serving up like cooks. Some will eat of one dish, and some of
another, so that there will not be a fragment left. Some will like
the strong solid roast-beef of the blasphemous libel. One honorable
member could not bear to see Christianity abused, because it was
part of the common law of England. This is substantial roast-beef
reasoning. One gentleman said he meant Mr. Wilkes's petition to be
the ground of expulsion; another, the message from the House of
Lords. "I come into this resolution," says a fourth, "because of his
censure upon the conduct of a great magistrate." "In times of danger," says a fifth, "I am afraid of doing anything that will shake
the government." These charges are all brought together to form an
accumulated offense, which may extend to the expulsion of every
other member of this House. This law, as it is now laid down, is
that any member who, at any time, has been guilty of writing a libel
will never be free from punishment. Is any man, when he takes up
his pen, certain that the day may not come when he may wish to be
a member of Parliament? This, sir, will put a last hand to the liberty
of the press.

It was not until his fourth election had been annulled that
Wilkes left prison. The persecution of the government had
turned him from an obscure member of Parliament into a
man of national prominence. As Junius said, "The rays of
the Royal indignation, collected upon him, served only to
illuminate, and could not consume." The people, unable to
send him to Parliament, made him Alderman and then Lord
Mayor of London, while Luttrell voted with the majority in

the Commons. At the next general election in 1774, Wilkes
was returned for Middlesex and allowed to take his seat, since
Massachusetts was causing too much trouble to encourage a
stirring up of old grievances at home. Thereafter, he sat without interruption, while the men who had expelled him brought
England to her lowest humiliation. In 1782 the resolution of
1769 declaring him incapable of election was expunged from
the records "as being subversive of the rights of the whole
body of electors of this kingdom."

2. VICTOR L. BERGER

> And if my words seem treason to the dullard and the
> tame,
> 'Tis but my Bay-State dialect — our fathers spake the
> same.   JAMES RUSSELL LOWELL,
> On the Capture of Fugitive Slaves near Washington.

The most prominent person convicted under the Espionage
Act, with the exception of Debs, was Victor L. Berger. He
was born in Austria in 1860, came to this country in 1878,
and was a founder of the Socialist Party in the United States,
editor of the *Milwaukee Leader*, and member of Congress,
1911–1913, the first Socialist to serve in Washington. The
left-wing Socialists always regarded him as a bourgeois member of the party. Before we entered the European War, he
gave vigorous expression to the orthodox Socialist views about
war, and employed many of the arguments in favor of American
neutrality which were used at that time by non-Socialists, for
instance, in President Wilson's note of December 18, 1916,
to all the belligerents, asking them to state their terms of
peace. Unlike the great majority of Americans, Berger and
other Socialists did not consider the German submarine campaign of February, 1917, a sufficient reason for changing their
minds, but maintained that war was justified only in case of
invasion. He was a member of the resolutions committee of
the Socialist Convention at St. Louis and signed the Proclamation and War Program of April 14, 1917,[4] which branded the
declaration of war as a crime against the people of the United

[4] See page 142, *supra*.

States and the nations of the world, and stated that in all modern history there had been no war more unjustifiable. Berger published this platform in the *Milwaukee Leader*, and poured out a stream of editorials, articles, and cartoons, denouncing the war policies of the government. He did not, however, urge any one to resist the draft, and indeed advised one Socialist conscientious objector to put on the uniform. Berger testified that several men in his immediate family volunteered, although his opposition would have prevented them from doing so. It is, of course, well known that the record of Wisconsin and Milwaukee in the war was very high; though Berger can take no credit for this, it tends to disprove that opposition to war produces violations of the draft act or other war laws.

In September, 1917, the *Leader* was deprived of its second-class mailing privilege for the future by a blanket order of the Postmaster General, and relief was subsequently denied by the courts.[5] The newspaper thus lost a daily circulation of approximately 15,000 subscribers. All first-class mail addressed to the *Leader* was returned to the sender. The District of Columbia Court of Appeals said of the articles on which the exclusion was based, and in this opinion the House of Representatives committee afterwards concurred:

No one can read them without becoming convinced that they were printed in a spirit of hostility to our own government and in a spirit of sympathy for the Central Powers; that through them, appellant sought to hinder and embarrass the government in the prosecution of the war.

The reader can determine the general character of the *Milwaukee Leader* from the passages abstracted in a later paragraph, and decide for himself whether the judicial and legislative comments quoted in this chapter are correct in concluding that Berger wanted to aid Germany. My own opinion is that they err in confusing opposition to the war with wishing the enemy to win. Whether Berger was within the terms of the Espionage Act or not, I find in his writings no desire that the militarism and autocracy of Germany should

[5] United States *ex rel.* Milwaukee Social Democrat Pub. Co. *v.* Burleson, 258 Fed. 282 (1919). The full record is in *Berger Hearings*, I, 503 ff. In 1921 the Supreme Court sustained the action of the Postmaster General. See Chapter VII, section II.

triumph, but rather a series of extremely bitter and cynical attacks upon what seemed to him the Junkerism and selfishness of all the governments on both sides of the war. They indicate that he wanted the war to end at once because in the absence of invasion he sincerely believed it unnecessary and a crushing burden upon the workers of America. I say this although I am repelled by the attitude of Berger. I can understand the abhorrence of Debs for a law which compels a man to kill fellow-workers because their rulers quarrel, and recognize that he speaks from the heart even while I disagree with him. But for Berger the war seems only an impersonal step in an economic argument. He sneers at the possibility of noble purposes in the conflict, and nowhere utters a word of praise or sympathy for those who gave up home and life with the desire that the world should not be made an armed camp and that oppressed nations should be free from military domination.

Despite all this, the fundamental question remains, whether it is for the advantage of government by public opinion and popular election that just because most of us consider a person's views detestable, he should be thrown into prison and American citizens should be denied the right to be represented by the man of their choice.

In February, 1918, Berger was indicted with four other Socialists for conspiracy under the Espionage Act. The indictment was brought in Chicago, because the defendants were alleged to have agreed there for the issue of publications in various places. The overt acts which Berger himself was said to have committed consisted of five editorials in the *Leader*, which were in substance as follows: (1) We were in the war because the Allies were at the end of their rope, and their obligations would otherwise be worthless; continued fighting would maintain the existing high prices of munition stocks; war meant absolute freedom from labor troubles, since strikes would be put down as treason; the plutocracy and its government in Washington would be enabled to establish autocracy as a war necessity; war would be a wonderful chance to establish a large permanent army; the commercial rivalry of Germany would be ended. The submarines, Belgium, invasion, and democracy had nothing to do with it. (2) There are many men driven insane at the front. (3) Young men do not talk as if they considered it an honor to be drafted. (4) Only big business men and their satellites are enthusiastic over the war, but they do not fight. (5) The Bible contains many passages which are opposed to war and must therefore be considered as treasonable.

Shortly before the indictment, Berger was nominated for the United States Senate on a Socialist platform announcing that if elected he would work for a speedy, general, democratic, and permanent peace without forcible annexations and punitive indemnities. War would ruin the country and could be ended by electing men pledged to end it. He was defeated, but in spite of the charges pending against him received over 100,000 votes.

In November, 1918, before the trial began, he was elected to Congress from the fifth district of Wisconsin, polling 17,920 votes against 12,450 for the Democratic candidate and 10,678 for the Republican. In December, he was put on trial before Judge Kenesaw Mountain Landis, convicted, and sentenced to twenty years imprisonment.[6] Berger appealed and was released on bail. On January 13, 1921, the United States Supreme Court reversed Berger's conviction because Judge Landis was disqualified by his prejudicial conduct before the trial.[7] The government then abandoned all charges against Berger. But this was long after the events now to be narrated.

When Berger presented himself to the House of Representatives in the spring of 1919 to be sworn in, it was charged that he was ineligible, and the question was referred to a special committee, which reported [8] for reasons hereafter stated that he was not entitled to take the oath of office or hold a seat as Representative. At the same time the candidate with the next highest number of votes, Joseph P. Carney, had claimed the seat, on the ground that since Berger was ineligible those persons who had voted for him should be considered to have deliberately thrown away their ballots — in the words of an English judge, just as if they had voted "for the man in the

---

[6] Volume II of *Berger Hearings* contains the full record of the trial.

[7] Berger *v.* United States, 255 U. S. 22 (1921), per McKenna, J.; Day, Pitney, and McReynolds, JJ., dissenting. See 21 *Columbia Law Review* 387.

[8] House of Representatives, 66th Cong., 1st Sess., Ho. Cal. No. 91, Rep. No. 413, hereafter called Berger Report. Voigt of Wisconsin dissented.

moon." [9] Fortunately Congressional practice does not thus disfranchise electors. So Carney did not have the luck of Luttrell. On November 11, 1919, the House of Representatives declared Berger's seat vacant.

The Governor of Wisconsin ordered a special election on December 19, 1919. The Republicans and Democrats nominated a fusion candidate and the German paper, the *Herold*, appealed to all German-Americans to support their compatriot against Berger. The Socialist vote was increased by nearly 8,000 over the first election, Berger receiving 25,802 ballots to 19,800 for his opponent. On January 10, 1920, the House again refused to seat him. This time, six Representatives voted in his favor, including Floor Manager James R. Mann, who said during the debate:

Mr. Berger has been elected anew to the House by a majority of those who vote in his district and to me the question is whether we shall maintain inviolate the representative form of government where people who desire changes in the fundamental or other laws of the land shall have the right to be represented on the floor of this House, when they control a majority of the votes in a Congressional district.

I do not share the views of Mr. Berger, but I am willing to meet his views in an argument before the people rather than to say we shall deny him the opportunity to be heard when selected by the people in the legal form and invite them, in effect, to resort to violence.

Has it come to the point that a man who believes certain things cannot be heard? His people, his constituents, desire him to represent them. It is not our duty to select a representative from this Congressional district. That is the duty of the people back at home.

Within an hour after Berger was unseated, the Socialist committee in Milwaukee announced his renomination for a third contest. However, he was not permitted to approach Wilkes's record, for the Governor of Wisconsin decided that another special election would be too expensive. Meanwhile, Berger was forbidden to speak in several cities, including that founded by Roger Williams, and Jersey City forcibly ran him out of town. Berger's enemies like those of Wilkes adopted

[9] Lord Campbell, C.J., in Regina *v.* Coaks, 3 E. & B. 249, 254 (1854). For absurd cases to the same effect, see Beresford-Hope *v.* Lady Sandhurst, 23 Q.B.D. 79 (1889); Madden *v.* Board of Election Commissioners, 251 Mass. 95 (1925). However, there are decisions to the contrary.

against him the very methods that vastly increased his influence.

Article I, section 5, of the Constitution provides: "Each House shall be the Judge of the Elections, Returns, and Qualifications of its own Members." This should be compared with the later clause: "Each House may . . . punish its Members for Disorderly Behaviour, and, with the Concurrence of two thirds, expel a Member."

The broad question raised by the Berger case is, whether (under the clause first quoted) a person who has received the highest number of votes in an election for Representative or Senator should be refused a seat because of his expression of unpopular opinions. More specifically, should he be excluded because during a past or pending war he opposed its continuance and the methods by which it was waged? Either way, the question is full of difficulties, which I shall content myself with sketching. These difficulties will be somewhat lessened if the main problem be split into several parts.

a. May the House reject a person for any reason the majority chooses?

At the outset, we are confronted with two extreme views. The first is that the constitutional provision first stated gives a majority of the House the unlimited right to exclude any elected person for any reasons it chooses to adopt. Since the House is the sole judge, it can act at its own sweet will. It is like a social club where anybody can blackball a candidate merely because he dislikes him. This was the view adopted by the House of Commons in regard to Wilkes, and repudiated by the ensuing events in England and the enthusiastic approval of liberals in the American colonies.

The second and opposing view is that the Constitution itself lists all the qualifications; and that if a district elects a man who conforms to its requirements, he must be seated, no matter how unfit for participation in law-making the rest of the House considers him. His unfitness is not a reason for exclusion by a majority vote, although, if it be continuing in its nature, it may justify his later expulsion by a two-thirds vote. I shall explain shortly what are the express constitutional requirements of a Representative, to which this second view permits nothing to be added.

The first view seems unsound. When the Constitution says that each House is to be "the Judge of the . . . Qualifications," this means that the House is to behave like a judge and not like a dining club or a dancer selecting a partner. The separation of powers is not absolute. A court sometimes makes laws, *viz.*, its own rules. Conversely, the Senate exercises judicial powers when hearing an impeachment; and so does either House in passing on the qualifications of a member. Hence, it must decide the facts by applying to them rules of law, and must not proceed arbitrarily. For instance, the majority has no right to exclude the minority by a new Pride's Purge. It is no answer to say that if the House of Representatives should exclude a man on some whimsical ground, no appeal would lie from its action. Neither is there any appeal from the Supreme Court. For this very reason the Court feels a grave responsibility to decide according to law. In the same way, the House has only the power to decide whether the man received the proper number of votes and satisfies the qualifications established by law; and it ought not to create new requirements for a particular case any more than a criminal judge ought to invent new crimes.

Let us assume, then, that the House should judge the facts of an exclusion case according to general rules of law, namely, the "Qualifications." It should not sit like a caliph in the *Arabian Nights* disposing of an individual according to personal notions of his unfitness. The elected person should be condemned only if he has violated standards which the House has already applied or expects to apply to any other man similarly situated.

Having accordingly rejected the first view stated above, are we thereby forced to adopt the second view? Or is there a middle ground available. We have explored the meaning of the constitutional word "Judge." Let us now try to interpret "Qualifications."

b. Are the "Qualifications" to be applied by the House limited to the constitutional requirements for membership?

What then are the lawful qualifications which an elected person must satisfy to be seated? On this point the second view already mentioned is adamant. It recognizes only five reasons (given by the Constitution itself) for refusing his seat to the man who has received the highest number of votes. Three of these are carefully listed for the House of Representatives in the original Constitution: [10]

No Person shall be a Representative who shall not have (1) attained to the Age of twenty-five Years, and (2) been seven Years a Citizen of the United States, and who shall not, (3) when elected, be an Inhabitant of the State in which he shall be chosen.

So also a Senator must be (1) thirty years old, (2) nine years a citizen of the United States, and (3) an inhabitant of the state for which he is elected. A fourth requirement for both Houses is clearly implied by the constitutional word "Elections." Bribery and corruption connected with the election disqualify the man with most votes, because they prevent him from being elected. Fraud vitiates all transactions, so no valid election has taken place. A fifth and last qualification, in which the italicized clause was important for Berger's case as we shall see later, was added in 1868 by section 3 of the Fourteenth Amendment:

No person shall be a Senator or Representative in Congress, . . . who, having previously taken an oath [as a federal or state legislator or officer] to support the Constitution of the United States, shall have engaged in insurrection or rebellion against the same, or *given aid or comfort to the enemies thereof.* But Congress may by a vote of two-thirds of each House, remove such disability.

There is much strength in Justice Story's position that nobody has power to add to these five constitutional requirements for eligibility: [11]

It would seem but fair reasoning, upon the plainest principles of interpretation, that when the Constitution established certain qualifications as necessary for office, it meant to exclude all others as prerequisites. From the very nature of such a provision, the affirma-

[10] United States Constitution, Art. I, § 2. Numerals inserted by me.
[11] 1 Story on the Constitution (5th ed.), § 625. Story was primarily concerned with attempts by the *states* to add qualifications, *e.g.*, that a Representative must live in his own district. Congress has always refused to recognize these state limitations as valid. Whether Congress itself can add requirements is a somewhat different question, but Story's position is sufficiently broad to deny such a Congressional power.

tion of these qualifications would seem to imply a negative of all others.

The power to judge "Qualifications," as thus construed, means only constitutional qualifications. The Constitution gives the voters of a district the inalienable right to choose any one they please who satisfies the requirements named in the Constitution. Representative government relies on the judgment of the people to pick fit men, not on the wisdom of a House of Congress or any other select group.

By this view even crime is no bar to membership, except treason by virtue of the Fourteenth Amendment. Unseating for bribery, as in the case of Senator Lorimer,[12] is not a disqualification for crime as such, but a decision that no valid election had taken place. In the improbable event that a district should elect a convicted murderer, he can act so long as he is at large. If the general welfare requires that this be made impossible, then the Constitution should be amended.

Despite some difficulties, this view has two great merits. First, it is definite. It tells Congress exactly how far it can go. Why adopt the dangerously loose view of unlimited qualifications because of the remote possibility that states will send murderers or idiots to Congress? A power in Congress to add new qualifications is equivalent to a power to change those prescribed by the fundamental law. If it can add crime or disloyal acts as bars, it can add profiteering as well. The House can exclude a Representative who does not reside in his district. A majority of elderly Senators can raise the minimum age to fifty. Either House can bar men of Jewish race. It can require that members must be already enrolled in either the Republican or the Democratic Party, or recognize only a single party entitled to nominate candidates. There is no line to be drawn, once the legislature is allowed to cross the constitutional limits. It can turn our democracy into an oligarchy by imposing high property qualifications, or into a dictatorship of the proletariat by declaring ineligible all persons deriving income from rents and invested capital.

The second advantage of this view is its objectivity. This was emphasized by Senator Knox of Pennsylvania when the

---

[12] Webb & Pierce, Senate Election Cases, 1002.

Senate debated the exclusion of Smoot of Utah because he was a Mormon.[13] Knox pointed out that the constitutional disqualifications do not in any way involve the moral qualities of a man. They relate to facts outside the realm of ethical consideration; and these facts are matters which Representatives and Senators are well fitted to decide out of their own experience, like a man's residence, counting the votes, and the honesty of the election. Such facts are quite different from determinations about disloyalty or the desirability of some organization to which the man belongs. As to all matters affecting a man's moral fitness, Knox urged, the states and the electors are to be the judges, subject to the power of the Senate or House to expel the member when an offense or offensive status extends into the period of service; and such a question cannot be raised until after the elected man has taken his seat. In short, the House or Senate should not let itself inquire into vague and speculative questions as reasons for disqualification, but should stick to familiar cold facts.

Yet, although the view of forbidding all additions to the five constitutional requirements seems to me the soundest policy, I must fairly concede that Congressional practice does not go so far. Neither Senator Beveridge nor several other Senators with whom I have talked about the matter would accept such a hard and fast position as Story's. They insisted that some additions to the constitutional qualifications must be possible. Otherwise, the great leaders of the Confederacy might have been eligible before the Fourteenth Amendment, or Brigham Young could have been elected and his forty wives have occupied the gallery to see him sworn in. Is a man to be brought from the felon's cell to the floor of the Senate? Could women be elected to Congress before they obtained the vote? In order to keep out an insane man, must the House resort to such subterfuges as expelling him after he is seated or finding him physically incapable of taking the oath? Suppose a Representative just before he is sworn in should create some outrageous disturbance in the House; if he cannot be disqualified, it will be necessary to go through the rigmarole of first swearing him in, and then expelling him. The duty of the Senate and the House to preserve the nation and carry on business is said

[13] 1 Hinds' Prec. 561–590; see *infra*, pp. 264–265, for this case.

not to be sufficiently safeguarded if the constitutional requirements are exclusive of all others.

The arguments against both of the extreme views mentioned
are so strong that the actual practice takes an intermediate
ground. As to elected persons satisfying all the requirements
in the Constitution, we are not forced to choose between giving
the House absolute power to unseat whomever it dislikes, and
giving the voters absolute power to seat whomever they elect.
A third alternative has been adopted, fairly close to the second
view. The constitutional qualifications ordinarily suffice; but
Congress has rather cautiously imposed some additional tests
by statute, and the House of Representatives or the Senate
has probably added a very few more qualifications by established usage (a sort of legislative common law) to cover certain
obvious cases of unfitness.

Before inquiring about the scope of these added disqualifications and whether they should include opposition to a war,
let us first ask whether such opposition violates the constitutional requirements of eligibility, inasmuch as the Berger
committee reported that these alone sufficed to unseat him.

*c. Is opposition to a war a disqualification under the Four-
teenth Amendment?*

Berger obviously satisfied the first four constitutional requirements, but the committee of the House of Representatives
held that he should be excluded because he had given "aid and
comfort to the enemy" and so was barred by the Fourteenth
Amendment. At the outset the committee decided not to be
governed by the action of the judge and jury at Chicago,
but to review all the evidence at that trial, the proceedings
about the exclusion of the *Leader* from the mails, and the fresh
testimony introduced at the hearings. The conclusions of fact
were in part as follows: [14]

   . . . the admitted acts, writings, and declarations of Victor L.
Berger and of the men with whom he was associated in the management and control of the Socialist Party from the time of the entrance
of this country into the war until their indictment by a Federal grand
jury . . . clearly establishes a conscious, deliberate and continuing
purpose and intent to obstruct, hinder, and embarrass the Govern-

[14] *Berger Report*, p. 7.

ment of the United States in the prosecution of the war and thus to give aid and comfort to the enemies of our country. The writings and activities of Mr. Berger and his associates could have had no other purpose. That Victor L. Berger was disloyal to the United States of America and did give aid and comfort to its enemies at a time when its existence as a free and independent Nation was at stake there can not be the slightest doubt.

I submit that this report is a serious misinterpretation of the legal phrase "aid and comfort to the enemy." The misinterpretation is so often made and so likely to recur in another war that its consequences go far beyond any injustice to Berger. For the sake of sound policies in the future, a decisive interpretation is demanded. We may well take to heart as a warning Warwick's speech to the Bishop of Beauvais in *Saint Joan* about the word "traitor":

It does not mean in England what it does in France. In your language traitor means betrayer: one who is perfidious, treacherous, unfaithful, disloyal. In our country it means simply one who is not wholly devoted to our English interests.

Berger's violation of the Espionage Act was not a bar under the Fourteenth Amendment because it did not amount to treason. It is an odd commentary on legislative justice that nearly every one involved in the Berger case assumed that "aid and comfort to the enemy" was synonymous with guilt under the Espionage Act. Of course, this phrase is often employed loosely in conversation and Congressional debates to include all sorts of language that is considered disloyal in war time, but legally these words have a technical significance. They are used in a statute or in the Fourteenth Amendment in the same sense as in the clause of the Constitution defining treason to "consist only in levying War against [the United States], or in adhering to their Enemies, giving them Aid and Comfort." [15] Therefore, the acts of aid and comfort which would disqualify Berger from serving in Congress under the Amendment (if section 3 be still in force)[16] must be of the same gen-

[15] The omission of adherence in the Fourteenth Amendment is immaterial. Charge to Grand Jury, 1 Bond (U. S.) 609, 611 (1861); United States *v.* Robinson, 259 Fed. 685, 690 (1919). See also Young *v.* United States, 97 U. S. 39, 62 (1877).

[16] This provision may relate to the Civil War only, like section 4 of the

eral character with those necessary to convict him of treason.

Was Berger guilty of treason? In answering this question, we must not be misled by colloquial usage. Theodore Roosevelt denounced the St. Louis Socialist platform as "treason," and "traitor" is a heart-warming conversational epithet for any one who wants a war stopped, but lawyers and legislators must be less vague in accusing a man of a crime that is punishable with death. Chief Justice Marshall said long ago that treason should not be extended by construction to doubtful cases, and there has never been a decision that talking against a war is treason. If it were, Vallandigham, Milligan, and the other Copperheads would surely have been prosecuted for this crime. The few writers who assert that the Espionage Act of 1917 created no new crimes, but that causing insubordination in the armed forces and obstructing enlistment are also treason,[17] are forced to rely on one or two sweeping judicial definitions, like Lord Reading's charge in the trial of Sir Roger Casement, that it is giving aid and comfort to the enemy to do any act which tends to strengthen them or tends to weaken the power of one's own country to resist. So broad a statement would if taken literally revive all the evils of constructive treason, but it must be limited with reference to the particular facts which the jury were considering. Casement had issued a proclamation to Irish prisoners in Germany urging them to form a regiment in the German army.[18] The use of words in an attempt to gain recruits for the enemy is absolutely differ-

---

same Amendment about pensions and Confederate debts. Also early in the Spanish war, in order to cement good feeling between North and South, both houses of Congress by the necessary two-thirds vote adopted a blanket resolution removing the disabilities imposed by section 3. However, the Berger committee held that section 3 still applied to subsequent disabilities.

[17] If so, the treason statute would have rendered the Espionage Act unnecessary. Instead the treason statute proved well-nigh useless during the war. See *supra*, Chapter II, note 4.

[18] Rex *v.* Casement, [1917] 1 K.B. 98. It is doubtful if even Casement's proclamation would be treason in American law, since no one did enlist in consequence of it. Compare Respublica *v.* Roberts, 1 Dall. 39 (Pa. 1778) with United States *v.* Robinson, 259 Fed. 685, 690 (1919). This point in the Casement trial received no attention from the Court of Appeal, which was entirely occupied with the question whether treason could be committed outside England, answered in the affirmative. It is interesting to Americans to find that one of the authorities relied on was a legal opinion rendered in 1775 that certain persons in New Hampshire could be prosecuted for treason.

ent from telling your fellow-citizens that they ought to stop fighting. It may be that the latter is so dangerous that it must be punished, but only as sedition, which consists of *words* creating disaffection. Treason requires overt *acts* of direct assistance to the enemy. The distinction is fundamental. It is inconceivable that the trivial utterances which were held criminal under the Espionage Act because of their bad tendency and the supposed intention to hinder the war were already subject under the treason statute to a death penalty.

This distinction is clearly brought out by the kind of conduct which has been held to be "giving aid and comfort to the enemy," for example, furnishing money, troops or arms, saltpeter for gunpowder, steamers for blockade running, delivering up deserters and prisoners, and actually joining the enemy in person. Contrast these acts, which advance the cause of the enemy by their immediate effect, with newspaper articles attacking the war, which may encourage the enemy but do not promote his success in any tangible or measurable way. The result is indirect and purely mental. It is true that words do sometimes constitute treason, as when a letter with invisible ink is sent to the enemy containing military information, or a wireless message. Here language has all the qualities of action, because it furnishes the enemy with something he can use. It is treason if he be given a gun to batter down a fort or a photograph of its plan or a written description. That the last is in words is immaterial. But if words are used in a speech demanding immediate peace, this is not assistance by acts at all, and furnishes the enemy with nothing but emotions of dubious value. Judges have frequently declared that expressions of opinion are not treason.

In the Berger case, however, the committee did not consider at all whether he was guilty of treason, and clearly he was not. There is nothing in the record to show any aid to Germany except by the indirect, intangible method of creating a body of opinion opposed to the continuance of the war. And this is a risk which a nation governed by public opinion must take, which ours has taken by guaranteeing freedom of speech. To call it treason is contrary not only to the First Amendment but to the law of treason. Therefore, Berger did not in any legal sense give aid and comfort to the enemy, and he was not

barred from the House of Representatives by the Fourteenth
Amendment.

Consequently, if his exclusion for spoken or written opposition to the war is to be justified, it can only be because of some
additional disqualification not mentioned in the Constitution.

*d. Was opposition to a war or other seditious speech a dis-
qualification for membership in Congress before the World
War?*

It is not an easy matter to decide what disqualifications have
been added by Congress to the five constitutional grounds of
ineligibility. The courts have uniformly denied that they have
any power to review either legislative expulsions or legislative
decisions on the qualifications of members inasmuch as the
Constitution expressly vests the sole jurisdiction in the chamber
involved. So practically all the precedents are legislative.
These precedents rarely afford a satisfactory formulation of
the principle on which the house acted, which can be automatically applied in subsequent cases after the manner of court
decisions. A legislature is not by nature a judicial body. Its
members are chosen and organized for carrying out policies,
and not, like judges, for the sole purpose of thinking together.
When they are called upon to perform judicial duties in trying
impeachments and charges of bribery, the most earnest efforts
to attain impartiality hardly prevent them from being swayed
by party motives, and their debates lack the training and the
restraints which mold the words of judges. The Lorimer case
brought out these qualities of a legislative trial. Moreover, the
basis of a legislative discussion is often obscure because of
the number of persons who join in the debate. Sometimes the
only certain fact is that the member was or was not unseated.
It is significant that the Wilkes case led Parliament to delegate the trial of controverted elections to a tribunal of judges.[19]
The Berger and New York Socialist cases might well lead us to
consider establishing a preliminary investigation by judges
instead of by a legislative committee, and thus obtaining the
benefit of a trained judicial opinion as the basis of the action
of the house.

[19] May, *Parliamentary Practice*, 12 ed., p. 581. This plan is already in force
in Pennsylvania. The Presidential Electoral Commission of 1877 affords an
analogy.

At all events, the range of new qualifications has been closely limited by Congress. In most instances, the precedents are inclined to agree with the outcome of the Wilkes controversy by insisting that causes of exclusion must be established by law, and that the resolution of one house of Congress cannot make law.[20] When a Representative was charged with having cruelly whipped negro soldiers under his command and bribing them not to testify against him before a military court, Garfield asked if anything in the Constitution and laws of the United States forbade that a moral monster should be elected to Congress. The House also refused to inquire into a charge of seduction, and the Senate into one of embezzlement. There is some authority that a man who has been convicted of crime *after* his election to the legislature should not be allowed to occupy his seat, but still there is a sharp disagreement whether he should be excluded or expelled. The reason for declaring the seat vacant is that his constituents should have the opportunity to reconsider their votes if they were cast in ignorance of a fact which so materially affects his fitness for the office. This argument supports the first exclusion of Berger (in 1919), but not the second (in 1920), for the overwhelming vote received by him at the second election, after his conviction, made it clear that the electorate considered guilt under the Espionage Act no disqualification for their representative in Congress. The Wilkes case established the principle that such a decisive expression of opinion given with full knowledge of the offense of sedition should not afterwards be overridden by one branch of the legislature. Indeed, the House of Representatives went one step farther than the House of Commons, for Wilkes when disqualified was in prison and wholly incapable of serving, but Berger was out on bail pending an appeal. His conviction might be reversed (as it was in 1921); and he was capable of taking his seat. An American precedent is Matthew Lyon, who was elected to Congress by voters who had full knowledge of his prosecution under the Sedition Act of 1798. He was allowed to qualify, and when he was subsequently convicted and imprisoned the House of Representatives by a close vote refused to expel him.[21]

Most of the exclusions from Congress before 1919 were for

[20] 1 Hinds' Prec. 488, 489, 570.   [21] 2 Hinds' Prec. 850.

offenses which had expressly been made a disqualification by Act of Congress.[22] The most important of these statutes was the Test Oath Act of July, 1862. At the outbreak of the Civil War several Southern Senators and Representatives were expelled for their treasonable conduct in remaining permanently absent from their Congressional duties and either taking up arms against the government or entering the Confederate lines and actively participating in the rebellion. On the other hand, both houses refused to expel members from border states who had committed no overt acts, but had vigorously opposed by speeches the prosecution of the war by the North. After more than a year of fighting, the matter was regularized by a statute obliging Representatives and Senators to swear before admission that they had never borne arms against the United States, given aid, countenance, or counsel to the enemy, or yielded a voluntary support to any government. It is noteworthy that although the terms of this statute included much more than treason, the ironclad oath was not used to bar members for personal disloyalty or passive sympathy with the rebellion, or speeches denouncing the war as an abolition war and opposing any further aid toward its prosecution. Thus, even in the heat of the Civil War, disloyalty was not a bar to an elected member of Congress, until it was expressly made so by a statute, and not then unless it was evidenced by actual aid to the enemy or words of acute virulence.

Some doubt was felt upon the validity of the Test Oath Act, and in 1868 it was virtually superseded by section 3 of the Fourteenth Amendment, on which the exclusion of Berger was wrongly based.

The Church of Jesus Christ of Latter-day Saints is a much more closely knit and powerful organization than the Socialist Party and instead of being legalized by statute has frequently been made the object of adverse legislation. Consequently, the decisions upon the admission of Mormons to Congress are much in point. The constitutional question was not squarely raised while Utah was still a territory because Delegates sit only by leave of the House. Nevertheless, the decisions of that

[22] In addition to the statutes mentioned, an act of 1853 disqualified for bribery. Since 1920 several Senators like Newberry have been forced out for election practices which were thought undesirable, even though not a violation of existing law. See *infra*, Chapter XIV, section x.

time make the distinction which I have emphasized between overt acts and mere opinions. In 1868 the election of a Delegate was contested on the ground that he represented the institution of polygamy and a community hostile to the other portions of the United States and was disqualified by a secret oath. Yet he was not excluded, for he had no plurality of wives. On the other hand, a Delegate who was himself a polygamist was unseated. Even in this case a strong minority protested against the assumption by the House of the arbitrary power to inquire into the moral fitness of candidates; and asked whether, if it was a bar for a Delegate to live with four women who were married to him, it would also be a bar if three of them were not.

After the admission of Utah as a state, the issue became acute. The Edmunds Act of 1882 had disqualified any polygamist, whether convicted or not, from office under the United States. A convicted polygamist, who was still living with three wives, was elected Representative in 1898, and was finally unseated after a thorough discussion from both points of view of the question whether Congress or the House could add qualifications to those specified in the Constitution. The majority relied to a large extent on his ineligibility under the Edmunds Act, so that the case supports the usual policy already stated, that any disqualification added to the Constitution should be embodied in a statute. The minority contended that Congress could not add any qualification to the Constitution, especially if it was not based upon a conviction of crime. This decision involved overt criminal acts and not opinions or party affiliations.

This distinction is clearly brought out by the refusal of the Senate in 1904 to exclude or expel Reed Smoot. He was not himself a polygamist or otherwise disqualified by statute, and had personally opposed polygamy in Utah, but he was one of the twelve apostles who together with the first president ruled over the Mormon hierarchy, and as a body encouraged the continuance of polygamous cohabitation (at least in long-standing marriages) and controlled the political affairs of Utah. According to the majority of the Committee, Mr. Smoot came there, "not as the accredited representative of the State of Utah, but as the choice of the hierarchy which controls the church and has usurped the functions of the State." Nevertheless, the Senate refused to look beyond the question of his personal guilt of crime or disbar him for the political and ethical purposes of the organization to which he belonged. This position limits the effect of the Test Oath cases and relegates them to the status of consequences of the extraordinary situation following the Civil War.

Therefore, the action of the House of Representatives in unseating Berger for mere words opposing the war was unprecedented. It only remains to consider the wisdom of following such a policy in the future.

e. Is it a wise policy to make opposition to a war or other seditious speech a disqualification for membership in Congress?

Some persons believe that sedition is more properly a disqualification than other crimes, because it involves a breach of allegiance. Sound policy points in just the opposite direction. The view just described is opposed to the outcome of the Wilkes controversy, to the action of the House of Representatives in letting Matthew Lyon keep his seat despite his violation of the Sedition Act of 1798, and to the distinction, repeatedly cited above from other precedents, between overt acts and mere expressions of opinion. The truth is that most violations of a sedition statute, and more especially of the Espionage Act of 1917 as it has been construed by the courts, are political offenses. They would so be classified by us if the utterances involved were spoken in another country. Now in dealing with foreign political offenses, which did not muddy our thinking by emotions, our law has always been careful to except such offenses from measures aimed against foreign criminals generally. For example, aliens can be kept out of the United States or deported for the conviction or commission of a crime involving moral turpitude, but nothing in this statute is to exclude an alien for "an offense purely political." [23] Again, our government has always refused to allow the extradition of persons charged by foreign nations with political crimes, even if the charge (as often happened with Russians) involved the advocacy of violence and revolution.[24]

[23] 18 U. S. C. A. § 136 (e).
[24] *Harvard Research in International Law*, Part I, Extradition, pp. 107–119

The opinion of American voters ignoring a candidate's conviction for a political crime is entitled to peculiar respect. Such crimes do not usually arise from an individual malevolence, as do murder and robbery, but from political, economic, or ethical views which are shared by a group, for instance, of pacifists or Socialists, and which are considered dangerous because they clash with the will of the majority. The election of such an offender is in effect an approval of these views by the voters of his district,[25] so that the legislature by excluding or expelling him denies expression to a political, economic, or ethical theory which is held by a considerable mass of the electorate. The tide of public opinion with regard to disloyal utterances is likely to vary with time and locality. The penalty affixed by the criminal statute sufficiently guards against their dangerous consequences in the emergency of war. If an additional penalty not included in the law is imposed by one branch of the legislature after hostilities have ceased, the result is to block changes in public opinion, whereas the theory of democratic government is that such changes shall find an immediate and ready expression through the ballot.

Lincoln's principle [26] that the nation must be able to protect itself in war against utterances which actually cause insubordination and obstruct the raising of armies may justify some of the Espionage Act convictions, but his policy was absolutely opposed to the annexation of political disqualifications when the emergency had passed. Berger's utterances were far less dangerous in their tendency than those expressed by many

---

(1935). See the state papers in Moore, *Digest of International Law*, IV, 332 ff. On the general subject, see Ferrari, "Political Crime," 20 *Columbia Law Review* 308 (1920).

[25] While Gitlow and Winitsky were in prison for long terms under the New York Anarchy Act, they were nominated in 1921 by the Workers' League for mayor of New York City and president of the board of aldermen respectively. They were denied a place on the ballot on the grounds that they could not serve if elected and that expensive election machinery is not run for a futile purpose. — Appeal of Lindgren, 232 N. Y. 59 (1921). Comment in 22 *Columbia Law Review* 373 observes: "The opinion did not consider the question of the policy of a protest vote. It was a doubtful exercise of discretion . . . to deny the mandamus when the concurrence of election and pardon, no matter how remote the possibility, before the term of office, would make the nomination anything but futile." Both prisoners were in fact pardoned by Governor Alfred E. Smith, but not until some time after the 1921 city election. See Chapter IX.

[26] Page 105, *supra*.

persons who took office unmolested during the Civil War. A large number of Democrats were elected to Congress in 1864 on a platform drafted by the notorious Vallandigham, which declared the war a failure.[27] The reasoning of the Berger committee would have allowed the Republican majority in Congress to exclude the Democratic minority. Apart from the fact of conviction, the conduct of these men furnishes a close analogy to Berger, much closer than the persons excluded under the Test Oath Act, most of whom had committed treason while a few others came from Border States and had definitely identified themselves with the South. The Mexican War affords more honorable precedents for the principle that men who oppose a war in public discussion should afterwards be sworn in at the National Capitol without question. Daniel Webster said at a public meeting in 1847: "We are, in my opinion, in a most unnecessary and therefore a most unjustifiable war." Henry Clay asked: "Must we blindly continue the conflict, without any visible object, or any prospect of a definite termination? . . . It is the privilege of the people in their primary assemblies, and of every private citizen, however humble, to express an opinion in regard to the purposes for which the war should be continued." Charles Sumner outdid Berger in vituperation: "The Mexican War is an enormity born of slavery. . . . Base in object, atrocious in beginning, immoral in all its influences, vainly prodigal of treasure and life; it is a war of infamy which must blot the pages of our history." [28] The additional element of conviction in the Berger case (aside from the appeal and possibility of later reversal) should be limited in its effect to the statutory penalty,[29] and should not overthrow the principle recognized in the cases just mentioned and many others, that variations of public opinion with respect to a war, especially if it is past, should be allowed to reflect themselves in the national legislature without interference. It is significant that all the Entente powers, except Japan, have admitted to their legislatures without any hesitation Socialists who op-

[27] J. F. Rhodes, *History of the United States*, IV, 522 ff.

[28] *Berger Hearings*, I, 712, 713. On the War of 1812, see Beveridge's *Marshall*, IV, c. I.

[29] See Cummings *v.* Missouri, 4 Wall. 277 (1866); *Ex parte* Garland, *id.* 333; Green *v.* Shumway, 39 N. Y. 418 (1868); Goetcheus *v.* Matthewson, 61 N. Y. 420 (1875).

268   PURIFYING THE LEGISLATURE

posed the war as vigorously as Berger, with the same intention to bring it to an immediate close. Indeed, some of the Italian Socialists were elected while serving prison sentences for their militant anti-war activities.

Therefore, although Berger's statements in the *Milwaukee Leader*, before the committee, and in Congress at the time of his exclusion, entitle him to no personal sympathy, nevertheless the twofold denial of his seat was, apart from all questions of legality, a great mistake and a wrong to the voters of the fifth district of Wisconsin.

The action of the House of Representatives has, however, still more serious and far-reaching aspects. If it had been based simply on Berger's conviction its effect would be limited to men who have been actually convicted under the Espionage Act. The great evil of the case is that the House of Representatives and its committee assumed the power to go behind the conviction, and expressed the view that without any conviction at all Berger could be deprived of his seat because of his opposition to the war. The chairman of the committee, Mr. Dallinger, said in the debate upon the first exclusion:

The one and only issue in this case is that of Americanism. It is whether a man who . . . took an oath . . . to support the Constitution . . . and who, when this country declared war . . . became the head and front of an organized conspiracy to hinder, obstruct, and embarrass the Government in its fight for existence, should be admitted to membership in this House simply because a constituency in one of our States has seen fit to give him a plurality of its vote. This issue is far broader than the question of a conviction for violation of a particular statute by a court in Chicago,[30] an appeal from which may be set aside by a higher court on technical grounds. . . . In our opinion the House expects it; the men who fought for their country in the great war expect it; the entire country expects it.

Therefore, though the precise legal ground of the Berger exclusion was the Fourteenth Amendment, the case gave public currency to the broad proposition that "disloyalty" during a war would bar a duly elected representative. Thus long after a war was over, a legislature could without any previous judi-

[30] On December 3, 1923, after the Department of Justice had dropped the Espionage Act charges against Berger, he at last took his seat in the House without a single dissenting voice.

cial condemnation conduct an inquiry into the mental state of
a man during the war and the tendency of his utterances to
discourage the national cause, just the kind of investigation
which is shown in my second chapter to have proved so vague
and unsatisfactory in the hands of an impartial judge and jury
and which was justified if at all only by the great necessi-
ties and dangers of the war. Furthermore, the conduct for which
Berger was convicted and excluded was said by him and regarded by many of his opponents to be that of the Socialist
Party generally, so that if conviction were an immaterial factor
as Mr. Dallinger said, Berger's ineligibility could naturally be
extended to any Socialist. Thus the popular impressions created by the Berger case paved the way for one of the most
astonishing episodes in American political life.

3. THE FIVE SOCIALIST MEMBERS OF THE NEW YORK ASSEMBLY

> *Then stood there up one in the council, a Pharisee,*
> *named Gamaliel, a doctor of the law, had in reputation*
> *among all the people, and said unto them: "Ye men of*
> *Israel, take heed to yourselves what ye intend to do as*
> *touching these men. Refrain from these men and let them*
> *alone: for if this counsel or this work be of men, it will*
> *come to nought; but if it be of God, ye can not over-*
> *throw it; lest haply ye be found even to fight against*
> *God."*
>
> — The Acts of the Apostles.

On January 7, 1920, just before the second exclusion of
Berger, and while the front pages of the press were still full
of the great conspiracy which would have overthrown the
nation had it not been for the New Year's round-up of four
thousand left-wing radicals, the New York Legislature opened
its session. Among the members of the Assembly or lower
house were five Socialists — Claessens, Solomon, Waldman,
De Witt, and Orr. The Socialist Party of New York was a
legally recognized party under the Election Law,[31] so that its
candidates had as much right on the ballot as Democrats or
Republicans. All these Socialists except De Witt had previously served in the Assembly. The opposition of the party to

[31] The Socialist candidate in 1918 received over 120,000 votes.

the war had aroused no objection to its representatives at any time during the conflict, even when ten of them took their seats at Albany just before the Spring Drive of 1918. And on this day, in 1920, the five members took office without interference, swearing that they would support the Constitution of the United States and that of New York, and discharge the duties of their office to the best of their ability, and that they had not influenced votes by bribe or promise. The New York Constitution, Article XIII, prescribes this oath and makes it all-sufficient:

No other oath, declaration or test shall be required as a qualification for any office of public trust.

They occupied their seats and for upwards of two hours entered into all the business of the day.

Suddenly the newly-elected Speaker, without notice or motion, directed the Sergeant-at-Arms to present the five Socialist members before the bar of the House. The surprised men were paraded down into the well of the Assembly chamber in front of the Speaker's rostrum, in full view of their fellow-members and hundreds of guests, who crowded the galleries and the floor to witness the ceremonies of the opening day. There they were lined up with the Sergeant-at-Arms on guard, while the Speaker addressed them:

You are seeking seats in this body, you who have been elected on a platform that is absolutely inimical to the best interests of the State of New York and of the United States.

He then declared that the Socialist Party was not truly a political party, but a subversive and unpatriotic organization,[32] and informed them that if the House should adopt a resolution declaring their places vacant they would be given an opportunity to appear before a tribunal to prove their rights to sit in the Assembly.

Next a resolution was presented to the Assembly, which had been drafted by the Attorney General as counsel for the Lusk

---

[32] This view of the Socialist Party was by no means confined to New York. A good indication of the prevailing emotional attitude during the winter of 1919–20 is an article by a distinguished Minneapolis lawyer, Rome G. Brown, "The Disloyalty of Socialism," 53 *American Law Review* 681 (September–October 1919).

Committee. Probing committees seem indigenous to New York. They had one in 1780 to detect and defeat conspiracies of Loyalists. On March 26, 1919, the legislature set up a joint committee of six under the chairmanship of Senator Lusk to investigate seditious activities and report to the legislature. Although in no sense a body for the prosecution of crime, it proceeded to conduct a series of spectacular illegal raids on the offices of the Rand School and other radical organizations, instigate prosecutions of radical leaders like Gitlow, and fill the press with a flow of terrorizing descriptions of the Red menace.[33] And now it was the moving spirit in ousting the Socialist Assemblymen.

The Lusk Committee's resolution did not even recite that the members were charged with certain offenses, but stated facts as if already proved, an Alice-in-Wonderland performance of "sentence first — verdict afterwards." It declared that they were members of the Socialist Party of America, which adhered to the revolutionary forces of Soviet Russia and endorsed the principles of the Communist International of Moscow, and this was pledged to the forcible and violent overthrow of all organized governments. The party by its St. Louis platform had opposed the war, and thereby stamped itself and all its members with an inimical attitude to the best interests of New York and the United States. These five members had subscribed to its principles and its aims and purposes against the government. They had been connected with an organization convicted of a violation of the Espionage Act. Therefore, it concluded, they were denied seats in the Assembly "pending determination of their qualifications and eligibility to their respective seats";[34] and the investigation of their qualifications and eligibility was referred to the Committee on Judiciary. The roll-call was then taken and the five Socialists were called upon to vote as members. After the passage of the resolution

---

[33] On the Rand School and Gitlow, see *infra* Chapters VIII and IX.

[34] This in itself is contrary to the usual practice. Persons certified as elected are entitled to participate in all legislative proceedings except their own case, until their ineligibility is adjudicated. Thus Senator Lorimer continued to sit until he was disqualified for bribery at his election. This is especially applicable to the New York Socialists, since they had taken the constitutional oath of office before any objection was made to their qualifications. See Chafee, *State House versus Pent House*, p. xi (1937).

they were hustled by the Sergeant-at-Arms out of the chamber, where their seats remained vacant for the remainder of the session, to the disfranchisement of sixty thousand voters of the City of New York.

In one of those magnificent decisions whereby the Supreme Court of the United States in former years fortified the civil liberties wrested from authority by the long struggles of the seventeenth and eighteenth centuries and proclaimed in the American Bill of Rights, Justice Bradley warned us that illegitimate and unconstitutional practices get their first footing by silent approaches and slight deviations from legal modes of procedure.[35] Since the 15th day of June, 1917, the nation had been led on by its panic-stricken fear of adverse opinion to abandon one national tradition after another. Every unheeded prediction of the handful of liberals was more than fulfilled. The Espionage Act was only to punish interference with recruiting and military discipline — but it was used against all prominent opposition to the war. Every one agreed that freedom of speech meant the absence of previous administrative restraint on political discussion — and the Postmaster General was allowed to establish a whimsical censorship of the political press and maintain it long after the last American soldier had been demobilized. Suppression was said to be only a war measure. The states prolonged it into peace, and the Attorney General of the United States begged Congress to imitate them. Radical aliens were put under control, and a similar law was demanded for radical citizens. One by one, the right of freedom of speech, the right of assembly, the right to petition, the right to protection against unreasonable searches and seizures, the right against arbitrary arrest, the right to a fair trial, the hatred of spies, the principle that guilt is personal, the principle that punishment should bear some proportion to the offense, had been sacrificed and ignored. Here and there a solitary and despised protest — the rest was silence. And now the waves of hysteria dashed against the very foundation of American life, the right of the people to elect their own rulers. Berger was excluded after he was convicted of crime, but these men were excluded without any conviction, without any crime, without any trial, from the offices which they had taken with

[35] Boyd v. U. S., 116 U. S. 616, 635 (1885).

all the qualifications and formalities prescribed by the fundamental law. At last the leaders of thought were awakened to the realization that a government cannot be saved, is not worth saving, at the cost of its own principles.

Woodrow Wilson, the successor of Jefferson, had taken no step to stop the encroachments on freedom of speech, had signed his name to both Espionage Acts, had allowed his officers without a reproach to censor and raid and arrest as they chose. It was reserved for the Republican presidential candidate at the election of 1916 to become the champion of Anglo-Saxon liberties. Charles Evans Hughes, leader of the American bar, former Governor of New York, former Associate Justice of the Supreme Court, within forty-eight hours of the Albany imbroglio, wrote Speaker Sweet that it was absolutely opposed to the fundamental principles of our government for a majority to undertake to deny representation to the minority through the men who had been elected by a ballot lawfully cast.[36]

If there was anything against these men as individuals, if they were deemed to be guilty of criminal offenses, they should have been charged accordingly. But I understand that the action is not directed against these five elected members as individuals but that the proceeding is virtually an attempt to indict a political party and to deny it representation in the Legislature. This is not, in my judgment, American government.

Are Socialists, unconvicted of crime, to be denied the ballot? If Socialists are permitted to vote, are they not permitted to vote for their own candidates? If their candidates are elected and are men against whom, as individuals, charges of disqualifying offenses cannot be laid, are they not entitled to their seats? . . .

I understand that it is said that the Socialists constitute a combination to overthrow the Government. The answer is plain. If public officers or private citizens have any evidence that any individuals, or group of individuals, are plotting revolution and seeking by violent measures to change our Government, let the evidence be laid before the proper authorities and swift action be taken for the protection of the community. Let every resource of inquiry, of pursuit, of prosecution be employed to ferret out and punish the guilty according to our laws. But I count it a most serious mistake to proceed, not against individuals charged with violation of law, but

[36] *New York Times*, January 10, 1920; Sweet's reply, January 11.

against masses of our citizens combined for political action, by denying them the only resource of peaceful government; that is, action
by the ballot box and through duly elected representatives in legislative bodies.

Speaker Sweet, after consultation with the Lusk Committee,
replied that the Socialists were not expelled, but merely subjected to an investigation by the body which was charged by
the Constitution with the authority to inquire into the fitness
of those who seek seats in the Assembly. The question presented squarely was whether the different organizations which
they sought to represent in the legislature advocated methods
and employed tactics to overthrow our form of government,
which would justify their exclusion from participating in legislative proceedings. He thus characterized the proceeding, as
did the Attorney General of New York, not as an inquiry into
the personal unfitness of these men or into the overt acts of
any one, but into the opinions and words of whole groups.
Finally he stated that criticism of the Assembly action without
full knowledge of the facts gave aid and comfort to those elements of our society which seek the destruction of our institutions.

Nevertheless, criticism poured in, not only from Socialists
and labor unions, but from large conservative groups like the
National Security League. The New York Board of Aldermen
refused to follow the example of the Assembly as to its Socialist
members. For once the *Tribune* and the conservative *Weekly
Review* stood shoulder to shoulder with the *New Republic* and
the *Nation*, and outdid them in the vigor of their condemnation. The Bar Association of the City of New York adopted
resolutions offered by Governor Hughes, opposing any attempt
to exclude legislators because of their affiliation with any political party, when they are seeking by constitutional and legal
methods to bring about any change in the Constitution and
laws. The Association appointed a committee of non-Socialists
to appear before the Judiciary Committee of the Assembly and
safeguard the principles of representative government. No
action could have done more to strengthen the confidence of
workingmen in the public spirit of the bar.

The Assembly paid no more attention to these protests than

the House of Commons to the remonstrances of Burke and the voters of England on behalf of Wilkes. The Assembly was past saving, but the nation was saved. The American people, long bedrugged by propaganda, were shaken out of their nightmare of revolution. The red terror became ridiculous on the lips of Speaker Sweet. A legislature trembling before five men — the long-lost American sense of humor revived and people began to laugh. That broke the spell. The light of day beat in not only upon the Assembly, but upon Congress and the Department of Justice. Never again did the hysteria of the past year return. The raids of January 2d were flood-tide, and with Governor Hughes' letter on the 9th, the ebb set in. Then followed the opposition of the conservative press and sober speakers to the pending federal sedition bills, the disclosures in the Colyer trial of the illegal character of the New Year's round-up, the decision of Secretary Wilson legalizing the Communist Labor Party, the wholesale cancellation of deportation warrants. The American people owe a lasting debt of gratitude to the New York Assembly.

But there was no return to sanity in Albany. On January 20th the investigation of the five members began before the Judiciary Committee, which was appointed by the Speaker who had taken such a definite stand against them. At the outset the Bar Association committee appeared, with Mr. Hughes as its chairman, but was not allowed to participate in the proceedings. Before withdrawing it filed a brief and these recommendations:

That the Judiciary Committee at once report to the Assembly that there is no question properly before the Judiciary Committee of any disqualification on the part of these members; that no charges against these members of any constitutional disqualification, or of any misconduct in office or of any violation of law on their part have been properly made, that the members under suspension should at once be restored to the privileges of their seats and that if it be desired to present any charges against them of any violation of law, such charges should be properly formulated, and that until such charges, properly laid, have been established by proof, after due opportunity to be heard, these members shall enjoy all the privileges of their seats in recognition of their own rights and of the rights of their constituencies.

This position was conclusively established by the Bar Association in its brief. The question was whether a legislature, especially in the absence of any disqualifying statute, can lawfully unseat a member for opinions and affiliations without overt acts. All the doubts raised as to Berger's exclusion were present here, and two more defects besides. The first was the constitutional prohibition already mentioned against any oath or test in addition to that already taken by the Socialist members. This clause had been held by the courts to forbid not merely new forms of test oaths, but all arbitrary requirements for voting or office-holding, particularly those based on opinions and party affiliations. Secondly, the five Socialists were not charged with violating any law.[37] They had been convicted of no crime, they were accused of no crime which could conceivably be a bar to office. They were proscribed for their beliefs and their membership in the Socialist Party.

The action of the Assembly must be characterized as a flagrant usurpation of power, only to be found in that "invisible government" of which Senator Root, who had good reason to know, said that for forty years it had been about as representative and responsible as the government of Venezuela:

It makes no difference what name you give, whether you call it Fenton or Conkling or Cornell or Arthur or Platt, or by the names of men now living. The ruler of the state during the greater part of the forty years of my acquaintance with the state government has not been any man authorized by the constitution or by the law.[38]

The conduct of the investigation was thoroughly in harmony with its illegality. It was not based on any definite charges nor was it even limited to the accusations in the Resolution of January 7th, 1920. The affair had all the characteristics of an accumulative crime as described by Burke in the Wilkes case.[39] Whenever the Attorney General or his associate counsel thought of some new offense with which the Socialist Party

<hr>

[37] There was a half-hearted allegation that they had violated the Espionage Act, but no evidence was given by the Assembly to support it. See note 40, *infra*.

[38] See 40 *Reports of the American Bar Association* 365 (1915); Elihu Root, *Addresses on Government and Citizenship*, p. 202 (at the New York Constitutional Convention of 1915).

[39] Page 246, *supra*.

could be taxed, it was lugged into the case and made a fresh
reason for exclusion. The Resolution was construed as a rov-
ing commission to the Judiciary Committee, to find as many
objectionable opinions of the Socialist Party as possible, on
the theory that twenty-seven bad grounds for exclusion might
be rolled together and make one good ground. Inasmuch as
there was no demarcation of counts in this rag-bag and ever-
reopened indictment, no single fact had to be proved to the
satisfaction of a majority of the Assembly. One member could
vote to exclude the five Socialists because he thought they were
as guilty under the Espionage Act as the three men who were
convicted at Syracuse;[40] another because he considered Socialism threatened the family; a third to protect the church;
a fourth, because Socialists sought to set up a Soviet in the
United States; some one else, because he disliked the vote of
Claessens against the military training of boys. Others might
object on the ground that the party fostered the claims of
conscientious objectors or worked for the repeal of the draft
or opposed the conscription of labor or voted against large
military appropriations. The range was large and every member could find a reason of his own. It was the Wilkes case
over again:[41]

> The very enumeration of so many grounds of expulsion implied
> their separate weakness and insufficiency; while it was designed to
> attract the support of members, influenced by different reasons for
> their votes.

Few legal documents furnish more delightful reading than
the *Outline*, as it was called, of "the case of the Assembly
against the five Socialist Assemblymen" — the title is a significant comment on the impartiality of a tribunal which constituted itself both judge and prosecutor. This made it clearer
than ever that the Socialists were excluded only for the supposed principles of their party. The nature of whatever
charges of personal unfitness were made may be gathered from
the following attempt to fasten overt acts on Solomon.

---

[40] See p. 104, *supra*. The whole of Judge Garvin's opinion in the Syracuse
case was reprinted in *Assembly Outline*. No facts or other reasons than this
were given to establish the guilt of the five members under the Espionage Act.

[41] May's *Constitutional History*, I, 316.

In 1692 the chief accusers of the Salem witches were a club of young girls who sent more than one old woman to her death by telling how they had seen her drink their blood or cause a yellow bird to sit on the minister's hat where it hung on a peg in the pulpit.[42] In 1920 a stenographer just under eighteen years old testified that three years before, when she was barely fifteen, she heard Solomon (one of the five members) make a speech in Brooklyn, with an American flag and a red flag flying on his stand. A detachment of soldiers rode up recruiting and asked to borrow his platform. She heard Solomon reply, "Lend you my platform? Can you borrow my platform? Huh; the gutter is good enough for you." They spoke from their jitney and went on. Nor was this the worst. A band of music came by on a trolley-car, stopped about three minutes, and struck up the "Star-Spangled Banner." And then in her presence and in the presence, she declared, of two policemen, "Mr. Solomon turned up his coat collar, put on his hat, and pulled it over his eyes, spit on the American flag and sat down." And the police did nothing.

The spy who is regularly employed by the government was brought into undesired publicity by the Colyer trial. The voluntary informer is also a recurrent feature of all prosecutions for opinion since the day of Titus Oates and beyond. The Attorney General's brief reprints the girl's testimony without question, although the two policemen attending Solomon's speech took the stand to swear that no such disloyal acts occurred.

The meat of the *Outline* is the portrayal of the iniquities of Socialism. This is a very different affair from the body of economic principles which is attacked by Carver, Taussig, and other economists, none of whom was summoned as an expert by the prosecution. The *Outline* conceives it as "a Revolutionary Party, having the single purpose of destroying our institutions and government and substituting the Russian-Soviet government, . . . an anti-national party whose allegiance is given to the Internationale and not to the United States."

[42] Palfrey, *History of New England*, IV, 102; Hutchinson, *History of the Province of Massachusetts Bay*, II, 27. Compare the testimony of the Edeau women in the prosecutions for the 1916 Preparedness Parade bomb in San Francisco. — *The Mooney-Billings Report*, pp. 145 ff. (New York: Gotham House, 1932).

Its purposes, mass action and the general strike, are treasonable. For its crimes the five members are responsible, and more than that, for the acts of any other person in that party, whether or not he belongs to their particular faction. As Mr. Stanchfield, for the prosecution, openly stated:

> The whole theory of this investigation rests upon the proposition that the Socialist Party, of which the five members under investigation are confessedly, concededly members, has embarked upon a program that calls for the overthrow of our form of government, some assert by constitutional means, others by violence. Now, assuming that that program is the basic charge under investigation, then my argument runs along this line: That every pamphlet, every declaration, every speech, every statement of every man who is affiliated with or belongs to that party, not necessarily in a technical sense of belonging to it, but everybody who upholds those claims, who supports those principles, who stands upon that platform, is bound by the speeches, the sentiments, the writings, the books, the publications of every other man affiliated with that association, whether they were present at the time when it was made or they were uttered, or whether they were absent.

No person who followed with any intelligence the proceedings of the Socialist Party at the convention of September, 1919, or May, 1920, could doubt that that party was as much divided into factions as any other. Nevertheless, the five members were held responsible on the principle just stated, not merely for the statements in the party platform, but also for the Debs speech at Canton, Ohio; for statements in the Moscow manifesto; for extracts from a book in Yiddish published by the Jewish Socialist Federation of America; for all the articles contributed to the *American Socialist*; for everything that was said by speakers at meetings at which one of the Socialist assemblymen was present; as well as for statements made in a letter by an organization to which he was bitterly opposed. This was guilt by association with a vengeance.

When such testimony and arguments were admitted, the result was a foregone conclusion. The Committee recommended expulsion, the Assembly characteristically waited until April 1st, which was too late for a reëlection, and then expelled the five members by an overwhelming vote. The Legislature next enacted several bills drafted by the triumphant Lusk

Committee, which throttled the Rand School and excluded from the ballot any organization which advocated "doctrines or policies that tend, if carried into effect, to the destruction, subversion, or endangering of the existing governments" of the state and nation, "and of the rights, privileges and institutions secured under such constitutions." Governor Alfred E. Smith vetoed all these Lusk bills in stinging messages.[43] And then, leaving the Governor's welfare bills untouched, the New York Legislature adjourned, and Speaker Sweet proclaimed the session "a victory for undivided Americanism."

Surely this event ought to free us from the tyranny of this word "Americanism" which seems like some magic helmet to render the true qualities of the wearer invisible to those around him. The men who use the ideals of the founders of our Republic, not as an inspiration for high-minded action on their own part but as a test by which they may condemn and imprison and disfranchise their fellow-citizens, are as unpardonable as the persecutors who used the teachings of the Gospels to consign men to the stake in this world and hell-fire in the next. Years ago William Graham Sumner commented:

> Who dares say that he is not "American"? Who dares repudiate what is declared to be Americanism? It follows that if anything is base and bogus it is always labeled American. If a thing is to be recommended which cannot be justified it is put under "Americanism." . . . Then we see what Americanism and patriotism are. They are the duty laid upon us all to applaud, follow, and obey whatever a ruling clique of newspapers or politicians chooses to say or want to do.[44]

The absurdity to which our greatest state descended in its frantic desire to suppress disloyalty cannot be entirely explained by the fear of Bolshevism, because the danger of that is far greater in European countries, which have large groups of Socialists in their legislatures unmolested. Nor was it entirely due to the activities of organizations like the Lusk

---

[43] *Progressive Democracy: Speeches and State Papers of Alfred E. Smith*, pp. 273–281 (1928). The bills restricting teachers became law under Governor Miller and were repealed after Smith was reëlected. See *infra* Chapter VIII. See also the New York legislation recommended in 1939 in the Report of the Lusk Committee's somewhat more restrained successor. — *Op. cit. supra*, Chapter V, note 31 (end), pp. 278 ff.

[44] Sumner, *Folkways*, p. 177.

Committee. Something more is needed to account for the statement of the *New York Times* that the expulsion of the Socialists was as clearly and demonstrably a measure of national defense as the declaration of war against Germany.[45] Speaker Sweet and his associates would not have acted as they did had they not been assured of wide support, especially in the rural districts. Much of the panic-stricken dread of Socialism is due to the sentiment that we must have unanimity of thought in this country. The surprising uniformity of American life has long excited attention from foreign observers.[46] Until recently we have had only a middle class without any proletariat or large group of extremely wealthy men. Since the issues of the Civil War died away, whatever few fundamental differences in opinion have existed have rarely coincided with party lines. A French writer in his biography of President Wilson remarks that a foreigner on coming to this country does not understand our political parties. In Europe every party has a platform which represents a definite policy, like monarchy, clericalism, Socialism. He finds nothing of the kind here. Why do we have two parties when they do not differ? Halévy explains that the Republican and Democratic parties are like two great department stores, such as the *Bon Marché* and the *Louvre*. Both sell very much the same things. Some people go entirely to one, some go entirely to the other, some go first to one and then to the other. They are there because they have always been there.[47] And somebody else has called them two bottles with different labels, both empty. But now a new party has entered the field which has real issues, vital one way or the other to all of us and hence the antagonism of its opponents is immediate and bitter. When it shows signs of gaining real strength then there is an energetic effort to stamp it out, which likes to base itself on patriotism and self-preservation.

It is not by such methods that the nation can be saved from the evil tendencies of any doctrine. The great strength of our argument against violent-talking radicals in the past has been that we could say to them: "It is true that in the countries

[45] Editorial of April 2, 1920.
[46] See Bryce's *American Commonwealth*, vol. II, chap. cxii.
[47] Daniel Halévy, *Le Président Wilson* (Paris, 1918), p. 109.

that you came from you naturally resorted to violence because you had no vote and could not abolish the abuses to which you objected. It is not so in this country. If you want a change, go and vote for it, vote for men who have promised to bring it to pass." The New York Assembly deprived us of this argument in the state where the left wing is strongest.[48] It appealed to force as the normal method for settling conflicts between ideas. It disfranchised 60,000 American citizens on the basis of a caricature of Socialism. It repudiated government by representation and substituted government by misrepresentation.

[48] Similar considerations apply to recent state statutes excluding the Communist Party and similar organizations from the ballot. See 37 *Columbia Law Review* 86 (1937); 54 *Harvard Law Review* 155 (1940). These statutes will be discussed in Chapter XII, section II.

PART II
THE FIRST DECADE OF PEACE
1920–1930

> *Far off I hear the crowing of the cocks,*
> *And through the opening door that time unlocks*
> *Feel the fresh breathing of Tomorrow creep.*

CHAPTER 7

THE LAST WAR CASES

I. STATES' RIGHTS AND OPPOSITION TO WAR:
GILBERT v. MINNESOTA [1]

> *The degree of tolerance obtainable at any moment depends on the strain under which society is maintaining its cohesion. . . . Under the strain of invasion the French Government in 1792 struck off 4000 heads, mostly on grounds that would not in time of settled peace have provoked any Government to chloroform a dog.*
>
> BERNARD SHAW, Preface to Saint Joan.

DURING the early years of the American Revolution several states felt the need of protecting Congress and flag against the Tory wits who asserted that Martha Washington had a yellow tom-cat with thirteen black stripes around his tail, which suggested to her the design for the flag.[2] Massachusetts accordingly passed a law fining any person who used expressions "in preaching or praying, or in public or private discourse or conversation, with an apparent design to discourage" people from supporting independence. Virginia had a similar statute, which came home to roost when that commonwealth denounced the Sedition Act of 1798 as a violation of freedom of speech. But state action was never used to curb opposition to subsequent wars, until 1917. It remained for our own day, when the doctrine of states' rights was supposed to be on its last legs, to establish by a Supreme Court decision

---

[1] 254 U. S. 325 (1920). The state war statutes are described in Chapter II, section VII. The actual decision involved only the Minnesota statute, but the majority opinion necessarily upheld the power of other states to punish opposition to war, although the more sweeping terms of some state laws left additional questions unsettled. A Texas war statute was upset by the state court as too broad. — *Ex parte* Meckel, 87 Tex. Cr. 120 (1920) On the Gilbert case, see *Holmes-Pollock Letters*, II, 61.

[2] See also Thompson, "Anti-Loyalist Legislation during the American Revolution," 3 *Illinois Law Review* 81, 147 (1908)

in December, 1920, several months after the events described in the last chapter, that the weapons which Massachusetts and Virginia used against the disloyal remain sharp and active in the hands of modern state governments and were not surrendered to the nation in 1789.

Inasmuch as the fighting had long been over and state wartime prisoners had been already or were soon released by expiration of their sentences or by pardons, this decision had no immediate practical importance, but it may produce serious consequences in our next war.

It is significant evidence of the altered attitude of Americans toward open discussion that during the World War eleven states and territories considered even the unprecedented severity of the federal Espionage Act of 1917 an insufficient protection against pamphlets and oratory, and supplemented it by the drastic local legislation mentioned in the second chapter. Thus Montana imposed a penalty of twenty years in prison for various insults to the Constitution, the uniform, and the flag, which were considered too trivial to be federal crimes, until Congress in 1918 inserted the whole Montana law into the middle of the Espionage Act. Nothing could show better the way state war legislation works than the fate of Starr of Montana, as described by a United States judge.[3] "He was in the hands of one of those too common mobs, bent upon vindicating its peculiar standard of patriotism and its odd concept of respect for the flag by compelling him to kiss the latter." In the excitement of resisting their efforts, Starr said: "What is this thing anyway? Nothing but a piece of cotton with a little paint on it and some other marks in the corner there. I will not kiss that thing. It might be covered with microbes." The state authorities did absolutely nothing to the mob, but they had Starr convicted under the Montana Sedition Act for using language "calculated to bring the flag into contempt and disrepute," and sentenced him to the penitentiary for not less than ten nor more than twenty years at hard labor.

The right of the states to enact and enforce such legislation was vindicated by the Supreme Court in 1920 in the case of

---

[3] *Ex parte* Starr, 263 Federal Reporter 145 (1920), Bourquin, J. On the Montana statute, see *supra* Chapter II, section 1.

the Minnesota statute.[4] This was enacted right after we entered the war, before Congress passed either the Draft Act or the Espionage Act. It made it unlawful to advocate by writing, print, or public talking, "that men should not enlist in the military or naval forces of the United States or the state of Minnesota," or "that citizens of this state should not aid or assist the United States in prosecuting or carrying on war with the public enemies of the United States." Any violator could be arrested without warrant, fined $100 to $500, and imprisoned three months to a year. Those penalties, though enough to deter all but the most militant pacifists, are unusually light for a war statute; but in 1919 Minnesota, eager to be ready for our next war, substituted a far more sweeping law [5] of the Montana type, imposing the maximum penalty of twenty years in the penitentiary without which no American sedition statute can be thought up-to-date.

The 1917 law, which alone concerns us, atoned for its want of severity by numerousness of prosecutions. On its face it seemed directed against the comparatively few men who urged prospective volunteers, "Don't enlist," and actually proposed resistance to the draft and other war laws. Not one such case appears among the eighteen prosecutions in the Minnesota Reports. The statute was used to reach a very different kind of language. These decisions, like the Espionage Act cases, pound home the truth so easily overlooked by high-minded advocates of a sedition law, that you never can tell from reading the law when enacted what sort of speeches and pamphlets will be suppressed by it six months later. The Minnesota courts held that this statute could be violated although not a single person was dissuaded from enlisting, without a word about enlisting, and even though the jury found and believed that the speaker had not the slightest intention of hindering enlistment or any other war service. It was enough for a conviction if "the natural and reasonable effect of the statements uttered was to deter those to whom they were made" from enlisting or giving aid in the war. Of course any discussion

---

[4] Minn. Laws, 1917, c. 463. See Chapter II, section VII. The decisions construing this statute are collected in 1 A. L. R. 331, 20 *id*. 1535. On the Townley trial and the Non-Partisan League, see *supra*, Chapter II, at n. 64.

[5] Minn. Laws, 1919, c. 93; now Mason's Minn. Stat., 1927, §§ 9972 ff.

opposing our entry into the war would easily have this effect, and also — what was more objectionable to the ruling powers of Minnesota — any bitter criticism, even by a man who favored the war, directed against the actual war methods of the federal government and of the official and unofficial persons who managed the war activities of Minnesota.

It is impossible to understand the operation of this statute and the vague test of guilt laid down by the courts without some mention of the Minnesota conditions which lay behind every prosecution and every verdict. The presence of a large number of farmers of German birth was part of the trouble, but a still more important factor is summarized by an acute and trustworthy observer, John Lord O'Brian, who as Assistant to Attorney General Gregory directed the enforcement of the Espionage Act:

The general condition in the grain-producing states was intensified by the traditional hostility of the farmer toward the commercial interests of the cities — a phase of agrarian discontent usually summed up in the claim that the townsmen profited unjustly at the expense of the consumers. This steadily showed itself in many rural districts in a form of hostility toward state, county, and local councils of defense, which, it was claimed, were usually dominated by business men, the boards of trade, commercial clubs, etc.[6]

Much resentment must have been caused in some parts of Minnesota by Liberty Bond committees who forced every one to file a complete inventory of his real and personal property, on the basis of which the committee, consisting partly of bankers, required him to buy bonds to an amount that necessitated his borrowing from these same bankers at an interest-rate which from the very outset was considerably higher than that of the coupons on the bonds. The hostility caused by such methods evoked sharp comments, which those in control were not reluctant to silence.[7]

Finally, the long-standing antagonism between farmers and business men had recently been crystallized by the formation of the Non-Partisan League. Whole counties were divided into Leaguers and opponents, with no neutrals, and the belief of

[6] 42 Rep. N. Y. St. Bar Assn. 297.
[7] For a similar situation in Wisconsin, see Charles D. Stewart, "Prussianizing Wisconsin," *Atlantic Monthly*, January, 1919.

these opponents in the seditious nature of the League was so strong that almost any public discussion of the war by a League member would lead to his conviction by a jury, which, naturally enough, would not contain members of the League.

It followed from these conditions that practically every speech or pamphlet prosecuted, instead of dealing with enlistment, was an expression of this hostility to "big business" or an exposition of the economic views of the League in such sentences as: "This war was arbitrarily declared against the will of the people to protect the investments of Wall Street in the bonds of the Allies." "It is an insult to the American farmer to ask him to raise more grain and then take our boys and send them over there." One man was convicted for saying that he agreed with the speech which had just been delivered by Gilbert (quoted below). These convictions were sustained on appeal; but those that were reversed as erroneous after the armistice had an equally terrorizing effect during the war, and show how such a statute may be used to stifle personal liberty. One such conviction was for a criticism of the food at a training camp; another for a statement to a Red Cross committee which visited a farmer at his house to solicit funds, that the government which had got us into an unnecessary war could get us out of it, and ought to supply the Red Cross by direct taxation instead of always sending men to ask for money. In addition to those cases, an attempt was made to have the whole war program of the League declared criminal, but without success.

From this background, familiar to many of us in the pages of Sinclair Lewis's *Main Street*, the scene shifts to Washington. Gilbert, a Nonpartisan leader, was indicted and convicted for the following words in a speech:

We are going over to Europe to make the world safe for democracy, but I tell you we had better make America safe for democracy first. You say, What is the matter with our democracy? I tell you what is the matter with it: Have you had anything to say as to who should be President? Have you had anything to say as to who should be Governor of this state? Have you had anything to say as to whether we would go into this war? You know you have not. If this is such a great democracy, for Heaven's sake why should we not vote on conscription of men? We were stampeded into this war by newspaper rot to pull England's chestnuts out of the fire for her. I tell you if they conscripted wealth like they have conscripted men, this war would not last over forty-eight hours.

This language should be compared with the terms of the Minnesota statute as a demonstration of sedition-law construction. The conviction was sustained by the United States Supreme Court, the Chief Justice and Justice Brandeis dissenting. Justice McKenna delivered the opinion of the court, but Justice Holmes concurred only in the result and not in the reasons. The dissenting judges based their objections to the constitutionality of the statute on two distinct grounds. Chief Justice White considered that interference with enlistment is a national matter within the exclusive war power of Congress, when this power is exerted; and Congress in passing the Espionage Act had occupied the whole field, leaving no room for state action. Here Chief Justice White, who was a Confederate drummer boy, supported national supremacy, while Justice Holmes, who fought in the Union army, upheld states' rights. Justice Brandeis took a somewhat similar position as the Chief Justice about the respective spheres of state and nation within our federal system and also held the statute a violation of freedom of speech.

Thus the validity of a state statute punishing opposition to war raises two important problems: (1) Does it encroach on the national war power? (2) Does it encroach on liberty of speech?

(1) May a state constitutionally punish opposition to war, especially if Congress legislates on the subject? It seemed possible that the offenses named in the Minnesota statute were, unless mere breaches of the peace, crimes against the United States, and therefore cognizable only in the federal courts. Of course, the same act may be both a federal and a state crime, for instance, counterfeiting, which injures United States money and is also a kind of cheating. Consequently, it was urged in support of these sedition statutes that a violation of the Espionage Act was also a breach of the duty of citizens of a state to assist the state in fulfilling its task of supporting the nation in war, and that sedition, although directly aimed at the federal government, must indirectly affect the security

of the state government. On the other hand, it has been held that treason against the United States cannot be prosecuted by the states; and interference with the federal war power is closely analogous. The argument that there was also interference with the states is open to question. They have no war powers; their control over the militia in so far as that was affected by any of the utterances prosecuted was taken out of their hands during the war; and although the state officers did render aid in the raising of troops, that did not make it a state function, any more than the assistance of a policeman in the arrest of a deserter from the army renders him amenable to state law. The control was entirely in the hands of the federal government.

Even though the crime could not properly be held to be exclusively within the jurisdiction of the United States, still this seemed like one of those cases where the state government had at the most a power concurrent with that of Congress, which must cease to operate when Congress had determined the proper laws to apply to the subject-matter. For example, a state would have power to grant immunity from civil suits to persons in military service so long as there was no federal law on the subject, but when Congress passed the Soldiers' and Sailors' Civil Relief Act, then a state law giving a less or a greater degree of protection became at once invalid.[8] The same principle might naturally apply to regulations about interference with the raising of armies.

However, Justice McKenna disposed of such arguments by saying that Congress alone can raise armies, but the states as well as the nation are intimately concerned in the outcome of a war. They must have power of coöperation against the enemies of all.

---

[8] Konkel v. State, 168 Wis. 335 (1919); see State v. Darwin, 102 Wash. 402 (1918). A similar statute was enacted on Oct. 17, 1940. Treason against the United States cannot be prosecuted by the states. — People v. Lynch, 11 Johns. (N. Y.) 549 (1814); Ex parte Quarrier, 2 W. Va. 569 (1866). See S. T. Ansell, "Status of State Militia under the Hay Bill," 30 Harvard Law Review 712 (1917). Cf. Halter v. Nebraska, 205 U. S. 34 (1907); Houston v. Moore, 5 Wheat. (U. S.) 1 (1820).

The dissenting opinions in State v. Tachin, 93 N. J. L. 485 (1919), raise the same point about a state war sedition statute, and also attack it as a violation of freedom of speech.

Whether to victory or defeat depends upon their morale, the spirit and determination that animates them — whether it is repellent and adverse or eager and militant; and to maintain it eager and militant against attempts at its debasement in aid of enemies of the United States is a service of patriotism; and from the contention that it encroaches upon or usurps any power of Congress, there is an instinctive and immediate revolt.

Justice Brandeis, on the other hand, maintained that the nation alone can limit discussion about the army and war. Even though the majority denied that this is required by the Constitution, the stubborn fact remained that it is the only sound policy. The undesirability of state war statutes is far more important than their unconstitutionality. The federal government has exclusive control over enlistments and the sole responsibility for the conduct of a war. When it determines that a man should not enter the army without the fullest consideration from every point of view of the consequences of his action, or when it decides to allow a fairly wide range of discussion to the opponents of a war either as a safety valve for discontent or for the sake of obtaining the advantage of their opinions, such national policies will be very seriously blocked if the various states see fit to run amuck and establish inconsistent limitations on discussion. These limitations will be enforced in the heated atmosphere of local fears and dissensions, and opinions will be suppressed which the nation thinks it wise to leave alone. If there is ever a time that the nation ought to act as a unit it is in war.

The injurious effects of state war laws upon a national policy toward such discussion are not a matter of conjecture. We know from Mr. O'Brian that the Department of Justice did not question the patriotism of the great mass of the membership of the Non-Partisan League, whatever the loyalty or disloyalty of its early leaders; and that the Minnesota policy was absolutely at variance with the national policy of treating guilt as personal and not "proscribing any class of individuals as a class." He tells us too that the severe enforcement of the Minnesota statute proved a cause of real embarrassment and danger to the federal government by increasing discontent in that state.[9]

[9] See the quotation from O'Brian in Chapter II, section VII.

If the war had lasted another year with uncertain prospects of victory, the continuance of this Minnesota policy might easily have embittered great masses of farmers and seriously hampered the production of grain and other war essentials.

In 1941, the authority of *Gilbert* v. *Minnesota* on this point of permitting the states to overlap national war legislation is somewhat weakened by the recent decision of the Supreme Court invalidating a Pennsylvania statute for the registration of aliens. Justice Black for the majority points out that Congress has subsequently enacted a complete scheme of regulation in its Alien Registration Act of 1940; and holds that the nature of the Congressional power and the character of the obligations imposed by such a law preclude the enforcement of state laws on the same subject. Although the national powers, which the states are here forbidden to invade, are listed by Justice Black as lying in the field of foreign affairs, whereas the Minnesota statute in the Gilbert case threatened to cripple the war powers of Congress, this does not appear to be a vital distinction. Certainly, such sentences as the following in his recent opinion are applicable *mutatis mutandis* to the Minnesota situation in 1917 and 1918:

We have already adverted to the conditions which make the treatment of aliens, in whatever state they may be located, a matter of national moment. And whether or not registration of aliens is of such a nature that the Constitution permits only of one uniform national system, it cannot be denied that the Congress might validly conclude that such uniformity is desirable. . . . Having the constitutional authority so to do, it has provided a standard for alien registration in a single integrated and all-embracing system in order to obtain the information deemed to be desirable in connection with aliens. When it made this addition to its uniform naturalization and immigration laws, it plainly manifested a purpose to do so in such a way as to protect the personal liberties of law-abiding aliens through one uniform national registration system, and to leave them free from the possibility of inquisitorial practices and police surveillance that might not only affect our international relations but might also generate the very disloyalty which the law has intended guarding against.[10]

---

[10] Hines *v.* Davidowitz, 312 U. S. 52, 73 (1941), Stone, J., dissenting with Hughes, C.J., and McReynolds, J. Justice Stone cited Gilbert *v.* Minnesota as favoring the validity of the Pennsylvania statute. On a different kind of in-

(2) We can now turn from this difficult problem of inter-governmental relations to the free-speech point in *Gilbert* v. *Minnesota*. Even if a state may validly overlap the Espionage Act, did the Minnesota statute or its application in this case go so far in limiting war-time discussion that it violated the United States Constitution?

This involved a very important preliminary question: Had the United States Supreme Court any power to reverse a state conviction because it unduly restricted freedom of speech? This power could not arise from the First Amendment, which says that *Congress* shall pass no law abridging freedom of speech. Indeed, it had long been settled that the whole group of ten amendments, which were added to the Constitution in 1791, restrict only federal action. For example, the guarantees of jury trial do not apply to state courts. Throughout Part I of this book, I discussed state sedition and anti-syndicalism laws with reference only to free-speech clauses in state constitutions. In 1920, when I first wrote those chapters, no thoughtful lawyer would have dared to make a firm assertion that the United States Constitution protects liberty of discussion against the states.[11]

The few attempts previously made to invoke the aid of the Supreme Court against state suppression had met with no success.[12] The attitude of the Court on these occasions might be humorously said to resemble that of a busy lawyer when consulted on a street-corner by a stranger: "This isn't the place to get advice on such a subject and it isn't any business of mine, but, so long as you've asked me, you haven't any case."

Now *Gilbert* v. *Minnesota* marked a slight change from this older attitude, and thus forecast its complete abandonment,

---

consistency between the Gilbert case and later Supreme Court decisions, see Brandeis, J., dissenting in Washington v. Dawson Co., 264 U. S. 219, 235 (1924); E. M. Dodd, "The New Doctrine of the Supremacy of Admiralty over the Common Law," 21 *Columbia Law Review* 647, 665 (1921).

[11] See Warren, "The New 'Liberty' under the Fourteenth Amendment," 39 *Harvard Law Review* 431 (1926).

[12] Patterson v. Colorado, 205 U. S. 454 (1907) (contempt for press criticism of state judge); Mutual Film Corp. v. Industrial Commn. of Ohio, 236 U. S. 230 (1915) (motion-picture censorship), see Chapter XIV, section v; Fox v. Washington, *id.* 273 (1915), see *supra*, Chapter IV, section v.

five years ahead.[13] Justice McKenna for the majority said to Gilbert in effect: "I don't know whether or not I have the power to review your conviction on free-speech grounds. Well, I'll assume for the sake of argument that I do have it. And so, after thinking over your whole case carefully, I'll have to decide against you on the facts anyway."

Still more significant is the opinion of Justice Brandeis. It may be a dissenting opinion, but its importance remains, because this is the first time that any member of the Court in any kind of published opinion squarely maintained that freedom of speech is protected against state action by the United States Constitution. Not, of course, by the original document of 1787, but by the Fourteenth Amendment, ratified in 1868, section 1 of which (with the most relevant words italicized) reads in part:

No State shall make or enforce any law which shall abridge the *privileges or immunities of citizens* of the United States; nor shall any State deprive any *person* of life, *liberty*, or property, without due process of law; nor deny to any person within its jurisdiction the equal protection of the laws.

Justice Brandeis gives very interesting reasons for his position that freedom to discuss national affairs is one of the "privileges or immunities" of citizens of the United States, which no state can abridge:

The right of a citizen of the United States to take part, for his own or the country's benefit, in the making of federal laws and in the conduct of the government, necessarily includes the right to speak or write about them; to endeavor to make his own opinion concerning laws existing or contemplated prevail; and, to this end, to teach the truth as he sees it. Were this not so, "the right of the people to assemble for the purpose of petitioning Congress for a redress of grievances, or for anything else connected with the powers or duties of the national government" would be a right totally without substance. Full and free exercise of this right by the citizen is ordinarily also his duty; for its exercise is more important to the nation than it is to himself. Like the course of the heavenly bodies, harmony in national life is a resultant of the struggle between contending forces. In frank expression of conflicting opinion lies the greatest promise of wisdom in governmental action; and in suppression lies ordinarily the greatest peril.

And then he states the principles which ought to govern when suppression becomes necessary:

There are times when those charged with the responsibility of government, faced with clear and present danger, may conclude that suppression of divergent opinion is imperative; because the emergency does not permit reliance upon the slower conquest of error by truth. And in such emergencies the power to suppress exists. But the responsibility for the maintenance of the army and navy, for the conduct of war and for the preservation of government, both state and federal, from "malice domestic and foreign levy" rests upon Congress. . . . Congress, being charged with responsibility for those functions of government, must determine whether a paramount interest of the nation demands that free discussion in relation to them should be curtailed. . . . No state may trench upon its province.

Justice Brandeis also suggests the possibility that liberty of speech is one type of "liberty" of which under another clause of the Fourteenth Amendment no person can be deprived without due process of law:

I have difficulty in believing that the liberty guaranteed by the Constitution, which has been held to protect against state denial the right of an employer to discriminate against a workman because he is a member of a trade union,[14] the right of a business man to conduct a private employment agency, or to contract outside the state for insurance of his property, although the legislature deems it inimical to the public welfare, does not include liberty to teach, either in the privacy of the home or publicly, the doctrine of pacifism; so long, at least, as Congress has not declared that the public safety demands its suppression. I cannot believe that the liberty guaranteed by the Fourteenth Amendment includes only liberty to acquire and to enjoy property.

In view of the test of freedom of speech declared by the unanimous opinion of the Supreme Court in the Schenck case,[15] it would seem clear that Gilbert was improperly convicted, since the Minnesota statute required no clear and present danger of interference with enlistment as a basis of guilt, nor did his speech create such a danger. Such was the view of Justice Brandeis. Nevertheless, the majority through Justice McKenna

---

[14] The cases so holding have since been overruled by decisions sustaining the Wagner National Labor Relations Act.　　　　　　[15] See *supra,* page 81.

held that even if freedom of speech cannot be wiped out by state action, it can be limited, and that a limitation was proper in this case:

> Gilbert's speech had the purpose they [the words of the Minnesota statute] denounce. The nation was at war with Germany, armies were recruiting, and the speech was the discouragement of that — its purpose was necessarily the discouragement of that. It was not an advocacy of policies or a censure of actions that a citizen had a right to make. The war was flagrant; it had been declared by the power constituted by the Constitution to declare it, and in the manner provided for by the Constitution. It was not declared in aggression, but in defense, in defense of our national honor, in vindication of the "most sacred rights of our nation and our people."
>
> This was known to Gilbert for he was informed in affairs and the operations of the government, and every word that he uttered in denunciation of the war was false, was deliberate misrepresentation of the motives which impelled it, and the objects for which it was prosecuted. He could have had no purpose other than that of which he was charged. It would be a travesty on the constitutional privilege he invokes to assign him its protection.

I would ask the reader to turn back once more to the speech on which Justice McKenna is commenting. Few of us would regard Gilbert as a sound exponent of all the motives which led us into war, but how many American citizens two years after the armistice, knowing all they did about the dissensions at Versailles, about the British appropriation of Mesopotamian oil, about the defaulted interest on the American loans to our Allies, about the Republican National Convention of 1920,[16] would have described that speech in the language of Justice McKenna? The experts on poison gas tell us that after the wind has swept it away from the levels of the battlefield, it still lurks for long in a few holes and crevices. Similar properties are apparently possessed by war emotion.

Nobody then realized that *Gilbert* v. *Minnesota* was the first glimmer of the new day which was to dawn with *Gitlow* v. *New York*.[17] At the time, the Gilbert case was only one more

[16] Beard, *Rise of American Civilization* (1927), p. 672, says about the months preceding the 1920 election: "In fact on all sides the canonical creed of the war, the enthralling idealism with which Wilson had sustained his grand crusade, was now attacked with relentless analysis — much to the amazement of the Socialists in jail for the objections they had so recently put on record in the court of opinion against the official hypothesis."

[17] Decided in 1925 and discussed in Chapter IX.

disappointment of the hopes that the Supreme Court would protect free speech against encroachment. The test of "clear and present danger," announced by a unanimous court in the Schenck case, had since been more honored in the breach than in the observance, but as yet it had not been expressly rejected, and it still stood as a landmark to which we might hold fast in future. Nevertheless, even with this test, the war taught the lesson that defined constitutional limits upon governmental power over discussion, though they have a real value for charging juries and setting aside verdicts, are of comparatively small service in the almost total absence from the national consciousness of any genuine belief in the usefulness of the open expression of unpopular ideas. President Wilson was a lover of Bagehot, but very little was seen during the Wilson administration of Bagehot's conviction of the value of toleration. Even tolerant officials administering the Espionage Act were continually hampered by the insistence of the people that conspicuous pro-Germans, pacifists, and socialists be prosecuted — otherwise they would be lynched. Those who still share Milton's confidence in the power of truth unguarded by sedition laws — "Let her and Falsehood grapple; who ever knew Truth put to the worse, in a free and open encounter?" — can best prepare for the next emergency by spreading the principles of the *Areopagitica* and Mill on *Liberty* through the minds of the American people.

II. NEWSPAPERS AND THE MAILS:
THE MILWAUKEE LEADER CASE

> *When men differ in opinion, both sides ought equally to have the advantage of being heard by the public; and when truth and error have fair play, the former is always an overmatch for the latter. Hence they cheerfully serve all contending writers that pay them well, without regarding on which side they are of the question in dispute.*
> BENJAMIN FRANKLIN, An Apology for Printers (1731).

No DECISION of the United States Supreme Court has gone so far in sustaining governmental powers over the press as its opinion on March 7, 1921, in *United States* ex rel. *Milwaukee*

Social Democratic Publishing Co. v. *Burleson*,[18] which upheld the former Postmaster General's order of October, 1917, deny-ing second-class mailing rates to Victor Berger's *Milwaukee Leader*. Although the case arose under the Espionage Act, its most important effect will probably be in extending the power of the Postmaster General to penalize discussion in time of peace.

The precise point decided may best be understood from a brief statement of the post-office statutes. Congress has speci-fied certain matter as non-mailable — for example, obscene literature, lottery prospectuses, and prize-fight films. Sending such matter is a crime, and the Postmaster General may exclude the offensive document from the mails by an administrative order issued without a jury trial and virtually uncontrolled by the courts. His decision that a letter or circular or issue of a magazine falls within a class forbidden by Congress will not be judicially reversed unless it is "clearly wrong." This has long been settled law. The Espionage Act of 1917 [19] merely added a new kind of non-mailable matter, unlawful opposition to war.

This is clearly previous restraint and might seem forbidden by the Blackstonian definition of freedom of speech,[20] which, however, is held not to apply to the postal power. This power, like the war power, ought to be subject to the requirements of free speech and due process of law, and there are statements by the Supreme Court that it is not unlimited.[21] Although the post-office may not be strictly a common carrier, it is in the nature of a public service company. The transportation of letters has been performed by private persons in the past, and

[18] 255 U. S. 407 (1921), affg. 258 Fed. 282 (D. C. App., 1919); discussed by H. M. Bates in 19 *Michigan Law Review* 728. For Postmaster General Bur-leson's censorship of the mails during the active period of war, see Chapter II, section VI. For the unsuccessful criminal prosecution of Berger and his ex-clusion from Congress, see Chapter VI, section II. See also Cohn, "The Censor-ship of Radical Materials by the Post Office," 17 *St. Louis Law Journal* 95 (1932); Deutsch, "Freedom of the Press and the Mails," 36 *Michigan Law Review* 703 (1938); 38 *Columbia Law Review* 474 (1938). For the English reactions to less drastic practices overseas, see 73 *Solicitors' Journal* 180 (1929); 74 *id.* 775 (1930).

[19] This statute is summarized *supra*, pp. 39, 98, note 102.

[20] See *supra*, pages 9 ff.

[21] *Ex parte* Jackson, 96 U. S. 727 (1927); Public Clearing House *v.* Coyne, 194 U. S. 497, 507 (1904).

if it were not unlawful, they would occasionally get some of this business now because they might offer greater speed in near-by deliveries. The carriage of parcels is still shared by private express companies. Now, it is certainly arguable that when the government furnishes services to its citizens for pay it should be judged by the ordinary standards applicable to other public utilities.[22] The business man who wishes to communicate with prospective buyers and sources of supply by letters is not a recipient of public bounty like an old-age pensioner or the occupant of free federal lands. Although he does make use of governmental machinery, he pays for what he gets; and in substance the transaction is like buying municipal water or riding on a national railway. If the United States should take over all the railroads, they ought not to make unreasonable discrimination among passengers and shippers any more than a private railroad corporation, and a somewhat similar limitation should apply to the postal power. The opportunity to obtain essential services is a condition of earning a livelihood and sometimes of life itself. If a city cuts off a man's water, he cannot dig a well; if he is kept off the trains, he cannot walk and may not be able to use a bus or a private automobile; and in the same way, the factory or newspaper which is excluded from the mails is denied any other practicable means of systematic intercourse. Even though it can deliver by express, it must use letters to solicit orders, obtain information, collect accounts, and so forth.[23] So the Postmaster's adverse decision virtually ruins its business.

Of course, this does not mean that there should be no statutory limits on the use of the mails. Nobody can quarrel with the legislation banning filthy publications and lottery tickets. Such Congressional restrictions as these may be considered as reasonable regulations in view of the nature of the service, like railroad rules excluding drunks and dynamite from trains. However, it is pushing matters much farther to say that the

[22] Leon Duguit, *Law in the Modern State*, translated by F. and H. J. Laski, New York, 1919. See H. J. Laski in 31 *Harvard Law Review* 186; and his *Authority in the Modern State*, p. 378.

[23] See the dissenting opinion of Justice Holmes (Justice Brandeis concurring) in Leach *v.* Carlile, 258 U. S. 138 (1922), on the harmfulness of denying practically any judicial review of the Postmaster General's finding that a business has used the mails fraudulently.

government is free to decide what it will transport just as much as a private automobile-owner can decide to what friends he will offer a ride and whether he will carry their suitcases as well; [24] or to argue that Congress can by loosely worded statutes empower the Postmaster General to keep out whatever discussion of public affairs he finds objectionable. A private power company must not refuse to sell electricity to an ardent supporter of the Tennessee Valley Authority. It is equally unfair for the government to deny its mail facilities to its leading critics, even in time of war, when criticism may perhaps improve the methods of fighting or accelerate a much-needed peace.

The advocates of unlimited control of the mails will do well to consider how such an argument will work out if the government should take over all broadcasting stations. Suppose that the administration thus denies the microphone to speakers of the opposite political party.

All questions of constitutionality aside, Congress ought to consider the advisability of continuing to place such a destructive power in the Postmaster General instead of in an impartial tribunal which would not be both judge and prosecuting attorney. Questions of the weight and physical contents of letters are administrative, like tariff valuations, where finality within the Department is desirable. The collection of the public revenues would become impossible if every dispute of fact over the value of an imported scarf or the income of a lawyer could be carried by the disgruntled taxpayer into the courts. But such frequent determinations of measurable facts do not furnish an analogy for post-office exclusion orders in borderline cases of possible indecency [25] or of alleged violations of the broad terms of the Espionage Act, without any previous adjudication of wrongfulness by a judge and jury. These controversies about objectionable language in the mails are comparatively

[24] A similar argument on behalf of arbitrary exclusions of speakers from city parks was rejected in the Hague case, discussed in Chapter XI, section VIII.
[25] 18 U. S. C. A. § 334. See the reversal of the post-office ruling in United States v. Dennett, 39 F. (2d) 564 (C. C. A. 2d, 1930), Judge A. N. Hand (sex instruction), discussed in Grant & Angoff, 10 *Boston University Law Review* at 502 (1930). Importation and interstate transportation by express are all made serious crimes. — 18 *id.* § 396; 19 *id.* § 1305. See Chapter IV, note 72, on exclusions of books by customs inspectors.

few, and similar in nature to questions which courts are accustomed to settle, besides being far-reaching in their consequences to the community as well as to the prohibited periodical. The publications totally excluded by Mr. Burleson from the mails during the war, as narrated in the second chapter, show the possibilities of danger when the attainment and dissemination of truth are regulated by the arbitrary will of one man.

The important feature of the *Milwaukee Leader* case is that the statutes made only those particular issues of the newspaper non-mailable which actually were found to violate law, but Mr. Burleson claimed the right to penalize subsequent issues of the same newspaper however innocent in character. For this purpose he made use of an entirely distinct post-office statute. The Mail Classification Act of 1879 provides four classes of post-office rates for different kinds of mail.[26] Second-class rates are granted to periodicals, which "must regularly be issued at stated intervals" and published "for the dissemination of information of a public character." Since these rates are from eight to fifteen times lower than the third-class rate for other printed matter, it is clear that the refusal of a second-class permit to a newspaper denies it any profitable use of the mails and places it at the mercy of competitors who enjoy the lower rates. The Postmaster General may withhold or revoke the permit if he finds that the publication does not fulfill the requirements of the Classification Act; for instance, that a newspaper has missed several issues, or that successive numbers of Frank Meriwether stories do not constitute a periodical.

These powers are wide but unquestioned. Mr. Burleson went much further. Although the Classification Act nowhere said that the existence of non-mailable matter in past issues forfeits second-class rates for future issues, he held that because the *Milwaukee Leader* had frequently violated the Espionage Act, its second-class permit should henceforth be revoked. His right to do this is sustained by a majority of the Supreme Court speaking through Justice Clarke, Justices Brandeis and Holmes dissenting.

The Court's finding that the *Leader* had been violating the Espionage Act before its suppression emphasizes the bad tendency of what was said, with no questioning as to its clear and

[26] Now 39 U. S. C. A. § 226.

present danger. "Articles denounced the draft law as unconstitutional, arbitrary, and oppressive, *with the implied counsel* [italics mine] that it should not be respected or obeyed." Soldiers in France were represented as becoming insane, and conveyed from the front in long trains of closed cars. (Dr. Thomas W. Salmon in the *American Legion Weekly* for January 28, 1921, reported over 7000 insane veterans in the United States.) "The Food Control law was denounced as 'Kaisering America' " — the same law denounced as unconstitutional by Chief Justice White only a week before the *Milwaukee Leader* decision.[27] As usual, the bad intention of the writers, although an essential element of the crime, was inferred from the bad tendency. "These publications," says Justice Clarke, "were not designed to secure amendment or repeal of the laws denounced in them as arbitrary and oppressive, but to create hostility to, and to encourage violation of, them."

Even if these particular issues of the *Leader* were properly held to violate the Espionage Act, this does not affect the main question — if the Postmaster General decides that a newspaper has published non-mailable matter in past issues, may he revoke its second-class permit for all future issues? Nothing in the statutes expressly gives him this drastic power. In the *Masses* case, Mr. Burleson contended that when one issue was barred from the mails, the magazine ceased to be a "regularly issued" periodical under the Classification Act.[28] This was obviously unsound, for the statutory requirement refers, not to the propriety of the reading matter, but to its intended and actual appearance at stated intervals. The *Masses* was issued even when it could not be mailed. Justice Clarke adopts different reasoning, that the second-class rates are granted on the assumption that the periodical will continue to conform to law, both to the requirements of the Classification Act and to prohibitions against printing non-mailable articles. A newspaper which has published such objectionable matter in several issues may reasonably be expected to continue violating the law. It would not be possible, he says, for the government to maintain a reader in every newspaper office in the country to approve every issue in advance. Consequently, an offending newspaper

[27] In United States *v.* Cohen Grocery Co., 255 U. S. 81 (1921).
[28] See *supra*, page 98.

must have its permit revoked until it submits satisfactory evidence of its repentance.[29] "Government is a practical institution, adapted to the practical conduct of public affairs."

There is force in this reasoning, and indeed most strong exercises of executive power are justified from the official point of view by the need of thorough enforcement of law. On the other hand our Constitution, with its Bill of Rights, recognizes the necessity for some sacrifice of administrative efficiency in order to prevent wrongs to individuals — hence it prohibits unreasonable searches and seizures, and guarantees trial by jury — and in order to maintain other purposes of society such as the discovery and dissemination of truth on public questions. Moreover, Justice Brandeis shows that it is practicable to exclude illegal matter without a revocation of second-class rates, for there is more opportunity to inspect this class of mail than any other. It is the only kind which has to be submitted to the local postmaster for examination before it is mailed. And however desirable the Postmaster General may consider the powers claimed in this case, the dissenting judges hold that Congress had not seen fit to grant them.

The correctness of this decision is far less important than its consequences. It is nowise limited to war cases, and enables the Postmaster General to suppress any newspaper with a few articles which are unmailable on any ground. In December, 1919, more than a year after the Armistice, Mr. Burleson refused to restore to the *New York Call* second-class mailing privileges which had been revoked in November, 1917, for what he found to be violation of the Espionage Act, though there had been no criminal conviction and, so far as I know, not even a prosecution. His action was held not to be reviewable by a court.[30] His order was partly based on another statutory provision, under which he found that the *Call*, an

[29] Somewhat similar reasoning was recently applied to an entirely different subject-matter in Milk Wagon Drivers Union *v.* Meadowmoor Dairies, 312 U. S. 287 (1941). Peaceful picketing in the future, though otherwise lawful, was held properly enjoined in view of several explosions and assaults in which the union had previously engaged. Justice Frankfurter said: "In such a setting it could justifiably be concluded that the momentum of fear generated by past violence would survive even though future picketing might be wholly peaceful." Justices Black, Reed, and Douglas dissented. Compare Warner *v.* Lilly, 265 U. S. 526 (1924); and Chafee, *The Inquiring Mind*, pp. 193–197.

[30] Burleson *v.* United States, 274 Fed. 749 (1921).

ordinary Socialist newspaper, tended "to incite arson, murder, or assassination." [31] And similarly without any jury, without any court, for it is rarely possible to say the Postmaster General is clearly wrong, he can punish by extinction a periodical which ventures to discuss problems of sex and family life which he considers obscene though many others think them valuable.

The wide powers exercised by the government in war prosecutions have been defended on the ground that the control over speech was in the hands of a jury, which was all that the founders meant by freedom of speech. The *Milwaukee Leader* decision gives no such chance for the expression of public opinion on the value of the periodical. Moreover, prosecutions come after the opinions and facts presented have reached the public, whereas a censorship may prevent the public from learning them at all. And the Postmaster General's powers are vague. They are like the law in Restoration France which allowed the government to suppress any journal "if the spirit resulting from a succession of articles would be of a nature to cause injury to the public peace and the stability of constitutional institutions." Such a law is utterly foreign to the tradition of English-speaking freedom.

Finally, if the Postmaster General is to possess these vast powers over opinion, his selection becomes a matter of great importance. Such powers can only be properly exercised by a man of judicial temper and training, confident of the value of freedom of thought. Such qualities can hardly be said to have distinguished Mr. Burleson. Will they be considered in the appointments of his successors? [32]

[31] See Chapter IV, note 64; 18 U. S. C. A. § 334, last sentence.

[32] Mr. Burleson's immediate successor, Mr. Hays, restored both the *Leader* and the *Call* to the second-class mail privilege. Berger's conviction under the Espionage Act was reversed by the Supreme Court nine months after the *Leader* decision, and all charges against him were dropped. See Chapter VI, section II.

CHAPTER 8

THE RAND SCHOOL CASE

Good-bye to the little red school-house.

I MAGINE a private educational institution in New York
City, ostensibly giving technical instruction in chemistry,
but actually teaching assassination. Suppose theoretical courses
in The Morality of Tyrannicide, and The History of Political
Killing from Jael and Sisera to Serajevo. Suppose practical
courses in Clockwork and Time Fuses, or The Comparative
Merits of Dynamite and TNT. Visualize the graduates of this
school going forth fanatical and expert bomb-makers, as eager
for a victim as a law-school graduate for his first client. Its
managers and teachers could be prosecuted for past instruction
under the Criminal Anarchy Act,[1] but must the government
wait until the pernicious doctrines have been absorbed by
immature minds? Should it not have power as soon as the aims
of the school are ascertained, before a single lecture is delivered,
to padlock the doors of this nursery of assassins?

It is only by conjuring up some such lurid picture that one
can understand the attitude of the supporters of the New
York 1921 legislation for the suppression of sedition in schools.
The two statutes were based on the recommendations of the
Lusk Committee for investigating seditious activities, which
had previously promoted the exclusion of the Socialists from
the New York Assembly and the prosecution of Gitlow and
his associates.[2] One law was aimed at those wolves in sheep's
clothing, revolutionary teachers in the public schools, and directed the expulsion of any teacher who had advocated "a
form of government other than the government of the United
States or of this state." [3] This statute was perhaps not open
to attack in the courts, but a vigorous contest over its enforcement was waged within the public school system.

---

[1] See Chapter IV, section v, *supra*.
[2] See Chapter VI, section III, and Chapter IX.
[3] N. Y. Laws, 1921, c. 666; repealed by Laws, 1923, c. 798.

The validity of the other statute, directed at private schools, was the issue in the Rand School case. Although the actual decision had little effect, because of the subsequent repeal of the legislation, it is worth while for us to consider the wisdom of the statute and the validity of the court's reasoning. History repeats itself. New legislative committees will investigate teaching in private institutions in New York and other states. They will be disturbed by radical or otherwise heterodox teaching. They will be tempted to follow in the footsteps of the Lusk Committee and propose some law to control, weed out, and padlock the private schools and colleges which they find distasteful. When such an occasion arises, it may be helpful for these committees and thoughtful members of the public to study the merits and operation of the Lusk Law for the licensing and supervision of private education in New York.

The provisions of this act [4] were simple. First, private education was brought within reach of the state broom. Nobody might conduct "any school, institution, class or course of instruction in any subject whatever" (construed to include only academic subjects and not classes in swimming or sewing) without a license from the regents of the state education board (legally entitled the University of the State of New York). The only exceptions were public schools, institutions — such as ordinary colleges — incorporated by the regents and thus already under their supervision, schools maintained by a religious denomination recognized as such in 1921 — like the Roman Catholic parochial schools — and classes teaching the rituals of fraternal orders. The application for a license must be made according to rules prescribed by the regents, and must state "the nature and extent and purpose of the instruction to be given."

Secondly, the state broom swept clean. "No license shall be granted . . . by the regents . . . where it shall appear that the instruction proposed to be given includes the teaching of the doctrine that organized governments shall be overthrown by force, violence or unlawful means." As this was judicially interpreted, the regents could refuse a license without giving the school a hearing. Furthermore, a license already granted must be revoked by the regents if the prohibited doctrines were

[4] N. Y. Laws, 1921, c. 667; repealed by Laws, 1923, c. 799.

taught. A licensed school or class was subject to visits by the regents or their employees. Observe that there was no provision for judicial review of the school's right to get or retain its license. Unless the action of the regents were unconstitutional or plainly outrageous, it had the same finality as the decision of a liquor board denying a license to a saloon.

What happened to a school, no matter how long established, which went on teaching without a license? Every teacher and officer was liable to $100 fine and sixty days in prison. And what was much more effective, the Attorney General might stop the unlicensed teaching at once by a court injunction.

Those who would unreservedly condemn such a statute should first ask themselves this question: "Do I want young people to be deliberately and systematically taught that the government of the United States ought to be forcibly overthrown?" Most sober-minded persons will answer by an emphatic "No." The real difference of opinion among such persons arises because some of them will prolong their reply as follows: "No; but though violent revolutionary instruction is an evil, still the danger of it is far less menacing to our society than the danger created by the methods enacted in this statute for ferreting out such instruction." For that reason the Lusk Laws were opposed by such conservative bodies as the Association of the Bar of the City of New York and vetoed by Governor Alfred E. Smith the year before they were again enacted and approved by his Republican successor, Governor Nathan Miller. The growing danger exemplified by these laws is monopoly of power in the hands of any single organization, whether a church, or a federation of powerful businesses, or the state. Through a monopoly of education the officials of the state can in time prevent the young from hearing any doctrine which they dislike. Whatever threatens the overthrow of these officials may readily be decided by them to be "advocacy of the overthrow of the government of the state by force and violence." In short, "the government" becomes identified with *their* government.

Governor Smith's veto message of May 18, 1920, related to substantially the same law, except that the 1920 bill allowed a license to be refused when the regents thought the proposed instruction "detrimental to the public interest," while the 1921 law framed the test in the narrower but none too specific words of the Criminal Anarchy Act. In this message Smith said:

This mere statement of the provisions of this bill [earlier in the message] is sufficient to demonstrate that in details it is wholly impossible of just enforcement. I prefer, however, to rest my disapproval of it not solely nor chiefly on that ground, but on the broader ground that in fundamental principle the bill is vicious. Its avowed purpose is to safeguard the institutions and traditions of the country. In effect, it strikes at the very foundation of one of the most cardinal institutions of our nation — the fundamental right of the people to enjoy full liberty in the domain of idea and speech. To this fundamental right there is and can be under our system of government but one limitation, namely, that the law of the land shall not be transgressed, and there is abundant statute law prohibiting the abuse of free speech. It is unthinkable that in a representative democracy there should be delegated to any body of men the absolute power to prohibit the teaching of any subject of which it may disapprove.

This bill seeks to bring within the power of prohibition of the Board of Regents every subject, political, ethical, religious, or scientific. Under its provisions they might decree that it was inimical to the public interest to give instruction on the theory of the single tax, on minimum wage, on child-labor laws and on public regulation of industry. It would then become a crime to instruct in any subject which, in the judgment of this Board, was inimical to the public interest. The free play of public opinion, resting upon freedom of instruction and discussion within the limits of the law, would be destroyed and we should have the whole sphere of education reduced to a formula prescribed by governmental agency.

The clash of conflicting opinions, from which progress arises more than from any other source, would be abolished by law, tolerance and intellectual freedom destroyed, and an intellectual autocracy imposed upon the people. . . . The proponents of these bills urge that they are essential to the protection of the community against radical opinion. I might rest upon the saying of Benjamin Franklin that "they that can give up essential liberty to obtain a little temporary safety deserve neither liberty nor safety." But I go further — the safety of this government and its institutions rests upon the reasoned and devoted loyalty of its people. It does not need for its defense a system of intellectual tyranny which, in the endeavor to choke error by force, must of necessity crush truth as well. The profound sanity of the American people has been demonstrated in many a crisis, and I, for one, do not believe that governmental dictation of what may and may not be taught is necessary to achieve a continuance of the patriotism of our citizenship and its loyal support of the government and its institutions.[5]

We have before us, therefore, not a contest in which the state or radicalism — according to the point of view — has all the argument on its side, but a problem of balancing two evils, violent ideas against a censorship. The New York Legislature of 1921 and Governor Miller pronounced censorship the smaller evil of the two, but the big issue still remains open: whether the people of New York (or any other state confronted in future with the same problem) did not definitely prefer to run the risk of dangerous teaching when they adopted the free-speech clause in their constitution.

The Rand School for Social Science was a Socialist and labor college maintained by the American Socialist Society at 7 East Fifteenth Street, near Fifth Avenue. It was established in 1906 and had over 5000 registered students. Its work was announced by its director as falling into two parts, opportunities for the general public to study Socialism, and systematic training to render Socialists more efficient workers for the Socialist party, trade unions, and coöperative societies. It also maintained a large public library and reading room, and a bookstore, doing a large mail-order business chiefly in material on social and labor questions. None of its activities had previously been held illegal, although its owner, the American Socialist Society, was convicted under the Espionage Act for publishing Nearing's *The Great Madness*, a matter unconnected with the school except that Nearing was a principal member of the teaching staff.[6]

A dozen years later, when the Rand School was about to close for lack of funds, an appeal to the public for help was sent out by John Dewey, the future mayor LaGuardia, Helen Keller, Charles A. Beard, Stuart Chase, Hendrik Willem Van Loon, Elmer Davis, and many other distinguished persons. This stated in the words of John Dewey: "It would be a calam-

---

[5] *Progressive Democracy: Addresses and State Papers of Alfred E. Smith* (Harcourt, Brace & Co., 1928), pp. 277 ff. See *supra*, Chapter VI, at note 43.

[6] United States *v.* American Socialist Society, 252 Fed. 223, 260 Fed. 885; Bulletins of the Department of Justice on the Interpretation of War Statutes, Nos. 129, 192, 198.

ity to intelligent untrammeled thought and speech everywhere.
. . . All sincere friends of sound adult education MUST JOIN
IN KEEPING THE RAND SCHOOL DOORS OPEN."

The litigation now discussed was only one stage in a running
fight between the School and the Lusk Committee. The School
was one of the objects of the series of spectacular raids conducted by the Committee in 1919. The Committee was alarmed
by the number of radicals on the teaching staff of the School,
the revolutionary character of some of the books and pamphlets
on sale in its store, and the incendiary nature of letters seized
from its files without much attempt to learn whether they were
addressed to the School by extremists or actually written by its
officers on School business. Thereupon, the Committee issued
startling reports to the press about this hive of revolutionists,
and induced the Attorney General to start proceedings to cancel
the School's charter. However, the School had broken no law
on the statute-book of 1919, and when Samuel Untermyer came
forward as its counsel the suit was promptly dropped. Some
new legislation was necessary to reach the institution, and the
licensing statute recommended by the Lusk Committee was
eventually enacted in 1921. This would abolish the Rand
School if actually teaching what the Committee charged, and
in any event make possible its supervision by the state. The
School refused to apply for a license, and the Attorney General,
assisted by the principal lawyer of the Committee, asked for an
injunction to stop its teaching.

The School suffered defeat in the first phases of the litigation,
for the injunction was granted and then affirmed by the Appellate Division, which is the next to the highest New York
court.[7] The question whether the Rand School was entitled
to a license was not raised. The case decided only that the
School must apply for a license, since the statute was constitutional. What the court did in this abortive litigation will aid
us to decide about the desirability of a similar future statute
for regulating or padlocking schools.

All private teaching of academic subjects was brought by
this Lusk Law under state supervision and visitation. Such
an extensive regulation of one of the oldest and most important

[7] People v. American Socialist Society, 202 N. Y. App. Div. 640 (1922).
Greenbaum, J., dissented.

human activities is a deprivation of liberty and property "without due process of law," in violation of the Fourteenth Amendment and the corresponding New York provision, unless the regulation may reasonably be interpreted to serve some public purpose so as to fall within the legitimate police power of the state.

In the past much social legislation restricting private enterprise had been held unconstitutional under these "due process" clauses, to the indignation of Socialists, labor leaders, and even such a staunch individualist as Theodore Roosevelt. The classrooms of the Rand School must have frequently echoed to denunciations of *Ives* v. *Railway Co.*, invalidating the first New York Workmen's Compensation Act, *Re* Jacobs, denying the state power to forbid the manufacture of cigars in crowded tenements, and *Lochner* v. *New York*, upsetting the ten-hour day in bakeshops.[8] It was amusing, therefore, to find the Rand School, a Socialist institution, striving on the authority of these very cases to *limit* governmental control over a private activity. After the School's foot was pinched by state regulation, its teachers may have understood better the irritation which other kinds of business feel under government regulation. And the emphasis placed by the School in this litigation upon the value of private initiative in education might well cause some qualms about "the coming epoch" when education and everything else are to be operated solely by a bureaucratic state.

By 1922 courts were taking a broader view of the police power than did the old cases just described; the due process clause no longer invalidates legislation promoting public safety. So the New York judges in the Rand School case considered that public safety is menaced by revolutionary schools as well as by exposed buzz-saws and dirty barber shops. They are grounds for prosecution, and so is advocacy of bloody rebellion under the Criminal Anarchy Act. But the state does not rest content with prosecution in the case of dirty barber shops. It inspects and closes them unless they conform to administrative regulations. The Lusk Law, according to these judges, had adopted the same policy in the case of private schools — an ounce of prevention is worth a pound of cure. The legislature

[8] These cases are reported in 201 N. Y. 271 (1911); 98 N. Y. 98 (1885); 198 U. S. 45 (1905).

and the court saw no distinction between dirty barber shops and revolutionary schools.

Perhaps there is no distinction, so long as we look only at the police power. However, that power is limited by another clause of the constitution of New York and other states, which Governor Smith had strongly stressed. Every citizen is free to "publish his sentiments on all subjects, being responsible for the abuse of that right; and no law shall be passed to restrain or abridge the liberty of speech."

Here is a difference between schools and barber shops, which may well take schools outside the legitimate field of state licensing. A school is engaged in the production of ideas and of intelligence, which are bound to suffer from bureaucratic supervision. An official may be trusted to recognize dirt or discriminate between dangerous and harmless machinery; he cannot be trusted to discriminate between dangerous and harmless ideas. Human nature has too strong a tendency to regard what one dislikes or disagrees with as a menace to the social order.

It may be objected that advocacy of the overthrow of organized government by violence is so plain that anybody can spot it at sight. The facts prove just the contrary, as this book has repeatedly shown.[9] Judge George W. Anderson ruled that the Communist Party did not profess that doctrine, but the Circuit Court of Appeals held that it did. Secretary of Labor Wilson likewise ruled that it did, but he ruled that the Communist Labor Party did not. Attorney General Palmer ruled that both parties were promulgating it, and his secret service agents helped several state prosecutors to land the two types of Communists in prison for long terms. When such sharp differences of opinion are exhibited by those in high authority about programs of social reconstruction, the task of determining whether a course on modern radical movements involves a bare intellectual interest in these programs, or approval, or exhortation to the students to put the principles studied into practice, is too delicate for any subordinate state official to undertake.

However, the New York judges did not discuss the free-

---

[9] See *supra*, Chapter IV, section VIII (*a*); Chapter V, sections III and V (*a*); and other passages. See also Swinburne Hale, "The Force and Violence Joker," *New Republic*, Jan. 21, 1920.

speech clause at all. The following passage indicates that they
thought the question was settled when it was previously decided that advocacy of violent revolution could be punished
under the Criminal Anarchy Act of 1902:

> The legislature has as much right to enact a salutary statute to
> prevent the promulgation of doctrines inimical to our form of govern-
> ment, the putting into effect of which would lead to the conviction
> of those who had adopted said doctrines under existing penal law,
> as to punish those who were guilty of violating such penal laws. A
> state has as much right to guard against the commission of an offense
> against its laws as to inflict punishment upon the offender after it
> shall have been committed.

This reasoning would equally justify a statute establishing a
censor for newspapers, with power to exclude any passages
which in his opinion would, if published, be held criminal by
a hypothetical jury. It gives no consideration to the fundamental difference between punishment by a jury and censorship
by an official.

Even Blackstone, the upholder of the powers that be, declared: "The liberty of the press . . . consists in laying no
previous restraints upon publication." And his view was whole-
heartedly adopted by an important New York decision (*Brand-
reth* v. *Lance*),[10] not cited in the Rand School case, which
declares that such a power of preventive justice "cannot safely
be entrusted to any tribunal consistently with the principles of
a free government." A jury is none too well fitted to pass on
the injurious nature of opinions, but at least it consists of twelve
men who represent the general views and the common sense of
the community and often appreciate the motives of the speaker
or writer whose punishment is sought. A censor, on the contrary, is a single individual with a professionalized and partisan
point of view. His interest lies in perpetuating the power of the
group which employs him, and any bitter criticism of the group
smacks to him of incitement to bloody revolution.

[10] 8 Paige 24 (1839). The doctrine of this case, that the injunction of defamatory writing violates liberty of speech, appears still to be law in New York.
Marlin Fire Arms Co. *v.* Shields, 171 N. Y. 384 (1902). The courts have
been insistent on the application of the free-speech guarantee to the one class
of cases where little or no social interest in the spread of truth is infringed.
See R. Pound's comment in 29 *Harvard Law Review* 640, 648.

When we look at a statute empowering officials to license, regulate, and close private schools in the light of decisions on the constitutionality of other types of censorship under the free-speech clauses, what do we find? On the one hand, a censorship of books, periodicals, etc., is almost always invalid, except under circumstances of extreme danger, as when a newspaper proposes to publish troop movements. In 1931 the United States Supreme Court in *Near* v. *Minnesota* [11] upset an injunction granted against a newspaper by a court after a hearing on the facts. This invalid censorship by a judge was much less arbitrary than the official censorship of schools without any hearing; and the objectionable nature of the Minneapolis scandal-sheet was much more obvious than the supposed dangerous qualities of the Rand School. On the other hand, a censorship of motion pictures was upheld by the Supreme Court in 1915.[12] Although the reasoning now seems questionable, we can agree that a photoplay differs in significant ways from a book or newspaper. The effect is more vivid and the possibilities of immorality are wider. Furthermore, a reader has considerable choice in selecting a book or a newspaper. He knows its tone in advance, and so cannot fairly claim governmental protection from its unwelcome opinions or statements of fact; whereas he goes to the motion picture theater for an evening's entertainment without knowing much about what is ahead of him, and feels aggrieved when the screen is suddenly occupied by a sequence which offends his moral or patriotic sensibilities. Finally, the ideas in books and newspapers are afterwards easily refuted or qualified by opponents in print and talk, while it is not easy to answer one movie by another movie. In other words, printed matter enters readily into the great process of continuous open discussion, which it is the purpose of free-speech clauses to promote and protect, in the belief that only through such a vigorous contest of views can truth and wise policies be satisfactorily discovered and spread abroad.

Where should we classify schools? With newspapers or with motion pictures? When the students are young children, it is arguable that the systematic character of the utterances, the impressionable nature of the listeners, their docility, their in-

[11] 283 U. S. 697, discussed *infra* Chapter XI, section III.
[12] See *infra*, Chapter XIV, section V.

ability to judge for themselves, create a peculiar situation analogous to motion pictures, though I can see strong reasons to the contrary. Be that as it may, when we come to mature students and especially adults, by whom institutions like the Rand School are largely attended, then I venture the following opinion, in the absence of any decision from the United States Supreme Court or a state court of last resort: Schools for advanced students are closely akin to newspapers and books, and very remote from motion pictures. Those who go to such schools do so with their eyes open. The instructor is really one of the students, and he is separated from the others merely by a desk. Very little he says is unquestioningly accepted. Here, if anywhere on earth, we get that steady free flow of discussion which was the ideal of Milton and Madison. The very readiness of radicals to differ among themselves proves this. Insofar as the general trend of a "labor school" is thought objectionable, the usual media for utterances are available for the other side to reach the students. It seems no more difficult to rebut or qualify the views imbibed by voters from attending an adult educational institution than it is to rebut or qualify the views they imbibe from reading *The Daily Worker*. The Constitution as construed in *Near* v. *Minnesota* forbids an administrative or even a judicial censorship of *The Daily Worker*. Does it not equally forbid an administrative censorship of a radical school for citizens, at least if they are over eighteen? A newspaper cannot be driven out of existence by officials or a court injunction, even after a hearing. Can a school be constitutionally driven out of existence by officials, who decline to listen to the school's lawyers and witnesses, and act merely on their own whimsical interpretation of its catalogue, the presence of some extremist books found in any well-stocked college library, and the reports of an emotional legislative investigating committee? An authoritative judicial answer to this question will be eagerly awaited, and meanwhile those who are terrified about these labor schools would do well to read and reread the veto message of Governor Smith.

The Rand School case was not ended by this decision of the Appellate Division in June, 1922. While the appeal was pending, Governor Miller, who signed the Lusk bills, was defeated in November, 1922, by Governor Alfred E. Smith, who had vetoed them. Smith's return to office was followed by the repeal of the Lusk legislation,[13] and the proceedings against the Rand School automatically lapsed. The cause of liberal education was won, not in the courts but at the polls.

In affixing his signature to the two acts removing the restrictions on public and private schools, Governor Smith said of the Lusk Laws:

They are repugnant to the fundamentals of American democracy. Under the laws repealed, teachers, in order to exercise their honorable calling, were in effect compelled to hold opinions as to governmental matters deemed by a State officer consistent with loyalty; and, further, no private school could be maintained in this State unless its teachings were similarly satisfactory to certain officials of the State. Freedom of opinion and freedom of speech were by these laws unduly shackled, and an unjust discrimination was made against the members of a great profession.

In signing these bills, I firmly believe that I am vindicating the principle that, within the limits of the penal law, every citizen may speak and teach what he believes.[14]

[13] See notes 3 and 4 *supra.*
[14] *Progressive Democracy*, p. 282.

CHAPTER 9

VICTORY OUT OF DEFEAT:
GITLOW *v.* NEW YORK

> *And not by eastern windows only,*
> *When daylight comes, comes in the light;*
> *In front the sun climbs slow, how slowly!*
> *But westward, look, the land is bright!*
> ARTHUR HUGH CLOUGH,
> "Say not the struggle naught availeth."

ATTORNEY GENERAL PALMER, laying a large quantity of revolutionary material before a committee of Congressmen, warned them, "It is not good reading late at night when you are at home in your own house. It gives you the creeps a little." No one need fear similar terrors from the Left Wing Manifesto, for publishing which Benjamin Gitlow's conviction was sustained by the Supreme Court of the United States in 1925.[1] After twenty pages of somniferous type telling the recent history of the world, it reaches its first incendiary passage: "Strikes are developing which verge on revolutionary action, and in which the suggestion of proletarian dictatorship is apparent, the strike-workers trying to usurp functions of municipal government as in Seattle and Winnipeg. The mass struggle of the proletariat is coming into being." And then fourteen pages more about destroying the bourgeois parliamentary state, with repeated exhortations to "mass strikes," "mass action," "expropriation of the bourgeoisie," and establishing "the dictatorship of the proletariat," until at last it winds up

---

[1] 268 U. S. 652 (1925). The state decisions upholding conviction are: People *v.* Gitlow, 111 N. Y. Misc. 641 (1920); 195 N. Y. App. Div. 773 (1921); 234 N. Y. 132, 539 (1922). Accounts of the original trial are found in the daily press. The decision of City Magistrate McAdoo holding Gitlow and his associates for the grand jury is reprinted in *Sedition, Hearing before the Committee on the Judiciary, House of Representatives* (Washington, 1920), p. 155. See also on the trial Swinburne Hale, "Criminal Anarchy," 21 *New Republic* 270, Jan. 28, 1920; A. Giovanitti, "Commercialism on Trial," *Liberator*, March, 1920.

by prophesying "a revolutionary struggle against Capitalism" that may last for tens of years before "the final act of conquest of power."[2]

Any agitator who read these thirty-four pages to a mob would not stir them to violence, except possibly against himself. This Manifesto would disperse them faster than the Riot Act. It is best described by recalling the Mouse in *Alice in Wonderland* reading about the Norman Conquest to dry off the Dodo and the Lory. " 'Ahem,' said the Mouse with an important air, 'are you all ready? This is the driest thing I know.' "

It is one more illustration of the irony of suppression that the numerous judges who considered the fugitive publication of this dull document in its entirety so objectionable that it merited five years in the penitentiary have thoughtfully winnowed out all the extremist passages and reprinted them in their opinions, so that they are permanently accessible to incipient revolutionists in brief and readable form at any lawyer's office.

In 1919 the Left Wing broke away from the Socialist Party with this manifesto, printed in the *Revolutionary Age*, of which Gitlow was business manager. The Lusk Committee (which itself published the manifesto with ever so much more extremist radical literature in full in its Report)[3] had Gitlow and others prosecuted for publishing it. A New York statute,[4] enacted in 1902 after McKinley's assassination, and a dead letter ever

[2] On the Secretary of Labor's interpretation of these documents for purposes of deportation, see Chapter V, section v (a).

[3] *Revolutionary Radicalism. . . . Report of the Joint Legislative Committee Investigating Seditious Activities* (Albany, 1920), in four volumes, at page 706 of vol. I. See also vol. II, p. 1322, which lists the names of the managing council of the *Revolutionary Age*, all of whom were indicted. Of these, Gitlow, Ignaz Mizher, Harry M. Winitzky, and Jim Larkin, the Irish labor leader, were convicted and imprisoned; the convictions of Isaac E. Ferguson and Charles E. Ruthenberg were reversed by the New York Court of Appeals because they were not proved responsible for the publication of the Left Wing Manifesto. — 199 N. Y. App. Div. 642 (1922), 234 N. Y. 159 (1925), Hogan, J., dissenting. The other four members, including John Reed, were never apprehended.

In 1939 the taxpayers of New York again paid a considerable sum for distributing on a large scale the kind of "inflammatory" documents for which the state had sent several men like Gitlow to hard labor in prison twenty years before. See Chapter V, note 31.

[4] N. Y. Penal Law, §§ 160–166. See *supra*, Chapter IV, section v. Besides the cases cited in notes 1 and 3, see *Re* Lithuanian Workers' Literary Society, 196 N. Y. App. Div. 262 (1921), refusing a charter to a socialist society; 21 *Columbia Law Review* 195.

since, was revived for this purpose. This statute punishes any advocacy of criminal anarchy, which is defined as "the doctrine that organized government should be overthrown by force or violence, or by assassination of the executive head or of any of the executive officials of government, or by any unlawful means."

Gitlow was convicted in January, 1920, and sentenced to hard labor from five to ten years, of which he served almost three. His conviction was upheld by the Appellate Division, by the Court of Appeals, Pound and Cardozo dissenting, and by the Supreme Court of the United States, Holmes and Brandeis dissenting.

In the Court of Appeals the constitutionality [5] of the Criminal Anarchy Act was upheld, but the main question on which the court split was its construction. This, after all, is not a wholly distinct issue, for a statute means what the judges say it means, and one judicial interpretation of a sedition law might give enough scope for political discussion to satisfy a liberal like John Stuart Mill, while another conceivable interpretation might limit speech and press with great rigidity. Consequently, the constitutional guarantees restrict not only legislative action but also judicial construction of what the legislature has done. It is also a serious restraint upon open discussion if speakers and writers are liable to find themselves subsequently held guilty of violating a sedition law which does not seem at the time applicable to what they are saying. When Gitlow published his manifesto, the Criminal Anarchy Act was generally supposed to punish anarchy, but the majority applied it to communism, which is at the opposite pole of political thought. They held that communism, which would bring all the activities of citizens under the control of the state, was not "a condition which could be fairly regarded as an organized government," and that to urge the achievement of such a régime through mass strikes was to advocate the overthrow of organized government by "unlawful means." Judge Pound's dissent, while strongly disapproving of the defendant's aims, insisted that organized government need not be representative or consti-

---

[5] The New York free speech clause is reprinted in Chapter I, note 2. On the decision in the Court of Appeals, see Note, 36 *Harvard Law Review* 199; *contra*, 32 *Yale Law Journal* 178.

GITLOW v. NEW YORK 321

tutional, but "is the political power in the state whose commands
the community is bound to obey and is the antithesis of government without such political power which is the unorganized or
anarchistic state." Since Gitlow had urged the dictatorship of
the proletariat and not anarchism, he was not within the terms
of this statute.

Although the defendant may be the worst of men; although Left
Wing socialism is a menace to organized government; the rights of
the best of men are secure only as the rights of the vilest and most
abhorrent are protected.

In the United States Supreme Court the only question was the
constitutionality of the Criminal Anarchy Act as thus construed
by the state courts. Unlike the Espionage Act free speech decisions, the case did not come up under the First Amendment,
which restricts only Congress, but under the Fourteenth:
". . . Nor shall any state deprive any person of . . . liberty
. . . without due process of law," that is, by arbitrary and
unreasonable legislation. In several cases the court had carefully refrained from deciding whether "liberty" protects liberty
of speech as well as liberty of the person and of contracts. The
possibility of an affirmative answer became stronger with
Gilbert v. *Minnesota* in 1920, as the seventh chapter has
pointed out. However, the question still stayed open, and as
late as 1922 Justice Pitney said that "the Constitution of the
United States imposes on the States no obligation to confer
upon those within their jurisdiction . . . the right of free
speech." [6] Then in 1923 the Supreme Court held that liberty
to teach a foreign language in private schools was within the
Fourteenth Amendment.[7] Just a week before deciding the
Gitlow case, the Court in the Oregon School case [8] invalidated

[6] Prudential Ins. Co. v. Cheek, 259 U. S. 530, at 538 and 543 (1922), discussed
in 36 *Harvard Law Review* 195 and 27 A. L. R. 39.

[7] Meyer v. Nebraska, 262 U. S. 390 (1923) (German language), per Mc-
Reynolds, J., Holmes and Sutherland, JJ., dissenting on the ground that the
statute might be considered reasonable. Protection to Japanese private schools
in Hawaii was given, after the Gitlow case, in Farrington v. Tokushige, 273
U. S. 284 (1927).

[8] Pierce v. Society of Sisters, 268 U. S. 510 (1925). It will be observed
that neither school case bore on the power of the state to regulate teaching
in public schools and universities, e.g. by anti-evolution laws. See Chafee, *The
Inquiring Mind*, pp. 33 ff.; *infra*, Appendix III, for the Tennessee and Mississippi
laws.

a law making it illegal for parents to send their children to private schools, and construed "liberty" to include the right of parents to direct the upbringing of their children. Although in both these cases the schools were deprived of property in the form of tuition fees, the decisions cleared the ground for a decision that liberty of thought without any property is protected under the Fourteenth Amendment. On the basis of such authorities, Walter Heilprin Pollak, who shared in the oral argument for Gitlow, persuaded the Supreme Court to settle the long-vexed issue at last by the unanimous statement that "we may and do assume that freedom of speech and of the press . . . are among the fundamental personal rights and 'liberties' protected . . . from impairment by the states." [9]

The majority of the Court, however, held, through Mr. Justice Sanford, that this statute did not wrongfully impair Gitlow's liberty of speech. The New York courts had expressly repudiated the test laid down by the Supreme Court in the Schenck case under the Espionage Act,[10] that words are punishable only when their nature and the surrounding circumstances created "a clear and present danger" of wrongful acts; and there was no evidence of such danger in this case. Consequently Gitlow's counsel contended that the state courts erred in rejecting the Schenck test, and that he had been punished merely for doctrines and words because of their supposed bad tendency to result at a remote time in acts. This bad-tendency test is an English eighteenth-century doctrine, wholly at variance with any true freedom of discussion, because it permits the government to go outside its proper field of acts, present or probable, into the field of ideas, and to condemn them by the judgment of a judge or jury, who, human nature being what it is, consider a doctrine they dislike to be so liable to cause harm some day that it had better be nipped in the bud. The danger test, on the other hand, leaves the doctrine to be proved or disproved by argument and the course of events. It avoids the risk of suppressing disagreeable truths, so long as there is no immediate risk of unlawful acts.

[9] For an able discussion of the background and implications of this holding, see Charles Warren, "The New 'Liberty' under the Fourteenth Amendment," 39 *Harvard Law Review* 431 (1926). *Cf.* the reply by J. P. Hall, 20 *Illinois Law Review* 809 (1926).

[10] 249 U. S. 47 (1919). See Chapter II, section v.

Justice Sanford virtually adopts the bad-tendency test. The words "tend" and "tending" are as frequent in his opinion as in an English charge during the prosecution of a reformer in the French Revolutionary Wars. As for the "clear and present danger" test, he declares that it merely served to decide how far the Espionage Act, which dealt primarily with acts, should be interpreted to extend to words. He rejects it altogether as a test of the constitutionality of a statute expressly directed against words of incitement which the legislature considers dangerous.[11] Thus words may be punished for their bad nature regardless of the court's opinion that there is no danger of bad acts. The injudicious choice of language becomes a crime:

A single revolutionary spark may kindle a fire that, smoldering for a time, may burst into sweeping and destructive conflagration. It cannot be said that the state is acting arbitrarily . . . when . . . it seeks to extinguish the spark without waiting until it has enkindled the flame or blazed into the conflagration.

The trouble is that in extinguishing the spark we cause much damage that might be avoided if the spark were left to go out by itself. There is no better way to increase discontent than to impose severe sentences for what the accused and his friends do not consider criminal at all.

Justice Holmes's brief dissent stands by the danger test, which cannot apply to suppress this manifesto concerned with an uprising only in some vague future.[12] To the majority view that it is punishable for the bad nature of the words, he replies:

It is said that this manifesto was more than a theory, that it was an incitement. Every idea is an incitement. It offers itself for belief, and, if believed, it is acted on unless some other belief outweighs it, or some failure of energy stifles the movement at its birth. The only difference between the expression of an opinion and an incitement in the narrower sense is the speaker's enthusiasm for the result.

---

[11] Fortunately, this narrowing of the Schenck test was not permanently adopted by the Supreme Court. See Chapters X and XI.

[12] See *Holmes-Pollock Letters*, II, 162–163, where Holmes says: "I am bothered by a case in which conscience and judgment are a little in doubt," probably as to the applicability of the Fourteenth Amendment; and later that he has dissented "in favor of the rights of an anarchist (so-called) to talk drool in favor of the proletarian dictatorship. But the prevailing notion of free speech seems to be that you may say what you choose if you don't shock *me*."

Eloquence may set fire to reason. But whatever may be thought of the redundant discourse before us, it had no chance of starting a present conflagration.

A profit and loss account of the Gitlow case immediately after it was decided showed one big gain, the possibility of federal protection against state suppression. Now that the Court's power to protect liberty of speech under the Fourteenth Amendment had been decisively established, that power was bound to be exercised sooner or later to reverse convictions. And so a more liberal Court could prevent the United States from becoming a checkerboard nation, with ultra-conservative states into which moderately radical Americans would come at peril of imprisonment for sedition. As yet, however, not much protection could be expected. Such extreme laws as the Tennessee evolution statute might be invalidated, but the intolerance of the California Syndicalism Act would not be checked by the existing Court. For the time, state freedom must be secured through state legislatures and state governors like Alfred E. Smith, who pardoned Gitlow and his associates soon after the Supreme Court decision and stopped further Anarchy Act prosecutions.

In 1925 the losses seemed much clearer than the gain. Without the danger test, which then appeared to be abandoned by the Gitlow case (though this fear was later proved unfounded),[13] freedom of speech means little more than the right to say what a considerable number of citizens regard as sound, which consequently is not likely to be prosecuted. For novel unpopular ideas, where alone it is really needed, it would no longer exist as a legal right.

We had also lost vision and courage. The Left Wing Manifesto was a tepid hash of the Communist Manifesto of Marx and Engels, which has been the program of influential parliamentary groups in every Continental country for over half a century. The terror which these dull and rusty phrases caused our prosecutors and judges would render them the laughingstock of European conservatives. The real danger in this country is not a conflagration but dry rot, "the slow smokeless burning of decay."[14] The ballot-box is not likely to be over-

---

[13] See note 11.   [14] Robert Frost, *The Wood-pile*.

thrown by force, but if non-voting goes on increasing, it may become as meaningless as the Electoral College. The clash of ideas is to be welcomed, not feared, even if it occasionally involves the intemperate exhortations of a manifesto. We may wisely ponder the comment of Junius, after the English sedition prosecutions: "The mass of the people is inert. The country has lost its passions."

The victories of liberty of speech must be won in the mind before they are won in the courts. In that battlefield of reason we possessed in 1925 new and powerful weapons, the dissenting opinions of Justices Holmes and Brandeis. Out of the long series of legal defeats had come a group of arguments for toleration that may fitly stand beside the *Areopagitica* and Mill's *Liberty*. The majority opinions determined the cases, but these dissenting opinions will determine the minds of the future.

And a Supreme Court comprising and influenced by men who really want to preserve the great American traditions of freedom of speech now has in its arsenal two weapons which were not available in 1917, Justice Holmes's test of "clear and present danger" and the Fourteenth Amendment, which was unused for the maintenance of open discussion until the Gitlow case. The nation which welcomed to its shores in the mid-nineteenth century two European scholars, Heilprin and Pollak, was amply repaid for its hospitality seventy-five years afterwards when their descendant placed forever in the hands of the Supreme Court this sharp sword with which to defend the ideals of Jefferson and Madison against local intolerance.

CHAPTER 10

CRIMINAL SYNDICALISM

I. THE CALIFORNIA I.W.W. INJUNCTION

In the Central Valley, temperatures are often very high.
California: A Guide to the Golden State.

BEFORE seeing how the Supreme Court exercised its new-found power to keep state sedition laws within bounds, let us go back to the states for a space and see how these laws had been operating there. The most interesting illustration is furnished by California.

After the Espionage Act showed the ease with which men can be punished for political and economic discussion which is distasteful to the majority of citizens, thirty-three states (as narrated in Chapter IV) made sedition in time of peace a serious crime. More than half these states adopted an almost uniform statute, which created the new crime of criminal syndicalism and was directed mainly against the Industrial Workers of the World.[1]

Thus the California statute passed in 1919 [2] begins by defining criminal syndicalism as

any doctrine or precept advocating, teaching or aiding and abetting the commission of crime, sabotage (which word is hereby defined as meaning willful and malicious physical damage or injury to physical property), or unlawful acts of force and violence or unlawful methods of terrorism as a means of accomplishing a change in industrial ownership or control, or effecting any political change.

Imprisonment from one to fourteen years may be inflicted upon any person who advocates, teaches, or aids and abets

---

[1] For a brief account of this organization, see Chapter V, section v (*b*).
[2] Cal. Gen. Laws (Deering, 1937) Act 8428. For very useful sketches of the history of the enforcement of this statute, see 10 *California Law Review* 512 (1922); 19 *id.* 64 (1930); 23 *id.* at 181 (1935).

criminal syndicalism; who wilfully attempts to justify it; who publishes or circulates any written or printed matter advocating or advising it; who organizes, assists in organizing, or knowingly becomes a member of any group organized to advocate it (without necessarily urging this doctrine himself); or who commits any act advocated by this doctrine with intent to effect a change in industrial ownership or any political change. Observe that the statute says nothing whatever about injunctions.

Although these Criminal Syndicalism Acts soon became a dead letter in most states, not so in California. In the five years following its enactment (until August 15, 1924), 504 persons were arrested and held for bail of $15,000 each, and 264 actually tried. At least thirty-four [3] cases have gone to appellate courts. One prosecution was used to bring another. When some I.W.W.'s were on trial and Miss Anita Whitney was produced as a witness for the defense to describe the aims of the organization, she was rejected because, not being a member, she had no expert knowledge. Consequently, other I.W.W.'s had to be brought in as witnesses. As soon as these left the courtroom after testifying, they were arrested on the ground that they had admitted being members of the proscribed organization, and they were also tried and convicted.

Nevertheless, the results secured by the criminal law proved unsatisfactory to the prosecuting officials. The Defense Committee said that "jurors are refusing to convict" on the evidence of "the self-confessed criminals whom the prosecutions have been in the habit of using as their chief witnesses." (Compare the nature of the witnesses' affidavits described later in this chapter.) However this might be, Attorney General U. S. Webb eventually adopted a very different method from trial by jury for breaking up the I.W.W. in California.

On July 16, 1923, he applied to the Superior Court in Sacramento County for an injunction against the Industrial Workers of the World, and various specified committees, officers, and members of the organization. The same day Judge Busick granted a restraining order in the terms requested

[3] Seventeen appeals are reported before the date of the injunction discussed in this chapter. For statistics of acquittals, reversals, etc., see 19 *California Law Review* at 66; 23 *id.* at 182.

by the Attorney General. The material clauses were as follows:

> It is further ordered, that the defendants, . . . their servants, agents, solicitors, attorneys, and all others acting in aid or assistance of the defendants, do absolutely desist and refrain from further conspiring with each other to carry out, and from attempting to carry out, their conspiracy to injure, destroy and damage property in the state of California and to take over and assume possession of the industries and properties in said state as well as the government thereof; and from knowingly circulating, selling, distributing and displaying books, pamphlets, papers or other written or printed matter advocating, teaching or suggesting criminal syndicalism, sabotage or the destruction of property for the purpose of taking over the industries [etc.] . . . or otherwise, and from advocating, by word of mouth or writing, the necessity, propriety and expediency of criminal syndicalism or sabotage, direct action, willful damage or injury to physical property and bodily injury to person or persons, and from justifying or attempting to justify, criminal syndicalism, crime, sabotage, violence or unlawful methods of terrorism with the intent to approve, advocate or further the doctrine of criminal syndicalism, and from organizing or aiding to organize or increase any assemblage or association of persons which teaches [etc.] . . . criminal syndicalism or the duty, necessity or propriety of committing crime, sabotage, violence or any unlawful method of terrorism as a means of accomplishing a change in industrial ownership or control, or effecting any political change, and from doing any acts to carry out the doctrines, theories and acts of criminal syndicalism and from in any manner whatsoever conspiring or confederating together for the carrying out of said purposes, or either thereof, until the further order of this court.

Of course, this injunction, if obeyed, would at once break up the I.W.W. in California. Observe that this drastic decree was not issued at the close of a painstaking investigation into the evidence, with ample opportunity for the defendants to cross-examine the state's witnesses, offer their own evidence, and present their reasons against the proposed injunction. Instead, it was granted at the very start of the litigation, before the defendants had even appeared in court. It is true that a month later, on August 23, they did have a chance to say something before Judge Busick continued the order as a temporary injunction; but such hearings are brief and nowise equivalent to a trial on the merits. The court acted largely on the basis of affidavits by former members of the I.W.W. submitted by the Attorney General, which will be described shortly. The usual policy of the law entitles both parties to say all they have to say before any decisive order is reached. Here the judge adopted the more expeditious practice of deciding the case first and trying it afterwards.

No doubt, temporary injunctions are sometimes granted in the early stages of other kinds of suits before the court hears the merits of the case: but this serious exception to the policy of knowing before deciding is properly used with caution, and a good judge takes care to safeguard the interests of both sides during the litigation, so as to avoid ending the dispute in the plaintiff's favor before the court is in a position to make a well-considered final determination. For this purpose, three principles are commonly kept in mind in weighing requests for temporary injunctions.

First, the plaintiff must show a real emergency. He must demonstrate that if he eventually wins the suit and has not been protected during its course, the defendant's acts meanwhile may cause him serious harm that cannot be cured or compensated by money damages. For example, A tells the court that B is threatening to cut down that very night an oak grove on a strip of land to which they both claim title; or A sues to establish a trust in a bank deposit standing in B's name, and says that B plans to draw out the money at once and decamp for parts unknown. In both cases, even though A succeeds in establishing his ownership of the disputed property he may gain only a barren victory; he cannot make the trees grow again or lay his hands on his vanished money. So the court will be likely to enjoin B's threatened action and tell B to wait till the case has been completely tried before doing his proposed acts. But if B is threatening merely to mow grass which will come up again, or if the alleged trustee has ample property of his own which the court can easily reach later on, then no emergency exists and the injunction may be refused. This principle is something like Holmes's test of "clear and present danger" for restrictions on freedom of speech, so that it is especially applicable to temporary injunctions which will interfere with expressions of opinion on vital economic and social matters. After the reader has considered what I tell below about the affidavits of renegade I.W.W.'s which formed the main proof of the alleged emergency, he can judge for himself whether irreparable disaster would have been suffered by the people of California if the trial court had taken time to let the organization defend itself before ordering it dissolved.

Secondly, the plaintiff must seek his temporary injunction promptly. He is in no situation to say to the court, "Hurry, hurry!" when he himself has let the matter slide for years. Later on I shall show that the state's affidavits largely described events several years before 1923, and the situation was then no more serious than for a long time previously. The state had waited for years without asking an injunction. Why could it not wait a few months longer and let the defendants continue their customary activities as before, subject of course to the criminal penalties of the Syndicalism Act, while they were trying to prove that the I.W.W. was a lawful union of laborers?

Thirdly, after considering the hardship to the plaintiff if the requested temporary injunction be refused, a normal court goes on to consider the hardship upon the defendant if the injunction be issued; and then the two hardships are weighed against each other. The judge ought not to cause a big irreparable harm to the defendant for the sake of preventing a little irreparable harm to the plaintiff. This is particularly true when there is considerable question whether the plaintiff will win in the end anyway; and this, we shall see, was the situation in the I.W.W. suit. Now, the principle just stated would probably not block a temporary injunction in the hypothetical cases of the oaks and the bank deposit. B will not suffer much if he cuts the oaks down after he has established ownership of the grove, instead of felling them tonight; and the alleged trustee can scrape along on other funds until he proves that the deposit belongs to him. Furthermore, the court can often safeguard the defendant against any risk of injury during the pendency of an injunction which is eventually set aside, by requiring the plaintiff to file a bond covering the defendant's possible damages caused by his obedience to the temporary injunction.

In the I.W.W. temporary injunction, this third principle received no attention whatever. No bond was required from the Attorney General to compensate the defendants if the order turned out not to be justified. Still more important, the effect of the injunction on the defendants was no matter of a temporary suspension of proposed future acts, like cutting down oaks or withdrawing a bank deposit. On the contrary, the injunction, if obeyed, stopped unionization practices which had long been going on, and killed the California organization once and for all. Even if the defendants won in the end after months of testimony and got the injunction dissolved, or if they appealed and got Judge Busick reversed next year, the I.W.W. would be gone. Whatever happened, it would be too late to put Humpty Dumpty together again.

So what Judge Busick did to the Industrial Workers of the World by his restraining order and later temporary injunction was a good deal like hanging a prisoner before he has been brought into the courtroom, hanging him again after half an hour's defense to snuff out the last whiffs of breath, and then telling his friends that they can have all the time they want to give in court their reasons for his acquittal. Perhaps there may be pressing emergencies when the best way to save society is thus to order an association shot at sunrise. Yet it is surely fair, before taking such unprecedented action, for the government to present at least a plausible picture of threatened immediate disaster and then support its allegations with unusually clear and convincing evidence that the community will be ruined if it gives the defendants the privileges allowed to a murderer caught red-handed — testimony, cross-examination, and well-prepared argument. And if California was so close to collapse as this, the time had come for martial law and not an injunction. Lincoln did not ask a United States judge to enjoin Lee's whole Army of Northern Virginia.

It is hardly surprising that some members of the I.W.W. decided to prolong the life of their organization in spite of Judge Busick's extraordinary injunction. One member who went ahead and procured new recruits was adjudged in contempt of court, fined, and then sent to jail to work out his fine. This man brought *habeas corpus*, but his release was refused by the Supreme Court of California.[4] The court merely decided

---

[4] *In re* Wood, 194 Cal. 49 (1924), adversely criticized by Professor H. W. Ballantine in 13 *California Law Review* 63; and also in 73 *University of Pennsylvania Law Review* 185. See State *v.* Howat, 109 Kan. 376 (1921); State *v.*

that the injunction was not void; that Judge Busick had the power to grant it. The court was not concerned with the possible erroneousness of the injunction, as it would have been had an appeal been taken when the injunction was issued.

This Sacramento injunction combined two significant legal tendencies of recent years: (1) governmental suppression of radical discussion and organizations; and (2) governmental use of the injunction instead of criminal prosecutions to maintain "law and order."

The first tendency raises the familiar problem of the desirability of using force against opinions. Such a policy of coercion is especially questionable as applied to the I.W.W. The organization thrives on discontent, and persecution is the best way to increase discontent. Carleton Parker showed this before the Syndicalist Acts were passed.[5] Professor D. D. Lescohier of Wisconsin reached the same conclusions in his first-hand observations of "The I.W.W. in the Wheat Lands": [6]

They are a social tragedy rather than a social menace. . . . The nation cannot avoid what the I.W.W. stands for by forcible suppression of the organization, and it should not try. It can avoid revolutionary organizations among the workers only by removing the economic and social disadvantages that are the source of revolutionary discontent.

The farmers of the Central Valley and their supporters had considerable provocation for demanding vigorous proceedings against sabotage of agricultural machinery, crop-burning, and other flagrant practices. It was only natural to believe that these elusive evils could be stamped out by suppressing the organization with which such acts were most associated. One must be tolerant of their intolerance. A journey through the Central Valley, one of the hottest places on earth where white men carry on normal processes of labor, makes it easy to under-

---

I.W.W., 113 Kan. 347 (1923) ; State *v.* Grady, 114 Wash. 692 (1921) ; 25 A. L. R. 1245 (1923). But compare People *v.* Steele, 4 Cal. App. (2d) 206 (1935). The New Hampshire Sedition Act of 1919 contains an injunction provision.

[5] "The I.W.W.," *Atlantic Monthly* (November, 1917), reprinted in his *The Casual Laborer and Other Essays* (New York, 1920).

[6] *Harper's Monthly* (August, 1923).

stand how passions once aroused there were bound to flare high among both workers and employers.

Yet, until the economic and social disadvantages causing discontent are dealt with directly, the use of the tremendous power of the state on behalf of employers and conservative unions, although it may produce a superficial weakening of revolutionary unionism, is sure to intensify its hostility to the state and the belief that government is only the organ of capital. The plight of the California farmers resembled that of the English farmers around 1830, when, vexed by persistent rick-burning, they persuaded the government to transport the "Dor-chester labourers" to Australia for attempting to form an agricultural union. But modern historians condemn the officials who treated so superficially the discontent which arose from low wages and from the unsettlement of rural workers by the recent enclosures of common lands, their former source of subsistence.[7] Similarly, the California field laborers who were enjoined by Judge Busick from continuing as members of their own peculiar union were not thereby turned into enthusiastic supporters of their country's laws or led to alter their economic views. They might even shift into more orthodox unions, where they would be safe from prosecution and could stir up violent sentiment with much more effect than if they were out in the open.

What happened to the I.W.W. after the injunction is sig-nificant in this connection. As an organization, it was con-siderably weaker. The wholesale prosecutions had effectively broken its strength for years and perhaps permanently. They forced it to concentrate its effort upon legal defense and cam-paigns for amnesty. Bitter internal quarrels broke out over the conditions on which amnesty should be accepted and the question of centralization of power within the organization. Between 1924 and 1930, there was not a single prosecution under the California Syndicalism Act, as against a previous yearly average of 100 persons indicted. The police continued to break up meetings by arrests, but then they released the prisoners at once. One might suppose that suppression had accomplished its purpose, for the I.W.W. in California seemed

[7] Hammond, *The Village Labourer*, 240 ff. (1919) ; *The Book of the Martyrs of Tolpuddle* (London Trades Union Cong. Gen. Council, 1934).

on its last legs. But where were the I.W.W.'s? Had they become happy-hearted pillars of society?

The answer is suggested by the only two California prosecutions reported since 1930. The judicial opinions describe each band of a dozen or so prisoners and their misdoings in familiar terms. They sound just like the I.W.W.'s of 1919–24. But they do not belong to the Industrial Workers of the World, they are all Communists. Apparently, the migratory laborers merely transferred their allegiance from a union which was always localized and sporadic to a fairly active revolutionary national party. A previously divided radicalism became more closely united. The great California clean-up had succeeded in brushing up the dust from under one bed and moving it over under another bed.[8]

It is a mistake to spend upon a mosquito-killing campaign the energy which might be used in draining the swamps where the insects breed. The I.W.W. is largely recruited from migratory laborers who wander haphazard from one seasonal crop to another. The situation of such laborers, imaginatively depicted in Steinbeck's *Grapes of Wrath*, is described with more restraint in the official guide to California: [9]

The heart of the great Central Valley [is] a desert of almost unbelievable fertility under irrigation. But irrigation demands unremitting toil; the omission of a single quarterly watering throughout might kill every tree and cultivated plant on the vast valley floor. Farming here is not farming as Easterners know it; most of the ranches are food factories . . . . Even the owners of small ranches

---

[8] People v. Horiuchi, 105 Cal. App. 714 (1930), 114 id. 415 (1931); People v. Chambers, 22 Cal. App. (2d) 687 (1937). Brissenden in 1932 reports the same tendency nationally: "Left wing strikes which in pre-war days would have been led by the I.W.W. are now led by Communists. Many prominent I.W.W. leaders, such as Haywood and William Z. Foster, joined the Communist party, and an appreciable proportion of this party's membership is composed of former members of the I.W.W." 8 *Encyclopaedia of the Social Sciences* at 16.

[9] *California: A Guide to the Golden State* (American Guide Series, 1939), pp. 440 ff. For a more elaborate account, which is considered by some to be exaggerated, see Carey McWilliams, *Factories in the Field* (1939). See also Brissenden, *The I.W.W.* (1920), pp. 10 ff., 338, and the I.W.W. songs on pp. 370 ff.; Brissenden, "Industrial Workers of the World," 8 *Encyclopaedia of the Social Sciences* 13 (1932); Goodrich, "Migratory Labor," 10 id. 441 (1933); Parker, *op. cit. supra* note 5. Judge Hart, who had decided several syndicalism cases, gave a measured opinion of the nature of the I.W.W. while invalidating a Eureka ordinance specifically directed against this organization.— *In re* Campbell, 64 Cal. App. 300 (1923).

usually concentrate on a single crop . . . . In addition to the permanent employees the valley uses a great deal of seasonal labor that forms a constant problem. The migratory worker, constantly on the move to catch the harvest seasons of one crop after the other — peaches, walnuts, apricots, grapes, celery — never stays long enough in any area to establish himself as a citizen. He lives apart from other residents, occasionally in barracks behind the fields and orchards, more often in crude shelters of his own devising along the river bottoms. Because there are too many who want work, the migrant cannot command an adequate return for his labor. The inhabitants of the towns do not know him and his family and local governments feel no responsibility for him. No one knows how to help him with his problems and no one knows how to get along without his help.

A good deal of the sabotage and other violence connected with this disconcerting situation might be ended if migratory laborers were encouraged to bargain collectively with the help of the National Labor Relations Board, and if they could live together in large model villages, where they could be with wives and children like normal human beings, and whence they could be carried by rail or motor-vehicles to the place where each successive seasonal crop is to be gathered. They might even be induced to alternate this temporary agricultural work with labor in city factories. In this connection, the practice of the Canadian government in transporting workers from industrial England to the wheat harvest is worthy of study. The federal government since 1933 has been trying to attack constructively the basic evil of homeless migratory labor.

The second legal tendency noted above, the use of the injunction instead of the criminal law, is also far-reaching in its possibilities of harm. Let us assume, though the defendants vigorously denied it, that the I.W.W. intended to do all the acts prohibited by this injunction. Even so, any violence they might commit could be severely punished under the ordinary Penal Code, and the Criminal Syndicalism Act contained sweeping provisions for the prosecution of speech that fell short of action. Why then did the Attorney General resort to an injunction? Because the actual violence was slight, and California jurymen no longer considered the I.W.W.'s worth convicting for anything else. So he wanted to get away from juries altogether.

How was this possible? The California constitution guarantees a jury trial to accused persons, but this does not apply to injunction suits in equity. Still courts of equity have no power to prevent crimes as such. They exist primarily to protect individual rights and not the state. B's factory is sending smoke into A's house. A gets an injunction forbidding B to continue the nuisance. If B disobeys, the court will order him imprisoned for contempt until he stops the smoke. The state is not a party to the proceeding. No chance as yet for the Attorney General to reach the members of the I.W.W.

However, the state may also get into equity as a property-owner. If B's factory is sending its smoke into the State House, the state may get an injunction just as A can, and it is immaterial that B's nuisance is also a criminal violation of a smoke ordinance. Perhaps the I.W.W.'s could be charged with threatening state property. What is still more important, a defendant may be injuring the public at large in a manner analogous to private nuisance. Suppose B's smoke contains poisonous fumes which are endangering the lives of the neighbors. Then the state may obtain an injunction, not only as a property owner, but also as the guardian of the health and general welfare of its citizens. On the same principle, in a California case [10] cited by the Attorney General as a precedent for enjoining the I.W.W.'s, one of his predecessors in office had mine-owners prohibited from casting large quantities of débris into a river, so as to obstruct the navigation and water supply of a district. This injunctive power has been extended by statute to objectionable establishments like disorderly houses or illegal saloons, which constitute a plague spot like the poison-spreading factory.

Before considering the expansion of these principles to cover the novel situation of the I.W.W. case, stop a moment to weigh the merits and demerits of the equitable proceedings just described. They have several advantages over the criminal law. They avoid juries, who are reluctant to impose punishment for these minor offenses. An injunction may be obtained on proof by a mere preponderance of the evidence; conviction

[10] People v. Gold Run Ditch, 66 Cal. 155 (1884).

requires proof beyond a reasonable doubt. And it is often desirable to get rid of a clearly illegal establishment by direct suppression of the thing itself without the crude and round-about method of imprisoning the human beings who operate it. Yet there are obvious disadvantages, which until the arrival of National Prohibition rendered courts very reluctant to ex-pand their injunctive power against public nuisances, especially in the absence of express legislative authority. If the defendant seriously disputes the illegality of his conduct and thus is liable to disobey the decree, he will be imprisoned for conduct which, unless it is really criminal, constitutes no proper cause for his confinement. He and his sympathizers in the community will reflect that he is in jail without a jury trial and at the will of a single judge, who both passed on the facts and determined the duration of confinement, and from whose decision the right of appeal is very limited. Lawyers may distinguish contempt from conviction, but the man himself sees little difference. The prison fare is the same in both cases, the prison walls are equally thick. If a judge, by the simple process of calling any crime a public nuisance, can throw into jail any person whom he con-siders to have violated his injunction, trial by jury for crimes becomes a virtual nullity.

Certainly a judge should not greatly expand so drastic and dubious a power and use it for the novel purpose of breaking up an association, especially an association of workers with some of the characteristics of a labor union, unless the legisla-ture expressly authorizes him to do so.[11]

From these general considerations we turn to the specific charges against the defendant I.W.W.'s which led the California judge to disregard all the considerations just set forth and issue his sweeping injunction. The complaint declared that the organ-ization to which the defendants belonged existed to teach crim-inal syndicalism, and was attempting "thereby to fan flames of discontent among all laboring men and women and all em-ployees" in the state; that the defendants were conspiring to advocate sabotage and crime and the breaking of employment contracts, for the purpose of accomplishing a political and eco-

[11] For authorities on public injunctions, see Chafee & Simpson, *Cases on Equity* (1934), I, 215–237.

nomic revolution in the state and nation; that they aimed at taking over the control of all industries and governments and "destroying all civilization as it now exists"; that many members had come into California during the two months preceding and conspired to cause a stoppage of work in the farms, mines, oil fields, and lumber industries of the state by syndicalism and sabotage; that if their purposes were accomplished, the health, lives, and property of the people would be endangered, and the production of the necessaries of life would be injured and decreased.

Aside from the allegations that the state was interested as a property owner, because its revenues from taxes would be diminished by these prospective injuries to its citizens' property, a ground obviously too remote for an injunction, the state's case must rest on the existence of a public nuisance by virtue of the threats summarized in the preceding paragraph. Yet the situation was entirely different from the recognized public nuisances like poisonous factories and illegal saloons. There was nothing you could put your finger on as a plague spot, only a vague congeries of prospective violations of the Criminal Syndicalism Act, which ought to have been dealt with, if at all, under the statute by the criminal proceedings which the legislature authorized, and not by an injunction without trial by jury which it did not authorize. So even if the charges in the complaint had been solidly proved true, the issuance of an injunction would have gone far beyond established precedents.

Compare with this I.W.W. case of 1923 the refusal of a California court in 1935 to let the same Attorney General use the injunction to break up an association of men whom he alleged to be menacing public health by treating the sick without passing medical examinations, in violation of a penal statute. The court stressed the absence of any legislative provision for the injunction:

[The Attorney General] urges the claimed disastrous consequences of our decision. It is sufficient to point out that if the legislature had deemed the remedy by injunction necessary to the enforcement of the acts governing the practice of healing arts it would have been an easy matter to provide therefor by statute.[12]

[12] People v. Steele, 4 Cal. App. (2d) 206 at 213 (1935). The court's dis-

And whether or not the suit presented any ground for equitable action after all the evidence had been heard, the granting of an injunction at the very outset of the proceedings was improper. A temporary injunction may properly be issued to preserve the *status quo* (the situation when the suit starts) during the trial of a case; this restraining order attempted to change the *status quo* by driving out of existence an organization which, whatever its merits, had been going on for years. Even if it be said that such an injunction does in rare instances alter the *status quo* when its continuance during the suit would work outrageous irreparable injury to the plaintiff,[13] no evidence was offered in this case to show that the situation with respect to the I.W.W. in California was any different from what it had been during the previous five years without fatal damage to lives and property.

So the judge ought not to have practically decided the case before hearing the defendants' whole story. Apart from that, let us see whether the state's evidence, taken as it stood without the usual test of cross-examination and answering testimony, bore out charges that the I.W.W. was trying to destroy all civilization.

The affidavits (on which a restraining order must be based) were only three in number. One, by a former deputy sheriff, merely stated the prevalence of incendiary fires in his neighborhood in 1917, without mentioning the I.W.W. The other two affidavits were by two former members of the I.W.W., whom the state used to trot out in almost every I.W.W. prosecution. Of these two renegades, the California Court of Appeal said, in a case the following year, that their testimony had been received in every case reviewed by that court in the past three or four years, and that they went over practically the same ground as in previous trials.[14] One of these witnesses is mentioned in ten appellate opinions as the chief witness for the state as to the criminal activities of the I.W.W., and the other in eight such opinions. Two other state witnesses, who were

tinction of the I.W.W. case apparently rests on the belief that practicing medicine without training is a much smaller menace to the public than belonging to an industrial union.

[13] An example would be the removal of a TNT factory which had been established on Park Avenue before the neighboring residents began suit.

[14] People *v.* Wright, 66 Cal. App. 782 (1924).

not in the injunction suit, appear by name in several appellate
cases. As one reads the testimony of these professional witnesses, he finds himself becoming very familiar with a few
destructive events attributed to the I.W.W., which took place
before 1919, when the Criminal Syndicalism Act was enacted.
I do not recall any appellate opinion in which a single prisoner
was charged by witnesses with himself committing or participating in the destruction of property or personal injuries, or
even with directly inciting such acts by speeches. His offense,
as alleged in the state's testimony, consisted either (1) in distributing the usual revolutionary documents of the I.W.W., or
(2) in being an organizer or member of the association which
issued such documents. It is always some other members of
the I.W.W. who are said to have committed or incited destructive acts, and not the prisoners at the bar. Even the
wording of the documents became milder after the statute was
passed, but the state met this by evidence that members of the
I.W.W. had said this was camouflage. In short the state of
California was using its Criminal Syndicalism Act, not to punish
actual sabotage or other unlawful acts, but to suppress general
printed discussions and stamp out this queer kind of industrial
union.

Aside from the suspicion which must always rest upon such
professional witnesses as formed the main basis of the California injunction, almost everything they said related to acts of
sabotage (including incendiary fires) in 1917 and 1918, none
of them committed by the present defendants, and the contents
of I.W.W. pamphlets which had been long in circulation. The
only statement that indicated the possibility of especial danger
in the immediate future was a single paragraph at the end of
the seven-page affidavit of one of these two renegades, a Los
Angeles policeman and thrice a former member of the I.W.W.,
who in another I.W.W. case stated on the witness-stand that
he "had never told the truth before in his life," "admitted participation in numberless atrocious offenses," and was judicially
characterized as showing himself to have been "one of the most
reprehensible characters thinkable." His sanity was at least
open to question.[15] This man, whom the California Court

---

[15] On these two witnesses, see People v. La Rue, 62 Cal. App. at 282 (1923);
People v. Cox, 66 Cal. App. at 293 (1924). Compare Oxman and Macdonald,
the two chief witnesses against Tom Mooney.

of Appeal afterwards described as "confessedly guilty of many despicable crimes," now said that in 1922 he was asked by several unnamed members to join an "Inner Circle . . . composed of trusted and desperate characters who would bind themselves under oath to assassinate jurists, prosecuting officers and others who were opposing the defendant organization . . . with the idea and purpose of so terrorizing officials and the public that they will cease to oppose the activities of the defendant organization, and cease to oppose its plans to take over all private property and overthrow the government."

There seems to be no reason why the I.W.W. and the existing state of affairs should not have been left alone until the suit was finished. In short, the charges at their face value did not justify an injunction; the defendants had no chance to answer them before being put in peril of prison; and the state's evidence did not support the charges. Yet anybody who remained an I.W.W. could now be sent to jail without a jury trial.

In conclusion, two points must be emphasized. First, aside from the validity of any particular injunction in these governmental suits, we are making a very grave mistake in allowing prosecuting officials to employ courts of equity in place of criminal courts. It is true that the criminal law has broken down in this country. The police will not or cannot arrest, magistrates release readily, district attorneys quash indictments or accept pleas of guilt for light offenses, rules of evidence furnish technical obstructions, juries refuse to convict.[16] The public turns with relief from this uncertainty to the automatic, hairtrigger action of a judicial restraining order. Once more, as in our failure to attack the causes of the I.W.W., we are evading the issue. Instead of setting ourselves diligently to reorganize the administration of criminal justice, we shrink from the difficult task and try to make the injunction do the same job of stamping out harmful enterprises and maintaining order in industrial disputes. Sooner or later we shall pay the price. In a jury trial, the responsibility is distributed. It does not all

[16] See Alfred Bettman, "Report on Prosecution — Criminal Justice Surveys Analysis," in 1 *Report of the National Commission on Law Observance & Enforcement* (Wickersham Commission, 1931). This invaluable study stresses the magistrates' courts and the prosecutors' offices as the critical points. Only a small proportion of prisoners ever reach a jury, and the acquittals are then much less frequent than is commonly supposed.

fall on the judge. The accused is convicted by men from the street, not very different from himself except in their freedom from crime. The jury takes up the slack, as it were. In a court of equity, there is nothing to take up the slack. The judiciary, the most delicate part of our political machinery, is subjected to a terrific strain when it is made to do unaided, and in highly controversial cases, work fitted for the rougher mechanism of the criminal law.

Finally, the efficiency of the governmental injunction in maintaining the normal processes of life during industrial disputes does not necessarily make it desirable. The natural wish of those in authority to make the government strong enough to meet the needs of the moment with rapidity may lead them to obtain efficiency by an undue sacrifice of freedom. Law and order are good, but they shade by imperceptible gradations into the order that "reigns in Warsaw." Experience has proved it wise that the public should have a fairly direct share in those functions of government that intimately affect the life of the average man; for instance, taxation, which may only be initiated by the branch of the legislature closest to the people, and punishment, which must be inflicted by a jury. The delays and uncertainties incident to such popular participation in government render men of action impatient. Charles I wanted taxes without Parliament, and the Star Chamber was instituted to suppress crime without a jury, and Strafford adopted his policy of "Thorough." The increased efficiency thereby secured was not adequately appreciated by the people at large. The use of the injunction to put men in prison without a jury trial for reasons that seem insufficient to a considerable body of their fellow-citizens is liable to produce a resentment that may eventually sweep away some judicial powers that had better be preserved, along with what can be spared.

Instead of these get-peace-quick methods, let us tighten up the machinery of criminal justice to punish violent acts with all the swiftness and sureness of which the jury system is capable; rely on reforms and carefully considered economic adjustments to eradicate large strikes and the revolutionary spirit; and keep courts of equity for the tasks for which they have been developed by long experience. An equity judge ought not to be turned into a super-policeman.

II. CRIMINAL SYNDICALISM REACHES THE SUPREME COURT

> *It has been said, in defence of [the Scotch Supreme Criminal Court in which the sedition trials of 1793 and 1794 were conducted by Braxfield and other judges], that the times were dangerous. So they were. But these are the very times in which the torch of justice should burn most purely. It has also been said that the prisoners were all guilty. Holding this to be true, had they not a right to be fairly tried? And lastly, it has been said, that after these trials there was no more sedition. The same thing might be said though they had been tried by the boot, and punished by the fire. Jeffreys and Kirke put down sedition, for the day, by their bloody assizes. But our exhibitions of judicial vigour, instead of eradicating the seditious propensity prolonged its inward vitality. Future outbreaks were only avoided by the course of events, which turned men's passions into other channels.*
>
> *These trials, however, sunk deep not merely into the popular mind, but into the minds of all men who thought. It was by these proceedings, more than by any other wrong, that the spirit of discontent justified itself throughout the rest of that age.*　　LORD HENRY COCKBURN,
> Memorials of His Time (1856).

WHEN the Supreme Court in the Gitlow case declared that freedom of speech may be protected against state laws by the Fourteenth Amendment, it created the hope that even though it had sustained the New York Anarchy Act, it might set aside convictions under the more sweeping criminal syndicalism acts like the California statute described in the last chapter. This hope was partly realized when important test cases on the constitutionality of such statutes were decided on May 16, 1927.

The first of these was brought against the California law by Miss Anita Whitney.[17] She was represented in the Supreme Court by Walter Pollak, who had helped establish the new doctrine of the Gitlow case. Miss Whitney was a woman nearing sixty, a Wellesley graduate long distinguished in philanthropic

[17] Whitney v. California, 274 U. S. 357 (1927), affg. 57 Cal. App. 449 (1922).

work. She joined the Socialist Party, and in 1919 when her "local" participated in the Left Wing secession at Chicago she became a temporary member of the new Communist Labor Party and went as a delegate to a convention at Oakland in November for organizing a California branch. Attorney General Palmer's raids on Communists had not yet occurred to warn the hundred delegates that they were engaging in an outlawed enterprise. If they were conscious of conspiring for the violent overthrow of the government, they took a strange way of going about it. The convention was openly held, reporters were present, and its deliberations were described in the next issues of the press. Miss Whitney vigorously supported a resolution that the new state party should aim to capture political power through the ballot. The convention voted this down, and adopted in its place the Chicago program of the national party, which in terms resembling Gitlow's Left Wing Manifesto (described in Chapter IX) urged the seizure of power by revolutionary industrial unionism and great strikes and commended the example of the I.W.W. "Notwithstanding her defeat," says the Governor of California, "Miss Whitney, as was perhaps natural, remained throughout the day of the convention, and, in fact, attended one or two committee meetings during the subsequent month. This, as far as the evidence discloses, marks the extent of her association with the Communist Labor Party, for membership in which she was afterwards convicted."

A special agent of the federal government who examined Miss Whitney's entire correspondence informed the Governor:

Neither in all of the letters from and to her and about her, nor in the investigations covering her activities, does there appear a single line or word tending to show that she ever advocated a violation of any law.

Nearly three weeks after the convention Miss Whitney was arrested as she was leaving a meeting of Oakland club women where she had been speaking on the condition of the American Negro. In January, 1920, she was tried under the recent Criminal Syndicalism Act, for teaching, advocating, and justifying violence; for herself committing acts of violence; and also under this clause:

Any person who . . . organizes or assists in organizing, or is or knowingly becomes a member of, any organization, society, group or assemblage of persons organized or assembled to advocate, teach or aid and abet criminal syndicalism . . . is guilty of a felony . . . .

Miss Whitney's defense was greatly hampered by the sudden death of her able counsel during the trial. As against more than twenty witnesses for the prosecution, she was almost the sole witness for the defense, and her direct testimony occupies only three pages of the thousand-page transcript. A very large part of the evidence against her, which in the Governor's opinion had most effect upon the jury, had to do, not with the Communist Labor Party which Miss Whitney had joined, but with the I.W.W., with which she was never connected. The testimony was largely composed of a recital of atrocities committed in California by the I.W.W., occurring years before the Oakland convention, and the reading of incendiary and blasphemous I.W.W. songs. This evidence was admitted because of a brief endorsement of the I.W.W., not by the state Communist Labor Party, but by the national convention at Chicago, which she had not attended, but whose program had been adopted by the California party. On her part, Miss Whitney testified that she was then a member of the Communist Labor Party, she did not intend this party to be an instrument of terrorism or violence, and it was not her purpose nor that of the state convention to violate any known law. The jury disagreed on the charges that she had herself taught, advocated, and committed violence; but she was convicted of organizing and joining an association believed by the jury to be prohibited by the statute. For this crime she was sentenced to San Quentin Prison for a term of one to fourteen years. Only two others of the hundred delegates to the convention were convicted; and these were found guilty, not merely of membership in the Communist Labor Party, but also of themselves advocating or aiding violence.

Thus in the case of Anita Whitney the Supreme Court had before it a conviction for being at a meeting and nothing more. This came very close to guilt by association, which will be discussed in a later chapter. However, the Court held that her presence at the Communist Labor Party convention was enough to keep her outside the shelter given to "liberty" by the Fourteenth Amendment. Justice Sanford, who spoke for the majority, discussed four points:

(1) To the argument that she could not properly be convicted merely for attending the convention and lacking a "prophetic" understanding of the unlawful purpose which would be given to the convention without her intention and against her will, he replied that her original membership in the national party, her failure to protest or withdraw from the convention, and her subsequent activities were evidence which the jury could weigh in determining her knowledge of the illegality of the organization.

(2) The Syndicalism Act is not unconstitutional for vagueness and uncertainty of definition. As applied here, it "required of the defendant no 'prophetic' understanding of its meaning." It "meets the essential requirement, that a penal statute be sufficiently explicit to inform those who are subject to it what conduct on their part will render them liable to its penalties, and be couched in terms that are not so vague that men of common intelligence must necessarily guess at its meaning and differ as to its application." Does it have any bearing, one ventures to ask, that Secretary of Labor Wilson did differ as to the application of similar words in the deportation statute, and held that they did not include this same Communist Labor Party.[18]

(3) It is no objection that the statute does not punish men who advocate violence as a means of *opposing* changes in industrial ownership or government, but only those who wish it to *accomplish* such changes. A law need not cover the whole field of possible abuses, and there is "nothing indicating any ground to apprehend that those desiring to maintain existing industrial and political conditions did or would advocate such methods." [19]

(4) The Syndicalism Act as applied in this case is not invalid as a restraint of the rights of free speech, assembly, and association. The Constitution does not confer an unrestricted and unbridled license giving immunity for every possible use of language. Those who themselves advocate crime may be pun-

[18] *Supra*, Chapter V, section v (a).
[19] But see *supra*, p. 223.

ished. By enacting this law the state legislature has declared that to be knowingly a member of an association for advocating crimes as described involves such danger to the public peace and the security of the state that membership should also be punished in the exercise of its police power. That determination must be given just weight, and the statute should not be declared unconstitutional inasmuch as it is neither arbitrary nor unreasonable.

The essence of the offense denounced by the act is the combining with others in an association for the accomplishment of the desired ends through the advocacy and use of criminal and unlawful methods. It partakes of the nature of a criminal conspiracy. That such united and joint action involves even greater danger to the public peace and security than the isolated utterances and acts of individuals, is clear.

Justice Brandeis filed a concurring opinion, in which Justice Holmes joined. He felt obligated to sustain the conviction because the constitutional issue had not been presented fully enough at the trial to bring the case within the Supreme Court's limited power of review in state criminal cases; but he disagreed sharply with the reasoning of the majority on freedom of speech and its application to the Syndicalism Act. The crime of membership in a society which this statute creates is, he pointed out, very unlike the old felony of conspiracy, which requires an act by at least one of the group approaching successful accomplishment of a serious crime which must be intended by all the conspirators. On the other hand, the new statute punishes a person for a step in preparation which, if it threatens the public order at all, does so only remotely. "The novelty in the prohibition introduced is that the statute aims, not at the practice of criminal syndicalism, nor even directly at the preaching of it, but at association with those who propose to preach it."

Justice Brandeis agrees with Justice Sanford that the fundamental rights of free speech and assembly are not in their nature absolute, but he demands a less vague test of the extent to which they may be restricted. The particular restriction proposed must in his opinion be necessary in order to save the state from destruction or from serious injury, political, economic, or moral, and this necessity does not exist unless speech would produce, or is intended to produce, a clear and present danger of such evils. This has been settled by the Schenck case, Justice Brandeis insists, in spite of the previous attempt of Justice Sanford in the Gitlow case to limit the application of the clear and present danger test to Congressional war statutes.[20] Though the legislature must decide in the first instance what is necessary, its decision is no more final when it denies liberty of speech than in the many cases where statutes have denied liberty of contract and been overthrown by the Supreme Court. In the end that court must decide whether there was a clear and present danger. True, it has not yet fixed the detailed rules for so deciding, but to reach sound conclusions on these matters we must bear in mind why a state is ordinarily denied the power to prohibit the dissemination of social, economic, and political doctrine which a vast majority of its citizens believe to be false and fraught with evil consequences.

Justice Brandeis then states the reasons for the traditional American policy of freedom of speech guaranteed by the Constitution, which he and Justice Holmes had been endeavoring to protect against the assaults of sedition laws and prosecutions encouraged by those who had been most eloquent in their appeals to the Constitution, even while they strove to reduce to a nullity one of its most vital clauses. These professed patriots are its most dangerous enemies, while among the strongest conservators of Americanism must be counted the author of the following words:

Those who won our independence believed that the final end of the state was to make men free to develop their faculties; and that in its government the deliberative forces should prevail over the arbitrary. They valued liberty both as an end and as a means. They believed liberty to be the secret of happiness and courage to be the secret of liberty. They believed that freedom to think as you will and to speak as you think are means indispensable to the discovery and spread of political truth; that without free speech and assembly discussion would be futile; that with them, discussion affords ordinarily adequate protection against the dissemination of noxious doctrine; that the greatest menace to freedom is an inert people; that

[20] See Chapter IX, note 11.

public discussion is a political duty; and that this should be a fundamental principle of the American government. They recognized the risks to which all human institutions are subject. But they knew that order cannot be secured merely through fear of punishment for its infraction; that it is hazardous to discourage thought, hope, and imagination; that fear breeds repression; that repression breeds hate; that hate menaces stable government; that the path of safety lies in the opportunity to discuss freely supposed grievances and proposed remedies; and that the fitting remedy for evil counsels is good ones. Believing in the power of reason as applied through public discussion, they eschewed silence coerced by law — the argument of force in its worst form. Recognizing the occasional tyrannies of governing majorities, they amended the Constitution so that free speech and assembly should be guaranteed.

If the words put into the Constitution by our forefathers are to mean anything, the danger arising from speech must not be checked by law unless it is imminent danger. Fear alone cannot justify suppression.

Those who won our independence by revolution were not cowards. They did not fear political change. They did not exalt order at the cost of liberty. To courageous, self-reliant men, with confidence in the power of free and fearless reasoning applied through the processes of popular government, no danger flowing from speech can be deemed clear and present, unless the incidence of the evil apprehended is so imminent that it may befall before there is opportunity for full discussion. If there be time to expose through discussion the falsehood and fallacies, to avert the evil by the processes of education, the remedy to be applied is more speech, not enforced silence. Only an emergency can justify repression. Such must be the rule if authority is to be reconciled with freedom. Such, in my opinion, is the command of the Constitution. It is, therefore, always open to Americans to challenge a law abridging free speech and assembly by showing that there was no emergency justifying it.

Moreover, even imminent danger cannot justify a prohibition of the functions essential to effective democracy unless the evil apprehended be relatively serious.

Prohibition of free speech and assembly is a measure so stringent that it would be inappropriate as the means for averting a relatively trivial harm to society. A police measure may be unconstitutional merely because the remedy, although effective as means of protection, is unduly harsh or oppressive. . . . Among freemen, the deterrents ordinarily to be applied to prevent crime are education and punishment for violations of the law, not abridgment of the rights of free speech and assembly.

After this statement of the theoretical reasons for maintaining the clear and present danger test, Justice Brandeis outlines the practical method for its application in a free speech trial.

Whenever the fundamental rights of free speech and assembly are alleged to have been invaded, it must remain open to a defendant to present the issue whether there actually did exist at the time a clear danger; whether the danger, if any, was imminent; and whether the evil apprehended was one so substantial as to justify the stringent restriction interposed by the legislature. . . . Whether, in 1919, when Miss Whitney did the things complained of, there was in California such clear and present danger of serious evil, might have been made the important issue in the case. She might have required that the issue be determined either by the court or the jury.

No such specific issue was raised by her, merely a general objection to the statute under the Fourteenth Amendment. Thus she lost the opportunity to secure an acquittal on this issue; and Justice Brandeis does not now feel able to decide it in her favor, since there was evidence on which the jury might have found that such a danger existed. He does not find such evidence in the mere fact of organizing the Communist Labor Party, for he thinks that "assembling with a political party, formed to advocate the desirability of a proletarian revolution by mass action at some date necessarily far in the future," is a right protected by the Fourteenth Amendment. What determines his decision against setting aside the conviction is the testimony about the I.W.W., which tended to establish a conspiracy on their part to commit present serious crimes and to show that such a conspiracy would be furthered by the activity of the Communist Labor Party, of which Miss Whitney was a member. Justice Brandeis may have believed that this testimony was either untrue or trivial, but he said he could not upset the conviction whatever his opinion on such matters, especially as the court's power to review the evidence in a state criminal case is narrowly confined to the constitutional issues.

Although the Supreme Court did not release Miss Whitney, freedom of speech profited by her resort to this tribunal, not only from the moral effect of the minority opinion but also from certain modifications made by Justice Sanford in the position he had taken in the Gitlow case.[21] There his opinion seemed to indicate that the state legislature was a final judge of the danger of the overthrow of the government, but in the Whitney case he stated that the statutory limitation of speech and assembly must not be arbitrary, unreasonable, or unwarrantable. Thus he approached somewhat Justice Brandeis' view of the limited powers of the state legislatures, although he did not reëstablish the clear and present danger test as the standard of what was arbitrary, etc., but left this matter open for future definition. At least his opinion made it plain that some sedition convictions may be set aside under the Fourteenth Amendment.

And this result was actually reached in another opinion filed by him the same day on behalf of a unanimous court. In *Fiske* v. *Kansas* [22] an I.W.W. organizer had been convicted under the Kansas statute, which is much like that in California, for advocating criminal syndicalism orally and through the distribution of printed matter, and for obtaining new members. The only evidence in the indictment or at the trial to show the unlawful purposes of the I.W.W. was the preamble to its constitution, which does not mention violence but urges a struggle between the working class and the employing class without peace until the workers take possession of the earth and the machinery of production and abolish the wage system; and that "instead of the conservative motto, 'A fair day's wage for a fair day's work,' we must inscribe on our banner the revolutionary watchword, 'Abolition of the wage system.' " The defendant testified at the trial that he had not advocated crime, sabotage, or other unlawful acts, and did not believe in criminal syndicalism or know it was supported by the society. The state court upheld his conviction, saying that although there was no expressed suggestion of crime in the preamble. the jury could read a sinister meaning between the lines and need not accept the defendant's testimony as a candid and accurate statement.

[21] See Chapter IX, note 11; 41 *Harvard Law Review* 527; 14 *California Law Review* 54.

[22] 274 U. S. 380; in the state court, 117 Kan. 69 (1924).

The Supreme Court set aside the conviction because a federal right had been denied "as the result of a finding shown by the record to be without evidence to support it." There was no suggestion in the testimony that any but lawful methods were to be used to accomplish the purposes of the I.W.W. Thus applied, the Kansas Syndicalism Act was "an arbitrary and unreasonable exercise of the police power of the state, unwarrantably infringing the liberty of the defendant."

The great importance of *Fiske* v. *Kansas* may easily be overlooked. The opinion contains no ringing phrases and does not even use the words, "freedom of speech and assembly." It might be assumed that the court did nothing more than declare that a man cannot be convicted for a crime which is neither charged nor proved. Yet the decision necessarily goes much further. The Supreme Court of the United States would not and could not set aside a state conviction for murder where the indictment and the evidence failed to show the necessary intent to kill. The defendant's liberty may be unjustly taken away in such a case, but the court has no general power to review all state criminal trials, nor does it want them to crowd its calendar. Fiske was heard and released because he was deprived of liberty of speech under a statute which, though constitutional in itself, had been construed to punish utterances which were now held to be immune under the United States Constitution. In *Fiske* v. *Kansas* the Supreme Court for the first time made freedom of speech mean something.

Brief mention may be made of a third decision the same day, *Burns* v. *United States*,[23] in which the Court through Justice Butler sustained a conviction of an I.W.W. organizer for a speech in Yosemite Park. Congress had brought the Park within the criminal law of California. Justice Brandeis dissented. This decision will be further discussed when I take up guilt by association.

The next event in order of time concerned the case of Anita Whitney. The majority of the Supreme Court was against her, but the minority was in fact victorious. Within a few months she was pardoned by Governor C. C. Young of California, who

[23] 274 U. S. 328 (1927). See Pillsbury, "Law Applicable to National Parks . . . within a State," 22 *California Law Review* 152 (1934); *infra*, Chapter XII, at n. 70.

in his statement of the reasons for his action repeatedly refers to the opinion of Justice Brandeis. The Governor approves his view that clear and present danger should be the vital issue of fact, and decides this issue in the Whitney case on the evidence before himself at the time of the pardon.

The Communist Labor Party has practically disappeared, not only in California, but also in other states where no criminal syndicalism law existed. It was a visionary attempt to plant a European radicalism upon an American soil, where it simply could not thrive. I am unable to learn of any activities of this party, in California at least, or possibly in America, which ever rendered it a danger to the state or a menace to our institutions. I am satisfied that, in the light of our present knowledge, no charge of criminal syndicalism would be now brought against its members.

After a full review of Miss Whitney's life and the trial, as to which he emphasizes her trial counsel's death and the misleading effect of the I.W.W. evidence, he sums up his impressive statement with a succession of reasons for the pardon, ending:

Because her imprisonment might easily serve a harmful purpose by reviving the waning spirits of radicals through making her a martyr; because whatever may be thought as to "the folly of her misdirected sympathies," Miss Whitney, lifelong friend of the unfortunate, is not in any true sense a "criminal," and to condemn her, at sixty years of age, to a felon's cell is an action which is absolutely unthinkable.

These three cases induce the following reflections:
First, they strengthened the principle that the constitutional line between permissible and punishable utterances will be fixed at the point where a clear and present danger of injurious acts is created. This test, though not automatic, is much more practicable than any other which has been authoritatively suggested.

Secondly, the easy acceptance by legislatures and courts of guilt by association should cause anxiety to others besides supporters of freedom of speech. When such elastic extensions of the crime of conspiracy become habitual, they may be applied to more than radical agitators. Business men may some day find the Sherman Anti-Trust Law amended to punish innocent shareholders of monopolistic corporations; and high-minded persons who had casually joined a society for the repeal of the Eighteenth Amendment were fortunate not to be tried on testimony that the officers of their society occasionally said nullification of Prohibition with the aid of bootleggers was the quickest way to secure its disappearance.

Thirdly, Miss Whitney's conviction shows the great danger of criminal syndicalism laws; though they seem at first sight to apply to thoroughly vicious persons, they can easily be interpreted by juries in times of excitement to include peaceable advocates of industrial or political change.

Finally, the ultimate disposition of her case emphasizes the truth that the only branch of the government which did much between 1917 and 1930 to preserve freedom of speech was the Executive. Legislatures hastily enacted sedition laws with sheep-like imitativeness. Three courts refused to release Miss Whitney, and the judicial records show many other instances where severe sentences were imposed and sustained against persons who urged no law-breaking. There were few majority opinions setting forth the importance of open discussion. Contrast the action of executives. Smith of New York vetoed the Lusk bills [24] in a strong message and pardoned all those convicted through the efforts of the Lusk Committee. Hunt of Arizona would not sign a sweeping sedition law. Small of Illinois pardoned William Bross Lloyd in reliance on a dissenting opinion in the state court.[25] Young of California pardoned Miss Whitney in reliance on a dissenting opinion by Justice Brandeis. Presidents Harding and Coolidge released all the war prisoners who had not served out their terms. Would that it were possible to add a greater name to this list, and that we might read in the official biography of Woodrow Wilson the President's statesmanlike reasons for vetoing the two Espionage Acts and his magnanimous decision not to imprison Eugene V. Debs.

[24] See *supra*, Chapter VI, at note 43.
[25] People *v.* Lloyd. 304 Ill. 23 (1922) ; Carter, J., dissenting at 106.

PART III

THE SECOND DECADE OF PEACE

1930–1940

> *For precept must be upon precept, precept upon precept; line upon line, line upon line; here a little, and there a little.*

CHAPTER 11

THE SUPREME COURT UNDER HUGHES

Nil desperandum Teucro duce et auspice Teucro; . . .
Cras ingens iterabimus aequor.   HORACE, Odes, I, 7.

O N February 3rd, 1930, Chief Justice Taft resigned and
on the same day President Hoover appointed in his place
Charles Evans Hughes. Ten days later he was confirmed by
the Senate, and he took the oath as Chief Justice of the United
States on February 24th. And so at the age of sixty-eight,
when most prosperous lawyers are deciding whether to retire
to Florida or California, Mr. Hughes began the most important
work of his life.

Half of the eight Associate Justices in 1930 had come on the
bench during the ten years since the Abrams case, but the old
divergences persisted. The two dissenting Justices, Holmes
and Brandeis, were still dissenting together in all sorts of cases,
on the opposite side from the two remaining members of the
majority, Justices Van Devanter and McReynolds. These last
were now frequently joined by President Harding's appointees,
Justices Sutherland and Butler. The position of the other two
Associate Justices was less certain. Justice Stone, named by
President Coolidge, had gone with the majority in upholding
the convictions of Gitlow and Anita Whitney, but had dissented
with Justices Holmes and Brandeis on different constitutional
issues. Justice Sanford was with them at times, as in the
Schwimmer case discussed later, but mostly with the majority;
he died in June, 1930, before any free speech cases came before
the new Chief Justice, and was replaced by Justice Roberts.

One must not assume a rigid dividing line between two groups
in the Supreme Court. The preceding paragraph illustrates the
way the alignment constantly varies from case to case. Justices are not bound to stick to one cause through thick and thin

like delegates at a presidential convention. There is nobody on earth who can give them orders how to vote. Few men are so completely their own masters. Still, there are intellectual trends in the bench like those in the world at large. The divided decisions of the nineteen-twenties showed that, within a margin of variation, the same four Justices would probably be found in the majority much of the time and the two from Massachusetts would probably be dissenting. Furthermore, the dividing line in the Court was not a party line. This has been true of divided decisions since Marshall's time. For example, not one of the numerous free speech decisions discussed in this book had all the Republican Justices on one side and all the Democratic Justices on the other. Holmes agreed with Brandeis. McReynolds agreed with McKenna earlier and Sutherland later. Although party affiliations have always been considered in connection with an appointment to the Court, it was clear by 1930 that they really deserve less attention than some other factor in the man, which will evidently exert a much greater force upon his determination of the issues coming before him as Justice.[1]

The Senate debate on the confirmation of Hughes as Chief Justice was a significant event in the history of the Court for its recognition of the problem just stated. Political affiliations were ignored as Senators tried to express and appraise this *something else* which was swaying Justices to one side or the other. Some of them were inclined to simplify the problem and insist that Mr. Hughes's representation of wealthy individuals and large corporate clients would mold his future outlook as a judge. Senator Norris, still a Republican like Mr. Hughes, said: "No man in public life so exemplifies the influence of powerful combinations in the political and financial world."

This was a risky attitude for liberals to take. After all, the right of every man to the service of a lawyer is as much a part of our Bill of Rights and American traditions as the right of free speech. The great service of the American Civil Liberties

[1] This problem is more fully discussed in "The Economic Interpretation of Judges," in *The Inquiring Mind*, p. 254; and "Liberal Trends in the Supreme Court," *Current History*, XXXV, 338 (December, 1931).

The mental processes and emotional inclinations of individual Justices of the Supreme Court have been subjected to penetrating and thorough analysis in numerous writings by Thomas Reed Powell.

Union consists in upholding both traditions in the face of malignant attacks. If the Union had not existed or been less efficient, hundreds of men would have gone defenseless,[2] with only a slim chance of obtaining liberty of speech or a fair trial. We liberals cannot have it both ways. If we blame a prominent lawyer like Mr. Hughes for some of his clients, we are merely chiming in with those who constantly call the American Civil Liberties Union communistic because it has represented Communists along with the great many other defendants. Senator Newberry and the St. Paul Reorganization Committee are as much entitled to an able presentation of their causes as Gitlow and the I.W.W.'s. Surely liberals and radicals, above everybody else, ought to realize the dangers of spreading the doctrine that no decent lawyer should take the case of a man accused of conduct which is considered to be especially antisocial. The doctrine of guilt by association is abhorrent enough in the criminal and deportation fields without being extended into the relation between lawyer and client.

Any lawyer who is eminent enough to be named to the Supreme Court of the United States has too able and complex a mind to admit of such an easy explanation. Probably the best place to look, if you want to guess his future attitude toward important cases, is not in his file of clients or in his safe-deposit box but at the books in his private library at home.

An important proof of the subtle nature of the problem is that the judicial grouping found in free speech cases often carries over to entirely different controversies, like the constitutionality of the Agricultural Adjustment Act or of an Oklahoma statute limiting dealers in ice. And here comes the most striking fact of all. The Justices who uphold wide legislative control over business are often the very same men who want to invalidate any wide legislative control over discussion. Justice Stone has made some illuminating observations on this apparent inconsistency.[3] The paradox admits of no simple explanation, like: "These judges don't know anything about the worries of business men. They were little fellows themselves, and so they're always on the side of the little fellow.

---

[2] See *infra* Chapter XIV, note 61. on the disbarment of some of the few individual lawyers who were available to represent radicals.

[3] United States *v.* Carolene Products Co., 304 U. S. 144, 151 note 4 (1938).

They're out for the under-dog, whether he's a mortgaged farmer or a soap-box orator." After all, Justice Stone came to Washington from one of the largest corporate law offices in New York, while Justice McReynolds hailed from Tennessee where under-dogs are said to be so plentiful as to require an expensive Experiment to take care of them. And the letters and non-legal essays of Justice Holmes reveal an aristocratic mind, much out of patience with the radicalism which his judicial opinions placed under the protection of the Constitution.

The true solution of the paradox is, I venture to think, somewhat as follows: Thoughtful lawyers in their attitudes toward social and economic problems fall roughly into three groups. The first is composed of men who are satisfied with the existing situation and anxious to keep things as they are. Since they see their path straight ahead, they are likely to succeed in practice and they often fill the higher places on the bench. Justices McReynolds and Butler seem to be of this type. At the opposite extreme are lawyers who are very much dissatisfied with existing conditions and anxious to change them. Such men are not likely to become judges. The legislature or some executive position offers them much greater opportunities for putting their ideas into action, although an occasional member of this group like Brandeis may care for judicial work. In between these two extremes falls an intermediate group of lawyers who, though reasonably comfortable themselves, are nevertheless troubled by inequalities in power and fortune and are skeptical as to the eternal merits of the present rules of the game. Perhaps they would not do much themselves to change the existing situation, for example, if they were legislators. Yet they are reluctant to stop other men from trying to make things better. They are not sure enough of their own ideas to be certain that the reformers are wrong. Hence these lawyers on becoming judges are willing to let men whose minds put them in my second class go considerably farther than they would themselves. This last group comprises Justices Holmes and Stone.

It is clear that judges in the second and third groups will be inclined to support a considerable range of legislative power over property and business. And the same conception of freedom for change extends beyond law-makers to speakers and writers. These judges know that statutes, to be sound and effective, must be preceded by abundant printed and oral controversy. Discussion is really legislation in the soft. Hence drastic restrictions on speeches and pamphlets are comparable to rigid constitutional limitations on lawmaking. A statute which prevents an orator from questioning the present distribution of property tends to crystallize that distribution in somewhat the same way as a rigid interpretation of the due process clause. Therefore, the critical judicial spirit which gives the legislature a wide scope in limiting the privileges of property owners will also tend to allow speakers and writers a wide scope in arguing against those privileges. So it is not really surprising that Justice Holmes dissented in both *Lochner* v. *New York* [4] and *Abrams* v. *United States*. Liberty for the discussion which may lead to the formation of a dominant opinion belongs side by side with the liberty of lawmakers to transform this dominant opinion into the statute that is its natural outcome.

However this may be, a deeper consideration of Mr. Hughes's record would have lessened the apprehensions of men like Senator Norris. Many acts of his political career were not those of a reactionary. During the life-insurance investigations of 1906, he was considered such a dangerous radical that the leading trustees of his own university were outraged at his being invited to give a Commencement address to the alumni and stayed away from the meeting to avoid hearing him speak. As Governor of New York he put the state into the forefront of progressive legislation. The best evidence of his qualifications for Chief Justice was the hundred and fifty opinions he had written as Associate Justice between 1910 and 1916 — the years when the national current had turned strongly toward social democracy and was bearing the Court along with it. Many of these opinions combined an intimate knowledge of economic problems with a forward outlook. Moreover his subsequent representation of large business interests in court was no sure indication of his position on the bench. An office lawyer may have some difficulty in ceasing to think like the heads of wealthy corporations with whom he has spent years in close collaboration, but Mr. Hughes took merely a few weeks preparing a case, presented it in court, and then turned to the

[4] 198 U. S. 45, 74 (1904).

affairs of a wholly different client like the United Mine Workers. Furthermore, this period of advocacy came long after his opinions had matured. It was unlikely that the liberalism of his earlier years was completely submerged by the arguments made after he resumed practice at sixty-two. Mr. Hughes was primarily a lawyer, and as such he felt it his duty to represent loyally the client for whom he happened to be working. While in the Republican administration he was its strongest advocate, at the bar he spoke for those who had retained him. On the bench his client is the people of the United States, and there has never been any danger that he would be inclined to represent any other.

On freedom of speech, his attitude was unmistakable. We last saw him in this book upholding the cause of the Socialist Assemblymen in New York. In an address to the graduates of Harvard Law School in June, 1920,[5] he took a strong stand in favor of maintaining the Bill of Rights and denounced deportation outrages about which his fellow-statesmen were preserving a discreet silence. And even the unkind characterization of him by a political opponent as "One of the best minds of the eighteenth century" was praise when applied to issues of liberty. The standards of individual freedom were set high by the century of Voltaire, Jefferson, and Madison.

I. THE RED FLAG SALUTE

For a year after the new Chief Justice took office no question of freedom of speech came before the Court. Indeed, there had been a lull since the three syndicalism cases of 1927, which had been disturbed only once, by the Schwimmer case in 1929 soon to be described. Then, on each of three successive Mondays in the late spring of 1931, Chief Justice Hughes read an opinion upholding freedom of speech and thought against governmental action. Twice he spoke for the Court. Only once was he dissenting, and even then he was in a bare minority of four. Something new and astonishing had happened. What had been the lonely views of Justices Holmes and Brandeis were becoming the views of the majority of the Supreme Court. It was the first

[5] Quoted *supra*, p. 102; Chapter V, note 14.

winter for many years in which neither of these men wrote a dissenting opinion.

The first of these three decisions was *Stromberg* v. *California*,[6] on May 18th, involving one of the post-war red flag statutes which state courts had invariably held valid under their own free speech clauses.[7] Now the attack was based on the Fourteenth Amendment.

In this case the sensible plan was adopted by prosecution and defense of submitting to the Supreme Court a short summary of the evidence at the trial, to which they both agreed. If this admirable device could be generally used in sedition cases, it would make them much easier to decide and discuss. It saves all concerned from the bother of thumbing over a voluminous record of trial testimony, avoids the danger of leaving out something material in boiling down this record, and greatly reduces speculation about the basis of the jury's verdict, so often a cause of trouble and controversy.[8]

Yetta Stromberg, an American-born girl of Russian parentage, was a supervisor of a summer camp in the foothills of the San Bernardino Mountains for children between ten and fifteen years old. She herself was nineteen and a member of the Young Communist League, which was affiliated with the Communist Party. She led the children in their daily study of history and economics, stressing class consciousness and the doctrine that "the workers of the world are of one blood and brothers all." The camp library contained a number of books and pamphlets, many of them hers; and quotations from these by the state court in affirming her conviction abundantly demonstrated that they contained incitements to violence and to "armed uprisings," teaching "the indispensability of a des-

---

[6] 283 U. S. 359 (1931), revg. People *v.* Mintz, 106 Cal. App. 725 (1930). See 19 *California Law Review* 64; 21 *Journal of Criminal Law and Criminology* 618. The indeterminate sentence had a five-year maximum.

The Stromberg and Near cases are discussed by Foster, "The 1931 Personal Liberty Cases," 9 *New York University Law Quarterly Review* 64; Sharp, "Movement in Supreme Court Adjudication, etc.," 46 *Harvard Law Review* 361. See also "The Bill of Rights and the Fourteenth Amendment," 31 *Columbia Law Review* 468.

[7] See *supra* Chapter IV, section IV. The state cases are collected in 20 A. L. R. 1548; 73 *id.* 1495. A red flag city ordinance was held void in one case. — *In re* Hartman, 182 Cal. 447 (1920).

[8] For examples, see Espionage Act cases of Frohwerk, Debs, and Abrams. *Supra* pp. 82–86, and Chapter III.

perate, bloody, destructive war as the immediate task of the coming action." It was agreed, however, that none of these books or pamphlets were used in the teaching at the camp. She testified that nothing in the library, and particularly none of the exhibits containing radical communist propaganda, was in any way brought to the attention of any child or any other person, and that no word of violence or anarchism or sedition was employed in her teaching of the children. There was no evidence to the contrary.

The only charge against Yetta Stromberg concerned a ceremony which began every camp day. Under her direction a red flag was run up bearing a hammer and sickle — a camp-made reproduction of the flag of Soviet Russia and the Communist Party in this country. During this daily flag-raising, the children stood at salute by their cots and recited in unison: "I pledge allegiance to the workers' red flag and to the cause for which it stands, one aim throughout our lives, freedom for the working class."

Readers who have dashed half-clad to compulsory college chapel can easily imagine the effect of this routine ritual upon a ten-year-old boy just aroused from sleep. Even the frequent religious services at New England church schools have not been conspicuously successful in rendering their graduates regular churchgoers in after life. So the men who governed California might well have questioned the educational importance of a compulsory flag salute.[9]

The California authorities reacted quite otherwise. They arrested Yetta Stromberg [10] under the statute which made it a felony to display a red flag (or any flag or device) in a public assembly "(1) as a sign, symbol or emblem of opposition to organized government, or (2) as an invitation or stimulus to anarchistic action, or (3) as an aid to propaganda that is of a seditious character." [11] The camp flag was charged with possessing all three characteristics, and the jury found her guilty without saying why.

[9] See the educational authorities quoted by Clark, J., in Minersville School District v. Gobitis, 108 F. (2d) at 691–2 (C. C. A. 3d, 1939).

[10] The other camp counsellors were also prosecuted and convicted; but they were released by the state appellate court, which found no conspiracy or personal participation on their part. — 106 Cal. App. 725.

[11] Cal. Penal Code, § 403a; numerals inserted by me.

In order to upset her conviction, the Supreme Court did not need to decide that the whole statute was unconstitutional. It was enough if the clause under which she was convicted was bad. Obviously the first clause about "opposition to organized government" was the most vulnerable. Was she convicted of violating that? The state appellate court thought not, and preferred to bring the flag within the more repulsive phrases about anarchism and seditious propaganda, although the evidence of such purposes was very weak. But the three clauses were presented to the jurymen without sharp lines of separation;[12] the prosecutor and the trial judge left them free to convict her under the first clause alone. They brought in a general verdict of "Guilty" without indicating what they considered to be the purpose of the flag. Therefore, so far as anybody could tell, Yetta Stromberg was convicted and sentenced to possibly five years in prison merely for displaying a flag which symbolized opposition to government, without being either anarchistic or seditious. Such was the view of the Chief Justice, shared by all his associates except Justices McReynolds and Butler.[13] Consequently, the Chief Justice expressly refused to pass on the validity of the last part of the statute,[14] and concentrated all his attention on the first clause.

The indefiniteness of the broad words "symbol of opposition to organized government" is shown by the fact that they were applied in this case to the flag of Soviet Russia, one of the most rigidly organized governments on earth. They might include peaceful and orderly opposition, by legal and constitutional means, to the present political system or even to continued con-

---

[12] See the remarks, in connection with the Abrams case, about the danger of unfairness in cumulative charges in sedition trials. *Supra*, p. 114, note 8.

[13] The majority comprised the two old dissenters Holmes and Brandeis; two other older Justices, Van Devanter and Sutherland; three recent members, the Chief Justice, Stone, and Roberts. In dissenting, Justices McReynolds and Butler agreed with the state court that she was convicted under either of the last two clauses, which they considered valid. Justice Butler also failed to see how the mere display of a flag fell within liberty of speech; and thought that "the anarchy that is certain to follow a successful 'opposition to organized government'" was a sufficient reason to uphold the first clause of the statute.

[14] He made some observations about the indefiniteness of "anarchism" and "seditious." Even if "seditious" be limited to advocacy of forcible overthrow of the government, as the state court contended, Chief Justice Hughes left open its constitutionality. This bears on section 2 of the Alien Registration Act of 1940, discussed in Chapter XII.

trol of the present system by the party in power.[15] The statute might be used to stifle evolution without revolution by punishing the display of a flag which was "recognized as a symbol of independent thought containing the promise of progress." So Yetta Stromberg's conviction was set aside as depriving her of the "liberty" guaranteed her by the Fourteenth Amendment. The first clause of the California statute is void, and so is similar language in other red flag laws. The Chief Justice said:

> The maintenance of the opportunity for free political discussion to the end that government may be responsive to the will of the people and that changes may be obtained by lawful means, an opportunity essential to the security of the Republic, is a fundamental principle of our constitutional system. A statute which upon its face, and as authoritatively construed, is so vague and indefinite as to permit the punishment of the fair use of this opportunity is repugnant to the guaranty of liberty contained in the Fourteenth Amendment.

The implications of the Stromberg decision extend beyond the precise issue of red flags. First, it holds that a criminal statute may be unconstitutional for indefiniteness, which, as Chapter IV showed, is a frequent characteristic of sedition laws.[16] Second, it throws doubts on the validity of the concept of guilt by association, to be discussed in the next chapter. In considering the purpose of the red flag, the Court paid no attention to the prisoner's communistic affiliations. Third, constitutional protection is extended beyond liberty of speech in the narrow sense. As Justice Butler was quick to observe, a flag is not speech. It does not talk. Now, if the Fourteenth Amendment includes the communication of ideas by a flag, how about pictures or motion-pictures? Art Young's cartoons played a prominent part in the exclusion of *The Masses* from the mails, and arbitrary film censorship may easily deprive citizens of a chief stimulus to progressive thought.[17]

---

[15] The phrase "overthrow of the government" in England or Continental Europe may merely mean a change of the ministry in power, while for us it has a sinister connotation of revolutionary destruction of the Constitution. This ambiguity has played some part in American interpretation of radical documents based on European ideas.

[16] A statute making it criminal to be a "gangster" was subsequently invalidated for vagueness. — Lanzetta *v.* New Jersey, 306 U. S. 451 (1939).

[17] Film censorship is discussed *infra* Chapter XIV, section v.

II. TWO UNDESIRABLE CITIZENS

A week later, on May 25th, came the Macintosh case.[18] All the other important free speech cases since 1930 involved state or municipal action, but this decision raised a problem of federal law: Was Professor Macintosh of the Yale Divinity School, a Canadian aged fifty-four, rightly denied naturalization because he would not promise to bear arms in defense of the United States unless he believed the war to be morally justified?

Macintosh was a Baptist minister, born in 1877. In 1914 he gave up teaching at Yale to serve as chaplain in the Canadian forces in France. He returned to this country to speak for the Allies. In 1918 he had charge of a Y.M.C.A. hut at the front until the armistice. Then he came back to Yale, where he was Dwight Professor of Theology and Chaplain of the Graduate School. In 1925 he filed his first papers. One would suppose that such a career would have made him exceptionally welcome among the ranks of American citizens. Quite otherwise. His courageous services in an actual war counted for nothing against his unwillingness when past military age to fight in every hypothetical future war, whatever its aims.

No Act of Congress stated that willingness to bear arms or support war was a prerequisite to naturalization.[19] Anarchists

---

[18] United States v. Macintosh, 283 U. S. 605 (1931); revg. 42 F. (2d) 845 (C. C. A. 2d, 1930), which differentiated the Schwimmer case.

On the same day as the Macintosh case, naturalization was also denied by a similarly divided Court to a Canadian woman, an Episcopalian who had served the government nine months in France nursing the sick and wounded, but refused to bear arms in defense of the United States. — United States v. Bland, 283 U. S. 636 (1931); revg. 42 F. (2d) 842 (C. C. A. 2d, 1930). A brief was filed on behalf of Bishop Parsons of California and others as friends of the Court.

A valuable Symposium on the Macintosh case by J. H. Wigmore, K. C. Sears, Ernst Freund, Frederick Green, and R. W. Hale is in 26 *Illinois Law Review* 375 and 681. See also E. Wambaugh in 6 *Tulane Law Review* 132; C. E. Carpenter in 10 *Oregon Law Review* 375; 11 *Boston University Law Review* 532; 3 *Dakota Law Review* 429; 30 *Michigan Law Review* 133; 80 *University of Pennsylvania Law Review* 275.

A Socialist was later denied citizenship by a district court, on the ground that he had advocated such extensive amendments of the Constitution that he was not attached to its principles. *In re* Saralieff, 59 F. (2d) 436 (Mo. 1932). See 18 *Cornell Law Quarterly* 251; 1 *George Washington Law Review* 124; 46 *Harvard Law Review* 325; 8 *Wisconsin Law Review* 378.

[19] 8 U. S. C. A. §§ 381, 382. See § 364, replaced in 1940 by § 705.

and polygamists were expressly barred, but not a word about pacifists. One statute required each petitioner before admission to citizenship to swear in open court,

that I will support and defend the Constitution of the United States against all enemies, foreign and domestic, that I will bear true faith and allegiance to the same; that I take this obligation freely, without any mental reservation or purpose of evasion.

The same oath is required by law from Senators, Representatives, and most federal officials,[20] and must have been taken conscientiously by hundreds of Quakers who were devoted servants of the nation without any realization that the words "defending . . . against all enemies" obliged them to sacrifice their religious scruples against war. Applicants for passports must also use these identical words. Macintosh was ready to take the oath of allegiance, which he interpreted as consistent with his views on war given below, but could not do so if the oath forced him to agree to fight under all conditions. Another statute provides that it must "appear to the satisfaction of the court" that for at least five years the applicant "has behaved as a man of good moral character, attached to the principles of the Constitution of the United States, and well disposed to the good order and happiness of the same." Offhand a Divinity School professor would seem to fulfill these conditions better than most men.

The obstacle to the Macintosh naturalization did not lie in the wording of these statutes, but in a question to be answered by each applicant, which was framed by the officials of the Bureau of Naturalization: "22. If necessary, are you willing to take up arms in defense of this country?" To this Macintosh replied: "Yes; but I should want to be free to judge of the necessity." I quote from his later expansion of this reply in a written memorandum, and from part of Justice Sutherland's summary of his statement at the court hearing:

I am willing to do what I judge to be in the best interests of my country, but only in so far as I can believe that this is not going to be against the best interests of humanity in the long run. I do not

---

[20] The President takes a different form of oath, prescribed by the Constitution, not by Congress.

undertake to support "my country, right or wrong" in any dispute which may arise, and I am not willing to promise beforehand, and without knowing the cause for which my country may go to war, either that I will or that I will not "take up arms in defense of this country" however "necessary" the war may seem to be to the government of the day. . . .

He said that he was not a pacifist . . . . He was ready to give to the United States all the allegiance he ever had given or ever could give to any country, but he could not put allegiance to the government of any country before allegiance to the will of God. He did not anticipate engaging in any propaganda against the prosecution of a war which the government had already declared and which it considered to be justified; but he preferred not to make any absolute promise at the time of the hearing, because of his ignorance of all the circumstances which might affect his judgment with reference to such a war. He did not question that the government under certain conditions could regulate and restrain the conduct of the individual citizen, even to the extent of imprisonment. He recognized the principle of the submission of the individual citizen to the opinion of the majority in a democratic country; but he did not believe in having his own moral problems solved for him by the majority. The position thus taken was the only one he could take consistently with his moral principles and with what he understood to be the moral principles of Christianity. He recognized, in short, the right of the government to restrain the freedom of the individual for the good of the social whole; but was convinced, on the other hand, that the individual citizen should have the right respectfully to withhold from the government military services (involving, as they probably would, the taking of human life), when his best moral judgment would compel him to do so. He was willing to support his country, even to the extent of bearing arms, if asked to do so by the government, in any war which he could regard as morally justified.

The United States District Court in Connecticut ruled that he was not "attached to the principles of the Constitution" and refused to admit him as a citizen. The Circuit Court of Appeals reversed this decision, and the government thereupon appealed to the Supreme Court.

This problem had already come before the Court two years before, under conditions somewhat less favorable to naturalization; Taft was then Chief Justice.[21] Rosika Schwimmer, a

[21] United States *v.* Schwimmer, 279 U. S. 644 (1929), revg. 27 F. (2d) 742 (C. C. A. 7th, 1928). The majority opinion was by Justice Butler, with the

Hungarian woman of fifty who wrote children's stories and books on public questions, had sought to obtain American citizenship. Besides being an uncompromising pacifist, she admitted having no nationalistic feeling, only a "cosmic consciousness of belonging to the human family, shared by all those who believe that all human beings are the children of God." She did not wish to remain a subject of dictator Horthy, and found the United States nearest of all countries to her ideals of a democratic republic. The District Court's refusal of naturalization was upheld by a six to three decision of the Supreme Court. Justice Butler recognized that she strongly desired to become a citizen, but declined to add her to the number of conscientious objectors disclosed by the war, especially as she was disposed to influence others to a similar opposition to bearing arms. This decision roused Justice Holmes to his last dissenting opinion in a free speech case:

The applicant seems to be a woman of superior character and intelligence, obviously more than ordinarily desirable as a citizen of the United States. . . . So far as the adequacy of her oath is concerned I hardly can see how that is affected by the statement, inasmuch as she is a woman over fifty years of age, and would not be allowed to bear arms if she wanted to. . . . Surely it cannot show lack of attachment to the principles of the Constitution that she thinks that it can be improved. I suppose that most intelligent people think that it might be. Her particular improvement looking to the abolition of war seems to me not materially different in its bearing on this case from a wish to establish cabinet government as in England, or a single house, or one term of seven years for the President. To touch a more burning question, only a judge mad with partisanship would exclude because the applicant thought that the Eighteenth Amendment should be repealed. . . .

She is an optimist and states . . . her belief that war will disappear and that the impending destiny of mankind is to unite in peace-

concurrence of Taft, C.J., and Van Devanter, McReynolds, Sutherland, and Stone, JJ. The dissenters were Holmes, Brandeis, and Sanford, JJ.

The government's attitude is ably presented, with a review of many earlier cases, by the Chief Counsel of the Bureau of Naturalization, Henry B. Hazard, " 'Attachment to the Principles of the Constitution' as Judicially Construed . . . ," 23 *American Journal of International Law* 783. For other comments, see R. C. Pugh in 3 *University of Cincinnati Law Review* 462; 18 *Georgetown Law Journal* 273; 5 *Indiana Law Journal* 521; 3 *Southern California Law Review* 224; 16 *Virginia Law Review* 169; 38 *Yale Law Journal* 673.

ful leagues. I do not share that optimism . . . . But most people who have known [war] regard it with horror, as a last resort, and even if not yet ready for cosmopolitan efforts, would welcome any practicable combinations that would increase the power on the side of peace. The notion that the applicant's optimistic anticipations would make her a worse citizen is sufficiently answered by her examination, which seems to me a better argument for her admission than any that I can offer. Some of her answers might excite popular prejudice, but if there is any principle of the Constitution that more imperatively calls for attachment than any other it is the principle of free thought — not free thought for those who agree with us but freedom for the thought that we hate. I think that we should adhere to that principle with regard to admission into, as well as to life within this country. And recurring to the opinion that bars this applicant's way, I would suggest that the Quakers have done their share to make the country what it is, that many citizens agree with the applicant's belief and that I had not supposed hitherto that we regretted our inability to expel them because they believe more than some of us do in the teachings of the Sermon on the Mount.

Despite the Schwimmer decision, Professor Macintosh's case for citizenship did not appear hopeless. The composition of the Court had altered meanwhile. Since Justice Holmes and Brandeis might naturally continue their former views, three more votes would be needed; and these could be obtained if the two new appointees, Chief Justice Hughes and Justice Roberts, and only one member of the Schwimmer majority — possibly Justice Stone — could be convinced that there were good reasons for distinguishing the Schwimmer decision. Macintosh presented a stronger case for citizenship than Rosika Schwimmer. He was not an internationalist like her, and his more qualified pacifism was very close to the attitude of many thoughtful native-born Americans, who are not normally called conscientious objectors. Finally, his position was deeply religious. In construing broad statutory language so as to exclude him and incidentally all Quakers from citizenship, the Bureau of Naturalization and a District Court ran counter to the spirit, at least, of the constitutional provisions against test-oaths and interference with religious liberty. Hence the Society of Friends obtained leave to file a brief as friends of the Court, opposing the narrow interpretation of the oath of allegiance and "attachment to the principles of the Constitution." The oral argument for Macintosh was made by John W. Davis.

All in vain. Four of the hoped-for Justices were convinced, including Justice Stone; but Justice Roberts was not. He and the surviving members of the Schwimmer majority [22] were enough to keep Professor Macintosh still a Canadian.

Justice Sutherland, speaking for the majority, held that Macintosh fell within the Schwimmer case; and saw no sufficient reasons for disturbing the conclusion of the examining official and the district judge, who saw the petitioner and heard the evidence. He pointed out that the war power is very broad and tolerates no qualifications, except those found in the Constitution or international law. Therefore, exemption from military service for Quakers and other objectors is not protected by the Constitution, but is merely a privilege conferred by Congress, which can withdraw it whenever it thinks necessary. But Macintosh was not willing to become a citizen with this understanding.

In effect, he offers to take the oath of allegiance only with the qualification that the question whether the war is necessary or morally justified must, so far as his support is concerned, be conclusively determined by reference to his opinion.

When he speaks of putting his allegiance to the will of God above his allegiance to the government, it is evident, in the light of his entire statement, that he means to make *his own interpretation* of the will of God the decisive test which shall conclude the government and stay its hand. . . .

If the attitude of this claimant, as shown by his statements and the inferences properly to be deduced from them, be held immaterial to the question of his fitness for admission to citizenship, where shall the line be drawn? Upon what ground of distinction may we hereafter reject another applicant who shall express his willingness to respect any particular principle of the Constitution or obey any future statute only upon the condition that he shall entertain the opinion that it is morally justified? The applicant's attitude, in effect, is a refusal to take the oath of allegiance except in an altered form. The qualifications upon which he insists, it is true, are made by parol and not by way of written amendment to the oath; but the substance is the same.

It is not within the province of the courts to make bargains with those who seek naturalization. They must accept the grant and take

[22] Justices Van Devanter, McReynolds, Sutherland, and Butler.

the oath in accordance with the terms fixed by the law, or forego the privilege of citizenship. There is no middle choice. If one qualification of the oath be allowed, the door is opened for others, with utter confusion as the probable final result.

Several observations are suggested by this reasoning of the majority. First, it mistakes the issue. The question was not whether the Constitution prevented Congress from denying naturalization to Macintosh, but simply whether Congress had in fact denied it. When we remember all that Quakers have brought into our national life, it was going very far for the officials to transform a few statutory generalizations into a drastic rule shutting out from citizenship the Quakers who have come from abroad in recent years and everybody ·else who even approaches their religious and moral principles about war.

Second, we find here that curious insistence, which crops up every once in a while, that a man is incapable of taking an oath unless it means to him exactly what some person in authority thinks the oath ought to mean. The very essence of an oath is that it comes from the heart of the swearer and not from outside himself. Chief Justice Hughes must have been reminded of the insistence of Speaker Sweet that the New York Socialist Assemblymen were incapable of taking the oath of office.

Third, it is hard to see how the government was asked to make a bargain with Macintosh had he been admitted to citizenship. It would not have been under the slightest obligation to exempt him from military service in the improbable event that a man over fifty was needed for fighting. Macintosh, like any other citizen, could have been subjected to the coercion of a draft statute.

Finally, we may doubt the wisdom of a policy in selecting a new citizen which lays such enormous stress upon a single aspect of the petitioner's character. Only persons of especial thoughtfulness are likely to express the scruples which Macintosh did, and men of such thoughtfulness may very well possess, like Macintosh himself, qualities of inestimable value to the country which far offset any possible embarrassment about inducting him into the army. There are other ways of serving the country besides learning to kill. How would the United

States have been any worse off if Macintosh had spent the ten years since 1931 teaching at Yale as an American citizen, and not as a Canadian? The nation might not have gained an additional soldier by naturalizing him, but neither has it done so by not naturalizing. And it seems absurd to suggest that his peaceable views constituted a danger of infection to others, especially as Congress has never seen fit to add pacifism to its long list of opinions that render an alien deportable. There is something humorous in the denial of American citizenship to persons of high intelligence, public spirit, and humanitarian sympathies like Douglas Macintosh and Rosika Schwimmer on the single ground of their unwillingness to bear arms, while during the same decade of Prohibition a considerable number of naturalized citizens were disturbing the country by their excessive willingness to bear arms, especially sawed-off shot-guns and machine guns. A wise naturalization policy should not make everything turn on a single opinion of the petitioner, especially when age or sex makes that opinion of little practical importance. Instead, it would seem that admission should depend on a total impression of the petitioner's personality and devotion to American ideals. His views on the war power or the Eighteenth Amendment or any other part of the Constitution should merely constitute factors to be weighed in combination with his career as part of the common-sense process of determining whether this individual and his descendants will or will not be productive and valued citizens.[23]

The full force of the arguments for citizenship for Macintosh can best be felt by reading the entire dissenting opinion of the Chief Justice. Pacifism is even less popular today than it was in 1931, which makes it all the more important for me to reprint the following passage:

Much has been said of the paramount duty to the State, a duty to be recognized, it is urged, even though it conflicts with convictions of duty to God. Undoubtedly that duty to the State exists within the domain of power, for government may enforce obedience to laws regardless of scruples. When one's belief collides with the power of the State, the latter is supreme within its sphere and submission or punishment follows. But, in the forum of conscience, duty to a moral

[23] See Ohlson, "Moral Character and the Naturalization Act," 13 *Boston University Law Review* 636 (1933).

power higher than the State has always been maintained. The reservation of that supreme obligation, as a matter of principle, would unquestionably be made by many of our conscientious and law-abiding citizens. The essence of religion is belief in a relation to God involving duties superior to those arising from any human relation. One cannot speak of religious liberty, with proper appreciation of its essential and historic significance, without assuming the existence of a belief in supreme allegiance to the will of God. Professor Macintosh, when pressed by the inquiries put to him, stated what is axiomatic in religious doctrine. And, putting aside dogmas with their particular conceptions of deity, freedom of conscience itself implies respect for an innate conviction of paramount duty. The battle for religious liberty has been fought and won with respect to religious beliefs and practices, which are not in conflict with good order, upon the very ground of the supremacy of conscience within its proper field. What that field is, under our system of government, presents in part a question of constitutional law and also, in part, one of legislative policy in avoiding unnecessary clashes with the dictates of conscience. There is abundant room for enforcing the requisite authority of law as it is enacted and requires obedience, and for maintaining the conception of the supremacy of law as essential to orderly government, without demanding that either citizens or applicants for citizenship shall assume by oath an obligation to regard allegiance to God as subordinate to allegiance to civil power. The attempt to exact such a promise, and thus to bind one's conscience by the taking of oaths or the submission to tests, has been the cause of many deplorable conflicts. The Congress has sought to avoid such conflicts in this country by respecting our happy tradition. In no sphere of legislation has the intention to prevent such clashes been more conspicuous than in relation to the bearing of arms. It would require strong evidence that the Congress intended a reversal of its policy in prescribing the general terms of the naturalization oath. I find no such evidence.

III. THE NEWSPAPER GAG LAW

On June 1st, 1931, just before the Supreme Court adjourned, the Chief Justice read his third opinion on freedom of speech, this time for the majority of the Court. For years much had been written about "previous restraint" as antagonistic to free speech, but *Near* v. *Minnesota* [24] was the first case in which the Supreme Court actually had to pass on this subject.

[21] 283 U. S. 697 (1931). See Foster, cited *supra* note 6; Shulman in 41 *Yale Law Journal* 262; 31 *Columbia Law Review* 1148; 17 *Cornell Law Quar-*

A Minnesota statute provided for the abatement, as a public nuisance, of a "malicious, scandalous, and defamatory" newspaper, magazine, or other periodical, and also of obscene periodicals. Truth was a defense only if "published with good motives and for justifiable ends." Temporary or permanent injunctions might be granted against a newspaper, etc., of the forbidden type, not only enjoining repetition of objectionable issues, but also stopping the newspaper entirely. Citizens could start such a suit if the county attorney failed to do so.[25] Violation of the injunction would of course be punished by imprisonment for contempt.

Observe that this Minnesota Gag Law was more drastic than a criminal sedition act in three respects: (1) It was previous restraint as to future issues, even if not so as to issues already published. (2) There was no jury trial as to responsibility for publication or the wrongful nature of the language used. (3) It was not directed at a particular wrongful passage, but at the entire life of the newspaper.

The *Saturday Press* of Minnesota in 1927 published articles stating that a Jewish gangster was in control of gambling, bootlegging, and racketeering; and charging gross neglect of duty on the part of the law-enforcing officials, including the county attorney. This same county attorney then sued to suppress the newspaper which was calling him to account, and alleged that it was largely devoted to "malicious, scandalous, and defamatory articles." He got a temporary order forbidding the defendants to publish, circulate or have in their possession any editions for two months back, any future editions of the same newspaper, and any publication by any other name containing malicious, scandalous, and defamatory matter. The objection of the manager, Near, that the statute was unconstitutional was overruled by the highest state court.[26] The question then went to trial to ascertain the criminal character of the newspaper. The only evidence consisted of several past issues. A permanent injunction was granted in the same terms as above, with findings of fact concluding the newspaper to be

terly 126; 22 *Journal of Criminal Law and Criminology* 909; 14 *Minnesota Law Review* 787; 16 *id.* 97; 4 *Southern California Law Review* 66.

[25] Minn. Laws 1925, c. 285.

[26] State *v.* Guilford, 174 Minn. 457 (1928).

a public nuisance and judgment that it be abated. This decree was also affirmed [27] and Near went to the United States Supreme Court invoking the Fourteenth Amendment.

If the Court had been disposed to draw the old-fashioned line between liberty and license, then the numerous quotations from the columns of this newspaper in Justice Butler's dissenting opinion show that it belonged far on the license side of the line. Here is just a sample: "Practically every vendor of vile hooch, every owner of a moonshine still, every snake-faced gangster and embryonic yegg in the Twin Cities is a JEW." But the Chief Justice stood firmly by that most important principle of freedom of speech, that "the rights of the best of men are secure only as the rights of the vilest and most abhorrent are protected." [28] The statute set up a new kind of censure of newspapers and magazines. If this scandal-sheet could be thus stamped out, so could less vituperative criticism of public officials. The offended officials only needed to find a judge who shared their opinion that the criticism passed legitimate bounds.

The Court invalidated the Minnesota statute as an improper deprivation of liberty of the press, by a five to four decision. The minority comprised members of the Gitlow and Whitney majorities — Justices Van Devanter, McReynolds, Sutherland, and Butler. Justice Butler's dissenting opinion emphasized the practical need for such legislation:

It is well known . . . that existing libel laws are inadequate effectively to suppress evils resulting from the kind of business and publications that are shown in this case. The doctrine that measures such as the one before us are invalid . . . as previous restraints . . . exposes the peace and good order of every community and the business and private affairs of every individual to the constant and protracted false and malicious assaults of any insolvent publisher who may have purpose and sufficient capacity to contrive and put into effect a scheme or program for oppression, blackmail, or extortion.

The Chief Justice's majority opinion was supported by the old-time dissenters, Justices Holmes and Brandeis, together with

[27] *Id.*, 179 Minn. 40 (1929).
[28] Pound, J., dissenting in People *v.* Gitlow, quoted *supra*, p. 321. For the same principle differently worded, see Holmes, J., dissenting in the Abrams and Schwimmer cases, *supra*, pp. 137, 371, and Lord Chatham, *supra*, p. 242.

the two latest appointees, Justices Stone and Roberts. The Chief Justice pointed out that the purpose of the statute was not punishment, but suppression. And it was directed, not simply at the circulation of defamatory statements about private citizens, but at the continued publication by newspapers of charges of corruption, malfeasance, or serious neglect of duty on the part of public officers. Such charges by their nature create a public scandal within the meaning of the statute. Therefore, since truth was not necessarily a defense, the law would have its normal operation against newspapers dealing with alleged derelictions of officials. A newspaper publisher who undertook to conduct a campaign to expose official misconduct must face, not only the possibility of an adverse jury verdict in a libel damage suit or a criminal libel prosecution, but also a single judge's determination that his newspaper was a public nuisance to be totally stopped. More than that. After his newspaper had been suppressed, he himself was put under an effective censorship. If he started a new publication he could go to jail for contempt unless he could satisfy the court as to its character. "Whether he would be permitted again to publish matter deemed to be derogatory to the same or other public officers would depend upon the court's ruling." So if we cut through mere details of procedure, the statute enabled the public authorities to bring before a judge the owner of any newspaper which attacked them; and unless he could produce enough evidence to satisfy the judge that his charges were true and published with motives the judge thought good and for ends the judge thought justifiable, his newspaper would be suppressed and he himself would have difficulty in staying in the newspaper business. "This is of the essence of censorship."

The next question was whether a statute so operating was consistent with liberty of the press as historically conceived and guaranteed. The Chief Justice reviewed the historical materials, some of which are set forth in the first chapter of this book. He relied strongly on Blackstone's statement that "the liberty of the press consists in laying no *previous* restraints upon publication." [29] Criticism of Blackstone's definition has been based on its failure to protect newspapers and books from

[29] See *supra*, pp. 9–12. The Chief Justice expressly left open the constitutionality of an injunction against a libel in a suit brought by the person defamed. See *supra*, p. 9; Chapter VIII, note 10.

subsequent punishment; nobody has objected that immunity from previous restraints does not deserve special emphasis. It is true that this immunity is not absolutely unlimited. But limitations have been recognized only in exceptional cases like disclosures of the sailing dates of transports or the location of troops. "On similar grounds, the primary requirements of decency may be enforced against obscene publications." And perhaps an injunction might be issued against incitements to acts of violence or the overthrow by force of orderly government. These limitations are not applicable in the Near case, and their exceptional nature places in a strong light "the general conception that liberty of the press, historically considered and taken up by the Federal Constitution, has meant, principally although not exclusively, immunity from previous restraints or censorship. The conception of the liberty of the press in this country had broadened with the exigencies of the colonial period and with the efforts to secure freedom from oppressive administration. That liberty was especially cherished for the immunity it afforded from previous restraint of the publication of censure of public officers and charges of official misconduct."

Madison is quoted:

Some degree of abuse is inseparable from the proper use of everything, and in no instance is this more true than in that of the press. It has accordingly been decided by the practice of the States, that it is better to leave a few of its noxious branches to their luxuriant growth, than, by pruning them away, to injure the vigour of those yielding the proper fruits. . . . Had "Sedition Acts" forbidding every publication that might bring the constituted agents into contempt or disrepute, or that might excite the hatred of the people against the authors of unjust or pernicious measures, been uniformly enforced against the press, might not the United States have been languishing at this day under the infirmities of a sickly Confederation? Might they not, possibly, be miserable colonies, groaning under a foreign yoke?

From this historical survey the Chief Justice goes on to emphasize the great value of immunity from previous restraint today:

The fact that for approximately one hundred and fifty years there has been almost an entire absence of attempts to impose previous restraints upon publications relating to the malfeasance of public officers is significant of the deep-seated conviction that such restraints would violate constitutional right. Public officers, whose character and conduct remain open to debate and free discussion in the press, find their remedies for false accusations in actions under libel laws providing for redress and punishment, and not in proceedings to restrain the publication of newspapers and periodicals. . . .

The importance of this immunity has not lessened. While reckless assaults upon public men, and efforts to bring obloquy upon those who are endeavoring faithfully to discharge official duties, exert a baleful influence and deserve the severest condemnation in public opinion, it cannot be said that this abuse is greater, and it is believed to be less, than that which characterized the period in which our institutions took shape. Meanwhile, the administration of government has become more complex, the opportunities for malfeasance and corruption have multiplied, crime has grown to most serious proportions, and the danger of its protection by unfaithful officials and of the impairment of the fundamental security of life and property by criminal alliances and official neglect, emphasizes the primary need of a vigilant and courageous press especially in great cities. The fact that the liberty of the press may be abused by miscreant purveyors of scandal does not make any the less necessary the immunity of the press from previous restraint in dealing with official misconduct. Subsequent punishment for such abuses as may exist is the appropriate remedy, consistent with constitutional privilege.

And finally the statute is not valid on the ground that it is designed to prevent scandal, breaches of the peace, assaults and so on.

. . . the theory of the constitutional guaranty is that even a more serious public evil would be caused by authority to prevent publication. . . . There is nothing new in the fact that charges of reprehensible conduct may create resentment and the disposition to resort to violent means of redress, but this well-understood tendency did not alter the determination to protect the press against censorship and restraint upon publication. . . . The danger of violent reactions becomes greater with effective organization of defiant groups resenting exposure, and if this consideration warranted legislative interference with the initial freedom of publication, the constitutional protection would be reduced to a mere form of words.

The Near case had no immediate effect beyond voiding the Minnesota statute, which is said to have grown out of a nasty

local situation. There had been no imitation of this Gag Law
in other states like the rapid spread of syndicalism acts. Still,
authorities are constantly subject to the temptation of imposing
some kind of rigid control on objectionable criticism. Here was
a new and very efficient device for that purpose. So probably it would soon have been copied elsewhere except for
this decision. And the broader implications of *Near* v. *Minnesota* make it one of the most important of all the free speech
cases in the Supreme Court. Its strong hostility to previous
restraints against the expression of ideas may conceivably
be applied to quite different forms of censorship, affecting
other media of communication besides the press. Newspapers,
books, pamphlets, and large meetings were for many centuries
the only means of public discussion, so that the need for their
protection has long been generally realized. On the other hand,
when additional methods for spreading facts and ideas were
introduced or greatly improved by modern inventions, writers
and judges had not got into the habit of being solicitous about
guarding their freedom. And so we have tolerated censorship
of the mails, the importation of foreign books, the stage, the
motion picture, and the radio. In an age when the film and the
broadcasting station have become rivals of the newspaper for
the transmission of news, the new judicial attitude evidenced in
Near v. *Minnesota* may have important consequences.[30] And it
may also affect sedition injunctions like those against the Rand
School and the I.W.W.

IV. TAXES ON KNOWLEDGE

After this rapid succession of free speech cases, five years
went by without any more coming before the Supreme Court.
Meanwhile, Justice Holmes resigned, and President Hoover
made his second appointment of an Associate Justice, Benjamin
Nathan Cardozo. In 1936 the Court was asked to consider an
entirely different sort of previous restraint on the press — a
heavy state tax on newspapers. Although the undesirability
of such "taxes on knowledge" had been frequently discussed
by historians, the judicial problem of their validity was almost
unprecedented.[31]

[30] See the excellent Note in 31 *Columbia Law Review* 1148 (1931).
[31] The few cases noted had all upheld newspaper taxes. Preston *v.* Finley,

The facts of *Grosjean* v. *American Press Co.*[32] were as follows: Louisiana had, in addition to all other taxes, imposed a 2 per cent tax on the gross receipts of any newspaper, magazine, etc., engaged in selling advertisements in the state and having a circulation of more than 20,000 per week. This figure had been neatly selected to hit the newspapers opposed to the Long dictatorship and exempt all the small papers which supported it. Instead of waiting to contest the validity of the tax after payment or incurring heavy penalties for non-payment, the nine newspaper publishers who fell within the law brought suit in the United States District Court to enjoin its enforcement. A permanent injunction was granted, and this was unanimously affirmed by the Supreme Court.

The tax was assailed on two grounds, as an abridgment of liberty of the press guaranteed by the due process clause of the Fourteenth Amendment, and as unfairly discriminating against large newspapers in violation of another clause of the same amendment entitling all persons to equal protection of the laws. If the Court had wished to avoid deciding the difficult free speech problem, it might easily have done so by declaring the tax bad on the second ground. Instead it took the bull by the horns, ignored the second ground of unfair discrimination against the larger newspapers, and based its decision squarely on liberty of the press.

In this case the opinion was written by Justice Sutherland. It contains a valuable review of the history of newspaper taxes. Parliament had repeatedly imposed heavy stamp taxes on newspapers with the undoubted purpose of suppressing criticisms objectionable to the government. These "taxes on knowledge" had the intended effect of curtailing the circulation of newspapers, and particularly the cheaper ones whose readers were generally found among the common people. A famous victim of such a law was William Cobbett's *Political*

---

72 Fed. 850 (C. C. Tex. 1896) ; New Orleans v. Crescent Newspaper, 14 La. Ann. 816 (1859) ; Information against Jager, 29 S. C. 438 (1888) ; Norfolk v. Norfolk Landmark Pub. Co., 95 Va. 564 (1898).

[32] 297 U. S. 233 (1936); affg. 10 F. Supp. 161 (La. 1935). See 5 *Brooklyn Law Review* 328; 49 *Harvard Law Review* 998; 20 *Minnesota Law Review* 671. On the procedural point of enjoining collection of the tax, see Deutsch, "Federal Equity Jurisdiction of Cases involving the Freedom of the Press," 25 *Virginia Law Review* 507 (1939).

Register, popularly called "Twopenny Trash."[33] Although
English liberals steadily fought against these stamp taxes, they
were not wholly removed until 1855. In 1785 the Massachusetts legislature had followed English precedents by imposing
a stamp tax on all newspapers and magazines, and the next
year an advertisement tax. Both met with violent opposition
and were soon repealed. These facts, Justice Sutherland says,
must be considered in construing the words "freedom of
the press" in the Constitution, which are now carried from the
First Amendment as part of the "liberty" guaranteed by the
Fourteenth. The framers of the First Amendment were familiar
with the English struggle, and with the controversy in Massachusetts. It is impossible, he thinks, that the framers intended
the words "freedom of the press" to adopt merely the narrow
view then embodied in English law that such freedom consisted
only in immunity from previous censorship; for this abuse had
then permanently disappeared from English practice. It is
equally impossible to believe that they did not intend to bring
within the reach of these words the modes of restraint on the
press which were accomplished by heavy newspaper taxes, in
view of the well-known purpose of such taxes and the general
hostility toward them in the colonies. Although sometimes a
constitutional provision should be construed in accordance with
contemporary common law, this is surely not so when the
common law rule was rejected by our ancestors as unsuited to
their civil or political conditions. This reasoning lends support
to the argument in my first chapter that the First Amendment
did not take over the English common law doctrines of sedition.

Of course, newspapers like any other business are subject
to the ordinary forms of taxation for support of the government,
but this is an unusual tax directed especially against newspapers, with a long history of hostile misuse against the freedom
of the press.

The predominant purpose of the grant of immunity here invoked
was to preserve an untrammeled press as a vital source of public
information. The newspapers, magazines and other journals of the
country, it is safe to say, have shed and continue to shed, more light
on the public and business affairs of the nation than any other instru-

[33] See Cole, *Life of William Cobbett*, pp. 80, 135, 207, 225, 239, 312, 350
(1924).

mentality of publicity; and since informed public opinion is the most potent of all restraints upon misgovernment, the suppression or abridgement of the publicity afforded by a free press cannot be regarded otherwise than with grave concern. The tax here involved is bad not because it takes money from the pockets of the appellees. If that were all, a wholly different question would be presented. It is bad because, in the light of its history and of its present setting, it is seen to be a deliberate and calculated device in the guise of a tax to limit the circulation of information to which the public is entitled in virtue of the constitutional guaranties. A free press stands as one of the great interpreters between the government and the people. To allow it to be fettered is to fetter ourselves.

V. THE LATEST SYNDICALISM CASE

De Jonge v. *Oregon*,[34] decided the next year, shows the way sedition laws actually operate in state courts.[35] The Communist Party in 1934 organized a public meeting in Portland, advertised by handbills, to protest against the shooting of striking longshoremen by the police and against illegal raids on workers' halls and homes. Some members estimated that not over 15 per cent of those present were Communists. The meeting was conducted in an orderly manner. De Jonge and the other speakers stuck closely to the subjects for which it was called, except for asking the audience to do more work in obtaining members for the party and to purchase some communist literature sold at the meeting; this did not advocate criminal syndicalism or any other unlawful conduct. While the meeting was in progress, it was raided by the police, who arrested De Jonge and several others who were conducting it These facts are taken from the agreed statement on which this case (like the Stromberg case) went to the Supreme Court, and from the admissions of the Attorney General during the oral argument.

De Jonge was indicted under the Oregon Syndicalism Act [36] on

[34] 299 U. S. 353 (1937); revg. 152 Ore. 315 (1936). See 25 *California Law Review* 496; 4 *University of Chicago Law Review* 489; 37 *Columbia Law Review* 857; 50 *Harvard Law Review* 689; 14 *New York University Law Quarterly Review* 369; C. E. Spencer, 16 *Oregon Law Review* 278; 46 *Yale Law Journal* 862.

[35] For another example from Oregon, see State *v.* Boloff, 138 Ore. 568 (1932), discussed in Chapter XII, at note 81.

[36] The Oregon Criminal Syndicalism Act was Code, 1930, §§ 14 — 3110–3113,

the ground that on this specified day he "did then and there
. . . conduct and assist in conducting an assemblage of persons, organization, society and group, to-wit: the Communist
Party, . . . which said assemblage of persons, organizations,
society and group did then and there . . . teach and advocate
the doctrine of criminal syndicalism and sabotage . . . ." His
defense was that the meeting was public and orderly and held
for a lawful purpose; and that neither criminal syndicalism
nor any unlawful conduct was taught or advocated at the
meeting either by him or by others. The evidence at the trial,
as already summarized, failed to show anything unlawful done
or spoken at the meeting. The prosecution proceeded to introduce communist literature found somewhere else to show that
the party advocated criminal syndicalism. De Jonge, on the
theory that the charge was that unlawful doctrines were urged
at the meeting, moved for an acquittal, which was denied. So
he was convicted and sentenced to seven years in prison. De
Jonge was a Communist anyhow, and that was enough. All
I can think of is the remark of an aristocratic Kentuckian in
post-Reconstruction days, that when he saw a Negro out after
dark he always shot him because he knew he wasn't out for
any good.

Offhand it looks as if De Jonge were indicted for unlawful
acts at a meeting, and then convicted for belonging to an unlawful party. Of course, that would not be due process of
law. But when he went with this contention to the highest
court in Oregon, the court said that was not the case at all —
the indictment did not refer to anything said or done at the
meeting, but to the advocacy of syndicalism and sabotage by
the Communist Party of America. Hence, all that was necessary
to show his guilt was that De Jonge had participated in a meeting called by the Communist Party, regardless of the innocence
of the meeting. So the conviction was sustained.

---

as amended by Laws, 1933, c. 459. This was repealed after the De Jonge decision by Laws, 1937, c. 362; and a simple conspiracy statute was substituted.
See *infra* Chapter XII, at note 82.

Syndicalism acts of the various states are collected in Appendix III. For
recent surveys of such legislation, see 35 *Columbia Law Review* 917 (1935);
84 *University of Pennsylvania Law Review* 390 (1936). A recent trial is described in "The Sacramento Criminal Syndicalism Cases," 4 *International Juridical Assn. Monthly Bulletin* No. 6, p. 4 (November 1935).

This dodging back and forth between the meeting and the party came to a sudden stop in the Unitel States Supreme Court. The unanimous decision [37] voiced by the Chief Justice accepted the state court's interpretation of the indictment, and boiled the issue down to this — Could a man be imprisoned for seven years for nothing else except assisting in the conduct of a meeting whose only alleged unlawfulness lay in its being called by the Communist Party?

The state of Oregon was ready to say just that. Its argument before the Court was as follows:

The State has determined, through its legislative body, that to preside at, conduct, or assist in conducting a meeting of an organization which has as its objective the advocacy, teaching or affirmative suggestion of crime, sabotage or violence as a means of effecting a change or revolution in industry or government, involves such dangers to the public peace and the security of the State, that these acts should be penalized in the exercise of its police power. . . .

The sole purpose of the Act is to prevent the advocacy or use of violence by forbidding anyone to preside at, conduct or assist in conducting a meeting of an organization which teaches it. Laws of this type are founded upon the principle that morons, especially those who are class conscious, and who believe that men in high places got there through imposition upon the toilers, are likely to translate into action the words of their voluble leaders. The will of the schemer is often carried out by the acts of the unthinking.

The Chief Justice gave these contentions short shrift. They amounted to saying that whenever the Communist Party called a meeting to discuss relief or the election of a candidate for Congress or the Presidency, every speaker at this meeting could be sent to jail.

That must not be. "Peaceable assembly for lawful discussion cannot be made a crime." It makes no difference whether the Communist Party advocates force and violence or not — a question which the Chief Justice expressly left open. If the right of assembly is to be preserved, the question is not as to the auspices under which the meeting is held, but its purpose; not as to the outside relations of the speakers, but whether they say anything unlawful. If De Jonge or anybody else at the meeting had committed a crime elsewhere, he could be

[37] Justice Stone took no part in this case.

prosecuted for that. If the state wanted to charge him with being a member of the Communist Party or soliciting members or distributing literature, let it do so in the proper way. If he was guilty of sabotage, then try him for it. But what the state must not do is to "seize upon mere participation in a peaceable assembly and a lawful public discussion as the basis for a criminal charge." Whatever the objectives of the Communist Party, the defendant was still "entitled to discuss the public issues of the day and in a lawful manner, without incitement to violence or crime, to seek redress of alleged grievances. That was of the essence of his guaranteed personal liberty."

The greater the importance of safeguarding the community from incitements to the overthrow of our institutions by force and violence, the more imperative is the need to preserve inviolate the constitutional rights of free speech, free press and free assembly in order to maintain the opportunity for free political discussion, to the end that government may be responsive to the will of the people and that changes, if desired, may be obtained by peaceful means. Therein lies the security of the Republic, the very foundation of constitutional government.

The De Jonge case pushes still farther the expansion of "liberty" in the Fourteenth Amendment, and throws new light on its relations to the first ten amendments, which were adopted in 1791 as the Federal Bill of Rights. More than a hundred years ago Chief Justice Marshall decided that these ten amendments, in spite of their general language, limit only the national government and not the states.[38] For a while after the Fourteenth Amendment was adopted, it was supposed that it imposed upon the states all the restrictions which the original Bill of Rights imposed upon the nation. However, it has long been settled that this is not altogether true. There are some liberties which the states can abridge although the federal government cannot. For example, a state can reduce the jury in a criminal case to eight men; it can bring pressure on the accused to take the stand at his trial; it can probably abolish jury trial in civil cases. And in the important recent case of *Palko* v. *Connecticut*,[39] Justice Cardozo held that a state can pass a statute

[38] Barron *v.* Baltimore, 7 Peters (U. S.) 243 (1833).
[39] 302 U. S. 319 (1937).

allowing it to appeal from an acquittal for crime; the prohibition of the Fifth Amendment against double jeopardy is not
carried over into the Fourteenth Amendment. At the same
time, he summarized several previous decisions holding that
the guarantee of liberty in the Fourteenth Amendment does
prevent the states from encroaching on many of the rights
which are specified in the first ten amendments. This strong protection is given to those rights which are, he said, "of the very
essence of a scheme of ordered liberty" and "so rooted in the
traditions and conscience of our people as to be ranked as
fundamental." Among these he named the rights guaranteed
by the First Amendment. One by one, the phrases of Madison
have been read into the simple word "liberty" in the amendment of 1868. The Gitlow case expanded "liberty" to include
"freedom of speech." The Near and Grosjean cases added "freedom of the press." And now the De Jonge case included among
those liberties which the state cannot take away "the right of
the people peaceably to assemble, and to petition the Government for a redress of grievances." Finally the Cantwell case
in 1940 brought in "the free exercise of religion."

VI. *ROUGE ET NOIR*

Herndon v. *Lowry* [40] was another sedition case of the same
year, the first to come to the Court from the South.

Angelo Herndon was a Communist Negro, who had gone as
a paid organizer to Atlanta where he enrolled at least five members and held three meetings. When arrested he carried under
his arm a box of membership blanks and pamphlets, and the
police found bundles of more in his room. The authorities
were especially concerned over a booklet named *The Communist Position on the Negro Question.* On its cover was a
map of the United States, with a dark belt across several
Southern states and the phrase "Self-Determination for the
Black Belt." Its author urged that the Black Belt should be
made one governmental unit, ruled by the negro majority.
This interstate domain was to be freed from class rule and
from American imperialism, even to the point of deciding its
foreign relations with other nations and with the government

---

[40] 301 U. S. 242 (1937), revg. 182 Ga. 582 (1936). See 34 *Columbia Law
Review* 1357; 50 *Harvard Law Review* 1313; 35 *Michigan Law Review* 1373.

of the United States. Lands of whites were to be confiscated for the benefit of negro farmers. It also advocated strikes, boycotts, and a revolutionary struggle for power against the white bourgeoisie, "even if the situation does not yet warrant the raising of the question of uprising." There was no evidence that he had distributed any of this material except membership blanks and two innocuous circulars about county relief.

Georgia has the distinction of being one of the few states that did not enact a sedition statute after the World War. However, the authorities dug up an old law which might serve to incarcerate such unwelcome visitors. Before the Civil War Georgia had a statute punishing with death anybody who attempted, by speech or writing, to excite an insurrection of slaves.[41] An accompanying provision imposed the same penalty on anybody who brought in printed matter calculated to excite a slave insurrection; this was to take care of Garrison's *Liberator* and other Abolitionist publications. After Appomattox, the legislature dropped out the references to slaves; but these laws stayed on the statute book, never enforced so far as reported cases show until the following section was invoked against Herndon and his fellow Communists: [42]

Any attempt, by persuasion or otherwise, to induce others to join in any combined resistance to the lawful authority of the State shåll constitute an attempt to incite insurrection.

The penalty is still death; but if the jury recommends mercy, then imprisonment for five to twenty years.

So a statute inspired by Nat Turner's Rebellion in 1832 was first used against Communist organizers in 1932. Herndon was indicted for attempting to incite an insurrection, with intent to overthrow the government of Georgia by open force.

[41] Ga. Code, 1861, § 4214.
[42] Ga. Code Ann., 1933, §26 —.902. This corresponds to Irwin's Rev. Code, 1868, § 4251, with slight changes made by Acts, 1871-2, pp. 19–20. The only other reported case under this statute took place the same year as the Herndon case, and the conviction was sustained by the state court on similar grounds. — Carr *v.* State, 176 Ga. 55 (1932); *id.* 747 (1933). About the same time Mary Dalton and other Communists were indicted under the different statute, which had originally been aimed at Garrison's *Liberator*, for circulating insurrectionary pamphlets and magazines including the *Daily Worker*, the Communist Manifesto by Marx and Engels, and *Woman in the Soviet Union*. — Dalton *v.* State, 176 Ga. 645 (1933), indictment held good.

The evidence at the trial was as already indicated.[43] The judge charged the jury that, in order to convict the defendant, "it must appear clearly by the evidence that *immediate violence* against the state of Georgia was to be expected or advocated." Herndon was convicted. The jury could have let him be hanged, but it recommended mercy and only sent him to prison for eighteen or twenty years.

Herndon claimed a new trial, for want of any evidence of his advocating the *immediate* violence required by the trial judge. The highest court in Georgia held that lack of this evidence was immaterial; the trial judge had construed the statute too narrowly; it really made him guilty if he intended insurrection "to happen *at any time*, as a result of his influence." On rehearing, the court said "at any time" meant *a reasonable time.* So the conviction was affirmed, inasmuch as the court found in the Black Belt booklets sufficient intention of a real revolution some day or other. It felt sure Herndon expected to distribute these booklets, else why did he have them around.[44] This unexpected broad interpretation of the law led Herndon to invoke the Fourteenth Amendment for the first time and try to get to the United States Supreme Court. His lateness made the task very difficult,[45] but at last a writ of *habeas corpus* was directed to Lowry, the sheriff.

Then the Supreme Court, by a bare majority, released Herndon. The Court's opinion was delivered by Justice Roberts, with the support of the Chief Justice and Justices Brandeis, Stone, and Cardozo.

Justice Roberts concentrated his attention on the two worst groups of evidence: (1) The membership blanks vaguely declared the Communist Party to be the party of the working class, personifying "proletarian revolutionary action." This, he concluded, "falls short of an attempt to bring about insurrection either immediately or within a reasonable time." More specific aims like unemployment insurance, emergency relief

---

[43] The indictment and evidence are briefly described here, because an adequate summary would cover several pages. Full information can readily be obtained from 301 United States Reports.

[44] Herndon v. State, 178 Ga. 832 (1934).

[45] The Supreme Court at first refused to consider the case at all. Herndon v. Georgia, 295 U. S. 441 (1935), affg. 179 Ga. 597 (1934). See 35 *Columbia Law Review* 1145; 49 *Harvard Law Review* 150; 30 *Illinois Law Review* 530; 20 *Minnesota Law Review* 216; 84 *University of Pennsylvania Law Review* 256.

for poor farmers, their exemption from taxes and debts, opposition to wage-cuts, and equal rights for Negroes, were not criminal upon their face. (2) The prosecution asserted that the demand for equal racial rights was rendered criminal by extrinsic facts like the Black Belt booklets in Herndon's possession, which showed the Communist Party aiming at forcible subversion of the lawful authority of Georgia. But Justice Roberts did not consider these booklets an attempt to cause insurrection. First, no evidence showed that Herndon distributed or even approved of them. Secondly, "the fantastic programme they envisaged" was no more than "an ultimate ideal." Nothing indicated that Herndon wanted to establish the Black Belt Free State at once or made it one of his principal aims. All he talked about, according to the state's proof, was relief.

To interject my own views for a moment, this old statute is valid in itself. A real attempt to cause a real insurrection in Georgia could of course be punished severely. But that does not mean that anything the community dislikes can be called an attempt. The word has a well-established meaning in our common law.[46] A criminal attempt requires more than a bad intention or even a slight overt act in pursuance thereof. The defendant must do enough to bring his unlawful intention reasonably near to a successfully completed crime. The attempt test, as Holmes's opinions show, is related to his free speech test of "clear and present danger." The evil-minded man must get well down the path toward his destination before he is guilty of an attempt as defined by the common law.[47] No matter how much Herndon intended to circulate his material, this was just looking along the path. It takes a good deal more than a war-map to make a victory.

Visualize a slave insurrection such as this statute was originally enacted to prevent, and then think of what Herndon did. It is hard to believe that anybody in Atlanta actually saw any

[46] See *supra* pp. 23, 47–48, 152. See also Hall, "The Substantive Law of Crimes — 1887–1936," 50 *Harvard Law Review* 616, 619–622 (1937).

[47] The legislature can, if it desires, expressly enlarge the common law scope of attempt and push the critical point back nearer the beginning of the path. — Commonwealth *v.* Mehales, 284 Mass. 412 (1933). But the Georgia statute merely used the word "attempt," with no qualifications, so it should be regarded as an expression of the common law of criminal attempts, especially when occurring in such an old statute.

resemblance. My guess is that the men concerned in this
prosecution were not worried in the slightest about any plotted
insurrection or the possibility of a new Liberia between the
Tennessee Valley Authority and the Gulf of Mexico. But they
were worried, I suspect, about something else that Herndon
really wanted — his demand for equal rights for Negroes. If
he got going with that, there was a clear and present danger
of racial friction and isolated acts of violence by individuals on
both sides. They were afraid, not that the United States Constitution would be overthrown, but that it might be enforced. Yet
you cannot indict a man for seeking to put the Fifteenth Amendment into wider effect. And the advocacy of other kinds of
racial equality, even of intermarriage, is not, I assume, a serious
crime in Georgia, if it be a crime at all. So the best way to
remove the dangers of colored assertiveness and racial friction
created by this outspoken Negro who would not let sleeping
dogs lie, was to seize on the Black Belt pamphlet and stretch
the old drastic statute to cover it. This the state court made
possible by saying that Herndon's documents had a "dangerous
tendency" to cause an insurrection. It was the fringe thus an-
nexed to the statute that the United States Supreme Court held
bad, not the statute itself.

The quoted phrase "dangerous *tendency*" brings us right
back to the fundamental principle of this book: The real issue
in every free speech controversy is this — whether the state can
punish all words which have some tendency, however remote,
to bring about acts in violation of law, or only words which
directly incite to acts in violation of law.[48] The whole first
chapter endeavors to show that the bad tendency test here
used by the Georgia court is fatal to the maintenance of open
discussion. It is the very essence of sedition as defined by the
English courts during the eighteenth century. Later chapters
showed this same tendency test cropping up in district court
cases under the Espionage Act, and it was occasionally coun-
tenanced by language in majority opinions of the Supreme
Court, so that I feared it had become embodied in our law.
Indeed, the Georgia court insisted that its test was upheld by
the Gitlow case.[49]

[48] *Supra*, p. 23.
[49] *Supra*, p. 323, for the influence of this test upon Justice Sanford's opinion.

Therefore, the most interesting point to me in the Herndon case is that Justice Roberts flatly repudiated this view. He said that the Gitlow decision furnished no warrant for the contention that under a law which described in general terms the mischief to be remedied and the actor's intent, "the standard of guilt may be made the 'dangerous tendency' of his words." He then went on:

> The power of a state to abridge freedom of speech and of assembly is the exception rather than the rule and the penalizing even of utterances of a defined character must find its justification in a reasonable apprehension of danger to organized government. The judgment of the legislature is not unfettered. The limitation upon individual liberty must have appropriate relation to the safety of the state. Legislation which goes beyond this need violates the principle of the Constitution. If, therefore, a state statute penalize innocent participation in a meeting held with an innocent purpose merely because the meeting was held under the auspices of an organization membership in which, or the advocacy of whose principles, is also denounced as criminal, the law, so construed and applied, goes beyond the power to restrict abuses of freedom of speech and arbitrarily denies that freedom. And, where a statute is so vague and uncertain as to make criminal an utterance or an act which may be innocently said or done with no intent to induce resort to violence or on the other hand may be said or done with a purpose violently to subvert government, a conviction under such a law cannot be sustained.

Herndon had a constitutional right to address meetings and organize parties unless he actually attempted to incite insurrection by violence. Since the evidence failed to show that he did so incite, then the application of this statute to him unreasonably limited freedom of speech and freedom of assembly.

Justice Roberts brings out better than anybody hitherto the importance of the procedure in a sedition prosecution. He says the statute, as construed by the Georgia court, is so vague and indefinite as to be bad under the Stromberg case. It does not furnish "a sufficient ascertainable standard of guilt." It does not, like the Espionage Act, pin the issue down to one particular activity of the government, and oblige the jury to decide whether the prisoner was urging interference with that single activity. It does not give the judge and jury any standard for appraising the circumstances and character of the defendant's utterances and conduct, so as to see whether they create "a clear and present danger of forcible obstruction of a particular state function." Nor does it make any specified conduct or utterance an offense.

Finally, he condemns the Georgia court's view that the accused was properly found guilty if he intended an insurrection to happen "at any time within which he might reasonably expect his influence to continue to be directly operative in causing such action by those whom he sought to induce." The consequences of such a view are so wide as to be fatal to open discussion. It raises the same procedural objection, that the jurymen are given no standard of guilt that they know how to apply. They are merely left free to punish the defendant terrifically if they happen to dislike his opinions.

If the jury conclude that the defendant should have contemplated that any act or utterance of his in opposition to the established order or advocating a change in that order, might, in the distant future, eventuate in a combination to offer forcible resistance to the State, or as the State says, if the jury believe he should have known that his words would have "a dangerous tendency" then he may be convicted. To be guilty under the law, as construed, a defendant need not advocate resort to force. He need not teach any particular doctrine to come within its purview. Indeed, he need not be active in the formation of a combination or group if he agitate for a change in the frame of government, however peaceful his own intent. If, by the exercise of prophecy, he can forecast that, as a result of a chain of causation, following his proposed action a group may arise at some future date which will resort to force, he is bound to make the prophecy and abstain, under pain of punishment, possibly of execution. Every person who attacks existing conditions, who agitates for a change in the form of government, must take the risk that if a jury should be of opinion he ought to have foreseen that his utterances might contribute in any measure to some future forcible resistance to the existing government he may be convicted of the offense of inciting insurrection. Proof that the accused in fact believed that his effort would cause a violent assault upon the state would not be necessary to conviction. It would be sufficient if the jury thought he reasonably might foretell that those he persuaded to join the party might, at some time in the indefinite future, resort to forcible resistance of government. The question thus proposed to a jury involves pure speculation as to future trends of thought and action. Within what time might one reasonably expect that an attempted organization of the Communist Party in the United States would result in violent action by that party? If a jury returned a special verdict saying twenty years or even fifty years the verdict could not be shown to be wrong. The law, as thus construed, licenses the jury to create its own standard in each case.[50] . . .

The statute, as construed and applied, amounts merely to a dragnet which may enmesh anyone who agitates for a change of government if a jury can be persuaded that he ought to have foreseen his words would have some effect in the future conduct of others. No reasonably ascertainable standard of guilt is prescribed. So vague and indeterminate are the boundaries thus set to the freedom of speech and assembly that the law necessarily violates the guarantees of liberty embodied in the Fourteenth Amendment.

Justices Van Devanter, McReynolds, Sutherland, and Butler once more dissented, the last time that they were all together in a free speech case, for within a few months Justice Van Devanter, who wrote the opinion, retired and was succeeded by Justice Black. To give only a few of his points, Justice Van Devanter felt sure that Herndon was planning to distribute the Black Belt booklets. Although there was no direct testimony to that effect, he never denied it; he was an active member of the party, sent to Atlanta as a paid organizer, and the literature was shipped to him for use in soliciting new members. Furthermore, he was not convicted just for urging reforms by lawful means. He approved of the party program and apparently brought it to the attention of others. He was a Negro getting Southern Negroes into the party, with a booklet in his hands which described measures that particularly appealed to such Negroes, like the establishment of an independent state for their benefit and the adoption of a fighting alliance with the revolutionary white proletariat. "Proposing these measures was nothing short of advising a resort to force and violence, for all know that such measures could not be effected otherwise."

There is a good deal of force in what Justice Van Devanter says. Why did Herndon have all this literature if he was not

---

[50] Here he quoted from United States *v.* Cohen, 255 U. S. 81 (1921), which held the Lever war-time food control law invalid as too indefinite. See *supra*, Chapter VII, at note 27.

planning to distribute it? That is what he was sent South for. Some of it was explosive stuff and he sounds like the kind of man to cause trouble. Perhaps a conviction would have been sustained if he had been specifically charged with possessing such printed material for distribution, under a statute with a light maximum penalty. But it is quite another thing to let printed words be called an attempt at insurrection like Dorr's Rebellion, the kind of crime that necessarily carries a heavy maximum punishment. Just as the Constitution will not allow the capital crime of "treason" to be stretched to cover mere words however violent, a similar stretch of the capital crime of "insurrection" is equally repugnant to American traditions. Speech and writing that amount at most to a breach of the peace ought not to be transformed into a major crime by the process of calling them big names. It is to be hoped that similar considerations will lead to a strict interpretation of the drastic provisions of Title I of the Alien Registration Act of 1940, which are discussed in the next chapter.

Furthermore, it was impossible to ignore the severity of Herndon's sentence, or the fact that if he was validly imprisoned the next Negro Communist to enter Georgia could be validly put to death under the same statute without having done a bit more than Herndon. Logically perhaps, the degree of the punishment ought not to influence an upper court's determination of errors of law below; but just the same it is bound to affect kindly men. In the Herndon case the Supreme Court was faced for the first time with the possibility that American citizens might be hanged or electrocuted for nothing except expressing objectionable opinions or owning objectionable books. They might not be burned at the stake as Giordano Bruno and Servetus were for equivalent crimes, but they would be just as dead. Something had to be done to prevent such disasters from occurring within these United States. It must be remembered, as I have insisted elsewhere,[51] that the Supreme Court (and usually a state appellate court) has no control over the severity of a sentence. Of that, the trial judge (or the jury as in this case) is complete master. So unless the Supreme Court held that no sentence could be imposed for what Herndon did, it would be obliged to approve whatever

[51] *Infra*, Chapter XII at note 83.

punishment a Georgia jury saw fit to impose upon Communists, including death. It was a case of all or nothing, and the Supreme Court chose nothing.

I have let my mind run over all the chief sedition defendants discussed in this book, from Debs down to date — Abrams, Berger, Gilbert, Gitlow, Miss Whitney, and the rest — and tried to decide which of them I myself honestly think did create a "clear and present danger" of unlawful acts under the circumstances surrounding his words. The upshot is, all but one seem to me fairly harmless. The one exception is Herndon. Not that there was clear and present danger of the insurrection for which he was indicted. Not that the Black Belt Free State could have suddenly emerged into being. But, given the unrest of Negroes, share croppers, mill-workers, his demands for equal racial rights, lavish relief, and the virtual abolition of debts might have produced some sort of disorder in the near future. Smoking is all right, but not in a powder magazine.

Yet that raises the question — if agitation which would be just blowing-off steam in the rest of the country is going to be forbidden in the South because of its peculiar kinds of unrest among the under-privileged, what legitimate hopeful alternatives are available to the unrestful and those that want to remove the causes of their unrest? Elsewhere one can urge the discontented classes to drop all thought of violence and try to remedy their grievances by the ballot. But how can you tell a Southern Negro to go and vote at state elections for the reforms he desires? The right so to vote is one of the main things a Negro agitator demands. The whites' fear of the consequences of success — and an outsider cannot call that fear unreasonable in view of Reconstruction experiences — is a big cause why men of Herndon's stamp are likely to bring about real trouble. In short, the very conditions that cause the grievances render agitation to remove the grievances dangerous.

Even for the discontented white groups in the South, the ballot is a less hopeful remedy than elsewhere. In a Northern or Western state, the discontented need win over only one of two political parties to favor the desired reforms, but in the South they must get control of a party that comprises almost the whole white population. This is a well-nigh insuperable

task. W. J. Cash in his *Mind of the South* [52] has shown how
time and time again the effort of the Populists and later radicals to accomplish their purposes by gaining control of the
Democratic Party has suddenly come to a halt, just as soon as
the strong opposition inside made it clear that a continuance
of their uphill fight would necessarily split the party. They
would not face the possibility of being read out of the Democratic Party and probably causing Negroes to be put into
office. Quarrels between various Democratic factions at the
primary do not offer a fruitful opportunity for threshing out a
contest over economic policies. They are not like a regularly
organized election campaign between two parties who are completely opposed to each other and anxious to prove that they
are different, instead of being constantly tempted (as factions
are) to pretend that conflicts of interest do not exist. In only
one instance, according to Mr. Cash, have the radicals succeeded in getting effective control of a state Democratic Party
in the South — when Louisiana was under Huey Long — and
the consequences do not encourage repetition. We cannot blink
the fact that one of the most delightful and promising parts of
the United States is almost as much a single-party country
as Italy or Russia or Germany. Despite the Americanism of
that party's aims, this situation upsets all the normal processes
of accomplishing reforms through political channels. It is.
significant that the only dictatorship which has ever occurred
in the United States was established in a Southern state, and it
is sinister that every method tried to end this dictatorship failed
except assassination.

When the possibility of reaching natural political objectives
by peaceful political methods is considerably impaired, this
encourages men like Herndon to use tactics close to the danger-
line. There ought to be a wider middle ground between speech
that is liable to cause outbreaks, and the helpless submission of
the under-privileged to their lot. And sedition prosecutions are
only likely to make matters worse.

VII. PEDDLERS OF IDEAS

The two remaining cases I shall discuss at length involved the
constitutionality of ordinances requiring permits for two dif-

[52] Pages 158–171, 283–287, 357 (1941).

ferent methods of communicating thought. The Court began with an ordinance of Griffin, Georgia, which forbade the distribution of advertising, and so-called literature of any kind, free or sold, without prior written permission from the City Manager; it directed the police to abate violations as a nuisance.[53]

Alma Lovell was the earliest arrival in the Supreme Court of Jehovah's Witnesses, a sect distinguished by great religious zeal and astonishing powers of annoyance.[54] Within two years it has called forth from our highest tribunal five separate decisions and many more denials of *certiorari*. Its members possess that quality of our Colonial ancestors which Burke described as "the dissidence of dissent and the protestantism of the Protestant religion." They accept the New Testament very literally, and their consequent pacifism got them into several Espionage Act cases. They apparently hold no church services, and are opposed to all organized religious systems as instruments of Satan and injurious to man. The Roman Catholic Church is singled out for particular and offensive condemnation, which has caused some nasty rows, one in Maine ending fatally. They are also unpopular with ritualists of quite another sort, because the young Jehovah's Witnesses in public schools conscientiously refuse to salute the flag. The German members are equally disliked by the Nazis and largely consigned to concentration camps. They are afraid of nothing, not even ridicule.

Jehovah's Witnesses seek adherents by speaking to pedestrians on the street and by house-to-house canvasses. In such ways they offer to sell their various booklets for small sums, tell about their faith, and solicit contributions. So Alma Lovell went around Griffin without applying to the City Manager 'or the permission required by the ordinance. She was speedily arrested, fined $50, and sent to jail for fifty days in default

---

[53] Lovell *v.* Griffin, 303 U. S. 444 (1938); revg. 55 Ga. App. 609 (1937). The best comments are in 5 *University of Chicago Law Review* 675 and 7 *George Washington Law Review* 94. See also 8 *Brooklyn Law Review* 236; 3 *University of Detroit Law Journal* 80; 27 *Georgetown Law Journal* 803; 3 *Legal Notes on Local Government* 351; 13 *St. John's Law Review* 81, 141; 25 *Virginia Law Review* 96, 625.

[54] For more information, see Gobitis *v.* Minersville School District, 108 F. (2d) 683, 685–6 (C. C. A. 3d, 1939); Cantwell *v.* Connecticut, *infra* note 62.

of payment. Having lost her appeal in the state court, she went up higher.

In order to understand the constitutional problem, we must start from the proposition that the complexities of modern life have led the law to require that permits (often called licenses) must be obtained for all sorts of activities which are thought capable of causing harm to the community unless subjected to supervision and inspection and a preliminary weeding out of unsuitable persons or things. The legislature may grant the requisite permission itself, as when it charters a railroad or a bank; but ordinarily it delegates its power to innumerable boards and officials supposedly skilled in their various fields, who license everything from abattoirs to zoos.[55] We are roused at dawn by a licensed milkman, go to work in a licensed taxicab, eat lunch in a licensed restaurant, drink a cocktail in a licensed bar, and a licensed broadcaster lulls us to sleep with a bed-time story of the latest horrors overseas.

It is helpful for this discussion to distinguish between two types: (1) a general permit granted once for all like admission to the bar or at long intervals like an automobile driving license; (2) a special permit, which is narrowly limited to a brief series of acts like carrying explosives between two cities on a specified day. Thus we are brought into the world by a doctor who has a general permit to practice, and wedded by a minister who needs a special permit from the Marriage Bureau. Obviously special permits enable the officials to exercise a much tighter supervision.

Such a ubiquitous governmental practice has naturally been extended over several activities concerned with the communication of facts and ideas, especially when they create an objective peril like fire-risk in public halls and theaters or confusion between wave-lengths of neighboring broadcasters. Occasionally the authorities lay hold of licensing to guard against some apprehended injury to the mind as well. For example, a statute may authorize renewal of a theater's license to be refused because of the obscenity of its productions. The Rand School case left unsettled the question whether a general permit can constitutionally be required for private teaching.

Previous restraint on speech exists whenever a license for

[55] See Chafee, *State House versus Pent House*, pp. 44 ff.

any method of communicating thought depends on somebody's judgment. So the problem always arises even with a general permit law, whether this particular method is one of the "exceptional" situations that Chief Justice Hughes spoke of in the Near case. He said in effect that the "clear and present danger" must be clearer than ordinary, in order to avoid the settled constitutional objection to previous restraints.

The possibility of invalidity becomes much greater when the permit is special as it was in the Griffin handbill ordinance. Special permits enable the officials to control what is said very rigorously. They come close to the old censorship of books. So such permits are less commonly required than general permits. A public hall or a theater has to be licensed annually, but the American law does not require a permit for every meeting or every play.[56] Even the Lusk Committee did not insist on approving each lecture at the Rand School before it could be delivered.

Still, special permits had become customary for some methods of communicating ideas, long before *Lovell* v. *Griffin*, and until that decision the courts had accepted them without question. The Supreme Court itself had upheld the censorship of motion pictures in 1915 and permits for speakers in city parks in 1897 — a problem which it would soon have to reconsider.[57] Special permits for the distribution of particular handbills had been sustained by numerous state courts.[58] So Alma Lovell's chances of escaping jail looked very slim indeed.

The argument for the validity of handbill ordinances was simple. Every free speech problem, as the first chapter brings out, involves a balancing of the individual and social interests in open discussion against some other interest, usually social, like national defense or domestic tranquility. When we are concerned with handbills like those of Jehovah's Witnesses, which have nothing to do with war or radicalism, the counterbalancing social interest is something quite different from anything we have yet considered. It is to keep the streets, gutters, and sidewalks clean. People who are given handbills and leaflets

---

[56] However, extra-legal special permits are sometimes issued or denied by mayors. See Chapter XIV, section III.

[57] See the Hague case, *infra* section VIII.

[58] The cases are collected in 22 A. L. R. 1484 (1923); 114 *id.* 1446 (1938).

often throw them away soon afterwards. Literature turns to litter.[59] This social interest in urban cleanliness was well presented by counsel for the city of Griffin, who urged that it outweighed whatever slight social interest in open discussion existed here:

This ordinance is a police measure . . . If it be kept in mind that every municipality is faced with a sanitary problem in removing from its streets papers, circulars and other like materials, the reasons for the adoption of such an ordinance become apparent. . . . Nothing in the ordinance is aimed at or relates to the right to worship as one may prefer, or the right to speak or write with complete freedom. The fact the appellant may have in her own mind associated her forbidden activities with her religious convictions does not establish any legal or constitutional connection between them. . . . Appellant is not a member of the press. The record in this case does not place her in the class of persons who are entitled to invoke the constitutional provisions touching the freedom of the press. Moreover, she was not convicted for anything she was speaking or writing. Neither does the ordinance prohibit her from speaking or writing as her judgment may dictate. The requirement of the ordinance that she is not to distribute printed matter which others have published, without a permit, involves in no way the constitutional right of free speech.

If a permit had been sought and denied without adequate reason, then, he said, her rights would have been infringed. The power was valid, and she suffered no legal wrong until it had been abused. There was no evidence for assuming that a permit would have been withheld. Until experience showed the contrary, the Court should presume that the permit would be granted to everybody lawfully entitled to it.

The Chief Justice, speaking for a unanimous Court,[60] held the ordinance invalid. The interest in cleanliness was not definitely promoted by it.

It covers every sort of circulation "either by hand or otherwise." There is thus no restriction in its application with respect to time or place. It is not limited to ways which might be regarded as inconsistent with the maintenance of public order or as involving disorderly

[59] See the police testimony from various cities in Schneider v. Irvington, 308 U. S. 147 (1939).

[60] Justice Reed had replaced Justice Sutherland before this decision. Justice Cardozo did not participate.

conduct, the molestation of the inhabitants, or the misuse or littering of the streets. The ordinance prohibits the distribution of literature of any kind at any time, at any place, and in any manner without a permit from the City Manager.

On the other hand, freedom of the press weighs very heavily in the scale —

We think that the ordinance is invalid on its face. Whatever the motive which induced its adoption, its character is such that it strikes at the very foundation of the freedom of the press by subjecting it to license and censorship. The struggle for the freedom of the press was primarily directed against the power of the licensor. . . . And the liberty of the press became initially a right to publish *"without* a license what formerly could be published only *with* one."* While this freedom from previous restraint upon publication cannot be regarded as exhausting the guaranty of liberty, the prevention of that restraint was a leading purpose in the adoption of the constitutional provision. . . .

The liberty of the press is not confined to newspapers and periodicals. It necessarily embraces pamphlets and leaflets. These indeed have been historic weapons in the defense of liberty, as the pamphlets of Thomas Paine and others in our own history abundantly attest. The press in its historic connotation comprehends every sort of publication which affords a vehicle of information and opinion. . . .

The ordinance cannot be saved because it relates to distribution and not to publication. "Liberty of circulating is as essential to that freedom as liberty of publishing; indeed, without the circulation, the publication would be of little value."

A few words must be added about the Handbill Cases [61] of 1939, which made the constitutional protection against ordinances still wider. Jehovah's Witnesses were concerned in one of these four cases; a drastic permit ordinance required the applicant to be photographed and fingerprinted so as to prevent people from soliciting money fraudulently or getting into houses for criminal purposes. The other three ordinances prohibited handbills absolutely, and were somewhat more specifi-

---

[61] Schneider *v.* Irvington, 308 U. S. 147 (1939), with which are grouped Young *v.* California, Snyder *v.* Milwaukee, and Nichols *v.* Massachusetts. See 40 *Columbia Law Review* 531; 8 *George Washington Law Review* 866; 28 *Georgetown Law Journal* 702; 53 *Harvard Law Review* 487; 35 *Illinois Law Review* 90; 15 *Indiana Law Journal* 312; 24 *Minnesota Law Review* 570; 25 *Washington University Law Quarterly Review* 611.

cally directed against littering the streets than the Griffin ordinance. The Court through Justice Roberts invalidated all four ordinances, Justice McReynolds dissenting. One case protected printed announcements of a meeting to discuss the war in Spain although the only expression of views was at the meeting itself. An invitation to discussion is more than commercial advertising; it is part of the process of making discussion effective.

The Court added still another liberty for Jehovah's Witnesses in *Cantwell* v. *Connecticut* in 1940.[62] Here several members went from house to house on a street ninety per cent populated by Roman Catholics carrying a phonograph with records attacking the Catholic Church. They would ask permission to play a record without disclosing its nature, and then request the listener to buy a booklet or make a contribution. As a result, they narrowly escaped a fist fight and landed in jail instead, under a statute against soliciting money for any religious or charitable purpose unless it was approved by a public welfare official, and also for a breach of the peace at common law. The statute was held invalid at least as to religious solicitations; and all the convictions were set aside, which ought to discourage the loose use of the breach of the peace prosecutions against unpopular speakers. Justice Roberts said:

In the realm of religious faith, and in that of political belief, sharp differences arise. In both fields the tenets of one man may seem the rankest error to his neighbor. To persuade others to his own point of view, the pleader, as we know, at times, resorts to exaggeration, to vilification of men who have been, or are, prominent in church or state, and even to false statement. But the people of this nation have ordained in the light of history, that, in spite of the probability of excesses and abuses, these liberties are, in the long view, essential to enlightened opinion and right conduct on the part of the citizens of a democracy.

The Court here completed the process of incorporating the whole of the First Amendment into the word "liberty" in the Fourteenth Amendment, for the decision rested almost entirely on religious freedom. However, this freedom is no more un-

[62] 310 U. S. 296 (1940). See 128 A. L. R. 1361; 130 *id.* 1504; 40 *Columbia Law Review* 1067; 15 *St. John's Law Review* 93; 14 *Southern California Law Review* 76.

limited than freedom of speech. If a man is impelled by his faith to commit polygamy, thuggery, or widow-burning, the Constitution will not protect him. Even devout non-action may bring disastrous consequences as we saw in the Macintosh case.[63] And a fortnight after the Cantwell case, the Court held, Justice Stone dissenting, that young Jehovah's Witnesses could be lawfully expelled from public school for refusing to join in what they felt to be idolatrous flag-worship.[64] Freedom of religion is not the subject of this book, so I shall merely say that if the phonograph and flag-salute cases had been decided in exactly the opposite way the combined results of the two decisions would give a scope to religious liberty closer to the ideals of the Chief Justice's Macintosh opinion, and to my conception of the life of the spirit.

Lovell v. *Griffin* marked a sharp turning-point in the law, and checked the use of permits for activities concerned with speech. The doctrine may some day serve as a protection from oppressive censorship of motion pictures and the radio, which communicate ideas more widely and persuasively than handbills and street phonographs. The broad language of the various opinions makes it plain that constitutional free speech is not limited to ancient forms of expression.

And yet, much as I like this broad language, there is something about the handbill and phonograph cases that makes me uncomfortable. The limitations they impose on governmental control of street distributions and solicitations look a bit fragile for a rough and tumble world. I wonder whether they can last, whether enforcement officials will not somehow or other circum-

---

[63] Conscientious objectors cannot obtain exemption from compulsory military training in a state university. — Hamilton *v.* Regents of the University of California, 293 U. S. 245 (1934).

[64] Minersville School Dist. *v.* Gobitis, 310 U. S. 586 (1940). See 127 A. L. R. 1502; and many comments in law reviews. The members of the Bill of Rights Committee of the American Bar Association, *infra* at n. 76, filed a brief as *amici curiae* against the flag-salute, which is reprinted as a supplement to 1 *Bill of Rights Review*, No. 1.

When similar children in New Hampshire were sentenced to the State Industrial School for their minorities as delinquent children, the sentence was reversed; and the children were remitted to the custody of their parents for such education as they can give them. State *v.* Lefebvre, 20 Atl. (2d) 185 (1941). The opinion of Justice Page should be read in full for its wise reflections on the cruelty of which patriotism is capable.

vent them. For example, before the handbill decisions, the police preferred to arrest the man who distributed papers as the primary cause of street litter. Justice Roberts, in stopping that practice, suggested — as an "obvious method" of accomplishing the same purpose — "the punishment of those who actually throw the papers in the streets." It seems unlikely that the police will carry out that policy, especially when the ideas in the handbill are as distasteful to them as to the discarders. In short, *Lovell* v. *Griffin* and its successors make it rather difficult for a city to frame an ordinance to keep its streets clean from communicative papers. Perhaps this does not greatly matter. Handbills are almost the only available way for poor men to express ideas to the public or announce a protest meeting. The talk about dirty streets and sidewalks often looks like just a pretense for suppressing unpopular causes. Think of all the present litter which lies outside the scope of such handbill ordinances — cigarette wrappers, matchcards, newspapers and so on. It may prove possible to promote the social interest in urban cleanliness by such non-legal methods as sidewalk rubbish cans, white-wings, and the formation of a civic pride in Spotless Town.

House to house canvassing raises more serious problems. Of all the methods of spreading unpopular ideas, this seems the least entitled to extensive protection. The possibilities of persuasion are slight compared with the certainties of annoyance. Great as is the value of exposing citizens to novel views, home is one place where a man ought to be able to shut himself up in his own ideas if he desires. There he should be free not only from unreasonable searches and seizures but also from hearing uninvited strangers expound distasteful doctrines. A doorbell cannot be disregarded like a handbill. It takes several minutes to ascertain the purpose of a propagandist and at least several more to get rid of him. Such an importunate caller seems as much subject to regulation as billboard advertising at a critical turn in the highway, which you have to look at whether you want to or not.[65] A man's house is his castle, and

---

[65] Perlmutter *v* Greene, 259 N. Y. 327 (1932). And billboard advertising of cigarettes, etc., may be validly singled out for prohibition. Justice Brandeis says: "Other forms of advertising are ordinarily seen as a matter of choice on the part of the observer. The young people as well as the adults have the

what is more important his wife's castle. A housewife may fairly claim some protection from being obliged to leave off bathing the baby and rush down to the door, only to be asked to listen to a sermon or a political speech. And this is not all. There is the risk of fraudulent solicitation of funds unless some trained person like the Connecticut licensing official distinguishes between honest and dishonest appeals. The Reverend Mr. Stiggins was unfortunately not the last clergyman to use religion for his own benefit. Moreover, hospitable housewives dislike to leave a visitor on a windy doorstep while he explains his errand, yet once he is inside the house robbery or worse may happen. So peddlers of ideas and salesmen of salvation in odd brands seem to call for regulation as much as the regular run of commercial canvassers. If the city government chooses to protect its citizens from the annoyances and risks just described, it can do so only by a complete prohibition of all systematic calls or by giving some official considerable discretion to weed out undesirables. All these social interests seem to be weighed rather lightly in the Handbill Cases and *Cantwell* v. *Connecticut*. Freedom of the home is as important as freedom of speech. I cannot help wondering whether the Justices of the Supreme Court are quite aware of the effect of organized front-door intrusions upon people who are not sheltered from zealots and impostors by a staff of servants or the locked entrance of an apartment house.

However, these decisions do not invalidate all ordinances that include within their scope sidewalk and doorway dissemination of thought. Several sentences in the opinions state that ordinances suitably designed to take care of legitimate social interests are not void. The Court does not undertake to frame such ordinances itself, but suggests some broad guiding principles, of which the most important is that the police power must not serve as a disguise for the suppression of unpopular persons and ideas. For example, an ordinance against playing phonograph records in the street would probably be upheld if its enforcement did not stop with Jehovah's Witnesses, but

message of the billboard thrust upon them . . . . In the case of newspapers and magazines, there must be some seeking by the one who is to see and read the advertisement. The radio can be turned off, but not so the billboard or street car placard." Packard Corp. *v.* Utah, 285 U. S. 105, 110 (1932).

also silenced the more loudly blaring sound-trucks of influential merchants. These decisions might possibly be regarded, not as specific rules for the management of streets, but rather as part of an educational process by which the Court seeks to impress on city officials the high value of freedom of thought. The Court kills an arbitrary ordinance once in a while "pour encourager les autres." In order to get a well-rounded understanding of the present state of the law, these few opinions upsetting convictions must be placed alongside a much larger number of memorandum decisions, where the Court allowed convictions under other permit ordinances to stand undisturbed by refusing to review them. It then seems that the Court has set its face against ordinances actually or easily used for suppression, and not against every permit ordinance that might conceivably stifle an unpopular group.

This is brought out by the latest of all the Jehovah's Witnesses cases,[66] which on March 31, 1941, upheld the conviction of several members for walking close together through the business district of Manchester in an "information march," each carrying a sign reading "Religion is a Snare and a Racket." In view of the New Hampshire court's non-discriminatory construction of the statute requiring permits for street parades, the Chief Justice sustained the limited authority conferred on the licensing board and said:

Civil liberties, as guaranteed by the Constitution, imply the existence of an organized society maintaining public order without which liberty itself would be lost in the excesses of unrestrained abuses. The authority of a municipality to impose regulations in order to assure the safety and convenience of the people in the use of public highways has never been regarded as inconsistent with civil liberties but rather as one of the means of safeguarding the good order upon which they ultimately depend. The control of travel on the streets of cities is the most familiar illustration of this recognition of social need. Where a restriction of the use of highways in that relation is designed to promote the public convenience in the interest of all, it cannot be disregarded by the attempted exercise of some civil right which in other circumstances would be entitled to protection. One would not be justified in ignoring the familiar red traffic light because he thought it his religious duty to disobey the municipal command

[66] Cox v. New Hampshire, 312 U.S. 569 (1941).

or sought by that means to direct public attention to an announcement of his opinions. As regulation of the use of the streets for parades and processions is a traditional exercise of control by local government, the question in a particular case is whether that control is exerted so as not to deny or unwarrantedly abridge the right of assembly and the opportunities for the communication of thought and the discussion of public questions immemorially associated with resort to public places.

VIII. FREEDOM OF ASSEMBLY

Hague v. *Committee for Industrial Organization*,[67] in 1939 soon after *Lovell* v. *Griffin*, involved the relation between freedom of assembly and a Jersey City ordinance requiring permits for speakers at meetings in streets and parks.

New Jersey has long been an area of industrial conflict. Its industries have been unionized more slowly than those of neighboring New York City, and the unions are constantly endeavoring to introduce the closed shop by sending in organizers, whose arrival is sometimes followed by strikes with accompanying disorders. These strikes or the fear of future strikes has frequently led governmental authorities to take steps against labor organizers and agitators and their meetings. Thus New Jersey had a peace-time sedition law as early as 1908 and

---

[67] 307 U. S. 496 (1939), affg. and modifying 101 F. (2d) 774 (C. C. A. 3d, 1939), Davis, J., dissenting, which affirmed and modified 25 F. Supp. 127 (N. J. 1938). The opinions below give more facts and deserve reading. The District Court's findings of fact and complete decree are essential to an understanding of the case, and appear in 101 F. (2d) at 791-797.

On the Hague decision as affecting the right of assembly, see 9 *Brooklyn Law Review* 201; 24 *Cornell Law Quarterly* 422; 7 *George Washington Law Review* 1026; 52 *Harvard Law Review* 320; 33 *Illinois Law Review* 845; 37 *Michigan Law Review* 609; 18 *North Carolina Law Review* 67; 14 *St. John's Law Review* 157; 48 *Yale Law Journal* 257.

On the right of assembly generally, see Chafee, "Assembly, Right of," 2 *Encyc. Soc. Sci.* 275 (1930), with bibliography; Dicey, *Law of the Constitution* (8th ed., 1923), p. 266; Goodhart, "Public Meetings and Processions," 6 *Cambridge Law Journal* 161 (1937); Loewenstein, "Legislative Control of Political Extremism in European Democracies," 38 *Columbia Law Review* 591 and 725 (1938); Jarret & Mund, "The Right of Assembly," 9 *New York University Law Quarterly Review* 1 (1931); Jennings, "Public Order," 8 *Political Quarterly* 7 (1937); 23 *California Law Review* 180 (1935); 42 *Harvard Law Review* 265 (1928); 47 *Yale Law Journal* 404 (1938) (valuable comparison of English and American law); 58 A. L. R. 751 (1929); 93 *id.* 737 (1934). Secret societies: 43 A. L. R. 914 (1926), 62 *id.* 798 (1929). Public wearing of uniforms of semi-official forces of foreign government: 53 *Harvard Law Review* 150 (1939).

enforced it several times before the World War.[68] Frequent
use was made of permit ordinances, laws against breaches of
the peace, etc. This suppression of labor meetings produced
meetings to protest against the suppression, and then the protest meetings were suppressed too. For example, Roger Baldwin, the Director of the American Civil Liberties Union, was
arrested in Paterson when he started to read the Declaration
of Independence in front of the city hall, and convicted with
others for holding an unlawful assembly.[69] And nowhere was
the ban so complete as in Jersey City.

Mayor Frank Hague fought the closed shop by establishing
the closed city. He made use of every possible administrative
device to prevent meetings from being held by any speakers
except those he approved. The owners of public halls were
deterred from renting them.[70] Permits for the distribution of
handbills were refused. And although many meetings of the
Mayor's supporters were allowed in the streets and parks and
public buildings, permits for such meetings were invariably
denied not only to organizers from the American Federation of
Labor and the Committee of Industrial Organization, but also
to several Congressmen and other advocates of free speech
such as Roger Baldwin, Norman Thomas, and Senator Borah.
The editor of *The Catholic Worker*, W. M. Callahan, was refused leave to hold a meeting to explain the Papal Encyclicals.
Prospective speakers who ventured into the city were promptly
put on ferry boats for New York. This policy had the strong
backing of Jersey City business men and voters generally, even
those who were otherwise opposed to the Mayor. It was also
sanctioned by the New Jersey courts. Norman Thomas brought
suit to compel the Mayor to give him a permit, and lost.[71] It

[68] N. J. Laws, 1908, c. 278, now N. J. S. A. 2:173 — 10, 11. Notice the
numerous other New Jersey sedition laws listed in Appendix III.

[69] A leading Republican lawyer, Mr. Arthur Vanderbilt, since President of
the American Bar Association, got the conviction reversed by the highest state
court. — State *v.* Butterworth, 104 N. J. L. 579 (E. & A. 1928) ; see 58 A. L. R.
751.

[70] For a similar device in Boston see Chapter XIV, section III.

[71] Thomas *v.* Casey, 121 N. J. L. 185 (Sup. 1938). The court relied on Har-
wood *v.* Trembley, 97 N. J. L. 173 (1922), with an interesting dissent by
Minturn, J. After the Hague case had made the ordinance void, the highest
New Jersey court refused to compel the issue of a permit to Norman Thomas
because he could speak anyway. — 123 *id.* 447 (1939).

was plain that only the United States courts could restore open discussion in Jersey City.

Although it was important to combat all the Mayor's devices for suppression, we are concerned only with his restriction of open-air meetings. He acted under a city ordinance forbidding any public assembly to take place in or upon the streets, parks, or public buildings of Jersey City unless a permit had been obtained three days ahead from the Director of Public Safety. The most important clause follows: [72]

The Director of Public Safety is hereby authorized to refuse to issue said permit when, after investigation of all of the facts and circumstances pertinent to said application, he believes it to be proper to refuse the issuance thereof; *provided, however, that said permit shall only be refused for the purpose of preventing riots, disturbances or disorderly assemblage.*

Violation was punishable by maximum fine of two hundred dollars or jail for ninety days or both.

The Jersey City officials relied on the italicized words of the ordinance. They insisted that if the proposed meetings were held disturbances were likely to follow, because the meetings would be attacked by opponents. The officials put in evidence protests against such meetings which had been received from the Chamber of Commerce, two organizations of veterans, and the Ladies of the Grand Army of the Republic. At least one threat of violence was voiced against the C.I.O. and its sympathizers — by a great mass meeting of three thousand persons, all of them veterans, who announced that if the authorities did not refuse a permit for an open-air C.I.O. meeting "the veterans would take the matter into their own hands and see to it that the meeting would be broken up." There was also evidence that Mayor Hague and his associates had inspired at least some of these protests. As the Circuit Court remarked, "Reversing the usual procedure, [Mayor Hague] troubled the waters in order to fish in them." [73]

Permit ordinances more or less like this have been adopted in many cities. For the most part they have been liberally

[72] The whole ordinance is quoted in 307 U. S. at 502, note 1. The italics are mine.

[73] 101 F. (2d) at 774, 784. For the threats by the veterans, see the dissenting opinion of Davis, J., at 806.

administered, for example, on Boston Common — though even that was closed to all meetings during the days preceding the execution of Sacco and Vanzetti.[74] In cases where permits had been refused, state courts almost invariably upheld the validity of the ordinance; and, as we shall see, Justice Holmes and the Supreme Court sanctioned the practice forty years ago. Even when the refusal was alleged to be arbitrary, many courts said that this was a practical question which the city official knew more about than they did, so that his determination of the undesirability of the meeting was necessarily final. Although a few cases did express willingness to grant a judicial review of unreasonable denials of a permit for a meeting, it is plain that this remedy is not very effective; even if the court decides that the permit ought to have been issued, this decision is not likely to come until after the date for which the meeting was planned.[75] Thus the whole trend of the law before the Hague case ran toward giving city authorities virtually complete control of open-air meetings except those held in vacant private lots.

Under these circumstances the prospective speakers in Jersey City were naturally reluctant to test the ordinance by violating it, getting arrested, going up through the state courts, and then spending several months in jail if the United States Supreme Court failed to upset the ordinance. So their lawyers, Morris Ernst and Dean Frazer of Newark Law School, adopted the safer tactics of the Grosjean case, and started off with a suit in the United States District Court to enjoin Mayor Hague and the other officials from enforcing the ordinance and the rest of his restrictions on discussion. The defendants were represented by Charles Hershenstein, personal counsel to Mayor Hague, and Edward J. O'Mara. Judge William Clark issued a

[74] *New York Times*, August 8, 14, 15, 22 (1927); Chafee, *The Inquiring Mind*, pp. 150–156.

[75] Cantwell *v.* Connecticut held that if the permit be otherwise void, it is not validated by an opportunity for judicial review.

State cases on permit ordinances for meetings are collected in the District Court's opinion and in references cited *supra* note 61. See, for example, Father Coughlin *v.* Chicago Park Dist., 364 Ill. 90 (1936); People *v.* Atwell, 232 N. Y. 96 (1921), Cardozo, J., concurring, and Pound, J., dissenting; Duquesne *v.* Fincke, 269 Pa. 112 (1920).

For the Supreme Court case sustaining the Massachusetts decision of Justice Holmes, see *infra* note 79.

sweeping injunction granting all the prayers of the plaintiffs, and the officials appealed.

At this point the newly established Bill of Rights Committee of the American Bar Association, under the chairmanship of Mr. Grenville Clark of New York, asked leave to intervene in the case because of its great public importance. Accordingly the members of the committee were allowed as friends of the court to file a brief in the Circuit Court of Appeals, and afterwards in the Supreme Court.[76]

The Court held the ordinance wholly invalid, and affirmed the injunction with one change hereafter described. The majority of five [77] comprised the Chief Justice and Justices Stone, Roberts, Black, and Reed (who had replaced Justice Suther-

[76] All the briefs of counsel are summarized, 307 U. S. 661. The Bill of Rights Committee brief is abridged in 25 *American Bar Association Journal* 7 (1939).

[77] The five majority Justices all took the same view as to the scope of freedom of assembly, but they differed on a procedural question, which bothered the Court a great deal and makes the majority opinions rather uninteresting to the general reader. This question concerned the extent to which a state's denial of freedom of assembly can be made the basis of an injunction. Congress has narrowly limited the scope of federal injunction suits against the enforcement of state laws, for fear that the lower courts would be overzealous in blocking the activities of state officials. For example, such a suit must as a general rule involve $3000 or more. The newspaper publishers in the Grosjean case could meet this requirement; but Norman Thomas and the other prospective speakers in Jersey City would lose at most a small lecture fee. So they had to bring themselves within statutes which dispense with any pecuniary minimum in certain exceptional situations involving the alleged invasion of civil rights under the Fourteenth Amendment.

The statutes define these situations very vaguely, hence the divergences of the majority Justices. The opinion of Justice Roberts, with which Justice Black concurred, affirmed the decree on the ground that the speakers had been deprived of their privilege as citizens of the United States to discuss the position of workers under the National Labor Relations Act; and left other kinds of meetings an open question. Justice Stone, supported by the Chief Justice and Justice Reed, had difficulty in finding evidence on the record that the meetings were to be about this statute; but they took a wider procedural view, and sustained the decree because the speakers were deprived of their liberty as *persons* to discuss any question of public importance, even though they did not concern a national question.

The practical differences between the two majority groups are brought out by the following illustrations: (1) The state authorities prevent a meeting to discuss a change in the state birth control laws; Justice Stone would grant a federal injunction, but Justice Roberts is uncertain whether Congress has authorized it. (2) An alien is prevented from addressing a meeting of aliens to discuss their rights under the federal deportation statutes; Justice Roberts would be doubtful about an injunction, because they are not deprived of "privileges or immunities of citizens of the United States"; Justice Stone would surely give

land before the Lovell case). Justices McReynolds and Butler dissented. The two latest Justices, Frankfurter and Douglas, took no part.

Since I was a member of the Bill of Rights Committee, I shall refrain from discussing the merits of the decision and instead set forth some of the reasoning of this group of lawyers about freedom of assembly and the two main obstacles that confronted them in seeking its protection in this case.[78]

"Freedom of assembly is an essential element of the American democratic system. At the root of this case lies the question of the *value* in American life of the citizen's right to meet face to face with others for the discussion of their ideas and problems — religious, political, economic or social. Public debate and discussion take many forms including the spoken and the printed word, the radio and the screen. But assemblies face to face perform a function of vital significance in the American system, and are no less important at the present time for the education of the public and the formation of opinion than they have been in our past history. The right of assembly lies at the foundation of our system of government. The cornerstone of that system is that government — all government, whether federal, state or local — shall be based on the consent of the governed. But 'the consent of the governed' implies not only that the consent shall be uncoerced but also that it shall be

the injunction because the state must not deprive "any person" of the liberty of assembly.

If the speakers had been convicted in the state courts for meeting without a permit and then gone directly to the United States Supreme Court, the five majority Justices would have set aside the conviction without any disagreements, since the procedural question just described would then have been immaterial.

On either theory the C.I.O. and the American Civil Liberties Union were thrown out as plaintiffs, for an association is not a "citizen" and was stated to have no "liberty." Yet newspaper corporations sued in the Grosjean case, *supra* section IV. Has a university no constitutional liberty of speech? See Snyder, "Freedom of the Press — Personal Liberty or *Property* Liberty?" 20 *Boston University Law Review* 1 (1940).

As to this procedural point, see 28 *California Law Review* 388; 39 *Columbia Law Review* 1237; 24 *Minnesota Law Review* 103; 14 *St. John's Law Review* 157; 13 *Southern California Law Review* 127.

[78] In the following quotations from the committee's brief, it has not seemed necessary to indicate omissions by dots. Paragraphs on pp. 414–428 not in quotation marks are either paraphrases of the brief or my separate views.

grounded on adequate information and discussion. Otherwise the consent would be illusory and a sham.

"No truth has been more strongly enforced by the history of recent years than that the suppression of discussion leads directly to tyranny and the loss of all other civil rights. On the other hand experience proves the necessity of a *constant process of open debate* if a free and democratic government is to function effectively. Satisfactory public opinion in a crisis is impossible unless both sides can present their contentions in meetings and through the press. Only in this way can public opinion take shape in legislation that will command the general support which will make it law in a real sense. Only so, also, can government on its administrative side be kept reasonably free from abuses. Only through free discussion, in short, can democracy function at all.

"These are old truths but they need constantly to be remembered and applied.

"There is a special aspect of free expression here present. The effort in this case was to suppress only *some* communications and *some* meetings. It is plain that the suppression was on the basis that the speakers and their probable utterances would be unpopular. And it is this very feature that gives a special importance to this case. What may be popular today may be unpopular tomorrow; and no principle could be more destructive of American free speech than to judge the permissibility of a public meeting by any standard of its popularity. The right to express unpopular opinions and to hold unpopular meetings is of the essence of American liberty. This is not only for reasons of principle but for practical reasons of government. If criticism, however severe and unpopular, of majority beliefs were suppressed, nothing is more certain than that the American system could not long survive.

"When all is said the preservation of free speech and assembly depends on ascribing a high *relative value* to these rights."

The next point is that the protection of freedom of assembly provided by the Hague injunction was in accord with the modern doctrine of the Supreme Court in its interpretation of liberty under the Fourteenth Amendment. Although none of the preceding cases had dealt specifically with the denial of permits for outdoor meetings, nevertheless this method of destroying the right of assembly was closely analogous to the suppression of unpopular meetings by criminal prosecutions, which was held invalid in the De Jonge case. And the invalidation of handbill permits in *Lovell* v. *Griffin* was a strong precedent.

So far the course seemed plain, but now it was necessary to overcome two serious difficulties: (1) There was an old decision of the Supreme Court right in the way of relief. (2) Threats and fear of disorder had been urged by the Jersey City authorities as the ground for their action, and the Supreme Court might hold that this was a practical question for the people on the spot to decide.

In raising the first of these objections, the Jersey City authorities contended that a city's ownership of streets and parks is as absolute as a man's ownership of his home, and that they consequently had the power to keep out anybody they pleased or close the streets and parks to meetings entirely. This position was supported by the great authority of Justice Holmes, who had said in Massachusetts while upholding a permit ordinance for Boston Common:

> For the legislature absolutely or conditionally to forbid public speaking in a highway or public park is no more an infringement of the rights of a member of the public than for the owner of a private house to forbid it in his house. When no proprietary rights interfere, the legislature may end the right of the public to enter upon the public place by putting an end to the dedication to public use. So it may take the less step of limiting the public use to certain purposes.

His decision was unanimously upheld by the United States Supreme Court in *Davis* v. *Massachusetts* in 1897.[79] Some way had to be found to get around this old decision in order to sustain the decree of the Circuit Court, which required the officials to keep the streets and parks open for public meetings

[79] 167 U. S. 43 (1897), affg. 162 Mass. 510 (1895). A New Jersey judge similarly said that Norman Thomas had no more right to speak in parks without a permit "than he has to invade a citizen's home without invitation." — Thomas *v.* Casey, *supra*, note 71.

without discrimination. One good reply was that the Boston Common case was decided long before the Gitlow case and its successors, by which the Court established the modern doctrine of protecting liberty of speech and assembly against state and municipal restrictions. And it was even stronger to go beyond technicalities and rest on the broad principle that thus to allow the city to suppress at will outdoor meetings of unpopular groups is a fatal impairment of freedom of assembly.

"We desire to stress the importance of open-air meetings as a means for public discussion and education. Outdoor public assemblies have a special function in the field of free expression that is fulfilled by no other medium. It is true that the press continues as a major vehicle of public discussion and that the new medium of the radio occupies a large part of the field. Yet it is also true that the open-air meeting still fills a major role, and is indispensable in giving free public debate its traditional scope. For this there are a number of reasons.

"The outdoor meeting is especially well adapted to the promotion of unpopular causes, since such causes are likely to command little financial support and therefore must often be promoted by persons who do not have the financial means to 'hire a hall' or purchase time on the radio.

"Moreover, the outdoor public meeting forms part of the tradition of American life. The Lincoln-Douglas debates were held in the open, and notwithstanding the development of the radio, it still remains true that a large part of our political, economic and social discussion goes on in outdoor meetings. Such meetings in public places are free not only to the speakers but to their audiences. Especially in summer, it is easier in many communities to attract an audience at an open-air meeting than in any other way. Outdoor meetings can be held in convenient neighborhoods so that long journeys to meeting halls are not required. It is worthy of note also that, offsetting the competition of the radio, other modern devices have widened the scope of the open-air meeting. The amplifier of the human voice enables a speaker to address several times as many people as a generation ago; and the development of the sound-truck has also been of importance. Nothing, therefore, could be more fallacious than to assume that the open-air meeting is now, or at any foreseeable time will be, outmoded as a major medium for public discussion and the formation of public opinion in the United States.

"The informal character of the outdoor meeting is often of advantage in developing questions and answers — one of the best ways of forming public opinion. For this and the other reasons just mentioned it may fairly be said that the outdoor meeting is the most *democratic* forum of expression.

"It is important to recognize that *as a practical matter* a city has a virtual monopoly of every open space at which a considerable outdoor meeting can be held, because vacant private land in cities has become scarce and expensive. If, therefore, a city can constitutionally close *both* its streets and its parks entirely to public meetings, the practical result would make impossible any open-air meetings in any large city. The effect would be to cut off a means of public discussion and education that, as above stated, has been of vast consequence to the American people. Such a result would, it seems plain, amount to an unconstitutional abridgement of the rights of free speech and assembly. It follows, we contend, that a city *must* make some reasonable provision for the holding of outdoor public meetings."

The question then arises as to the best ways to carry out this basic objective. Although parks and streets serve the diverse purpose of traffic and recreation, the most statesman-like and workable approach is to regard the availability of streets and parks for meeting-places as but two parts of a single problem which should be handled as a unit. This problem is that of reconciling the city's function of providing for the exigencies of traffic in its streets and for the recreation of the public in its parks, with its other fundamental obligation of providing adequate places for public discussion in order to safeguard the guaranteed right of public assembly. Various possibilities present themselves, depending on the conditions in particular cities. For example, it may well develop that the most feasible solution of this problem in many cities will be the establishment of "Hyde Parks" of sufficient number and so located as to provide effectively for free outdoor public discussion. These considerations led to the suggestion (perhaps not accepted by the Hague decision) that the constitutional doctrine which should control this problem is that a city *must* in *some* adequate manner provide places on its property for public meetings — as distinguished from a more rigid doctrine that would *compel* both its streets and its ordinary parks to be made available. This doctrine would protect freedom of assembly without imposing rigid specific requirements as to either streets or parks that might in practice prove difficult or unworkable. Thus, while we stressed the vital importance of upholding the principle that a city must safeguard the right of assembly in open-air meetings, we also suggested that *in respect of ways and means* to that end, the rule should be reasonably flexible.

This importance of streets and parks for public assembly undermines the assumption of Justice Holmes that a city owns its parks in the same sense and with the same rights as a private owner owns his real estate, with the right to exclude or admit anyone he pleases.

"The parks are held for the public. A man's house is primarily for himself and his family, and if he chooses to admit strangers, that is his incidental right. But the primary purpose of a park is to provide generally for the use and recreation of the people. An essential difference between a city and the private owner is that the latter can admit some outsiders and exclude others on any whimsical basis he wishes. But surely a city has no such right in respect of the parks. A city may regulate reasonably in this respect but may not arbitrarily discriminate. This does not mean that the city is unable to make any choices. Thus it can keep adults out of children's playgrounds. But it cannot keep out red-headed children while admitting youthful blondes and brunettes, nor can it limit the park benches to members of one political party.

"Accordingly, though it is doubtless true that a city can regulate its property in order to serve its public purposes, there is, we submit, a constitutional difference between reasonable regulation and arbitrary exclusion. In short, the right of a city in respect of its parks resembles other governmental rights in that it must be administered for the benefit of the public and not in an arbitrary manner. There are many different kinds of public benefits to be derived from parks, and one of the most important is the constitutional right of assembly therein. The parks are held by the city subject to this right.

It can be regulated in a reasonable manner; it must not be denied.

"The danger of the private ownership theory of public property, represented by *Davis* v. *Massachusetts*, becomes particularly impressive at a time like the present when acquisitions of large amounts of property are being made by government and it is carrying on enormous activities, such as those conducted by the Tennessee Valley Authority. If these properties can be administered with the arbitrary power to exclude anybody who happens to be disliked by officials or politically influential groups, then those who oppose the governmental policies of the moment would find many aspects of their lives at the mercy of a property owner (nation, state or city), possessed of vast and arbitrary power. They could be shut out at the will of the executive or the legislature, not only from parks or libraries or museums, but from mailing or receiving letters; from purchasing electric current or water power or goods manufactured in government plants; from riding on municipal trolley cars or buses; from selling their products to the government or from doing work for it in fields where there might no longer be any other customer worth mentioning. A private owner can ordinarily admit whom he pleases, sell to whom he pleases, buy from whom he pleases. But surely, the Constitution does not confer upon government a similar uncontrolled choice.

"The true analogy to government ownership of parks and other property dedicated to public uses is furnished by a public utility, which must give service to all so long as this is consistent with the performance of its functions.[80] It can regulate, but not discriminate. It can refuse to deal with those who interfere with its functions or with other users of its service, or when the available services are exhausted. We already recognize this principle as applied to governmental substitutes for private utilities. Thus a municipal street railway can eject 'drunks' and set a limit on overcrowding, but nobody contends that it can refuse to transport members of unpopular groups even if other passengers express a dislike for them.

"In the same way, the parks can be regulated in a manner

---

[80] The same analogy is applicable to the mails. See *supra*, Chapter VII at note 22; T. R. Powell, "The Right to Work for the State," 16 *Columbia Law Review* 99 (1916).

consistent with their purposes, one of the most important of which is the right of free assembly therein for public discussion at reasonable times and places. Disorderly persons can be excluded, because they interfere with peaceable users of the parks like drunks in the municipal trolley car. Open-air meetings can be assigned to a particular park or a particular area, just as passengers can be assigned to particular seats or told to move away from the door. If all the available space is occupied and there is no more room for meetings, permits can stop, just as a full municipal streetcar can refuse to take on passengers. But we submit that law-abiding Democrats or Republicans or Communists or unionists or members of the American Civil Liberties Union can no more be constitutionally kept out of empty park spaces reasonably suitable for open-air meetings than they can be excluded from an empty municipal trolley car, or be refused current from a municipal power plant.

"In sum, a city is required to furnish its municipal services to all, subject only to reasonable rules. Surely this principle is no less applicable when those services include the making available of space for open-air meetings, in pursuance of the right of assembly that is guaranteed by the Constitution of the United States.

"The basis of the right of assembly is the substitution of the expression of opinion and belief by talk rather than force; and this means talk for all and by all."

For somewhat the same reasons, the majority of the Court held that the Boston Common case did not apply.[81] Justice Roberts said:

Wherever the title of streets and parks may rest, they have immemorially been held in trust for the use of the public and, time out of mind, have been used for purposes of assembly, communicating thoughts between citizens, and discussing public questions. Such use of the streets and public places has, from ancient times, been a part of the privileges, immunities, rights, and liberties of citizens. The privilege of a citizen of the United States to use the streets and parks for communication of views on national questions may be regulated in the interest of all; it is not absolute, but relative, and must be

---

[81] The dissenting opinion of Justice Butler saw no distinction from Davis v. Massachusetts.

exercised in subordination to the general comfort and convenience, and in consonance with peace and good order; but it must not, in the guise of regulation, be abridged or denied.

Our second difficulty now presents itself: Does the right of reasonable regulation of public meetings which the city officials must possess in the interests of public welfare — traffic in streets, recreation in parks, and so on — also include the power to forbid in advance a meeting which, in their opinion, threatens disorder? The alternative view obliges the officials to let the meeting go on until disorder actually occurs or is just around the corner — the "clear and present danger" test once more. In the absence of permit legislation, this latter view is part of the English and American law of assembly; previous restraint is forbidden by the common law, as shown earlier in this book.[82] The meeting must not be forbidden or broken up until a real disturbance of the peace arises and a magistrate "reads the Riot Act." But can this rule be validly changed by a statute or ordinance like that in Jersey City, which authorizes the permit to be refused "for the purpose of preventing riots, disturbances or disorderly assemblage"?

There are three conceivable answers to this problem: (1) The officials are charged with the safety of the city and they must have final power to judge of the danger which may make meetings undesirable. This was the view of numerous state courts, and if it was accepted by the Supreme Court the plaintiffs were bound to lose the chance to speak in Jersey City. (2) A permit cannot be refused to law-abiding persons because of official apprehension of disorder, however genuine and well-founded. Then the ordinance was invalid on its face and the plaintiffs would surely win. This was the view of the Circuit Court. (3) The plaintiffs could also win by an intermediate solution of the problem — the officials can prohibit a proposed meeting if and only if this is necessary to avoid a clear and present danger of real disorder. Hence the permit ordinance is valid if it be carefully worded or interpreted so as to require a genuine fear based on substantial evidence. Since this was obviously

[82] Chapter IV, section IV. See also Chafee, *op. cit. supra* note 67, last paragraph; state statutes on unlawful assembly listed in Appendix III.

lacking in Jersey City, the ordinance had been unconstitutionally construed by the officials so as to infringe freedom of assembly, just as the Georgia insurrection statute was unconstitutionally construed by the state authorities in the Herndon case. Such was the view of the District Court, who thought that the power to refuse permits ought to exist in the interests of public safety, but that the power had been grossly abused by Mayor Hague and his associates.

The solution can best be reached by a full discussion of the control of outdoor meetings, which shall frankly realize the difficulties facing city authorities in time of stress and the dangers against which it is their duty to safeguard the public. We must consider if this duty can best be performed by heading off a troublesome meeting or otherwise. The members of the Bill of Rights Committee felt doubtful whether the Supreme Court would hold the ordinance invalid *per se*, or whether such a result should be urged as desirable. Perhaps it was wiser to leave the officials with some power to disallow meetings when there was a genuine and well-founded fear of disorder with which the authorities might be unable to cope. At the same time it is vital that such a power should be administered fairly and without discrimination against unpopular persons or causes. Consequently, the committee took the position that the third view, at least, was essential, leaving open the wisdom of the second view. Whether or not the ordinance was unconstitutional on its face, such threats and alleged apprehension of disorder as appeared in this case did not justify the refusal of a permit. The ordinance had been unconstitutionally administered in that the officials adopted a standard under which permits were denied because of threatened disorder without reference to the possibility of controlling such disorder through police protection of the meeting, or to the source of the threats. If their contention were upheld by the Court, then a precedent would be established whereby, as a practical matter, free speech through open-air meetings might be suppressed in every city of the country. Such a result would be a blow to constitutional liberties in a vital spot.

We do not minimize the importance of the maintenance of public order and of reasonable public tranquility. The right of public assembly, like freedom of speech or even religious liberty, has some limitations in the interest of public decency and order. However, it was unnecessary to speculate as to theoretical conditions which might conceivably make it impossible to provide adequate police protection. No such extreme state of facts was shown to exist in Jersey City. No evidence whatever of police helplessness was adduced. A mere threat of disorder was said to be enough.

"In this matter of public meetings, a process of mutual adjustment, of give-and-take, is required on both sides. Public order and the protection of property are precious, but freedom of discussion is precious also. If the latter is to be preserved, some danger of disorder must be faced for the sake of the constitutional right of free assembly. It is natural that threats of trouble should often accompany meetings on controversial questions. But it is not consistent with American principles to suppress the meetings on that account. The practice under ordinary conditions in our large cities is for the authorities to arrange with the applicants to put the meeting in a suitable place, and have enough policemen on hand to quell apprehended disturbances." [83]

"The requirement that a permit must be applied for on reasonable notice gives the city authorities the opportunity to ascertain the danger of disturbances and then to provide a sufficient police force to meet any such danger. Moreover, this procedure makes it possible, if permits are sought for several meetings on the same day, for each to be assigned an appropriate place. All this would be in accordance with the give-and-take principle of our constitutional system; but no such course was followed in Jersey City."

Thus far the threat of disorder has been considered without regard to its source. There was, however, a special circumstance in this case: the findings indicated no tendency to disorder on the part of the speakers at any forbidden meeting or that their *supporters* would promote disorder. At most it appeared that *opponents* of the speakers had threatened to break up the meetings; and there was no evidence that these threats could not have been successfully resisted if the city officials had desired to provide adequate police protection.

[83] Such a practice was adopted by Arthur Woods when police commissioner of New York City, as described *supra*, pp. 156–157.

But nothing showed any *bona fide* intention or effort to protect the proposed meetings.

On this state of facts the real question at issue is whether *any* disorder, even though only by opponents of the speakers, excuses the suppression of open-air meetings through the denial of permits. If the Supreme Court had so held, the constitutional right of free assembly would to a large extent have become a mockery. Such a doctrine could only mean that a constitutional right is subject to destruction by an arbitrary official decision, notwithstanding that a basic object of the Bill of Rights is to protect citizens from arbitrary action of that very character.

The doctrine urged by the Jersey City officials, that the mere threat of disorder is a valid constitutional ground for refusing a permit, would be appropriate only to a nation of Timid Souls. But as Mr. Justice Brandeis said of the generation that included the framers of the First Amendment:

> Those who won our independence by revolution were not cowards. They did not fear political change. They did not exalt order at the cost of liberty.[84]

The sound constitutional doctrine is that the public authorities have the obligation to provide police protection against threatened disorder at lawful public meetings in all reasonable circumstances. It is their duty to make the right of free assembly prevail over the forces of disorder if by any reasonable effort or means they can possibly do so.

"In no other way can the right of free assembly be made a reality. Surely it must be clear that in order to 'secure'[85] the rights of free speech and assembly against 'abridgement,' it is essential not to yield to threats of disorder. Otherwise these rights of the people to meet and of speakers to address the citizens so gathered, could not merely be 'abridged' but could be destroyed by the action of a small minority of persons hostile to the speakers or to the views they would be likely to express.[86]

[84] Whitney *v.* California, 274 U. S. 357, 377 (1927).

[85] The brief shows by a quotation from Franklin that the word "secure" as used in the Constitution — "to secure the blessings of liberty to ourselves and our posterity" — means "make safe" rather than "acquire" or "obtain."

[86] See the case of the Salvation Army and the Skeleton Army, *supra*, pages 160–161.

426 THE SUPREME COURT UNDER HUGHES

"The doctrine invoked by the Jersey City officials seems to be the opposite of that just stated. In essence, it is that if the city authorities do not approve the speakers or the purpose of the meeting, and if some of the community object and threaten disorder, these circumstances alone justify the suppression of the meeting. It is apparent that this doctrine, if upheld, would place the rights of free speech and assembly in open-air meetings at the mercy of any faction even though a small one. But in the view for which we contend, it is immaterial whether the faction or opposition is small or great. It is the duty of the officials to prevent or suppress the threatened disorder with a firm hand instead of timidly yielding to threats.[87]

" 'The right of the people peaceably to assemble' cannot mean that the right ceases unless everybody present, including opponents of the speakers, is certain to be peaceable. Law-abiding speakers and their supporters should not be deprived of the great American institution of assemblage in the open air because other persons are intolerant and ready to violate the law against assault and battery. Such a doctrine would mean that a citizen loses his constitutional rights because his opponent threatens to commit crimes.

"Surely a speaker ought not to be suppressed because his opponents propose to use violence. It is they who should suffer for their lawlessness, not he. Let the threateners be arrested for assault, or at least put under bonds to keep the peace.

"If a permit can constitutionally be refused on the grounds relied upon by the defendants, a small number of lawless men by passing the word around that they intend to start a riot could prevent any kind of meeting, not only of radicals or Socialists or trade unionists, but also of Negroes, of Jews, of Catholics, of Protestants, of supporters of German refugees, of Republicans in a Democratic community or *vice versa*. Indeed, on any such theory, a gathering which expressed the sentiment of a majority of law-abiding citizens would be forbidden merely because a small gang of hoodlums threatened to break up the meeting. The only proper remedy for such situations, small or serious, is the police protection to which

[87] This is true *a fortiori* if there be collusion between the officials and the threateners, as both the lower courts held in this case.

citizens are entitled in public places, whether they are there singly or in groups."

An argument to the contrary was made by Judge Bodine of New Jersey in the Norman Thomas case:

That the police could quell any disorder is no reason to grant a permit which might lead to disorder and a possible injury to innocent persons. The public are entitled to their tranquillity, and the discretion to issue the permit in question is vested in the chosen representatives of the city.[88]

But the assertion of the predominance of a "right to tranquillity" over the right of free discussion amounts to saying that a man can be denied freedom because of the intolerance of his opponent.

The question of the constitutionality of the ordinance on its face must now be considered. The question is important as bearing upon the validity of other ordinances of like general purpose in many cities requiring permits for meetings in streets and parks. Few, if any, of these may contain language like that of the Jersey City ordinance with reference to the refusal of permits to prevent riots and disorders. However, this omission might make numerous ordinances conceivably more drastic than that of Jersey City in that they might be interpreted as purporting to give the licensing authority a virtually unlimited discretion to refuse permits for any reason. In view of the doubts raised on this score by the Circuit Court, the Bill of Rights Committee hoped that the Supreme Court would find it advisable to deal with the question in order to inform cities as to what sort of ordinances are valid.

Suppose that the Jersey City ordinance were interpreted so as to remove some of the previous objections by adding what the italicized words say — that the official is authorized to refuse the permit *for the time being* when, after investigating all the circumstances, he *reasonably* believes *on the basis of substantial evidence* that such refusal is *necessary* for the purpose of preventing disturbances, etc., *of so serious a character as to be beyond control.*[89] Would this conflict with freedom of assembly? There would still be serious doubts. For

[88] Thomas v. Casey, 121 N. J. L. at 192.
[89] Compare the actual language of the ordinance, *supra*, at note 72.

one thing, an official could always refuse the permit and let the prospective speaker kick his heels until after the date set for the non-existence of the italicized conditions.

"The argument for its constitutionality would be that it is reasonable to allow denial of a permit as a necessary means of preventing rioting so serious as to be uncontrollable, having in mind that (except in case of outright insurrection) such denial would amount only to a postponement pending arrival of the militia or other forces necessary to protect the meeting. The contrary argument would be that, even when so construed, the ordinance would empower an administrative official to impose a previous restraint upon a meeting merely in antici- pation of an uncontrollable riot that in fact might not occur. In support of such a contention, it can be argued that the in- stances in which the police force of a city, properly warned and organized, would be unable to suppress any attempted disorder at a public meeting would be so rare as to furnish no justification for arming any official with power to pass judg- ment *in advance* to the effect that the police force of the city would be unable to cope with the situation."

The Supreme Court went the whole distance and held the Jersey City ordinance void upon its face. Justice Roberts said:

It does not make comfort or convenience in the use of streets or parks the standard of official action. It enables the Director of Safety to refuse a permit on his mere opinion that such refusal will prevent "riots, disturbances or disorderly assemblage." It can thus, as the record discloses, be made the instrument of arbitrary suppression of free expression of views on national affairs, for the prohibition of all speaking will undoubtedly "prevent" such eventualities. But uncon- trolled official suppression of the privilege cannot be made a substi- tute for the duty to maintain order in connection with the exercise of the right.

On the other hand·Justice McReynolds in his brief dissent- ing opinion raised a very cogent objection:

The District Court should have refused to interfere by injunction with the essential rights of the municipality to control its own parks and streets. Wise management of such intimate local affairs, gen- erally at least, is beyond the competency of federal courts, and essays in that direction should be avoided.

This warning brings out an important difference here from isolated cases of sedition convictions like those of Herndon and De Jonge. In the Hague case, as in the Lovell case, the Supreme Court was concerning itself with a recurring nation-wide problem of city government. It was not just a question of releasing a single prisoner. The decision necessarily altered a settled municipal practice all over the country. The court undertook, in some measure, to direct cities in the management of parks and streets.

Indeed, the lower courts, besides telling Jersey City what it must not do, had undertaken to tell it what it might legiti-mately do. The decree below enumerated the conditions under which a permit for park meetings might be granted or denied.[90] Here Justice Roberts called a halt. He said that the decree should not do more than declare the old ordinance void and enjoin its enforcement. Then the prospective speakers would have everything they were entitled to. "They are free to hold meetings without a permit and without regard to the terms of the void ordinance. The Court cannot rewrite the ordinance, as the decree in effect does."

This is an extremely interesting statement. In other parts of the law, the Court had sometimes undertaken to tell a past wrongdoer, not only what he must not do in future in order to avoid further wrongs, but also what he might legitimately do. As Justice Holmes said in a Sherman Act case, "the de-fendants ought to be informed as accurately as the case per-mits."[91] Thus a copper company which had been pouring clouds of sulphurous smoke over neighboring territory was instructed as to the maximum amount of sulphur which might be allowed to escape from its chimneys, and obliged to keep daily records and report periodically to the Court, with the possibility that the permitted amount of sulphur might be increased or diminished in accordance with subsequent experi-ence.[92] In such cases courts may be said to have undertaken the continuous supervision of a business so as to be sure that

[90] See the District Court's decree as to public meetings, paragraph 4 (a)–(e) in 101 F. (2d) 795–6, as modified by the omission in *id*. 787 and note 2.

[91] Swift *v*. United States, 196 U. S. 375, 401 (1905).

[92] Georgia *v*. Tennessee Copper Co., 206 U. S. 230 (1907); 237 U. S. 474 and 678 (1915); 240 U. S. 650 (1916). See also Arizona Copper Co. *v*. Gillespie, 230 U. S. 46 (1913), affg. 12 Ariz. 190, 206 (1909).

it was run harmlessly. However, the United States courts would be assuming a stupendous and inappropriate task if they undertook a similar supervision of municipalities all over the country. It was much wiser to leave the job of framing park and street ordinances to the city solicitors of the various municipalities. The Court was not ready to do more than lay down a general standard. In other words, the Court cast upon the municipal official who framed the ordinance "the burden . . . of deciding for himself how near he may with safety drive to the edge of the precipice, and whether it be not better for him to keep as far from it as possible." [93] The cities of the United States must be governed by themselves and not by the United States courts.

Mayor Hague loyally accepted the Supreme Court decision by having the ordinance repealed almost immediately and a satisfactory substitute framed.[94] The American Civil Liberties Union held a large victory meeting in Journal Square, where Norman Thomas hailed the decision on the very spot whence he had been ejected by the police a year before. In contrast to the unruly turmoil when he was thus prevented from speaking, now a mildly curious crowd of five thousand with fifty or more policemen listened without interruption except from some salesmen of Father Coughlin's *Social Justice*, who also led a jeering crowd of young hoodlums to jostle the speakers into the tube after the meeting. A fortnight later the C.I.O. held an orderly rally on Pershing Field without a permit. The police were on their guard this time. Everything was orderly except for a little booing and the inaccurate throwing of three eggs. The meeting closed with thanks from the speakers to the police, who escorted them to their cars followed by two thousand cheerers.[95]

The result of the Hague decision seems to be that speakers

[93] Jenkins, J., in Hires Co. *v.* Consumers' Co., 100 Fed. 809, 813 (C. C. A. 7th, 1900). (I admire the language but not the result of this unfair competition case.) For valuable discussion of the desirability of specific guiding decrees, see Durfee, "Nebulous Injunctions," 19 *Michigan Law Review* 83 (1920), 23 *id.* 53 (1924).

[94] *New York Times*, June 20, 21; July 7, 12 (1939).

[95] *Id.* June 13, 14 (editorial), 19 (Thomas remonstrates to Coughlin), 28; July 2, 1939.

are free to talk without previous permission from anybody, but remain fully responsible for what they say. If it be thought there is danger that without a permit the police would not know of the speech so as to be on hand in case of trouble it would be practicable to adopt a plan which worked well in Republican France. The prospective speaker does not apply for a permit, he merely notifies the city authorities that he is going to speak. They then send him a receipt, which they can be legally compelled by him to do if they will not send it voluntarily. This receipt can be shown to any policeman as evidence that the meeting is legal. His notice serves as a warning to the city to have as many policemen on hand as seem desirable under the circumstances, and allows them to assign a suitable place for the meeting. Notice that under this system there is no censorship, no control by officials. Any man is free to speak. No permission in advance is necessary. And the public safety is amply protected.

There are still several problems as to proper limitations on the right of assembly upon which the Hague case does not touch. Something was said in Chapter IV about the point at which the police may lawfully break up a meeting; and public control over privately owned halls will be discussed in Chapter XIV. For other problems — meetings in vacant lots, street parades, secret societies, private drilling, uniforms, colored shirts, masked gatherings in the Ku Klux style, and so on — exigencies of space and time oblige me to send the reader elsewhere.[96] One question, however, he is sure to ask now, in the spring of 1941, and it must not be left unanswered.

Should meetings of organizations affiliated with foreign governments be unsuppressed? To take the most conspicuous example, should the authorities tolerate a meeting of the Nazi Bund, where American citizens hail in unison the ruler of another nation whose ideas are hostile to our institutions?

My reply to this question assumes that Congress has not declared war, because there is no sense in repeating here the discussion of war-time problems in earlier chapters. So suppose whatever amount of international unfriendliness you please but no war. And I refuse to base legal distinctions on

[96] See the references cited *supra* note 67, last paragraph.

talk about our being "practically in the war now," for that would be a flat disregard of the Constitution of the United States.[97] If Congress has not declared war, the United States are at peace.

Of course, varying degrees of national peril in peace time must affect the constitutional aspects of any free speech problem, as well as its practical aspects. If a "clear and present danger" is actually created by a meeting of the sort described, then state legislation specifically forbidding such a meeting to be held would be valid under the Fourteenth Amendment; and a similar federal statute would satisfy the First Amendment, granted the affirmative power of Congress to regulate such a local meeting. But there is no such legislation now.

So unless the proposed meeting falls within the general terms of a permit ordinance which is valid under the Hague decision, the authorities cannot exercise previous restraint. They must let the meeting take place. However, they can have a large force of police in attendance to maintain order. These policemen can arrest immediately any speaker who says anything in violation of the state sedition act or other local law or the Alien Registration Act described in the next chapter. And when such speeches are made at the meeting or actual disorder occurs or is imminent, then the police can order the assembly to disperse at once. Furthermore, other persons who are responsible for the unlawful character of the meeting can probably be prosecuted under a conspiracy statute or otherwise.

Some persons may deplore this state of the law and say that it leaves us defenseless in the face of insidious forces impelled from foreign capitals. This amounts to wishing that we had a different kind of Constitution. The framers of the First Amendment preferred to run these risks rather than incur the opposite danger of having a government immune from criticism. While the Hague decision stands, the Constitution requires this sort of meeting to be tolerated so long as the police can maintain control. Certainly those who wish that such a meeting could be suppressed because the speakers want to overthrow our Constitution cannot very well take the position

[97] Article I, section 8, clause 11: "The Congress shall have Power . . . To declare War . . ."

that we ought to toss the Constitution into the wastepaper basket ourselves.

When the situation becomes such that this sort of meeting will be beyond the powers of police if it be held, then we had better not be fooling around with permit ordinances and sedition laws. It is high time to call out the National Guard and the United States Army and perhaps to establish martial law. Justice Reed says:[98]

Free speech may be absolutely prohibited only under the most pressing national emergencies. Those emergencies must be of the kind that justify the suspension of the writ of habeas corpus or the suppression of the right of trial by jury.

As long as the normal processes of civil government are operating, then the privilege of holding public meetings, which is an essential part of those processes, should be operating too.

Wisdom is even more important than constitutionality, as I have said so often in this book. So let us assume that a proposed Bund meeting can be validly forbidden, and consider only whether its suppression would be desirable. No all-embracing answer can be given to this question, because so much depends upon the circumstances at the particular time. In order to decide an issue of fact, you have to know the facts. Hence I shall only set forth two broad considerations of policy, which ought to make the authorities think a long while before they forbid the meeting. In the first place, it is very important to bring a subversive movement out into the open, and a public meeting serves this purpose admirably. Instead of speculating about mysterious forces, the police can see who are there, how many, what they are like, what they are doing. That is just what we need to know. We can find out who are the leaders, and take their names. We can arrest them if they have done or said anything unlawful. Popular imagination sometimes exaggerates the strength of a subversive movement. If in fact it consists of comparatively few and mostly unimpressive members, then to let people see this fact allays their fears and

<hr>

[98] Milk Wagon Drivers Union *v.* Meadowmoor Dairies, 312 U. S. 287, 320 (1941). Although this was spoken in a dissenting opinion, it seems unlikely that the majority of the Court disagreed with this particular statement.

discourages potential members from joining. In short, if an organization has dangerous leaders, don't go for the meetings — go for the leaders. Hit the bull's eye and not the outer rings.

Sometimes it is said that such meetings ought to be suppressed because they are actuated by foreign emissaries in our midst. The same line of reasoning applies here. We ought to follow Holmes's great maxim, "Go for the jugular." Instead of suppressing meetings on the chance of discouraging the emissaries, why not hit at the emissaries directly? We can do so much more effectively by taking advantage of recent federal legislation which is aimed at just such unwelcome foreigners. One Act of Congress passed in 1938 and recently amended requires anybody who acts in the United States as an agent of a foreign government (with certain exceptions for diplomatic and consular representatives, etc.) to register beforehand with the Secretary of State. This also applies to "agents of foreign principals," and such principals include organizations like a German propaganda society or the Third International.[99] Another law, of October, 1940, requires registration with the Attorney General on the part of any organization in this country "subject to foreign control," if it is engaging in political activity or civilian military activity or aims to control, seize, or overthrow the government of the United States or of a state by force or military measures.[100] If anybody within these two statutes fails so to register before acting, he incurs severe criminal penalties. Here again you get publicity. You bring the dangerous people out into the light where you can see them and keep track of them, instead of driving them underground to accomplish their objectionable purposes in the dark.

And finally, a curtailment of freedom of discussion is an abandonment of a most important part of the Constitution, as the Supreme Court has repeatedly declared. Such a withdrawal should be undertaken only as a last resort in the face of great danger. We can conceive of a situation so serious that some of the Constitution must be given up for the sake

[99] 22 U. S. C. A. (1940 Supplement) §§ 233–233g. See 41 *Columbia Law Review* 159 (1941).
[100] 18 U. S. C. A. (1941 Supplement) §§ 14–17.

of saving the rest. Lincoln faced such a choice frankly in his famous letter to Horace Greeley during dark days of the Civil War. But such a policy is as tragic as if our army gave up New England and fell back beyond the Hudson River in order to get a better defense line against an invading enemy. We might hope that the abandonment was only temporary, but there is always the risk of its being permanent. Certainly it is a policy to be adopted with the greatest reluctance.

We need not be frightened by the experiences of European governments, at least those which like France and the Weimar Republic were riddled from top to bottom with disloyalty and economic conflicts so that it seems unlikely that the most rigorous suppression of public meetings could have prolonged their lives. Maggots live in rotten meat. A weak government may not be able to maintain a constitutional policy of free speech, any more than a weak person can safely go outdoors. But we are concerned with a strong government, the government of the United States, which is still today what Thomas Jefferson pronounced it when Napoleon held the mouth of the Mississippi — "The strongest government on earth." [101]

This finishes my survey of leading decisions under Chief Justice Hughes. As Justice Frankfurter says,[102] "The whole series of cases defining the scope of free speech under the Fourteenth Amendment are facets of the same principle in that they all safeguard modes appropriate for assuring the right to utterance in different situations."

Since he and Justice Murphy joined the Court, still another kind of situation has been brought within the scope of liberty of speech by a group of decisions beginning with *Thornhill* v. *Alabama*.[103] These cases recognize that "peaceful picketing is the working man's means of communication." Justice Murphy was the first to express the doctrine that this means of com-

[101] See *supra*, page 141.

[102] See the Meadowmoor case, 312 U. S. at 293.

[103] 310 U. S. 88 *per* Murphy, J., with McReynolds, J., dissenting (April 22, 1940). See also Carlson *v.* California, *id.* 106 (decided the same day similarly); the Meadowmoor case, 312 U. S. 287, *per* Frankfurter, J., with Black, Douglas, and Reed, JJ., dissenting; and American Federation of Labor *v.* Swing, *id.* 321 *per* Frankfurter, J., with Roberts, J., and the Chief Justice dissenting (both decided February 10, 1941). *Cf.* Senn *v.* Tile Layers' Protective Union, 301 U. S. 468 (1937).

munication is still another type of "liberty" within the Fourteenth Amendment: [104]

Freedom of discussion, if it would fulfill its historic function in this
nation, must embrace all issues about which information is needed
or appropriate to enable the members of society to cope with the
exigencies of their period. In the circumstances of our times the
dissemination of information concerning the facts of a labor dispute
must be regarded as within that area of free discussion that is guaranteed by the Constitution.

Besides invalidating state statutes that rendered peaceful
picketing criminal, the Court in February, 1941, used the same
doctrine to dissolve a state injunction which was so sweepingly drawn as to include peaceful picketing or persuasion
on the part of the defendants. As Justice Black put it,[105]
"There is every reason why we should look at the injunction
as we would a statute, and if upon its face it abridges the
constitutional guaranties of freedom of expression, it should
be stricken down. . . . The injunction, like a statute, stands
as an overhanging threat of future punishment." These decisions involve the relation between free speech and social interests entirely different from any previously dealt with in
this book. Any adequate presentation would require a knowledge of the law of labor injunctions which I do not possess.
Hence I must ask the reader to be content with the foregoing
brief summary of these important cases.

In a sense the wheel has turned full circle during the twenty-
four years narrated in this book, and we are back again where
we were in the opening chapters. Again we are involved in a
war in Europe, again numerous persons inside Congress and
out are gravely disturbed by pro-Germans and pro-Russians
and other heterodox groups in the United States. Bigger and
better deportations are once more demanded, and new state
sedition legislation. The federal peace-time sedition law, which
was almost obtained by Attorney General Palmer, is now on
the statute book, as the next chapter will show. Therefore,

---

[104] Thornhill v. Alabama, 310 U. S. at 102.

[105] Meadowmoor case, 312 U. S. at 308. Although this was said in a dissenting
opinion, the majority merely took a different view of the facts, and Justice
Black's principle was evidently applied by the Court in the Swing case cited
supra note 103.

those who believe that freedom of speech is a great tradition of American life have grave reasons for apprehension.

And yet we have in 1941 three reasons for hope which we did not have in 1917, three factors which may enable us to surmount this crisis more wisely than the last. In the first place, the very mistakes of 1917–1920 serve to warn us against repeating them. We know so much better than we did then, how a statute that seems on its face to hit only really dangerous men can be loosely construed in practice so as to stifle much-needed discussion. Secondly, we have in Europe a terrible warning against the evils of intolerance. And finally, the scope and the limits of the phrase "freedom of speech" in the First Amendment are no longer a matter of speculation as they were in 1917. In that year the only judicial interpretations of the phrase were meager and scattered and of little help. When Walter Nelles became the pioneer in exploring this constitutional domain, he had to cut his own way. His pamphlet on the *Espionage Act Cases*, without which this book could never have been written, had to be built up by hard thinking from an erroneous statement of Blackstone, a short passage in Cooley, and a few analogies from the law of criminal attempt and solicitation. So likewise Judge Learned Hand in writing his opinion in the *Masses* case had to go, not to judicial precedents, but to Milton and Mill. And Justice Holmes drew his views from the well of his own mind. "Others have labored, and we have entered into their labors." Specific problems have been analyzed by numberless legal writers and judges. And in decision after decision the Justices of the United States Supreme Court have mapped the territory for us, first the solitary dissenters, then the hesitating majority in the Gitlow case, and finally the authoritative opinions of Chief Justice Hughes, followed by one Associate Justice after another as they too expressed in diverse situations their fundamental beliefs. It is not just a question of particular situations. Through them all runs a new philosophy of the importance of open discussion in American life, which stems from the great dissent of Justice Holmes in *Abrams* v. *United States*.[106] A

[106] I regret that I have not the space to quote many of these general statements. Some of the most eloquent expressions are in both the majority and the minority opinions in the picketing cases, cited in note 103.

German refugee lawyer of distinction compares American thought to the harmonies of an orchestra of many diverse instruments, whereas totalitarian Germany is like the Indianapolis concert a few years ago with two hundred pianos. The same characteristic of Americanism is more formally expressed by Justice Roberts:

The essential characteristic of these liberties is, that under their shield many types of life, character, opinion and belief can develop unmolested and unobstructed.[107]

And the whole process of "freedom broadening down from precedent to precedent" under Chief Justice Hughes is thus described by the same Associate Justice:

This court has characterized the freedom of speech and that of the press as fundamental personal rights and liberties. The phrase is not an empty one and was not lightly used. It reflects the belief of the framers of the Constitution that exercise of the rights lies at the foundation of free government by free men.[108]

[107] Cantwell v. Connecticut, 310 U. S. 296, 310 (1940).
[108] Schneider v. State (Town of Irvington), 308 U. S. 147, 161 (1939).

CHAPTER 12

MORE LEGISLATION AGAINST SEDITION

> *I think it is clear today that the enemies of American democracy, whoever they are, are not advocating its violent overthrow. In the field of speech, they are talking about the vices of England, or of the Jews, or the folly of war or the advantages of trading with a victorious Germany. In the field of action, their eye is not on the overthrow of the government but on retarding production for defense . . . The legislation which speaks in terms of advocacy of violent overthrow falls patently wide of the mark. It represents an uncritical acceptance of a formula devised during the days when the Communist manifesto represented the technique of revolution; when revolutionaries operated by declaring rather than disguising their principles.* PROFESSOR HERBERT WECHSLER.

ALTHOUGH the Supreme Court during the ten years since 1931 has been giving us more liberty, yet toward the end of the decade Congress and state legislatures began giving us less. Fears of Communism suddenly revived and inspired several unprecedented statutory restrictions on freedom of speech, press, and teaching. This tendency is by no means the result of the national defense program or German conquests or alarm about Trojan horses. Hearings on our first federal peace-time sedition law since 1798 began in 1935, while the Rhineland was still neutralized; the bill was thoroughly debated and passed the House by an overwhelming majority in July 1939, a month before German troops entered Poland; the brief debates in June 1940 made not the slightest reference to the fall of France or fears of foreign attack. And a nation which had successfully passed through six wars unprotected by teachers' oaths and the compulsory flag salutes of school children found them sweeping state after state like an epidemic, at least two years before anybody had ever heard of a "fifth column."

Whatever the cause, novel forms of statutory suppression have arrived and are apparently here to stay. They are too numerous to receive full treatment in this book. For example, nothing more will be said about the education rituals just mentioned, about the Dies Committee and the successors to the Lusk Committee in New York, or about the details of recent anti-alien laws. Only two subjects will be discussed at length, both of which affect citizens. One is the new Federal Sedition Act, somewhat misleadingly named the Alien Registration Act of 1940; the other is the exclusion of Communists in many states from the ballot.

I. CITIZENS IN THE ALIEN REGISTRATION ACT OF 1940

> *Not guns nor battleships will ultimately preserve democracy, but the devotion of a people who have the good sense to realize that intolerance is no respecter of persons — that once unleashed it has no regard for religion or race or economic status; or, least of all, for that dignity of the individual which lies at the basis of our civilization. Democracy in America will be saved if as a people we are wise enough to know that if we do not respect others' faiths the day may come when other men will not respect our faiths.* JUSTICE MURPHY, Address to the National Conference for Palestine, January 8, 1940.

On June 28, 1940, the Alien Registration Act became law.[1] Its official title would make us expect a statute concerned only with finger-printing foreigners and such administrative matters.

[1] 54 Stat. 670. The main bill was H. R. 5138, into which several other bills were merged. Important documents are: (1) To Make Better Provision for the Government of the Military and Naval Forces . . . by the Suppression of Attempts to Incite . . . to Disobedience: Hearings before House Committee on Military Affairs, 74th Cong., 1st Sess., on H. R. 5845 (McCormack bill like §§ 1, 4, March, 1935), cited herein as 1935 House Hearings. (2) Crime to Promote the Overthrow of Government: Hearing before Subcommittee of House Judiciary Committee, 76th Cong., 1st Sess., on H. R. 5138 (April, 1939), cited herein as 1939 House Hearings. (3) Subversive Activities in Army and Navy: Hearing before Senate Naval Affairs Committee, 76th Cong., 1st Sess., on S. 1677 (July, 1939), cited herein as 1939 Senate Hearings. (4) 74th Cong., 1st Sess., House Report No. 1603, To Punish for Exerting Mutinous Influence upon Army and Navy, from Committee on Military Affairs, to accompany S. 2253 (July 22, 1935), cited herein as 1935 House Report. (5) 76th Cong., 1st Sess., House Report No. 994, Suppression of Certain Subversive Activities, from Judiciary Committee, to accompany H. R. 5138 (June 29, 1939), cited herein as 1939 House Report. (6) 76th Cong., 1st Sess., Senate Report No. 732, Suppression of Attempts to Incite the Members of Army and Navy to Disobedience,

Indeed, that was the impression received from the newspapers at the time of its passage. Not until months later did I for one realize that this statute contains the most drastic restrictions on freedom of speech ever enacted in the United 'States during peace. It is no more limited to the registration of aliens than the Espionage Act of 1917 was limited to spying. Most of the Alien Registration Act is not concerned with registration, and the very first part of it has nothing particular to do with aliens. Just as the 1917 Act gave us a war-time sedition law, so the 1940 Act gives us a peace-time sedition law — for everybody, especially United States citizens.

The five purposes of the statute, as set forth in the report of the Senate Judiciary Committee, are as follows:

(1) To prohibit the advocacy of insubordination, disloyalty, mutiny, or refusal of duty in the military or naval forces of the United States.

(2) To prohibit the advocacy of the overthrow or destruction of any government in the United States by force or violence.

(3) To add several additional grounds for the deportation of aliens to those already provided by law.

(4) To permit the suspension, subject to congressional review, of deportation of aliens in certain "hardship cases" when the ground for deportation is technical in nature and the alien proves good moral character.

(5) To require the registration and fingerprinting of aliens.[2]

---

from Committee on Naval Affairs, to accompany S. 1677 (July 6, 1939), cited herein as 1939 Senate Report. (7) 76th Cong., 3d Sess., Senate Report No. 1796, Prevention of Subversive Activities and Registration of Aliens, from Judiciary Committee, to accompany substitute amendment to H. R. 5138 (June 10, 1940), cited herein as 1940 Senate Report. (8) Senate debates and passage of S. 1677 (Walsh bill, substantially section 1 of statute) — no roll call, 84 Cong. Rec. 2121, 9360 (March 2, July 18, 1939). (9) House debates and passage of Mc-Cormack amendment to H. R. 6075 (substantially section 2 of statute), id. 6605 (June 5, 1939). (10) House debates and passage of H. R. 5138 (substantially whole statute except alien registration, section 2 put in on July 29th on floor), id. 9532–40, 10345–85, 10445–56 (July 19, 28, 29, 1939). (11) Senate debates and passage of H. R. 5138 (present statute with alien registration inserted) — no roll call, 86 Cong. Rec. (temporary) 12615–22 (June 15, 1940). (12) House debates on conference bill, id. 13465 ff. (June 22, 1940). (13) Senate debates on conference bill — no roll call, id. 13565–13566 (June 22, 1940).

See 35 *Columbia Law Review* 917 (1935); 41 *id.* 159 (1941); Oppenheimer, "The Constitutional Rights of Aliens," 1 *Bill of Rights Review* 100 (1941); Wechsler, Solicitor General Biddle, and others, "Symposium on Civil Liberties," 9 *American Law School Review* 881 (1941).

[2] 1940 Senate Report, pp. 1–2.

It will be observed that the official name of the Act applies to only the last of these five subjects. The first two, which concern us, are covered by Title I. This is in fact an omnibus statute combining in somewhat mitigated form a number of separate bills directed against aliens and subversive activities. Representative Howard W. Smith of Virginia introduced the bill (H.R. 5138) which eventually became law, after numerous changes and amendments; his honors for Title I are shared by Representatives Hobbs of Alabama and McCormack of Massachusetts, and for section 1 by Senator Walsh.

A. Mitchell Palmer is dead, but the Federal Sedition Act he so eagerly desired is at last on the statute-books. The host of over forty alien and sedition bills [3] in Congress in 1939 and 1940 recalls the similar situation exactly twenty years before, but there is one astonishing contrast. In 1919–20, Palmer's bill and its companion measures encountered a powerful opposition in the hearings and in the press. Samuel Gompers, head of the American Federation of Labor, appeared at two hearings and talked against it for nearly two hours each time. Alongside him were Jackson H. Ralston, well-known attorney for the American Federation of Labor, the American Newspaper Association, committees of the Society of Friends, the Farmers' National Council, the National Association for the Advancement of the Colored People, and Alfred Bettman, who had been in charge of Espionage Act cases during the war. The subject was threshed out pro and con all winter long in editorials and public meetings over the country. Yet in the hearings on the present law, which came in April 1939 — a year before the fall of France — the only opponents of its sedition sections were Osmond Fraenkel for the American Civil Liberties Union, Ralph Emerson for the C.I.O. Maritime Unions, and Paul Scharrenberg for the American Federation of Labor.[4]

---

[3] Thirty-nine such bills were listed on July 19, 1939, 84 *Congressional Record* 953; and many more were introduced later. Even the enactment of the Alien Registration Act did not satisfy the thirst for sedition legislation, and the bills still pour in. One of the latest proposals is to make Communists *per se* deportable and punishable.

[4] At the 1935 House Hearings on the earlier McCormack bill (*supra* note 1) the opposition was not much larger. Charles A. Beard, the historian, Professor Karl N. Llewellyn of Columbia Law School, and Congressmen Maury Maverick

The supporters of sedition legislation tried to draw the usual red herring across the main issue of constitutional free speech by smearing the Civil Liberties Union as communistic. Also the opponents were characterized as "mealy-mouthed Americans" by Congressman Dempsey, who was thereupon advised by Mr. Emerson not to use that expression along the water-fronts.[5] Outside of Congress very little was said against this and other pending sedition bills, either in the newspapers or in public halls or over the radio. Indeed one hardly realized during 1939 and 1940 that any such legislation was in prospect. What had happened to our love of freedom in those twenty years?

Frankly, I cannot explain the comparative silence in the face of this drastic proposal for suppression of discussion. Perhaps one reason was that there were so many bills that everybody got confused. Another may be that the public is far less critical of its government before a war than after a war. Still another was the emphasis on the restrictions on aliens.

A few words must be devoted to the deportation provisions, mainly because of their influence on the sedition provisions. The Deportation Act of 1918, whose enforcement was described in Chapter V of this book, was made still more sweeping in 1920. As it then stood, it was characterized by John Lord O'Brian, a former Assistant Attorney General in charge of Espionage Act cases during the war, as an "extraordinary

---

and Vito Marcantonio appeared in opposition to what is now section 1 of the statute, besides the American Civil Liberties Union, which was then represented by Mr. Allan S. Olmsted, 2d, and Mr. Frederick A. Ballard. Labor was unrepresented.

[5] 1939 House Hearings, 27, 38. On the Civil Liberties Union see *id*. 27, 42–43. The statement about advocating murder and assassination, which is attributed there (p. 42) and elsewhere to Roger Baldwin, director of the Union, is a garbled account in the Fish Committee Report of Baldwin's testimony before this committee. 71st Cong., 3d Sess., H. Rep. 2290 on Investigation of Communist Propaganda (January 17, 1931 under H. Res. 220), pp. 56–57. Baldwin's complete testimony, set forth in the printed Hearings, shows that his views are entirely different from the impression given by these garbled extracts and that they in fact correspond to the views of Justices Holmes and Brandeis. See Investigation of Communist Propaganda, Hearings before House Special Committee, 71st Cong., 2d Sess. under H. Res. 220 (December, 1930), pt. I, vol. IV, pp. 405–417; reprinted in *Who's Un-American?* (A. C. L. U., 1935).

statute," which "presents a distinct anomaly in our jurisprudence." [6]

Yet this 1920 statute was not severe enough to satisfy Congress in 1940, when the number of resident foreigners was small
compared to what it had been twenty years before. There
would seem to be little satisfaction nowadays in telling an
unpopular alien: "Go back to the place you came from that
isn't there any more." However, Congressmen have taken
a savage joy in demanding bigger and better deportations. I
never realized how Nazis feel toward Jews until I read what
Congressmen say about radical aliens. Indeed, the Smith bill
as originally sent to the House Judiciary Committee in April
1939 included provisions for the deportation of any alien who
"advises a change in the form of government of the United
States" (with no violence whatever), or "engages in any way
in domestic political agitation" (like attending a Democratic
rally or a trade-union meeting to urge the passage of a wages
and hours law); and of any alien who should not within a year
declare his intention to become a citizen. Furthermore, concentration camps were to be established for deportable aliens.
Fortunately, these plans for concentration camps, compulsory
naturalization, and the complete suppression of political activities among the unnaturalized were abandoned in committee,
but the spirit which put them into this and similar bills will
very likely obtain their enactment before the present crisis
ends.

Symptomatic of the present temper of Congress is a bill
introduced in May 1940 by Representative Leland M. Ford
of California to deport any alien who has used or uses the
support of Communists, whether individuals or organizations,
so as to interfere "with the good order and happiness of any
local community, or with the established democratic, economic,
or domestic relations within this Republic." [7] And an influential coalition of one hundred and fifteen "patriotic" societies
is persistently advocating the suspension of all immigration for
ten years, absolute prohibition of the admission of refugees,

---

[6] "The Menace of Administrative Law," 25 *Reports of the Maryland State
Bar Association* 161, 163 (1920). See *supra* Chapter V, note 4.

[7] H. R. 8310 in 86 *Congressional Record* (temporary) 9291, 9689 (May 14,
17, 1940).

and "the prompt deportation of all foreigners in the United States whose presence is inimical to the public interest." [8]

A main purpose of the deportation provisions enacted in 1940 was to do away with the effect of the recent Supreme Court decision in the Strecker case.[9] This held that an alien, formerly a member of a forbidden organization, was not deportable when his membership had ceased eight months before the issue of the warrant for his arrest. The new statute accordingly provides for deportation if the alien ever belonged to a proscribed class of radicals, "wholly without regard to the place, time, length, or character of his membership. It being the intent . . . that membership . . . at any time, of no matter how short duration or how far in the past, irrespective of its termination or of how it may have ceased, shall require deportation." The giving, lending, or promising of money for any doctrine or organization constitutes affiliation therewith. It matters not how distant the alien's sin, how complete his repentance, how great his present merits. Suppose an Italian was brought to this country as a child. In college in his ebullient youth he contributed two dollars to a Communist club, but decided not to join it. That was eight years ago. Now he is the conservative president of a bank, a pillar of society, married to an American woman and the father of four American citizens. Out he goes automatically — to Mussolini and a country where he knows nobody and whose language he has forgotten. Useless to blame him for not becoming naturalized, because Congress has made this impossible on account of his former Communist affiliation.[10] Furthermore, the discretion possessed by the Attorney General to grant respites from deportation in certain cases of hardship [11] is expressly denied by Congress when deportability is due to forbidden ideas, even in the distant past. This Italian banker is unpardonable along with prostitutes and cocaine addicts. And a retroactive de-

[8] 1939 House Hearings, p. 87.

[9] Kessler v. Strecker, 307 U. S. 22 (1939) (Justices McReynolds and Butler dissenting); affg. 95 F. (2d) 976, 96 id. 1020 (C. C. A. 5th, 1938). See 52 Harvard Law Review 157; Note, 48 Yale Law Journal 111; 19 Boston University Law Review 477 (adverse); 37 Michigan Law Review 1296 (same); 18 Oregon Law Review 335.

[10] 8 U. S. C. A. § 705, last sentence (Oct. 14, 1940).

[11] Alien Registration Act, § 20; now 8 U. S. C. A. § 155 (c) (d), as amended.

portation statute is not invalidated by the constitutional prohibition against *ex post facto* laws.[12]

Once Congress had lashed itself into such anger against
supposedly subversive aliens, it is small wonder that it made
a clean job by throwing citizens into the statute too. Representative T. F. Ford of California remarked during the debates:

The mood of the House is such that if you brought in the Ten
Commandments today and asked for their repeal and attached to
that request an alien law, you could get it.[13]

The federal Sedition Act of 1940 is Title I of the so-called
Alien Registration Act. It will be simplest to discuss the provisions section by section.

Section 1. (a) It shall be unlawful for any person, with intent
to interfere with, impair, or influence the loyalty, morale, or discipline of the military or naval forces of the United States —

(1) to advise, counsel, urge, or in any manner cause insubordination, disloyalty, mutiny, or refusal of duty by any member of
the military or naval forces of the United States; or

---

[12] Article I, § 9: "No Bill of Attainder or *ex post facto* Law shall be passed."
The leading case on "*ex post facto* law" in this connection is Bugajewitz *v.*
Adams, 228 U. S. 585 (1913), Holmes, J. See also *Ex parte* Cardonnel, 197
Fed. 774 (Cal. 1912); United States *v.* Day, 42 F. (2d) 127 (C. C. A. 2d, 1930).
Yet tearing a long-resident alien up by the roots for conduct years before the
statute seems harsher than several of the criminal laws invalidated under this
clause.

How about the other prohibition, against a "Bill of Attainder"? The problem whether this includes a specific deportation act was presented in 1940 by
H. R. 9776, which merely directed the Secretary of Labor "to take into custody
and deport to Australia the alien, Harry Renton Bridges." Compare the bill
of attainder in the Long Parliament, ordering the Earl of Strafford put to death
with no prior adjudication of guilt. The Bridges bill passed the House on June
13th by a vote of 330–42, but was dropped when the retroactive deportation
provisions of the Alien Registration Act became law. See text and debates in
86 *Congressional Record* (temporary) 12380–12407 (June 13, 1940). There is
no decision on specific legislation as a bill of attainder. For some discussion,
see *Ex parte* Garland, 4 Wall. (U. S.) 333, 386 (1867); *In re* De Giacomo, 12
Blatchf. (U. S.) 391 (C. C. N. Y. 1874); *In re* Yung Sing Hee, 36 Fed. 437
(C. C. Ore. 1888).

[13] 84 *Congressional Record* 10370 (July 28, 1939). At the end of the House
debates on the conference bill, Representative Celler, previously in opposition,
said: "Candidly, I am informed that if we do not accept this bill, we will get
one far worse. Any bill containing dreadful provisions against the alien would
pass this House with no substantial opposition. In common parlance, it would
go through 'like a dose of salts.' I am, therefore, endeavoring to be practical.
In fear of a worse bill, we must accept this bill." — 86 *Congressional Record*
(temporary) 13469 (June 22, 1940).

(2) to distribute any written or printed matter which advises, counsels, or urges insubordination, disloyalty, mutiny, or refusal of duty by any member of the military or naval forces of the United States.

(b) For the purposes of this section, the term "military or naval forces of the United States" includes the Army . . . , the Navy, Marine Corps, Coast Guard, Naval Reserve, and Marine Corps Reserve . . . [and the seamen on merchant vessels when in the service of the Army or Navy].

These provisions are substantially similar to the Espionage Act of 1917, discussed in Chapter II. The Navy Department drafted this section as a separate bill as far back as 1935; and it was approved by the War Department. Search warrant provisions now in section 4 were included. The House Committee on Military Affairs recommended the bill by a divided vote. Nothing much happened for four years, but in 1939 the Navy Department requested the same measure. It was thereupon inserted in the Smith bill (which became the Alien Registration Act) and referred to the House Judiciary Committee. A bill corresponding to sections 1 and 4 was also favorably reported by Senator Walsh in 1939 from the Senate Committee on Naval Affairs. The reasons for section 1 were concisely stated by Acting Secretary of the Navy Edison:

Literature of a subversive character has been distributed in increasing quantities in recent years to the personnel of the Army and Navy. The literature, apparently emanating from Communist organizations, seeks to undermine the morale of the services by urging disloyalty and disobedience of laws and regulations for the government of the armed forces.[14]

As an example of what went on, Commander Clement of the Navy during the 1935 Hearings thus described the Communist tactics when battleships were in San Francisco on Navy Day in 1934:

Small groups, consisting of, say 2 men and 3 girls, will come aboard ship with the regular crowd of visitors and sightseers. The men of this group will circulate about the decks, stuffing their handbills into boats, behind ventilators, and so forth, where members of the crew eventually find them, read them, *and then generally turn*

---

[14] Letter quoted by Senator Walsh, 84 *Congressional Record* 2122 (March 2, 1939); the same wording appears in 1939 Senate Report, p. 1.

them over to the executive or the officer of the deck. Meanwhile the girls of the group — chosen for their good looks — will be picking out promising appearing enlisted men, engaging them in conversation with the object of making dates with them ashore and working on them there to convert them to the "cause" and thus gain a recruit within the ship's company. Once gained, a cell is formed through which others may be talked over into joining.[15]

The economy pay-cuts at the start of the Roosevelt administration were causing some unrest in the ranks of the Navy, and among officers as well. Some of the Communist leaflets played considerably on such resentments; and also urged sailors to demand decent food and housing conditions, the right to receive working-class literature, civil trials instead of courts martial, abolition of the compulsory salute when off duty, and equality between officers and enlisted men. Samples of the most extreme passages are:

You must refuse to fight in the interests of the bosses! When you are called into war, follow the example of the Russian soldiers and sailors. Use your military training against your real enemy, the capitalist class that exploits us and plunges us into wars! You must refuse to fight against the Soviet Union.

Young sailors, you are our class brothers, although the bosses try to use you against your class. We call upon you to be loyal to your class brothers, whether in this country or abroad — to follow the glorious tradition of the French sailors in 1918, who refused to attack the Soviet Union, and the Kronstadt sailors who were the driving force that carried through the glorious Russian revolution, which built the first workers' and farmers' government.

The following extract from the *Epworth Herald* goes farther than any Communist publication quoted:

Accept the draft, take the drill, go into the camps and onto the battlefield, or into the munitions factories and transportation work — but sabotage war preparations and war. Be agitators for sabotage. Down tools when the order is to make and load munitions. Spoil war materials and machinery.

Plans in Communist magazines for missionary work among the armed forces were put in evidence, but not stated to have

[15] 1935 House Hearings, p. 19; italics mine. See also the account of the shore card-party in 1935 House Report, p. 10. Several of the leaflets are reprinted in 1935 House Hearings.

reached any soldiers or sailors. None of the leaflets said to have been distributed among them relate to any specific mutiny or disobedience, or to the formation of Communist cells in the army or navy. This is corroborated by the subsequent testimony of Lieutenant Ira H. Nunn, U.S.N., from the Office of the Judge Advocate General:

It is noteworthy that the handbills distributed by the agitators that we wish to reach never advocate open rebellion or insurrection. The nature of these handbills is that they exhort the enlisted men to dissatisfaction with their lot. They represent that authority is embodied in the officer class as representatives of the capitalist class, and create in the minds of the men, or endeavor to create in the minds of the men, a debate as to whether or not they should, in the event of emergency, obey their orders or do otherwise. There is no open rebellion advocated, and of course, none has occurred.[16]

In the spring of 1935 pacifism still appeared capable of realization. The Kellogg Pact had not yet died in obscurity. Influential groups among the Methodists and other respectable quarters were urging less military training and a reduction of naval construction.[17] The proposed statute offered hopes of stifling such agitation. Thus Major General Amos Fries, U.S.A. retired, testified in favor of the bill that these attacks on citizens' military training "influenced appropriations." "They try to bring influence upon you people in Congress, and they in that way indirectly affect the services." Furthermore, he told how a great outcry had been raised against chemical warfare, which he had traced back to pacifists and Communists, whom he evidently regarded as much the same thing.[18]

When asked about the effect of these documents on the soldiers and sailors, the supporters of the bill testified as follows:

GENERAL H. E. KNIGHT (Army General Staff): While there has been much effort for several years on the part of the subversive groups to penetrate the armed forces, it appears that their efforts have not met with a great deal of success.

[16] 1939 House Hearings, p. 30.
[17] See the extracts from votes of Methodist Conferences in Hamilton v. Regents, 293 U. S. at 251–253.
[18] 1935 House Hearings, pp. 31–32.

Q. Have they made any headway at all, General?

A. Very little, sir.

Q. How does that manifest itself?

A. A very few men have been discharged because they were known to have communistic ideas. There have been a couple of cases of men tried by court martial . . . . The ordinary soldier does not kick. He is treated too well.

Q. As a rule he will resent it [this propaganda], will he not?

A. Yes, sir. . . . Even the C. C. C., those boys have resented it. . . .

Q. And you found no tendency on the part of any of these boys to fall for this kind of propaganda?

A. None whatever.

ASSISTANT SECRETARY OF THE NAVY H. L. ROOSEVELT: The Navy Department has every confidence in the loyalty of its personnel. . . .

Q. Do you think there is any likelihood of there being a mutiny under the present situation?

A. No, but I think if you keep hammering at the enlisted personnel, it might have some result in time, and it is to prevent that that we are interested.

GENERAL D. C. McDOUGAL (Marine Corps): It has made no headway whatever.[19]

When the Navy Department again asked for section 1 in 1939, it made efforts, which I shall now fully describe, to show that the need for such legislation had "grown to the acute stage" during the intervening four years. The chief evidence was the following statement by Lieutenant Nunn, which impressed the supporters of this section in Congress so much that they quoted it several times:

Whereas the last time we came before Congress with this request we were forced to say there had been no apparent damage done, I am afraid now, gentlemen, that we have to report that damage is being done, and that it is the reason this measure was renewed after it was allowed to lie dormant during the Seventy-fifth Congress. We are having some trouble, a little trouble, and . . . I believe that our comparative freedom from things of this kind can be laid directly to the high character and the intelligence of the men that make up our armed forces. They are a fine bunch of men, the most loyal people I

[19] 1935 House Hearings, pp. 17, 11, 58, 36.

have ever known, but there exists a slight difficulty, which certainly will grow worse if not corrected.[20]

Lieutenant Nunn also testified that in recent months some enlisted men — "I do not know the number" — had been discharged for membership in subversive organizations. "At least one of these men was discharged because he would not fight." Although courts martial against such men might be possible, the Navy Department did not wish to proceed in that way. (A 1935 witness said that "a few men" had been court-martialed for spreading communistic propaganda.[21] How few was not stated.) No figures were given by anybody of the number of disciplinary cases in the Navy or Army because of outside propaganda, or to prove that these cases had actually become more frequent since 1935 or the beginning of the Communist Party or any other date.

The only further evidence in support of section 1 was as follows: (1) Some new communistic literature circulated in ships and navy yards was given to the committee, but not reprinted. (2) An extract was read from a Los Angeles newspaper three years old (February 25, 1936) about two women who were picked up aboard a battleship distributing circulars describing an alleged mutiny in the British Navy and "more or less suggesting and implying that our men should do likewise." Although this was the third time that such an incident had occurred on this battleship within two years, the women had to be released because no statute could be found under which they could be prosecuted. (3) Commander A. M. Bledsoe of the Bureau of Navigation, after speaking generally of reports that subversive organizations were attempting to undermine the loyalty, morale, and discipline of the Navy by leaflets and personal contact, said:

In all fairness I must state that I do not believe these organizations have been very successful, but I think that this lack of success is due more to the type of men that we are recruiting nowadays than to lack of effort on the part of these organizations. We know they attempt, or have attempted with some small measure of success, to establish committees aboard our ships, as well as aboard our mer-

[20] 1939 House Hearings, p. 35.
[21] McCormack, 1935 House Hearings, p. 64. Other proponents were equally vague.

chant ships. In several cases it has been necessary to separate from the Navy men who have joined these organizations or become pacifists.[22]

Such was the evidence of danger of disaffection in the armed forces which called forth section 1. Representative Sam Hobbs submitted a brief unanimous report in favor of this section, which was referred to the Committee of the Whole House on the state of the Union.

The best statement in favor of section 1 was made in the majority report of the 1935 Military Affairs Committee, submitted by Chairman J. J. McSwain of South Carolina:

It must be carefully noted that this legislation is not addressed to propaganda circulating among the citizenry generally. It is addressed solely and exclusively to a sort of "intellectual insulation against disloyalty" of the men who have specially contracted to be instantly prepared, in mind and in body, for the defense of the Government of the United States against its foes, whether foreign or domestic. . . . These men are being paid, fed, housed, and clothed by the Government in order that they may be constantly prepared to perform their mission. Therefore, if they are to be kept in a constant state of mental agitation, if their minds are to be constant debating societies as to their duty to obey orders, rules, regulations, and laws, if any influences are permitted to reach them to reduce their feeling of loyalty, to cause them to question their duty to the Government, to make possible, if not merely probable, their actual disloyalty in an emergency, to the end that they may throw down their arms rather than defend their government, even if they should not use their arms in joining the ranks of those who might seek to invade our country or overthrow our Government, then our Army and Navy would be seriously reduced in efficiency, the expenditures we are making might prove futile, and in fact, we might be building up and training a Frankenstein to destroy our Government. No sane government could tolerate such condition. Ships, guns, rifles, tanks, airplanes, and munitions would all be worse than useless, without loyal soldiers and sailors to employ them. Loyalty is the very essence of an army and navy. We all know that loyalty can be undermined and destroyed by subtle, sinister, and subversive propaganda. . . .

Therefore, since national defense forces are necessary, we must punish those who deliberately seek by subtle and sinister persuasion to undermine the loyalty and sense of duty of our soldiers and sailors.[23]

[22] 1939 House Hearings, p. 28.   [23] 1935 House Report, pp. 2–4.

A vigorous minority report by Maury Maverick of Texas and P. J. Kvale of Minnesota raised such objections as these:

Twenty-eight thousand communists overthrowing the Army and the Navy! Worse than being nonsense, however, is the fact that it is a direct insult to the patriotism of the enlisted men of the Army and Navy. Are we about to have a revolution? Is our Army seething with sedition? Is our Navy likely to have mutiny at sea? To even intimate such a thing is the worst kind of folly.

The mere reporting out of a bill like this morally weakens the national defenses of our country. It gives the impression that the Congress of the United States is suspicious of the Army and the Navy. It says that we do not trust our soldiers and sailors and implies that we do not trust our own citizens. . . .

What will come if such a bill is passed? Cross-currents of persecutions, hunts by hysterical false "patriots"; newspaper raids, brutal arrests on unfounded gossip; censorship by intimidatory actions, head-crackings, bloodshed, unconstitutional searches and seizures, suspicions, industrial warfare — bringing chaos rather than halting it.[24]

The debates in the House on the Alien Registration Act were prolonged and extremely interesting. The proponents talked mostly about the provisions against aliens, but occasionally section 1 got attention. The arguments in its favor are sufficiently represented by the following speech of Mr. Hobbs:

To my mind it is one of the most important bills that has ever been presented in this body. There is no security in this country for life, liberty, the pursuit of happiness, or property without adequate national defense. There can be no adequate national defense as long as subversive influences threaten to undermine the loyalty and devotion of our fighting forces. . . .

The officers testified before our committee that they were loath to ask for this provision in peacetime but that conditions had become worse, that propagandists were now gaining a foothold to some extent among the enlisted men of our Army and Navy, and that but for the high character and splendid loyalty that has always obtained among the rank and file of our men they would have had to ask for the enactment of this bill much sooner.[25]

[24] *Id.* pp. 15, 17.
[25] 84 *Congressional Record* 10357 (July 28, 1939). See also Blackney of Michigan, *id.* 10365; Robsion of Kentucky, *id.* 10366.

MORE SEDITION LEGISLATION

The opponents attacked section 1 as unnecessary and likely to have an unexpectedly wide scope. It might be used against the recent Methodist manifestos on pacifism or to punish civilians objecting to the use of troops in a strike. It took away the liberty of soldiers and sailors to read. It was a confession of Congressional lack of confidence in the personnel of the army and navy — "that we believe the boys are so weak that they will fall for any propaganda that may be presented to them." Mr. Izac of California, who had served in the navy for ten years, called section 1 the "Army and Navy wet-nurse bill." [26]

The high spot of the debates came when Mr. O'Toole of New York moved to amend section 1 to read:

It shall be unlawful for any person connected in any capacity with the Army, Navy, or the Coast Guard of the United States to read any newspaper, book, magazine, or other publication, including the Bible and Congressional Record, while in said service.[27]

Of course, this amendment was not offered to pass, but only as a *reductio ad absurdum* of the policy of section 1, that graduates of West Point and Annapolis were to have their reading censored by Congress. Indignant members at once arose and eloquently denounced this amendment as a Communist attempt to deny the word of God to our soldiers and sailors, and to destroy religion as it had been destroyed in Russia. The O'Toole amendment was defeated, 117–1.

Mr. Izac thereafter moved to strike out all of Title I, which at this stage related only to the incitement of disaffection in the armed forces. It was an insult to say to these young men: "We trust you to be soldiers and sailors, but we cannot trust you to be loyal Americans." [28] When Mr. Izac's motion was lost, 115–30, the passage of section 1 was a foregone conclusion. It went through the House next day with the rest of the bill by a vote of 272–48.[29]

26 84 *Congressional Record* 9540, 10379, 10381.
[27] *Id.* 10376.
[28] *Id.* 10379.
[29] See the list of those voting, 84 *Congressional Record* 10455 (July 29, 1939). The conference bill passed the House on June 22, 1940, by 382–4 (Marcantonio, O'Day, Professor T. V. Smith of Chicago University, Sweeney). There were no roll calls in the Senate.

The whole world has changed since these debates in July 1939. When the nation is on a war footing as now, disaffection in the army and navy ceases to be a peace-time problem. If we were legally at war, the Espionage Act of 1917 would be in force. Hence a fresh argument can now be made for section 1, that it is only a natural extension of the 1917 Act to take care of the present warlike crisis. The weakness in this argument is that section 1 is not limited to the national defense emergency. If it were, or if it expired at the end of two years like the Sedition Act of 1798, then it would not be unprecedented legislation. On the contrary, section 1 will remain enforceable during the peaceful future for which we hope. Therefore, in the long run it must be judged for what it is, a law abridging freedom of speech and of the press in times of peace.

Even as an emergency measure, section 1 is dangerous be-because it is liable in periods of excitement to produce the sort of prosecutions that occurred in the District Courts under the Espionage Act.[30] The very statute which was an example to be avoided even in war has been chosen by Congress as a model to imitate in peace.

In addition to what has been quoted from others, I shall by way of summary make four comments on the disaffection section of the Alien Registration Act.

First, it is difficult to see any need for it that offsets in the slightest all the trouble it may cause. Of course, disloyalty in the armed forces is bad, but we have hitherto avoided it without this statute. Trying to turn soldiers into pacifists is like inviting Harvard medical students to join the Christian Scientists. The army and navy have been able to take care of themselves for a century and a half. It will take a good deal more than the unimpressive evidence submitted at the Hearings to convince me that soldiers and sailors suddenly have to be protected by policemen.

Moreover, plenty of legislation was available before 1940 to cope with any serious danger of disloyalty in the armed forces, if it should ever exist. To begin with, we have the two Civil War conspiracy statutes,[31] section 6 for conspiracies

[30] See *supra* Chapter II, section III.
[31] Sections 6 and 37 of the Criminal Code are quoted *supra* Chapter IV, section I. For decisions thereunder see 18 U. S. C. A. §§ 6, 88.

contemplating force and section 37 for those which do not. No plan to demoralize troops and sailors is worth losing sleep over unless it involves two or more persons; but if it does, it will be conspiracy within one of those statutes whenever it is a really dangerous plan. Now, it may be true, as several government officials stated,[32] that the two conspiracy statutes cannot be used to reach the dissemination of such leaflets as I have previously quoted or the casual propaganda described in the testimony of Commander Clement and other naval officers. That is just the point — this whole business is not serious enough to be a conspiracy. Then why worry so much about it?

At first, we are told that the Communists are engaged in a great conspiracy to overthrow the government by wholesale slaughter, and they are going to begin by disarming our armed forces and taking over the guns and warships themselves; [33] then, when the government legal advisers say that the evidence shows nothing which a court would call conspiracy, we are authoritatively informed that this shows the law is helpless in the face of Communism — the red flag will be waving over the Capitol before we know it, unless a sedition act is passed right away. And they have got us so worked up by their picture of horror that we really believe them. Now there either is a conspiracy or there is not. If there is not a conspiracy they are simply like the Fat Boy in Pickwick and want to make our flesh creep. And if there is a conspiracy, the Civil War conspiracy statutes are on the books just where they have always been, ready for any emergency which may arrive. Nobody who has glanced over the hundreds of cases under sections 6 and

[32] Attorney General Cummings wrote Secretary of the Navy Swanson on June 1, 1935, that section 6 would not be applicable to the circulation of subversive literature in the navy, because it requires the conspiracy to contemplate the use of force against government officials. — 1935 House Hearings, p. 81. It is of course not necessary for a violation of section 6 that the contemplated force shall have actually been used. Any really dangerous plot against the navy or army would naturally involve the use of force, so that section 6 seems then available. Section 37, which involves no force, is not mentioned by Mr. Cummings. See also on the conspiracy statutes, Lieutenant Nunn, 1939 House Hearings, pp. 29–31. As to the availability of these and other statutes against any real danger of disaffection, see Ballard, 1935 House Hearings, pp. 73–76; Llewellyn, id., pp. 68–69; Maverick and Kvale, 1935 House Report, pp. 17–19.

[33] See Lt. Col. Orvel Johnson, of the R. O. T. C. Assn., 1935 House Hearings, p. 31.

37 will be apprehensive that they will be narrowly construed or that any leaflets by a real conspirator can keep away from these sections merely by being "carefully worded." [34] It would be like trying to fool the customs officers in the days of Prohibition by tying bottles of Canadian whiskey to the brakerods under a car. For example, if Communists are actually planning to form cells on battleships in violation of naval regulations, their slightest overt act toward recruiting members would be enough to constitute a conspiracy "to commit an offense against the United States" within section 37. If they frame a plot to incite a regiment to mutiny, they are guilty under section 6 of conspiring "by force to prevent the execution of a law of the United States." Finally if the Communist Party, as Mr. Hamilton Fish Jr. and other Congressmen would have us believe, is really an organization of "fanatical, desperate men and women," who aim to "strike at strategic points and key industries, and to inaugurate a reign of terrorism and bring about an armed uprising," if the Party has "only one real object in view, . . . to establish by force and violence in the United States a 'soviet socialist republic,' " [35] then the Department of Justice ought to have had the leaders of this frightful plot indicted and tried for conspiracy years ago,[36] which would have saved us from all the endless fussing around with deportations and raids and innumerable sedition bills and costly Congressional investigations of subversive activities and trying to pass laws to arrest pretty girls on battleships.

Still other statutes take care of military disaffection. Any soldier or sailor who is actually persuaded by propaganda to spread some himself or disobey a superior officer or attempt to mutiny can be court-martialed.[37] Enticing desertion from army, navy, arsenal, or armory is a crime.[38] Particularly important statutes [39] give the President and the military authorities wide powers to make regulations governing civilians while they are on military reservations, naval vessels, and defensive

[34] The contrary is assumed in 1939 Senate Report, p. 1.
[35] Fish Committee Report, cited *supra* note 5, p. 66.
[36] Judge George W. Anderson suggested this course as far back as 1920. — Colyer *v.* Skeffington, 265 Fed. at 64 (Mass. 1920).
[37] 10 U. S. C. A. §§ 1538–1539; 18 *id.* §§ 483–484; 34 *id.* § 1200, Articles of War, No. 4.
[38] 18 U. S. C. A. §§ 94, 95.   [39] *Id.* §§ 96, 97.

sea areas; and impose penalties for violation. The President can establish sea areas in his discretion for purposes of national defense. Of course such regulations cannot reach civilian propaganda off government property, but this seems one of the smaller risks run by soldiers and sailors on leave. It would be a fairly easy matter to establish such new rules as may be necessary to check the worst practices described at the hearings, like the dissemination of leaflets on warships. Why not make a direct military attack on the evil, instead of asking civilians to operate a costly far-flung campaign of sedition prosecutions? When we wanted to get rid of spitting on the sidewalk, we did not do so by making it a state's prison offense for anybody to open his mouth on the street. We just passed an ordinance against spitting on the sidewalk. Is it really impossible to control leaflets on warships by making a regulation against leaflets on warships? And so as to military reservations. Simply give the authorities discretion to issue or refuse a permit in advance for the distribution of printed matter, whatever its nature. Anything brought by civilian visitors, without a permit, would be subjected to summary seizure at the entrance to government property, and anybody violating the regulation could be given a fine and a jail sentence appropriate to the offense.[40] The liberty given handbills by recent Supreme Court cases hardly extends over battleships and army camps.

Second, even if such regulations would not be a satisfactory solution and a broader statute like section 1 is needed to fill an existing legal gap between conspiracies and harmless conduct, the penalties for the new crimes need careful consideration. Since the big argument in favor of section 1 is that this propaganda is not serious enough to be reached by the Civil War conspiracy statutes, we should naturally expect the punishments in the 1940 Act to be correspondingly lighter. But the actual law is just the opposite. Conspiring to overthrow the United States government by force gets at most six years,[41] whereas stuffing leaflets into ventilators of battleships can get

[40] My guess is that if the offense were defined specifically, instead of being covered by the big words of the Alien Registration Act, most people would think $100 and 30 days about right.

[41] 18 U. S. C. A. § 6. And the fine is $5,000 as against twice as much under the Alien Registration Act. The penalty for a conspiracy without force is two years in prison or $10,000 fine, or both. — 18 U. S. C. A. § 88.

ten years.[42] Section 1 of the 1940 Act "proposes, in effect, to use a twelve-inch gun to kill a gnat." [43]

The truth is, that the precedent of the Espionage Act has thrown federal and state punishments for sedition badly out of line with the rest of our penal system. What most astonished Sir Frederick Pollock about the Abrams case was "The monstrously excessive sentence — twenty years for an offense on which the sentence would have been about six months in England, or twelve at most." [44] In the same way, the Alien Registration Act punishes conduct pretty close to breaches of the peace with maximum prison sentences which in other parts of the Criminal Code are reserved for such crimes as the embezzlement of government arms and ammunition, counterfeiting silver money, mutiny on a merchant vessel, the misconduct of a steamship officer causing loss of life, and homicide in a sudden quarrel. The imprisonment is twice as long as for a postal employee stealing mail, interstate transportation of stolen automobiles, maltreatment of a vessel's crew by her officers, and embezzlement of public moneys. Three years is enough for a federal official accepting a bribe, but it needs the prospect of ten years in Atlanta to deter a Communist girl from making dates with sailors for political purposes.[45]

Third, there is grave danger that section 1, although enacted to protect soldiers and sailors, will be used in times of excitement to suppress the discussion of public affairs among civilians. The words of the statute do not indicate such a result, but neither did the similar words of the Espionage Act of 1917. It is an outstanding feature of every sedition act that the way it is enforced differs from the way it looks in print as much as a gypsy moth differs from the worm from which it has grown. For example, who would have expected an English statute inspired like section 1 by the fear of naval mutinies to be used to break up a trade-union of farm workers? [46] The possibility of sweeping judicial interpretation of the provisions of sec-

[42] Any reader who thinks that judges will refrain from imposing sentences close to the maximum for such trivial offenses, please turn back to page 79.

[43] Maverick and Kvale, 1935 House Report, p. 13.

[44] *Holmes-Pollock Letters*, II, 31.

[45] Ten-year sentences: 18 U. S. C. A. §§ 87, 277, 484, 461, 453. Five-year sentences: *id.* §§ 317, 318, 408, 482, 100. Three-year sentence, *id.* § 467.

[46] For the case of the Dorchester Labourers see Chapter X, note 7.

tion 1 is no mere conjecture, because we know exactly what happened to the same provisions in the Espionage Act. The decisions of 1917–1919 will serve as precedents for the construction of section 1.

Chapter II of this book shows what is only too liable to happen. Without repeating what is said there, I shall briefly state three ways in which the Military Disaffection Act of 1940 may easily be expanded beyond its precise wording. (1) The language of the speeches or pamphlets which are prosecuted need not say anything about the army or the navy, but may merely consist of expressions of opinion about the merits and conduct of our national defense policy or even of English policy. This point will be elaborated in connection with section 4. (2) The clause requiring "intent to interfere with the loyalty" of the armed forces does not prevent the application of section 1 to discussion among civilians. The Espionage Act cases show that a wicked intent can always be inferred from the nature of the words, if the jury considers those to be objectionable. All that really counts is the jury's opinion of the language used by the speaker or writer. Thus the statute may easily be used to imprison an unpopular author of a letter to a newspaper stating that a certain type of army airplanes is killing too many American pilots or a minister who preaches a pacifist sermon to his congregation. And the formulation of war aims through constant argument and counter-argument may be as much impeded as it was in 1918, unless the Attorney General takes stringent steps to prevent his subordinates from bringing the same kinds of prosecutions. (3) These expressions of opinion will not need to be specifically addressed to soldiers or sailors or to men on the eve of entering service. If some of them happen to be among a large body of listeners or readers, so much the worse for the defendant, but it is enough that the words may conceivably reach men actually or potentially in uniform. Notice that section 1 punishes anybody who distributes printed matter which might cause objectionable military conduct, but it does not say that the distribution must be made to soldiers or sailors. Nor is there any requirement that the forbidden oral remarks must be spoken to members of the armed forces.

The range of section 1 was soon greatly increased by the

enactment of our first peace-time Selective Service Act. Every male citizen between twenty-one and thirty-five is now potentially a member of the army, and at least one such person is likely to participate in all but the most private discussions of public affairs. Hence it will be difficult to express any critical view of the government's defense policies without violating section 1, unless it be interpreted very differently from the Espionage Act. Indeed, an audience of young women will not be much safer if contemporary judges apply Justice Pitney's views about the criminality of bringing home to the sisters, wives, and sweethearts of drafted men a sense of impending personal loss.[47]

Fourth, the law may easily be administered in such a way as to lessen the intellectual activity of drafted men and the rest of the armed forces, especially officers. Very likely they will suffer no serious harm by being deprived of Communist leaflets like those produced at the hearings. The trouble is that the language used by Congress to reach these leaflets is so wide that it can be made to include some of the most important contemporary writing on national issues as well. Think of the books shut out of the mails under the Espionage Act.[48] It was all very well in 1900 for Bernard Shaw's officer to say "I never expect a soldier to think"; but that theory seems less successful forty years later. Brains are a necessary item of equipment for the varied problems of mechanized warfare. The old military principle, "Theirs not to reason why, Theirs but to do or die," if followed today is likely to result in much more dying than doing. It is indeed fortunate that British generals are no longer what H. G. Wells called them, "the duller members of a mentally understimulated class." By and large, the more reading, the more thinking. However, most contemporary writers on live subjects who are worth their salt are bound to say some things which have a discouraging effect on

---

[47] See *supra* p. 94; also Judge Van Valkenburgh *supra* p. 52.

To make assurance doubly sure with respect to drafted men, the Selective Service Act of 1940 contains provisions against outside interference with conscription, thus overlapping section 1 of the Alien Registration Act. These provisions (§ 11) punish anybody who "knowingly counsels, aids, or abets another to evade registration or service in the land or naval forces or any of the requirements of this Act, or of said rules, regulations, or directions, . . ."

[48] *Supra*, pp. 98–99.

blindly optimistic patriots. Some of them will wrench such passages from their context and use them against the books. Even if such books are not prosecuted, they will tend to go under cover as soon as some other writers are indicted. An atmosphere of suppression dampens down everything. Thus "the intellectual insulation against disloyalty," which Congress desired this statute to create in the Army and Navy,[49] may readily prove to be so heavy that it will keep out a good deal else besides. Some military leaders of unquestioned patriotism worry much more about the possibility of intellectual insulation in the armed forces than about the remote menace of Communism. An army and navy which are not part of the nation's life with all its stresses and strains are likely to become either an inefficient instrument of democracy or an unsympathetic group disturbing to its safety.

Disaffection in the armed forces is indeed dangerous, but the only sure safeguard against it is the men themselves. I believe that the Army and the Navy and the great mass of our people are intensely loyal to the government and that one reason for this loyalty is the scope which our laws permit for freedom of discussion. Any real plot to bring about a mutiny can be severely dealt with under the two conspiracy statutes. As for the speeches and leaflets which are not sufficiently serious to fall within those statutes, we can well afford to run whatever slight risk of trouble they create for the sake of the freedom which Thomas Jefferson believed to be the most precious possession of this country.

Section 2. (a) It shall be unlawful for any person —

(1) to knowingly or willfully advocate, abet, advise, or teach the duty, necessity, desirability, or propriety of overthrowing or destroying any government in the United States by force or violence, or by the assassination of any officer of any such government;

(2) with the intent to cause the overthrow or destruction of any government in the United States, to print, publish, edit, issue, circulate, sell, distribute, or publicly display any written or printed matter advocating, advising, or teaching the duty, necessity, desirability, or propriety of overthrowing or destroying any government in the United States by force or violence;

[49] Representative McSwain, quoted *supra* at note 23.

(3) to organize or help to organize any society, group, or assembly of persons who teach, advocate, or encourage the overthrow or destruction of any government in the United States by force or violence; or to be or become a member of, or affiliate with, any such society, group, or assembly of persons, knowing the purposes thereof.

(b) For the purposes of this section, the term "government in the United States" means the Government of the United States, the government of any State, Territory, or possession of the United States, the government of the District of Columbia, or the government of any political subdivision of any of them.

Even if the previous section can be classed as an army and navy law within the war powers, the clauses above quoted are a full-fledged sedition law, which does not rest on any express power in the Constitution. Section 2 resembles the New York Anarchy Act under which Gitlow was convicted and pardoned, and it is almost as broad as the California Syndicalism Act, under which Anita Whitney was convicted and pardoned. Here at last is the federal peace-time sedition law which A. Mitchell Palmer and his associated patrioteers tried to scare the country into passing twenty years ago without success. Not a spark of evidence was introduced in committee or in Congress to show any more need for such a federal statute now than in 1920. No proof was offered of any evil which had to be remedied by the unprecedented provisions of section 2. The plain reason for it is, that the persons and organizations who have been hankering for such a measure during the last two decades took advantage of the passion against immigrants to write into an anti-alien statute the first federal peace-time restrictions on speaking and writing by American citizens since the ill-fated Sedition Act of 1798.

So far as I can ascertain, the provisions of section 2 never received a favorable report from any committee of the Seventy-Sixth Congress that had subjected them to the test of a public hearing.[50] First, they were in our Smith Bill (H. R. 5138)

[50] The Senate Judiciary Committee did recommend section 2, but had held no hearings thereon and gave no arguments for it beyond a formal statement; at this late stage the main task was to rearrange the whole complex statute. I have found no hearings in the 76th Congress on the McCormack Amendment, and have not searched for hearings in earlier Congresses. The 1935 Disaffection Bill did not contain this section.

when it went to the House Judiciary Committee, where they encountered considerable opposition at the hearings. Then they were brought up on the floor of the House by Mr. Mc-Cormack of Massachusetts as an amendment to an entirely different bill, to punish spies on forts, naval vessels, etc.[51] Although he did not describe any situation that called for this sedition law, his amendment passed the House 357 to 17, after brief speeches in which Congressmen said they were "on the side of American institutions and government." Next came the committee report on the Smith Bill, which omitted the section in question without comment on its desirability, merely saying that it overlapped the McCormack Amendment which had already passed the House.[52] Finally, after long debates on the Smith Bill, section 2 suddenly bobbed up again. This time it was Mr. Smith who offered it as an amendment, for fear the Senate might not pass the McCormack Amendment (as it did not). He then argued that the House might as well do to citizens what it had already done in the deportation sections to aliens:

We have heard a lot of talk here about abusing the poor alien. The gentlemen who have been talking that way cannot complain about this section. We have laws against aliens who advocate the overthrow of this Government by force, but do you know that there is nothing in the world to prevent a treasonable American citizen from doing so? He can advocate revolution, the overthrow of the Government by force, anarchy, and everything else, and there is nothing in the law to stop it.[53]

Nothing could better illustrate the insidious progress of intolerance than the insertion of this anti-citizen section into the anti-alien bill of 1940. First, Congress started out to limit the speech of radical aliens on the ground that they were merely guests; of course we should never think of imposing similar

[51] The McCormack Amendment was to H. R. 6075, a bill to increase the penalties in § 1 of the Espionage Act of 1917, which deals with spies and is not limited to war time. 84 *Congressional Record* 6604 ff. (June 5, 1939). H. R. 6075 never passed the Senate. However, a similar Senate Bill (S. 1398) containing only the spy clauses did pass both houses, and became law on March 28, 1940 (50 U. S. C. A. § 31 as so amended). This footnote is just one example of the confusing maze of multiple overlapping spy and sedition bills in the 76th Congress.

[52] 1939 House Hearings, p. 1; 1939 House Report, p. 4.

[53] 84 *Congressional Record* 10452 (July 29, 1939).

regulations on the freedom of speech of citizens.[54] Next, section 1, which did apply to citizens, was justified because it was not directed to the entire civilian population; it was an effort to protect a paid, specially organized group — it dealt with the Army and Navy, and they were different from the general public.[55] Finally, section 2, which did deal with the general public and the entire civilian population, got into the bill at a late stage, and the circle of suppression was complete. *Facilis descensus Averno.*

One further extension still remains possible, which may be much less agreeable to the sponsors of section 2. Its provisions, which were put permanently on the statute-book in order to hit radicals, may some day be turned against conservatives. This was shrewdly pointed out by Representative Hinshaw of California, whose opposition to the amendment evidently surprised a good many of his fellow Congressmen.

We can look back into the history of the United States and see times of turmoil, times of strife among the people. . . . I speak to my colleagues on the Republican side, . . . as well as many on the Democratic side, who would favor this amendment, and I call attention to the fact that it is quite conceivable that at some time in the future of the United States a government might come into power that was not at all to their liking, and it might come there by ballot. I refer to such a government as a virtual dictatorship, supported by a Congress as supine as the German Reichstag. There might be those among you who would feel that the persons who were in command of the United States through such a government should not be there, and I suggest that you consider whether it is not a fact that in some words that you might speak, you yourselves might be subjected to the conditions of this title which it is proposed to have inserted in the bill. . . .

I submit to you that . . . some word or thought that we as citizens might express offhand, without intending to violate the law, might be taken under this title to mean something very serious, and a man could be subjected to persecution and to the heavy penalties of this act. I do not think it is right, I do not think it is fair . . . I do not believe in meeting intolerance with injustice. I value my liberty as did my ancestors who fought to set this country free.[56]

[54] See, for example, Hobbs, *id.* 10359.
[55] McCormack in 1935 House Hearings, pp. 26, 62.
[56] 84 *Congressional Record* 10453.

After a few other remarks, the Smith Amendment embodying section 2 passed 79 to 32, a narrow margin when compared with the overwhelming votes behind other sections of the Alien Registration Act.

Such was the manner in which Congress slipped easily into a repetition of the Sedition Act of 1798. This comparison may seem unjustified to some supporters of section 2 of the 1940 act, because its wording is quite different from that of 1798. One of the striking features of a sedition law is that it always is said to be different — its proponents are sure to contend that they are not repeating the mistakes of last time. Thus Blackstone defended the seditious libel prosecutions of his day because they were not the same as the censorship; and the Six Acts of 1819 were not the same as those libel prosecutions; and the Defense of the Realm Act under which Bertrand Russell went to prison was not the same as the Six Acts.

There are fashions in sedition laws as in everything else. The draftsmen of 1798 went for a model to the English seditious libel prosecutions just ahead of their day,[57] and imported into their statute phrases like "intent to bring the government into contempt or disrepute." [58] The draftsmen of 1940 likewise found their model in the sedition laws just ahead of them, which happened to be the New York Anarchy Act and the Criminal Syndicalism Acts. Aside from greater severity of sentences, the only big change during the intervening hundred odd years is in phraseology. Instead of saying "to excite against the government the hatred of the good people of the United States," sedition laws now say, "to advocate the overthrow of the government by force or violence." Yet the new words work out in much the same way as the old words. This book has shown again and again *ad nauseam* that "advocate force and violence" can be stretched in practice to imprison people who do not resemble at all the desperate revolutionists of whom one naturally thinks on reading these words for the first time.[59] Courts and juries will find that the overthrow of the government by force is necessarily involved in the expression of many ideas which are essential to a fruitful discussion

[57] See *infra* Chapter XIII.
[58] 1 Stat. 596 (1798).
[59] See, for example, *supra*, pp. 182–187, 206–208, 223–224.

of public affairs, or else harmless.[60] Consequently, the operation of the twentieth-century state statutes against Gitlow and Anita Whitney was substantially the same as the operation of the Sedition Act of 1798 against Matthew Lyon. The utterances for which they were all convicted came to be regarded as merely intemperate political and economic controversy; Gitlow and Miss Whitney were pardoned and Lyon's fine was repaid. Section 2 of the 1940 Act has exactly the same possibilities of unexpectedly wide application. Can we rely on the present administration to construe it narrowly and use it only against really dangerous men?

The truth is that the precise language of a sedition law is like the inscription on a sword. What matters is the existence of the weapon. Once the sword is placed in the hands of the people in power, then, whatever it says, they will be able to reach and slash at almost any unpopular person who is speaking or writing anything that they consider objectionable criticism of their policies.

Section 2 is almost identical with the hypothetical peacetime sedition bill which I envisaged in 1920 [61] and used earlier in this book as the basis for discussing the constitutionality and desirability of such a law. Consequently, the reader is asked to turn back to the last two sections of Chapter IV and apply what is written there to these provisions of the 1940 Act. The same considerations and my next few paragraphs also apply *mutatis mutandis* to section 1.

The doubts expressed in Chapter IV as to the constitutionality of a law like section 2 under the First Amendment are somewhat strengthened by the recent Supreme Court decisions reviewed in Chapter XI. A pamphlet advocating the overthrow of the government by a vague revolution in the remote future would pretty clearly fall within the terms of section 2 because it was covered by the similar language of the New York Anarchy Act in the Gitlow case. Legislation so construed was held constitutional there and in the Whitney case.[62] But would the same constitutional view be taken today? Although those two cases have never been overruled, the dis-

---

[60] See the remarks of Fraenkel and Scharrenberg in 1939 House Hearings, pp. 11, 69.

[61] *Supra* pp. 169–170.   [62] *Supra* Chapters IX, X.

senting opinions of Justices Holmes and Brandeis therein insisted that this interpretation of sedition statutes violated liberty of speech; and the general attitude of these two dissenters toward the value of open discussion now appears frequently in majority opinions. Consequently, it is very possible that orotund hints at far-distant uprisings under circumstances which create no clear and present danger of harmful acts will be held immune from punishment under section 2. If I am right in so supposing, then this section is valid only to the extent that it is used against a speaker or writer who definitely urges others to engage in an insurrection in the near future. Hence, any convictions under section 2 for distributing the I.W.W. Preamble and the Communist Manifesto of 1848 and similar disquisitions will be set aside. In short, although section 2 may not be wholly unconstitutional, still the Court may confine it within much narrower limits than were desired by the Congressmen who so persistently obtained its enactment.

However, the actual operation of section 2 during the next two years will not be much affected by the Supreme Court. If we get into a period of excitement, prosecutors and trial judges and juries may enforce section 2 vigorously against the discussion just described. Such was the use of similar phraseology in state anarchy and syndicalism acts. If meetings of what may be called soft revolutionists are broken up by numerous arrests, and their pamphlets are seized under search warrants, and a series of successful prosecutions against some radicals scares the rest into silence, then section 2 will have accomplished a sweeping suppression, whatever happens to it when it gets to the Supreme Court. Indeed, it may never get there at all. The Court never passed on the validity of the Sedition Act of 1798 or on most of the clauses of the 1918 amendment to the Espionage Act, and it has not yet considered the membership clauses of state sedition laws, although these were enacted twenty years ago and have been abundantly enforced since. Thus what counts during the immediate months of emergency ahead of us is probably not the attitude of the Supreme Court, but the attitude of policemen, prosecutors, trial judges, and the United States commissioners who issue search warrants. Hence it is highly important for the maintenance of open discussion that those people should limit section 2 to the really wicked man who is trying to stir up dangerous acts here and now.

It is significant that during the hearings and debates some proponents of these two sections were not much disturbed by problems of constitutionality. They admitted that the provisions might be too sweepingly construed in practice, but considered that Congress should nevertheless enact them and leave it to the courts to lop off whatever about them was excessive.[63] A similar position may easily be taken by prosecutors and other men charged with the enforcement of the statute. Their impulse during a crisis may be to go to the limit of the terms of the statute in suppressing ideas and agitators considered by them to be objectionable, and leave the Constitution to the Supreme Court.

At this point a very interesting constitutional question arises. May not section 2 be entirely invalid, because of this danger that the practical application of its wording will discourage desirable discussion? It may be like an egg — if it's partly bad, then it's all bad.[64] This possibility is suggested by the opinion of Justice Murphy in *Thornhill* v. *Alabama*, decided a few months before the enactment of section 2. The loose scope of that section may very well bring it within the condemnation which Justice Murphy visited upon a different sort of sweeping statute:

> The power of the licensor . . . is pernicious not merely by reason of the censure of particular comments but by reason of the threat to censure comments on matters of public concern. It is not merely the sporadic abuse of power by the censor but the pervasive threat inherent in its very existence that constitutes the danger to freedom of discussion. . . . A like threat is inherent in a penal statute . . . which does not aim specifically at evils within the allowable area of state control but, on the contrary, sweeps within its ambit other activities that in ordinary circumstances constitute an exercise of freedom of speech or of the press. *The existence of such a statute, which readily lends itself to harsh and discriminatory enforcement by local prosecuting officials, against particular groups deemed to*

[63] See 1939 House Hearings, pp. 33 (Lieutenant Nunn), 71 (Representative Smith); 86 *Congressional Record* (temporary) 12620 (Senator Danaher).

[64] The usual separability provision in section 40 of the act will not necessarily save any portion of section 2, because the good and the bad parts seem inextricably mingled. See Smith *v.* Cahoon, 283 U. S. 553, 562–565 (1931).

merit their displeasure, results in a continuous and pervasive restraint on all freedom of discussion that might reasonably be regarded as within its purview. It is not any less effective or, if the restraint is not permissible, less pernicious than the restraint on freedom of discussion imposed by the threat of censorship. . . . Where regulations of the liberty of free discussion are concerned, there are special reasons for observing the rule that *it is the statute,* and not the accusation or the evidence under it, *which prescribes the limits of permissible conduct and warns against transgression.*[65]

Special attention must be given to the most drastic portion of section 2, namely clause (a) (3). This makes it a crime for a man to be a member of an organization which is subsequently found to advocate the overthrow of the government by force, regardless of what he himself says or does. This idea that guilt is not necessarily personal, but can result from association, is absolutely abhorrent to every American tradition or conception of criminal justice before 1918. Unfortunately, in that hysterical period it got into our deportation statutes and state syndicalism acts; but the operation of both kinds of laws is not a cause for pride,[66] and might well have deterred Congress from passing this part of section 2. It is the first time that guilt by association was ever introduced into a federal criminal law. Neither the Sedition Act of 1798 nor the Espionage Acts of 1917 and 1918 included such a conception. We got safely through the Civil War and the World War without finding it necessary to create group guilt outside the limits of an actual conspiracy.

It is noteworthy that both the eminent lawyers charged by the Department of Justice with the enforcement of the Espionage Act during the World War have publicly condemned statutes penalizing men for mere membership in an organization.[67] Alfred Bettman, in opposing one of the federal peacetime sedition bills of 1920 which made membership criminal just like section 2, pronounced this an "absolutely complete departure from our traditional democratic doctrines," and con-

[65] 310 U. S. 88, 97–98 (1940). Italics mine.
[66] *Supra* Chapter V, section III; Chapter X, section I.
[67] Alfred Bettman in Hearings before the Committee on Rules, 66th Cong., 2d Sess., on H. Res. 438, Wash., 1920, pp. 125–128; John Lord O'Brian, "The Menace of Administrative Law," 25 *Reports of the Maryland State Bar Association,* 1920, at p. 163.

tinued: "One of the fundamental conceptions of Anglo-Saxon law is that guilt is personal and not by association." And John Lord O'Brian declared that "the abandonment of the doctrine of personal guilt" in our deportation statutes presented "an anomaly in our jurisprudence."

The provisions thus attacked present serious constitutional questions.[68] Probably the wide powers of Congress over immigration enable it to deport an alien for what somebody else does, but it is quite another matter to imprison a citizen for what somebody else does. If they are fellow-conspirators they must share the responsibility for whatever is planned, but this clause of the Alien Registration Act is intended to reach membership in organizations that are not conspiracies; otherwise it is rendered unnecessary by the conspiracy statutes discussed earlier. None of the Supreme Court cases on state sedition acts has squarely involved guilt by association. The nearest to it was the case of Anita Whitney.[69] She was held properly convicted for what was said at a meeting in which she took no active part; but the majority opinion by Justice Sanford emphasized her failure to leave the hall when she heard extremist speeches and declared that the offense "partakes of the nature of a criminal conspiracy." The conviction of Burns was also sustained, although the evidence against him consisted largely of what the I.W.W. had done, but Burns was an active organizer and distributor of literature. He was more than a mere member.[70] On the other hand, Justice Brandeis, whose views now carry great weight in the Supreme Court, dissented in the Burns case and disagreed with the conviction of Anita Whitney. Furthermore, the recent decisions discussed in Chapter XI on Stromberg, Herndon, and De Jonge all concentrate their attention on what the prisoner himself did, and throw out of the case the literature and additional evidence of what was done by the Communist Party or by other members thereof. And the Chief Justice said in 1920, when opposing the expulsion of the Socialist Assemblymen: "It is of the

---

[68] The fullest discussion of the constitutional point is in 45 *Harvard Law Review* 927 (1932), which discusses a state decision upholding a conviction merely for membership in the Communist Party. Three judges out of seven dissented. — State *v.* Boloff, 138 Ore. 568 (1932), discussed *infra* at n. 81.

[69] 274 U. S. 357 (1927), discussed in Chapter X, section II.

[70] 274 U. S. 328 (1927), discussed in Chapter X, section II.

essence of the institutions of liberty that it be recognized that guilt is personal . . ." Consequently, it seems possible that the Court may hold that the mere existence of that party or some similar radical organization does not present a situation of clear and present danger so as to deprive every member of the protection of the First Amendment.

Whatever be thought about constitutionality, the wisdom of clause (a) (3) of section 2 presents a much more important question. History provides us with numerous attempts by the governments of other countries to introduce this same conception of guilt by association into their law in order to break up some objectionable organization. For example, Congress can find a precedent for its action in Imperial Germany. In 1878, after two attempts had been made upon the Emperor's life, Bismarck secured a law "against the generally dangerous efforts of Social Democracy," a party which then advocated the doctrine that the existing capitalistic society must be overthrown by forcible revolution. This law made men offenders, not for anything they individually did or said, but simply by reason of their membership in an association which aimed at the overthrow of the existing order of government or society. The party throve and prospered under this law as never before. When it was repealed, the party became conservative.[71] Similar legislative measures were adopted in England during the hysteria of the French Revolution against associations which advocated universal manhood suffrage, although as May says, the few men who were really guilty of sedition and treason would have met with no sympathy among a loyal people. A statute was passed suppressing by name the "Societies of United Englishmen, United Scotchmen, United Britons, United Irishmen, and The London Corresponding Society" and enacting that any person who thereafter became or continued a member of any such society should be deemed guilty of an unlawful combination and confederacy and upon conviction might be transported for seven years.[72] Other societies were broken up by a general statute punishing any one concerned in taking oaths to engage in any "seditious pur-

[71] Ernst Freund, *The Police Power*, p. 513 note; Stephen, *History of the Criminal Law*, II, 395. Alfred Bettman, *supra* note 67.

[72] 39 Geo. III, c. 79 (1799).

pose." This was the statute used nearly forty years later to punish the Dorchester labourers for membership in an agricultural union.[73]

May's description of England in 1792 applies to this country today, and should stand as a warning:

> In ordinary times the insignificance of these societies would have caused contempt rather than alarm; but as clubs and demagogues, originally not more formidable, had obtained a terrible ascendancy in France, they aroused apprehensions out of proportion to their real danger. . . . The Government gave too ready a credence to the reports of their agents; and invested the doings of a small knot of democrats, chiefly workingmen, with the dignity of a widespread conspiracy to overturn the constitution. Ruling over a free State, they learned to dread the people, in the spirit of tyrants. Instead of relying upon the sober judgment of the country, they appealed to its fears; and in repressing seditious practices they were prepared to sacrifice liberty of opinion. Their policy, dictated by the circumstances of a time of strange and untried danger, was approved by the prevailing sentiment of their contemporaries, but has not been justified in an age of greater freedom by the maturer judgment of posterity.[74]

Ireland is another country where the policy of guilt by association has been a favorite with the government. In 1825 the Catholic Association, which advocated the admission of Roman Catholics to full civil and political rights, was suppressed by an Act of Parliament declaring unlawful every society acting for more than fourteen days for the purpose of procuring the redress of grievances in church or state, and making membership thereafter a misdemeanor punishable by fine and imprisonment in the discretion of the court. The Catholic Association was dissolved, and its former members started a new society every fourteen days to do exactly the same things. When the statute expired after three years, the Catholic Association immediately revived. In 1829 it was suppressed again by name, but it had accomplished its object of securing Catholic Emancipation.[75] In 1881 the British Cabinet repeated this policy with what Morley, who ought to know,

[73] 37 Geo. III, c. 123 (1797); 20 *Columbia Law Review* 234 (1920); *supra* Chapter X, note 7.

[74] May, *Constitutional History of England*, II, 32–34.

[75] 6 Geo. IV, c. 4 (1825); 10 Geo. IV, c. 1 (1829); May, II, 88–93.

calls "about the most egregious failure in the whole history of exceptional law." Parnell's Land League was suppressed by proclamation under authority of a Coercion Act, and hundreds of suspects, including Parnell himself, were arrested and imprisoned; "but the only effect of these measures was largely to increase agrarian crime in Ireland and to strengthen the malign influence of the instigators to violence who had to some real extent been held in check by the imprisoned leaders." [76]

It is this policy of guilt by association which our government now proposes to imitate. The American policy was always different until 1918. A man has not been visited with legal penalties because he had bad companions. He has not been imprisoned except for acts which he himself did or injurious words which he himself uttered. An alien was not expelled before the war unless after investigation of his individual qualities he was found undesirable. Even with treason, the most dangerous crime of all, a man is not guilty just because he associates with treasonable persons. Chief Justice Marshall held in the case of Aaron Burr that he must himself commit overt acts of treason.[77] Unless a man is a member of a conspiracy he is not responsible for the acts of others which are not authorized by him. And no one can soberly contend that the Communist Party is a conspiracy. The Supreme Court held unanimously in 1920 that the president and treasurer of the Philadelphia *Tageblatt* could not lawfully be convicted for items in its columns violating the Espionage Act, which were put in by their associates on the newspaper, since they were in no way responsible for the publications complained of.[78] The same principle applies to the rank and file of the Communist Party.

The Alien Registration Act brings into our federal criminal law the European principle that a man is known by the company he keeps and that guilt is not personal.

Some of the obnoxious European statutes just mentioned were milder than the Alien Registration Act in one way — they proscribed the Social Democratic Party or the Catholic Association by name and so told the members exactly what

[76] 44 Vic., c. 4 (1881); May, III, 160; Morley, *Recollections*, II, 318.
[77] Beveridge, *Marshall*, III, chap. ix.
[78] Schaefer *v.* United States, 251 U. S. 468; see p. 87 *supra*.

they were in for if they did not immediately resign. It is much harsher to force the members of hundreds of organizations to guess whether they belong to something unlawful, at the peril of ten years in prison if they guess wrong. In other words, an actual or prospective member of some unpopular association is not told in advance by section 2 (a) (3) that the association advocates the overthrow of the government by force. The first authoritative determination of that fact may come at the moment when he stands in the dock and hears the jury bring in a verdict of "Guilty." How many members of radical organizations can fairly be supposed to have known on June 28th, 1940, that their organization was within that new statute? After all, the purposes of an organization do not stand out like a sore thumb. One can read through the whole platform and campaign handbook of a party, without being sure what its real purposes are. They are concealed behind a printed compromise designed to reconcile the widely divergent groups which make up any political party. Were the real purposes of the Republican Party in 1928 those of Andrew Mellon or Herbert Hoover or George Norris? As for the Democrats, remember the Madison Square Convention. What is true of the major parties is *a fortiori* true of radical organizations. A radical by his very nature tends to keep on splitting off. Brissenden's book on the I.W.W. is largely a history of factional fights. How can any member of such an organization be sure precisely what it stands for? Joining the Communist Party is not like joining a cocktail party, where everybody knows its purpose.

To impose imprisonment on the members of a group without any warning except the elastic language of section 2 (a) (3) recalls Bentham's discussion of the uncertainties of the criminal law of his time, much of which was not written out in statutes but merely defined by judicial decisions that might come after the prisoner had been arrested. Bentham complained that the criminal judges gave laws to the poor just as a man makes laws for his dog. "When your dog does anything you want to break him of, you wait until he does it and then you beat him for it. That is the way you make laws for your dog," and that is the way we are making laws for our radical workmen.

Somebody may object that no member of an unlawful organization can be punished if he was ignorant of its unlawfulness, because the last words of clause (a) (3) limit the crime to persons who are members *"knowing its purposes."* This contention about the scope of the statutory defense may be true, but it is by no means certain. My doubts must be explained at the risk of being somewhat technical, for the problem is sure to be very important if any prosecutions are brought under the membership clause.

The persons on the membership lists of the Communist Party fall roughly into four different groups. Let us typify them by four prisoners who have been indicted under clause (a) (3) — Algernon, Ben, Christabel, and Delilah. Suppose that the federal jury first decides what so many state juries have decided, that the Communist Party advocates the overthrow of the government by force. Next it is faced with the question — which of the four prisoners can properly be convicted as "knowing its purposes"? The testimony by the respective defendants is as follows: Algernon says he did not even know he was a member; his only contact with Communists is that he once heard Granville Hicks lecture on Walt Whitman and somebody must have put his name on a mailing list. Ben is an illiterate colored man, who joined the party because it had a Negro on the ticket, but he never read anything or went to meetings or listened to speeches. Christabel went to many meetings and perused all the programs and manifestos, which she found rather puzzling; she understood them to urge better conditions for workers and the equal distribution of wealth, but she did not like violence or infer anything of the sort from what she read and heard. Delilah was a fanatical revolutionist, who thought the party would give her just what she wanted — a guillotine by which to knit.

If this testimony of the prisoners is uncontradicted, what ought the jury to do? Algernon and Ben should clearly be acquitted. Delilah is plainly within the critical phrase "knowing its purposes," and the jurymen will convict her unless they are sick of sedition prosecutions or like her looks. Christabel is the problem. She knew what the party leaders said, but she did not interpret their language in the same way as the jury. It seems to me very probable that she will be convicted, and that her conviction will be sustained by the Circuit Court of Appeals. The court is likely to hold that she knew the purposes of the party, although she did not know their unlawfulness. Very likely the court will quote in its opinion that misleading adage, "Every one is presumed to know the law."

Now, the moral of this story is that a very large number of Communists are substantially in the situation of Christabel. It is obviously contrary to common sense to say that every man and woman who voted the Communist ticket last November knew, as he did so, that the party advocates "the overthrow of the government by force or violence." If my conjectures about the narrow scope of the defense prove correct, then the Christabels and not the Delilahs will furnish most of the grist for the sedition mill.

Even if the critical statutory phrase be more leniently construed to mean, in effect, "knowing its unlawful purposes," Christabel will probably go to prison just the same, whenever the evidence of her ignorance is not quite so clean-cut as I have supposed. After all, there is no sure proof of what was inside her head; as the jurymen themselves consider that the manifestos urge violence, they may easily conclude that Christabel thought so too, whatever she now says to the contrary. And if the appellate court takes the same view of the party as the jurymen do, it will probably say that Christabel's knowledge of the unlawfulness was a question of fact for the jury. Remember that you and I never can be sure that a prisoner really had the mental state which a statute requires.[79] We only know what some tribunal finds that mental state to be. And when the person unquestionably belongs to an organization which the tribunal regards as very dangerous, then it will very probably infer her guilty state of mind from the fact that she joined such a subversive group. The emotional drive will be to stamp out the Communist Party.

So Christabel and the thousands like her, who read the Communist documents without realizing force lurks therein, have little solace from the "knowing its purposes" clause. All that really counts is whether the party is unlawful within clause (a) (3). On that question, also, the jury's verdict may be final, because the court may say that the issue whether an

[79] See *supra* pp. 61–63.

organization does advocate forbidden doctrines is a jury question, so long as the evidence is conflicting.[80]

Now come back for a minute to Ben. He too has a poor chance of escape, once the prosecutions get into full swing. His defense like Christabel's depends on his mental state, and if there is any evidence that he attended meetings the jury may not believe his tale of ignorance of the party program.

If anybody thinks I am exaggerating the possibilities of clause (a) (3), let him look at the case of Ben Boloff, under the similar phraseology of the Oregon Syndicalism Act.[81] Boloff was a sewer digger who had come from Russia as a boy of eighteen and resided in Oregon for twenty years. Never before had he been convicted of any crime. He had not attended school for a single day and could not read or write, nor could he speak English. All he knew was hard work — how to dig a ditch or lay sewer pipe. In 1930 he came to Portland in search of work. After he had walked the streets for a few days vainly looking for a job, he was arrested for vagrancy. This charge was dismissed, but two days later the police arrested him again for violating the Syndicalism Act because they had found in his pocket a Communist membership card. This showed that he had belonged for eight years, and during less than half that time had paid monthly dues of at most fifty cents, which the majority opinion described as "substantial sums of money." He had attended meetings in the local hall where the red flag was constantly on display and he could see quantities of literature profusely illustrated with pictures of men bearing arms and engaged in violence. One of the witnesses "felt quite certain" that Boloff had attended at least one meeting where the use of violence was advocated by the speakers. Boloff admitted that he was a frequenter of the Plaza in Portland where the Communist Party speakers held forth. He testified that he understood that the organization of

[80] See Chapter XIII, note 5.
[81] State v. Boloff, 138 Ore. 568 (1932), three out of seven judges dissenting; noted in 45 Harvard Law Review 927 as upholding the constitutionality of guilt by association. The statute was Oregon Code, 1930, § 14 — 3, 112, enacted in 1921. Although its membership clause did not contain the express requirement of knowledge, which is in the Alien Registration Act, the text shows that this requirement has little material importance. See also State v. Hennessy, 114 Wash. 351, 366 (1921); references cited supra, p. 385, note, last paragraph.

which he was a member was a workingmen's society which was endeavoring to better conditions for the working man. This was all that Boloff himself did or said. The trial judge refused to submit to the jury the question whether the defendant did or did not know the nature of the Communist Party. The evidence against him consisted mainly of a large amount of Communist literature, much of it carried through the mail as second-class matter, and of testimony about what had been said at Communist meetings and conventions without proof that the statements of the most rabid speaker were ratified by the organization. The chief witness for the prosecution was a police officer who had joined the Portland Communist local a few months before to learn its nature, and had risen rapidly to become secretary and its delegate to two regional conventions. He and an immigration official gave expert testimony of the purposes of the Communist Party, and stated that it aimed "to bring about an armed revolution at the very first opportunity." On this testimony Boloff was convicted and given the maximum imprisonment of ten years in the state penitentiary, but was mercifully exempted from paying a fine. This sentence was affirmed on appeal by a bare majority of the Supreme Court of Oregon. Even the writer of the majority opinion said:

It is difficult to understand why this humble offender who obviously occupies an obscure place in life should receive a penalty which is almost the maximum. Benjamin Franklin once declared, "Punishment inflicted beyond the merit of the offense is so much punishment of innocence."

Judge Belt in dissenting said:

Ten years in the penitentiary! What a price to pay for warped ideas! Who is this man Ben Boloff that he should thus be considered such a menace to society? . . .

Let it be borne in mind that the charge in the indictment is predicated solely upon the mere act of the defendant in joining the Communist Party. Aside from his membership in this organization, there is not a scintilla of evidence that he ever said or did anything to teach or advocate crime or physical violence. . . . Indeed, the evidence well warrants the inference that Boloff did not know that he was joining an organization having an unlawful purpose. . . . In the light of the above record it is utterly absurd that this ignorant defendant, who does not know what it is all about, will, by reason of his ideas, constitute an imminent danger to the welfare of our government. . . .

The State, having shown that the defendant joined the Communist Party, apparently sought, under the theory of a conspiracy, to hold him responsible for all of the strange doctrines and teachings that any member of such organization ever advocated — whether the defendant believes in or even knows of the same. Applying the same logic, if some Democrat should go so far as to assert in a public speech that all Republicans should be shot at sunrise, then every member of the Democratic party would be guilty of crime.

Fortunately Boloff was released and the entire Criminal Syndicalism Act was repealed and replaced by provisions imposing a three-year sentence for conspiracy to commit a felony,[82] substantially the equivalent of section 37 of the Federal Criminal Code. Congress might well follow the example of the Oregon legislature, by repealing section 2 of the Alien Registration Act and falling back on the federal conspiracy laws, which were considered adequate to protect the government when Lee was within a hundred miles of Washington.

Nothing could illustrate better than the Boloff case the danger of putting long maximum sentences in sedition statutes. Kindly conservatives complacently assume that the maximum will be reserved for dangerous fanatics, and the rest will be let off with three months or so. It just doesn't work out that way. A trial judge entrusted with a ten-year maximum sedition act behaves like a fifteen-year-old boy behind the wheel of a car that can reach eighty miles an hour. It does. And this judge has practically final power over the sentence. A United States Circuit Court of Appeals and most state appellate courts cannot reduce the sentence, as in England.[83] Unless they find errors of law justifying a new trial, they have no choice except to send the prisoner to serve out the original sentence.[84]

[82] Oregon Laws, 1937, c. 362.

[83] *American Law Institute: Code of Criminal Procedure* (official draft, 1930), pp. 168, 1297; L. Hall, "Reduction of Criminal Sentences on Appeal," 37 *Columbia Law Review* 521, 762 (1937); Orfield, *Criminal Appeals in America* (1939), pp. 101–121. See also *supra* Chapter XI at note 51. A few states have statutes allowing their appellate courts to revise sentences.

[84] The constitutional guarantee against "cruel and unusual punishment" was held not to be infringed by the sentence in the Boloff case or in the Hennessy case, *supra* note 81. — Weems *v.* United States, 217 U. S. 349 (1910), involved an unusual situation and has had no influence on sedition appeals.

Some people may try to brush aside the injustice of the Boloff case by saying, "Oh, well, he was pardoned!" Such people ignore the misery of the defendant and his family when they listen to the long sentence from the mouth of the trial judge, or when the prison doors clang to. How can they know he will not be shut up for the full time? And those who argue thus have no notion of the labor a pardon or commutation requires from busy men, on top of all the expense and work of obtaining the conviction. In a crisis like this, we all have something better to do with our time than march up the hill and then march down again.

The basic assumption of the framers of section 2 (a) (3) of the Alien Registration Act is, that "Everybody knows the Communist Party advocates force and violence." Consequently, if any member who does not resign at once goes to prison later, it is his own fault. In other words, uneducated workmen like Boloff know the answer to a question which has puzzled men of high intelligence ever since the Deportation Act of 1918. United States Circuit Judges and Cabinet officers could not agree about it in 1920.[85] We have had two decades since then in which to make up our minds, and the problem is still unsolved. Dean Landis in the Bridges case and the Supreme Court in the Strecker case deliberately left it unanswered. Why should a citizen in 1941 be bound by a decision of Secretary Wilson against an alien in 1920, that the party urges bloody revolution? You cannot find that ruling in most well-stocked county law libraries. Much more recent and much more accessible is the 1938 decision of Hutcheson, one of our ablest federal judges, that the party is seeking to remake the United States according to its heart's desire by political means, not violence.[86] When doctors disagree, how can a patient be expected to know poison when he sees it?

Those who blithely accept this clause of the Alien Registration Act because of their hatred for Communists would be wiser to remember that its scope is not limited to the Communist Party by any means. There are dozens of other organi-

[85] See Chapter V, section v (a).

[86] Strecker v. Kessler, 95 F. (2d) 976 (C. C. A. 1st, 1938). The Supreme Court refused to express any opinion on this question, but affirmed the decision on the ground that Strecker had ceased to be a member before his arrest. See *supra* note 9; 48 *Yale Law Journal* 111.

zations which the Act's supporters are very eager to dissolve. One backer condemned as "un-American groups connected with pink, red, and scarlet activities" the C.I.O., the American Civil Liberties Union, the Survey Associates, the New School for Social Research, the coöperative movement, and the Brookings Institution.[87] Put a man like that in as United States attorney, and the membership clause may very well be used to arrest several old-fashioned liberals. It may not stop there, either. Conservatives are not necessarily immune. A Congressman of radical proclivities added to the list of subversive organizations the League for Constitutional Government, the American Defense Society, James True Industrial Reports, and Edmonson's Economic Service.[88] Some New Dealers would be highly delighted to get after numerous manufacturers who have paid out money to these enterprises. Clause (a) (3) is like a cannon cracker, liable to go off at both ends.

Attorney General Jackson has recently sought to avoid these embarrassing difficulties of determining the purposes of an organization by the short-cut of outlawing the Communist Party. Probably this means that criminal penalties will be threatened against future recruits and any present members who neglect to resign, with deportation thrown in as usual for alien members.[89] Such a measure would have the merit of giving Communists a sharp warning instead of leaving them to puzzle out the perplexing purposes of the party. But it raises a fresh crop of difficulties. In the first place, would a statute declaring a whole political party unlawful be constitutional? Perhaps the Supreme Court would hold it reasonable to single out this party for destruction because of the readiness of its leaders and newspaper writers to obey the Master's Voice in Moscow. However, the fate of the corresponding British at-

[87] Mr. Thorkelson of Montana, 84 *Congressional Record* 10384 (July 28, 1939). The Fish Committee Report is similarly comprehensive. See also Dilling, *The Red Network* (1934).

[88] Mr. Dickstein of New York, 86 *Congressional Record* (temporary) 18695 (Sept. 19, 1940).

[89] A bill with similar provisions (H. R. 3455) was introduced on Feb. 18, 1941 by Mr. L. M. Ford of California and referred to the Judicial Committee. For some objections to such a law from conservative sources, see Mr. Hobbs, 86 *Congressional Record* (temporary) 13469 ff. (June 22, 1940); and Mr. McCormack's condemnation of the Sedition Act of 1798 as "an effort by one political party to destroy another one," 1935 House Hearings, p. 62.

tempt to break up the Catholic Association in Ireland by naming it does not augur success. What if the scattered members of the Communist Party simply adopt a different name, or else re-form their ranks within some larger party — for example, that to which the Attorney General belongs? Further reasons why this sort of law might be unwise can be gathered from the last section of the present chapter. Burke said in his speech on the Conciliation of a certain rebellious people, when his opponents wanted a bill "with teeth in it," that you cannot draw an indictment against a whole nation. You cannot draw it against a whole party either.

Those Republicans and Democrats who shout for the imprisonment of the entire Communist Party because of certain clauses in its platform might recover their sense of humor long enough to ask themselves if they ever endorsed every plank in their respective party platforms. Even Congressmen, party leaders, and Presidents have been known to disregard some such principles. It is an arduous task to capture and convict men who are personally dangerous. Have we so little to do that we can afford to take time off and butcher the Boloffs to make an American holiday? Let us punish men for the injuries they do, or even, if we must, for what they say, but stop condemning them for the grandiose phrases of a party creed.

The final argument of the advocates of guilt by association is that we must take unprecedented steps to meet unprecedented perils.[90] Clause (a) (3) is defended because we can use it to break up Foreign Legions in our midst, which according to them is something we never had before. Have these men forgotten the events which led up to the Sedition Act of 1798 — the Reign of Terror in France, and the hordes of French sympathizers in the United States, whose activities were directed by the French Ambassador himself? Yet the passage of a mild statute then to combat subversive influences closely affiliated with a foreign revolutionary government was condemned at the time by men so diverse as Hamilton and Jefferson, and has been considered ever since one of the biggest

---

[90] See Loewenstein, "Legislative Control of Political Extremism in European Democracies," 38 *Columbia Law Review* 591, 725 (1938). The last sentence of this paragraph is based on the statement of Representative Hobbs, 84 *Congressional Record* 10447 (July 29, 1939), and on correspondence with the Department of Justice.

blunders of our national history. It is all very well to say that we need a sedition law to use against Nazis and Fascists, but if the Alien Registration Act of 1940 is thus employed, it will be almost the first time to my knowledge that a sedition act has been enforced against powerful men with money. The lamentable truth, which as a former employer I hate to admit, is that sedition laws operate in practice as a device to keep down the agitation of discontented workmen. Think of the Dorchester labourers, Abrams, and the I.W.W.'s jailed under the Espionage Act and the California Syndicalism Act. This truth is hammered home by the present crisis. Many of the prominent Nazis and Fascists in the United States are aliens. If they are really within clause (a) (3), then they could have been reached long ago by the membership clauses of the Deportation Act. For if there are any organizations on earth that advocate the overthrow of the government of the United States by force, it is the organizations with which these men are affiliated. And yet, what has happened? Hundreds of Communist workmen have been rounded up by immigration officials and deported. So far as I can ascertain, not one Nazi and not one Fascist has been arrested and shipped over seas.

Section 3. It shall be unlawful for any person to attempt to commit, or to conspire to commit, any of the acts prohibited by the provisions of this title.

This and the two remaining sections of Title I are only auxiliary to the main sections, 1 and 2. It was natural to insert a conspiracy clause, as in the Espionage Act, but the consequences of section 3 carry us very far away from unlawful acts.[91] For example, if we read it into section 1 (a) (3), we see that a man can be imprisoned for ten years if he attempts to advise a soldier to refuse to perform his duties. If we hitch it to section 2(a) (3), just discussed, it is a crime to attempt to help to organize any society to encourage others to overthrow the government. I am reminded of the lazy old colored man lying abed at noon, who said that he was beginning to commence to start to get up. It will be remembered that William M. Evarts attacked section 6 of the Criminal Code, which is far closer to forceful acts than this modern con-

[91] See Representative Coffee, 84 *Congressional Record* 9536 (July 19, 1939).

spiracy section, because "in the extravagance of its comprehension, it may include much more than should be made
criminal, except in times of public danger." [92] The penalty
under this Civil War statute is six years in prison, and under
the 1940 Act it is ten years. If the extent of the danger can
be measured by the size of the punishments, a conspiracy to
overthrow the government by force is only about half as dangerous as a conspiracy to advocate its overthrow.

Section 4. Any written or printed matter of the character described in section 1 or section 2 of this Act, which is intended for
use in violation of this Act, may be taken from any house or other
place in which it may be found, or from any person in whose possession it may be, under a search warrant issued pursuant to the provisions of title XI [of the Espionage Act of 1917].

The portion of the Espionage Act here mentioned [93] is the
general federal statute regulating searches and seizures. Under
its provisions, a search warrant may be issued by a United
States district judge or a United States commissioner upon
probable cause, supported by affidavit, naming or describing
the person and particularly describing the property and the
place to be searched. The judge or commissioner must, before
issuing the warrant, examine on oath the complainant and any
witness he may produce and require their affidavits or deposi-
tions. Such affidavits, etc., must set forth the facts tending to
establish the grounds of the application or probable cause for
believing that they exist, *e.g.*, that a certain house contains
Communist leaflets designed to produce disaffection in the
Navy. If the judge or commissioner is satisfied that these
grounds exist or that there is probable cause to believe their
existence, he issues a search warrant to a United States marshal or other officer. This states the particular grounds or
probable cause and the names of the persons who gave affidavits; and commands the officer forthwith to search the specified person or place for the specified property and bring it
before the judge or commissioner. The officer may break in
doors or windows of a house or room to execute the warrant,

[92] *Arguments and Speeches of W. M. Evarts*, I, 470 (1919). See *supra* Chapter IV, section 1.
[93] 18 U. S. C. A. §§ 611–633.

if, after notice of his authority and purpose, he is refused admittance. Service at night is restricted. After making the search, the officer returns the warrant with an inventory of what he seized, and the person from whom it was taken can have a copy. Suppose the grounds of the seizure are disputed. The judge or commissioner then hears testimony. If the property or papers taken are not what the warrant describes or if the warrant was issued without probable cause, then the property must be restored to its former possessor; but otherwise it is retained by the government or disposed of according to law.[94]

Wrongful searches and seizures are punishable — for example, if an officer wilfully exceeds the authority given him by the search warrant, or if he seizes property without a warrant unless in the course of making a lawful arrest. It is a crime for anybody to get a search warrant issued maliciously and without probable cause. Making false affidavits, etc., is perjury. On the other hand, penalties are imposed for resisting the execution of a search warrant or assaulting the officer.[95]

Thus section 4 of the Alien Registration Act authorizes searches, so regulated, to be made for the new classes of criminal objects created by the earlier sections. For example, it was intended to make possible the seizure of quantities of Communist leaflets, such as those described during the hearings about section 1. Obviously, the scope of the search warrant may be as wide as the interpretation placed upon sections 1 and 2 by the judge or commissioner who issues the warrant and passes subsequently upon the validity of the seizure. Pretty much everything depends on the judgment, for there is no jury and the books and pamphlets seized are not likely to be worth the trouble and expense of an appeal. Any printed matter or manuscript which this one man believes to come within section 1 or 2 can be ferreted out by smashing down the doors and windows of private houses, and then kept by the government. All this can be done in advance of prosecution, and there may never be any prosecution. Is such previous restraint based on a "clear and present danger" of unlawful acts much greater than the harmfulness of the Minneapolis scandal-sheet in *Near* v. *Minnesota*?

[94] On searches and seizures generally, see Chapter XIV, note 5.
[95] 18 U. S. C. A. §§ 53a, 628–631.

What is most important is the actual administration of the issue of search warrants. It remains to be seen whether district judges scrutinize affidavits very closely, whether they are more cautious in their decisions about supposedly seditious pamphlets than they were in the prosecutions of 1917 and 1918, and whether their rulings about books will be wiser than those of Postmaster General Burleson. And the power to issue warrants and validate seizures can also be exercised by United States commissioners, who are practising lawyers as well and might be subjected to more local emotion and pressure than a judge.

The safeguards laid down by the long statute summarized in preceding paragraphs are impressive, and yet it was under this very statute that the government in 1917 searched and destroyed the motion picture film called *The Spirit of '76*, because it depicted in an unfavorable light the conduct of British soldiers during the Revolution.[96] Consider the effect during the present emergency if judges or commissioners follow Judge Bledsoe's reasons:

Great Britain is an ally of the United States. . . . this is no time . . . for the exploitation of those things that may have the tendency . . . of creating animosity or want of confidence between us and our allies, because so to do weakens our efforts, weakens the chance of our success, impairs our solidarity . . . . And it is not at all necessary that it should be shown to have such effect [of inciting hatred of England] ; it is enough if it is calculated reasonably so to excite or inflame the passions of our people, or some of them, as that they will be deterred from giving that full measure of co-operation, sympathy, assistance, and sacrifice which is due to Great Britain, simply because . . . Great Britain . . . is working with us to fight the battle which we think strikes at our very existence as a nation.

By such reasoning a book or pamphlet will be seizable under the 1940 Act if it criticizes the conduct of the British government during the Munich crisis, doubts the complete purity of England's war aims, suggests defects in her military and diplomatic strategy, revives memories of the Easter Rebellion or Amritsar, disapproves of British policy in India, or mentions the war-debts.

The clause requiring the searched-for matter to be "in-

[96] United States *v. Spirit of '76*, 252 Fed. 946 (Cal. 1917) ; see *supra* pp. 10, 55.

tended for use in violation of this Act" may not prevent far-ranging seizures. So long as the book is found to have been written or published with intent to cause disaffection in the armed forces or advocate the forceful overthrow of our government, this is enough as I understand the section. And remember that the intent of the author or publisher need not be proved; it can be inferred from what the judge (or commissioner) considers objectionable in the language of the book. If I am right in my interpretation, then no matter how innocent the mind of its present possessor, it can be seized in his house or office. For example, a collection of the publications of Communists or Bunds or Continental governments hostile to the United States might be validly carried off from the house of a professor of history or the shelves of a university library. The same thing might happen to any books in their possession which are critical of Great Britain or of our own military and economic defense policies.

Even if I am wrong in thinking the intent of the possessor not material, the law also permits *his* intent to be inferred from the fact that he keeps on hand such pernicious books (as the judge or commissioner thinks them). So the seizures may still be extensive.

Fears of this sort led to sober objections to the bill on the floor of the House. Thus Representative Eberharter of Pennsylvania, a Reserve Officer in the Army, pointed out that a Congressman receives a lot of letters. Suppose that a constituent wrote him that the President was trying to force the country into war, as had been charged in Congress, and that Eberharter ought to resign from the Reserve immediately. This would be within section 1, since it urged disloyalty to his oath. According to Mr. Eberharter's view and mine, the intent of the writer and not that of the recipient is what counts. Consequently, a warrant would lie to search Mr. Eberharter's office and his person in order to get possession of that letter.[97] Representative Ferguson of Oklahoma, who was also a Reserve Officer, opposed the whole of Title I for similar reasons.

Am I to understand that my office, my mail, is to be constantly scrutinized to see whether I am subjected to propaganda urging that

[97] 84 *Congressional Record* 10381 (July 28, 1939). Representative Hobbs contested this interpretation, but Mr. Eberharter was clearly right.

I disobey the commands of my superior officers? . . . Am I to be held responsible for having that in my possession which comes entirely unsolicited? [Representative Hobbs replied that a judge or commissioner would pass on the issuance of the search warrant.]

But it undoubtedly sets up some one as a judge of what I am capable of reading, who passes on the intent. I cannot quite conceive how the intent and the contents of the article can be separated . . .

We certainly have some well-educated officers in our service. I can well imagine under a very narrow interpretation of this bill that an officer's quarters might be searched and the officer be very severely embarrassed because he had a copy of Karl Marx's book on Capital in his library. It could be easily carried that far and it has been carried that far in times of hysteria in all countries.[98]

Section 5. (a) Any person who violates any of the provisions of this title shall, upon conviction thereof, be fined not more than $10,000 or imprisoned for not more than ten years, or both.

(b) No person convicted of violating any of the provisions of this title shall, during the five years next following his conviction, be eligible for employment by the United States, or by any department or agency thereof (including any corporation the stock of which is wholly owned by the United States).

The maximum punishment for the violation of the Sedition Act of 1798 was imprisonment for two years and a fine of $2000.[99]

If the Attorney General treats Title I of the Alien Registration Act like a revolver to be kept in his desk if any burglar ever shows up, then it will not cause trouble. But if he lets all of his district attorneys take it out and play with it, then some of them may start sniping at soapbox orators by the front gate. And if the burglar should ever come, as I assuredly hope not, then the Attorney General may find the old Civil War rifle section 6 a more effective protection than this new-fangled weapon which tends to spread its bullets in all directions.

The worst feature of a law like this is that it encourages spies, persecution, and hysteria. It is too bad that during the present crisis when, as Mr. Fraenkel aptly says,[100] "Now is the

[98] *Id.* pp. 10378, 10381. See also Marcantonio, *id.* p. 10372; Beard, 1935 House Hearings, pp. 51–52; 1935 House Report (minority).

[99] 1 Stat. 597, § 2 (1798).

[100] 1939 House Hearings, p. 11.

time for us to keep our heads clear and cool," Congress has seen fit to subject us to the same dangers which Edward Livingston correctly predicted from the Sedition Act of 1798:

The country will swarm with informers, spies, delators, and all the odious reptile tribe that breed in the sunshine of despotic power. The hours of the most unsuspected confidence, the intimacies of friendship, or the recesses of domestic retirement afford no security.[101]

And I am wondering, along with a representative of labor at the hearings on this sedition law [102] — If the First Congress of the United States had passed such a bill as this, just how many of us would be here today?

II. EXCLUDING COMMUNISTS FROM THE BALLOT

> *You can catch more flies with molasses than you can with vinegar.*   New England Proverb.

The desire to outlaw Communists, already mentioned, has led several states to exclude them from the ballot.[103] California has enacted a statute, effective in 1941, which eliminates from primaries and elections any party which "uses . . . as part of its party designation the word 'communist' or any derivative"; and any party which is "directly or indirectly affiliated, by any means whatsoever," with the Communist Party, the Third International, or any other foreign organization, government, etc. Then a general clause bans any party which advocates the overthrow of the government by violence. Other states have merely enacted this general provision, and left it to the election officers to apply it to Communists. In some states with no statutory exclusion the Secretary of State has kept Communists off the ballot, on the ground that they could not honestly take an oath to support the government which they are in fact seeking to overthrow. We are back in the days of Speaker Sweet and the New York Socialist Assemblymen. Bills of this sort are pressing into every legislature that meets and

[101] Quoted by Representative Celler in 84 *Congressional Record* p. 10362 (July 28, 1939).

[102] Emerson, 1939 House Hearings, p. 40.

[103] See 54 *Harvard Law Review* 155 (1940); 37 *Columbia Law Review* 86 (1937). The statutes are listed in Appendix III *infra*.

also into Congress. Whether such statutes are constitutional or not, I shall not stop to inquire.[104]

From the point of view of conservatives, it seems to me very unwise to keep these people off the ballot, much as we dislike them. There are several reasons for this position.

In the first place, their desire to be on the ballot is a departure from the basic principle of their creed, and we should encourage them to carry that departure as far as possible. The out-and-out Communist despises action through parliaments and legislatures. He wants the government overthrown by general strikes, assassination, and bloody revolution. Now here we have a group of men who call themselves Communists and yet are eager to behave like ordinary citizens by using the ballot and running for office. Although it is true that some of the aims they hope to accomplish if they ever get to the legislature do seem very objectionable to us, the fact remains that they are anxious to accomplish these ends and many others which are entirely legitimate by the very methods of which we highly approve. In short, when they want to behave like American citizens, we ought to let them behave like American citizens. On the other hand, if we refuse to let them be candidates and thus virtually make it useless for them to vote (for the writing-in privilege amounts to little), then we are strengthening the hands of the few consistent Communists who are trying to persuade the others that they ought to stick to the tactics of Lenin and Trotsky, plan a bloody revolution, and leave "all this nonsense" of voting and trying to get elected alone as so much rubbish.

In the case of the rank and file of the Communists, we are not confronted with persons whom it is impossible to convert to American ideals. Their minds are not made up for life. They have become Communists for various reasons; perhaps out of resentment over unjust treatment by an employer or a foreman, perhaps because of their own poverty and their indignation at wasteful displays of great wealth, perhaps because they emigrated from Russia and naturally preserve some sympathies with the friends and relatives whom they left behind who have profited by the Russian Revolution, and perhaps

[104] Doubts are raised by Nixon *v.* Herndon, 273 U. S. 536 (1927); Nixon *v.* Condon, 286 U. S. 73 (1932).

merely because they are young and enthusiastic and crammed with partially digested knowledge. A good Italian proverb says that the man who is not a radical at twenty will be a spy at forty. Whatever the cause of their calling themselves Communists, there is always, I feel very strongly, a good chance of reconciling them to American ways. Many European countries like France have had parties whose labels sounded very extreme, and yet which developed into groups favoring mild progressive legislation less advanced than some of the New Deal statutes. The name does not make a great deal of difference if we can only dilute the violent ideas.

I think there is a very good prospect of doing that. For several years the Russian Revolution was the symbol of a better world. It was assumed to be a heaven on earth. As time went by it became increasingly difficult for those who dreamed of a City of God to ignore the facts in Moscow. With the invasion of Finland, the gap between the dream and the reality became so wide that Russia can easily cease to be such a symbol, except for a few persons in whom the habit or obsession clings on obstinately. Radicals of my acquaintance who used to speak of Russia as a land of hope are now reduced to saying that it is no worse than any other country. In other words, the idealistic driving force of Communism is no longer there. The dream which began when Lenin and Trotsky landed at the Finland Station in St. Petersburg came to an end when bombers crossed the Finland frontier. The hopes for a better world which formerly found their symbol in Russia can now be redirected toward Mr. Roosevelt's promises of an America where all can be happy and prosperous, and their resentment can be gradually removed by high wages, an electric refrigerator, and a second-hand Ford. So, to sum up this argument, it is a terrible mistake to outlaw these people at the very moment when there is a better prospect of making them loyal Americans than we have had for years.

In the second place, if Communists go on the ballot the authorities will receive an accurate knowledge of the true size of this group. It is very easy to know how many people voted Communist at the last election. Of course there are some Communists who prefer to vote for a Democrat, since he might be elected and would carry out some of their wishes, whereas any practical Communist knows that a vote for his own candidate has no chance of success. Even so, the number of electors who actually vote Communist does gives a valuable indication of the size of the membership. Now if you throw this party off the ballot, you have absolutely no way of telling the size of the group. They may be very few, they may be very numerous. Who can say? Easily frightened persons will think that they are very numerous, whereas the present voting strength indicates that we have no serious cause for anxiety since the numbers are so small. In short, if we are scared about the possibility of Communists under the bed, let us cling hard to the existing system which encourages most of them to get on the bed where we can see them.

Thirdly, if you outlaw the Communist Party, some Communists will become Democrats or join a new party like LaGuardia's group in New York. Consequently, candidates will be found who will promise extreme measures in order to satisfy these new left-wing members of the lawful party.

Fourth. The prime cause of all dangerous political agitation is discontent. Outlawing the Communists will double their discontent, especially that of the members who will thenceforth not vote at all. Now, they can say, "This isn't such a bad country after all, for at least it does give us a chance to vote for the man we want to." But if you outlaw the Communists, then they can say, "This country won't let us earn a decent living and now it won't even let us vote. So let's try something else."

PART IV

WIDER HORIZONS

A new point of view, one which allows the investigator to see things the other way around.

EMILE DUCLAUX, Pasteur.

CHAPTER 13

HISTORY OF THE LAW OF SEDITION[1]

> *From all sedition, privy conspiracy, and rebellion; from
> all false doctrine, heresy, and schism; from hardness of
> heart, and contempt of Thy Word and Commandment,
> Good Lord, deliver us.*
>
> The Litany, in The Book of Common Prayer.

FOR purposes of comparison with twentieth-century American legislation on sedition, it is worth while to summarize the historical growth of sedition law with emphasis on earlier periods and other English-speaking countries. To some extent this chapter will draw together matters which have been scatteringly mentioned elsewhere.

The term sedition has come to be applied to practices which tend to disturb internal public tranquility by deed, word, or writing, but which do not amount to treason and are not accompanied by or conducive to open violence. There is some doubt in England whether the noun describes a crime, but the courts have recognized as misdemeanors at common law seditious words, seditious libels, and seditious conspiracies. The use of the adjective signifies that the practices are accompanied by a seditious intent, the legal definition of which has changed, however, with the development of toleration and political rights.

Offenses thus described as seditious were originally punishable by death as treason. Thus in the fifteenth century it was treason to accuse the king of murder, call him a fool, and suggest that his horse might stumble and break his neck; to

---

[1] This chapter consists mainly of parts of my article on Sedition in 13 *Encyclopaedia of the Social Sciences*, 636 (1934), published by The Macmillan Co. of New York, who have kindly authorized me to reprint it here. Passages are also taken from my contribution to *Freedom in the Modern World*, published in 1928 by Coward-McCann, Inc., of New York, by whose permission I am using this material. For bibliography, see 13 *Encyclopaedia of the Social Sciences* at 639. For odd early cases, see also Black, "Imagining the King's Death," 30 *Law Notes* (N. Y.) 149 (1926).

make astrological calculations to predict the time of the king's death; or to publish poems and ballads to the disgrace of the king and his council. By the reign of Henry VIII treason was confined to more dangerous offenses and was no longer charged when men were indicted (and presumably imprisoned) for saying: "I like not the proceedings of this realm, I trust to see a change of the world"; or for answering a fellow-drinker's "God save the King!" with "God save the cup of good ale, for King Henry shall be hanged!" or for remarking when shooting at the butts, "I would the King's body had been there as the arrow did light!" By the reign of Charles I it was definitely held not to be treason to call the king unwise and say, "He is no more fit to be King than Hickwright," a simple old shepherd; or to describe His Majesty as "the greatest whoremonger and drunkard in the Kingdom." Henceforth it was no more than a misdemeanor to say, "Damn the Queen!" or to drink a health to the pious memory of an executed traitor. In Queen Anne's reign a tanner "in indifferent circumstances" was merely stood in the pillory twice for remarking that Charles I was rightly served in having his head cut off.

Trials for political libel were common in the sixteenth and seventeenth centuries, and in the latter prosecutions for seditious words also took place frequently. However, so far as printed books were concerned, the government had a much stronger control through the censorship.[2] This was exercised at first by the Crown and then taken over by the Long Parliament, an example of the persistency of legal machinery through changes of political rule which is paralleled in the continuance of the Russian Czarist censorship by the Soviets. The opposition to this censorship is forever associated with the name of John Milton. Despite his *Areopagitica*, however, this form of control lasted until after the Revolution of 1688, and the method of its abolition in 1695 is very significant. The House of Commons in stating the reasons for terminating the censorship asserted no broad principle like the French Declaration of Rights, that "the free communication of thoughts and opinions is one of the most valuable of the rights of man."

---

[2] Holdsworth, "Press Control and Copyright in the 16th and 17th Centuries," 29 *Yale Law Journal* 841 (1920); *id.*, *History of English Law*, VI, 360 ff. (1927).

Instead, the members devoted themselves to the bad features of the existing legal machinery. To quote Macaulay:

The Licensing Act is condemned, not as a thing essentially evil, but on account of the petty grievances, the exactions, the jobs, the commercial restrictions, the domiciliary visits, which were incidental to it. It is pronounced mischievous because it enables the Company of Stationers to extort money from publishers, because it empowers the agents of the government to search houses under the authority of general warrants, because it confines the foreign book trade to the port of London; because it detains valuable packages of books at the Custom House till the pages are mildewed. The Commons complain that the amount of the fee which the licenser may demand is not fixed. They complain that it is made penal in an officer of the Customs to open a box of books from abroad, except in the presence of one of the censors of the press. How, it is very sensibly asked, is the officer to know that there are books in the box till he has opened it? Such are the arguments which did what Milton's *Areopagitica* failed to do.[3]

With this termination of the censorship in England, and soon after in the American colonies, began the second stage of sedition, which lasted for about a hundred years until the close of the eighteenth century. The publication of books was so free that Continental writers like Voltaire printed in England, and newspapers sprang up in abundance. However, the law covering seditious libel, which consisted of written or printed matter found by the court to have been published with a seditious intent, became the chief weapon of the government against the advocacy of political reforms; and successful prosecutions were frequently directed against what would now be considered mild anti-administration editorials. Famous cases were those of Zenger in New York for adversely criticizing the royal governor, and of Wilkes and the Junius letters in England.

The outcome of these prosecutions turned largely on two controversial legal doctrines.

In the first place, conviction was made much easier because true criticism of the government could be punished as well as false. Thus, the truth of the charges made by Junius or other writers against the King's ministers was not allowed to be an issue at all, because of the doctrine that prevailed in crim-

[3] Macaulay, *Works* (Trevelyan edition), IV, 125. See *supra* p. 18.

inal libel cases, "The greater the truth the greater the libel."
On the other hand, those who thought that public opinion was
legislation in the soft felt that truthful criticism should be
protected as the best way to obtain wiser laws and wiser administration of existing laws.

Secondly, inasmuch as the judges were appointees of the
Crown and natural supporters of the existing political system
while the juries were drawn from the commercial classes who
suffered from misgovernment and corruption, the result of a
prosecution depended much on the question whether the main
issue should be decided by the jury, who would probably acquit
the critic of an unpopular official, or by the judge, who would
probably convict. The courts did permit the jury to determine the undoubted question of fact — whether the defendant
had actually written, printed, or published the book (or pamphlet or newspaper) and so was responsible for it; this was often
difficult to decide because of the secrecy with which opponents
of the government surrounded the production of their newspapers and pamphlets, so that even today the identity of Junius
is not surely established.[4] However, the courts kept for the
judge the still more important question — whether the book,
etc., was "seditious," which as then defined meant tending to
stir up disaffection against the king or his ministers or the
established institutions of government. For example, everybody agreed that the jury should decide whether Woodfall
printed Junius' Letter to the Duke of Grafton. But as to the
question whether it was seditious to say to a Cabinet minister,
"I do not give you to posterity as a pattern to imitate, but as
an example to deter," the judges asserted that this was an issue
of law for them to decide; and the defense lawyers argued that
it was an issue of fact for the jury.

The hottest fight was waged about the form of the jury's
verdict. In prosecutions for most crimes, for example murder,
the jury has power to bring in a general verdict of "Guilty" or
"Not guilty." Although the jury is sworn to take the law
from the judge, nevertheless the jurymen are practically free

[4] An apparently unnoticed indication of the authorship of these letters is
the contemporary use of an English Etymology by a Dutch scholar, Francis
Junius. May not the juxtaposition of his own last name with the *cognomen*
of Brutus, the foe of tyrants, have caught the eye of Sir Philip Francis? (See
Boswell's *Johnson* for 1748 as to F. Junius.)

to disregard the judge's charge and acquit a prisoner who has in reality violated the rules of law which the judge laid down. And so it was evident to both sides that if in a seditious libel prosecution the jury could bring in a general verdict of "Not guilty," then the virtual control of sedition cases would belong to the jury, and critics of Cabinet ministers would be frequently acquitted. The judges strove to avoid this lamentable result by a technical device. They merely allowed the jury to bring in a limited or special verdict on the issue of publication. For instance, in the Junius case, the jury could only decide whether Woodfall did or did not print the Letter to the Duke of Grafton; if the verdict found him thus responsible for it, then the jury-men could not acquit him although they thought the letter unobjectionable; the jury dropped out and the judge could enter a judgment of conviction and send Woodfall to prison if, as was probable, the judge considered that such criticism of the Duke was dangerous to the nation. Of course, the defense lawyers opposed this practice and urged that the jury had the right to bring in a general verdict of "Not guilty" as in other crimes; and thus the jurymen could acquit Woodfall if they liked the letter.

Gallons of ink were poured out and hundreds of pamphlets published on both sides of this controversy. We can see now that both sides were partly wrong. The vital issue about the seditious nature of the words used by a defendant was neither a question of law nor a question of fact. It was not a question of law, because it did not involve the formulation of a general rule; the definition of the crime of sedition was accepted for the time being by all concerned. Neither was this vital issue a question of fact, because it did not relate to occurrences in the outside world of persons and things and actions, like "Did Wilkes write No. 45 *North Briton*?" or "Who was Junius?" The truth of the matter is that trials involve three kinds of issues: (1) questions of law; (2) questions of fact; (3) questions of the application of a legal standard to the facts.[5] And

[5] For this concept of legal standards as a separate category, I am indebted to Roscoe Pound. See, for example, his *Interpretations of Legal History*, 154–155 (1923). In my explanation of the controversy leading up to Fox's Libel Act, I have ventured to differ from the eminent authority of Lord Blackburn in Capital & Counties Bank *v*. Henty, L. R. 7 A. C. 741, 771–776 (1882), because he still thought of only two categories — questions of law and questions of

the problem of the seditious nature of words belongs in the third class.

The law is full of similar situations. Examples of legal standards are negligence, proximate cause, probable cause, unreasonable restraint of trade, and (in private libel suits) bringing the plaintiff into hatred, ridicule, or contempt. In sedition prosecutions, the courts had already established the standard of what is sedition; the facts in the external world about printing, etc., were determined by the jury; and the book with all it said was in court before everybody's eyes. But the third question still remained, who should apply this standard to these facts?

With other standards, the practice varies. The standard of negligence is applied to the facts of an automobile accident by the jurymen; they decide whether the motorist's conduct was what an average reasonable man would have done under the same circumstances. On the other hand, a standard is sometimes applied by the court. Suppose after a waitress has been prosecuted by her former employer for stealing silver spoons and acquitted, she turns round and sues him for damages for malicious prosecution. To recover, she must establish (among other things) that the facts known to the employer gave him no "probable cause" to have her arrested and tried. The jurymen decide what those facts were, but not whether they constituted proper grounds for prosecuting the waitress. That issue is handled by the judge. If there is no dispute about the evidence in the employer's possession, the judge rules that it did or

---

fact — and was not aware of the possibility of a third category of legal standards.

The same concept of legal standards is also useful in administrative law, in demarcating the respective spheres of administrative finality and judicial review. For example, "advocacy of force and violence" in the Deportation Act is neither a question of law for the courts nor a question of fact for the immigration officials. It is a standard to be applied to the facts found by the officials. Who then can better apply this standard of criminality of an organization? In practice the officials usually ɑo the job, but the question whether they are as well fitted as United States judges for this task deserves more consideration from Congress and the Supreme Court than it has yet received. See *supra* Chapter V; 48 *Yale Law Journal* 111 (1938). Compare Colyer *v.* Skeffington, 265 Fed. 17 (1920) with the C. C. A. opinion in 277 Fed. 129 (1922). In disputes about imported books, Congress in 1929 transferred the application of the standards of obscenity, etc., from the customs officials to the Circuit Courts of Appeals. — *Supra* Chapter IV, note 72.

did not justify prosecution. If the facts are disputed, he instructs the jury: "If you find that the facts were so-and-so, then there was probable cause for the prosecution and you must find for the defendant. But if you find that the facts were this-and-that, then the employer should not have prosecuted the waitress, and, if you decide that the other essentials of the wrong existed, then you should find for the plaintiff and assess her damages." The governing principle is that the duty of applying a particular standard to the established or admitted facts should be entrusted to whoever can do the job better. Is it more appropriate for an expert trained in the law or for twelve representatives of the community? Jurymen can tell from their own experience whether a motorist has been unduly careless, but they are unfamiliar with starting prosecutions. Furthermore, the judge, who is used to administering justice, knows that unless recoveries are very cautiously permitted in malicious prosecution suits, a good many other people who ought to file complaints of crimes with the district attorney will be scared off, to the injury of public order. So the standard of negligence is applied by the jury, and the standard of "probable cause" by the court.

Who then will do a better job with the standard of sedition, the judge or the jury? Much depends on the political outlook of the man who answers this question. If he wants a strong government by those in the seats of the mighty, he will think that the judge will understand the dangers of disaffection better than a jury. If he wants a government guided by an informed public opinion and liable to be called to account for errors and misdeeds, then he will think that twelve men drawn from the community can safely decide whether a given piece of political discussion is what the public needs to hear or not. In short, as pointed out in the first chapter, this technical controversy between judge and jury was only like waves thrown up from the deep whirlpool of conflicting currents as to whether the government of England and the colonies should be more democratic or not.

Conservatives like Blackstone supported these drastic limitations on political discussion by saying that freedom of speech meant only the absence of restraint before publication, and did not affect prosecutions after publication, so that in their opinion complete liberty had been secured with the disappearance of the censorship. Their opponents, the liberals on both sides of the Atlantic, recognized that a censor who passed on all material that came from the press was indeed more objectionable than an occasional prosecution before a judge who was not so liable to be arbitrary; but they preferred even more the decision of twelve men drawn at random from the community and thus applying its views of the type of discussion desired by citizens. On the whole, this liberal view seems the sounder, for the dangerous effect of utterances upon common people is a practical question like negligence, more appropriate to a jury of common people than to a professionalized judge. In this struggle for jury control the leadership was taken by Thomas Erskine, who was counsel for the defense in many of these cases.

Eventually the liberals were victorious. Charles James Fox's Libel Act of 1792,[6] copied throughout the United States, allowed the jury to bring in a general verdict, thus giving the jurymen complete power to acquit the writer or publisher whenever they thought that the book was not seditious; and in this country constitutions or statutes made truth a defense in all criminal libel cases if published with good motives. It has been argued that the contemporaneous free speech guarantees in our constitutions were intended to effect the same reforms, but American courts continued to take the old position until specific constitutional or statutory provisions gave the juries power over all aspects of the prosecutions. The solidity of the new procedure is shown by the Sedition Act of 1798, designed to punish attacks on the federal administration, which with all its sweeping provisions made truth a defense and let the jury determine all the issues.

After almost complete control over sedition prosecutions had thus been vested in the jury, it was expected that ordinary political discussion would no longer be punished. However, during the excitement of the French Revolution and the Napoleonic Wars juries showed themselves eager to convict men for urging parliamentary reform or for attacking flogging in the

---

[6] Quoted *supra* p. 23, n. 50. On similar American legislation, see p. 22, n. 48. Numerous English prosecutions, mostly before 1792, are collected in 19 A. L. R. at 1511 ff. On truth as a defense, see *supra* p. 5, n. 2.

army. The first English prosecution for seditious conspiracy took place in 1795. In the United States juries proved equally drastic under the Sedition Act of 1798. In short the jurymen became, for the time being, as ardent supporters of strong government as the judges had been a few years before. Thus the procedural changes of the late eighteenth century did not immediately produce their full effect. This did not happen until they were reënforced by new political ideals, which were rapidly developing under the influence of the Liberals and Bentham in Great Britain, and of Jefferson, Madison, and the Bills of Rights in the United States.

Once men came to believe in their hearts that plain citizens should play a large part in the business of government through choosing, criticizing, and displacing legislators and executives, once it was understood that newspapers and pamphlets and oral discussion were essential to this control of the people over their rulers, then the new-found power of the people's representatives to render political discussion immune from suppression was freely exercised. Sedition was not merely tried differently; it became defined differently, as we shall soon see, and within much narrower limits. Thus the technical shift of control from judge to jury was followed, after an interval of about time enough for a new generation to grow up, by a tremendous shift of the line that separated permissible from punishable speech. Most expression of ideas and facts of public significance became lawful, and the long series of sedition prosecutions came to an end.

The succeeding third period, in the nineteenth century, was the freest in modern times. Since the Reform Bill of 1832 English prosecutions for seditious offenses have been very infrequent and usually unsuccessful. There were a few cases against the Chartists, and in 1886 John Burns, later a cabinet minister, was prosecuted for uttering seditious words at a large meeting of unemployed in Trafalgar Square which was followed by rioting. In his charge to the jury [7] Judge Cave adopted Stephen's definition of seditious intention, which is very interesting as a revelation of the great change which had taken place in the substantive law. The first sentence was

[7] Regina v. Burns, 16 Cox. C. C. 355 (1886).

based on eighteenth-century conservative conceptions and was taken substantially from a statute of 1819, during the last gasp of suppression in the unrest after the Napoleonic Wars. In this sentence, Judge Cave started to define seditious intention as

> an intention to bring into hatred or contempt, or to excite disaffection against the person of Her Majesty, her heirs or successors, or the government and constitution of the United Kingdom, as by law established, or either House of Parliament, or the administration of justice or to excite Her Majesty's subjects to attempt, otherwise than by lawful means, the alteration of any matter in Church or State by law established, or to raise discontent or disaffection amongst Her Majesty's subjects, or to promote feelings of ill-will and hostility between different classes of such subjects.

But then Judge Cave added this very important qualifying sentence, which shows significantly the influence of Fox's Libel Act and political development since the Reform Bill:

> An intention to show that Her Majesty has been misled or mistaken in her measures, or to point out errors or defects in the government or constitution as by law established, with a view to their reformation, or to excite Her Majesty's subjects to attempt by lawful means the alteration of any matter in Church or State by law established, or to point out, in order to their removal, matters which are producing or have a tendency to produce, feelings of hatred and ill-will between classes of Her Majesty's subjects, is not a seditious intention.

John Burns was acquitted and lived to help save his country in the World War. Judge Cave's qualified definition has been accepted as authoritative in England ever since it was declared. However, it is so loose that guilt or innocence must obviously depend on public sentiment at the time of the trial.

A still greater freedom prevailed in the United States during the whole of the nineteenth century. The common law of seditious offenses had probably been abolished by the free speech clauses of the federal and state constitutions, as explained in the first chapter of this book. Only one state case since 1800 has ever suggested that seditious libel remained a common-law crime; and in this Pennsylvania trial in 1805 the defendant was acquitted.[8] In any event there are no common-law federal crimes, so that the United States government cannot punish seditious practices unless it prohibits them by statute. After the Sedition Act of 1798 expired in two years, there was no such federal legislation until 1917, with the possible exception of the conspiracy sections of the Criminal Code,[9] which are not violated by the use of seditious words unaccompanied by some overt act. In the states likewise, old penalties for heterodox opinions were gradually removed and very little fresh legislation against them was enacted. Although Mr. Leon Whipple in his *Story of Civil Liberty in the United States* [10] has collected many instances of the violation of liberty before 1900, these were mostly acts by mobs or by officials, police, and soldiers, committed under old laws or no laws at all. Except for the statutes against Mormon polygamy, I recall no new nineteenth-century legislation against minorities, and in this case behavior was involved rather than opinions.

Not only were there few prosecutions in English-speaking countries during this period, but also immigrants with strange views for which they had suffered on the Continent of Europe were given asylum and welcome in England and the United States; and socialistic communities were established in our midst and even permitted without legal interference to pursue experiments in relations between the sexes. In short, the prevailing doctrine of *laissez faire* was extended to the field of discussion. The outstanding representative of the liberty of the time was John Stuart Mill.

Unfortunately, Mill's arguments did not become deeply ingrained in popular consciousness in this country. Freedom of speech was a cherished tradition, but remained without specific content. Perhaps the very absence of interference allowed the philosophical and political principles which underlay the constitutional guarantees to be forgotten for lack of constant assertion and examination of them. Consequently, these guarantees proved of slight use against the growing tendency to

[8] *Respublica v.* Dennie, 4 Yeates 267 (Pa. 1805). See a few later cases of criminal libel prosecutions for criticism of officials in 19 A. L. R. at 1511 ff.; and two decisions cited *infra* Chapter XIV, note 7.

[9] See Chapter IV, section 1, *supra*.

[10] New York: Vanguard Press, 1927.

resort to governmental action for the limitation of individual liberty in the field of discussion as well as in other departments of life. It seems odd to link together the legal restrictions on business and wealth enacted by collectivists at the opening of the twentieth century and the sedition laws enacted against collectivists since the war. Yet I think the antagonistic factions in a bitter political and economic struggle are moved by the same impulse, entirely alien to the principles of Benthamite individualism, namely, an increasing insistence on the interests of the community and on their protection by the state.[11]

This new tendency became articulate in proposing restrictions on free discussion in the late 1880's. The Haymarket bomb may serve to mark the turning-point of toleration for extremists,[12] and after the assassination of McKinley the new spirit emerged into legislation with the New York Criminal Anarchy Act of 1902 and the federal statute of 1903 excluding anarchists from our shores. More serious suppressions were forecast in industrial disputes — for instance, the prohibition of street meetings in San Diego in 1912 — so that the Espionage Act and the sedition laws after the war did not come out of a clear sky. The year 1917 certainly found us in a fourth period, when the scope of freedom of speech once more became a burning issue. In this period we are still living.

On the one side are those who contend that liberty of discussion has not been violated by the Espionage Act cases and state sedition prosecutions. Just as Blackstone defended the suppressions of his time by saying that freedom of speech was preserved years before when the censorship had been abolished, so the conservatives today insist that it was made sufficiently secure a century ago when juries were given control of sedition prosecutions. Thus Professor Corwin of Princeton writes:

The cause of freedom of speech and press is largely in the custody of legislative majorities and of juries, which, so far as there is evi-

---

[11] A similar idea is expressed by H. F. Goodrich, in his article, "Does the Constitution Protect Free Speech?" 19 *Michigan Law Review* 487, 499 (1921).

[12] Note the contrast in temper between Spies *v.* People, 122 Ill. 1 (1887), and the life of Albert R. Parsons, one of those executed for very remote connection with the bomb, in 14 *Dictionary of American Biography* 264 (1934). See Zeisler, "Reminiscences of the Anarchist Case," 21 *Illinois Law Review* 224 (1926).

dence to show, is just where the framers of the Constitution intended it to be.[13]

On the other side are those who maintain that freedom of speech means more than the abolition of the censorship and the right to trial by jury; that the fear of severe sentences may kill open discussion without any legal previous restraint; and that although juries will safeguard the criticism of the government by spokesmen of views popular among the electorate, they are far less likely to acquit men who hold unpopular opinions, which nevertheless for the public good ought to be allowed expression. Therefore, they want the reviewing power of the Supreme Court to become an effective legal machinery for the protection of freedom. They urge that the Constitution to be vital must be interpreted so as to impose limits on legislation against speech, beyond which statutes become invalid and juries are not permitted to convict. In this still existing fourth period, the struggle is for a reformulation of the definition of freedom of speech which shall make it possible to prevent the government from suppressing valuable discussion by a censor or punishment or any other method. According to the participants in this endeavor, the Constitution embodies prohibition of the censorship and Fox's Libel Act, and much more besides. These are but two procedural devices to safeguard a principle,[14] and it is that principle which is affirmed by the Constitution. I have spoken of Milton and Erskine and Mill as leaders in the three previous periods. In the fourth period the one name which belongs with theirs is that of Oliver Wendell Holmes.

The principle thus enforced by the Constitution is the interest of the community in the discovery and dissemination of truth. In this book, I have emphasized the need of sound opinions, but Mr. Walter Lippmann's *Liberty and the News* and his *Public Opinion* show that still greater importance at-

[13] E. S. Corwin, "Freedom of Speech and Press under the First Amendment: A Résumé," 30 *Yale Law Journal* 48, 55 (1920). To the same effect is Day Kimball in Note, 33 *Harvard Law Review* 442 (1920), discussed in Chapter III, *supra*; see other conservatives cited in Pound, *Cases on Equitable Relief against Defamation* (2d ed. by Chafee), p. 17 note (1930).

[14] Thus a third and entirely different safeguard of liberty of discussion was recently established by the Supreme Court in Grosjean *v.* American Press Co., 297 U. S. 233 (1936), discussed in Chapter XI, section IV.

taches to the ascertainment and spread of the actual facts. The process of reformulating the definition of freedom of speech, which is fully described in my first chapter, consists in treating each free speech problem as a conflict between the interests of the community in national safety from external or internal violence, in morality, and so forth, on one side, and on the other side the individual interest in speaking out coupled with this social interest in the gains from open discussion, which should be the biggest weight in the scale. After making such a balance by an exercise of informed and thoughtful judgment, we can better determine in each situation where the line should lie that divides punishable sedition from legitimate though perhaps distasteful speech. Justice Holmes and the Supreme Court have placed the line at the place where speech creates a "clear and present danger" of unlawful acts. The detailed application of these considerations to the numerous state and federal sedition laws enacted in the United States since 1917 has been undertaken throughout this book.

In England, also, the twentieth century has witnessed an increased control over speech and writing, but for the most part through fresh legislation. The recent English tendency is to ignore the common law of seditious offenses. For example, when Edward F. Mylius was prosecuted in 1911 for a printed statement that King George V had contracted a morganatic marriage before he married Queen Mary, the charge was criminal libel and not seditious libel.[15] The only reported English case of sedition since 1886 occurred in 1909 when Aldred was convicted for proclaiming a Hindu assassin a martyr in the cause of political independence.[16]

Although the common law of sedition has become almost obsolete in England, statutes still make punishable certain specific offenses of a related nature. During the World War pacifists were imprisoned under administrative regulations authorized by Parliament "for securing the public safety and the defence of the realm." Such regulations might even ignore Magna Charta.[17] This sweeping power to issue Orders in

---

[15] *The Times*, London, Feb. 2, 1911.   [16] 22 Cox. C. C. 1 (1909).

[17] See King *v.* Halliday, [1917] A. C. 260, Shaw dissenting, discussed by Laski, Note, 31 *Harvard Law Review* 296; and in his *Authority in the Modern State*, p. 101.

Council has been revived during the present war.[18] The Seditious Meetings Act, passed in 1817,[19] and directed against meetings of more than fifty persons within a mile of the Houses of Parliament for the purpose of considering political changes, was invoked in 1932 against Mann and Llewellyn. The Unlawful Oaths Act of 1797 [20] subjects to seven years' imprisonment members of a secret society who are bound by oath to obey its orders or not to disclose its secrets, unless the society is authorized by Parliament. This statute, enacted after the naval mutiny on the Nore, was used in 1834 to transport the "Dorchester labourers" to Australia for belonging to an agricultural union; and it is still unrepealed. Under the Incitement to Mutiny Act of 1797,[21] anyone who endeavors maliciously to seduce from his duty any person serving in His Majesty's forces or to incite any act of mutiny may be imprisoned for life. Somewhat the same offense is punishable much more lightly under the Incitement to Disaffection Act of 1934,[22] which also authorizes the seizure under search warrant of any document of such a nature that its dissemination among members of the army or navy would constitute this offense and makes the person in possession of the document an offender. Observe the resemblance to section 1 of our Alien Registration Act of 1940, discussed in the preceding chapter. The Police Act of 1919 [23] makes it a misdemeanor for any person to cause or attempt to cause disaffection among the members of any police force. Under the Aliens Restriction (Amendment) Act of 1919,[24] it is a misdemeanor for an alien to attempt to cause sedition or disaffection among the forces of the Crown or the civilian population or to promote industrial unrest in an industry in which he has not been engaged for the two preceding years. Unlawful drilling and the sale of arms for illegal purposes are common-law offenses.

The most extensive recent British peace-time statute is the

[18] Defence of the Realm Act, 2 & 3 Geo. VI, c. 62, § 1 (1939). See Cecil T. Carr, "Crisis Legislation in Britain," 40 *Columbia Law Review* 1309 (1940).

[19] 57 Geo. III, c. 19, § 23.

[20] 37 Geo. III, c. 123, § 1. For the Dorchester Labourers, see Chapter X, note 7.

[21] 37 Geo. III, c. 70, § 1.

[22] 24 & 25 Geo. V, c. 56.

[23] 9 & 10 Geo. V, c. 46, § 3.   [24] 9 & 10 Geo. V, c. 92, § 3.

Public Order Act of 1936,[25] aimed primarily at the British Union of Fascists led by Sir Oswald Mosley. A provision against the use of "threatening, abusive or insulting words . . . whereby a breach of the peace may be occasioned" was employed to give a month at hard labor to a young Communist who complained because the government had initially suppressed the facts concerning the former King Edward VIII and Mrs. Simpson; and two months to a Fascist who asserted that "England will never be England again" until all the Jews are expelled. Other important clauses regulate meetings in streets and private dwellings, private armies, and parades, considerably cutting down the right of assembly.

The outstanding characteristic of the English peace-time legislation of late years, as compared with our own federal and state sedition law, is its much greater definiteness. Specific offenses are described, except for the rather vague phrase "breach of the peace."

It is too soon to speak of the British handling of speech and publication during the present war.[26]

The sedition law of important Dominions in the British Empire differs at least in its administration from the English common law of seditious offenses. Sections 132 and 134 of the Canadian Criminal Code, against seditious words, libels or conspiracies, were harshly interpreted to suppress opposition in Canada to the World War. An Alberta judge remarked in 1916: "There have been more prosecutions for seditious words in Alberta in the past two years than in all the history of England for over one hundred years and England has had numerous and critical wars in that time." [27] Lately there have been a number of Canadian prosecutions of Communists and other radicals for seditious offenses. Section 124–A of the Indian Penal Code, which punishes as sedition any attempt to excite disaffection toward the government of British India, has

[25] 1 Edw. VIII & 1 Geo. VI, c. 6. See "Public Order and the Right of Assembly in the United States: A Comparative Study," 47 *Yale Law Journal* 404 (1938).

[26] See note 18.

[27] Rex *v.* Trainor, 27 Canadian Criminal Cases, 241. See also 17 *Columbia Law Review* 432 (1917); "The Montreal Sedition Cases," 9 *Canadian Bar Review* 756 (1931); Brewin, "Civil Liberties in Canada during Wartime," 1 *Bill of Rights Review* 112 (1941).

been invoked in recent years in a considerable number of cases. The Union of South Africa makes sedition a crime under the Roman-Dutch common law, but this law defines sedition more narrowly than does the English common law, and the offense must involve something in the nature of an insurrection.

The Continent of Europe lies outside my province. Professor Karl Loewenstein of Amherst has given a valuable account of legislation against Nazis and Communists in the years before the present war in his articles on "Legislative Control of Political Extremism in European Democracies." [28]

The foregoing survey of past English and American attempts to end sedition by severe penalties brings out four points:

(1) The persons punished were for the most part unimportant and comparatively harmless, like the indiscreet ale-drinker under Henry VIII, London workmen sympathetic with the French Revolution, the Dorchester labourers, the Abrams group in their Harlem third-floor back, the war-time scoffer who said "No soldier ever sees those socks," the herded Boston Communists who proposed (as Judge Anderson remarked) "to finance a revolution on dues of twenty-five cents a week," and hundreds of ragged migratory workers in California. Sedition laws do not seem to catch any really dangerous leaders. Thus the Sedition Act of 1798 sent to jail a few Jeffersonian newspaper editors in such promising foci of insurrection as Vermont; but neither Jefferson nor Madison nor their associates in putting through the Virginia and Kentucky Resolutions was touched, although these declarations of states' rights may have actually imperiled the newly created Union. Beard says of the "immense inquisitorial activities" under the Espionage Act of 1917: "Not a single first-class German spy or revolutionary workingman was caught and convicted of an overt act designed to give direct aid or comfort to the enemy." The few prominent persons convicted of sedition in this country since 1917 — Debs, Berger, Anita Whitney — were famous for other reasons than any near-success in heading a movement to overthrow the government of the United States. Every time an epidemic of prosecutions takes place, the list of apprehended radicals

[28] 38 *Columbia Law Review* 591, 725 (1938).

mekes a pretty sorry showing. The net is always flung wide, numberless little fish are dragged in, but the big ones break through the meshes and escape — if indeed there are any big fish there outside the usual piscatorial imagination, which later historians frequently doubt.[29]

(2) The suppressions of one period are condemned a generation afterwards — or much sooner — as unnecessary, unwise, and cruel. The sentence on Joan of Arc was revoked within twenty-five years of her death. The resolution declaring Wilkes incapable of election to the House of Commons was expunged from its records thirteen years later as "subversive." The names of the Scotch victims of Braxfield were carried on the banners at the Edinburgh celebrations of the Reform Bill forty years after they were transported to Australia. Congress repaid the fines imposed under the Sedition Act of 1798. Berger resumed his seat in Congress in 1923 without a single objection, even from the able committee chairman who had denounced Berger in 1919 as "the head and front of an organized conspiracy to hinder the government in its fight for existence."

(3) The main principles of the speeches and pamphlets which a government made vigorous attempts to suppress are often put into force within a few decades. Of course, the extreme measures advocated by some of these agitators are fortunately not accepted. However, if we strip off from the condemned manifestos and pamphlets all the vague claptrap about violent revolution, we are likely in each period to find two solid things at the core. First, there is a proposal for reforming specific governmental arrangements and practices which are attacked as unjust; and secondly, as a more generalized cause of these resentments, we find some sort of economic desperation — what Bacon in his *Essay of Seditions and Troubles* calls "that material cause of sedition . . . want and poverty in the estate." Now, the significant fact is that the specific proposals just mentioned, which were so intemperately urged by the agitators, do eventually prevail under the direction of their calmer successors. And, furthermore, this victory of their concrete ideas is often accompanied by a

"The net's not spread to catch the hawk or kite
Who do us wrong, but for the innocent birds
Who do us none at all." — Terence, *Phormio*.

financial betterment of the group whose discontent they voiced.
So that within a few years the discontent has vanished and
the proposals that seemed revolutionary are taken for granted
as commonplaces. In short, the victims of state trials are
frequently the precursors of statesmen. For example, the supposedly dangerous English political societies of the 1790's and
the days of the Six Acts were broken up chiefly for advocating
the end of rotten boroughs, the extension of the franchise, and
a greater responsibility of the government of England to the
great mass of her citizens. Behind these proposals and the vituperative language in which they were phrased lay "the condition of England"; how bad that was is revealed in the
most delightful of all books by radical agitators, Cobbett's
Rural Rides. The specific aims approached realization in the
Reform Bill of 1832, and the economic causes of discontent
disappeared under the leadership of Sir Robert Peel. The
Jeffersonian editors of 1798 wanted an active opposition party,
whereas the Federalists denounced bipartisan politics as "faction." The beliefs of the editors were accepted and the economic distress of their aroused readers was drained off with
the advent of Jeffersonian and Jacksonian Democracy and the
opening of free land in the West. Many of the criticisms which
the Socialists and the Nonpartisan League in 1917 directed
against large loans to belligerents and other alleged economic
causes of our entry into the World War were embodied in the
Neutrality Act of 1939 and preceding legislation. The industrial unionism of the I.W.W., though not its revolutionary
philosophy, has a legal status today under the National Labor
Relations Act in the much larger and more powerful C.I.O.
As for the two Communist parties of 1919, we began only
fourteen years later to feel abundant "proletarian mass pressure on the bourgeois state," which has by no means ended.
Their denunciatory platforms and manifestoes against capitalism and its attendant wrongdoings seem wordy and futile
generalities when compared with speeches since 1933 from
high officials and the deadly precision of the Securities and
Exchange Act or the remodeled Frazier-Lemke Act, or many
another statute produced by the very "bourgeois parliamentarism" which these imprisoned prophets affected to despise.
And when we look back to the economic unrest which was

voiced by the platforms and activities of the I.W.W. and the Left-Wing Socialists of the period after 1917, we are indeed living in a different world. The wildest dreams of remote revolution in the hearts of the mortgaged farmers and low-paid workers of twenty years ago are but the unsubstantial fabric of a vision beside the governmental generosity of the Wages and Hours Bill or the huge sums paid out on Farm Relief. Bacon must have foreseen our time when he urged as the wisest means to stop sedition:

Above all things, good policy is to be used, that the treasure and moneys in a state be not gathered into few hands. For otherwise a state may have a great stock, and yet starve. And money is like muck, not good except it be spread. This is done chiefly by suppressing, or at the least keeping a strait hand upon the devouring trades of usury, engrossing, great pasturages, and the like.

(4) History shows that sedition is often the symptom and not the cause of serious unrest. Hence, though it is indeed a cause for anxiety, there is usually some better cure for sedition than sedition laws. The three centuries of occasional outbreaks of violent criticism of government which have elapsed since the first publication of *The Essayes* have confirmed the wisdom of the following sentence, whose parenthetical clause seems to anticipate the "clear and present danger" test of Justice Holmes:

The surest way to prevent seditions (if the times do bear it) is to take away the matter of them.

CHAPTER 14

METHODS OF CONTROLLING
DISCUSSION IN PEACE TIME[1]

*Substantive law has at first the look of being gradually
secreted in the interstices of procedure.*

SIR HENRY MAINE.

EARLY in this book I took a procedural approach toward
the Espionage Acts and described the operations of the
human machinery employed in war-time suppression.[2] I now
propose to use a somewhat similar approach to the problems
of various kinds of peace-time control of speech and writing.
I hope that nobody will mind if I go over a good deal of
familiar ground. At this day there are no new principles of
freedom of speech. All the essentials have been said many
times, but the trouble is that people pay very little attention
to them.

Because of our constitutional form of government we are
too apt to approach legal problems by considerations of
phraseology. We attach overmuch significance to the presence
of certain words in a fundamental document. It is far from
my intention to belittle the influence on the minds, both of
those who enforce law and of the citizens at large, which comes
from the noble language of our Bills of Rights. They make it
possible for us, when liberty is in danger, to strengthen our
appeal to reason and common sense by calling into play the
associations which attach to the constitutions that were framed
with so much thought by the founders of our government.
Nevertheless, we cannot afford to forget that the guarantees of

[1] This chapter is in large part taken from an address contributed by me to
Freedom in the Modern World, edited by H. M. Kallen and published in 1928
by Coward-McCann, Inc., New York, who have kindly permitted me to reprint
the material here. The discussion of Control of Plays and Books was first published in 1 *Bill of Rights Review* 16 (1940), and is here reprinted by consent.

[2] See Chapter II, section IV.

liberty in the Bills of Rights do not of themselves operate to preserve liberty. They are brought actively into our lives by the intervention of human beings in ways which must be determined by specific legal rules. Dicey in his *Law of the Constitution* has shown that in England, where there are no constitutional guarantees at all, good legal machinery has made possible a large measure of liberty, but that the eloquent language of the French Declaration of the Rights of Man in 1791 was followed by some of the worst deprivations of liberty in modern history because of the lack of efficient remedies which a citizen could invoke for his protection.

This point may be illustrated by the fate of some of our other constitutional rights. The right not to be imprisoned illegally is rarely violated because our statutes provide with much detail the remedy of *habeas corpus*, by which an imprisoned person can have the legality of his detention investigated by a court with great speed.[3] Macaulay called the Habeas Corpus Act "the most stringent curb that ever legislation imposed on tyranny." On the other hand, the constitutional right to bear arms is practically meaningless because there is no method provided by law for asserting it.[4] The constitutional immunity from unlawful searches and seizures is very important, as anybody can testify who has been forced to submit to the humiliating experience of a search of his person; but numerous American judicial opinions in recent years show that this right has been repeatedly disregarded by officials who were zealous to enforce the criminal law. In England such violations are rarer. The reason is plain. Both countries provide in theory the same remedy for protecting the right, a civil action for damages against the officials who carry out the unlawful search or seizure. In England, however, this machinery works because juries have brought in heavy verdicts against the officials, and they in turn have become law-abiding, whereas I do not recall any case in this country where substantial damages have been given. In the United States courts the judges have without legislation pro-

---

[3] 4 *Reports of the National Commission on Law Observance and Enforcement* (Wickersham Commission) 34 (1931).

[4] See Chafee, "Arms, Right to Bear," 2 *Encyclopaedia of the Social Sciences* 209 (1930).

vided a different remedy, the exclusion of the evidence which has been unlawfully obtained, but state officials are subject to no such practical check.[5]

Again, consider the divergent strength of the same fundamental right under different circumstances. The various constitutions declare that no one shall be compelled to incriminate himself. In the courtroom this right is effectively protected, because judges have developed specific rules limiting the duty of a man to take the stand or testify when this might result in his condemnation for what he says. Possibly he receives too much protection, but there is no doubt that the legal machinery secures his liberty. Contrast the same right in the stage between arrest and trial. The accused is frequently subjected to the "third degree," consisting of prolonged questioning by relays of police officials and deprivation of sleep, perhaps of food. The legal machinery does exclude a confession thus obtained, but this does not prevent the officials from following up clues furnished by the confession, so that these violations of the right continue.[6] We need to consider new machinery — for instance, a better-organized police force trained and equipped to use lawful methods with skill and efficiency.

These instances show that the constitutional definition of a given liberty is less important than the legal machinery which determines the scope of the liberty in a particular case, that is, which demarcates the line between permissible and forbidden governmental action and which forces the government not to cross that line. Consequently it is essential, in discussing any situation where freedom of speech or some other form of liberty is involved, to examine the existing legal machinery; and, if this be unsatisfactory, to canvass the merits of possible alternatives. Four aspects, at least, of such machinery are important: (1) its nature; (2) the persons who constitute it

[5] On searches and seizures generally, see 2 Willoughby, *Constitutional Law* (2d ed.) § 720 (1929); 8 Wigmore, *Evidence* (3d ed.) § 2183 ff. (1940); Lasson, *History and Development of the Fourth Amendment* (1937); Fraenkel, "Concerning Searches and Seizures," 34 *Harvard Law Review* 361 (1921); Chafee, "Progress of the Law — Evidence," 35 *id.* at 694–704 (1922); Note, 46 *id.* 1307 (1933). See also *supra*, pp. 204–205, 311, 485–489.

[6] *Op. cit. supra* note 3, *passim*; Chafee, "Remedies for the Third Degree," 148 *Atlantic Monthly* 621 (1931); Warner, "How Can the Third Degree be Eliminated?" 1 *Bill of Rights Review* 24 (1940).

and draw the line in the particular case, for we should keep reminding ourselves that we have no mechanical devices for detecting unpermissible speech and writings but must always rely on human beings; (3) the time when the line is drawn; (4) the speed and expense and risks with which the line is drawn.

First, the nature of the machinery, which is extremely varied. Often, it operates in at least two stages, the initial power of restricting liberty and an independent check on abuses of the initial power. Under our constitutional system, for instance, the initial stage of arrest under a sedition statute is followed by intermediate stages of indictment, jury trial, sentence, culminating in the independent check of a determination by the Supreme Court of the United States as to the possible unconstitutionality of the statute. As already indicated, we have focused our attention too exclusively on this type of check, which is peculiar to this country. Other types have already been suggested, such as a civil action for damages against the official, or the exclusion of evidence illegally obtained. Where the initial stage consists of a determination by an administrative official, who refuses to license a play or to admit a book to the mails, a check may conceivably be furnished by a review of his decision in the courts. Finally — and this is a very important point — we shall find in certain free speech situations that the machinery which actually operates to restrict discussion is very different from the machinery set out in the statute-books. We are much more interested in what officials do than in what legislators say.

Secondly, the persons who compose the legal machinery. Whenever we authorize a particular restriction on liberty we ought not to forget that we are entrusting to fallible human beings a power over the minds of others. Benjamin Franklin (or a Philadelphia contemporary) stated the problem in saying that the desirability of stamping out evil thoughts is obvious, but the question remains whether any human being is good and wise enough to exercise it. And Milton asked, "How shall the licensers themselves be confided in, unless we can confer upon them, or they assume themselves above all others in the land, the grace of infallibility and uncorruptedness?" It is true that sometimes in our modern society we have to run the risk of abuses in the limitation of various kinds of liberty, because the evils we aim to avoid are so serious. For instance, freedom of action is restricted in all sorts of ways through administrative boards. These compel parents to vaccinate their children and send them to school; inspect food offered for sale; license street musicians; and order rotten tenements torn down. Some similar limitations on liberty of discussion may be necessary. However, the risk of human error ought to be weighed in each case; and even when this risk is run it ought to be minimized as far as possible through the selection of persons who by training, habits, social background, are least apt to act mistakenly or unjustly. For example, our building inspectors ought to have some architectural training; and the censorship of plays will vary enormously, accordingly as it is exercised by a student of literature or by a police official who has devoted his best years to the suppression of burglars and the regulation of motor traffic.

Thirdly, when is the line drawn by the men who possess power to demarcate permissible and illegal ideas? Do they make their decision before or after communication to the public — for example, the sale of a book or the production of a play or the delivery of a speech? If they can decide in advance, the interference with freedom of speech is likely to be considerably greater. Hence the long-lived hostility to censorship and Blackstone's rule against "previous restraint," considered in the first chapter. Yet we saw there that the fear of subsequent punishment may often choke those who would otherwise speak out. Indeed, this question of the time of drawing the line often provokes a sharp conflict of interests between the diverse groups of persons affected by suppression. On the one hand, the people who hear speeches, read books, and see plays and films gain by the absence of a censorship, for then they have a chance to get at the facts and ideas even if somebody is later put in prison for spreading them. On the other hand, the persons who would thus go to prison may look at the matter quite differently. They may prefer to be told ahead exactly what they can or cannot do. Such a preference was apparently rare in the seventeenth and eighteenth centuries when the disseminators of borderline books and pamphlets operated sporadically or on a small scale, when the theater was not a highly organized business and motion-pictures were undreamed of. Nowadays, however, millions of dollars and hundreds of persons may be involved in a metropolitan newspaper or a photoplay, so that the impulse to play safe becomes much stronger than it was for a Fleet Street bookseller or John Wilkes or John Peter Zenger. A few successful prosecutions for obscenity or sedition will spell ruin for the modern incorporated purveyor of facts and ideas. Goldstein went to prison in 1917 for putting *The Spirit of '76* on the screen, but such a sacrifice to artistic integrity will probably stand alone in the history of the motion-picture industry. And the owner of a syndicated press chain is not likely to share the eagerness of Socrates to speak the truth even if he must die. The balance-sheet becomes a more important document than the editorial page, and it seems wiser to keep them both out of the red. Therefore, the old hatred of censorship appears to be weakening. In several of the concrete situations which we are about to examine, the businesses concerned are acquiescing in a systematic weeding-out before the material is offered to the eyes and ears of the public. Whether this previous restraint be performed by a government censor as in theaters generally, or by non-official representatives of the whole industry as in motion-pictures, or by the particular purveyor as in radio broadcasting stations, the loss to open discussion is much the same.

Fourth, what are the speed and expense and risks of a given method of drawing the line between permitted and forbidden utterances?

By the speed and expense of the legal machinery, I mean the rapidity and cheapness with which initial abuses are checked by a subsequent independent decision. The effectiveness of *habeas corpus* is due in large measure to the summary fashion in which the writ may be at once obtained from any judge. On the other hand, although an erroneous injunction against peaceful persuasion by strikers may be corrected by an appeal to a higher court, the time which intervenes is often so long that it amounts practically to no check at all. Thus in the Tri-City case the Supreme Court of the United States lopped off certain clauses of the injunction seven years after it was granted, whereas the strike had probably ended within a few months so that an appeal was not worth waiting for. Similarly, the severe sentence imposed on Rose Pastor Stokes under the Espionage Act was not reversed until after the war was over, so that though wrong it maintained its deterrent effect on other pacifists until the question had become academic. In like manner the process of carrying appeals from convictions or injunctions through the state courts and perhaps to Washington may be so expensive that no use will be made of it. When the determination of the scope of liberty is of immediate importance, a slow and costly review is equal to no review, and the initial stage becomes of vastly greater importance as to both methods and personnel.

The risks of a particular method of determining the illegality of a presentation of facts and ideas form a very important factor in the operation of that method. What are the consequences of an unfavorable decision upon the persons directly affected, *e.g.*, the theater-owner, the motion-picture producer? This question is closely connected with the element of time, which constituted my third point. As we shall soon see, numerous purveyors of ideas think the adverse ruling of a censor to be less objectionable than conviction by a jury.

Let us now consider several points at which liberty of discussion is subject to restriction by law, and the existing or appropriate legal machinery for demarcating the limits of liberty, keeping always in mind the four aspects of the legal machinery already indicated.

I. PROSECUTIONS WITH A JURY

These may be brought for sedition, indecency, blasphemy (a topic which would seem to be forbidden by the "clear and present danger" test), and libels so outrageous as to make breaches of the peace probable.[7] In these prosecutions, the human machinery includes the legislature which enacts the law, and legislators have of late years become curiously sub-

[7] On criminal libel generally, see 19 A. L. R. 1470. For an extreme example of punishment, see Commonwealth *v.* Canter, 269 Mass. 359 (1929), adversely criticized in 43 *Harvard Law Review* 663. For a careful opinion, see Wheeler, J., in State *v.* Pape, 90 Conn. 98 (1916). On blasphemy, see 14 A. L. R. 880; 19 *id.* at 1510. For a recent case under the Massachusetts Blasphemy Act, see Chafee, *The Inquiring Mind*, p. 108.

ject to statutory epidemics, borrowing suppressive statutes from other states without regard to local conditions; then the prosecuting attorney, who starts proceedings and whose powers are very much greater than is generally realized; then the jury, whose method of selection is material; and the trial judge, who either is elected and so risks being sensitive to waves of popular indignation, or is appointed on the recommendation of the Department of Justice, which also may aid in speeding or retarding his promotion; finally, as a check, the appellate court. Under our system this check is imperfect, for unlike the English Court of Criminal Appeal it usually cannot reduce unduly long sentences if the conviction itself was proper, so that the personality of the trial judge who fixes sentences is very important. And even if the convicted agitator obtains a reversal from the United States Supreme Court or the highest state court, it will come too late to do much good for his particular agitation, whatever the beneficial effect of the decision upon his successors.

II. PETTY OFFENSES

A charge of using language likely to cause a breach of the peace is a convenient catchall to hold unpopular soapbox orators. The sale of indecent books and periodicals may be so tried in some jurisdictions. Here the trial judge, who has entire control, has been selected to deal with drunkards, traffic violators, etc., and naturally has had little experience with issues of free speech. Furthermore, these police judges are more independent of one another than Superior or Supreme Court judges, so that we get odd incidents like the acquittal of H. L. Mencken for selling a copy of the *American Mercury* in Boston, and the conviction of a newsdealer for selling the same number in Cambridge.[8] Some method of unification is necessary as in the cases of the federal district attorneys during the war; and it would be better if freedom of the press

---

[8] See *infra* note 14. On wide divergences among New York police judges in treating drunkenness, vagrancy, etc., see Everson, "The Human Element in Justice," 10 *Journal of Criminal Law & Criminology* 90 (1919). On the invalidity of loose construction of vagrancy statutes, see 45 *Harvard Law Review* 184 (1931); 27 *Illinois Law Review* 67 (1932). As to breaches of the peace and freedom of speech, see Cantwell *v.* Connecticut, *supra* Chapter XI at n. 62.

were taken out of the hands of police judges and placed in the jury trial courts. True, there is in all cases an appeal for a jury trial after a conviction in the police court, but this check is not sufficient because the penalties are too small to make it worth while to incur the expense.

III. INDOOR AND OUTDOOR MEETINGS

The police have a very wide power to stop agitators for such vague offenses as obstructing traffic, sauntering and loitering, picketing, carrying placards, distributing handbills, parading without a license.[9] The initial stage is in their hands, so that the superintendent of police really determines the limits of expression of opinion in the streets. According to the words of the law a later stage is provided in the courts; but practically such a check on the police is useless since it operates long after the day when the street demonstration would have been effective. Consequently, if the superintendent decides to stop a demonstration, he can go ahead even though the courts may later overrule him. The additional check of a suit against the arresting official for damages is worthless because juries will not bring in a substantial verdict.

Another method of restriction on open-air agitation is to require a permit from the mayor or some other official for speakers in a street or park, which may be arbitrarily refused. He then constitutes the entire legal machinery. The legality of such permit requirements was made dubious in 1939 by the Supreme Court decision against Mayor Hague of Jersey City, discussed in Chapter XI; but the method appears to remain still in use in many American cities.

Indoor agitation is usually less restricted, because it does not interfere with the general use of public areas. On the other hand, listeners are more liable to be excited in a crowded room than in the open air. Even without such a danger, a city mayor is impelled by other reasons to bar certain meetings in privately owned halls,[10] especially when these meetings are open to the public *gratis* or for a small charge. Whenever the

[9] See *The Inquiring Mind*, pp. 156–161; *supra* Chapter XI, section VII and note 103.

[10] Publicly-owned buildings, such as municipal auditoriums and schoolhouses, are not here considered. If wisely managed, these offer a new opportunity for

subject announced for discussion is distasteful to the mayor, *e.g.*, birth control, he is tempted to use every means in his power to prevent the meeting.

How does he do so? Often the statutes and ordinances merely provide that persons uttering obscene or seditious words can be punished *after* the speeches; and no law authorizes the mayor to forbid any meeting in advance because of its purpose, or to punish the owner of a hall for permitting a meeting against the mayor's orders. Yet in actual practice a mayor has often exercised such a power by threatening halls where forbidden meetings are held with proceedings for structural defects. The mayor can usually find a statute authorizing him to revoke the license of a hall because of such defects as insufficient fire exits or too narrow staircases or improper building materials. Past mayors of Boston have used such a statute to prohibit meetings to promote the Ku Klux Klan or advocate the repeal of the Massachusetts law against birth control. No owners of halls dared disobey the mayor, since no matter how much care had been taken in the construction and repairs of a hall, some violation of the complicated building regulations probably existed, for which the mayor could if defied revoke the owner's license and deprive him of all profits from his investment for some time to come. No hall-owner cared to risk everything on the chance that a court would eventually restore his license. So the law actually in operation for controversial meetings in halls was not the law about such meetings on the statute-book, but the personal will of the mayor.

There is something humorous in this mayoral solicitude about the danger from fire to radicals and Ku Kluxers and birth-control supporters, although no anxiety whatever was shown about building conditions in the same halls when meetings were held there by the mayor's own side. It seems much more natural to protect one's friends from conflagrations and collapsing floors than one's enemies.[11]

the formation of well-considered opinion among citizens about public affairs and an additional safety-valve for blowing off discontent.

[11] A similar device was used by the police in Vienna before 1914. — Wickham Steed, *The Hapsburg Monarchy* (1914), p. 76, quoted in *The Inquiring Mind*, p. 144.

The tests outlined in the beginning of this chapter must be applied to this actual human machinery for regulating the subjects of meetings in public halls, regardless of the unused judge and jury set up by the statutes for this same purpose. When we consider the fitness of the machinery for its task, it makes little difference whether the mayor acts alone or as one member of a building commission including real estate men, architects, and builders. The persons thus empowered by the legislature to revoke the licenses of halls are thoroughly trained to judge whether stairs are strong enough to hold the crowd, whether there are large enough exits, or too few fire escapes. Those are things that can be weighed and measured and figured, and they know how to do it. But who can be trusted to weigh the wisdom of an idea? Who has the experience that qualifies him to say that a statute is so essential to the welfare of the community that any advocate of its repeal must be forbidden to speak? Men measure and weigh with footrules and scales whose accuracy is determined beforehand by scientific tests and impartial persons. There is no foot-rule to measure the hurtfulness of an argument or whether a group is antagonistic to our system, no scale to weigh the permanent value of a statute whose repeal is sought. The censor will have to measure and weigh with his own mind. His prejudices, his bias, his personal views, however well considered, must be the standard of decision, for he has no other.

Moreover, the authorities in charge of architectural defects do more than make the initial decision as to the desirability of the subject-matter of meetings in halls. Their initial decision is also the final decision for all practical purposes. Even if an adventurous hall-owner should carry the matter into the courts, he could not get judicial relief until long after the day set for the meeting. And in fact no court ever does pass on these questions, because no hall-owner wants to go to the trouble, expense, and danger of fighting the officials who can so easily put him out of business.

The danger is not in the suppression of any particular doctrine or group, but in the very existence of suppression. Let no one remain content with the thought that he dislikes the particular victims of these decisions by mayors against public meetings. Intolerance is the most contagious of all diseases, and no party or creed is immune. The suppression of opponents has the same delightful fascination in our day that cutting off their heads had in the French Revolution. But the moderate republicans who first rejoiced in that method soon found it employed by *their* opponents, and the control of the guillotine shifted from group to group, of increasingly extreme views, until finally the conservatives seized it and beheaded Robespierre. So with the weapon of intolerance. Substantial citizens of St. Paul who urged the banishment of radical professors from the University of Minnesota were outraged when the Non-Partisan League in North Dakota purged the critics of public ownership from their State University Faculty. Roman Catholics who acquiesce in the suppression of birth-control or Ku Klux meetings in Boston should watch the same spirit of intolerance infecting Protestants and leading to laws against the teaching of evolution in Tennessee and Mississippi, against the existence of parochial schools in Oregon. Nor is it just a matter of legislation. Intolerance can work by more subtle and sinister but equally effective methods. Probably no true construction of any statute or ordinance enables most mayors to prevent public discussions of what they object to, but they do it. No statute in Ohio authorizes the exclusion of Roman Catholic school teachers from the public schools, but it has been stated that in some districts an inquisition into the religious views of teachers is conducted in violation of law, and only Protestants get positions. Intolerance can always find some crevice in the administration of the law through which to creep and accomplish its purpose. The only remedy is to build up every day and every hour the opposite spirit, a firm faith that all varieties and shades of opinion must be given a chance to be heard, that the decision between truth and error cannot be made by human beings, but only by time and the test of open argument and counter-argument, so that each citizen may judge for himself.

Of late years, whenever any controversy has arisen over discussion, constitutional free speech seems to be always just around the corner. People praise this magnificent fundamental right and then deny that it is applicable to this particular agitator or minority group. We are like Oliver Cromwell when he was besieging a Roman Catholic town in Ireland, which

offered to surrender on the one condition of freedom of conscience. Cromwell replied:

As to freedom of conscience, I meddle with no man's conscience;
but if you mean by that, liberty to celebrate the mass, I would have
you understand that in no place where the power of the Parliament
of England prevails shall that be permitted.[12]

We should do much better to imitate a contemporary Englishman, Lord Justice Scrutton, who freed an Irishman from
illegal arrest with these words:

The law of this country has been very jealous of any infringement
of personal liberty. This care is not to be exercised less vigilantly,
because the subject whose liberty is in question may not be particularly meritorious. It is indeed one test of belief in principles if you
apply them to cases with which you have no sympathy at all. You
really believe in freedom of speech if you are willing to allow it to
men whose opinions seem to you wrong and even dangerous.[13]

IV. PLAYS AND BOOKS [14]

Laws against indecent publications and plays have a peculiar
interest for law-abiding citizens, because they are more apt
to restrict the liberties of such citizens than perhaps any other
part of our criminal statutes. Although such people are not
very likely to be punished for selling obscene books or acting
in lewd plays, nevertheless, these laws may be used by the
authorities to suppress books and plays which law-abiding
citizens want to read or see. It is not hard for officials to
create a virtual censorship against significant fiction and
drama, which may easily impoverish the intellectual life of
the community.

Most of us agree that the law must draw some line between
decency and indecency, a line between permitted art and art
that can be punished or suppressed. Some writers, it is true,
contest this whole position. They believe that the law should
keep its hands off all questions of decency and leave them to

[12] Quoted by W. M. Evarts, *Arguments and Speeches*, I, 464.
[13] Rex *v.* Secretary of State, *Ex parte* O'Brien, [1923] 2 K. B. 382.
[14] See the much more detailed and informative studies by Grant and Angoff:
"Massachusetts and Censorship," 10 *Boston University Law Review* 36, 147;
"Recent Developments in Censorship," *id.* 488 (1930).

the judgment of the readers and playgoers themselves insofar as they are adults, while children can be kept away from objectionable books or sights by their parents.[15] But this extreme view is not likely to be accepted by any considerable group of legislators. They and the great majority of their constituents will continue to insist for a long time to come that there must be some limit on the literary discussion of the relation between the sexes, and that when this limit is passed the police or other government officials must take vigorous measures.

However, the recognition that there must be a legal line between decency and indecency does not end the matter. The real problem remains — where and how is the line to be drawn? It cannot be drawn by statutes. For example, look at typical statutes now in force in Massachusetts. A bookseller can be severely punished for selling a book or magazine if it is "obscene, indecent or impure, or manifestly tends to corrupt the morals of youth." [16] Drama is covered by another section, by which the producer and actors can be fined and imprisoned if a play is "lewd, obscene, indecent, immoral or impure, . . . or . . . suggestive of lewdness, obscenity, indecency, immorality or impurity, or . . . manifestly tending to corrupt the morals of youth." [17] An additional penalty is imposed on Boston theater owners by a different statute, under which the mayor, the police commissioner, and a member of the city art commission may by a majority vote revoke or suspend the license of any theater, after holding a hearing, if they object to a play on grounds of "public morality or decency." [18] Nothing here tells law-enforcing officials and jurymen on which side of the line they ought to place *Measure for Measure* or the story of Joseph and Potiphar's wife. A bookseller gets no help from these words in deciding whether he can safely put *Anthony Adverse* on his shelves. The statute-book does not tell Miss

---

[15] For example, see Ernst & Seagle, *To the Pure: A Study of Obscenity and the Censor* (1928). For a more moderate view, see Cairns, "Freedom of Expression in Literature," 200 *Annals of the American Academy of Political & Social Science* 76 (1938). See also Glenn, "Censorship at Common Law and under Modern Dispensation," 82 *University of Pennsylvania Law Review* 114 (1933).

[16] Mass. Gen. Laws, 1932, c. 272, § 28.

[17] *Id.*, § 32.

[18] Mass. Acts, 1936, c. 340, amending statutes of 1908 and 1915.

Helen Hayes whether she will run the risk of spending several months in jail for acting *Coquette*, because the heroine makes it unmistakably clear that she was seduced between the acts.

Such vagueness is avoided by many other parts of the criminal law. Thus burglary is entering a dwelling-house with the intent to steal between one hour after sunset and one hour before sunrise. And statutes make it fairly plain to both police and citizens what is forbidden and what is allowed on Sunday.

Anybody can see that the facts affecting indecency are too varied to permit a precise definition to be framed by the legislature to cover books and plays for many years ahead. The statutes can hardly do more than lay down a general standard. And the courts do little to make the standard more precise. In the leading case on the Massachusetts book statute, which decided that the jury should not read the book as a whole but merely pass on the portions alleged to be obscene, the court refused to define "obscene" "indecent" "impure" "manifestly," saying: "They are common words and may be assumed to be understood in their common meaning by an ordinary jury." [19] Lord Cockburn thus interpreted "obscene" in the corresponding English statute: "I think the test of obscenity is this, whether the tendency of the matter charged as obscenity is to deprave and corrupt those whose minds are open to such immoral influences, and into whose hands a publication of this sort may fall." [20]

Therefore the line between permissible and forbidden books or plays is not drawn once for all in the statutes or by judges. The line is drawn afresh during the course of every proceeding directed against a particular book or play. Hence, it makes very little difference what words are used in the statute. The really important question concerns the procedure by which the statute is enforced in actual life. What legal machinery is now available to the person who is forbidden to express ideas on the stage or in books, when he believes that those ideas are not criminal? How can he test the alleged illegality? If he now has no effective remedy, what changes in the law or in administrative practice are desirable to give him such a remedy?

If the criminal statutes just set forth be invoked against

[19] Commonwealth *v.* Buckley, 200 Mass. 346, 352 (1909).
[20] Regina *v.* Hicklin, L. R. 3 Q. B. 360, 371 (1868).

plays and books, the same procedure is used as in other obscenity prosecutions, and this has been already described. However, we shall soon see that the usual methods of control are quite different. The technique suggested at the outset of this chapter can in this problem be reduced to three questions: (1) What persons draw the line? (2) When do they draw it? (3) What are the consequences of an unfavorable decision upon the persons concerned, who for plays include theater owner, producer, and actors, and for books publisher and bookseller? I shall first discuss these questions at length in connection with the theater; and then deal more briefly with their application to the control of books. Motion-pictures will be treated under a separate heading, since they raise special problems.

What persons draw the line as to the indecency of plays? Whatever the statutory definition of "obscene," it must be applied to each play by human beings who are liable to err. There is no litmus paper, no foot-rule, no thermometer, which will scientifically demonstrate too much indecency in a play. We must rely on fallible human opinions. What sort of men are least apt to make serious mistakes?

One method is to set up a permanent dramatic censor. This is virtually the method now used in Boston. The theaters rarely subject themselves to prosecutions in court for reasons to be stressed later, and they avoid interference with their licenses by the statutory board of three officials described above by complying with the orders of a city censor appointed by the mayor. I do not get the impression that the holder of this office is usually a man of extensive literary training with an established reputation as a dramatic critic. Familiarity with the *Oedipus Rex* of Sophocles or the *Hippolytus* of Euripides might lessen his fears that a total collapse of family life will be caused by the presentation of incest on the stage in O'Neill's *Desire under the Elms*. And even when a trained writer is chosen censor, as in England, he makes some peculiar rulings. There is always danger of warped judgment caused by the fact that most people do not like such a job, so that you are liable to get volunteers of the Comstock temperament who are morbidly sensitive about the morals of others. Constant preoccupation with questionable books or plays is not good for any man. It throws him off his balance, and takes away his sense of proportion.

Would the situation be better if a statutory board of three officials exercised direct oversight of all doubtful plays? These officials are not wholly preoccupied with indecency, and there is a chance that interruption by other matters will keep their minds healthy. On the other hand, a mayor and a police commissioner are not ordinarily selected on the basis of wide reading and literary judgment. They have other duties, which require other qualities. They may lack the training of the permanent censor, and yet run the same risk of being arbitrary and bureaucratic. An art commissioner comes closer to the mark, but after all plays are quite different from statues and public buildings. If we are to run the risks of individual judgment, the head of a public library seems the best qualified for a censor's job. Still the whimsical way in which librarians keep some famous literary masterpieces on locked shelves does not augur well for the freedom of the drama, if they are to pass upon plays as well as 'books.

A different proposal would empower the trial judge to enjoin plays which he considers indecent. This involves the same risks as control by a single official censor. A judge is not chosen for his dramatic training. Everything would be left to the chance experience and prejudices of a single man.

On the whole, the best tribunal to pass on plays is a jury. There you get not one man but twelve. They are, or for this kind of case ought to be, selected from the kind of people who go to plays. Thus you get the judgment of a number of men fresh from life, about the kind of plays they want to be shown. Therefore, in considering personnel I favor decision of indecency by a jury, who might be required to have higher qualifications than ordinary jurors, for example, a high school education.

When is the line drawn? A censor decides before publication, and a criminal prosecution comes after publication. This is a main reason why the historic struggle for freedom of the press has been so largely directed against censorship. The public does not like to have its reading systematically stifled in advance. Even if a prosecution comes later, at least those who wanted to read the book or newspaper have been able to do so. On the other hand, the producers of a play like to find out in advance just where they stand. They could get the advantages of a jury in the ordinary criminal prosecution, but the trouble is that a verdict that a play is decent would come too late to be of any use. It might not be reached for a year or more after the play began to run. The manager cannot afford to wait for so long a time. Hence, the theaters prefer to get an immediate decision from the police or a district attorney or a mayor or a censor, because then either they know that they can go ahead safely or else they withdraw the doubtful play ahead of time and substitute something else. Consequently, to get the advantages of a jury verdict, it ought to come at the beginning of the run. How can this be arranged?

What are the consequences of an adverse decision? Here we meet another disadvantage of a jury verdict in a prosecution. If the jury finds the play obscene, there is a heavy fine, and perhaps prison sentences for the producer and some of the actors, followed probably by termination of the theater license. They cannot afford to take this chance, and, for this reason also, prefer to leave the question to an official, whose adverse decision has no worse consequences than the stopping of the particular play. Another trouble with the prosecution method, as the *Captive* case in New York brought out, is that even if some eager actors want to test their "indecency" by the legal method of a jury trial, they cannot force the authorities to prosecute.[21] Prosecutions are merely threatened, and that scares the theater owners and producers enough to keep the play off the boards.

The true solution, I venture to suggest, was indicated by the procedure used by the mayor of Quincy, Massachusetts, when *Strange Interlude* was banned in Boston. Informally, he assembled a jury who witnessed a dress rehearsal of the play, and then he accepted the jury's verdict that it was not indecent. Play juries of this sort could be made official by new statutes which would allow test cases to determine whether a play is decent. These test cases would be decided by juries with proper educational qualifications, called at once, who

[21] Liveright *v.* Waldorf Theatres Corp., 220 App. Div. 182 (N. Y. 1927). See Hays, *Let Freedom Ring*, pp. 237 ff. (1928) ; review by Chafee, 42 *Harvard Law Review* 142 (1928).

would witness a sample performance, hear arguments, and bring in a verdict. The statutes might provide that if the play was already performing in another city, the jury could travel there to see it at the expense of the theatrical people; this would be cheaper than bringing actors and scenery on later and then having the play banned. If the jury in the test case declared the play indecent, there would be no fine or imprisonment; the play would simply not appear publicly in the city where it had been thus condemned. Of course, if the play should go on in defiance of the jury's findings, all participants in the condemned production should be liable to a criminal prosecution of the usual sort with heavy penalties after conviction.

One important point still remains as to the theater — who may take the initiative to determine the decency or indecency of a particular drama? Thus far I have assumed that the proper public authorities may institute the suit to submit the drama to a play jury, just as in the past they have instituted prosecutions or proceedings to revoke a theater license. However, the initiative should not be a monopoly of the public authorities. They should no longer be able, as in the past, to coerce the theater owner, producer, and actors by threats without facilitating settlement of the issue of decency by a legal tribunal. Therefore, the theater owner or the producer should also be authorized by the proposed statutes to institute proceedings for a play jury.

In substance, this would be a suit for a declaratory judgment. Consequently, such a suit may be possible under existing declaratory judgment statutes, even if no specific legislation for the theater problem is enacted. The suggested play jury may fall within the usual provisions of such statutes allowing a jury trial on issues of fact. However, the broad terms of a declaratory judgment statute have been held inapplicable in New York to suits for a declaration that the plaintiff is not guilty of a crime,[22] although relief of this sort has frequently been given elsewhere.[23] On this account, some courts might

[22] Reed v. Littleton, 275 N. Y. 150 (1937), adversely criticized in 6 *Brooklyn Law Review* 472 and Note, 46 *Yale Law Journal* 855; see also 14 *New York University Law Quarterly* 398 and 11 *St. John's Law Review* 320.

[23] Borchard, "Declaratory Judgments, 1939," 9 *Brooklyn Law Review* 1 (1939); Chafee, *Cases on Equitable Remedies*, p. 471, n. 2 (1938).

refuse to give a declaration that a play was decent.[24] Hence, it would be desirable to enact new statutes specifically authorizing play juries, and enabling suits to be instituted by any person interested in putting on the play as well as by the public authorities.

The control of indecent books raises somewhat different questions than the problem of indecent plays. Although an advance proceeding like the play jury might be desirable for books, there are, as it will be seen, special constitutional difficulties.

The law concerning books reads very simply on paper. According to the statutes, the decision about the indecency of a book must always be made by a jury. The time for this decision is in a criminal prosecution after the book has been published or has been sold by a bookseller. The consequence of an adverse decision is the severe punishment of the defendant by imprisonment or fine.

This law usually operates the way it reads if the accused is a publisher; but it operates very differently if he is a bookseller. When a publisher with a large general line of books is charged with bringing out an indecent book but believes that he is giving readers a work of real literary merit, then the publisher can often afford to fight. If he faces prosecution and is acquitted, he may win large financial returns. Many New York publishers have been willing to test the legality of their books in the criminal courts, and they have secured an impressive list of acquittals during the last twenty years.[25] Convictions against publishers have been obtained in only three New York cases since 1920, and those three books went pretty far. Consequently, the authorities are not eager to get into hot water by attacking powerful publishers, unless the case against the book is very strong.

On the other hand, a bookseller is in a weak position. He

[24] See Dreiser v. John Lane Co., 183 App. Div. 773 (1918), in which before the Declaratory Judgments Act a court refused to pass on the decency of a book, *The American Tragedy*, in advance of a criminal prosecution; and *supra* note 21. For a successful prosecution of a Boston bookseller for selling the same book, see Commonwealth v. Friede, 271 Mass. 318 (1930); Grant & Angoff, 10 *Boston University Law Review* at 496 ff.

[25] See Cairns, *op. cit. supra*, note 15, at p. 82.

cannot expect to make enough money from selling copies of single books to pay a fine or even his lawyer's bill for defending a criminal prosecution. If he is convicted, the fine will take a considerable share of the profits from his other books. Furthermore, a conviction will scare away reputable patrons for the future. Hence, so far as booksellers are concerned, the determination of the indecency of a book is not likely to be left to a criminal jury. A bookseller is very anxious for a decision about the book before he commits a possible crime by selling it. Therefore, he will readily acquiesce in a ruling by persons who have no statutory standing, so long as they assure him that he will be left alone if he abides by their ruling.

In some cities, the district attorney issues a list of prohibited books or announces that a particular book is banned. In other cities, the task of literary criticism is performed by the police while they are resting from active duty on the beat. In Boston, the Watch & Ward Society, a private organization, has at times charged itself with the compilation of a blacklist. Through its coöperation with the police, the Society can warn any bookseller that if he sells a book on the list his arrest will follow promptly.[26] At other times, the booksellers have set up a committee of their own to issue the Index Expurgatorius. Whichever of these methods be used, the obvious result is a virtual censorship unauthorized by statute. Whenever a book is put on the blacklist in the particular city, it disappears at once from the shelves of all reputable booksellers there, no matter how great its merits or how extensive its sales in other parts of the United States.

The decisions of such a censor or body of censors are almost always final. They are reviewed by no court, except in the few instances where the publisher chooses to come to the booksellers' aid, as when H. L. Mencken defeated the suppression in Boston of an issue of the *American Mercury*.[27] This uncontrolled censorship is likely to be far more sweeping than convictions by juries. The Boston booksellers were deterred by

---

[26] The practice is described in American Mercury v. Chase, 13 F. (2d) 224 (D. Mass. 1926), noted in 75 *University of Pennsylvania Law Review* 258, and in 25 *Michigan Law Review* 74. See also Hays, *Let Freedom Ring*, pp. 160 ff. (1928); Chafee, *The Inquiring Mind*, pp. 136 ff. (1928); Commonwealth v. DeLacey, 271 Mass. 327 (1930); Grant & Angoff, *op. cit. supra*, note 14.

[27] See the references in note 26.

the threats of the blacklist from selling well-known books like
*All Quiet on the Western Front, A Farewell to Arms, The
World of William Clissold,* and *Manhattan Transfer,*[28] although
none of the publishers of these books was prosecuted in New
York, much less convicted. The situation is at its worst when
a prosecutor or a policeman acts as censor. It is not much
better when control is vested in a private organization like the
Watch & Ward Society, where the actual decision is likely to
be made by elderly men morbidly interested in reading obscene
books so that they can keep them away from others or by
zealous employees anxious to exhibit activity in order to hold
their jobs. When the booksellers do the censoring themselves,
the public at least gets the benefit of literary training; but the
booksellers are bound to be timid because they know that
they will lose their privilege if they pass a few books which
are subsequently denounced by local clergymen and moralists.

Since there is little book publishing outside New York and
three or four other large cities, the law of most states against
indecent books is largely directed at booksellers. Thus the
situation just described represents law in action in nearly all
the United States. Plainly it is not at all the same as the law
in the statute-books. Yet, unsatisfactory as this law in action
is, we shall go on having it so long as the law on paper seems
even more undesirable to the booksellers.

Unfortunately, it is not easy to devise a better statute. One
ideal is to permit an advance decision on the indecency of a
book, so that the booksellers will not risk prison or a heavy
fine if the book is found obscene. For this purpose, the Boston
booksellers introduced a bill in the legislature some years ago
providing for suit against the book rather than the bookseller.[29]
If a judge sitting in equity decided the book to be indecent,
he could enjoin the book; and booksellers would not be prosecuted, unless they sold after such an injunction. This plan
resembled the old practice of having books burned by the common hangman, which has recently been revived by the Nazis.

This Massachusetts bill, which was not enacted, had the

[28] See the list of books banned in Boston in Ernst & Seagle, *To The Pure,*
p. 295 (1928) ; Cairns, *op. cit. supra,* note 15, at 83.

[29] See detailed discussion by Grant & Angoff, 10 *Boston University Law
Review* at 488 ff.; *The Inquiring Mind,* p. 140 and note.

advantages of giving warning to the booksellers before sale and of taking control away from police, prosecutors, and private organizations of vice-hunters. However, it failed to attain a second important ideal — that the decision about indecency should be made by a jury. A decision by a legally trained judge after due proof and argument is better than an unauthorized official or private censorship, but a jury trial for restrictions on the sale of books is probably required by both sound policy and the constitutional guaranty of freedom of the press. Here is where books differ from plays. The Constitution may not prohibit censorship of plays,[30] but the whole history of the free press clause shows that it certainly concerns books. Suppression of a newspaper by injunction was held unconstitutional in *Near* v. *Minnesota*.[31] Freedom of the press cannot be confined to newspapers; indeed the attack on the English censorship centered around books at a time when there were hardly any newspapers. Therefore, it seems that a jury is even more necessary to pass on books than on plays.

Both ideals would be fulfilled by a plan for books resembling the play jury. A statute might allow proceedings for a declaration as to the decency of a particular book to be instituted either by the public authorities or a group of citizens or a bookseller. A jury would then be impaneled to read the book, and approve it or condemn it. The statute could require that booksellers who withheld the questioned book from sale during the proceeding should not be arrested or prosecuted for previously selling the book. And if the book was declared by the jury to be decent, subsequent sales should be lawful. This would be far better than the existing informal censorship.

However, we should have to consider carefully the constitutionality of such a proceeding under such cases as *Near* v. *Minnesota*.[32] Does the prohibition of censorship merely mean an assurance of jury trial, or does it also forbid advance decisions against the sale of books? One of the main arguments against censorship of the press is that the public shall have the advantage of reading the book or newspaper, even if the

[30] See Mutual Film Corp. *v.* Industrial Commn., 236 U. S. 230, 241 (1915). On the question whether this case has been shaken by Near *v.* Minnesota, *infra* note 31, see the discussion of film censorship in section v of this chapter.

[31] 283 U. S. 697 (1931), discussed in Chapter XI, section III.

[32] *Supra*, note 31.

publisher or bookseller is subsequently convicted. We must remember that the suppressed book may not be wholly bad. Even though some parts are found to be obscene, the result of a removal of the book from sale in pursuance of the suggested jury verdict will be that the public will be deprived of the decent portions of the book. So it is arguable that the law cannot constitutionally act against a book until after it is sold.

Suppose that a statute required all books to be submitted to a jury before publication, and provided that if the jury condemned the book as indecent all copies could thereafter be destroyed by officials and anybody who distributed the book could be convicted without a further contest as to its decency. Might not such a statute violate the constitutional guaranty against censorship even though twelve jurymen acted as censors? If this be true of advance control of publication, may it not also apply to advance control of sales by booksellers? On the other hand, it can be urged that the bookseller may waive this constitutional right if he institutes the proceeding for a declaratory judgment through a jury verdict. The question still remains whether he should be permitted to waive the interest of the public in reading the unobjectionable parts of the book. All this requires careful thought, but at least the plan seems worth further consideration.

Accordingly, my conclusion, both as to plays and books, is that decisions on the issue of indecency should be made by the citizens themselves through qualified juries. The practical problem is to make such jury verdicts more convenient than in the ordinary criminal prosecution, so as to lessen the risk of honest theater owners, producers, publishers, and booksellers who are anxious to obtain a legal determination before going ahead.

V. MOVING PICTURES [33]

Censorship of motion pictures by a board of officials exists in six states — Kansas, Maryland, New York, Ohio, Pennsylvania, and Virginia. The action of any one of these six states

[33] My chief source for this topic is "Censorship of Motion Pictures," an admirable Note in 49 *Yale Law Journal* 87 (1939). Censorship statutes are listed in Appendix III.

against all or part of a picture may affect its appearance in neighboring non-censor states within the territory served by the same distribution agency. Deletions from a given talking picture in one state may thus spoil the plot sequence for audiences in several states. In addition, many cities in non-censor states have set up their own boards of policemen or policewomen to supervise films, and such boards are apt to be more capricious than state censors, because they are infinitely more susceptible to the influence of any locally powerful religious, social, or patriotic organization. For example, Charlie Chaplin's stroke of genius, *The Great Dictator*, was recently banned in Chicago, apparently out of deference to its large German population; and photoplays based on the Spanish Civil War have been cut or forbidden in numerous cities because of certain church groups who regard Franco the bomber of Basques as a bulwark of Christianity. The ordinary criminal law punishing obscene entertainments is also applicable, but prosecutions are rare, probably because threats or direct censorship are sufficient to keep the theaters on their good behavior.

If some form of legal censorship be necessary, a centralized federal board would avoid the present multiplicity of state and municipal authorities. As yet, however, federal regulation is limited to criminal statutes punishing the transportation of lascivious films and pictures of prize-fights, and a section of the Tariff Act prohibiting the importation of any picture which is immoral or advocates treason or insurrection.[34] Even though a film has been passed by the customs officials, this does not exempt it from being banned by a state board of censors.[35]

In short, any controversial motion picture, after satisfying the uncrowned kings of movie morals, Mr. Will H. Hays and Mr. Joseph Ignatius Breen, must run the gauntlet of a host of big and little despots, each of whom is just as immune from court interference as the Secretary of Labor deporting an alien or the Postmaster General depriving the *Milwaukee Leader* of cheap postal rates.[36] And finally the picture is subjected to

[34] 18 U. S. C. A. §§ 396, 405; 19 *id.* § 1305.

[35] Eureka Productions, Inc. *v.* Lehman, 17 F. Supp. 259 (S. D. N. Y. 1936), affd. by memo., 302 U. S. 634 (1937).

[36] See Chapter V, section II; Chapter VII. On the very narrow scope of

the critical gaze of audiences, who, if displeased by whatever has outlived the numerous censors, can rapidly render it a heavy financial loss.

The result is what might be expected. The maxim of the industry is said to be: "Thou shalt not offend any one, anywhere, at any time." And so it has almost ended by boring every one everywhere. It is a wonder that we get some of the magnificent films we do. An able writer in the *Yale Law Journal* attacks the desirability of this whole system of multiple official and self-imposed censors.[37] It would seem that the informal control by audiences would be sufficient, in view of their power by voluntary boycotts to ruin both the producer and the theater if really objectionable pictures are forced on them. Furthermore, if the films are clearly filthy, both these responsible persons can readily be punished by state and federal prosecutions.

For the sake of brevity, I shall confine myself to the operation of the machinery set up by state laws. What sort of men make the decisions? Some states give the power to members of the state department of education and the statutes sometimes call for persons "well qualified by education and experience." Pennsylvania formerly obtained the services of an eminent writer of American history, Mr. E. P. Oberholtzer, who later published a book on *The Morals of the Movies*. Yet the salaries are too low to attract many men of his ability, even if they be willing to sacrifice time from writing good books in order to look at bad films. When we examine the output of the machinery, we find odd products coming from the unreviewable judgments of censorious censors. Ohio and Kansas banned newsreels considered pro-labor. Kansas ordered a speech by Senator Wheeler opposing the bill for enlarging the Supreme Court to be cut from the *March of Time* as "partisan and biased," until popular outcry forced a reversal. Virginia and New York banned *The Birth of a Baby*. New York prohibited the French film *Harvest* for a time.[38] Kipling's *Without Benefit of Clergy* did not pass muster until

judicial review of film censors' orders and its futility, see 49 *Yale Law Journal* at 96–97.
[37] See *supra*, note 33.
[38] See other examples in 49 *Yale Law Journal* at 94 ff.

the couple had been married. An early version of *Carmen* was condemned in three states on three different grounds. The Ohio censor objected because cigarette-girls smoked cigarettes in public. The Pennsylvania censor disapproved the duration of a kiss — "No kiss over five feet long." And the California censor was indignant because at the end of the film the hero stabbed the heroine. It was permissible for a woman to kill a man on the screen, for "Girls will be girls," but what would the world come to if the process were reversed?

Most of the arguments commonly advanced for film censorship are the same as those urged in the seventeenth century for continuing the censorship of books and periodicals. Suppressing newsreels is much the same as suppressing newspapers.[39] Yet we have long since removed from the statute-book all previous restraints on printed publications, leaving it largely to the reader, as Milton says, to "consider vice with all her baits and seeming pleasures, and yet abstain, and yet distinguish, and yet prefer that which is truly better." All the objections to a press censorship apply as well to film censorship, especially in an age when more persons probably go to the movies than read books. Are not grown men and women to be trusted to tell bad from good when it is in plain sight? Why is it dangerous for them to witness on the screen the great problems which they are accustomed to find in the writings of Tolstoy or Eugene O'Neill or Shakespeare without apparently going to the dogs in consequence?

That brings us to the main defense of film censorship, the children. Its vigorous supporters urge that every photoplay must be suitable for the youthful eyes and ears which might be in the audience. And so they would have us reduce the subject-matter of all films to the level of a twelve-year-old child. Instead, we might better order the motion-picture houses to exclude youngsters from certain plays, and thus let adults chew occasionally on intellectual and artistic nourishment too tough for milk-teeth. Also we can rely on groups of parents and other unofficial bodies to classify films according to their suitability for various ages. Or we might even go back to *laissez-faire*, and trust sensible parents to keep their children

[39] As to the validity and extent of newsreel censorship, see 49 *Yale Law Journal* at 93–95.

at home from mature films. As for the children of foolish parents, they know so much already that it is doubtful whether celluloid and sound-tracks can make them any worse. At all events, it is arguable that much of our film censorship is a left-over from the era of Prohibition. As the writer mentioned above says, "No longer is there any belief that the American people can be legislated into sainthood."

The validity of state motion-picture censorship was upheld by the United States Supreme Court in 1915.[40] In those early days of films, long before talking pictures and newsreels, movies were regarded as merely an entertainment, in a class with vaudeville and the *Black Crook*. The Court could not then realize the importance of this new method for communicating facts and ideas to great masses of the public. In spite of the deeply rooted Anglo-Saxon antagonism to censorship of the press, the Justices were willing to distinguish films and let them be subjected to the previous restraint which even Blackstone regarded as inconsistent with free discussion. Justice Holmes is said to have expressed regret, many years afterwards, that he ever concurred in this decision and that he did not sense its consequences.

Much water has run under the bridge in the last quarter-century. Now that the desirability of legal censorship of motion pictures is seriously questioned, it might be possible to persuade the Supreme Court to overrule its 1915 decision and declare that state film censorship violates the Fourteenth Amendment.[41] The value of motion pictures to the thought of the nation is obvious today. The Gitlow case has given the Amendment an extensive application to state encroachments on free speech, which men never dreamed of in 1915. *Near* v. *Minnesota*[42] in 1931 invalidated previous restraints against a newspaper which was far more scandalous than most of the films which have fallen under the censor's ban. Certainly, if an order deleting items from a newsreel like the *March of Time* should be carried to the Supreme Court, we might hope for an illuminating reconsideration of the place of the film in a

[40] Mutual Film Corp. *v.* Industrial Commn. of Ohio, 236 U. S. 230 (1915), *per* McKenna, J. Many state cases to the same effect under state free-speech clauses are collected in 64 A. L. R. 505 (1929).

[41] See 49 *Yale Law Journal* at 110 for lines of attack.

[42] 283 U. S. 697 (1931), discussed with other relevant cases in Chapter XI.

modern society. In *Thornhill* v. *Alabama* in 1940, Justice Murphy said for the majority of the Court:

> Those who won our independence had confidence in the power of free and fearless reasoning and communication of ideas to discover and spread political and economic truth. Noxious doctrines in those fields may be refuted and their evil averted by the courageous exercise of the right of free discussion.[43]

In an age when "commerce" in the Constitution has been construed to include airplanes and electromagnetic waves, "freedom of speech" in the First Amendment and "liberty" in the Fourteenth should be similarly applied to new media for the communication of ideas and facts. Freedom of speech should not be limited to the air-borne voice, the pen, and the printing press, any more than interstate commerce is limited to stagecoaches and sailing vessels.

Newsreels and political addresses on the screen are already exempted by the statutes of Kansas, New York, and Pennsylvania. It is much to be hoped that other state legislatures will follow their example without waiting for a Supreme Court decision.

And the immunity of motion pictures from state censorship should not be confined to current-events films. Freedom of speech covers much more than political ideas. It embraces all discussion which enriches human life and helps it to be more wisely led. Thus, in our first national statement of the subject by the Continental Congress in 1774,[44] this freedom was declared to include "the advancement of truth, science, morality, and *arts* in general." Motion pictures have already taken their place beside the novel and the stage drama as one of the great arts.

Let us consider for a moment the chief function hitherto performed by the novel and the theater. Aside from entertainment, mystery, and romance, they can offer us a criticism of life. The greatest novels and dramas examine the basic conceptions of the community and ascertain how far they are true and sound, and whether they should be retained or modi-

---

[43] 310 U. S. 88 at 95 (1940), McReynolds, J., dissenting.
[44] *Supra* p. 17. Italics mine. The ideas in this paragraph and those succeeding are partly derived from an address by Dr. Abraham Myerson.

fied or rejected for something better. Just as Socrates went up and down Athens stinging men's minds into fresh activity about such ideas as "virtue," "knowledge," "justice," which had become stale like old hay for want of an occasional turning over and loosening up in the sunlight, so a great writer arouses us from our dogmatic slumbers and forces us to reconsider conceptions we and many previous societies have been inclined to take for granted. Among these complacently accepted generalizations are the following: the supremacy of settled rules of law, reshaped in the *Antigone* of Sophocles and Galsworthy's *Justice*; that the rulers of society are upright, denounced by *King Lear*; that the people always make wise decisions, probed in *Coriolanus*; that high ideals lead to success in this world, doubted in *Julius Caesar* and *An Enemy of the People*; that any marriage is worth preserving, examined in Ibsen's *Doll's House*; that a woman's virtue should be kept at any cost, tested and affirmed in *Measure for Measure*; that no good can ever come from a *liaison*, scrutinized in Henry James's *Ambassadors*; that the relationship between parent and child is always beautiful, subjected to biting acids in Butler's *Way of All Flesh*; that the enjoyment of wealth is essential to happiness, challenged in *War and Peace*; that innocent men are never convicted, queried in *The Brothers Karamazov*; that right and wrong are clearly distinguishable to us though not in older times, held up to the light in Shaw's *Saint Joan*; that God's in His heaven and all's right with the world, and the wicked do not flourish like a green bay tree, and wrong is always on the scaffold, right forever on the throne, proved untrue in the *Oedipus Rex*, *Othello*, *Candide*, *The Newcomes*, and *There Shall Be No More Night*, and of course in the Psalms. An even deeper assumption, that life is worth living, is brought into the laboratory in *Hamlet* and *The Three Sisters*, which make us ask "What's it all about, anyway?"

Oftentimes the examination accomplished by tragedy does not upset the old conception, but (as in *Measure for Measure*) it reëstablishes it on good reasons instead of outworn claptrap. The structure of society does not tumble down when we probe its framework, but it may collapse if we fail to do so. The probing may reveal an occasional timber that needs to be mended or replaced; but it also convinces us that the others are sound, only some of them rest on supports which are rotting away or riddled by termites. And so we can confidently rebuild the house or even expand it to meet our growing needs.

Now, every one of the complacent maxims mentioned above is commonly embodied in screenplays. In particular, the proposition that the wicked do not flourish like a green bay tree and virtue always gets tangible rewards recurs in the happy endings of most films, so often false both to life and the printed source of the scenario. And yet the motion picture has the same opportunity for conveying the lessons of tragedy as the novel and the theater, indeed a greater opportunity because of the superior vividness of the seen picture and the heard voice over cold type and because the film reaches a tremendously greater audience. It can enable a far larger number of men and women to reshape their chief ideas so as to be a better foundation for living. The consummate ability which has given us the marvelous pictures of recent years like *David Copperfield* and *Mutiny on the Bounty* and *Fantasia* can probe the framework of society if it chooses. Already the French film *Grande Illusion* tests as vigorously as the *Trojan Women* of Euripides the persistent belief that war and a decent civilization can coexist. And beside his *Bacchae* may be placed Charlie Chaplin's *Modern Times*. Both plays question the moral of the fable of the ant and the grasshopper — so popular in our age of machinery and efficiency — that a steady attention to productive output is all of life. Sooner or later the picturesque queens of England will be used up, and sea mutinies and storms will run dry. Then the public will demand from the screen more of what they get from the best novels and dramas.

At that point the censor, if he still exists, will become more active than ever. Plays of the *Gertie's Garter* type, full of bare legs and *doubles entendres*, do not bother him much. They are like firecrackers set off by mischievous boys outside the front-gate. But a play like *Grande Illusion* or *Strange Interlude*, which questions the complacent assumptions of our society, is to him like a dynamite cartridge placed under the foundations of the house. Such a photoplay may easily be banned though it contain not one word to raise a blush on the cheeks of the unmolested readers of the *New Yorker* and *Esquire*.

Therefore, if we are to have unhampered criticism of life

from motion pictures, the state censorship should be completely abolished, either by a decision of the United States Supreme Court or better yet by legislative repeal of the existing statutes.[45]

VI. DAMAGES FOR LIBEL AND SLANDER [46]

Defamation suits protect the reputation of the plaintiff rather than a social interest. Here we have a possible deterrent on speech by heavy damages which might be very serious if abused, but the issues are decided by a jury which represents community opinion on what is defamatory — juries are retained for this purpose in England though generally abandoned in civil cases — and there is a check by the appellate court. Expressions by a writer of his opinions' on public matters like the merits of a book or play are protected though erroneous if *bona fide*, and truth is a defense if proved — sometimes a difficult task even if it actually exists. In England, juries are more ready to give substantial damages than in this country, and this greater sensitiveness to the value of reputation may be the indication of a more civilized community.

VII. CONTEMPT PROCEEDINGS

A judge has power to fine or imprison men for violation of his injunction against supposedly intimidating or boycotting speech or for criticism of his judicial acts. Injunctions have been extensively used, not only against strikers but also to break up the I.W.W.[47] The effect of lack of speed of appeal, which makes a single equity judge virtually the final arbiter of the fate of the strike, has not been sufficiently appreciated.

[45] See *Progressive Democracy: Addresses and State Papers of Alfred E. Smith*, p. 282, for his message opposing the New York motion-picture censorship as "a step away from that liberty which the Constitution guaranteed." He said in part: "As all crimes are predicated upon sins, no persons should be held guilty of sin under the law until they can be convicted of a crime. The Bill of Rights throws every possible safeguard around the individual and the fullest possible presumption of innocence is constitutionally established until the contrary is proven beyond reasonable doubt. The danger to the future of our liberty lies in our apparent willingness at times to compromise with this principle. Once this avenue is opened nobody can, with any degree of certainty, predict where it may lead."

[46] Freedom of speech is frequently regarded as a bar to injunctions against libel and slander. See *supra*, Chapter VIII, note 10.

[47] See *supra* Chapter X, section 1; Chapter XI at note 105.

Provisions are much needed for a rapid review of his rulings on questions of law. Even the theoretical working of the machinery is not satisfactory, and Professor Eugene Wambaugh suggested three changes: (1) the judge who issues the injunction should not try the question of whether it is violated, since he may naturally be somewhat prejudiced, but should send this issue to another judge; (2) there should be an appeal on the facts and not merely on law as at present; (3) there should be some limit on the penalty which may be imposed. No matter how high it is, there ought to be some limit; but now the severity of the judge is absolutely uncontrolled except by his own discretion. There is also need for investigation of the power exercised by some judges to punish adverse criticisms of their rulings as contempt of court even after the case is closed and there is no longer the slightest danger of interference with the proper conduct of the litigation.[48]

VIII. FEDERAL ADMINISTRATIVE PROCEEDINGS

The post-office has great power to limit the liberty of the press, as we have seen.[49] It can exclude publications from the mail altogether, or it can deprive a newspaper or magazine of its second-class postal rates, thereby virtually driving it out of business. The courts refuse to review the departmental finding that a book is obscene, a business circular fraudulent, or the circulation of a newspaper falsely stated, so long as this finding is supported by some evidence, no matter how insufficient. Thus there is a very inadequate check on the legal machinery of the post-office. When we examine the nature of this machinery, we find that there is no satisfactory hearing. Moreover, the publisher receives no warning before his book or periodical is definitely excluded from the mails. Unlike the old-time censors, the Postmaster General will not give a ruling in advance of publication. Thus the publisher loses the advantages of a censorship, which at least gave warning before the imposition of penalties, and he gets all its disadvantages. It is difficult to tell who are the officials who make the actual deci-

---

[48] Two important decisions on contempt in the United States Supreme Court are Times-Mirror Co. v. Superior Court of California, and Bridges v. California, both printed in 62 Sup. Ct. Rep. 190 (Dec. 8, 1941). See 48 *Yale Law Journal* 54 (1938); Elisha Hanson, 37 *Cornell Law Quarterly* 165 (1942).

[49] Chapter II, section vi; Chapter VII, section ii.

sions, and there is no indication that the government requires
them to be educationally qualified for their delicate task. The
requisite of speed is conspicuously lacking, for even the limited
review in the courts comes much too late for the publisher to
mail out the forbidden issue of his periodical on time. It is
true that the post-office has performed a valuable service in
stamping out the commercialized exploitation of the young by
vicious advertisements, but beyond this its powers over speech
are very questionable. Certainly the fitness of its machinery
should be fully investigated by the President and Congress.

The control of the Bureau of Immigration over the admission
of aliens into the United States depends not only on the usual
social interests in public safety and order but also on the interest of the nation in the character of its population. A policy
of drastic restriction has resulted, under which neither Mazzini
nor Marx would probably be admitted to the United States
today. There is practically no judicial check. Even on the
issue of citizenship the departmental ruling is final, and a native
American can be forever barred without a day in court, so long
as there is some evidence against him.[50] The administrative
machinery is adapted to the numerous questions of racial origin,
health, sanity, and earning power, which have to be decided rapidly. The officials are chosen for determining such questions
rather than for their ability to discriminate between various
types of radical European thought. Even if the national interest
in the character of our population justifies the exclusion of heterodox aliens who would not dwell comfortably in our midst, it
does not apply to temporary visitors who propose to exchange
ideas with us for a few months and then depart. Yet the same
hostile policy is exercised toward these, and the nation which
welcomed Kossuth was afraid to admit Karolyi, his successor
in the leadership of Hungarian Liberals.

The deportation from the United States of aliens who have
already made a home here (discussed at length in the fifth chapter) is a much more serious restriction on liberty, but it is
subject to a similar administrative power with slightly more

[50] United States v. Ju Toy, 198 U. S. 253 (1905). But a person already in
the United States and threatened with deportation is entitled to have his claim
of citizenship decided by a United States court. — Ng Fung Ho v. United States,
259 U. S. 276 (1922).

restrictions. It is an interesting question whether the decrease of immigration under our recent quota laws will diminish the desire to deport radical aliens as they become a proportionately small element in the population; or whether the feeling against them will grow stronger as the rest of our inhabitants acquire approximate homogeneity in political, social, and economic outlooks.

Liberty of thought may also be restricted by the discretionary power of judges to refuse naturalization to radicals and pacifists, and by the denaturalization of such persons on the technical ground that they originally obtained their citizenship without loyalty to the United States.[51]

IX. GOVERNMENTAL CONTROL OF EDUCATION

In the public schools the social interest in the spread of truth may be restricted by the natural desire of the community to determine the purposes for which it will spend its own money. The legal machinery is ordinarily operated by school officials with very little check by the courts. Usually the only check is an appeal from the official immediately in charge to some higher educational board. The nature of the machinery for the selection and promotion of teachers raises difficult problems such as security of tenure, adequate hearings before dismissal, and the disqualification of teachers for heterodox views, either expressly through a licensing system such as formerly existed in New York under the influence of the Lusk Committee,[52] or indirectly through the necessarily wide powers of officials to find that a teacher is inefficient, when occasionally the real objection to him may be heresy. The personnel of the officials who control freedom of thought in the schools is fortunately better adapted for the investigation of such issues than in other departments of the government. Here the officials are or should be chosen for their fitness to understand intellectual questions. If they fail to deal wisely with liberty it is probably because they are not well qualified to have charge of education at all. On the contrary, a police superintendent or an immigration official may conduct his

[51] Naturalization and denaturalization are discussed in Chapter II, section vi; Chapter IV, section vi; Chapter V at note 38; Chapter XI, section ii.

[52] See Chapter VIII on the Rand School Case.

ordinary tasks admirably, and yet have no capacity to discriminate between thoroughly vicious ideas and those which should have a chance to be heard.

The arrangement of the curriculum and the selection of textbooks could best be performed by the teachers themselves, but financial reasons often bring these questions under official control. It seems doubtful whether men who are selected for their ability to regulate expenditures are also qualified to determine the probable validity of the evolutionary hypothesis or the accuracy of historical discussions of the American Revolution.

In private schools the liberty of teaching is greater, for the state cannot base its interference on its control of its own funds, but only upon the general interest of the community in the training of the young. This reason has been held by the Supreme Court not to justify the total abolition of private schools by legislation.[53] Some governmental regulation of their curriculum will be permitted for the sake of public safety, but teaching a foreign language is not dangerous enough to be constitutionally prohibited.[54] The Lusk Committee sought to bring private schools under strict state control through a system of licenses, but the statute was repealed before its validity was finally adjudicated in the litigation brought by the Rand School.[55] If public school teaching is to be rigorously restricted by officials, the need for free private schools is all the greater. Somebody should be able to experiment. In so far as such schools are regulated, the powers and training of the public officials who supervise them become a matter of great importance.

X. CONTROL BY THE GOVERNMENT OF ITS OWN OFFICERS

The earliest form of freedom of speech secured by the English Parliament was the immunity of its members from responsibility to the King or in the courts for what they said in debates. Our constitutions give a similar protection to American legislators. They are accountable only to the body to which

[53] Pierce v. Society of Sisters, 268 U. S. 510 (1925).

[54] Meyer v. Nebraska, 262 U. S. 390 (1923), Holmes and Sutherland, JJ., dissenting.

[55] See note 52.

they belong.[56] This notable right does not, however, insure complete liberty of thought in legislatures. Whether properly or not, the legislative powers of exclusion and expulsion are sometimes exercised against a member because of his heterodox views. The exclusion of Victor Berger from Congress and of the five Socialists from the New York Assembly showed that legislatures are no more likely than courts to investigate men's opinions in an enlightened and impartial spirit.[57] Little as I like the election methods of Vare and others, who were excluded from the Senate in the nineteen-twenties for large campaign expenses, still if either house of Congress can create an extra-constitutional requirement of fitness in such cases, there is some danger that it may also feel entitled to impose its own standards of loyalty and orthodoxy in the future upon men whose views, however unacceptable, have been approved by the majority of the voters in the state which elected them.

The responsibility of government employees for adverse criticism of their superiors is a difficult question, which deserves more discussion than it has received. The advantages of thoroughgoing loyalty in a military or a civilian subordinate officer are obvious, and most people feel that if such a person is dissatisfied with the conduct of affairs he should resign before having his say. Still, not every officer can afford to throw up his job; and the result of an enforced silence within the service may be, that inefficiency or corruption on the part of men higher up will continue unchecked because honest persons who know the facts do not dare tell them to the public. And proposals by brilliant younger men for needed reforms may be unduly delayed if they can be considered only by conservative insiders; the fate of General De Gaulle's plan for mechanizing the French army illustrates the dangers. Certainly, if subordinate officials must address all their adverse criticisms to their superiors, great care should be taken to provide adequate machinery by which such a criticism shall receive thoughtful attention, shall not be suppressed by the

[56] For instance, U. S. Constitution, Article I, section 6. See 1 Willoughby, *Constitutional Law* (2d ed.) § 342 (1929). Although an outsider cannot recover damages from a legislator who has defamed him on the floor of the House, he can talk back without liability himself. Turn about is fair play. — Duncan *v.* Record Pub. Co., 131 S. C. 485 (1925).

[57] See Chapter VI for these cases.

554 WAYS OF CONTROLLING DISCUSSION

very superior against whom it is directed, and shall not be a cause for dismissal of the critic or his loss of promotion.

Space does not permit comment on other topics affecting liberty of discussion, such as the law of copyrights; [58] deprivations of the constitutional right to petition Congress or the state legislature; [59] unreasonable searches and seizures; [60] the liability of lawyers to be disbarred for radicalism after they have defended radicals, which makes it hard for the accused to get any counsel, as conservative lawyers may refuse their cases; [61] the relation of liberty of the press to the legal position of large news agencies like the Associated Press; [62] and the governmental regulation of radio broadcasting stations so as to promote or discourage the opportunity for all kinds of political parties and social groups to present their respective views to the public.[63] The foregoing survey of the various types of legal machinery affecting the scope of liberty is far from complete, but it may at least have suggested some of the problems and difficulties involved.

The actual conflicts are not so acute now as they were twenty years ago. Yet I do not think we have become more tolerant. We are simply more indifferent and less frightened. Yet excitement is bound to come again and the time of tranquility

[58] See Rogers, "Copyright and Morals," 18 *Michigan Law Review* 390 (1920).

[59] See Spayd v. Ringing Rock Lodge, 270 Pa. 67 (1921), discussed in 35 *Harvard Law Review* 332, in 43 *id.* at 1016 ff., in 6 *Minnesota Law Review* 241, and in 14 A. L. R. 1446; *supra*, pp. 58–59.

[60] See Chapter XIV, note 5.

[61] See "Disbarment for Disloyalty or Sedition," 24 *Law Notes* (N. Y.) 145 (1920); 8 A. L. R. 1262; 9 *id.* at 201; 12 *id.* 1189; 19 *id.* 936; 43 *id.* at 110.

[62] See International News Service v. Associated Press, 248 U. S. 215 (1918), discussed by Kocourek in 13 *Illinois Law Review* 708; Sinclair, *The Brass Check: A Study of American Journalism* (1920), which a successful radical journalist explained to me by saying: "Sinclair didn't know how to get on with the boys."

[63] See Caldwell, "Censorship of Radio Programs," 1 *Journal of Radio Law* 441 (1931); "Indirect Censorship of Radio Programs," 40 *Yale Law Journal* 967 (1931); F. R. C. v. Nelson Bros. Bond & Mtge. Co., 289 U. S. 266 (1933); KFKB Bdctg. Assn. v. F. R. C., 47 F. (2d) 670 (D. C. App. 1931) (medical question box); Duncan v. United States, 48 F. (2d) 128 (C. C. A. 9th, 1931) (profanity); Trinity Methodist Church v. F. R. C., 62 F. (2d) 850 (D. C. App. 1932) (vituperative vice-hunting).

should be used to overhaul and improve the numerous kinds of legal machinery. Nor should we be content with adjusting the negative forces which restrain liberty. We should also consider the development of positive forces which will encourage it and remove the sluggishness of thought into which we all easily lapse even without any prohibitions upon opinion. We cannot afford to neglect methods for obtaining livelier oral discussion and places available for it, and for encouraging fuller presentation of all sides of international and industrial controversies in the press, on the screen, and over the radio.

The experiences of suppression since 1917 have been destructive of any passive confidence that liberty will go on of its own accord. Its price still remains eternal vigilance. Freedom requires much tiresome labor over the technicalities with which I have dealt, for it cannot be maintained by eloquent expositions alone. Yet in the end such expositions furnish the main strength of liberty. A people gets sooner or later as much freedom as it wants. This want is not created by us lawyers but by the prophets who influence the minds of legislators and administrators, and the minds of the public to whom members of the government react with extreme sensitiveness. The best safeguard against repetition of the errors of 1917 lies in the ferment in the thoughts of the young and of those who do not let themselves grow old. The persecutions have not been wholly without gain. They have made us look to the neglected defenses of liberty.

PART V

1941

> *Society is dissolving every moment, and the question is, How shall the reconstruction of authority in the minds and lives of men be made? In the past largely by the authoritarian process, by taboo, superstition, ignorance, and force. In our day this is still largely true, perhaps, but there is also an increasing process in which authority is maintained by recreating appreciation of and agreement with the values that are transmitted, with allowance for shifting values and attitudes and interests. That order of things whether social, economic, or political, is now most secure which constantly recreates the loyalty and obedience of its members, which constantly redevelops the sources of its interest and power from interest and reflection. That order is weakest which must largely depend upon authority and force with suppression of discussion and reason and criticism.* CHARLES E. MERRIAM.

CHAPTER 15

FREE SPEECH TODAY

> *My God there is need today of people who can say straight things in a straight way, and not all coated over with sugar.* An Englishwoman's letter, written between air raids, in January, 1941.

SPEECH should be fruitful as well as free. Our experience introduces this qualification into the classical argument of Milton and John Stuart Mill, that only through open discussion is truth discovered and spread. In their simpler times, they thought it enough to remove legal obstacles like the censorship and sedition prosecutions. Mill assumed that if men were only left alone, their reasoning powers would eventually impel them to choose the best ideas and the wisest course of action. To us this policy is too exclusively negative. For example, what is the use of telling an unpopular speaker that he will incur no criminal penalties by his proposed address, so long as every hall owner in the city declines to rent him space for his meeting and there are no vacant lots available? There should be municipal auditoriums, schoolhouses out of school hours, church forums, parks in summer, all open to thresh out every question of public importance, with just as few restrictions as possible; for otherwise the subjects that most need to be discussed will be the very subjects that will be ruled out as unsuitable for discussion.

We must do more than remove the discouragements to open discussion. We must exert ourselves to supply active encouragements.

Physical space and lack of interference alone will not make discussion fruitful. We must take affirmative steps to improve the methods by which discussion is carried on. Of late years the argument of Milton and Mill has been questioned, because truth does not seem to emerge from a controversy in the automatic way their logic would lead us to expect. For one thing, reason is less praised nowadays than a century ago; instead, emotions conscious and unconscious are commonly said to dominate the conduct of men. Is it any longer possible to discover truth amid the clashing blares of advertisements, loud speakers, gigantic billboards, party programs, propaganda of a hundred kinds? To sift the truth from all these half-truths seems to demand a statistical investigation beyond the limits of anybody's time and money. So some modern thinkers despairingly conclude that the great mass of voters cannot be trusted to detect the fallacies in emotional arguments by Communists and so on, and hence must be prevented from hearing them. Even the intellectuals do not seem to do much better in reaching Truth by conflicting arguments. For example, take controversies between professors. They talk and talk, and at the end each sticks to his initial position. On which side does Truth stand? We still do not know. Then, too, the emergencies seem greater and more pressing than of yore. We are less willing to await the outcome of prolonged verbal contests. Perhaps Truth will win in the long run; but in the long run, as Walter Lippmann says, we shall all be dead — and perhaps not peacefully in our beds either. Debating is only fiddling while Rome burns. Away with all this talk; let's have action — now.

Nevertheless, the main argument of Milton and Mill still holds good. All that this disappointment means is that friction is a much bigger drag on the progress of Truth than they supposed. Efforts to lessen that friction are essential to the success of freedom of speech. It is a problem, not for law, but for education in the wide sense that includes more than schools and youngsters. The conflict of oral evidence and arguments can be made increasingly profitable by wise improvements in technique. Anybody who has attended a forum knows how much depends on an able chairman and on sensible rules enforced by him. Journalists and other writers value accuracy of facts far more than formerly — we can expect even more from them in future. None of us can get rid of our emotions, but we can learn to drive them in harness. As for blazing propaganda on both sides, young Americans can be trained to keep alive the gumption which comes down to us from Colonial farmers; this will make them distrust all men who conceal greed or a lust for power behind any flag, whether red or red-white-and-blue.

Reason is more imperfect than we used to believe. Yet it still remains the best guide we have, better than our emotions, better even than patriotism, better than any single human guide, however exalted his position.

A second point deserves renewed emphasis. The effect of suppression extends far beyond the agitators actually put in jail, far beyond the pamphlets physically destroyed. A favorite argument against free speech is that the men who are thus conspicuously silenced had little to say that was worth hearing. Concede for the moment that the public would suffer no serious loss if every communist leaflet were burned or if some prominent pacifist were imprisoned, as perhaps he might be under the loose language of the unprecedented federal sedition law passed last year, for discouraging drafted men by talk about plowing every fourth boy under. Even so, my contention is that the pertinacious orators and writers who get hauled up are merely extremist spokesmen for a mass of more thoughtful and more retiring men and women, who share in varying degrees the same critical attitude toward prevailing policies and institutions. When you put the hotheads in jail, these cooler people do not get arrested — they just keep quiet. And so we lose things they could tell us, which would be very advantageous for the future course of the nation. Once the prosecutions begin, then the hush-hush begins too. Discussion becomes one-sided and artificial. Questions that need to be threshed out do not get threshed out.

The evils of such a policy of suppression are especially acute during a national emergency like the World War or the present rapid development of national defense. Because of the 1956 prosecutions brought under the Espionage Act, tens of thousands among those "forward-looking men and women" to whom President Wilson had appealed in earlier years were bewildered and depressed and silenced by the negation of freedom in the twenty-year sentences requested by his legal subordinates from complacent judges. So we had plenty of patriotism and very little criticism, except of the slowness of munition production. Wrong courses were followed like the despatch of troops to Archangel in 1918, which fatally alienated

Russia from Wilson's aims for a peaceful Europe. Harmful facts like the secret treaties were concealed while they could have been cured, only to bob up later and wreck everything. What was equally disastrous, right positions, like our support of the League of Nations before the armistice, were taken unthinkingly merely because the President favored them; then they collapsed as soon as the excitement was over, because they had no depth and had never been hardened by the hammer-blows of open discussion. And so when we attained military victory, we did not know what to do with it. No well-informed public opinion existed to carry through Wilson's war aims for a new world order to render impossible the recurrence of disaster.

In 1941 the same problem confronts us, only it is infinitely more difficult. The task of today is to produce airplanes, guns, and battleships. The task of tomorrow is to throw out the half-crazed ruler who threatens to destroy the civilization pain-fully built up since Marathon. The task of the day after to-morrow is to rebuild that civilization far more solidly than in 1919.

It is this task of the day after tomorrow which most re-quires free flow of discussion. Suppose Hitler is gone, what then? What is to be done with the Germans? Are they to be exterminated, or split into little duchies like Weimar and Saxe-Coburg-Gotha, or made equal partners in an association of free peoples? Who is to rule Italy in place of Mussolini? How about totalitarian Russia? Are Czechoslovakia and Poland to be set up again? It is going to be ever so much harder to answer these questions than to write the Treaty of Versailles. In 1919, there was some chance of sorting out the old pieces and making a go of it. After all, the League came very near success. If Stresemann had lived a few years longer, if Hin-denburg had died a few years sooner, if there had been no Ruhr invasion and resultant inflation to ruin the German middle class, it might have worked. But in 1942 there will be no old pieces. New materials will have to be laboriously fashioned.

In this tremendous task of the day after tomorrow, the United States will be forced to take a major share. We can-not afford to turn away from it in disgust as in 1920, and let

Europe plunge eventually into a third and still more frightful disaster in 1960. The Atlantic will then be more easily crossed by bombers than the English Channel is now. The American arsenal of munitions will be the first enemy objective. In short, so long as we permit Europe to be divided into competing armed groups, we shall be inevitably obliged to save the British Empire every other decade at increasing cost to ourselves in money and blood. Adequate national defense under such conditions will absorb most of the national life.

If we are to use the opportunity of Hitler's collapse so as to prevent such recurring calamities, a great many people must be constantly thinking and talking and writing about this day after tomorrow. Nobody in America or in Europe has yet given it anywhere near the thought which Wilson gave it before we entered the World War. These gigantic problems will remain unsolved unless we insist on surrounding our busy factories and navy yards and camps with a steady atmosphere of free, temperate, and enlightened discussion which shall gradually shape the terms of a lasting peace, without which victory will be only a little better than defeat.

The Supreme Court, though much more anxious to support liberty of speech than it was twenty years ago, can do nothing to keep discussion open during an emergency. Cases of suppression will get to Washington long after the emergency is over. What counts is what the local United States judges do. Still more important is the attitude of the prosecutors and police, because they can stifle free speech by breaking up meetings by arrests and confiscating pamphlets, and then not bothering to bring many persons to trial. Above all, the maintenance of open discussion depends on all the great body of unofficial citizens. If a community does not respect liberty for unpopular ideas, it can easily drive such ideas underground by persistent discouragement and sneers, by social ostracism, by boycotts of newspapers and magazines, by refusal to rent halls, by objections to the use of municipal auditoriums and schoolhouses, by discharging teachers and professors and journalists, by mobs and threats of lynching. On the other hand, an atmosphere of open and unimpeded controversy may be made as fully a part of the life of a community as any other American tradition. The law plays only a small part in either suppression or freedom. In the long run the public gets just as much freedom of speech as it really wants.

This brings me to my final argument for freedom of speech. It creates the happiest kind of country. It is the best way to make men and women love their country. Mill says:

A State which dwarfs its men, in order that they may be more docile instruments in its hands even for beneficial purposes, will find that with small men no great thing can really be accomplished.

And Arthur Garfield Hays tells the story of a liberated slave who met his former master on the street. The master asked, "Are you as well off as before you were free?" The Negro admitted that his clothes were frayed, his house leaked, and his meals were nothing like the food on the old plantation. "Well, wouldn't you rather be a slave again?" "No, massa. There's a sort of a looseness about this here freedom that I likes."

Doubtless it was an inspiring sight to see the Piazza Venezia in Rome full of well-drilled blackshirts in serried ranks cheering Mussolini, or to watch Nuremberg thronged with hundreds of thousands of Nazis raising their arms in perfect unison at the first glimpse of Hitler. In contrast our easy-going crowds seem sloppy and purposeless, going hither and thither about their own tasks and amusements. But we do not have the other side of the picture — when every knock on the door may mean that the father of the family is to be dragged off to a concentration camp from which no word returns; great newspapers reduced to mere echoes of the master's voice; the professorships of universities that once led the world filled as we fill third-class postmasterships; the devoted love of young men and women broken up by racial hatreds; the exiles; the boycotts; and what is perhaps worst of all, those who conform to the will of the men in power in order to avoid financial ruin or worse, and yet, even while holding their jobs, live days and nights in the uneasy fear of calamity and the shamefaced consciousness that they have had to sell out their minds and souls. Once commit ourselves to the ideal of enforced national unanimity, and all this logically and easily follows.

Behind the dozens of sedition bills in Congress last session, behind teachers' oaths and compulsory flag salutes, is a desire to make our citizens loyal to their government. Loyalty is a beautiful idea, but you cannot create it by compulsion and force. A government is at bottom the officials who carry it on: legislators and prosecutors, school superintendents and police. If it is composed of legislators who pass shortsighted sedition laws by overwhelming majorities, of narrow-minded school superintendents who oust thoughtful teachers of American history and eight-year-old children whose rooted religious convictions prevent them from sharing in a brief ceremony — a government of snoopers and spies and secret police — how can you expect love and loyalty? You make men love their government and their country by giving them the kind of government and the kind of country that inspire respect and love: a country that is free and unafraid, that lets the discontented talk in order to learn the causes for their discontent and end those causes, that refuses to impel men to spy on their neighbors, that protects its citizens vigorously from harmful acts while it leaves the remedies for objectionable ideas to counter-argument and time.

Plutarch's Lives were the favorite reading of the men who framed and ratified our Constitution. There they found the story of Timoleon who saved his native city of Syracuse from the Carthaginian tyrants. In later years young hotheads used to get up in the public assembly and abuse Timoleon as an old fossil. His friends urged him just to say the word, and they would soon silence his detractors. But Timoleon insisted on letting the vituperative youngsters have their say. "He had taken all the extreme pains and labor he had done, and had passed so many dangers, in order that every citizen and inhabitant of Syracuse might frankly use the liberty of their laws. He thanked the gods that they had granted him the thing he had so oft requested of them in his prayers, which was, that he might some day see the Syracusans have full power and liberty to say what they pleased."

It is such a spirit that makes us love the United States of America. With all the shortcomings of economic organization, with all the narrowness and ignorance of politicians, we know that we are still immeasurably freer than we should be in Italy, Germany, or Russia to say what we think and write what we believe and do what we want. "There's a looseness about this here freedom that I likes."

Let us not in our anxiety to protect ourselves from foreign tyrants imitate some of their worst acts, and sacrifice in the process of national defense the very liberties which we are defending.

APPENDICES

APPENDIX I

BIBLIOGRAPHICAL NOTE

THE SOURCES for each chapter are indicated in the footnotes thereto; and a fuller account of the sources for Part I is contained in Appendix I of my *Freedom of Speech* (1920). Particular attention is called to the article by J. P. Hall cited *supra*, p. 108, note 3, as it seems to me the best criticism of my position on the war-time prosecutions.

This Appendix is designed to suggest some material on the general subject of free speech for those who wish to read more. It is by no means exhaustive.

The legal meaning of freedom of speech cannot properly be determined without a knowledge of the political and philosophical basis of such freedom. Four writings on this problem may be mentioned as invaluable: Plato's *Apology of Socrates*; Milton's *Areopagitica*; the second chapter of Mill, *On Liberty*; and Walter Bagehot's essay, "The Metaphysical Basis of Toleration." [1] The second chapter of J. F. Stephen, *Liberty, Equality, Fraternity*, has an important critique on Mill. Two stimulating books by Walter Lippmann are his *Liberty and the News* (New York, 1920) and *Public Opinion* (New York, 1922).

English events are narrated in T. Erskine May, *Constitutional History of England* (2d ed. 1912), especially chapters ix and x. English law is well analyzed by James Paterson, *The Liberty of the Press, Speech and Public Worship* (London, 1880).

For events in the United States, with more attention to suppressions before 1900 than I have given, see Leon Whipple, *The Story of Civil Liberty in the United States* (New York, 1927). A good recent book is G. J. Patterson, *Free Speech and a Free Press* (Boston, 1939).

This subject lends itself very well to the exchange of divergent views in symposia. Three of these are excellent: (1) "Freedom of Communication," 9 *Publications of the American Sociological Society* 1 (1914); the important contribution by Henry Schofield is reprinted in his *Essays on Equity and Constitutional Law* (1922) II, 510. (2) "Freedom of Inquiry and Expression," edited by E. P. Cheyney, 200 *Annals of American Academy of Political and Social*

[1] *The Works and Life of Walter Bagehot*, edited by Mrs. Russell Barrington, VI, 219.

Science (November, 1938). (3) "Symposium on Civil Liberties," by H. Wechsler, Solicitor General Biddle, etc., *Handbook of Association of American Law Schools and Proceedings of 38th Annual Meeting* (December, 1940), pp. 52–86; reprinted in part in 9 *American Law School Review* 881–901 (1941).

Three useful continuing sources for current decisions and events are: (1) The frequent pamphlets issued by the American Civil Liberties Union, which can be obtained from its New York office or local committees. (2) *American Law Reports, Annotated* (A.L.R.); this series reprints judicial decisions with extensive notes, which are brought down to date by a supplementary volume, and it will be found in most county bar libraries. (3) *Index to Legal Periodicals*, where valuable articles and comments on decisions and legislation can be run down under such headings as "Constitutional Law" and "Freedom of Speech"; this comes out several times a year and can be consulted in the same libraries.

Possibly some readers will be interested in a list of my own published writings on civil liberties which it seemed best to omit from the present book:

(1) The discussion of searches and seizures and the account of the Lusk Committee's raids on the Rand School and the office of the unrecognized Soviet government (*Freedom of Speech*, pp. 296–311) have been omitted because the subject is greatly affected by numerous subsequent decisions, especially under National Prohibition. I have given some attention to searches and seizures in an article, "Progress of the Law — Evidence," in 35 *Harvard Law Review* at 694–704 (1922).

(2) The chapter on "Freedom and Initiative in the Schools" (*Freedom of Speech*, chapter 7) and two essays on schools and colleges in *The Inquiring Mind* had to be sacrificed for the sake of space. Eventually I hope to reprint these with added material in another book on Liberty and Learning.

(3) Two essays on events in Boston in *The Inquiring Mind* seemed too local to include: "The Bimba Case," a blasphemy trial; and "The Freedom of the City." However, much of the latter essay has been used in Chapter XIV.

(4) The labor essays in *The Inquiring Mind* are: "The Interchurch Steel Report"; "Company Towns in the Soft-coal Fields"; "The Labor Injunction"; "Strike Injunctions Obtained by Coal Operators"; and "Strike Injunctions Obtained by the United States." Some of these present interesting facts, but they are isolated phases of the broad subject of labor law, which I am not competent to treat

in the large. For the same reason, I have refrained from extended discussion of the recent Supreme Court decisions on the effect of freedom of speech upon statutes and injunctions against picketing.

(5) Three book reviews in *The Inquiring Mind* affect free speech, but are too slight to reprint: "The State and its Rivals"; "Liberty under Socialism"; and "Mill Today."

(6) "Propaganda and Conscription of Opinion," *Harvard Public Alumni Bulletin*, XXVII, 339–344 (1924), reprinted in *The Next War* (Cambridge, 1925). Since much of this is still applicable, I regret that it could not be reprinted, but parts were too obsolete to make this desirable. However, I have used a few passages.

(7) "Arms, Right to Bear," 2 *Encyclopaedia of Social Sciences* 209 (1930); and "Assembly, Right of," *id.* 275.

(8) *The Report on Lawlessness in Law Enforcement*, which was prepared by Walter H. Pollak, Carl S. Stern, and myself for the Wickersham Commission, comprises the third degree and unfairness in prosecutions (June 25, 1931). This appears in Volume IV of the bound *Reports of the National Commission on Law Observance and Enforcement*, and is also published separately as Report Number 11. My unofficial comments on "Remedies for the Third Degree" are printed in the *Atlantic Monthly*, CXLVIII, 621–630 (1931). See also my Preface to E. J. Hopkins, *Our Lawless Police* (1931). By Judge Kenyon's directions, Pollak, Stern, and I also submitted a report on the prosecutions of Mooney and Billings in California. This was ready just before the life of the Wickersham Commission came to an end, and the Commission very reasonably concluded that a review of such highly controversial cases ought not to be officially published unless the Commission had plenty of time to read over and weigh our conclusions. Hence, I do not think it right to describe this report as "suppressed." However, I have every confidence in the accuracy and soundness of this report, which was mainly prepared by Pollak with the assistance of Thomas A. Halleran. It has since been published as *The Mooney-Billings Report* (Gotham House, New York, 1932).

(9) Introduction to *Civil Liberty* edited by Edith M. Phelps (H. W. Wilson Co., New York, 1927), pp. 45–49.

(10) *State House versus Pent House: Legal Problems of the Rhode Island Racetrack Row* (The Booke Shop, Providence, R. I., 1937).

(11) Some collaboration on Brief of Bill of Rights Committee of American Bar Association in Gobitis *v.* Minersville School Dist. (Flag Salute Case), reprinted as supplement to 1 *Bill of Rights Review*, No. 1 (1940).

APPENDIX II

PRESENT FEDERAL STATUTES AFFECTING
FREEDOM OF SPEECH

NOTE: The federal statutes were collected in 1926 into the United States Code, where they are arranged alphabetically under fifty numbered titles, *e.g.*, Aliens, War. This large volume is in most large public libraries, lawyers' offices, etc. Supplements contain legislation since 1926. The Code is also published in many volumes called United States Code Annotated (frequently cited in my footnotes as U.S.C.A.), which contains exhaustive notes on the history of each statute and the judicial decisions interpreting it. At the back of each volume is inserted a pocket supplement bringing statutes and cases down to date. This publication can be consulted in many county law libraries.

Each item in the following list begins with a brief indication of the nature of the particular statute. Next the original date of enactment is given in parentheses with occasional information about amendments. (Little attempt has been made to run dates back of the Revised Statutes of 1874.) Then follows the reference to the United States Code; the title-number comes before the colon and the section-number after it. (For example, the Espionage Act of 1917 is 50:33, 34, which means Title 50, sections 33 and 34.) Finally, reference is made to the places in this book where the statute is discussed with some fullness.

The list does not include expired or repealed statutes such as the Alien and Sedition Laws of 1798 or the Espionage Act amendment of 1918. For these see the Index. Furthermore, many statutes are here omitted which punish unlawful acts such as spying, photographing fortifications, etc.

A. Interference with the United States government.
    Treason (before 1874). 18:1, 2. (Chapter II, note 4; Chapter IV, at note 5 and section VII; Chapter VI, section II.)
    Inciting insurrection that takes place (before 1874). 18:4. (Chapter IV, at note 5.)
    Espionage Act, in effect in war only (1917). 50:33, 34. (Chapter II.)
    Interference with the draft. Selective Service Act, § 11 (1940). 50:311. (Chapter XII, note 47.)

Punishment of soldiers and sailors for spreading disaffection in armed forces, inciting to mutiny,, etc. (various dates). 10:1538–1539; 18:483–484; 34:1200, Articles of War, No. 4. (Chapter XII, at note 37.)

Enticing desertion (before 1874). 18:94, 95. (Chapter XII, at note 38.)

Power to make regulations governing civilians in military and naval areas (1909). 18:96, 97. (Chapter XII, at note 39.)

Accessories to crime actually committed. Criminal Code, § 332 (1874). 18:550. (Chapter II, at note 18.)

Seditious conspiracy to use force against government. Criminal Code, § 6 (1861). 18:6. (Chapter II, at note 3; Chapter IV, section 1; Chapter XII, section 1.)

Conspiracy to commit offense against government with overt act, no force required. Criminal Code, § 37 (1867). 18:88. (Chapter II, at note 3; Chapter IV, section 1; Chapter XII, at note 31.)

Alien Registration Act (1940). 18:9–13. Chapter IV, sections VII, VIII; Chapter XI, note 14; Chapter XII, section 1.)

Threats to kill the President (1917). 18:89. (Chapter IV, at notes 50 and 64.)

Sabotage in war and peace (1918, am. 1940). 50:101–103. (Chapter III, note 33; Chapter IV, note 1.)

Explosives manufactured, possessed, etc., in war (1917). 50:121–143. (Chapter IV, note 12.)

Explosives manufactured, possessed, etc., in peace (1939). 22:245j—11. (Chapter IV, note 12.)

B. Objectionable Foreign Influences.

Correspondence to influence conduct of foreign government. (1799, am. 1932). 18:5. (Chapter IV, note 5.)

Registration of agents of foreign government or foreign principal (1938). 22:233–233g. (Chapter XI, at note 99.)

Registration of organization subject to foreign control (1940). 18:14–17. (Chapter XI, at note 100.)

C. Aliens.

Deportation of radicals (1903, am. 1918, 1920, 1940). 8:137, 155, 157. (Chapter V; Chapter XII, section 1.)

Naturalization requirements (1906, am. 1938 and 1939). 8:381, 382. (Chapter XI, section II.)

No naturalization for certain radicals (Oct. 11, 1940). 8:705. (Chapter XII, at note 10.)

D. Mails.

Matter non-mailable which violates Espionage Act, or advocates treason, insurrection, or forcible resistance to law of U. S. (1917). 18:343, 344. (Chapter II, at note 8 and sections III, VI; Chapter VII, section II.)

Matter non-mailable if obscene, or tending to incite arson, murder or assassination (1874). 18:334. (Chapter IV, note 64; Chapter VII, notes 25, 31.)

Rates for second-class mail matter (1879). 39:226. (Chapter VII, at note 26.)

E. Importation and Interstate Transportation.

Imported books, films, etc., seizable for obscenity, advocacy of treason, etc. (1930). 19:1305. (Chapter IV, note 72; Chapter XIV, at note 34.)

No interstate transportation of obscene matter, films, etc. (1897, am. 1920). 18:396. (Chapter VII, note 25; Chapter XIV, at note 34.)

F. Search Warrants.

Form and requirements for search warrants (1917). 18:611–633. (Chapter II, at note 8; Chapter V, notes 11, 18; Chapter XII, at note 93.)

Search warrants in aid of judicial proceedings (1789). 28:377. (Chapter V, note 11.)

Search warrants for matter violating Alien Registration Act (1940). 18:12. (Chapter IV at note 71; Chapter XII, section 1.)

APPENDIX III

STATE WAR AND PEACE STATUTES AFFECTING FREEDOM OF SPEECH

NOTE: The information here given ends in 1940. Statutes on attempts, breach of the peace. picketing, permits for meetings, etc., may affect free speech, but are not here listed.

SUMMARY OF STATUTES BY SUBJECTS

I. Statutes against Opposition to War. (See Chapter II, section VII; Chapter VII, section II.)

> Alaska, Fla., Hawaii, Iowa, La., Minn., Mo., Mont., Neb., N.H., N.J., Pa., Tex., W. Va., Wis.

II. Statutes not Limited to War.

   A. Against Red Flags and other Insignia. (See Chapter IV, section IV; Chapter XI, section I.)

   > Ala., Ariz., Ark., Cal., Colo., Conn., Del., Ida., Ill., Ind., Iowa, Kans., Ky., Mass., Mich., Minn., Mont., Neb., N.J., N.M., N.Y., N.D., Ohio, Okla., Ore., Pa., R.I., S.D., Utah, Vt., Wash., W. Va., Wis.

   B. Against Conspiracy. (Mostly before 1917. Common law crime in some states. See Chapter IV, sections I–III.)

   > Statutes in all states and territories except Alaska, Conn., Del., D C., Ga., Ill., Kans., Ky., N.H., Ohio, Pa., Tex., Vt.

   C. Against Incitement to Crime Generally. (See Chapter IV, sections I–III. Besides the few states listed, some punish incitement under their attempt statutes, not here listed. and in some it is a common law crime.)

   > Alaska, Ariz., Cal., Ida., Mont., Nev., N.H., Okla., S.D.. Wash., Wyo.

   D. Against Incitement to Specific Acts of Violence. (See Chapter IV, section V; Chapter XI, section VI. In this group, the statutes are narrower in scope than sedition, anarchy, and syndicalism acts, though somewhat overlapping them.

Most of these statutes were enacted before 1917, some of them during the Civil War period or earlier.)

Conn., Fla., Ga., Ill., Md., N.J., N.C., Tenn.

E. Against Sedition. (See Chapter IV, section v. In this group I have placed all broad statutes against radical uttterances, except those which are entitled anarchy acts or syndicalism acts. The subject-matter also overlaps group D, and perhaps the old Florida, Illinois, and Maryland statutes belong in this group. See also Wyoming statute on incitement to crime generally.)

Ark., Colo., Conn., Del., Hawaii, Ill., Ind., Iowa, Ky., La., Mich., Mont., N.H., N.J., N.M., Pa., Tenn., W. Va.

F. Against Criminal Anarchy. (See Chapter IV, section v; Chapter IX. This group derives from the New York act of 1902, and is pre-war except for the Massachusetts and Vermont acts, which are narrower and might be classed under D, above. See also Colorado sedition statute.)

Mass., N.J., N.Y., Vt., Wash., Wis.

G. Against Criminal Syndicalism. (See Chapter IV, section v; Chapter X; Chapter XI, section v. These conform to the usual type described on p. 165 *supra*, unless otherwise indicated in the List of States below.)

Alaska, Ariz., Cal., Hawaii, Ida., Iowa, Kans., Ky., Mich., Minn., Mont., Neb., Nev., Ohio, Okla., Ore., R.I., S.D., Utah, Wash.

H. Against Unlawful Assembly. (See Chapter IV, section IV; Chapter XI, section VIII. The language varies in different states, sometimes overlapping or equaling riot. In some states it is a common law crime. The statutes are older than 1917.)

Statutes in all states and territories except Ark., Ind., Md., Miss., Okla., Tenn.

Special statute directed against Ku Klux Klan and similar groups: N.Y., N.C., Ohio, Tex., Wash. See also conspiracy statutes in Tenn., Va., W. Va.

Special statute for meetings in English: Neb.

Special statute for licensing parades: N.H. and perhaps elsewhere.

I. Exclusion of certain Radicals from the Ballot. (See Chapter XII, section II. These statutes are very recent. Bills are pending in other states in 1941.)

Ark., Cal., Del., Ind., Tenn.

J. Motion Pictures. (See Chapter XIV, section v.)

Censorship in Conn., Fla., Kans., La., Md., N.Y., Ohio, Pa., Va.; defeated in Mass.

Special statute in W. Va.

K. Regulation of Schools, Teachers, Public Officers, etc. (See Chapter VIII.)

New York (probably some other states overlooked).

L. Teaching of Evolution Forbidden.

Miss., Tenn.

M. Scandalous Newspapers to be Enjoined. (See Chapter XI, section III.)

Minn.

ALPHABETICAL LIST OF STATES AND TERRITORIES WITH THE STATUTES OF EACH

NOTE: An asterisk shows that the particular statute has been discussed in this book (see name of state in Index).

The date of enactment of each statute is given in parentheses, followed by the reference to the latest book of revised (collected) statutes in the state. These books usually list the court decisions on the constitutionality or interpretation of each statute. Remember that the cases so listed are only appellate court decisions; many prosecutions and convictions never reach such a court.

As some of the statutes have varying penalties, only the punishment for the most serious offense is mentioned; this will indicate the relative severity of these laws. Fines may operate as a term of imprisonment if the defendant is obliged to work them out when too poor to pay. Sentences for more than a year are usually served in the state penitentiary, and those under a year in the county jail.

A statute placed between brackets is believed to be no longer in force, because it has expired or been repealed or been held invalid in the decision here cited.

Alabama

Red flags, etc. (1919). Code, 1928, §§ 4104–7. $500–$5,000.

Conspiracy (before 1852). *Id.* §§ 3571–2 (to commit felony or misdemeanor). 6 mos., $1,000.

Unlawful assembly (1919). *Id.* §§ 920–4, 5439, 5444.

Alaska

War opposition (1917). Comp. Laws, 1933, §§ 4912–13 (utter any seditious matter or *tending* to excite discontent, etc.; fair and honest criticism excepted). 1 yr. or $1,000.

Incitement to crime generally (1913). *Id.* § 5045 (soliciting misdemeanor). 6 mos., $500.

Criminal syndicalism (1919). *Id.* §§ 4914–17. 10 yrs., $5,000.

Unlawful assembly (1899). *Id.* § 4904–5. 1 yr., $50–$500.

Arizona

Red flags, etc. (1919). Code Ann., 1939, § 43—2402. 6 mos., $100–$300.

Conspiracy (1901). *Id.* §§ 43—1101–2, 44—1813 (to commit any crime, or any act injurious to public health or morals). 1 yr., $1,000.

Incitement to crime generally (1901). *Id.* § 43—6104 (counseling misdemeanor). 6 mos., $300.

[Criminal syndicalism (1918 sp., c. 13). 10 yrs., $5,000. Message of Governor Hunt, refusing to sign this act, *id.* 49; Senate and House Resolutions denouncing the I.W.W., *id.* 55, 67. REPEALED in 1928.]

Unlawful assembly (before 1901). Code Ann., 1939, § 43—1304. 6 mos., $100–$300.

Arkansas

Red flags, etc. (1919). Pope's Dig. Stat., 1937, § 2945. 6 mos., $1,000.

Conspiracy (1873). *Id.* § 3571 (to usurp or overthrow government of state). 1–15 yrs.

(1837). §§ 3572, 3952 (to commit any felony). 1 yr., $250.

Sedition (1919). *Id.* § 2944 (language encouraging inflicting of personal injury or destruction of property, propaganda which tends to overthrow the present form of government by any violence or unlawful means). 6 mos., $10–$1,000.

Exclusion from ballot (1935). *Id.* §§ 4910–11 (group advocating overthrow of government by force or violence, or carrying on program of sedition or treason by radio, speech or press).

California

*Red flags, etc. [(1919). Penal Code, Deering, 1937. § 403a (symbol, etc., of opposition to organized government, or stimulus to anarchistic action, or aid to seditious propaganda.) 6 mos.–5 yrs. First clause UNCONSTITUTIONAL, Stromberg *v.* California (1931); see Chapter XI, section 1. REPEALED in 1933, and replaced by next item.]

(1933). Deering's Codes, 1937, Military and Veterans Code, § 616 (symbol, etc. of *forceful or violent* opposition to organized government, or stimulus to anarchistic action, or aid to propaganda advocating *overthrow of government by force*). 6 mos.–5 yrs.

[Los Angeles Red Flag Ordinance held UNCONSTITUTIONAL, *In re* Hartman, 182 Cal. 447 (1920).]

Conspiracy (1872). Penal Code, Deering 1937, §§ 182–4 (any crime, or any act injurious to public health or morals). Same penalty as crime or act planned.

Incitement to crime generally (1872). Penal Code, Deering 1937, § 659 (soliciting misdemeanor). 6 mos., $500.

*Criminal syndicalism (1919). Gen. Laws, Deering 1937, Act 8428. 1–14 yrs.

Unlawful assembly (1872). Penal Code, Deering 1937, §§ 407–410. 6 mos., $500.

*Exclusion from ballot (1940). Elections Code, §§ 2540.3–4 (no party using "communist" in its name or affiliated with Communist Party of United States, etc.).

Colorado

Red flags, etc. (1919). Stat. Ann., 1935, c. 48, §§ 18–20 (any display of red flag). 1–10 yrs.

Conspiracy (1861). *Id.* c. 48, § 177 (to do any unlawful act). 10 yrs., $1,000.

Sedition (1919). *Id.* c. 48, §§ 21–29 (anarchy and sedition to advocate forcible resistance to constituted government in general or government or laws of U.S. or Colo., or their overthrow; advocate personal injury or unlawful destruction of property, "either as a general principle or in particular instances as a means of affecting governmental, industrial, social, or economic conditions"; membership clauses; distribution of pamphlets or possession for distribution). 20 yrs., $10,000.

Unlawful assembly (before 1908). *Id.* c. 48, §§ 193–4. 3 mos., $50.

Connecticut

Red flags, etc. (1919). Gen. Stat., 1930, § 6041. 6 mos., $200.

New Haven Red Flag Ordinance (1919), 29 *Yale Law Journal* 108.

Incitement to specific acts of violence (1923). Gen. Stat., 1930, § 6072 (soliciting unlawful injury to public or private property, assault on army, natl. guard, or police, killing or injuring any class or body of persons). 10 yrs., $5,000.

(1918). *Id.* § 6085 (directly or indirectly encouraging use of explosives to injure person or property). 20 yrs., $5,000.

Sedition (1919). *Id.* § 6039 (disloyal, scurrilous or abusive matter about form of government of U.S., military forces, etc., or matter intended to bring them into contempt, or which creates or fosters opposition to organized government). 5 yrs., $500.

(1919). *Id.* § 6040 (public advocacy of "any measure, doctrine, proposal or propaganda intended to injuriously affect the government" of U.S. or Conn). 3 yrs., $1,000.

Unlawful assembly (before 1902). *Id.* §§ 6186–8. 6 mos., $100.

[Motion picture censorship. Public Acts, 1925, c. 177, § 2 (tax statute; tax commr. to revoke permit for any film he finds "immoral or of a character to offend the racial or religious sensibilities of any element of society"). REPEALED in 1927.]

Delaware

Red flags, etc. (1919). Rev. Code, 1935, § 5155. 15 yrs., $2,000.

Sedition (1931). *Id.* § 5156 (advocating change by violence in form of government; membership clauses). 20 yrs., $100–$10,000.

Unlawful assembly (before 1915). *Id.* § 5179. 6 mos., $20–$200.

Exclusion from ballot (1935). *Id.* § 1810 (like Arkansas).

District of Columbia

Unlawful assembly (1892). Code, 1929, Title 6, § 117. $25.

Florida

War opposition (1917). Comp. Gen. Laws, 1927, §§ 2076–7 (persuading or publicly attempting to persuade a person not to enlist in war or when "our foreign relations tend to indicate an impending war or state of war"). 90 days, $200.

Conspiracy (1868). *Id.* § 7541 (to commit any offense, or any act injurious to public health or morals). 1 yr., $5,000.

Incitement to specific acts of violence (1866). *Id.* § 7133 (attempt by writing or speaking to "excite an insurrection or sedition"). 20 yrs.

Unlawful assembly (1868). *Id.* § 7175. 6 mos., $500.

Motion picture censorship (1921). *Id.* §§ 3584–6, 7719. Held UNCONSTITUTIONAL by lower court. 49 *Yale Law Journal* 93, n. 41.

Georgia

*Incitement to specific acts of violence (1871–2, modifying statute before Civil War). Code, Ann., 1936, §§ 26—902–3 (attempt to incite insurrection, etc. Death, or 5–20 yrs. UNCONSTITUTIONAL as applied in Herndon *v.* Lowry (1937); see Chapter XI, section VI.

*(1866, modifying statute before Civil War). *Id.* § 26—904 (introducing or circulating writings inciting insurrection, etc.). 5–20 yrs.

Unlawful assembly (before 1851). *Id.* § 26—5301. 12 mos. in chain gang, $1,000.

Hawaii

War opposition (1918). Rev. Laws, 1935, §§ 5491–4 ("language calculated or *tending* to discourage or prevent the vigorous prosecution of the war"; "disrespect to any flag of the United States"; "contemptuous or abusive language about any allied nation or its flag or uniform"). 1 yr., $1,000.

Conspiracy (1869). §§ 5720–30 (to commit any offense or instigate any one thereto). 10 yrs., $1,000.

Sedition (1918). *Id.* § 5790 (contemptuous or disloyal language about government of U.S., armed forces, flag, etc., or calculated to bring them into disrepute or contempt). 10 yrs., $1,000.

(1921). *Id.* § 5600 (printing or circulating any writing "intended to advocate or incite" any act of violence, "such as sabotage, sedition, anarchy, rioting"; or "which by deliberate misrepresentation shall be designed to create or *have the effect of creating* distrust or dissension between different races or between citizens and aliens"; anti-boycott clause). 1 yr., $1,000; more for 2d offense.

Criminal syndicalism (1919). *Id.* §§ 5601–4. 10 yrs., $5,000.

Unlawful assembly (1870). *Id.* §§ 6170–80. 20 yrs., $1,000.

Idaho

Red flags, etc. (1919). Code Ann., 1932, § 17—4609. 1–10 yrs., $1,000.

Conspiracy (1864). *Id.* § 17—1027 (like California). 1 yr., $1,000.

Incitement to crime generally (1887). *Id.* § 17—304 (counseling misdemeanor). 6 mos., $300.

Criminal syndicalism (1917). *Id.* §§ 17—4401–4. 10 yrs., $5,000.

Unlawful assembly (1864). *Id.* §§ 17—3304–5. 6 mos., $300.

Illinois

Red flags, etc. (1919). Rev. Stat., State Bar Assn. ed., 1939, c. 38, §§ 563–4. 1–10 yrs.

Incitement to specific acts of violence (1861). *Id.* c. 134, §§ 10–11 (telegraphing to incite or aid insurrection). 10 yrs.

Sedition (1919). *Id.* c. 38, §§ 558–560, 564 (advocating reformation or overthrow of present representative form of government by violence or other unlawful means; issuing books, etc.; membership in society, etc.). 1–10 yrs.

Unlawful assembly (1845). *Id.* c. 38, § 506. $100.

Indiana

Red flags, etc. (1919). Burns Stat. Ann., 1933, §§ 10—1301–3 (preamble referring to Russia). 5 yrs., $5,000.

Conspiracy (1905). *Id.* § 10—1101 (to commit felony). 2–14 yrs., $25–$5,000.

Sedition (1919). *Id.* §§ 10—1302–3 (advocating, or circulating any document advocating, overthrow of government of U.S., Ind., or of all governments, by force or physical injury to personal property, or "by the general cessation of industry"). 5 yrs., $5,000.

Exclusion from ballot (1935). *Id.* (Supp. 1940) § 29—1015 (like Arkansas).

Iowa

War opposition (no express war statute, but sedition statute below applied in 189 Ia. 1212).

Red flags, etc. (1919). Code, 1939, §§ 12901–2. 6 mos., $1,000.

Conspiracy (1851). *Id.* § 13162 (to commit any felony, any illegal act injurious to public trade, health, morals, or police). 3 yrs.

Sedition (1917). *Id.* § 12900 (attempt by writing, speaking, etc., to excite "an insurrection or sedition"). 20 yrs., $1,000–$10,000.

(1917). *Id.* §§ 12904–5 (advocating subversion or destruction by force of Ia. or U.S. government; attempting to excite hostility or opposition to them; membership clauses). 6 mos.–1 yr., $300–$1,000.

Criminal syndicalism (1919). *Id.* §§ 12906–9. 10 yrs., $5,000.

Unlawful assembly (1851). *Id.* § 13339. 30 days, $100.

Kansas

Red flags, etc. (1919). Gen. Stat., 1935, §§ 21—1304–6 (red flag or banner "distinctive of bolshevism, anarchy, or radical socialism," or showing sympathy with enemies of U.S.). 18 mos.–3 yrs.

*Criminal syndicalism (1920). *Id.* §§ 21—301–4 (adds "or for profit"). 1–10 yrs., $1,000. Applied UNCONSTITUTIONALLY in Fiske *v.* Kansas (1927); see Chapter X, section II.

Unlawful assembly (1868). *Id.* §§ 21—1001–2. $200.

Motion picture censorship (1913, amended in 1917). *Id.* §§ 51—101–12, 74—2201–9.

Kentucky

[Red flags. Laws, 1920, c. 100, § 10. 21 yrs., $10,000. REPEALED in 1922.]

Sedition and criminal syndicalism (1920). Carroll's Stat., Baldwin's 1936 Revision, §§ 1148a—1–14. 21 yrs., $10,000.

[Clauses for dispersal of assembly by peace officer and punishing incitement of enmity between classes, etc., REPEALED in 1922. Severability clause REPEALED in 1940.]

Unlawful assembly (1893). *Id.* § 1268. 5–50 days, 1 cent–$100.

Louisiana

War opposition (1918). Code Crim. Proc., Dart 1932, §§ 1188–9 (resembles contempt part of Espionage Act of 1918; speech or writing "reasonably calculated to bring into disrepute the entry or continuance of the U.S. in the war"). 5 yrs., $50–$5,000.

(See sedition statutes, below.)

Conspiracy (1870). *Id.* §§ 837–9 (to commit murder, arson, battery, etc.). 2 yrs., $1,000.

Sedition (1917). *Id.* §§ 1193–7 (publishing or circulating writing or print advocating that men should not enlist in armed forces of U.S. or La., or orally advocating same in public place or before more than 5 persons; any advocating that citizens of La. should not aid U.S. in carrying on war). 3 mos.–1 yr., $100–$500.

(1917). *Id.* §§ 1185–7 (like Ia. statutes of 1917 with same penalties).

(1918). *Id.* § 1190 (cause contempt of flag of U.S. or any of its officers by words or act). 5 yrs., $50–$5,000.

Unlawful assembly (1872). *Id.* § 885. 3–6 mos., $100–$500.

Motion picture censorship (1935). Gen. Stat., Dart Ann. 1939, §§ 9594.11–17, transferred to Board of Education by Wilson Supp. 1940, §§ 7789.52, 7789.154. See 49 *Yale Law Journal* 91, note 31.

Maine

Conspiracy (before 1857). Rev. Stat., 1930, c. 138, § 26 (to commit any illegal act injurious to public trade, health, morals, police, or a crime punishable by prison sentence). 3 yrs., $1,000.

Unlawful assembly (1840). *Id.* c. 134, §§ 3–4. 1 yr., $500.

Maryland

Conspiracy (1927). Flack Ann. Code, 1939, Art. 27, § 42. 10 yrs., $2,000.

Incitement to specific acts of violence (1862). *Id.* Art. 27, § 608 (secret or public meeting, or secret club, to encourage secession of Md. from U.S.). 2–6 yrs., $500–$3,000.

Motion picture censorship (1916, am. 1922). *Id.* Art. 66A.

Massachusetts

[*Red flags, etc. (1913). Laws, 1913, c. 678, § 2. 6 mos., $100. REPEALED in 1915.]

Conspiracy (common law crime). Gen. Laws, Tercentenary Edition 1932, c. 277, Forms p. 3250. See c. 279, § 5, on punishment.

*Criminal anarchy (1919). *Id.* c. 264, § 11 (speech, writing, picture, etc., advocating assault on public official, killing any person, unlawful destruction of property, overthrow of Mass. government by force or violence). 3 yrs., $1,000.

Unlawful assembly (common law crime). As to dispersal, see *Id.* c. 41, § 98; c. 269, §§ 1–8. See c. 279, § 5, on punishment.

[Motion picture censorship. DEFEATED in referendum in 1922; 49 *Yale Law Journal* 91, n. 31.]

Michigan

Red flags, etc. (1919). Stat. Ann. 1938, c. 286A, § 28.237 (red flag in any public assembly). 4 yrs., $2,000.

Conspiracy (common law crime). *Id.* § 28.984, Forms. 5 yrs., $2,500; see *Id.* § 28.773.

Sedition (1935). *Id.* §§ 28.241–3 (advocacy of overthrow of government of U.S. or any state by force or violence; not to be construed to abridge free speech or press or peaceful picketing). 5 yrs., $5,000.

Criminal syndicalism (1919). *Id.* §§ 28.235–6. 10 yrs., $5,000.

Unlawful assembly (common law crime). As to dispersal, see §§ 28.789–796.

Minnesota

War opposition [*(1917). Laws, 1917, c. 463 (text is *supra*, p. 100). 1 yr., $100–$500. SUPERSEDED in 1919 by next item.]

(1919). Mason's Stat. 1927, §§ 9972–5 (copies practically all of Espionage Acts of 1917 and 1918). 20 yrs., $10,000.

Red flags, etc. (1919). *Id.* §§ 10510–13 (excepts signal by railroad employee or warning of obstruction on public highway). 1–7 yrs., $1,000.

Conspiracy (before 1894). *Id.* §§ 10055–6 (to commit a crime, any act injurious to public health, morals, etc.). 3 mos., $100.

Criminal syndicalism (1917). *Id.* §§ 10057–60. 1–10 yrs., $5,000.

Unlawful assembly (before 1894). *Id.* §§ 10282–3. 3 mos., $100.

[Scandalous newspapers (1925). *Id.* §§ 10123—1–3 (may be enjoined as nuisance). 12 mos., $1,000, for contempt. UNCONSTITUTIONAL by Near *v.* Minnesota (1931); see Chapter XI, section III.]

Mississippi

Conspiracy (1892). Code 1930 Ann., § 830 (to commit crime, or act injurious to public health, morals, etc.). 1–6 mos., $25 minimum.

Evolution not to be taught in public school, state college, etc. (1926). *Id.* §§ 7315–16. $500 and loss of position.

Missouri

War opposition (1845). Stat. Ann. 1932, Crimes, p. 2736, § 3875 (counsel another to give aid or comfort to enemies of state here or elsewhere). 10 yrs., $1,000–$5,000.

Conspiracy (1845). *Id.* p. 2736, § 3876 (to usurp or overturn government of state, interfere forcibly with its administration). 4 mos., $500–$5,000.

(before 1899). *Id.* p. 2963, § 4243 (to commit any offense, or any act injurious to public health or morals). 1 yr., $1,000.

Unlawful assembly (before 1899). 1 yr., $1,000.

Montana

War opposition [(1918). Laws, 1918 extraordinary sess., c. 11 (model for Espionage Act of 1918). 20 yrs., $20,000. Probably REPEALED by implication by next item.]

(1919). Rev. Codes, 1935, §§ 10737–8 (copies for war Espionage Act of 1917 and munitions curtailment clause of U.S. Act of 1918; rest of 1918 Act for all times). 1–20 yrs., $200–$20,000.

Red flags, etc. (1919). *Id.* §§ 10745–6. 6 mos.–5 yrs., $500.

Conspiracy (before 1879). *Id.* §§ 10898–10900 (to commit any crime, or any act injurious to public health and morals). 1 yr., $1,000.

Incitement to crime generally (1895). *Id.* § 11586 (counseling misdemeanor). 6 mos., $500.

Sedition (1919). *Id.* §§ 10737–8 (most of U.S. 1918 Espionage Act effective in peace; see War opposition, *supra*). 1–20 yrs., $200–$20,000.

Criminal syndicalism (1918). *Id.* §§ 10740–4. 1–5 yrs., $200–$1,000.

Unlawful assembly (before 1879). *Id.* §§ 11288–91. 1 yr., $1,000.

Nebraska

[War opposition (1918). Comp. Stat., 1929, §§ 28—104–112 (very wide; punishes concealment of knowledge that sedition has been committed; also any violation of U.S. Act of 1917; bars accused from teaching, lecturing, editing, preaching, or serving as priest during prosecution; allows private citizen to start prosecution). 20 yrs., $10,000. REPEALED in 1933.]

Red flags, etc. (1919). *Id.* §§ 28—1104–7 (black flag; red flag except for railroad signals and highway obstructions; flag or sign with "inscription antagonistic to existing government of Neb. or U.S."). 3 yrs., $1,000.

Conspiracy (1919). *Id.* § 28—301 (to commit any felony). 2 yrs., $10,000.

Criminal syndicalism (1919). *Id.* §§ 28—815–17 (adds "or for profit"). 1–10 yrs., $1,000.

Unlawful assembly (1899). *Id.* §§ 28—804–7. 3 mos., $100.

(1919). *Id.* §§ 28—741–2 (all public meetings to be conducted in English). $10–$100.

Nevada

Conspiracy (1912). Comp. Laws, 1929, §§ 10061–2 (to commit a crime, or act injurious to public health, morals, etc.). 1 yr., $500–$1,000.

Incitement to crime generally (1912). *Id.* §§ 10300–1 (publish or circulate written or printed matter "having a *tendency* to encourage or incite" the commission of any crime, breach of peace, violent act, disrespect for law). 1 yr., $500–$1,000.

Criminal syndicalism (1919). *Id.* §§ 10560–3. 10 yrs., $5,000.

Unlawful assembly (1912). *Id.* § 10278. 3 mos., $200.

New Hampshire

War opposition (1917). Public Laws, 1926, c. 380, § 28 (influence any person not to work in any factory or munition plant, or encourage or attempt to encourage strike therein, so long as such establishment is making supplies for armed forces). 9 mos., $500–$1,000.

Incitement to crime generally (1919). *Id.* c. 394, §§ 27–8, 30 (do or assist in doing any act or thing which advocates or *tends* to incite or encourage violation of any law of U.S. or state). 10 yrs., $5,000.

Sedition (1919). *Id.* c. 394, §§ 26, 28–30 (advocating overthrow or change in government of U.S. or N.H. or interference with any public or private right by force or unlawful means; assembling for advocating this; introducing into state, publishing, distributing, possession for distribution of any matter, including pictures, advocating this). 10 yrs., $5,000; injunction provision; destruction of books, pictures, etc.

Unlawful assembly (1850). *Id.* c. 374, § 9. 1 yr., $500.

*(1919). *Id.* c. 145, §§ 2–5 (parades to be licensed). $500.

New Jersey

War opposition (1918). N.J.S.A. 2:173—22 (like Minnesota, 1917). 7 yrs., $100–$2,000.

Red flags, etc. (1919). *Id.* 2:173—20–21 (red or black flag, or emblem of any organization opposed to organized government, for purpose of inciting hostility or opposition to or destruction of any and all government). 15 yrs., $2,000.

[(1920). Laws, 1920, c. 235, § 3 (flag, emblem, etc., which in any way incites, etc., hostility to government of U.S. or N.J.). 7 yrs., $2,000. AMENDED in 1934 by next item.]

(1934). N.J.S.A. 2:173—21 (flag, etc., inciting subversion or destruction by force of any and all government, or government of U.S. or N.J.). 7 yrs., $2,000.

Conspiracy (1898). *Id.* 2:119—1 (to commit a crime). 3 yrs., $1,000.

*Incitement to specific acts of violence (1908). *Id.* 2:173—10–11 (advocating unlawful destruction of public or private property, assaults on army, natl. guard, or police, killing or injuring any class of persons or individual; publishing or circulating book, etc., advocating or *tending* to incite this). 7 yrs., $2,000.

Sedition (1918). *Id.* 2:173—12 (inciting or attempting to incite an insurrection or sedition among any class or portion of population). 20 yrs., $10,000.

[(1918). Laws, 1918, c. 44, § 2 (advocating in public or private, by speech, writing, etc., subversion or destruction by force of government of U.S. or N.J., or attempt by speech, writing, etc., to incite *"hostility or opposition"* to government of U.S. or N.J.). 10 yrs., $2,000. AMENDED in 1934 by N.J.S.A. 2:173—13 below, replacing italicized words.]

[(1918). *Id.* § 3 (membership in society or attendance at meeting for purpose of inciting, etc., *"hostility or opposition"* to government of U.S. or N.J.). 10 yrs., $2,000. UNCONSTITUTIONAL by State *v.* Gabriel, 95 N.J.L. 337 (Sup. 1921). REPEALED in 1930. See 1934 statute, N.J.S.A. 2:173—14 below.]

[(1920). Laws, 1920, c. 235, §§ 1, 2, 4, 5, 6 (printing, writing, multigraphing, etc., book, pamphlet, etc., advocating *"hostility"* to government of U.S. or N.J., or constitution, by-laws, etc., of society advocating this, or picture symbolizing this; possession for distribution, distributing, or exhibiting, etc., said material; letting or hiring building or room to society, meeting, etc., advocating this, or permitting use of premises). 7 yrs., $2,000. AMENDED in 1934 by N.J.S.A. 2:173—15-19 below, replacing italicized word.]

(1934) N.J.S.A. 2:173—13 (changes italicized words of § 2 of 1918 statute to punish attempt to incite *"the subversion or destruction by force"* of government of U.S. or N.J.). 10 yrs., $2,000.

(1934). *Id.* 2:173—14 (changes italicized words of § 3 of 1918 statute to punish society or meeting to incite *"the subversion or destruction by force"* of government of U.S. or N.J.). 10 yrs., $2,000.

(1934). *Id.* 2:173—15-19 (changes italicized word of 1920 statute to punish printing material, letting rooms, etc., in connection with advocacy of *"the subversion or destruction by force"* of government of U.S. or N.J.). 7 yrs., $2,000.

Criminal anarchy (1902). *Id.* 2:173—7-9 (advocating subversion or destruction by force of any and all government; joining society or meeting, introducing or circulating printed matter within state for such purposes). 15 yrs., $2,000.

*Unlawful assembly (1898). *Id.* 2:103—1 (common law crime). 3 yrs., $1,000. UNCONSTITUTIONALLY applied in State *v.* Butterworth, 104 N.J.L. 579 (E. & A. 1928). See also State *v.* Haywood, 36 N.J.L.J. 146 (1913).

New Mexico

Red flags, etc. (1919). Stat. Ann., 1929 Compilation, § 35—3302 (red or black flag, or emblem of organization "opposed to organized government"). 6 mos., $25–$100.

Conspiracy (1919). *Id.* § 35—201 (to commit a felony). 1–14 yrs., $25–$5,000.

[Sedition (1919). *Id.* §§ 35—3101–5 (any act aiming at destruction of, or which is "antagonistic to or in opposition to organized government, inciting revolution or opposition to such government; employers knowingly employing persons engaged in such advocacy are punishable). 10 yrs., $1,000. UNCONSTITUTIONAL by State *v.* Diamond, 27 N.M. 477 (1921).]

Unlawful assembly (1853–4). *Id.* § 35—3201. 6 mos., $200.

New York

[Red flags, etc. (1919). Consol. Laws Ann., McKinney 1938, Penal Law, § 2095–a (text *supra* p. 159). 1 yr., $500. UNCONSTITUTIONAL by People *v.* Altman, 241 App. Div. 858 (1934).]

Conspiracy (1881). *Id.* Penal Law, § 580 (to commit a crime, or any act injurious to public health, morals, etc.). 1 yr., $500.

*Criminal anarchy (1902). *Id.* Penal Law, §§ 160–6 (stated *supra*, p. 163). 10 yrs., $5,000 (less for permitting assemblage).

Schools, public offices, etc. (1917). *Id.* Civil Service Law, § 23–a; Education Law, § 568; Public Officers Law, § 35–a (removal of civil service employees, public school teachers, public officers, etc., for treasonable or seditious word or act).

(1918). *Id.* Education Law, § 674 (elimination of public school text-books containing seditious or disloyal matter, or favorable to country with which U.S. at war; commission to examine text-books; teacher using disapproved book punishable). 1 yr., $500.

[*(1921). Laws, 1921, c. 666 (public school teachers must obtain certificate of loyalty; none issued to advocates of "a form of government other than the government of the U.S. or of this state"). REPEALED in 1923.]

[*(1921). Laws, 1921, c. 667 (every private school must obtain license from state; none issued if instruction includes teaching of doctrine "that organized governments shall be overthrown by force, violence, or unlawful means"). 60 days, $100. Injunction provision. REPEALED in 1923.]

(1939, am. 1940). Consol. Laws Ann., McKinney 1938, Civil Service Law, § 12–a; Laws, 1940, c. 564 (no person to be appointed or continue as public officer, civil servant, teacher in public school or other state educational institution, if he advocates by speech, writing, circulation of writings, etc., that government of U.S. or any state be overthrown by force, violence, or any unlawful means, or organizes or joins group which so advocates; judicial review).

Unlawful assembly (1881). *Id.* Penal Law, § 2092. 1 yr., $500.

(1909). *Id.* Penal Law, §§ 710–1 (assembly of persons masked, except licensed masquerade ball). 2 yrs., $1,000–$5,000.

(1923). *Id.* Civil Rights Law, §§ 53–56 (oath-bound societies obliged to register constitution, membership list, etc.). $1,000–$10,000. Applied to Ku Klux Klan, 241 N.Y. 405 (1926), 278 U.S. 63 (1928).

*Motion picture censorship (1921, am. in 1926, 1927). *Id.* Education Law, §§ 1080–92.

North Carolina

Conspiracy (1868). Code Ann., 1939, § 4179 (by force to overthrow government of N.C., oppose its authority, delay the execution of any law, etc.). 10 yrs., $5,000.

Incitement to specific acts of violence (1861). *Id.* § 4178 (incite rebellion or insurrection). 15 yrs., $10,000.

Unlawful assembly (1868–9). *Id.* § 4547 (aiding dispersal).

(1868–9). *Id.* § 4180 (oath-bound secret political or military association; disguises, etc.). 4 mos.–10 yrs., $10–$100.

North Dakota

Red flags, etc. (1921, initiative). Supp. to Comp. Laws, 1913–25, §§ 9790a2–3 (public display of red or black flag, or banner antagonistic to existing government of U.S. or N.D. or *tending* to occasion breach of peace). 30 days, $100.

Conspiracy (1877). Comp. Laws, 1913, § 9441 (to commit a crime, or any act injurious to public health, morals, etc.). 1 yr., $500.

Unlawful assembly (1877). *Id.* §§ 9810–11. 1 yr., $500.

Ohio

Red flags, etc. (1919). Throckmorton's Code Ann., Baldwin's Rev. 1940, §§ 12398—1–2 (red or black flag, banner with inscription "opposed to organized government," flag of "anarchistic society"). $100.

Criminal syndicalism (1919). *Id.* §§ 13421—23–26. 10 yrs., $5,000.

Unlawful assembly (1831). *Id.* § 12809. 30 days, $500, and bonds to keep peace.

(1889). *Id.* § 12910 (unite to commit misdemeanor wearing white caps, masks or other disguise). 2–10 yrs., $2,000.

Motion picture censorship (1913). *Id.* §§ 871—48–53, 154—47.

Oklahoma

Red flags, etc. (1919). 21 Stat. Ann., 1937, § 374. 10 yrs., $1,000.

Conspiracy (1890). *Id.* §§ 421–3 (to commit any crime, any act injurious to public health, morals, etc.). 1 yr., $500.

(1915). *Id.* § 424 (to commit any offense). 2 yrs., $10,000.

Incitement to crime generally (1890). *Id.* § 28 (counseling misdemeanor). 1 yr., $500.

Criminal syndicalism (1919). *Id.* §§ 1261–4 (adds "or for profit"). 10 yrs., $5,000.

Oregon

Red flags, etc. (1919). Comp. Laws Ann., 1940, § 23—1071. 10 yrs., $1,000.

*Conspiracy (1937). *Id.* § 23—1309 (to commit any felony). 3 yrs., $1,000. Replaced next item.

[*Criminal syndicalism (1919). Laws, 1919, c. 12 (adds "or for profit"). 1–10 yrs., $1,000. Replaced by Laws, 1921, c. 34, which was UNCONSTITUTIONALLY applied in De Jonge *v.* Oregon (1937); see Chapter XI, section v. Amended by Laws, 1933, c. 459, and then REPEALED in 1937 and replaced by conspiracy statute above.]

Unlawful assembly (1864). Comp. Laws Ann., 1940, § 23—801–2. 3 mos.–1 yr., $50–$500.

Pennsylvania

War opposition (1861, am. 1939). Purdon's Stat. Ann., 1940 Supp., § 4203 (persuading person from entering service of U.S. or Pa., with intent to oppose or subvert government of U.S. or Pa.; perhaps not limited to war). 10 yrs., $5,000.

Red flags, etc. (1895, am. 1939). *Id.* § 4209 (red flag in public procession). 3 mos., $20.

Sedition (1919, am. 1921, 1939). *Id.* § 4207 (any publication, utterance, or conduct, the *intent* of which is to cause any outbreak of violence, "to encourage any person to take any measure with a view of attempting to overthrow by threat of force" the government of Pa. or U.S., to encourage any person to commit any overt act with a view of bringing such government into hatred or contempt, etc.; membership clause). 20 yrs., $10,000.

Unlawful assembly (1860, am. 1939). *Id.* 1940 Supp., § 4401. 3 yrs., $1,000.

Motion picture censorship (1911, am. 1915). 4 Purdon's Stat. Ann., §§ 41–58, 71 *id.* §§ 119, 356.

Rhode Island

Red flags, etc. (1914). Gen. Laws, 1938, c. 612, § 49 (public display of flag, being in itself, or having upon it any inscription "opposed to organized government"). 3 mos., $100.

(1919). *Id.* c. 604, § 1 (any flag as "emblematic of a form of government proposed by its supporters as preferable to the form of government" of U.S.). 10 yrs., $10,000.

Conspiracy (common law crime). *Id.*, c. 625, § 3, clause 5 (form).

Criminal syndicalism (1919). *Id.* c. 604 (special wording; "language intended to incite a disregard of the constitution or laws of R.I. or U.S."; advocacy of any change in form of government except as constitution or laws provide, etc.; membership and conspiracy clauses; meeting for such purposes is unlawful assembly, subject to dispersal). 10 yrs., $10,000.

Unlawful assembly (before 1872). c. 607, §§ 1–3 (dispersal). See preceding item.

South Carolina

Conspiracy (common law crime). Code of Laws, 1932, § 1380. 6 mos.–3 yrs., $100–$2,000.

Unlawful assembly (before 1902). *Id.* § 1737. 30 days, $100.

South Dakota

Red flags, etc. (1919). Code, 1939, § 13.0806. 30 days, $100.

Conspiracy (before 1901). *Id.* § 13.0301 (to commit any crime, etc.). 1 yr., $500.

Incitement to crime generally (before 1901). *Id.* § 13.0303 (counseling commission of misdemeanor). 1 yr., $500.

Criminal syndicalism (1918). *Id.* §§ 13.0801–4. 1–25 yrs., $1,000–$10,000.

Unlawful assembly (before 1901). *Id.* § 13.1402–7. 1 yr., $500.

Tennessee

Conspiracy (1932). Michie's Code, 1938, § 11063 (to commit any offense against the state). 5 yrs., $1,000.

(1857–8). *Id.* § 11064 (to commit any indictable offense, or any act injurious to public health, morals, etc.). 1 yr., $1,000.

(1897). *Id.* §§ 11068–9 (to take human life or engage in any act "reasonably calculated to cause the loss of life," whether generally or of a class or of any individual; to burn, to destroy or feloniously take property of class or individual; encouraging any one to become or remain a member of such conspiracy). 3–21 yrs.

Incitement to specific acts of violence (1915). *Id.* § 11038 (advising night-riding). 3–15 yrs.

(See preceding item and next item.)

Sedition (1857–8). *Id.* § 11026 (uttering seditious words, dispersing scurrilous libels against state or general government; instigating others to cabal and meet together to contrive rebellious conspiracies, riots, etc.; concealing such practices). 1 yr., $1,000; bonds to keep peace; ineligibility for office for 3 yrs.

Exclusion from ballot (1935). *Id.* § 1936(1) (like Arkansas).

Evolution not to be taught in public school, state college, etc. (1925). *Id.* §§ 2344–5. $100–$500.

Texas

[War opposition (1918). Vernon's Penal Code, 1938, Arts. 153, 155 (like Louisiana). 2–25 yrs. UNCONSTITUTIONAL by *Ex parte* Meckel, 87 Tex. Cr. 120 (1920).]

Unlawful assembly (1857). *Id.* Arts. 439, 454. $500.

(1925). *Id.* Arts. 454a–g (wearing masks in public place or entering house to frighten). 6 mos., $100–$500.

Utah

Red flags, etc. (1919). Rev. Stat., 1933, § 103—26—84 (flag intended to proclaim disloyalty to U.S. government or belief in anarchy). 1–10 yrs., $1,000.

Conspiracy (1876). *Id.* §§ 103—11—1–3 (like California). 1 yr., $1,000.

Criminal syndicalism (1919). *Id.* §§ 103—54—1–5. 1–5 yrs., $200–$1,000.

Unlawful assembly (1876). *Id.* §§ 103—50—5–6. 6 mos., $300.

Vermont

Red flags, etc. (1919). Pub. Laws, 1933, § 8733 (red flag except as danger signal, black flag except as weather signal, or banner with inscription opposed to organized government). 6 mos., $200.

Criminal anarchy (1919). *Id.* § 8370 (like Massachusetts, but has "directly or indirectly"). 3 yrs., $1,000.

Unlawful assembly (before 1862). *Id.* § 8586. 6 mos., $100.

Virginia

Conspiracy (1877–8). Code, 1936, § 4392 (to incite colored population to violence against whites, or *vice versa*). 5–10 yrs.

(1934). *Id.* § 4483b (to murder, rob, burn, etc.). 1–10 yrs.

Unlawful assembly (1877–8). *Id.* § 4532. 1 yr., $500.

Motion picture censorship (1922, am. 1930). *Id.* §§ 378b–j.

Washington

Red flags, etc. (1919). Remington's Rev. Stat. Ann., 1932, §§ 2563—7–9 (flag suggestive of any group espousing any principle antagonistic to the constitution or laws of U.S. or Washington). 10 yrs., $5,000.

Conspiracy (1909). *Id.* § 2382 (like California). 1 yr., $1,000.

*Incitement to crime generally (1909). *Id.* § 2564 (printing or circulating any book, etc., having a *tendency* to encourage any crime, breach of peace, violent act, or disrespect for law). 1 yr., $1,000.

Criminal anarchy (1909). *Id.* §§ 2562–2563 (like New York). 10 yrs., $5,000.

Criminal syndicalism [(1919). Laws, 1919, c. 3 (usual form). 10 yrs., $5,000. Vetoed in March, 1917; passed over veto in January, 1919. REPEALED in March, 1919, and replaced by next item.]

(1919). Remington's Rev. Stat. Ann., 1932, §§ 2563—1–2 (special wording; advocating "crime, sedition, violence, intimidation or injury" as a means of change; membership clauses). 10 yrs., $5,000.

(1919). *Id.* § 2563—3–6 (special wording, advocating sabotage; membership clauses). 10 yrs., $5,000.

(The last two items combined cover the same ground as the usual syndicalism act. Washington is the only state with statutes against both anarchy and syndicalism.)

Unlawful assembly (1909). *Id.* §§ 2550–2551. 1 yr., $1,000.

(1909). *Id.* §§ 2553–4 (assembly of disguised or masked persons, except at masquerade ball). 1 yr., $1,000.

West Virginia

War opposition (1863). Code Ann., 1937, § 5911 (justifying armed invasion or organized insurrection in state by speaking, writing, etc., during its continuance). 1 yr., $1,000.

*Red flags, etc. *Id.* §§ 5913–14 (text is *supra* pp. 159–160). 1 yr., $100–$500 (1st offense); 1–5 yrs. (2d offense).

Conspiracy (1882). *Id.* §§ 6033–6 (Red Men's Act — conspire to inflict bodily injury on any person or destroy, injure, or carry away property). 1–12 mos.

Sedition (1919). *Id.* § 5912 (text is *supra* p. 165). 1 yr., $100–$500 (1st offense); 1–5 yrs. (2d offense).

Unlawful assembly (1849). *Id.* §§ 6027, 6032. 12 mos., $500.

Motion pictures (1919). *Id.* § 6109 (any picture or theatrical act injuriously reflecting upon progress, status, etc., of any race or class, calculated to arouse prejudice or feelings of one race or class against any other). 30 days, $100–$1,000.

Wisconsin

[War opposition (1918). Laws, 1918 (spec. sess.), c. 13 (like Minnesota, 1917). 3 mos., $100–$1,000. EXPIRED at end of the war.]

Red flags, etc. (1919). Stat., 1939, § 348.485. $10–$100 (30 days on default of payment).

Conspiracy (common law crime). *Id.* 348.40. 1 yr., $500.

Criminal anarchy (1903). *Id.* §§ 347.14–18 (like New York). 3–10 yrs., $5,000.

Unlawful assembly (1878). *Id.* § 347.02–3. 1 yr., $500.

Wyoming

Conspiracy (1876). Rev. Stat., 1931, § 33—818.

Incitement to crime generally (1919). *Id.* § 32—103 (advocating or suggesting crime as means of coercion or accomplishing political or industrial reform or purpose here or abroad). 5 yrs., $5,000; bonds to keep peace.

Unlawful assembly (1890). *Id.* § 32—404. 3 mos., $100.

INDEX

(Note: Prosecutions, etc., are indexed under the name of the defendant. The Appendices are not indexed.)

INDEX

De Jonge v. *Oregon*, 384–388; see also
83*n.*, 416, 429, 471.
DEMPSEY, Representative, 443.
DENATURALIZATION, 551; of Pro-Germans, 100; under sedition bills, 169;
of I.W.W., 226; of philosophical
anarchist, 231 and *n.*
Dennett, United States v., 301*n.*
Dennie, Respublica v., 507*n.*
DEPORTATIONS, Chapter V, 196–240,
550–551:
  Statutes: Act of 1798, 3, 16*n.*, 27,
99; of 1918, 99–100, 197–198 (text);
of 1920, 198*n.*, 443–444; Alien Registration Act of 1940, viii, 198*n.*,
441, 443–446; federal power, 171,
196–197, 235–236; ex post facto and
attainder clause, 446 and *n.*
  Administrative machinery, 198–
204, 550–551; no time-limit, 198 and
n., 445; references, 201*n.*; test by
officials, 199–202; right to public
trial, counsel, etc., 202–204; arrest
warrants, 204, 211; searches and
seizures, 204, 205 and *n.*, 212; fair
administrative trial, 205, 212–213;
finality of administrative decision,
199, 205*n.*, 219*n.*
  Raids of January, 1920, viii, x,
196, 204–215, 240; arrest of citizens,
169, 206, 210–214 *passim*, 223–224,
550*n.*; treatment of women, 206–
207; use of government spies, 215–
218.
  *Types of persons deported from
U. S.*, 197–198, 218–231; war opponents, 99–100, 140*n.*, 198*n.*; punishment for sedition, 169; Communists, 219–224; I.W.W., 224–228;
violent and philosophical anarchists,
228–231; no Nazis or Fascists, 483*n.*,
484.
  Constitutionality and wisdom,
232–240.
  Miscellaneous topics: Bisbee, 41
and *n.*; from Jersey City, 410; from
Russia, 155; of Americans from
other countries, 237 and *n.*; in history of persecution, 234–235; effect
of economic views of judges, 75;
Strecker case and resulting inclusion of ex-members of forbidden
classes, 445–446; Bridges, 446*n.*

See also ALIENS; COMMUNISTS;
DENATURALIZATION.
DESILVER, Albert, x.
DETROIT, deportations, 208*n.*, 213 and
n., 237.
DEUTSCH, on post-office censorship,
299*n.*; on enjoining state restrictions on free press, 382*n.*
DEWEY, John, appeal for Rand School,
310–311.
DE WITT, S. A., N. Y. Socialist assemblyman, 269.
Dial, 77*n.*
DIAMOND, state sedition case, 167*n.*
DICEY, A. V., 6*n.*, 70 and *n.*, 160*n.*,
409*n.*, 518.
DICKENS, Charles, 123, 456, 547.
DICTAGRAPH, used to prosecute for conversations, 54*n.*
Dictionary of American Biography,
84*n.*, 508*n.*
DIES COMMITTEE, 440.
DILLING, *Red Network*, 482*n.*
DISBARMENT, of radical lawyers, 359*n.*,
554.
DISORDERLY CONDUCT, pacifism punished as, 68 and *n.*, 93*n.*, 100*n.*, 526.
See also BREACH OF THE PEACE.
DISQUE, Colonel, 102, 143.
DISTRICT ATTORNEYS, United States.
See PROSECUTING ATTORNEYS.
DISTRICT COURTS, UNITED STATES, administration of Espionage Act, ix,
51–60; juries in, 70–73; judges in,
74–79. See also ESPIONAGE ACT.
DODD, E. M., 294*n.*
DOE, J. P., prosecution, 54–55, 61.
DORCHESTER LABOURERS, 333 and *n.*,
459 and *n.*, 473, 484, 511, 513.
DORR WAR, 145, 396.
DOUGLAS, William O., Justice, 304*n.*,
414, 435*n.*
DRAFT. See CONSCRIPTION.
DRAKARD, John, English prosecution,
25–26.
DREISER, Theodore, 536*n.*
DREYFUS, Alfred, 104, 120.
DUCLAUX, Émile, quoted, 495.
DUE PROCESS OF LAW, involves balancing, 32, 35; applies to deportation
proceedings, 199, 205 and *n.*, 208,
232–233; to postal power, 299; in
Rand School case, 311–313. See also

defendants' past misconduct, 303, 304 and *n.*

Federal injunctions against state statutes violating freedom of speech, etc., 382 and *n.*, 412, 413 and *n.*, 414*n.*

Contempt proceedings, 548–549.

INSURRECTION, normal law against, 144–149; exclusion from mails of matter advocating, 39; Georgia statute and Herndon case, 389–398.

INTENTION, bad, not punishable *per se*, 46, 78; doctrine of constructive intent, 24, 26–28, 49–51, 57–64, 89, 118–121, 160, 181, 185–187, 477, 488; in Sedition Law of 1798, 27–28; in Espionage Act, see same; in Alien Registration Act, 476–480, 488; in state sedition laws, 160.

Specific intent, 115, 125–126, 129–135.

INTERESTS, principle of social and individual, 31–35, 149–150, 158–159, 235–236, 401–403.

INTERNATIONAL, COMMUNIST. See COMMUNISTS.

International Juridical Association Monthly Bulletin, 385*n.*

INTERNATIONAL LAW, armed intervention, 140*n.*; mistreatment of races, 235; arbitrary expulsions, 237; extradition of political offenders, 265–266. See also FOREIGN GOVERNMENT.

Investigation Activities of the Department of Justice, cited, 147*n.*, 216*n.*

IRELAND, 186, 287; discussion of, in war, as crime in U. S., 99, 118, 135, 487; suppression in, 181, 473–474, 483, 528–529. See also CASEMENT.

Irish World, excluded from mails, 99.

ISAIAH, 355; prosecution for quoting, 186.

ITALY, 33*n.*, 34*n.*, 215, 268, 562, 564, 565.

I.W.W. See INDUSTRIAL WORKERS OF THE WORLD.

IZAC, Representative (Cal.), 454.

Jackson, Ex parte, I.W.W. case, 205*n.*, 227.

JACKSON, Robert H., Attorney General (now Justice), 482–483.

JAPAN, 267.

JARRET, on right of assembly, 409*n.*

JEFFERSON, Thomas, 195, 273, 325, 362, 462, 505; Virginia Statute of Toleration, 17, 28–29, 61, 185; on Sedition Act of 1798, 27, 28, 50, 483, 513; First Inaugural, 141–142, 435; encouragement of revolution, 191.

JEFFREYS, Judge, 182, 202, 343.

JEHOVAH'S WITNESSES, war prosecutions, 76*n.*, 399; handbills and street canvassing, 398–409; refusal to salute flag, 364*n.*, 399, 405 and *n.*; street parade, 408. See also RUTHERFORD.

JENKINS' EAR, cause of war, 102.

JENNINGS, on right of assembly, 409*n.*

JERSEY CITY, 251; regulation of meetings before Hague case, 410–412; after decision, 430. See also *Hague v. C.I.O.*

JESUS, a crime to quote against war, 51, 55–56; called reformer and anarchist, 112, 127; Sermon on the Mount, 49, 106–107, 371.

JEWS, 76, 99, 113, 174*n.*, 233, 234, 235 and *n.*, 238*n.*, 239, 255, 376–377, 426, 444, 512.

JOAN OF ARC, 258, 514.

JOHNSON, C. R., 71*n.*

JOHNSON, Samuel, 11*n.*, 106*n.*, 151*n.*, 154*n.*, 238.

Journal of Criminal Law and Criminology, 363*n.*, 376*n.*

JOYCE, James, 191*n.*

JUDGES, effect of free speech clauses on, 6; Federalist judges, see FEDERALIST JUDGES; function in libel and sedition prosecutions, see JURY, FOX'S LIBEL ACT.

Interpretation of Espionage Act, 42–51, 51–66; administration of trials under Act, 74–79, 84, 89, 91, 250; in Abrams case, 112–128; jesting with prisoners, 126–128; unfitness to determine bad intention and bad tendency, 120, 139, and elsewhere; attitude toward radicals, 75–77, 112–113, 359–361; sentences, 79; see also SENTENCES.

Questioning witnesses, 122 and *n.*; unfairness by judges, 76*n.*; as substitutes for policemen, 341–342; eco-

as test of guilt, 57–64, 160, 181, 185–187, see INTENTION; of multiplication of overlapping charges, 114*n.*, 365; of culling sentences from long pamphlet or book, 91–92, 93, 188–192.

Right to counsel, 202–204, 358–359; prisoner's address to jury, 77*n.*; good trial record, 82–84, 202–203, 363, 384; publicity of trial, 202–204; promptness of appellate review, 53, 80, 468–469, 522–523, 548–549; narrow range of prosecutors' discretion, 68–69.

See also ASSOCIATION, GUILT BY; HUMAN MACHINERY.

Procès de tendance, 159.

PROFANITY, 149–152.

PROFITEERS, discussion of criminal, 45, 52–53, 62, 87, 93, 94, 106, 193, 249–250; possible ground of legislative exclusion, 255.

PRO-GERMANS, 4, 53*n.*, 57, 64, 65 and *n.*, 66, 86–92, 98, 168, 184, 193, 243.

PROHIBITION, 61*n.*, 103, 178, 205*n.*, 212, 337, 354, 370, 374, 544.

PROPAGANDA, organized disloyal, 38, 40, 434. See also FOREIGN GOVERNMENT.

PROSECUTING ATTORNEYS, effect of free speech clause on, 6; in the war with Germany, 59–60, 67–69; under Sedition Act of 1798, 71; in Abrams case, 112–128, 140.

PROSECUTIONS, with jury, 523–524; for petty offenses without jury, 524–525.

PROTESTANTS, 399, 426.

PROUDHON, 189.

PROVERBS, quoted, 181–182, 215, 306, 490.

Prudential Insurance Co. v. *Cheek*, 321*n.*

Public, excluded from the mails, 98.

PUBLIC UTILITY, state-like, 299–301, 419–422.

PUGH, R. C., on naturalization, 370*n.*

PURIFYING LEGISLATURE, 241–280. See also LEGISLATIVE EXCLUSIONS.

QUAKERS, 230; naturalization of, 368–375.

QUEBEC, address to people of, 16–17, 150, 545. See also CANADA.

RACE RIOTS, and friction, 174 and *n.*, 392, 397–398. See also NEGROES; RIOTS.

RADICALS, freedom of speech for, 3–4, see also AGITATORS, MINORITIES, SPEECH, FREEDOM OF, *Meaning*; duty of restraint, 162–163; mob violence against, see MOB VIOLENCE, RAIDS; under Espionage Act, 71, 75*ff.*, 80–97, 108–140, 142–143; prevalent after the war, 141–144; relation to the criminal law in peace, 141–195, see SEDITION and succeeding entries; deportation, 196–240; exclusion from legislatures, 269–280; from ballot, 491–493; disbarment, see DISBARMENT; charge of radicalism as libel, 163*n.* See also ANARCHISTS; COMMUNISTS; INDUSTRIAL WORKERS OF THE WORLD; REVOLUTION; SOCIALISTS.

RADIO, censorship of, 381, 405, 554 and *n.*

RAI, Lajpat, book on India excluded from mails, 99.

RAIDS, on radicals, 144, 181; on Communists, 204–215, 240; on I.W.W., 181, 205*n.*, 207, 227; time of Wilkes, 243–244; in war, 39, 104; by Lusk Committee, 271, 311. See also SEARCHES AND SEIZURES.

RAND SCHOOL, 306–317; see also 174, 220*n.*, 271, 280, 381, 400, 401, 551–552.

RANDOLPH, John, 21.

RAY, Judge, 13*n.*, 184.

READING, Lord, 259.

RECHT, Charles, 228*n.*

RECORD, of trial, importance, 82–84, 202–203, 363, 384.

RED CROSS, criticism of, punished, 51; refusal of contributions, punished, 100, 289.

RED FLAG LAWS, 159–163, 181; validity, 163*n.*, 362–366.

"RED MENACE," 144, 168, 275.

REED, John, 319*n.*

REED, Stanley, Justice, 304*n.*, 402*n.*, 414 and *n.*, 433, 435*n.*

REFERENDUM, before war, discussion criminal, 51, 58.

Relation between the Army and the Press, 90.

RELIGION, toleration, 4, 150, 151, 155–

Atheneum Paperbacks

HISTORY—AMERICAN

Atheneum Paperbacks

HISTORY

HISTORY—ASIA

THE NEW YORK TIMES BYLINE BOOKS

Atheneum Paperbacks

STUDIES IN AMERICAN NEGRO LIFE

LAW AND GOVERNMENT

Atheneum Paperbacks